With love,
4/22/04
Arthur

The Shepherd and the Rock
Origins, Development,
and Mission of the Papacy

J. Michael Miller, C.S.B.

Our Sunday Visitor Publishing Division
Our Sunday Visitor, Inc.
Huntington, Indiana 46750

Nihil Obstat: Reverend Richard J. Schiefen, C.S.B.
Censor Deputatus

Imprimatur: Most Reverend Joseph A. Fiorenza
Bishop of Galveston-Houston
September 20, 1994

The nihil obstat and imprimatur are official declarations that a book or pamphlet is free of doctrinal or moral error. No implication is contained therein that those who have granted the nihil obstat and the imprimatur agree with the content, opinions or statements expressed.

Copyright © 1995 by Our Sunday Visitor Publishing Division
Our Sunday Visitor, Inc.
ALL RIGHTS RESERVED
Scripture text from *The New Oxford Annotated Bible with the Apocrypha,* Revised Standard Version, Old Testament Section, ©1952; New Testament Section, Second Edition, © 1971 by the Division of Christian Education of the National Council of the Churches of Christ in the U.S.A. The Oxford Annotated Apocrypha, © 1977 by Oxford University Press, Inc.
Excerpts from *Vatican Council II: The Conciliar and Post Conciliar Documents,* New Revised Edition edited by Austin Flannery, O.P., copyright ©1992, Costello Publishing Company, Inc., Northport, NY are used by permission of the publisher, all rights reserved. No part of these excerpts may be reproduced, stored in a retrieval system, or transmitted in any form or by any means — electronic, mechanical, photocopying, recording or otherwise, without express permission of Costello Publishing Company.
Other sources from which material has been excerpted or has served (either quoted verbatim or paraphrased) as the basis for portions of this work are cited in the endnotes of each chapter. References to "[Unnamed authority]" are taken from *L'Osservatore Romano* and are written by Vatican officials. If any copyrighted materials have been inadvertently used in this book without proper credit being given, please notify Our Sunday Visitor in writing so that future printings of this work may be corrected accordingly.
With the exception of short excerpts for critical reviews, no part of this book may be reproduced or transmitted in any form or by any means, electronic or mechanical, including photocopying, recording, or by any information storage or retrieval system, without permission in writing from the publisher. Write: Our Sunday Visitor Publishing Division, Our Sunday Visitor, Inc., 200 Noll Plaza, Huntington, Indiana 46750

ISBN: 0-87973-735-2
LCCCN: 94-68606
PRINTED IN THE UNITED STATES OF AMERICA

Cover design by Rebecca J. Heaston
Cover photo Vatican Museums; "Christ Consigns the Keys to Peter," after Raphael.
735

*To the memory of Katharine Robb Miller
true daughter of the Reform
who loved the pope
but never understood the papacy*

ABBREVIATIONS

AA *Apostolicam actuositatem.* Vatican II, Decree on the Apostolate of Lay People. 1965.
AG *Ad gentes.* Vatican II, Decree on the Church's Missionary Activity. 1965.
CCC *Catechism of the Catholic Church.* 1994 (English translation).
CD *Christus Dominus.* Vatican II, Decree on the Pastoral Office of Bishops in the Church. 1965.
CIC *Codex Iuris Canonici.* Code of Canon Law. 1983.
CN *Communionis notio.* Congregation for the Doctrine of the Faith, Letter to the Bishops of the Catholic Church on Some Aspects of the Church Understood as Communion. 1992.
DH *Dignitatis humanae.* Vatican II, Declaration on Religious Liberty. 1965.
DS Denziger-Schönmetzer. Henry Denziger and Adolf Schönmetzer, eds., *Enchiridion symbolorum, definitionum et declarationum de rebus fidei et morum.* 33rd ed. Freiburg im Breisgau: Herder, 1964.
DV *Dei verbum.* Vatican II, Dogmatic Constitution on Divine Revelation. 1965.
DVE *Donum veritatis.* Congregation for the Doctrine of the Faith, Instruction on the Ecclesial Vocation of the Theologian. 1990.
GS *Gaudium et spes.* Vatican II, Pastoral Constitution on the Church in the Modern World. 1965.
IM *Inter mirifica.* Vatican II, Decree on the Means of Social Communication. 1963.
LG *Lumen gentium.* Vatican II, Dogmatic Constitution on the Church. 1964.
M Mansi. Giovanni Domenico Mansi, ed., *Sacrorum conciliorum nova et amplissima collectio.* 31 volumes. Florence-Venice, 1757-1798. Reprint and continuation by L. Petit and J.- B. Martin, 60 volumes. Paris, 1899-1927.
ME *Mysterium ecclesiae.* Congregation for the Doctrine of the Faith, Declaration in Defence of the Catholic Doctrine of the Church against Certain Errors of the Present Day. 1973.
NEP *Nota explicativa praevia.* Preliminary Explanatory Note of the Theological Commission attached to *Lumen gentium.* 1964.
OE *Orientalium ecclesiarum.* Vatican II, Decree on the Catholic Eastern Churches. 1964.
OT *Optatam totius.* Vatican II, Decree on the Training of Priests. 1965.
PB *Pastor bonus.* John Paul II, Apostolic Constitution on the Roman Curia. 1988.
PG *Patrologia Graeca.* J. P. Migne, ed. Paris, 1857-1866. 162 volumes.
PL *Patrologia Latina.* J. P. Migne, ed. Paris, 1844-1864. 221 volumes.
PO *Presbyterorum ordinis.* Vatican II, Decree on the Ministry and Life of Priests. 1965.
RPE *Romano pontifici eligendo.* Paul VI, Apostolic Constitution on the Vacancy of the

Apostolic See and the Election of the Roman Pontiff. 1975.
SOE *Sollicitudo omnium ecclesiarum.* Paul VI, Apostolic Letter on the Duties of Papal Representatives. 1969.
UR *Unitatis redintegratio.* Vatican II, Decree on Ecumenism. 1964.

Table of Contents

Introduction 9

Chapter one
JESUS AND PETER 12
    Rock, Keys, Binding and Loosing 13
    Jesus' Prayer for Peter 20
    Peter as Shepherd of the Flock 22
    A Weak and Sinful Man 25

Chapter two
PETER AND THE APOSTOLIC COMMUNITY 31
    First Witness to the Risen Lord 31
    Leader of the Early Community 33
    Peter and the Other Apostles 37
    Peter and Paul 40
    Images of Peter in the Later New Testament 43

Chapter three
SUCCESSION TO PETER'S MINISTRY 50
    From Jerusalem to Rome 50
    Apostolic Succession 54
    Petrine Succession 60
    The Bishop of Rome as Successor to Peter 63

Chapter four
EARLY DEVELOPMENT OF ROMAN PRIMACY 71
    Papal Primacy and the Development of Doctrine 71
    Early Interventions of the Roman Church 73
    Recognition of Roman Primacy 75
    Testimony of Irenaeus 78
    Primacy of the Roman Bishop 80
    Petrinitas 81
    Leo the Great 84

Chapter five
FROM THE EARLY MIDDLE AGES TO THE CATHOLIC REFORM 93
    The Pope's Role in Temporal Affairs 93
    Monarchical Vision of the Papacy 96
    Conciliarism: Council Over Pope? 104
    The Reformation: Church Without a Pope 106
    The Catholic Reform 109

Chapter six
THE PAPACY AND THE EAST ... 115
- Peter and the Bishop of Rome ... 115
- Eastern Ecclesiology and the Pope ... 118
- What Kind of Roman Primacy? ... 123
- Separation of East and West ... 127
- Orthodoxy and Papal Primacy ... 130
- Councils of Reunion ... 132

Chapter seven
PRIMACY OF JURISDICTION ... 139
- First Vatican Council ... 139
- Institution of Petrine Primacy ... 141
- Permanence of the Primacy ... 142
- Purpose of Jurisdiction ... 145
- Nature of Papal Authority ... 148
- Limits to Papal Authority ... 154

Chapter eight
ORDINARY PAPAL TEACHING ... 162
- From Testimony to Teaching ... 162
- Characteristics of the Everyday Magisterium ... 166
- Purpose of the Pope's Ordinary Magisterium ... 170
- Documents and Degrees of Authoritative Teaching ... 173
- Encyclicals ... 177
- Assent to Ordinary Papal Teaching ... 180

Chapter nine
PAPAL INFALLIBILITY ... 188
- Gift to the Church ... 188
- Origins of the Doctrine ... 191
- Definition of Vatican I ... 193
- Object of Papal Infallibility ... 197
- Response to Extraordinary Papal Teaching ... 200
- Conditions for Exercising Papal Infallibility ... 201
- Consultation, Consent, and Reception ... 203

Chapter ten
PAPACY AND EPISCOPACY AT VATICAN II ... 212
- Reception of Vatican I's Teaching on the Papacy ... 212
- Origins of Collegiality ... 217
- Characteristics of the Episcopal College ... 220
- Subject of Supreme Authority in the Church ... 225

Chapter eleven
COLLEGIALITY AND THE PAPAL OFFICE 234
Ecumenical Councils 235
Collegial Action of the Dispersed Episcopate 237
Synod of Bishops 238
College of Cardinals 241
Episcopal Conferences 244
Ad Limina Visits of Bishops 248
Pastoral Visits of the Pope 250

Chapter twelve
PETRINE MINISTRY AND PARTICULAR CHURCHES 257
Universal and Particular Church 257
The Pope and the Local Church 259
Guardian of Unity and Advocate of Catholicity 263
Papal Intervention in the Particular Church 266

Chapter thirteen
THE POPE'S TENURE OF OFFICE 278
Historical Models of Papal Election 278
Cardinal Electors 283
Electoral Procedures 286
End of a Pope's Tenure: Resignation and Illness 289
Loss of the Papal Office Through Heresy 291
"Bad" Popes 293

Chapter fourteen
THE ROMAN CURIA AND THE PETRINE MINISTRY 299
Origin 299
Participation in the Petrine Charism 303
Organizational Structure 305
Papal Representatives 312
Proposals for Reforming the Papal Bureaucracy 316

Chapter fifteen
THE HOLY SEE AND PAPAL POLITICS 322
Vatican City State and the Holy See 322
World Politics and the Pope 325
Instruments of Papal Politics 326
Objectives of Papal Diplomacy 333
Evaluation of Papal Diplomacy 339

Chapter sixteen
FACING THE FUTURE: 21 THESES ON THE PAPAL MINISTRY 346
Index 371

Introduction

The market is flooded with books on popes, the history of the papacy, and a massive number of specialized monographs and articles that analyze every detail of this fascinating institution. Theologians and religious commentators seem to have left very few stones unturned. Haven't we had enough? Why another book on the papacy? In its own way, the abundance of materials creates its own problems: too many stones, no broad picture of the pivotal historical and religious importance of the papacy. This book is an attempt to pull together for nonspecialists what is most significant about Catholic teaching and practice on the pope's Petrine ministry.

In his essay on Leopold von Ranke's *History of the Popes*, the English historian Thomas Babington Macaulay expressed why the papacy captivates anyone interested in Western civilization, whether believer or not:

> The proudest royal houses are but of yesterday, when compared with the line of the Supreme Pontiffs. That line we trace back in an unbroken series, from the Pope who crowned Napoleon in the nineteenth century to the Pope who crowned Pepin in the eighth; and far beyond the time of Pepin the august dynasty extends, till it is lost in the twilight of fable. The republic of Venice came next in antiquity. But the republic of Venice was modern when compared with the Papacy; and the republic of Venice is gone, and the Papacy remains. The Papacy remains, not in decay, not a mere antique, but full of life and youthful vigour.... Nor do we see any sign which indicates that the term of her long dominion is approaching. She saw the commencement of all the governments and of all the ecclesiastical establishments that now exist in the world; and we feel no assurance that she is not destined to see the end of them all.[1]

This admiration and attraction remain. Another historian, Arnold Toynbee, called it "the greatest of all Western institutions."[2] The papacy does not just inspire the spilling of seas of ink but also compels media attention, even if much of it is critical and begrudging. The eyes of the world focus on Rome and its bishop, whom Catholics believe to be the successor of St. Peter.

Without the popes, it is hard to imagine Western history, at least as we know it. The papacy has proved to be an incredibly durable institution. It is a survivor. To survive, however, it has taken various historical forms at different times. In the first centuries, the Roman pontiffs headed congregations not much larger than a middle-size parish in an urban metropolis today. Many were martyred for their belief in Christ. Later popes, like monarchs, led armies into battle, deposed kings, and patronized artists. The distance separating St. Peter from the fifteenth-century Borgia pope, Alexander VI, is enormous. Popes have been slaves and penniless; they have also held immense temporal power and wealth. Nevertheless, all are in the long line of what is the oldest institution in the Western world with an unbroken existence. Fascinating as such a tale is, this book is neither a history of the papacy nor an account of any particular pontiff. Rather, its focus is the office which each pope has held, the Petrine function embodied in so many different ways in the institutional papacy as it has evolved in the course of history.

Every Catholic girl or boy who has ever argued with a non-Catholic playmate has quickly learned that not all popes were good men. Some were avaricious, others were bellicose, others lustful. The seven deadly sins have swept through the Vatican. The "Holy" Father has, at times, been anything but holy. The excesses of anti-Catholic polemics notwithstanding, it is undeniable that in the course of two millennia, unworthy men have held the Church's highest office. Although we cannot rejoice in evil, a study of the papacy sheds light on an essential truth of faith: that the Church belongs to Christ, not to us or the pope, and that the mystery of iniquity spares no office or institution, even the bride of Christ. Bad popes, for all their ugliness and betrayal, tell us that despite our infidelity, God remains faithful to his people.

A further reason for the particular fascination which inspired this book is the authority and prestige which the papacy still enjoys. At the beginning of the *Annuario Pontificio*, the Vatican handbook or directory containing an amazing amount of information on the Church's central government, John Paul II is given an imposing list of titles: Bishop of Rome, Vicar of Jesus Christ, Successor of the Prince of the Apostles, Supreme Pontiff of the Universal Church, Patriarch of the West, Primate of Italy, Archbishop and Metropolitan of the Roman Province, Sovereign of Vatican City State, and Servant of the Servants of God. In a democratic age, when authority is exercised only with the consent of the governed, the papacy seems out-of-step, although it is also the oldest elected office in the West.

This book also reflects an apologetic interest: to help Catholics to understand the Church's doctrine and to be able to answer intelligently the innumerable questions raised about the papacy. Precisely because of its importance and power, other Christians have frequently expressed their abhorrence of the papacy. In the words of John Wesley's hymn, so opponents argue, "the Church's one foundation is Jesus Christ her Lord" — and nobody else! Some have held that the papacy is an "invention of the devil" and that the pope is the antichrist.

More positively, in the past thirty years, relations between the Catholic Church and churches or ecclesial communities which do not accept the papacy as Catholics do have improved remarkably. Despite some vestiges of pope-bashing, serious theologians have been engaged in many discussions and official dialogues concerning Peter's continuing office in the Church. While Catholics have been open to a critical evaluation of the papacy, many Orthodox, Anglicans, Lutherans, and others have expressed their interest in a ministry of unity serving the universal Church. Although Catholics and their dialogue partners have not yet fully capitalized on such initiatives, the slow process of becoming reconciled in our diversity has begun.

I also hope that this book contributes to dispelling a kind of sourness about the papacy which has crept into some Catholic circles. Few, it is true, express direct contempt either for the pope or his office. Still, it has become more common to manifest dislike for the pope, to criticize bitterly his disciplinary decisions and teachings, and to call into question various dimensions of the doctrine and practice of the Petrine ministry. Others, coming to the defense, have perhaps exaggerated the papacy's role in the Church. Several years ago, Eugene Kennedy divided American Catholics into two "cultures," two ways of looking at and living their experience of the Church. One culture, he said, remains attached to the institutional dimension of the Church.[3] Catholics of this tradition respect the pope, accept his teaching authority, support Peter's Pence, place Vatican flags in their churches' sanctuaries, and want the pope's picture on their Catholic calendar. On the other hand, says Kennedy, there is another culture in which Catholics say that the pope "remains their father but they now see themselves as adults."[4] My reading is that this latter group is becoming increasingly indifferent to the papacy and to what the pope says. I hope that a clear presentation of the truth of Catholic teaching on the papacy will help to close this rift.

With so many scriptural, historical, canonical, dogmatic, and political studies available, I have tried to make a judicious selection of material. To keep the book readable, descriptions of lengthy scholarly differences of opinion are kept to a minimum, in favor of what I believe to be the "common opinion" among Catholic scholars.

The object of this book, then, is to present Catholic teaching on the ministry of Peter which continues to serve the Church in the office of the pope. Not every historical form taken by the papacy in the course of its two millennia belongs to the essential nucleus of the office of Peter. Throughout the book I have sought to answer one single question: What was Christ's will for the Petrine ministry, and how has the Spirit guided its historical development down to the present day?

Notes for the Introduction

1. Cited in Hans Küng, *The Church*, trans. Ray and Rosaleen Ockenden (New York: Sheed & Ward, 1967), 24-25.
2. Arnold Joseph Toynbee, *A Study of History*, vol. 4 (London, 1939), 512.
3. Eugene Kennedy, *Tomorrow's Catholics, Yesterday's Church: The Two Cultures of American Catholicism* (San Francisco: Harper & Row, 1988), 100.
4. Kennedy, *Tomorrow's Catholics*, 178.

Chapter one
JESUS AND PETER

The purpose of the first two chapters is to identify the scriptural foundations for the ministry Christ entrusted to Peter. Since Catholics believe that the pope is the successor of Peter, we must first ask who Peter was. This means going back to first-century Palestine. Although we cannot expect the New Testament to use present-day terminology about the papacy, the roots of the office are there. Later developments in the papal office can therefore be judged according to their continuity with these origins.

The New Testament has principally a twofold value. It is both a historical record and an inspired document which contains "firmly, faithfully and without error . . . that truth which God, for the sake of our salvation, wished to see confided to the sacred Scriptures" (DV 11). As a historical record, it recounts events in the life of Jesus and the early Church. As an inspired document, it interprets and reveals the inner meaning of the events described. These two factors must be kept in mind when examining the New Testament origins of Peter's role in the early community.

The gospels are a collection of different kinds of writings concerned with the sayings and deeds of Jesus and others, based on the memory of individuals and communities. The apostolic community recorded its teaching about Jesus and, in doing so, preserved numerous references to Peter's relationship with Jesus and his ministry in the community. After Jesus, Peter is the person most frequently mentioned in the New Testament: 114 times in the gospels and 57 times in Acts.[1] Without denying the underlying unity of the biblical portrayal of Peter, we can point out many nuances. Each evangelist selected what he wanted from both the oral and written traditions, interpreting the meaning of the events from his own standpoint and for his own particular audience. The views gathered from these different lenses provide a well-defined scriptural portrait of Peter.

Scripture witnesses to an early tradition that Jesus designated a unique role for Peter during his public ministry. While any particular reference may be inconclusive by itself, when taken together, they furnish proof for Peter's preeminence in the apostolic group. The New Testament contains what the early Church, in her formative apostolic age, believed about the vocation and mission of Peter and "thus the role which was being given to Peter at the time the particular New Testament books were written."[2] Illumined by the Spirit, the community interpreted and transmitted its experience and understanding of Peter's function. This apostolic interpretation is normative for all subsequent generations of believers. Underlying my approach to these texts is the basic theological principle stated by Dominican theologian J. M. R. Tillard: "what the Church *of apostolic times*, led by the Spirit of Pentecost, understood of its own nature and in consequence allowed to be produced in its life, belongs to the Gospel events."[3] In other words, how the early Church comprehended and lived the ministry given to Peter belongs to the foundational period of divine revelation, an age whose teaching remains permanently binding for the Church.

Rather than draw a full profile of Peter, I shall limit my treatment in this chapter to those texts which have had an enduring influence in all discussions regarding the origins of the papal ministry. On three different occasions, Jesus picked out Peter *alone* and confided to him a unique role among his followers. The evangelists record these dialogues in the *Petrine texts* found in Matthew 16:18-19, Luke 22:31-32 and John 21:15-17, each of which is without direct parallels in the other gospels. The person of Peter and his mission belong to the essential structure of the Church's primitive preaching, and witnesses to this fact are present in the different biblical traditions which developed. From very early times, these three texts have shaped the Church's understanding of Peter's ministry. Not only Catholics but increasingly Protestants as well interpret them as giving Peter a "primacy" among the original apostles, that is, a specific function or leadership role in the community.

Rock, Keys, Binding and Loosing

Emblazoned in three-foot-high black letters on a gold mosaic field around the base of Michelangelo's cupola in St. Peter's Basilica in Rome are Christ's words to the Galilean fisherman: "You are Peter, and on this rock I will build my Church, and I will give you the keys of the kingdom of heaven." No text is more crucial for understanding the origins of the papacy than the following:

> Now when Jesus came into the district of Caesarea Philippi, he asked his disciples, "Who do men say that the Son of man is?" And they said, "Some say John the Baptist, others say Elijah, and others Jeremiah or one of the prophets." He said to them, "But who do you say that I am?" Simon Peter replied, "You are the Christ, the Son of the living God." And Jesus answered him, "Blessed are you, Simon Bar-Jonah! For flesh and blood has not revealed this to you, but my Father who is in heaven. And I tell you, you are Peter, and on this rock I will build my church, and the powers of death shall not prevail against it. I will give you the keys of the kingdom of heaven, and whatever you bind on earth shall be bound in heaven, and whatever you loose on earth shall be loosed in heaven (Mt 16:13-19).

Authenticity and Setting

Because these verses provide the strongest argument to justify the Catholic belief that the papacy is rooted in Jesus' will, until recently many Protestants disputed their authenticity. They maintained that Matthew 16:18-19 was a Roman forgery, inserted into Matthew's original gospel in order to legitimate the primacy exercised by the bishop of Rome. This theory has not withstood the test of time. As the Lutheran-Catholic ecumenical study *Peter in the New Testament* has concluded, today nearly all exegetes recognize that these verses, found in every ancient manuscript and translation, belong to the original text of Matthew's gospel.[4]

Given the strongly Aramaic substructure of the passage (Aramaic was the language of Palestine at the time of Jesus), a convincing argument can be made that the early Christian community passed on its memory of this dialogue from original witnesses.

Every verse suggests the dialogue's Aramaic source, reflecting "a precise recollection guarded in the corporate memory of the apostles of an event in the actual life of Jesus."[5] The play on words with "rock" ("you are Peter [Rock] and on this rock") works perfectly in Aramaic, where *kepha* appears in both places. The noun *kepha* means simply "rock" or "stone."[6] The Greek text, most probably the original language of Matthew's gospel, requires a change of gender between *Petros* (Peter) and *petra* (rock). Other Aramaicisms in the passage betraying the text's Palestinian origin include "powers of death," "flesh and blood," and "Simon Bar-Jonah."[7] It is therefore reasonable to conclude that the passage comes from an Aramaic setting, recalling an encounter between Jesus and Peter.

The history of exegesis has raised yet another question. Could the text be an editorial addition of Matthew himself rather than a memory of Jesus' words to Peter? Unquestionably the passage bears traces of the evangelist's editorial hand; the "blessed are you" and "Father who is in heaven" are typical of his style. Even so, most scholars deny, for reasons which we shall examine, that Jesus' reply was later fabricated to justify Peter's role in the apostolic community.

Another objection is raised by the phrase "my Church" in the passage. Reform biblical scholar Oscar Cullmann notes that "this is the main objection which has always been brought against the saying's [Mt 16:18] authenticity."[8] These critics maintain that Jesus expected the imminent coming of the reign of God and therefore could not have planned for a community which was to endure. Whatever Jesus' precise eschatological expectations, most scholars today recognize that such hopes for the coming reign of God are in harmony with his desire to form a messianic community. The idea of a messianic community was known to Jewish thought in Jesus' day and is reconcilable with his preaching on the reign of God.[9] Consequently, scholars are very reluctant to deny the text's historicity on these grounds alone. As German theologian Johann Auer points out, the root problem is theological: "Only if one acknowledges that the earthly Jesus of the gospels possessed a messianic consciousness can one understand why he would speak about 'his church.' Only on this basis can one understand, further, that he would promise the office of universal shepherd and the power to bind and to loose to the apostle Peter."[10]

Scholars continue to disagree, however, whether the passage comes from Jesus' public ministry, from the last supper, as Cullmann has argued,[11] or from a post-resurrection appearance, as many contemporary exegetes propose. The latter group maintains that the dialogue should be transferred to one of the "Church-founding" appearances of the risen Lord.[12] John P. Meier states that "the original context of vv.17-19 may have been the Easter appearance (Lk 24:34; 1 Cor 15:3) of Christ to Peter."[13] Whatever the conclusions of this exegetical discussion, the text's basic meaning and importance remain unchanged. Its truth is unaffected by the occasion when the original dialogue actually took place. Even if we were to grant that Peter's confession and Jesus' promise took place during a post-Easter appearance, this would not weaken the passage's foundational importance for Peter's vocation rooted in Christ's will. In fact, it might strengthen its significance by removing it from being connected with Jesus' following harsh rebuke of Peter as a "hindrance" (Mt 16:23).

From Simon to Peter

John's gospel records that Simon received a new name when he first met Jesus: " 'So you are Simon the son of John? You shall be called Cephas' (which means Peter)" (Jn 1:42). Similarly, in recording their lists of the Twelve, Mark and Luke note that at some point Christ renamed Simon (cf. Mk 3:16; Lk 6:14). It is, however, Matthew who provides the classic dialogue on the change of name.

Caesarea Philippi, a Roman town flaunting the splendors of Hellenistic culture to nearby Jews, had as its backdrop a broad rocky cliff with an almost vertical fall of about two hundred feet. The Temple of Jupiter, a symbol of the pagan world's power, crowned the rock. And so, writes theologian and scientist Stanley Jaki, the rock at Caesarea Philippi "was a most appropriate stage for Christ's eliciting Peter's confession and for His own reply to it."[14]

Within sight of this rock on the road to town, Jesus asked his disciples who they thought he was. Simon answered Jesus' question, "Who do men say that the Son of man is?" (Mt 16:13), with his confession of faith, "You are the Christ, the Son of the living God" (Mt 16:16; cf. Mk 8:29; Lk 9:20). With solemn and deliberate authority, indicated by beginning his response with the phrase "and I tell you," Jesus then changed his disciple's name to *Kepha* or *Cephas* (in transliterated Greek): "you are Peter, and on this rock I will build my church" (Mt 16:18).

The Jewish Scriptures shed light on what Jesus would have meant by calling Simon "Rock." The Old Testament refers to God as "the Rock of Israel" (2 Sam 23:3) because he assures salvation for his people. Other designations, such as "fortress" (2 Sam 22:2), "rock of refuge" (Ps 31:2), and "stronghold" (Ps 144:2), are closely related to calling God a rock. He is trustworthy because he is "an everlasting rock" (Is 26:4); there is no other rock (cf. Is 44:8). Generations of Jews prayed, "I love thee, O LORD, my strength. The LORD is my rock, and my fortress, and my deliverer, my God, my rock, in whom I take refuge" (Ps 18:1-2). In a stony land, God was the people's rock and sure foundation. The Jews also called God their father, lord, king, and judge. Others were also given these latter titles; not so with "rock."

Because their tradition so forcefully emphasized that God alone was the Rock, the only Rock, no Jew was ever given this name.[15] When Jesus called Simon *Kepha*, therefore, this designation would undoubtedly have struck his Jewish listeners as irreverent. This fact is all the more striking, commented German theologian Karl Adam, "because neither the Greek *Petros*, nor the Aramaic *Kepha*, had been employed as proper names before the time of Christ."[16] The name *Kepha*, until then attributed exclusively to the Lord of Israel, "could not help but evoke in pious Jews, as all the Twelve were, a sentiment of awe and reverence"[17] when Jesus gave it to Simon.

Since before this dialogue Peter was unknown as a proper name, Jesus' naming him *Kepha* implies that, like Yahweh of old, he assigned a new mission to the apostle. Within Judaism the giving of a new name marked a decisive point in salvation history. When God changed someone's name, it signified that he was intervening in order to alter the course of historical events so that his plan would be realized. For example, he changed

Abram's name to Abraham (cf. Gen 17:5), Sarai's to Sarah (cf. Gen 17:15), and Jacob's to Israel (cf. Gen 32:28). God gave them new names to indicate that he was taking possession of their lives, accompanying his intervention with promises regarding the future of his people and with particular tasks for the individuals concerned. He chose whom he willed and created what he wanted.[18] Both divine choice and grace were evident in these name changes which transformed those chosen, giving them a new identity.

After Simon professed who Jesus was, Jesus declared who Simon was. Following the example of the Old Testament, Jesus designated Simon as "Rock," assigning him a new position in the community which Jesus himself was in the process of establishing. Election and grace were likewise evident in Peter's case. Simon did not ask to have his name changed. Nor did the other apostles designate him as Rock on their own initiative. Moreover, according to Cullmann, "this name cannot be explained exclusively in terms of Peter's character."[19] Courageous, spontaneous, and good-natured, Simon was also fickle and unsure — anything but a candidate for the nickname Rock. His confession of Jesus' messiahship was not his own doing; it was not due to "flesh and blood." Peter was illumined with inspiration from on high, from the One whom Jesus called "my Father who is in heaven."

Yet another argument confirms what Jesus wanted to signify by changing Simon's name: the conferral on him of a new function in the community. Nicknames were known and used among the Jews. The brothers James and John, for example, were called Boanerges, that is "sons of thunder" (Mk 3:17), a nickname which fitted their personalities (cf. Lk 9:54). It did not stick, however, and never replaced their original names.[20] It is improbable that Jesus meant *Kepha* as a nickname. Had it meant "Rocky," it would surely have prompted joking or taunting from the apostles. At first, the title Peter did not replace the name Simon. Jesus continued to address Simon by his original name. The evangelists usually called him Simon Peter or simply Peter. In the early Church, the apostle's original name eventually fell completely into disuse, and Peter, designating his function, replaced it.[21] The community's memory preserved the name Peter as coming from Jesus himself. The four gospels, therefore, unanimously agree that Jesus himself designated Simon as *Kepha* (Peter/Rock), even though they identify different occasions for the event. More than a new name, "Peter" was a title designating an office or mission which Simon was to discharge.

Upon This Rock

The words "and on this rock I will build my Church" (Mt 16:18) have been the subject of endless debate, frequently provoked more by polemics concerning the papacy than by any ambiguity inherent in the text itself. This ancient controversy revolves around the question who or what the "rock" was, upon which Christ promised to build his Church.[22] Since the Reformation, Protestant exegetes have favored interpreting this second *kepha* as a reference to Peter's faith. The Church, they contend, was founded on the faith which Peter confessed. However, critics now generally agree that this second "rock" refers to the first "Rock," the man Peter.[23] According to Cullmann, the parallelism between "you are Rock" and "on this rock," shows that the second rock can only be the same as the first.[24]

By calling Simon "Rock" after his confession of faith, Jesus intended to emphasize a relation between that faith and the apostle's function as rock. Even so, the role of rock was attributed to the person of Simon and not merely to his faith. Simon's personal confession of faith was the reason why Jesus made him a solid rock. Peter, then, was designated the foundation stone of the new messianic community, the rock upon which Christ promised to build his Church, because he confessed the true faith concerning Jesus' identity.[25] In the words of Joseph Ratzinger, "Peter becomes the Church's rock as the bearer of its creed."[26]

Biblical, rabbinic, and Essene texts exist which show that the idea of a messianic community built on the rock of truth was familiar to the Jews. Because of his faith, Abraham, for example, was considered such a rock, a foundation on which the chosen people were supported.[27] A rabbinical text enlightens this view of Abraham, our father in faith: "Yahweh said, 'How can I create the world, when these godless people will rise up and revolt against me?' But when God saw Abraham who was to come, he said, 'Look, I have found a rock on which I can construct and establish the world.' For this reason he called Abraham a rock, 'Look to the rock from which you were hewn' (Is 51:1-2)."[28] Similarly, Peter's faith can be compared with Abraham's. Consequently, Peter, too, has a foundational role for the new community.

Other New Testament texts also help us to understand the mission Peter received when he was designated *Kepha*. Christ is described as the "living stone" (1 Pet 2:4), the capstone which insures the Church's ultimate stability: " 'The very stone which the builders rejected has become the head of the corner' " (1 Pet 2:7). Only Christ is the absolute ground of creation, since "in him all things were created" (Col 1:16). Indeed, Jesus Christ is the reason the Church's foundation can never weaken. What the Son received from the Father "he delegates to his designated representative during the time when he himself will be with the Father."[29] Jesus made Simon a sharer in his own mission to found the Church on solid rock, stronger than the powers of evil. Christ is her builder and cornerstone, and the edifice of "living stones" (1 Pet 2:5) is his work.

In his promise to Peter, Jesus used the image of a building. So that it would be durable, its foundation had to be rock-like. Moreover, since Christ was referring to a community of persons, that role, too, had to be personal. The only function in the personal realm which is capable of giving a community unshakable stability, support, and permanence is leadership.[30] Peter was commissioned to provide the whole community with a stability which he derived from sharing in divine steadfastness. By giving the apostle a share in his own solidity, Jesus acted "like a man building a house, who dug deep, and laid the foundation upon rock" (Lk 6:48). Peter was made a solid rock by Christ who was "like a wise man who built his house upon the rock" (Mt 7:24). As the rock-foundation dependent upon Christ, Peter would guarantee the Church's endurance against the "powers of death" (Mt 16:18).

Keys of the Kingdom

In the same dialogue, Matthew also records that Jesus entrusted to Peter, precisely as the Church's foundation, the "keys of the kingdom of heaven." These keys symbolized the "power" of the faith he professed.[31] According to the New Testament, only Peter receives the keys. Christ used this metaphor to explain to his apostles the mission which he was assigning to Simon. In this instance, too, the locale can shed light on what Christ intended. Anyone approaching Caesarea Philippi from the principal road would have glimpsed its main gate with its massive locks. Therefore, the metaphor of the keys of the kingdom of heaven "in front of a city gate symbolizing the powers of a world which Christ often and emphatically denounced was a pedagogy that almost imposed itself."[32]

In Judaism keys and doors were the source of many common metaphors. Keys symbolized the power of the one who administered a house or a possession. If they were those to a house, the keys referred to the authority of the majordomo. If they were to a palace, then they referred to that of the prime minister. When Jesus mentioned "keys," therefore, the apostles would have had in mind this connotation of administrative authority. Keys designated the power which a master confided to his deputy who was to take care of his master's possessions during his absence.[33]

Furthermore, Jesus and his listeners would also have known the biblical passages which referred to "keys." Isaiah, for example, recounts the transfer of power from Shebna, the prime minister of King Hezekiah of Judah, to Eliakim, who deposed and replaced him. On Eliakim's shoulder, Isaiah said, God would place "the key of the house of David; he shall open, and none shall shut; and he shall shut, and none shall open" (Is 22:22). The new prime minister, whose symbol of power was the keys, controlled access to the palace, and therefore to the king. In Jesus' day, this text was frequently interpreted as a prophecy which would be fulfilled in the messianic age. At that time, it was said, the "key" would open the kingdom of heaven itself and not just the house of David.

In light of this scriptural background, what Jesus intended by the "keys of the kingdom" becomes more intelligible. While the scribes and Pharisees "shut the kingdom of heaven against men" (Mt 23:13), Peter received the keys to lead people to the kingdom. Just as Jesus transferred a share in his steadfastness to Simon, so did he hand over the keys of his heavenly house to his designated steward.

The later New Testament description of the risen Christ as he "who has the key of David, who opens and no one shall shut, who shuts and no one opens" (Rev 3:7, cf. 1:18) also helps to clarify the meaning of the keys. Christ alone has the power to introduce his people into the kingdom of heaven. "In light of this passage," writes Auer, "the saying about the keys given to Peter would mean that Christ wanted to give to him, and through and in him to the Church built upon him, the key to God's eschatological royal rule."[34] When Christ handed the keys to Peter, he provided him with the authority to open the door to all those who wanted to belong to the kingdom and to close it in the face of enemies. Jesus made Peter its gatekeeper, the majordomo who could open or close the gates of the heavenly city.

The Shepherd and the Rock

Among the Jews of Jesus' time, keys also called to mind another practice. The act of handing over keys was a well-known rabbinic ritual. When young rabbis completed their training for office, they received a key from their teachers. This gesture symbolized that they had received authority to teach God's word.[35] Those who held the keys in a community possessed spiritual authority. The rabbis also had these keys sewn into their robes or carried them in their girdle, reminding them of the authority and mission they had assumed as teachers.[36] According to German theologian Michael Schmaus, the teachers of the law exercised authority, "by proclaiming the will of God set forth in the Torah through preaching, teaching and judging."[37] The transmission of keys therefore involved the transferral of specific power, a gesture which the apostles would have easily understood. When Jesus gave to Peter alone "the keys of the kingdom of heaven," his gesture signified that the apostle received a singular authority among the apostles. As steward of the kingdom, Peter was entrusted with deciding what was permitted or forbidden according to God's will. In the visible Church, Peter was assigned a mission regarding what Christians were to believe and how they were to act.

Binding and Loosing

Closely coupled with the metaphor of the keys is Jesus' promise to Peter that "whatever you bind on earth shall be bound in heaven, and whatever you loose on earth shall be loosed in heaven" (Mt 16:19). Unlike the keys which Peter alone received, later all the apostles together received the power of binding and loosing (cf. Mt 18:18). In this case, too, Jesus used an idea known to his listeners. The Jews were already familiar with binding and loosing, a concept to which Christ gave a new significance.

In technical rabbinic use, the terms "binding" and "loosing" had primarily a disciplinary meaning. As a reminder of the mission they had received, rabbis carried keys in their garments. They held the authority to "bind" or condemn people to excommunication; they could also "loose" or remove them from the penalty of forceful separation from the community of believers. The *Catechism of the Catholic Church* explains the meaning of "binding" and "loosing" in this way: "whomever you exclude from your communion, will be excluded from communion with God; whomever you receive anew into your communion, God will welcome back into his" (CCC 1445). Included in the idea of binding and loosing is the power to forgive sins by excommunication and reconciliation (cf. Mt 18:18; Jn 20:23).

The terms also had a secondary meaning which related to doctrinal decisions. Rabbis had the right to declare a teaching either licit or prohibited; they could approve or disapprove it. Consequently, they could "loose" or "bind" the consciences of individual community members.[38] Within Judaism, spiritual authority involved not only the disciplinary action of expelling someone from the community or readmitting him into it, but also the ability to distinguish between true and false doctrine.

According to traditional Catholic theology, Peter received an investiture that conferred on him a power to teach, sanctify, and direct the whole Christian people.[39] "The power to 'bind and loose' connotes the authority to absolve sins, to pronounce doctrinal judgments, and to make disciplinary decisions in the Church" (CCC 553). As the only recipient of the keys of the kingdom of heaven, Peter enjoyed a unique ministry in the Church. He was to bind and loose in a privileged way, corresponding to his particular authority. This power embraced the decision-making necessary for the community's well-being. Jesus told Peter that his decisions "on earth" would have value "in heaven," that is, in God's sight. God would bind and loose whatever Peter did.

This promise is related to Jesus' later pledge at the last supper to send the Spirit of truth to the Church. "But the Counselor, the Holy Spirit, whom the Father will send in my name, he will teach you all things, and bring to your remembrance all that I have said to you" (Jn 14:26, cf. 14:16-17). The Holy Spirit would communicate his decisions to Peter, who would ratify them and make them known.[40] The early community might well have interpreted Jesus' words about the "keys of the kingdom of heaven" and "binding and loosing" in such a way that they regarded Peter as empowered to act like a chief rabbi. As holder of the keys, he, too, could promulgate binding disciplinary rules and make authoritative doctrinal decisions.

Jesus' Prayer for Peter

Like Matthew, Luke also records Peter's privileged position in his gospel, probably written in the early 80s. Luke, for instance, omits any reference to Andrew when he narrates Jesus' call of the first disciples. In Mark and Matthew, the call of the first disciples is recounted straightforwardly. Jesus told the fishermen, "Follow me and I will make you become fishers of men"(Mk 1:17; cf. Mt 4:19). Luke's longer narrative highlights Peter as the first one whom Jesus called; Jesus engaged him alone in dialogue (cf. Lk 5:1-11). Though Simon's partners would also be fishermen, Jesus directed his promise to Peter personally: "Do not be afraid; henceforth you will be catching men" (Lk 5:10). In this way, Christ hinted that Peter would have a special community function. In his account, Luke looks forward to Peter's missionary role which he later documents in his second book, the Acts of the Apostles.

For the most part, Luke draws a very positive picture of Peter. He, too, puts Simon at the head of his list of the Twelve, noting that Jesus himself had named him Peter (cf. Lk 6:14). American Scripture scholar Raymond Brown notes that "as part of his general tendency to polish the image of the Twelve, Luke either omits or modifies some of the Marcan scenes most unfavorable to Peter."[41] Unlike Mark and Matthew, the third evangelist omits any references to Peter's refusal to accept Jesus' prediction of his upcoming passion and to his subsequent rebuke (cf. Mk 8:33; Mt 16:23). Furthermore, according to Luke, Peter is more modest in his protests that he would not deny Jesus (cf. Lk 22:33), saying it only once and not twice, as in Mark (cf. 14:29, 31). These Lucan nuances suggest that the evangelist, knowing Peter's role in the early community which he described in Acts, refrains as much as possible from drawing attention to any details which would tarnish the apostle's image.

Promise of Special Prayer

Taken from the last supper account, the second Petrine text is found only in Luke. It, too, records that Peter received a mission for the community's welfare. During the meal, Jesus confided to his disciples that they would soon be greatly agitated and spiritually tried ("sifted like wheat"). As God had allowed Satan to tempt Job (cf. Job 1:6-12), so would he permit Christ's disciples to undergo the upcoming violent temptations posed by the imminent catastrophe of the crucifixion. Luke contrasts the effects of Satan's attacks on Peter with those on Judas. The former repents; the latter despairs. Suddenly, in the midst of his concern for the disciples, Jesus turned to Peter and addressed him personally. As in the dialogue at Caesarea Philippi, here, too, Christ's words coupled a promise with a mission:

> "Simon, Simon, behold, Satan demanded to have you, that he might sift you [all] like wheat, but I have prayed for you that your faith may not fail; and when you have turned again, strengthen your brethren" (Lk 22:31-32).

Although Jesus prayed for all his followers, including those who would come afterward (cf. Jn 17:9-11, 20), he singled out Peter as the beneficiary of his special prayer. Foretelling the apostle's denial (cf. Lk 22:34), Jesus was aware of his weakness. Nonetheless, he did not spare him the temptations and trials endured by the other apostles. Christ prayed that Peter would persevere in faith and that in the time of trial, Satan would not prevail over Peter's confidence. Here Jesus promised to share his victory with Peter who, as a result, received a singular mission. Peter's faith was to be decisive for all.

Strengthening the Brethren

Peter received his privileges so that he might carry out a mission for the good of others. After he had acknowledged that Jesus' prayer had upheld him, Peter was to share that same strength, which had saved him, with his brothers. Whenever their faith would be threatened or weakened, the apostle was to support them with the power which he had received from Christ. Jesus assigned to Simon Peter the function of supporting the other apostles' faith. This call to "strengthen" them no doubt reminded the listeners at the table of the dialogue at Caesarea Philippi.[42] Peter's own experience of weakness and subsequent conversion, his "turning again," provided him with an experience of grace which would allow him to serve others in times of similar trial.

Just as Jesus gave Peter a share in his own steadfastness, so his prayer would enable the apostle to strengthen and encourage others to put their trust in God and the power of his grace, especially in the crisis provoked by Jesus' passion and crucifixion. Despite human weakness, God's power would be effective through Peter so that the community would endure. The "brethren" he is commanded to strengthen include not only the other apostles, but all who have a claim to discipleship. In Luke's view the "brethren" are the whole community (cf. Acts 1:15, 6:3, etc.).[43] All believers, therefore, were to benefit from Peter's ministry.

Peter as Shepherd of the Flock

Most likely written toward the end of the first century, the gospel of John is later than that of either Matthew or Luke. It was intended for a community familiar with both speculative Hellenistic thought and Jewish tradition. The fourth evangelist's presentation of Peter agrees with the general portrait in the synoptic gospels, containing evident parallels in the "naming" (cf. Jn 1:41-42) and "confession" scenes (cf. Jn 6:67-69). Nonetheless, John has his own concerns, including Peter's relation to the "beloved disciple." Like the synoptic writers, he understood that the story of Jesus and the early Church was intelligible only if it included Peter. Mentioning Peter more than any other evangelist, John records the apostle's misunderstanding of Jesus' act of washing the disciples' feet (cf. Jn 13:6-11), his readiness to protect Jesus at the time of his arrest (cf. Jn 18:10-11), and his impetuousness (cf. Jn 21:7-8). In keeping with his favorable portrait, John omits any reference to Peter as a hindrance or "stumbling block." According to Ratzinger, the Johannine tradition "offers us an absolutely clear witness for knowing that privileged position of Peter which derives from the Lord."[44]

In John's account of Peter's call, he is not the first one invited to be a disciple. Jesus first summoned Andrew, who then brought his brother Simon to him. Looking at this second recruit, Christ said to him: " 'So you are Simon the son of John? You shall be called Cephas' (which means Peter)" (Jn 1:42). The preservation of the Greek transliteration of the Aramaic *Kepha* probably reflects the dialogue at Caesarea Philippi, where Jesus changed Simon's name. Here the name change also follows upon a confession of faith, though John attributes it to Andrew, who announces it to Peter: "'We have found the Messiah' (which means Christ)" (Jn 1:41).

Later, however, Peter also confessed his faith in Jesus. Toward the end of the Eucharistic discourse (cf. Jn 6:1-71), Jesus posed a question to his followers about their willingness to accept the amazing doctrine of his flesh as "food indeed" and his blood as "drink indeed" (Jn 6:55). He then asked them, "Do you also wish to go away?" (Jn 6:67). Peter answered for the group: "Lord, to whom shall we go? You have the words of eternal life; and we have believed, and have come to know, that you are the Holy One of God" (Jn 6:68-69). Unlike the synoptic accounts, John does not here record that Jesus gave a particular mission to Peter.

Jesus' Forgiveness and Peter's Love

Though chapter twenty-one appears to be an addendum to John's original gospel, this closing chapter confirms both the role of the beloved disciple and that of Peter. The opening narrative records an appearance of the risen Jesus to the apostles at the Sea of Tiberias (cf. Jn 21:1-14). Like the similar account in Luke (cf. 5:1-11), John depicts Peter as a great missionary who was to "fish for men" in abundance. The fourth evangelist, however, also uses the narrative to tell of the beloved disciple's profound love for Christ. Because of his love, he had an intuitive insight into Jesus, recognizing him as the man on the beach who was giving the apostles instructions on how to fish. "It is the Lord!" (Jn 21:7), he exclaimed. Despite the beloved disciple's undisputed love for Jesus — he had stood by him at Calvary (cf. Jn 19:16-27) — it was not to him that Christ confided the care of his flock.

The third Petrine text records the lakeside conversation between Jesus and Peter after they had finished breakfast. Here the risen Jesus fulfills his promises to Peter. On the shore, Christ confirmed his earlier promise at Caesarea Philippi that he would grant Peter "the keys of the kingdom of heaven." Whereas Matthew's text announces Jesus' intention to found his Church (cf. Mt 16:18-19), here John proclaims its fulfillment. Like the other two Petrine texts, this one also narrates that Jesus engaged Peter personally in conversation and assigned him a particular mission:

> When they had finished breakfast, Jesus said to Simon Peter, "Simon, son of John, do you love me more than these?" He said to him, "Yes, Lord; you know that I love you." He said to him, "Feed my lambs." A second time he said to him, "Simon, son of John, do you love me?" He said to him, "Yes, Lord; you know that I love you." He said to him, "Tend my sheep." He said to him the third time, "Simon, son of John, do you love me?" Peter was grieved because he said to him the third time, "Do you love me?" And he said to him, "Lord, you know everything; you know that I love you." Jesus said to him, "Feed my sheep" (Jn 21:15-17).

Because Jesus wanted to know how intense Peter's love for him was, he asked him three times, "do you love me?" (Jn 21:15,16,17). When asking this question, he selected Peter from the other apostles, impressing upon his listeners that love of God was the condition for exercising ministry in the Church. It was because Peter loved Jesus that the Lord entrusted him with his flock. In transforming Simon into Peter, Jesus spared the apostle no humiliation. Wanting even greater love from him, Jesus asked, "Do you love me *more than these?*" (Jn 21:15). Peter had to learn how uncompromising Christ's desire for love was, so that he would be able to teach its demands to others.[45] Since Peter had no way of knowing whether he loved Jesus *more*, he replied three times, "Yes, Lord; you know that I love you."

Like Matthew and Luke, John also highlights Peter's spiritual frailty. Christ's triple question echoed the apostle's threefold denial (cf. Jn 18:17, 25-27), each protestation of love recalling an earlier act of betrayal. For every denial Jesus exacted a pledge of love. After each of Peter's affirmations, he confided him with a mission: "Feed my lambs . . . Tend my sheep . . . Feed my sheep" (Jn 21:15-17). Because each of Peter's declarations showed that he had turned back (cf. Lk 22:32), he was now ready to receive his office.

Pastor of Jesus' Sheep

This interchange between Jesus and Peter is not, however, only a touching scene of personal forgiveness. For John, it has implications for the whole community. The dialogue's structure and juridical language also suggest a formal exchange between them, one with important ramifications for all believers. Just as the rabbis used a formula that was repeated three times in the act of solemnly transferring authority, in the same way, Jesus revealed his will about the community's future. The threefold question and answer was a rite of installation, and here "in solemn juridical manner the risen Christ entrusts to Peter the care of his flock."[46]

In John's account, Jesus relied on the familiar imagery of "shepherding" to convey his intention about Peter's role in the community. The literature of antiquity often referred to the person responsible for guiding a community as a shepherd. Likewise, the Scriptures frequently described Yahweh himself as the shepherd of his people. Individuals invoked him as "my shepherd" (Ps 23:1), and the community prayed to him as the "Shepherd of Israel" (Ps 80:1). Rebuking the abuses in office of the kings of Israel, Jeremiah referred to them as wicked shepherds (cf. Jer 23:1-3). So, too, did Ezekiel. In reproaching the nation's leaders, he said: "Ho, shepherds of Israel who have been feeding yourselves! Should not shepherds feed the sheep?" (Ez 34:2) At the same time, the prophets looked forward to a time when God himself would pasture his people in place of the unfaithful guides: "He will feed his flock like a shepherd, he will gather the lambs in his arms, he will carry them in his bosom, and gently lead those that are with young" (Is 40:11; cf. Jer 31:10; Ez 34:11). Matthew records Micah's prophecy about Bethlehem: " 'for from you shall come a ruler who will govern [shepherd] my people Israel' " (Mt 2:6; cf. Mic 5:2).

Versed in the Jewish Scriptures, Jesus frequently used pastoral imagery during his public ministry. In the parable of the lost sheep he described God's care for his people (cf. Lk 15:4-7). He also spoke of his own mission "only to the lost sheep of the house of Israel" (Mt 15:24). John records that Jesus himself proclaimed that he fulfilled Israel's hope for the coming of the good shepherd: "I am the good shepherd. The good shepherd lays down his life for the sheep" (Jn 10:11).

In his gospel, John writes that Jesus chose Peter to tend his entire flock, entrusting him with a ministry to all the sheep. The sheep, however, remain Christ's: "feed *my* lambs . . . tend *my* sheep." He is the one who laid down his life for them. Totally dependent upon the Master who remains "the Shepherd and Guardian" of souls (1 Pet 2:25) and "the great shepherd of the sheep" (Heb 13:20), Peter was named visible shepherd of the community, the custodian with obligations.

What duties were implied in assigning Peter this pastoral ministry over Christ's flock? The two orders of Jesus, "feed" and "tend," are almost synonymous. While the former suggests the idea of nurturing, the latter implies leading or guiding. Together they connote that "feeding the sheep" should be understood as doing everything needed to safeguard those committed to the shepherd's care. In the background is the ideal good shepherd whom Jesus had described (cf. Jn 10:9-16). The pastor is to combine self-sacrificing love with the organizational ability and decision making necessary for tending the flock. In the Old Testament, "to tend" the sheep often implied the prerogatives of government (cf. 2 Sam 5:2; Is 40:11). Just as Jesus provides for his sheep, so must Peter, his pastoral vicar. According to the New Testament, the image of the shepherd "expresses great authority and responsibility."[47] Nourishing the flock means that the shepherd must protect them from heresy, ever ready to defend the sheep from marauders: "Take heed to yourselves and to all the flock, in which the Holy Spirit has made you overseers, to care for the church of God which he obtained with the blood of his own Son. I know that after my departure fierce wolves will come in among you, not sparing the flock" (Acts 20:28-29).

For the evangelist John, the pastor must be ready to give up his life as Christ did. Jesus, in fact, foretold that Peter would do this: " 'But when you are old, you will stretch out your hands, and another will gird you and carry you where you do not wish to go.' (This he said to show by what death he was to glorify God)" (Jn 21:18-19). Following the example of the Good Shepherd who gave his sheep eternal life, Peter was to be a means of leading to eternal life the flock entrusted to his care. His ministry was to be one of total self-dedication so that the disciples might "have life, and have it abundantly" (Jn 10:10).

As he shared in Jesus' steadfastness, so did Peter share in his pastoring. The risen Christ delegated Peter to take his place on earth. As shepherd, Peter was to represent the heavenly and exalted Lord. By the Sea of Tiberias, the Good Shepherd, as it were, handed over his pastoral staff to Peter, his chosen disciple, authorizing him to be his vicar. This was Christ's last command to the Church: he named Peter the shepherd of his flock. The apostle was to be the community's visible head. Entrusted to him were all who belong to Christ. As no one was excluded from Jesus' flock, so no one was excluded from Peter's care. His was a universal charge. And since the flock of Christ remains his after the apostle's death, this dialogue is directed not only to Peter personally but also to the pastoral ministry he embodied.[48]

A Weak and Sinful Man

A complete picture of Peter in the New Testament must take into account the narratives that betray his weakness and sinfulness. Closely associated with each of the Petrine texts describing Peter's greatness is a text recalling his frailty. Simon Peter fulfilled his ministry in the fullness of a humanity in need of mercy. For all the prominence the evangelists give to Peter, they do not ignore his fragile faith, denials, and the biting rebukes he received from Jesus. The fact that the tradition recalls these memories so straightforwardly testifies convincingly in favor of accepting that these accounts record events from Jesus' ministry and a post-resurrection appearance. They confirm Peter's foundational role in the Church, without in any way annulling or diminishing his authority. Because Christ had transformed Simon into the Rock for his community, the record of his failures does not undermine that role. Instead, it witnesses to the power of Jesus' prayer for Peter. Convinced that Jesus had chosen Peter for a special ministry, the evangelists can serenely recall his dark moments.

Although Mark describes Peter as the spokesman for the disciples (cf. Mk 1:35-38, 3:14-16, 9:2-13, 14:29-42), he also depicts him as embodying their failures (cf. Mk 8:27-33; 14:66-72). When Mark recounts the dialogue at Caesarea Philippi, Jesus does not reply to Peter's confession of faith by changing his name or making any promises. Instead, the evangelist passes immediately to Jesus' foretelling of the passion (cf. Mk 8:31-32) and his harsh rebuke to Peter: "Get behind me, Satan! For you are not on the side of God, but of men" (Mk 8:33). By his refusal to accept that the Messiah had to suffer, Peter misunderstood the implications of his confession.

Origins, Development, and Mission of the Papacy

Matthew likewise records Jesus' reprimand to Peter, adding the phrase, "You are a hindrance to me" (Mt 16:23). Whereas divine revelation had enabled Peter to recognize Jesus as the Christ, it was "flesh and blood" (Mt 16:17) that replied to Jesus' prophecy of the passion and of the kind of Messiah he was to be. Consequently, Peter was called "Satan" (Mt 16:23) insofar as he challenged Jesus' plans.

As the mainstay of the Church, Peter can carry out his function only by sharing in the human drama of faith with all its doubts and temptations. Matthew does not portray Peter as perfect but as a real man with problems and difficulties. While he was still a Protestant theologian, Max Thurian suggested that the painful memory of Peter's failures reminds the community that Jesus is the cornerstone on which the Rock rests. "Perhaps," he wrote, "Matthew feared that Peter would be over-idealized by the ecclesial community and that it would be given a sense of security more by the force of a human authority than by the faith of a frail being who has no other power than the constant support of Jesus Christ."[49] The Church is a place of forgiveness, and Peter "represents this fact in his own person since he, who can be the holder of the keys, although having fallen into temptation, is also capable of confessing his fault and is restored by means of forgiveness."[50] The apostle's fear-driven denial of Jesus later led to repentance and pardon.

Luke's dialogue between Jesus and Peter at the last supper emphasizes that the apostle is elected for a mission despite his own weakness (cf. Lk 22:31-32). During this conversation Jesus drew attention to the power of evil. Speaking about Satan's "sifting" the apostles (cf. Lk 22:31), he situated Peter's mission within the realm of spiritual combat. Jesus answered Peter's protestation of fidelity to death, "Lord, I am ready to go with you to prison and to death!" (Lk 22:33), with a rebuke: "I tell you, Peter, the cock will not crow this day, until you three times deny that you know me" (Lk 22:34).

Assailed by temptation, the apostle experienced a moment of weakness but did not lose his faith in Christ. Peter's faith was put to a difficult test. So was that of the other apostles (cf. Mt 26:30-35). In a realistic and dramatic way, Peter shared in their trials. He was thereby enabled and entrusted with strengthening the disciples' fidelity.[51] Thurian comments that "in Peter, therefore, the Church recognizes a man who had been tempted to weaken in his faith, but who was liberated by the efficacious prayer of Jesus and charged with the great mission of helping the other leaders of the Church not to fall into the same temptation of discouragement, not to abandon their faith, and to remain firmly in communion with Christ."[52]

In describing Peter's weakness in Gethsemane, the synoptics are unsparing. Jesus asked Peter, James, and John to "remain here, and watch" (Mk 14:34; cf. Mt 26:38). He later returned and said to Peter: "Simon, are you asleep? Could you not watch one hour? Watch and pray that you may not enter into temptation; the spirit indeed is willing, but the flesh is weak" (Mk 14:37-38; cf. Mt 26:40-41). Twice more he found the threesome sleeping. At the moment of Jesus' agony, Peter was anything but rock-like.

The passion narratives highlight Peter's denials. They were, as Swiss theologian Hans Urs von Balthasar wrote, "the last in a series of embarrassing misunderstandings about the real significance of Christ's existence."[53] Only with Jesus' assistance could

Simon be transformed into the promised Rock: "And the Lord turned and looked at Peter. And Peter remembered the word of the Lord" (Lk 22: 61). After his threefold denial of Christ, Peter wept bitterly (cf. Mt 26:75; Mk 14:72; Lk 22:62). His proud claim, "If I must die with you, I will not deny you" (Mk 14:31), had not resisted the accusations of a servant girl and other bystanders (cf. Mk 14:66-71). The apostle's tears betray that he was a truly repentant sinner.

John's Petrine text does more than just painfully recall the apostle's denial through Jesus' threefold question. It also contains a rebuke. When inquiring about the future of the beloved disciple, Peter asked, " 'Lord, what about this man?' Jesus said to him, 'If it is my will that he remain until I come, what is that to you? Follow me!' " (Jn 21:21). Peter was not to presume to make demands on Christ that were not associated with his mission.

Peter's human pretensions to steadfastness and fidelity floundered. This experience of sinfulness enabled Peter to put his trust neither in himself nor anything human, but only in Christ. Jesus did not promise to prevent Peter's denial and sin but to pray that the apostle's faith would never fail. Grace triumphed only through Christ's special prayer. God alone, not "flesh and blood," bridged the gap between Peter's good intentions and his human frailty. In John's seaside scene, Peter's ministry is situated within the order of grace.

John presents Peter as a man embodying both the need for reconciliation and the restoration to divine grace. Although holding the keys of the kingdom, the shepherd must ask for and receive forgiveness. Independently of any personal quality or merit, Christ conferred a specific ministry on Peter.

The gospels reveal that Peter was not only sometimes childishly impetuous (cf. Jn 13:9), lacking faith (cf. Mt 14:28-31), and a self-confessed "sinful man" (Lk 5:8), but also that he failed, at least initially, to comprehend Jesus' identity.[54] Only by divine Providence was Peter a solid rock. On his own he was an obstacle, a stumbling block, and a betrayer. Even so, Peter's personal weaknesses did not annul the ministry Christ assigned to him. Instead, they disclose that the apostle's role in the primitive Church was independent of the force of his personality or strength of his virtue. It was due to "a formal disposition by Christ," writes French theologian Louis Bouyer, "and therefore of an assured, unequaled, and corresponding charism."[55] As in the case of Paul (cf. 2 Cor 12:9), "grace is sufficient to Peter to achieve his fulfillment; the power of God is at its best in his weakness as a man."[56] The shadows surrounding the Petrine texts vividly proclaim the mystery of grace which is the core of Christ's message and redemptive sacrifice.

◆

Despite their exegetical difficulties, when the three Petrine texts are taken together, they provide a converging, convincing biblical witness that Jesus conferred on Peter a distinctive ministry. The Scriptures testify that a unique bond was forged between Jesus and the Galilean fisherman from Bethsaida. More than friendship, it involved Christ's entrusting specific responsibilities to his chosen apostle. We can distinguish three aspects of the office assigned: Peter was to be the keeper of the keys, the strengthener in the faith, and the pastor of the flock.

Origins, Development, and Mission of the Papacy

The singular mission confided to Peter is the foundation of later theological justifications for papal primacy. When the prerogatives from Matthew's gospel, couched in the images of rock, keys, and binding and loosing, are taken together, they lead to the conclusion that Jesus himself singled out Peter, delegating to him particular duties in the community. Notwithstanding discrepancies regarding the circumstances, the four evangelists record that Christ gave to Peter alone among the Twelve a new name, changing Simon's name to *Kepha* or Rock. Summarizing the significance of this divine action, Paul VI wrote: it allowed Peter to "be assimilated to Christ, his visible vicar, as we say, in the function of foundation, to support the building of which Christ says he wants to be the builder, the architect and the artist."[57] Because of the faith he confessed, Peter was chosen to provide the visible community with the stability of an unshakable rock.

Although the power of binding and loosing is closely linked to that of holding the keys and controlling access to the kingdom of God, the two are not identical. The keys specify a more comprehensive power than that of binding and loosing, especially since the latter responsibility also refers to the power given to all the apostles (cf. Mt 18:18). As gatekeeper, the only holder of the "keys of the kingdom of heaven," Peter was promised wider powers than those common to the other apostles.

Luke records that at the last supper Jesus promised to pray for Peter so that he might strengthen others (cf. Lk 22:32), the "all" for whom he gave his life. Despite his betrayal of the Master, Peter remained Jesus' chosen one. The apostle was therefore assigned the task of confirming the community's faith. Upheld by Jesus' own sustaining prayer, Peter was to share with others the divine strength he had received in time of trial.

In the third Petrine text, which John situates by the Sea of Tiberias after the resurrection, Peter was commissioned to be pastor of Jesus' flock (cf. Jn 21:15-17). As the one who sacrificed himself to defend and save his flock, Jesus remains the true pastor who alone knows how to guide his sheep. Nonetheless, John records that in the absence of the Good Shepherd, Peter was to tend the Master's flock. Furthermore, as St. Augustine comments, this ministry of feeding Christ's flock was to be carried out as "a duty of love."[58]

According to the Petrine texts, Peter receives *first* and *in a special way* a sharing in the messianic privileges which are later also communicated to others, as we shall see in the next chapter. This is true of his power to bind and loose, to strengthen his brothers, and to pastor the sheep. Peter's functions as the Church's rock-like foundation and holder of the keys are, however, unique.

The three classical texts provide a scriptural basis for holding that Jesus himself distinguished Peter among the Twelve, giving him a preeminent function in the early community. They point positively in the direction of the historical papacy which later developed from the leadership role that Jesus promised to Peter during his ministry and conferred after his resurrection. At the same time, in describing Peter's sinfulness, the New Testament also reveals the disproportion between the office and its incumbent. The evangelists emphasize that Peter was a sinner, capable of making mistakes. Even so, his personal weaknesses did not diminish the authority Christ conferred on him. In assigning to sinful Simon and his successors the function of being a rock, Jesus "makes it clear that it is not these men who sustain the Church, but only he who accomplishes it *in spite of* men, rather than *through* them."[59]

The Shepherd and the Rock

Notes for Chapter one

1. Johann Auer, *The Church: The Universal Sacrament of Salvation*, Dogmatic Theology, trans. Michael Waldstein. vol. 8 (Washington, D.C.: Catholic University of America Press, 1993), 228.
2. Raymond E. Brown, Karl P. Donfield, and John Reumann, eds., *Peter in the New Testament* (Minneapolis: Augsburg Publishing House, 1973), 19-20.
3. J. M. R. Tillard, *The Bishop of Rome*, trans. John de Satgé (Wilmington: Michael Glazier, 1983), 105.
4. Brown et al., *Peter in the New Testament*, 85, n. 192.
5. Tillard, *Bishop of Rome*, 108.
6. Oscar Cullmann, "Petros, Kephas," *Theological Dictionary of the New Testament*, ed. Gerhard Friedrich, trans. Geoffrey W. Bromiley, vol. 6 (Grand Rapids: Wm. B. Eerdmans Publishing Company, 1968), 100.
7. Karl Adam, *The Spirit of Catholicism*, rev. ed., trans. Justin McCann, (Garden City: Doubleday & Company, 1954), 91.
8. Cullmann, "Petros," 106.
9. Yves Congar, "La Chiesa è apostolica," in *L'evento salvifico nella comunità di Gesù Cristo*, Mysterium Salutis ed., Johannes Feiner and Magnus Löhrer, trans. Giovanni Moretto, Dino Pezzetta, and Gino Stefani, vol. 7 (Brescia: Queriniana, 1972), 685; cf. Leo Scheffczyk, *Il ministero di Pietro*, trans. Franco Ardusso (Turin: Marietti, 1975), 23-24.
10. Auer, *The Church*, 242.
11. Cullmann, "Petros," 105.
12. Brown et al., *Peter in the New Testament*, 92.
13. John P. Meier, *On Matthew* (Wilmington: Michael Glazier, 1980), 179.
14. Stanley L. Jaki, *The Keys of the Kingdom* (Chicago: Franciscan Herald Press, 1986), 39.
15. Stanley L. Jaki, *And on This Rock*, 2nd ed. (Manassas: Trinity Communications, 1987), 73-74.
16. Adam, *Spirit of Catholicism*, 94.
17. Jaki, *And on This Rock*, 77.
18. Congar, "La Chiesa è apostolica," 684.
19. Cullmann, "Petros," 103.
20. Congar, "La Chiesa è apostolica," 684.
21. Michael Schmaus, *The Church: Its Origin and Structure*, Dogma 4, trans. Mary Ledderer (New York: Sheed and Ward, 1972), 35-36.
22. For a list of patristic interpretations of the "rock," see J. M. R. Tillard, "The Presence of Peter in the Ministry of the Bishop of Rome," *One in Christ*, 27:2 (1991), 101, n. 1.
23. Otto Karrer, *Peter and the Church*, trans. Ronald Walls (New York: Herder and Herder, 1970), 17-18.
24. Cullmann, "Petros," 108.
25. J. M. R. Tillard, *Church of Churches: The Ecclesiology of Communion*, trans. R. C. De Peaux (Collegeville: Liturgical Press, 1992), 300.
26. Joseph Ratzinger, *Church, Ecumenism and Politics*, trans. Robert Nowell (New York: Crossroad Publishing Company, 1988), 35.
27. Congar, "La Chiesa è apostolica," 686; cf. Cullmann "Petros," 106.
28. Cited in Joseph Ratzinger, "The Primacy of Peter," *L'Osservatore Romano*, 27 (July 8, 1991), 5.

29. Karrer, *Peter and the Church*, 18.
30. Schmaus, *The Church*, 36.
31. Tillard, *Church of Churches*, 301.
32. Jaki, *Keys of the Kingdom*, 42.
33. Congar, "La Chiesa è apostolica," 687.
34. Auer, *The Church*, 269-270.
35. Jaki, *Keys of the Kingdom*, 43.
36. Jaki, *Keys of the Kingdom*, 43.
37. Schmaus, *The Church*, 36.
38. Congar, "La Chiesa è apostolica," 688.
39. Paul VI, *Insegnamenti di Paolo VI*, vol. 10 (Vatican City: Polyglot Press, 1973), 690.
40. Veselin Kesich, "Peter's Primacy in the New Testament and the Early Tradition," in John Meyendorff, ed., *The Primacy of Peter* (Crestwood, 1992), 51.
41. Raymond E. Brown, *Biblical Reflections on Crises Facing the Church* (New York: Paulist Press, 1975), 71.
42. Adam, *Spirit of Catholicism*, 95.
43. Rudolf Schnackenburg, *The Church in the New Testament*, trans. W. J. O'Hara (London: Burns & Oates, 1974), 68.
44. Ratzinger, "Primacy of Peter," 5.
45. Hans Urs von Balthasar, *The Office of Peter and the Structure of the Church*, trans. Andrée Emery (San Francisco: Ignatius Press, 1986), 20.
46. Schmaus, *The Church*, 38.
47. Auer, *The Church*, 275.
48. Auer, *The Church*, 245.
49. Max Thurian, "The Ministry of Unity of the Bishop of Rome to the Whole Church," *Bulletin/Centro Pro Unione*, 29 (Spring 1986), 10.
50. Ratzinger, "Primacy of Peter," 7.
51. Tillard, *Church of Churches*, 298.
52. Thurian, "Ministry of Unity," 12.
53. Hans Urs von Balthasar, *Elucidations*, trans. John Riches (London: SPCK, 1975), 100.
54. Brown et al., *Peter in the New Testament*, 160.
55. Louis Bouyer, *The Church of God*, trans. Charles Underhill Quinn (Chicago: Franciscan Herald Press, 1982), 379.
56. Thurian, "Ministry of Unity," 10.
57. Paul VI, *Insegnamenti di Paulo VI*, vol. 4 (Vatican City: Polyglot Press, 1967), 763.
58. Augustine, *Homilies on John*, 123.5
59. Ratzinger, "Primacy of Peter," 8.

Chapter two
PETER AND THE APOSTOLIC COMMUNITY

The three Petrine texts do not tell the whole story about Peter's vocation and mission in the early Church. The description of his role during Christ's public ministry is doubtlessly "colored" by later preaching and the editorial concerns of the New Testament writers. Nonetheless, the evangelists confirm that the apostle held a prominent position in the post-apostolic community.[1] They remembered and passed on in writing a remarkable portrait of Peter. This preferential treatment of the apostle by Jesus prepared the way for his function in the post-resurrection community.

In the early Church, did Peter claim by word or action, either explicitly or implicitly, any special functions? If he fulfilled a leadership role, did others accept it? By addressing these questions, I hope to shed light on the role of Peter in the apostolic Church and further identify the biblical foundation for a Petrine ministry.

After Jesus' ascension, Peter began to assert his ministry more forcefully. He began to exercise authority in the community. Besides being the spokesman and representative among the Twelve, functions which he had carried out during Jesus' lifetime, the apostle became the community's leader. Endowed by the Spirit with power and strength at Pentecost, Peter guided the Church's mission to both Jews and Gentiles. By examining the New Testament texts which recount the life of the first Christian communities, the implications of the exchanges between Jesus and Peter for the early Church become evident.

First Witness to the Risen Lord

Christ's post-resurrection appearance to Peter, recorded by Luke (24:34) and Paul (1 Cor 15:5), was decisive for the development of the chief apostle's ministry. Among the disciples, he "took the primary role as official proclaimer of the Lord's resurrection."[2] Peter's encounter with the risen Christ stands between his faltering confession at Caesarea Philippi and his bold proclamation on Pentecost. This experience "had the effect of ripening Peter's faith," says J. M. R. Tillard, "and so of transforming the place which he had held during the ministry of Jesus into an authentic primacy."[3] Peter's "primacy of faith" in the risen Lord complements his original confession of faith (cf. Mt 16:17).

Luke narrates that when two of Jesus' disciples rushed back from Emmaus to Jerusalem, anxious to tell the others what they had experienced on their journey, the Eleven met them with the announcement: "The Lord has risen indeed, and has appeared to Simon!" (Lk 24:34). No evangelist describes this appearance, but "it must have occurred in the Jerusalem area between Peter's Easter morning visit to the tomb when he did *not* see Jesus (cf. 24:12,24) and the evening return of the two disciples to Jerusalem."[4] Without drawing any attention to it, Luke inserts this kerygmatic proclamation into his narrative. Most probably he introduced it as a bridge to his Acts of the Apostles, preparing the reader for Peter's future role in the early Church as the primary official witness to the resurrection. Luke's announcement also calls to mind that Jesus' promised prayer for Peter had been efficacious. His betrayal forgiven, the apostle was now empowered to strengthen his brothers (cf. Lk 22:32) with the news that Jesus had triumphed over death.

Paul confirms the reliability of this Lucan tradition of an appearance to Peter. Writing in the early 50s to the Corinthians, Paul passed on to them a solemn creedal formula which he had received from the community. Composed within a decade of Christ's death, this primitive summary of the faith declared that "he was raised on the third day in accordance with the scriptures, and that he appeared to Cephas, then to the twelve" (1 Cor 15:4-5). It is probable that this appearance to Peter refers to the same one which Luke inserted into his gospel.

As in Matthew's account (cf. 16:18), Simon is given the Aramaic name *Kepha*, transliterated into Greek as *Cephas*. It is likely therefore that this ancient summary of the Church's *kerygma* originated in Palestine. Passing on this traditional formula, Paul places Peter's name at the head of the list of witnesses to the risen Jesus. Because Paul wanted to give the kerygma the value of a legal testimony, he omitted the women's testimony of a post-resurrection appearance to them (cf. Mt 28:9-10; Mk 16:9-11; Jn 20:14-18). Since their testimony would have been inadmissible in Jewish courts, for apologetic purposes the list begins with those who could serve as official witnesses. French Dominican theologian Yves Congar describes this order as "more qualitative than chronological."[5] Instead of emphasizing the temporal priority of Jesus' appearance to Peter, the creedal statement stresses the weightier value of his testimony. As Karl Adam notes, "St. Peter's pre-eminence as a witness is not to be explained by his being the first to believe in the Resurrection, but contrariwise it is by his already recognized pre-eminence that we must explain the special value which his testimony enjoyed."[6]

Although Luke and Paul most clearly describe this "firstness" or "primacy" of Peter as a witness to the risen Christ, John and Mark also tentatively hint at some kind of Petrine prerogative in this regard. John records that after Mary Magdalene had seen the stone removed from the tomb, she "went to Simon Peter and the other disciple" (Jn 20:2). The fourth evangelist notes, too, that the beloved disciple, upon arriving at the tomb on Easter morning, stepped aside to allow Peter to enter: "They both ran, but the other disciple outran Peter and reached the tomb first; . . . but he did not go in. Then Simon Peter came, following him, and went into the tomb" (Jn 20:4-6). Mark's gospel names Peter specifically as one to whom Christ would appear. His account of the angelic greeting to the women, "But go, tell his disciples and Peter that he is going before you to Galilee" (Mk 16:7), likewise suggests something unique about Peter's relation to the post-resurrection appearances. Called to strengthen the faith of his brothers, Peter sees the risen Lord before them (cf. CCC 641).

A strong biblical tradition exists, therefore, for affirming that Peter, who had first confessed Jesus as the Christ, is also the first official witness to his resurrection from the dead. Singled out by Jesus for unique responsibilities, Peter "received confirmation of this commission through the first appearance of the Lord after the resurrection," affirms

The Shepherd and the Rock

Oscar Cullmann, "so that he was properly instituted as the first leader of the Christian community."[7] Witness to Jesus' resurrection was essential to apostleship (cf. Acts 1:22). As the first one privileged, Peter was the first official bearer of the faith which created the Church. In this sense he was the "primate" in what was necessary to being an apostle — witnessing to the resurrection.[8] This priority corresponds to Peter's mission of strengthening his brothers in the faith (cf. Lk 22:32).[9] "Founded on faith in the resurrection," writes Tillard, "[Peter's] primacy will become a means of serving that faith."[10]

Leader of the Early Community

Written by Luke, probably during the 80s, the Acts of the Apostles narrates the story of early Christianity and its spread from Jerusalem to Rome. Without Peter, Luke could not have told this story of the Church's beginnings. Cullmann writes that "Acts tells us how Peter, after the death of Jesus, carries out the commission which he had received."[11] The first half of Acts presents Peter as the community's principal personage; the second half casts Paul in that role. Even after Paul's evangelizing activity had begun, however, Luke takes pains to stress that his missionary work was made possible through Peter.[12]

According to Acts, Peter both assumed and was accorded leadership in the early Church. He proved this leadership by being the "first" preacher, missionary, and healer. Primarily, however, he showed it by making decisions which demonstrated his authority as the keeper of the keys whose authority could bind and loose.

Among the apostles gathered in the upper room awaiting the coming of the Holy Spirit, Luke names Peter first (cf. Acts 1:13). This list follows the synoptic pattern cataloging the names of the Twelve, each of which mentions Peter first and Judas last; the remaining names are not in identical order (cf. Mt 10:2-4; Mk 3:16-19; Lk 6:13-16). Matthew is the most emphatic in expressing a priority for Peter. He begins his list by putting the adverb "first" before naming him: "The names of the twelve apostles are these: first, Simon, who is called Peter" (Mt 10:2). Mark and Luke record Peter's firstness less forcefully: "And he appointed twelve, to be with him . . . Simon whom he surnamed Peter" (Mk 3:14,16); and "he called his disciples, and chose from them twelve, whom he named apostles; Simon, whom he named Peter" (Lk 6:13-14).

Preacher

Peter first exercised leadership when he preached the great sermon on Pentecost: "But Peter, standing with the eleven, lifted up his voice and addressed them" (Acts 2:14). In the name of all who had been witnesses with him, Peter proclaimed that "this Jesus God raised up" (Acts 2:32). Furthermore, when the crowd wished to know how to respond to the good news, it was Peter who replied: "Repent, and be baptized every one of you in the name of Jesus Christ" (Acts 2:38). Like Christ, Peter initiated his own ministry with a call to conversion (cf. Mk 1:15). This Pentecost homily was the first of a series which he addressed to the crowds. Through his preaching Peter fulfilled Jesus' prophecy that his future role would be "catching men" (Lk 5:10).

Peter also defended the faith before the rulers of the people and elders in Jerusalem.

Origins, Development, and Mission of the Papacy

Filled "with the Holy Spirit" (Acts 4:8), he preached that salvation came only from Jesus (cf. Acts 4:12). Just as Peter had been the apostles' spokesman during the public ministry, he later carried out the same task on their behalf before the authorities (cf. Acts 4:19-20, 5:29-32). As leader of the early Christians, Peter guided the community's evangelizing effort, disobeying the authorities' orders not to teach in Jesus' name. When the apostles were arrested a second time, Luke writes that he again defended them: "But Peter and the apostles answered, 'We must obey God rather than men' " (Acts 5:29). This bold statement illustrates that Peter overcame the temptation to which he had succumbed during Jesus' ministry, when he was rebuked for setting his mind on human rather than divine things (cf. Mt 16:23).

Besides being the most active of the Twelve in Jerusalem during the Church's first years, Peter was also her greatest missionary. After going to Samaria with John (cf. Acts 8:14), he made the first missionary journeys to Lydda (cf. Acts 9:32) and to Caesarea (cf. Acts 10:1). His ministry later extended beyond Palestine, including Antioch (cf. Gal 2:11) and Rome, probably Corinth, and possibly Asia Minor (cf. 1 Pet 1:1). In writing to the Corinthians, Paul refers to a pro-Cephas party in their community (cf. 1 Cor 1:12). This group arose either because of a visit of Peter to that church or because some members had a special allegiance to him.[13] When addressing the Galatians, a predominantly Gentile community which he had himself evangelized, Paul simply assumes that they know who Peter is. He mentions Cephas' presence at Jerusalem and Antioch with no introductory explanation. Whenever Paul preached the gospel, Peter's role was part of the story.[14]

Miracle Worker

Acts also recognizes that Peter was the first miracle worker in the community. The cure at the Beautiful Gate of the cripple from birth shows this Petrine priority (cf. Acts 3:1-10). Accompanied by John, Peter addressed the cripple. Convinced that Christ had given him the power, he took the lame man by the hand to cure him: "But Peter said, 'I have no silver and gold, but I give you what I have; in the name of Jesus Christ of Nazareth, walk' " (Acts 3:6). The literary and theological similarity with the healing miracles of Jesus is apparent. A comparison between Peter's raising of Tabitha (cf. Acts 9:36-41) and Jesus' raising of the young girl (cf. Mk 5:38-42) illustrates the same point. The crowds also seemed to expect Peter, more than the other apostles, to perform miracles. They laid out their sick on cots and mats in order that "as Peter came by at least his shadow might fall on some of them" (Acts 5:15). In the Acts of the Apostles, Luke deliberately describes Peter as similar to Christ, "who was a prophet mighty in deed and word" (Lk 24:19).

Decision Maker

According to Luke, Peter took the initiative in resolving critical questions in the early Church, thereby assuming his position as the leader of the Twelve: in the election of Matthias, the confrontation with Ananias and Sapphira, the baptism of Cornelius, and the intervention at the council of Jerusalem.

• *CHOICE OF MATTHIAS* Immediately after Christ's ascension, the core group of apostles had to deal with the vacancy in their number left by Judas' betrayal and death. They were conscious of the symbolism that the Twelve, as the New Israel superseding the Old, were to render eschatological judgment seated on their thrones (cf. Lk 22:29-30). Peter assumed the authority to reconstitute the group as the Twelve. He noted the vacancy, called the election for a replacement, and established the criteria to be used for the choice: "In those days Peter stood up among the brethren . . . and said . . . 'So one of the men who have accompanied us during all the time that the Lord Jesus went in and out among us, beginning from the baptism of John until the day when he was taken up from us — one of these men must become with us a witness to his resurrection' " (Acts 1:15,21). Accepting his intervention, the Eleven carried out Peter's decision by casting lots and in that way added Matthias to their group (cf. Acts 1:26). As Jesus had called the Twelve from among his many disciples, so Peter assumed responsibility for maintaining the symbolic number of the Twelve originally designated by Jesus.

• *AUTHORITY TO JUDGE* Peter showed his singular disciplinary authority, his power in the Holy Spirit to bind and loose, within the young community. In the chilling tale of Ananias and Sapphira, who lied about the purchase price of some land and presented only part of the money to the apostles, Peter displayed his prophetic power (cf. Acts 5:1-11). Endowed with special insight, he perceived their avarice and desire to cheat the community (cf. Acts 5:3-4). Because of the impurity of their motives, the apostle pronounced divine judgment upon the couple. For Peter, lying to him was lying to the Holy Spirit: "You have not lied to men but to God" (Acts 5:4). As a punishment for their sins, both husband and wife died in front of him. Their sudden death, comments Stanley Jaki, "symbolized the supreme rule of the power of death" outside the kingdom of God whose keys Peter held.[15] Such awesome authority would not be understandable if it did not derive from Christ. In the case of Simon the Magician, Peter again judged motives, telling him, "your heart is not right before God" (Acts 8:21). According to Oscar Cullmann, both narratives are instances of the power of binding that Jesus gave Peter. When Peter judged, he did so in the name of God.[16]

• *EVANGELIZATION OF THE GENTILES* Still more expressive of Peter's authority was his resolution to open the Church to the Gentiles. He was the first to baptize pagans without making them accept the Jewish law beforehand. By making this decision, he initiated the evangelizing mission among the pagans. Acts narrates the event. One day Peter had a vision of ritually impure food which he was three times told to eat (cf. Acts 10:16). As well as echoing Jesus' threefold command to pastor his flock (cf. Jn 21:15-17), this detail also suggests, following standard Old Testament indications, that he was the recipient of supernatural revelation.[17] The Spirit bade Peter to overcome his obedience to Jewish ritual prescriptions (cf. Acts 10:19-20), ordering him to put aside his observance of the law.

Peter went to Caesarea, where he brought the good news to the pagan friends and relatives of the pagan Cornelius. While preaching to the Gentile centurion and his household, "the Holy Spirit fell on all who heard the word" (Acts 10:44). Peter recognized that this gift of the Spirit was the same as that given to the Jews. Consequently, "he

Origins, Development, and Mission of the Papacy

commanded them to be baptized in the name of Jesus Christ" (Acts 10:48). Convinced "that God shows no partiality" (Acts 10:34) and that he gives the pagans "the same gift" (Acts 11:17) offered to the Jews, the apostle was able to defend himself against the Jewish Christians who criticized his action. Judging Peter's account to be convincing, they subsequently sanctioned his unprecedented step: "When they heard this, they were silenced. And they glorified God, saying, 'Then to the Gentiles also God has granted repentance unto life' " (Acts 11:18). Peter carried the whole Church with his inspired decision. It was not Paul, the great apostle to the Gentiles, who began the mission to the pagans, but Peter, whose own evangelizing was confined primarily to the Jews.[18]

Enlightened by the divine light given in a vision, Peter resolved that the gospel should also be preached to the pagans, without requiring the demands of the Jewish law. This illumination, given personally to Peter so that he would make a decision in conformity with God's plan, guided and supported him in carrying out his revolutionary gesture.[19] Divine revelation inspired Peter's resolution to accept God's plan: the Gentiles did not first have to become Jewish proselytes, subject to the Mosaic law, before receiving baptism. Just as Peter's confession of faith in Jesus depended on "my father who is in heaven" (Mt 16:17), so was his decision to baptize Cornelius dependent on supernatural intervention. In both instances the Holy Spirit used Peter as his instrument, assuring that God was acting through him in what he said or did.

• *INTERVENTION AT JERUSALEM* At the Jerusalem council Peter also played a critical role (cf. Acts 15:1-29). Here the apostles and presbyters authoritatively resolved the question of the freedom of all Christians from the ritual practices of the law. In his speech, the first one for the event which Acts records, Peter began by recalling that "in the early days God made choice among you, that by my mouth the Gentiles should hear the word of the gospel and believe" (Acts 15:7). He then went on to speak in favor of freedom from Jewish ritual law. Against the Judaizing efforts of some converted Pharisees, he persuaded the assembly to confirm the earlier decision not to impose circumcision on the Gentile converts: "Now therefore why do you make trial of God by putting a yoke upon the neck of the disciples which neither our fathers nor we have been able to bear? But we believe that we shall be saved through the grace of the Lord Jesus, just as they will" (Acts 15:10-11).

By evoking the example of baptizing Cornelius, Peter's witness was determinative. After his intervention, the whole assembly fell silent (cf. Acts 15:12). Even James, who was not one of the Twelve but "the Lord's brother" (Gal 1:19) and head of the Jewish-Christian community at Jerusalem, realized that God had looked favorably on the Gentiles, admitting that Peter's position agreed with the words of the prophet (cf. Acts 15:14-21). At Jerusalem, Peter's authority was crucial in resolving a question essential to the Church's development. Despite his prominence at the meeting, he was, however, not the only important figure in the debate. James, the other apostles, and the elders also played a role in reaching the decision. Together the assembly exhibited their "one accord" (Acts 15:25). James pronounced the decisive judgment (cf. Acts 15:19-20), and the apostles and elders gave the sentence enforcing the decision (cf. Acts 15:23).[20]

Acceptance of Peter's Ministry

When Peter took charge in these numerous ways, the community calmly acquiesced to his direction. The apostles, who had been so jealous about occupying the first places in the kingdom (cf. Mt 20:20-28; Mk 10:35-45; Lk 22:24-27), accepted his leadership without argument. No outcries that Peter had abusively assumed authority greeted his functions as preacher, healer, and leader in the early Church. On the contrary, the community responded to his authority by offering special prayers on his behalf. When he was imprisoned by Herod, "earnest prayer for him was made to God by the church" (Acts 12:5). This prayer arose from the conviction that Peter was uniquely important to the Church's life.

In addition to receiving the support of the community's prayers, Acts also recounts that Peter enjoyed special divine protection. Twice he was rescued from prison. The first time, other apostles were arrested with him: "But at night an angel of the Lord opened the prison doors" (Acts 5:19). On the second occasion, King Herod put him in jail. The evening before his trial, an angel miraculously led Peter, who had been bound with chains, to freedom. At first he thought he was seeing a vision. But once free, Peter exclaimed: "Now I am sure that the Lord has sent his angel and rescued me" (Acts 12:11).

However Acts may reinterpret the events of the early Christian community in light of a later theology, the preeminence it attributes to Peter in its early chapters has historically solid roots.[21] Raymond Brown does not hesitate to affirm that "everywhere among Christian communities in the period of the 60s Peter's name would have been known and he would have been looked on as a figure of importance."[22]

Peter and the Other Apostles

Catholic theology underscores the three Petrine texts in the gospels as the primary sources for a biblical foundation for the papacy. They record Jesus' conversations with Peter *alone*, when he promised and conferred *unique* responsibilities on the apostle. Even so, they should not be interpreted in a way which separates Peter from the other members of the apostolic group. Jesus enjoyed rich relationships, living in a profound communion of persons, which included Mary, Joseph, John the Baptist, and the Twelve. Peter likewise lived in communion with the other apostles. He was, writes German theologian Hermann Pottmeyer, "determined through his 'being with' Jesus Christ, with Mary, and with the other apostles and disciples. . . . [T]he mission of Peter is intrinsically co-determined by the other callings."[23] As the first apostle, the Scriptures portray Peter as intimately associated with his companions in carrying out his apostolic tasks.

"Firstness"

Though Peter was the first of the apostles to be graced with a post-resurrection appearance, bringing the paschal faith to others, he was not the only official witness among them. Beginning on Easter evening, Jesus appeared several times to the Eleven as a group. Peter himself referred to these appearances, when he preached that "we are witnesses" (Acts 3:15) to the risen Christ. Paul confirms Peter's testimony when he reports that many other witnesses joined Peter in experiencing a post-resurrection appearance (cf. 1 Cor 15:6-8).

While undoubtedly testifying to Peter's singular mission, the Petrine texts are echoed in other biblical passages which refer to the apostles. A certain structure is evident in these texts: what is first given to Peter is then shared with the others. Some of them originate with Jesus himself; others come from the early community. Let us now look at the texts of Matthew, Luke, and John in the context which brings into focus the relation of Peter to the other apostles.

Although Jesus did not give the functional title "Rock" to his disciples as a group, the New Testament alludes to all the apostles as the foundation upon which the Church is built: "You are fellow citizens with the saints and members of the household of God, built upon the foundation of the apostles and prophets, Christ Jesus himself being the cornerstone" (Eph 2:19-20). They are the "twelve foundations" of the heavenly Jerusalem, having "on them the twelve names of the twelve apostles of the Lamb" (Rev 21:14). Jesus also gave to all the apostles the power to bind and loose: "Truly I say to you [plural], whatever you bind on earth shall be bound in heaven, and whatever you loose on earth shall be loosed in heaven" (Mt 18:18). They, too, had the power to make authoritative decisions, declaring something forbidden or permitted, and to teach authoritatively.[24]

Nor was Peter the only leader who assumed a responsibility for "strengthening" the community as Jesus had charged him at the last supper. Others, like Paul and Barnabas, did likewise; they returned to Lystra, Iconium, and Antioch "strengthening the souls of the disciples, exhorting them to continue in the faith" (Acts 14:22, cf. 18:23; Rom 1:11). Similarly, after the council in Jerusalem, "Judas and Silas, who were themselves prophets, exhorted the brethren with many words and strengthened them" (Acts 15:32).

Moreover, besides Peter, others carried out duties in the community for which they were fittingly called "shepherds." Luke relates Paul's words to the elders at Miletus: "Take heed to yourselves and to all the flock, in which the Holy Spirit has made you overseers, to care for the church of God which he obtained with the blood of his own son" (Acts 20:28). The letter to the Ephesians refers to the gift that some were "pastors" in the community (Eph 4:11; cf. 1 Pet 5:2). Peter was the first, but not the only, pastor. He was " 'first' but in solidarity and *communion* with all the Apostles," writes Tillard, " 'first' in what all the others have and are."[25] They, too, received their calling and mission directly from Christ.

Solidarity With the Twelve

According to the gospels, Peter acted in solidarity with the other apostles during Jesus' public ministry. The evangelists frequently present Peter as the apostles' spokesman: he answered questions directed to all of them, as at Caesarea Philippi (cf. Mt 16:16; Mk 8:29; Lk 9:20); he responded to Jesus' query about who touched the fringe of his cloak (cf. Lk 8:45); he expressed their astonishment after the miraculous catch of fish (cf. Lk 5:8); and he verbalized their doubts and critical questions (cf. Mt 15:15; Lk 12:41).

Outsiders to the group, like the tax collector, also turned to Peter as the group's representative (cf. Mt 17:24). The synoptic writers convey this primacy of Peter by referring to "Simon and those who were with him" (Mk 1:36) or to "Peter and those who were with him" (Lk 9:32). Moreover, with James and John, Peter formed a trio to which the evangelists give special prominence. They alone were present at two crucial moments of Jesus' life: at his transfiguration (cf. Mt 17:1-9; Mk 9:2-10; Lk 9:28-36) and in Gethsemane (cf. Mt 26:36-46; Mk 14:32-42; Lk 22:40-46). Even among this threesome, however, Peter stood out. He was the spokesman at the transfiguration and the one whom Jesus addressed in the garden.[26] These texts tell us that Peter had a special position during Jesus' public ministry. Nonetheless, as long as Christ was present, he was not yet fully the apostles' leader.[27]

John's gospel presents yet another example of Peter's apostolic solidarity. In the Johannine tradition, Peter was not the "first in everything": neither the first to follow Jesus nor to confess his messiahship. Nor was he first in the order of love.[28] John compares Peter to the disciple whom Jesus loved (cf. Jn 13:23-26, 18:15-16, 20:2-10, 21:1-23). The beloved disciple enjoyed a "primacy of love." This disciple was quicker to see, understand, and believe. He and Peter often appear together. Yet the beloved disciple is a kind of foil for Peter as the leader. Cullmann concludes that "the special position of Peter is not contested . . . [and] proves how firm was the tradition about the precedence of Peter among the disciples."[29] Brown thinks that the contrast between Peter and the beloved disciple is "a backhanded attestation to the importance of Peter as the apostolic witness best known to the Church at large."[30] While enjoying his own kind of primacy, the beloved disciple accepts Peter as the primary bearer of pastoral responsibility in the community.

Following the Johannine tradition, Luke's account in Acts describes Peter and John acting like a team after Pentecost.[31] Jointly they performed the first miracle in the apostolic Church (cf. Acts 3:1-11), and later the Jewish leaders arrested them together (cf. Acts 4:1-22). The Jerusalem apostles also sent Peter and John as a twosome to visit the recently baptized converts in Samaria (cf. Acts 8:14).

Like the gospel traditions, Acts frequently mentions Peter along with the other apostles (cf. Acts 2:37, 5:29). It also lists him first when naming members of the Twelve (cf. Acts 1:13, 3:1, 4:11,19). In its various traditions, the New Testament recognizes the close relationship of Peter both to other individual apostles and to them as a group.

Peter exercised his particular ministry from within the apostolic college and as a member of it. He "does not appear as a 'super apostle'," says Louis Bouyer, "but as the apostle in whom is found, personally reunited, everything that is shared or possessed in common by the whole apostolic college."[32] Still, his ministry was distinct. Because of his singular call by Christ and the unique tasks he received, Peter shared in the authority belonging to the Messiah himself.[33] Within the Twelve, he held a "special messianic vicariate." Peter received first, personally, and fully the mission and power which the other apostles received collectively.

Origins, Development, and Mission of the Papacy

Peter and Paul

The relation between Peter and Paul sheds further light on the Petrine ministry in the first generation. As the second great figure of early Christianity, Paul's attitude to Peter is particularly relevant to understanding the origin of the Petrine office.

Concerned with defending his own title as an apostle, "not from men nor through man, but through Jesus Christ and God the Father" (Gal 1:1), Paul referred to Peter only secondarily. Nevertheless, in Galatians and in 1 Corinthians, Paul mentions Peter frequently enough so that his attitude to Cephas emerges with notable clarity. Many Protestant scholars invoke Paul's dealings with Peter to argue against the existence of an authoritative Petrine ministry in the early Church. According to William Farmer, however, Paul passed on "a pro-Petrine if not an implicit Petrine-primacy tradition."[34] In order to support this thesis, several questions about Paul's recognition of Peter's role merit close examination.

In his letter to the Galatians, Paul wrote to a community in which there were Judaizers who insisted on circumcising Gentile converts before their baptism. It appears that these Judaizers invoked Peter's authority to justify this practice, trying to present him as one of their supporters. This was the "different gospel" (Gal 1:6) Paul so vehemently opposed. He addressed the Galatians to set the record straight: the Judaizers had no basis for appealing to Peter's authority to support their views. To prove his point, Paul described his encounters with Peter: two at Jerusalem and one at Antioch.[35] Despite the real difficulties between them, which he did not hide, Paul was satisfied that their disagreements had been resolved. His lively interchanges with Peter could not be used, he argued, to legitimate a practice which pitted one apostle against the other. Let us now look at these three meetings.

Paul's First Visit to See Peter

Paul was adamant that he had received the gospel from God himself (cf. Gal 1:11-12). Sent by the risen Christ, Paul had his apostolic credentials and authority from him. He began his mission without first conferring with any one or going up "to Jerusalem to those who were apostles" (Gal 1:17) before him. Even so, he was not an independent apostle. Paul knew about Peter, whom he always called by his functional title "Cephas." Three years after his conversion, he went to see him.[36]

Paul set out for Jerusalem "to visit Cephas and remained with him fifteen days" (Gal 1:18). Paul undertook this visit, which was not merely a courtesy call or a get-acquainted visit, without yet knowing Peter personally. During this first visit, Paul wanted to get more than the elementary facts about Jesus. This information he undoubtedly already had from his days of persecuting the Church, when he would have familiarized himself with Jesus' teaching.

Though his faith was already firmly grounded from his own revelatory experience, in his "apostolic concern to 'get it right' "[37] from an eyewitness, Paul went to question Peter. The recent convert wanted to get first-hand information about Jesus. It was "most likely that Paul questioned at length the chief eyewitness of the earthly life of Jesus and the first witness of the risen Christ about those traditions whose truth Paul considered central to his preaching."[38] This two-week stay, a rather long time for a visit, equipped Paul to "leave informed and ready to report to others on the results of his inquiry."[39] By making his visit to Jerusalem, the Apostle to the Gentiles recognized the desirability of having Peter's authority confirm his work of evangelization.

Communion With "the Pillars"

Some time later, "by revelation" (Gal 2:2), Paul set out for a second meeting with Peter: "Then after fourteen years I went up again to Jerusalem" (Gal 2:1). Having preached the gospel to the Gentiles, without requiring their circumcision before entry into the Church, Paul wanted to be certain that he was acting in accord with the Jerusalem authorities. He was anxious that these leaders, including Peter, approve his preaching the gospel unencumbered by the law. Consequently he went to visit "those who were of repute . . . lest somehow I should be running or had run in vain" (Gal 2:2). Paul narrates this encounter because he was eager to remind the Galatians that the highest possible authorities had cleared him for his mission to the Gentiles.

Whatever Paul's feelings about James, Cephas, and John, he went to Jerusalem owing to their prominence in the community. At least some Christians referred to these three as "pillars" (Gal 2:9), and Paul himself took them seriously.[40] He knew that he could be certain of preaching the authentic gospel only if it agreed with that of the "pillars"; they were its criterion.[41]

The order in which Paul mentions the three is deliberate: "James and Cephas and John" (Gal 2:9). James was the leader of the local community at Jerusalem, deserving first place for that reason alone. He was also the foremost among those who favored imposing the law on Gentiles admitted to the Church. Cephas was listed second. Does Paul mean to suggest James' superiority to Peter? Not at all. Paul knew that Peter was the first witness to the *kerygma* of Jesus' resurrection (cf. 1 Cor 15:5), before James (cf. 1 Cor 15:7), a tradition he scrupulously transmitted. Furthermore, Paul looked to Peter, not to James, as a model for his own gospel (cf. Gal 2:7-8). Therefore, even though Paul referred to James first, he was not arguing for Peter's subordination to James.

Realizing that the leaders in Jerusalem had the power to break communion with him, Paul was cautious and respectful. He had no intention of dividing the followers of Christ.[42] During this second visit, the Jerusalem "pillars" acknowledged that Paul had received the grace to undertake an apostolic mission to the Gentiles, just as Peter had for the Jews (cf. Gal 2:7). Because Paul took these leaders seriously, he reported that they "gave to me and Barnabas the right hand of fellowship" (Gal 2:9). Paul interpreted this handshake of *koinonia* as legitimating his mission. Offered by Peter, along with James and John, it was "the sign and the effective means of realizing the collegial unity of all the apostles of Jesus Christ."[43]

Confrontation at Antioch

After recounting his second visit to Jerusalem, Paul then narrated his encounter with Peter at Antioch. Both apostles went there after the council at Jerusalem. Here the Apostle to the Gentiles says that he "opposed him [Peter] to his face, because he stood condemned" (Gal 2:11). This incident, in which Paul reprimanded Peter for being in the wrong, is frequently adduced by those who claim that Paul denied Peter's authority by this admonition. What are the facts?

Some Christians coming from Jerusalem, "from James," wanted to impose on Gentile converts the dietary regulations of the Mosaic law, though not circumcision, a matter which had already been settled (cf. Acts 15:1-12; Gal 2:3-9). Peter, who had formerly fraternized with Gentile converts and enjoyed table fellowship with them, apparently changed his mind: "For before certain men came from James, he ate with the Gentiles; but when they came he drew back and separated himself, fearing the circumcision party" (Gal 2:12).

Others, Paul says, also "acted insincerely" (Gal 2:13). This defection, even of Paul's companion Barnabas, alludes to the high esteem in which Peter was held and how seriously his positions were taken.[44] Peter's behavior threatened both the unity of the Antiochene community and the freedom of all Christians from Jewish dietary law. Paul believed that his action compromised "the truth of the gospel" (Gal 2:14). Significantly he delivered his rebuke not to Barnabas, but only to Peter. Furthermore, Paul was little concerned with the opposition of James or his group. They provoked only his sarcasm.

Knowing that Peter had previously agreed otherwise, Paul called him to account for concealing his true convictions. Both apostles had already come to an understanding: evangelizing the Gentiles would not require submission to the requirements of the Mosaic law, whether circumcision or dietary rules. The fact that Peter acted as if he had changed his mind about the "freedom which we have in Christ Jesus" (Gal 2:4) troubled Paul. Peter's gesture implied that he was going back on the agreement reached by the Church. And what Peter allowed and did mattered to Paul. He rebuked Peter for his dishonesty in believing one thing — the unity of Jews and Gentiles — and doing another. "But when I saw that they were not straightforward about the truth of the gospel, I said to Cephas before them all, 'If you, though a Jew, live like a Gentile and not like a Jew, how can you compel the Gentiles to live like Jews?' " (Gal 2:14).

At Antioch, Paul thought that Peter's concession to the Judaizers was ambiguous and full of dangers.[45] It played into the hands of those wishing to saddle Gentile converts with the whole Mosaic law. Precisely because Peter's authority was exceptional, a public settlement with him was called for.[46] According to Bouyer, this incident reveals that Paul's relations with Peter "were not burdened with modern ecclesiastical protocol" and that "Peter's authority, in what he said and in what he would allow to be believed, was of capital importance for Paul."[47] However great Peter's recognized authority, he, too, stood under the judgment of the gospel.[48] For this reason, Paul demanded that the practice previously agreed upon be reconfirmed.

Scripture does not tell us why Peter acted as he did. It could be, as Otto Karrer suggests, that he wanted to keep peace with the Jewish Christians, finding a way out of the problem they presented. After all, Paul himself had let Timothy be circumcised for a similar reason (cf. Acts 16:3), for the sake of peace. Paul did not wholly or relentlessly

The Shepherd and the Rock

exclude every concession to those who continued to accept certain demands of the law. He had proclaimed that "to those under the law I became as one under the law" (1 Cor 9:20). It is very possible that Peter, like Paul, had the best of intentions, trying as far as possible to avoid open conflict with the Judaizers.[49] When challenged by Paul, who thought his position was cowardly, Peter allowed his behavior to be corrected.

Paul rebuked Peter because he wanted to correct a faltering brother, not because of a doctrinal divergence between them. "For if there is one thing that is certain in church history," writes Farmer, "it is that in spite of any pig-headedness on the part of either or both of these great apostles, they did stand together on the fundamental theological basis of the faith."[50] Paul's opposition to Peter centered "not on Cephas as a person claiming undue authority but on Cephas as acting without principle."[51] While never doubting his own apostolic authority, Paul nonetheless accepted the place which Peter held in the community, while ever ready to judge his actions and decisions. He rejected forcefully any suggestion that people were to choose between him and Peter (cf. 1 Cor 1:12, 3:22). For his part, Peter never had misgivings about the full apostolicity claimed by Paul and recognized his mission to the Gentiles (cf. Gal 2:7).[52]

Despite Peter's function as the rock-apostle, he remained vulnerable to the personal weakness and temptations of Simon. The Apostle to the Gentiles reproved Peter's way of acting, but without questioning his leadership role in the Church.

Images of Peter in the Later New Testament

The facts of Peter's life do not exhaust all that the New Testament writers had to say about his mission in the early community. Also significant are the "images" of Peter which they put together to form a portrait of him. These different impressions developed as the community grew. They form a sequence "in which the various images of the apostle reinforce, modify, and interpret each other."[53] Even before his death, but increasingly so afterward, Peter was a symbol of pastoral leadership in the Church. The series of images evolved in the apostolic age, showing that Peter's mission was increasingly recognized as the Church moved away from the first generation. Early Christians were not only interested in Peter's historical person but also in the continuing Petrine function which he personally embodied. For the biblical portrait of Peter to be complete, these Petrine images should be delineated.[54] In some way, each one points to the later functions that would be attached to the Petrine ministry.

The two New Testament letters, 1 and 2 Peter, put the final touches on the portrait of the apostle that was emerging in the early Church. Although scholars are divided about whether Peter himself authored the first letter attributed to him, nearly all reject that he wrote 2 Peter.[55] Nonetheless, whoever their author was, these letters provide valuable testimony to the continuing influence which second-generation Christians attributed to Peter. The very fact that his name was attached to these letters (cf. 1 Pet 1:1; 2 Pet 1:1, 3:1), which give instructions to other churches, shows that great authority derived from being associated with Peter's name. They witness to a widespread and living Petrine authority.[56]

Origins, Development, and Mission of the Papacy

These two canonical letters provide yet another illustration of an evolving Petrine tradition in the early community. This tradition moved in the direction of attributing to Peter an increasingly influential role. As time passed, Peter's stature grew in the Church. Building on the original events of Jesus' public ministry and of the early community, second-generation Christians not only preserved but also magnified their portrait of the apostle and his mission. As the outstanding witness to the earthly and risen life of Jesus, Peter emerged as the prototype of the guarantor and teacher of the tradition and as the symbolic figure of the community's leader and pastor.[57]

The following four images of Peter, drawn from different New Testament traditions, summarize the preeminent position assigned to Peter as described in the last decades of the first century and the early decades of the second century.

Evangelizer

Unlike most of the other members of the Twelve, Peter had a great missionary career, both to the Gentiles (cf. Acts 10:1-11:18) and the Jews (cf. Gal 2:7-8). With the passing of time, the community increasingly emphasized his evangelizing function. According to 1 Peter, the apostle was a zealous preacher of the gospel. By addressing "the exiles of the Dispersion in Pontus, Galatia, Cappadocia, Asia, and Bithynia" (1 Pet 1:1), the epistle reinforces Peter's image as a missionary. In more symbolic fashion, chapter twenty-one of John's gospel records Peter's initiative in going fishing and hauling ashore the net full of fish, bringing them to Jesus. The community remembered Peter as the one who, through Jesus' power, would be "catching men" (Lk 5:10), a fact testified to by his successful evangelizing endeavors.

Shepherd

After the first tumultuous years, as it became clearer that the age of the Church was to be prolonged, the community settled down to a more stable existence. Consequently, it turned its attention to permanent ministries. When the missionary enterprise was foremost, Peter emerged as the model evangelizer. Later, when pastoral concerns also moved to the forefront of the community's concerns, Peter was described as the most prominent of those entrusted with pastoral care of the flock. In the New Testament, the symbol of the shepherd increasingly indicated this pastoral task, complementing, even replacing, the image of an evangelizing fisherman. "The shift from fisherman to shepherd," writes Brown, "may well reflect the history of Peter's image in the Church."[58] Commenting on this powerful image of shepherding, Anglican theologian John de Satgé says: "Self-sacrificing care is mixed with organizing ability, decision-making, and the management of men. The image is physical as well as spiritual and implies structure, control, adaptability, continuity. It suggests not simply people, but people living in social structures. The sheep are not scattered but gathered into a fold."[59] Shepherd symbolism was well adapted to the attention which the community more and more gave to being guided by its leaders.

The two Petrine letters confirm the growing relevance of this pastoral imagery. Peter's first letter presents the chief apostle as the model elder or pastor who assumed the right, in fraternal fashion, to instruct others about their duties: "So I exhort the elders among you, as a fellow elder and a witness of the sufferings of Christ . . . Tend the flock of God that is your charge" (1 Pet 5:1-2). Peter counsels the elders, just as he had been counseled by Christ (cf. Jn 21:15-17). But in this letter he does not present himself as their equal. Instead, he uses "a polite stratagem of benevolence" in addressing them.[60] Mindful that Jesus was "the chief Shepherd" (1 Pet 5:4) and "the Shepherd and Guardian" of their souls (1 Pet 2:25), the second-generation community nevertheless acknowledged that Peter rightfully assumed the mantle of pastoral direction over them, a responsibility deriving from the memory of Jesus' commission to the apostle.

Martyr

Closely linked to the image of Peter as shepherd is that as martyr. Jesus had foretold that he would follow in the footsteps of the Good Shepherd who laid down his life for his sheep (cf. Jn 13:36, 21:18).[61] John's editorial comment on Jesus' prediction that Peter would be led where he would rather not go ("This he said to show by what death he [Peter] was to glorify God" [Jn 21:19]) implies that the evangelist already knew about the apostle's martyrdom when he wrote his gospel.

Second-generation Christians recognized that martyrdom was intrinsic to Peter's mission in the community. Since he shared uniquely in Jesus' authority, he was obliged "specially to participate in Jesus' spirit of service and his readiness to suffer."[62] Peter fulfilled his role as rock and keybearer by his willingness to follow Jesus' example in accepting the cross. Martyrdom was the culmination and seal of his office which embodied the mission of Jesus, the chief Shepherd.[63] Peter gave an example as "a witness of the sufferings of Christ" (1 Pet 5:1), providing a model for all other pastors of that love unto death which they were to show to their flocks.

Guardian of the Faith

In the gospel accounts of Jesus' public ministry, Peter is presented as the great confessor of faith in Jesus as the Messiah (cf. Mt 16:17; Mk 8:29; Lk 9:20; Jn 6:69). Dependent upon divine inspiration, he is the first and representative recipient of the truth that "no one can say 'Jesus is Lord' except by the Holy Spirit" (1 Cor 12:3). Building on this tradition, the later New Testament books regard Peter as the guardian of orthodox faith against false teaching. They link this custodial role of safeguarding doctrine with the power of authoritative teaching implied by binding and loosing.

Probably the last written New Testament book, 2 Peter testifies to the doctrinal responsibility associated with Peter's mission. The letter emphasizes the need to maintain the Petrine tradition of witnessing to the truth about Jesus, even after the apostle's death: "Therefore I intend always to remind you of these things. . . . And I will see to it that after my departure you may be able at any time to recall these things" (2 Pet 1:12, 15). Endeavoring to preserve the legacy of true teaching, the author cites Peter as an eye-witness able to guarantee the authenticity of the message in face of "cleverly devised myths" (2 Pet 1:16).

Origins, Development, and Mission of the Papacy

In describing Peter's mission in the Church, the pseudonymous author of 2 Peter assumes that the apostle had the right to interpret Scriptures, especially prophecies (cf. 2 Pet 1:19-21). The letter also represents Peter as guarding the faith against false teaching, correcting those who were misinterpreting Paul's letters and instructions: "There are some things in them hard to understand, which the ignorant and unstable twist to their own destruction, as they do the other scriptures. You therefore, beloved, knowing this beforehand, beware lest you be carried away with the error of lawless men and lose your own stability" (2 Pet 3:16-17); 2 Peter "implies that it is Peter who holds the key to the right interpretation of the Pauline corpus,"[64] even daring to correct the misinterpretations of other apostles. Brown concludes that its author "calls upon the authority of Peter who speaks magisterially as the interpreter of sacred writings against false prophets (1:20ff)."[65] The sequence of images that began with Peter's recognition of Jesus as the Christ ends with the apostle protecting the orthodoxy of the faith.

◆

According to the witness of sacred Scripture, during the public ministry Peter was the spokesman and representative of the disciples. Jesus' story cannot be told without encountering Peter at its key moments. After the resurrection, Peter was recognized as the most esteemed and influential among the Twelve, becoming the central figure who directed the community's early life. Exegetical studies have reached a surprising conclusion in recent years: from the beginning, Peter exercised decisive authority in the Church.

The reasons justifying Peter's special ministry are found in the Bible. He received from Jesus, along with special friendship, a unique commission. Not merely the recipient of personal privileges, Peter, whose very name indicates his function, was entrusted with a special mission in the Church. He was appointed the rock-foundation of Christ's messianic community and the keeper of the keys of the kingdom of heaven. Sustained by Jesus' prayer, Peter was to pass on this strength to others, pastoring Christ's own flock.

After Pentecost, Peter carried out the duties of leadership in the Church. In describing the fulfillment of Jesus' promises to Peter, the Acts of the Apostles shows "the primacy in action."[66] He was "vicar" for his Master through his preaching, miracles, and authority. Indicative of Peter's leadership was the authority he exercised in dealing with Ananias and Sapphira (cf. Acts 5:1-11) and Simon the Magician (cf. Acts 8:9-24). In addition, his decision to admit pagans into the Church (cf. Acts 10:1-11:18) and his crucial intervention at the council of Jerusalem (cf. Acts 15:6-12) confirmed his singular function in the community.

The apostle would not have dared to assume a guiding role, nor would the Church have so calmly accepted it, if Jesus had not established it. Even when Peter's personal conduct shows signs of the old Simon, as at Antioch, his preeminence remains uncompromised. This role derives in substance, if not in every detail, from the promise and commission of Christ which the earliest Christian community ratified through its practice.

Despite the uniqueness of his own duties, Peter maintained close fellowship with his fellow apostles. The biblical testimony affirms that Peter was both one of the Twelve and also its leader. He exercised his "firstness" without breaching his solidarity with the apostles. Nonetheless, because of his own mission and power, Peter often took the initiative in deciding matters for the Church.

The New Testament presents Peter's special function as both the will of Jesus expressed during his ministry and that of the risen Lord. It provides sufficient basis for a divinely-given Petrine ministry directed to the care of all Christians. Several decades after Jesus' death, "the Christian community has, in the Spirit, the firm conviction that the role played by Peter after Pentecost is not explained by accidental circumstances," concludes Tillard, but instead "it comes from the design of Jesus himself."[67] Nonetheless, this divine plan contained no clear model regarding how it was to be carried out in the Church's later life. Scripture presents the essential components of Peter's office, but leaves open future developments. The structural elements of such a function, by no means fully realized in the early community, included the task of consolidating the Church, authoritatively guiding her, reinforcing her faith, and pastoring her for Christ. The subsequent office, which we call the papacy, grew from its roots in Peter's ministry as rock, keybearer, supporter, missionary, shepherd, martyr, confessor, and guardian of the faith.

Catholics believe, therefore, that the seeds of the papal ministry are in the Bible. It contains a dynamic series of functions linked to Peter's mission which eventually became embodied in the papacy. This biblical profile of Petrine responsibility provides the outline against which all later developments can be judged insofar as they are in continuity or discontinuity with these origins. To the shape that Peter's ministry took after his death we shall now turn.

Notes for Chapter two

1. Raymond E. Brown, *Responses to 101 Questions on the Bible* (New York: Paulist Press, 1990), 128.
2. Gerald O'Collins, *Jesus Risen* (New York: Paulist Press, 1987), 162.
3. J. M. R. Tillard, *The Bishop of Rome*, trans. John de Satgé (Wilmington: Michael Glazier, 1983), 113.
4. Raymond E. Brown, Karl P. Donfried, and John Reumann, eds., *Peter in the New Testament*, (Minneapolis: Augsburg Publishing House, 1973), 125-126.
5. Yves Congar, "La Chiesa è apostolica," in *L'evento salvifico nella comunità di Gesù Cristo*, Mysterium Salutis, ed. Johannes Feiner and Magnus Löhrer, trans. Giovanni Moretto, Dino Pezzetta, and Gino Stefani, vol. 7 (Brescia: Queriniana, 1972), 682.
6. Karl Adam, *The Spirit of Catholicism*, rev. ed., trans. Justin McCann (Garden City: Doubleday & Company, 1954), 104.
7. Oscar Cullmann, "Petros, Kephas," *Theological Dictionary of the New Testament*, ed. Gerhard Friedrich, trans. Geoffrey W. Bromiley, vol. 6 (Grand Rapids: Wm. B. Eerdmans, 1968), 104.
8. Congar, "La Chiesa è apostolica," 696.
9. John Paul II, Discourse, December 16, 1992, *L'Osservatore Romano*, 51/52 (December 23/30, 1992), 9.

10. Tillard, *Bishop of Rome*, 113.
11. Cullmann, "Petros," 109.
12. John de Satgé, *Peter and the Single Church* (London: SPCK, 1981), 11.
13. Cullmann, "Petros," 111.
14. Raymond E. Brown, *Biblical Reflections on Crises Facing the Church* (New York: Paulist Press, 1975), 69.
15. Stanley L. Jaki, *The Keys of the Kingdom* (Chicago: Franciscan Herald Press, 1986), 49.
16. Oscar Cullmann, *San Pietro: Discepolo, Apostolo, Martire* [1960] in *Il Primato di Pietro*, ed. Oscar Cullmann et al. (Bologna: Mulino, 1968), 39.
17. De Satgé, *Peter and the Single Church*, 18.
18. De Satgé, *Peter and the Single Church*, 27.
19. John Paul II, Discourse, January 13, 1993, *L'Osservatore Romano*, 3 (January 20, 1993), 11.
20. Brown et al., *Peter in the New Testament*, 50.
21. De Satgé, *Peter and the Single Church*, 30.
22. Brown, *Responses to 101 Questions on the Bible*, 128.
23. Hermann J. Pottmeyer, "Why Does the Church Need a Pope?" *Communio*, 18:3 (1991), 309.
24. Francis A. Sullivan, *The Church We Believe In: One, Holy, Catholic and Apostolic* (New York: Paulist Press, 1988), 159.
25. J. M. R. Tillard, *Church of Churches: The Ecclesiology of Communion*, trans. R. C. De Peaux (Collegeville: Liturgical Press, 1992), 295.
26. Joseph Ratzinger, "The Primacy of Peter," *L'Osservatore Romano*, 27 (July 8, 1991), 5-6.
27. Rudolf Schnackenburg, "Die Stellung des Petrus zu den anderen Aposteln," in *Petrus und Papst*, ed. Albert Brandenburg and Hans Jörg Urban (Münster: Aschendorff, 1977), 26.
28. Tillard, *Church of Churches*, 295-296.
29. Cullmann, "Petros," 102.
30. Brown, *Biblical Reflections on Crises Facing the Church*, 75.
31. Brown et al., *Peter in the New Testament*, 161.
32. Louis Bouyer, *The Church of God*, trans. Charles Underhill Quinn (Chicago: Franciscan Herald Press, 1982), 379.
33. Leo Scheffczyk, *Il ministero di Pietro*, trans. Franco Ardusso (Turin: Marietti, 1975), 29.
34. William R. Farmer and Roch Kereszty, *Peter and Paul in the Church of Rome* (New York: Paulist Press, 1990), 47.
35. Brown et al., *Peter in the New Testament*, 25-26.
36. Johann Auer, *The Church: The Universal Sacrament of Salvation*, Dogmatic Theology, trans. Michael Waldstein, vol. 8 (Washington, D.C.: Catholic University of America Press, 1993), 233.
37. Farmer and Kereszty, *Peter and Paul in the Church of Rome*, 36.
38. Farmer and Kereszty, *Peter and Paul in the Church of Rome*, 6.
39. Farmer and Kereszty, *Peter and Paul in the Church of Rome*, 39.
40. Brown et al., *Peter in the New Testament*, 29.
41. Ratzinger, "Primacy of Peter," 5.
42. Brown, *Responses to 101 Questions on the Bible*, 131.
43. Farmer and Kereszty, *Peter and Paul in the Church of Rome*, 124.
44. De Satgé, *Peter and the Single Church*, 29.
45. Congar, "La Chiesa è apostolica," 694.

46. Adam, *Spirit of Catholicism*, 102.
47. Bouyer, *Church of God*, 380.
48. Tillard, *Bishop of Rome*, 116.
49. Otto Karrer, *Peter and the Church*, trans. Ronald Walls (New York: Herder and Herder, 1970), 44.
50. Farmer and Kereszty, *Peter and Paul in the Church of Rome*, 49.
51. Brown et al., *Peter in the New Testament*, 30.
52. Jean-Jacques von Allmen, *La primauté de l'église de Pierre et Paul* (Paris: Cerf, 1977), 67.
53. De Satgé, *Peter and the Single Church*, 17.
54. Edward Yarnold, "Theological Trends: The Papacy I," *The Way*, 19:3 (1979), 221.
55. Brown et al., *Peter in the New Testament*, 16, 149-152, 154-155.
56. Schnackenburg, "Die Stellung des Petrus," 33.
57. Pottmeyer, "Why Does the Church Need a Pope?" 308.
58. Brown, *Biblical Reflections on Crises Facing the Church*, 74.
59. De Satgé, *Peter and the Single Church*, 21.
60. Brown et al., *Peter in the New Testament*, 152.
61. Brown et al., *Peter in the New Testament*, 164.
62. Hans Urs von Balthasar, *The Office of Peter and the Structure of the Church*, trans. Andrée Emery (San Francisco: Ignatius Press, 1986), 142.
63. Farmer and Kereszty, *Peter and Paul in the Church of Rome*, 8.
64. Farmer and Kereszty, *Peter and Paul in the Church of Rome*, 7.
65. Brown, *Biblical Reflections on Crises Facing the Church*, 76.
66. De Satgé, *Peter and the Single Church*, 28.
67. Tillard, *Church of Churches*, 299.

Chapter three
SUCCESSION TO PETER'S MINISTRY

A study of Peter's historical career and the subsequent aggrandizing Petrine tradition leaves open the question of his importance for the later Church. Scripture alone cannot decide whether later developments were in line with Jesus' intentions.[1] As the people of God, the Church is aware that "the Spirit of truth" promised her (Jn 16:13, cf. 14:26) helps her understand and interpret Scripture through the ages. An ever-deepening and progressive clarification of revelation marks the Church which, as Vatican II states, "is always advancing towards the plenitude of divine truth" (DV 8).

After following Peter's steps to Rome, I shall propose three distinct, though interrelated, questions which will be addressed in this chapter. First, did Christ intend the apostles to have successors? Second, did Peter have any successors to his particular ministry? Third, if Peter had successors, who are they?

From Jerusalem to Rome

Among the best founded traditions coming to us from antiquity is that of Peter's martyrdom in Rome. While the Scriptures give no conclusive proof about Peter's sojourn in Rome, documentary and archaeological evidence abound in favor of the authenticity of this tradition.

Scripture

There is no explicit scriptural evidence that Peter ever went to Rome, nor any for the route he traveled, the time of his arrival, the length of his stay there, or his role in the community. A few biblical hints for a Roman sojourn, nonetheless, have been suggested.

After his arrest in Jerusalem by Herod Agrippa I in the early 40s, Peter was miraculously released from prison (cf. Acts 12:1-17). Acts ends the account by recording that "he departed and went to another place" (Acts 12:17b). Though this text is sometimes interpreted to mean Peter's departure for Rome, the evidence is inconclusive. In writing to the Romans, Paul says that he does not intend to proclaim the good news there, lest he "build on another man's foundation" (Rom 15:20). Some have taken this as implying that Peter had previously preached in Rome.

In its closing greeting, 1 Peter strongly supports a Roman sojourn for the apostle, where the author writes: "She who is at Babylon, who is likewise chosen, sends you greetings" (1 Pet 5:13). In the Old Testament, Babylon symbolized a power inimical to God. Following this tradition, early Christians used it as a code name for Rome (cf. Rev 14:8, 16:19). Like Babylon, the capital of the Roman Empire epitomized corruption and worldly might. Even if Peter himself was not the author of this letter, the writer claiming his authority thought it was appropriate to identify Rome as the place from which Peter wrote to other churches.

Nonbiblical Documents

Early nonbiblical sources, however, provide solid evidence that Peter passed his closing years in Rome before his martyrdom, which probably occurred during the Neronian persecution of 64. It is impossible to affirm with any certainty how long he spent in Rome. A third-century legend recounts a twenty-five year stay in the city. More likely, however, is the opinion that Peter spent no long period of time in Rome before 58, when Paul wrote to the Romans. He may have arrived there only in the 60s, shortly before his martyrdom. Peter, then, was not the original missionary who brought Christianity to Rome.[2]

Written in the mid-90s, the *First Letter to the Corinthians* is the most important first-century document outside the New Testament. Although not explicitly indicating the author's identity, it is commonly attributed to Pope St. Clement (88-97), the head of the Roman community.[3] In writing to the Corinthians, Clement says that among the Christians who suffered ill-treatment and death, probably during the persecution of Nero, were Sts. Peter and Paul. Of Peter's death he says: "There was Peter, who because of unjust envy suffered tribulations not once or twice but many times, and thus became a witness and passed on to the place of glory which was his due."[4] The letter does not specify either the date, place, or manner of Peter's death, but the context implies that it was at Rome. Right from the outset, Peter's "witness" or martyrdom is associated with Paul's.

About a decade later, on his journey to the capital, St. Ignatius of Antioch (†107) wrote ahead to the Roman Christians, begging them not to deprive him of the grace of martyrdom. About the tradition of Peter's sojourn in Rome he says: "Not as Peter and Paul do I send you instructions. For they were apostles; I am a condemned man. They were free; I am now a slave."[5] This passage presupposes that Ignatius knew about a relation between the two apostles which associated them with Rome.

By the end of the second century, conventional wisdom held that Peter preached and died in Rome. Eusebius (†340), often referred to as the Father of Church History, records a letter written by Dionysius, bishop of Corinth (†170): "In this way by your impressive admonition you have bound together all that has grown from the seed which Peter and Paul sowed in Romans and Corinthians alike. For both of them sowed in our Corinth and taught us jointly; in Italy too they taught jointly in the same city, and were martyred at the same time."[6]

By the early third century, the common tradition maintained that Peter, along with Paul, founded the Roman church. Tertullian (†225) provides the strongest witness for linking this founding with the apostles' martyrdom there: "How happy is that church on which the apostles poured forth all their teaching together with their blood! Where Peter endured a passion like his Lord's! Where Paul won his crown in a death like John [the Baptist]'s!"[7] This tradition of Peter's presence and martyrdom at Rome continued unchallenged throughout the third century. No one ever claimed that Peter had died anywhere other than Rome; no voice was raised in favor of a rival tradition.[8]

To this trustworthy documentary evidence should also be added the numerous apocryphal writings which, beginning in the early third century, claimed to provide accounts of Peter's teaching and career. Acts of his preaching, deeds, and journeys abounded in the ancient world. In uncritical fashion, they express a naive faith ever anxious to glorify the apostle. Among the best known legends were the *quo vadis?* story and that of Peter's encounter with Simon the Magician in Rome. While these writings might contain some fact buried beneath the fiction, they are unreliable as historical testimony to Peter's stay and martyrdom in Rome. Nonetheless, they were widely cited by authoritative authors and contributed to the emerging portrait of Peter as a grandiose and inspiring figure associated with the Roman church.[9]

Archaeological Evidence

Besides this documentary testimony, impressive archaeological evidence now supports the fact that Peter was buried in Rome. Eusebius's *History of the Church* chronicles a statement of the Roman presbyter Gaius, whose testimony goes back to about 200. Regarding the tombs of Sts. Peter and Paul, Gaius wrote: "I can point out the monuments of the victorious apostles. If you will go as far as the Vatican or the Ostian Way, you will find the monuments of those who founded this church."[10] Though this statement brings us only to the beginning of the third century, it is reasonable to accept that the Church would have preserved the memory of this venerable site. When fear of persecution lessened, the faithful placed small commemorative markers to indicate the spot of the apostle's martyrdom.

Over this modest monument above Peter's tomb the Constantinian basilica was erected in the early fourth century and, in the sixteenth century, the present basilica. The Emperor Constantine (†337) decided to remedy this plain center of Christian cult by erecting a church over it. The fact that the original basilica was built on this very difficult and sloping site "is explained solely by the fact that the monument with niches was considered by the Christian community of Rome to be Peter's tomb."[11] For centuries Christians believed that Peter had been buried on this site, but they had no proof of the fact.

Beginning in 1939, extensive excavations were carried out under St. Peter's Basilica which led to the widely accepted conclusion that the cupola of Michelangelo rises over the site of Peter's tomb. Underneath the basilica's present crypt lies a grandiose pagan necropolis built on the Vatican Hill. Within this necropolis, which contained many lavish mausolea, the early Christians maintained a few poor graves. About a hundred years after Peter's death, they marked his grave with a small *aedicula* or monument, the so-called "trophy." A little more than forty years ago, archaeologists found this small burial monument, which many have identified, though not without controversy, as the apostle's place of burial.[12]

In 1950, Pius XII (1939-1958) announced to the world the astounding discoveries of the previous decade. "Has the tomb of St. Peter really been found?" he asked. "To that question the answer is beyond all doubt, *yes*. . . . A second question, subordinate to the first, refers to the relics of St. Peter. Have they been found? At the side of the tomb remains of human bones have been discovered. However, it is impossible to prove with certainty that they belong to the body of the apostle."[13] Further study showed that these particular bones could not have been those of the apostle.

Later, however, the archaeologists found other bones, which Paul VI (1963-1978) declared to be the skeletal remains of Peter. Guided by archaeological and scientific evidence, the Pope said that "the relics of St. Peter have been identified in a manner which we find convincing . . . very patient and accurate investigations were made with a result which we believe positive."[14] Although the authenticity of these bones as Peter's cannot be a matter of faith, the ancient testimonies, confirmed by recent archeological study, lead to the morally certain conclusion that Peter went to Rome and was martyred there.

Jerusalem: the Church Peter Left Behind

After Pentecost, Peter combined his role as the principal guide of the early Church with that of the leadership of the Jerusalem community. When he left the city after escaping from prison, the leadership of the *local* church at Jerusalem passed into the hands of James, "the Lord's brother" (Gal 1:19). Though he was not among the Twelve, he had seen the risen Lord (cf. 1 Cor 15:7). At first, James was head of the Hebrew section of the Jerusalem church. After Peter's departure, he assumed the leadership of the whole mother church at Jerusalem (cf. Acts 12:17, 21:18), where he presided at the apostolic council (cf. Acts 15:13). James exercised an authority that probably extended as far as Palestine and Syria. Even so, because the awaited conversion of Israel did not take place, Jerusalem lost "its significance as the center of the new people of God."[15]

When Peter left Jerusalem to dedicate himself to itinerant missionary work, did he keep his primacy of oversight and teaching in the *universal* Church or did he transfer it to James along with his leadership of the Jerusalem church? Whatever ecclesial primacy Christ intended, most Protestants maintain, remained with James in the mother church at Jerusalem, and not with Peter.

While it is true that James assumed the directive role at Jerusalem, he did so as the leader of a particular community, not as heir to Peter's universal authority. Commenting on Oscar Cullmann's thesis that Peter left James the government both of the church at Jerusalem and of the universal Church, Louis Bouyer concludes: "Nothing in the New Testament texts is capable of establishing that Peter saw things in this light, or that this opinion was generally admitted in the primitive Church."[16] Moreover, no biblical evidence even hints that Peter carried out his missionary activity as a subordinate of James.[17] Peter made crucial decisions, as we have seen, without James, who was a "pillar" of the Jerusalem church. While Peter thought it wise to justify his baptism of Cornelius to the Jerusalem community, this action did not compromise his authority as pastor of the flock. In the spirit of the Master's love, the apostle was willing to give an account of his actions to his brothers in the community.

Even after Peter's departure, Jerusalem remained the respected origin of all other churches, since it was the initial point of departure for the Church's evangelizing mission. Neither Antioch nor Rome could replace Jerusalem as the holy city of the Lord's paschal mystery, where the apostolic community first witnessed to its faith (cf. Acts 1:8). Paul's collection for the Jerusalem community (cf. Rom 15:25-28; 1 Cor 16:1-4; 2 Cor 8-9) testifies to its historically inalienable status. Nonetheless, Jerusalem was not destined to remain the center of the Church. Peter's transfer of local pastoral leadership to James, "far from signifying the handing over of leadership of the whole Church, implied the fact that the People of God no longer had, and could no longer have, their center in Jerusalem."[18] Using later terminology, we can say that James' authority in Jerusalem was without universal outreach but was instead limited to the specific flock of a particular church.[19]

An even more decisive argument for maintaining that Peter kept his special ministry is the unlikelihood that he would have "resigned" his apostolic office in order to carry out its universal responsibilities. Jesus commissioned him to pastor all his sheep rather than to head a local community. "Peter would have been bound to regard it as a betrayal of his commission, as faithlessness to the Lord who had commissioned him," writes Otto Karrer, "if he had resigned from the responsibility for the Church given to him personally, unless induced to do so by a specific fresh revelation."[20] Not a shred of evidence exists for any such revelation. As long as he was still alive, Peter was unable to pass on his ministry to anyone else, so intimately was it linked to Christ's personal delegation. When Peter left Jerusalem, he took with him in his person, so to speak, the responsibilities of his pastoral office.

Apostolic Succession

While not fully describing the teaching on apostolic succession, we must sketch its essential outlines so as to understand the doctrine of Petrine succession. The apostolicity of the Church is expressed in three ways. First, the Church is apostolic in her *origin*, "built upon the foundation of the apostles and prophets" (Eph 2:20). Second, in her *doctrine* she must remain ever faithful to the original apostolic witness, "the truth that has been entrusted to you by the Holy Spirit who dwells within us" (2 Tim 1:14). Third, the Church is apostolic in her *ministerial structure*; she continues to be taught, governed, and sanctified by bishops who succeed to the apostles (cf. CCC 857).

Original "Apostolate"

As eternally begotten of the Father, the Son's intra-trinitarian procession is historically manifested in his Incarnation and redemptive mission. The Son is the primary "apostle" or "one sent" by the Father: "My food is to do the will of him who sent me, and to accomplish his work" (Jn 4:34). The incarnate Son, in turn, sent the Twelve on their mission: "As the Father has sent me, even so I send you" (Jn 20:21, cf. 17:18). Because the one who sends is present in the one sent (cf. Jn 17:21), Jesus said to the disciples: "He who hears you hears me, and he who rejects you rejects me, and he who rejects me rejects him who sent me" (Lk 10:16). The apostles, then, are the living instruments through whom Christ continues to accomplish the work of redemption.

Unlike other rabbis, Jesus deliberately chose the Twelve from among the wider group of disciples: "And he went up into the hills and called to him those whom he desired; and they came to him" (Mk 3:13). His sovereign will, not their own choice, made them his apostles. Christ bound the Twelve to himself as a community "to be with him" (Mk 3:14).

The Twelve also received Jesus' special teaching, since "to his own disciples he explained everything" (Mk 4:34). Seeing to it that they would be like scribes "trained for the kingdom of heaven" (Mt 13:52), he prepared them for their future ministry. Sent by Jesus to share in preaching the kingdom of God and healing the sick (cf. Mk 6:7-13; Mt 10:5-8; Lk 9:1-6), they were confirmed as primary witnesses to his life, teaching, and paschal mystery only after his resurrection (cf. Mt 28:18-20; Mk 16:15-16; Lk 24:45-49; Jn 20:21-23; Acts 1:8). The apostles' mission to bear witness to the farthest extremities of the world (cf. Acts 1:7-8) was founded on Christ's specific call and command rather than on personal gifts or talents.

To equip them for their duty, Jesus gave the Twelve a share in his own authority, which he intended to perpetuate in the community through them.[21] In the apostles Jesus really, though "mystically," became present by means of their ministry so that salvation could reach others.[22] They were truly "ministers of a new covenant" (2 Cor 3:6), "ambassadors for Christ" (2 Cor 5:20), and "stewards of the mysteries of God" (1 Cor 4:1).

Co-workers in the Apostolic Ministry

While the Twelve were still alive and active, no one succeeded to the apostolic ministry which Jesus had confided to them. His teaching contains nothing explicit regarding the need for either co-workers or successors to the apostles; as far as we know, he never gave any such instructions. Already during the Church's first generation, however, helpers and co-workers appeared on the scene.

Despite the difficulty of discovering Christ's *implicit* will, good reasons exist for interpreting his commission to "go into all the world and preach the gospel to the whole creation" (Mk 16:15; cf. Mt 28:19; Lk 24:47) as implying a future need to include collaborators with, and successors to, the apostles' ministry. His command suggests that there should always be proclaimers and baptizers. Because Christ's revelation is definitive and unsurpassable, the provisions he made for continuing his saving work should last. The Word entrusted himself to living people, and people are added to the Church when they encounter a preacher (cf. Rom 10:14-17). Christ's personal presence in his body, the Church, continues through representatives who make him and his saving grace available to all people.

During the lifetime of the Twelve, with whom Paul became identified, this original group soon chose certain men to be, as Vatican II states, "helpers in their ministry" (LG 20). The Twelve, writes Jesuit theologian Francis Sullivan, "made decisions about Church structures as the need arose, and . . . they felt guided by the Spirit in such decisions."[23] Since theirs was primarily a missionary charge, the Twelve entrusted others with assuming responsibility for the on-the-spot pastoral care of the new communities. At the Church's beginning, different communities were internally organized in diverse ways.

Depending on the local situation and tradition, various names were given to the

Origins, Development, and Mission of the Papacy

community leaders. While there is much fluidity in terminology, these "fellow workers for the kingdom of God" (Col 4:11) included deacons (cf. Acts 6:2-6), elders or *presbyteroi* (cf. Acts 11:30, 14:23, 15:6), and overseers or *episkopoi* (cf. Phil 1:1). In this very early period, the distinction between elders and overseers (bishops) was not yet well defined, and the terms were sometimes used interchangeably for the same individuals (cf. Acts 20:17, 28; Titus 1:5, 7). For this reason, many modern scholars refer to the "presbyters/bishops" of the first generation. Always, however, it was the Holy Spirit who empowered men for their official ministry (cf. Acts 20:28). All office was a gift from the Lord, which only he could give, because through it he gave himself to the chosen individual for the community.[24]

In the New Testament Church, "apostolic authority embraced all that was meant in the first century by episcopal and presbyteral authority and in the second century by the authority of a bishop."[25] The "apostolic men" shared in the authority Christ had given to the apostles. "Whatever the method by which they were chosen, whether through the authority of the Twelve or Paul or some link with them," says the International Theological Commission, "they share in the authority of the apostles who were instituted by Christ and who maintain for all time their unique character."[26] Yet the role of these co-workers was different from that of the Twelve. Without a direct mandate from the risen Lord, they remained subject to higher apostolic authority. Nevertheless, these co-workers shared in the apostolic ministry of teaching and pastoring.

While most of "the apostolic men" remained itinerant missionary preachers, some founded churches, assuming settled pastoral responsibilities. These collaborators in the apostolic ministry were representatives of the apostles in the various tasks they carried out: preaching the gospel, directing liturgical services, and guiding the community.[27] Sharing in the apostolic ministry was always collegial, a lived experience of ecclesial communion: "first among the original apostles, then with their co-workers, and then with all those who were called and appointed to pastoral ministry in the churches."[28]

Successors of the Apostles

In the years after the traveling apostles founded the first Christian communities, there was "a tendency to assert and strengthen the ministry of teaching and leadership."[29] Faced by the centrifugal forces of false teachers and doctrine, which sought to compromise a church's unity, believers increasingly attributed greater authority to their pastors.[30] This strengthening of authority, already begun in the very early period, led in the post-New Testament period to recognizing a resident office of apostolic ministry as normative for a church's life. As long as the apostles lived, they could keep some control over the local communities, whether by directly intervening or by serving as an instance of recourse. Once they could no longer be present, however, apostolic *episkope* passed into the hands of others.[31]

With the definitive passing away of the apostolic generation, it became necessary, due to Christ's will that the Church was to last "to the close of the age" (Mt 28:20), for men to succeed to, and not just collaborate with, the apostles. "The Gospel, which they were charged to hand on," teaches the Second Vatican Council, "is, for the Church, the principle of all her life for all time" (LG 20). Before their deaths, the apostles understood that Christ wanted them to provide for successors. They had "the deliberate intention," writes German Jesuit theologian Karl Rahner, "of transmitting formally their office and their mission."[32] In the words of *Lumen gentium*, "they consigned, by will and testament, as it were, to their immediate collaborators the duty of completing and consolidating the work they had begun" (LG 20). As the apostles' heirs and representatives, these men continued their mission with the assured help of the Spirit. While such successors were to pastor the communities, preserve ecclesial unity, and monitor sound doctrine, their principal duty was to provide for the Eucharistic celebration which flowed from the proclamation of the gospel.

The Pastoral Letters contain evidence of the apostles' desire to preserve their mission through succession. Timothy and Titus, disciples and co-workers of Paul during his lifetime, both carried on his work after his death, having authority to "appoint elders in every town" (Titus 1:5). A principal obligation of Timothy and Titus was to guarantee the Church's continuity and expansion by choosing suitable men to exercise pastoral ministry in local communities (cf. 1 Tim 3:1-13, 5:22; Titus 1:5-9). The first apostles and disciples associated them with the apostolic ministry by the laying-on of hands (cf. 1 Tim 4:14; 2 Tim 1:6). Those associated with Paul's ministry either directly or through his co-workers were the "elders" and/or "bishops" who were recognized as successors to Paul in teaching and leadership. Regardless of the terminology used, only those who were duly appointed and carried out the fullness of apostolic ministry are true successors to the apostolic mission.

That succession to the apostles occurred is indisputable. *How* it happened throughout the Church is obscure because documentation is lacking. Between the original apostles and the bishops who later emerged as heads of local communities "is a kind of tunnel in which we are unable to discern," writes Bouyer, "the details of a transmission which may have been conducted in rather complex forms."[33]

By the mid-second century, ecclesiastical writers maintained that bishops succeeded to the place of the apostles. The earliest witness, from before the end of the first century, is Clement's *First Letter to the Corinthians*: "Our apostles knew through our Lord Jesus Christ that there would be strife for the office of bishop. For this reason, therefore, having received perfect foreknowledge, they appointed those who have already been mentioned, and afterwards added the further provision that, if they should die, other approved men should succeed to their ministry."[34]

Less than a century later, in order to preserve authentic teaching against the heresies of the gnostics who claimed to possess private sources for their teaching, St. Irenaeus (†200) formulated the classic statement on apostolic succession. He held that true doctrine could be known and guaranteed only by referring to the episcopal teaching of those who had received it publicly through a direct historical succession traceable to the apostles: "Those who wish to see the truth can observe in every church the tradition of the apostles made manifest in the whole world. We can enumerate those who were appointed bishops in the churches by the apostles, and their successors down to our day."[35] Yves Congar sums up the ancient belief that doctrine was transmitted through episcopal succession: "Ever since Christians first wrote their history, they conceived it as the continuity of a movement of communication of the divine life which, begun in God, was propagated on earth, after Christ, through the apostles and the succession of bishops."[36]

Pulling together the various threads of the early tradition, Vatican II proposes Catholic teaching on apostolic succession: "In order that the mission assigned to them [apostles] might continue after their death, they passed on to their immediate cooperators, as it were, in the form of a testament, the duty of confirming and finishing the work begun by themselves . . . they therefore appointed such men, and gave them the order that, when they should have died, other approved men would take up their ministry" (LG 20).

After the apostles' death, the Church had the spontaneous conviction that other "envoys" should exercise the same ministry carried out by apostles, even though they were not those who had seen, heard, or touched with their hands the Word of life (cf. 1 Jn 1:1). The primary holders of apostolic authority all came to be called bishops. According to the Second Vatican Council, the office of shepherding in the Church, first received by the apostles, continues in the episcopal ministry: "The sacred synod consequently teaches that the bishops have by divine institution taken the place of the apostles as pastors of the Church" (LG 20).

Bishops ≠ Apostles

The bishops are not, however, new or recycled apostles. The early Church carefully preserved the distinction between apostles and bishops. To their unique foundational roles, the apostles could have no successors. Their extraordinary charisms of apostleship were not transmissible.[37]

First, bishops are not eyewitnesses to revelation, as the Twelve were; instead, they are ministerial heads of communities who give authoritative testimony to the deposit of faith which has already been formed. Only the original apostles are the Church's irreplaceable foundation (cf. Eph 2:20), the foundation of the new Jerusalem (cf. Rev 21:14). Second, because of the Spirit's unique presence in the apostolic Church, the apostles' teaching itself constituted the deposit of faith which later generations were to preserve. Unlike the apostles, bishops are not themselves vessels of revelation. Third, the apostles individually enjoyed the charism of preaching the gospel without error. Bishops, however, possess this charism only as a collegial body. Lastly, except for the pope, no bishop succeeds to a particular apostle, though he might succeed to an apostolic see. Instead, each bishop is accepted as a member of the episcopal college which succeeds as a body to the apostolic college.[38]

Besides these nontransferable privileges, the apostles also received the mission of authoritative teaching and pastoral leadership. It is this mission which can be handed on to successors. Those who succeed to the apostles enjoy the same ministry of teaching and pastoring, thereby sharing in Christ's own authority. Bouyer suggests that instead of calling bishops "successors" of the apostles, it might be better to say that the apostles "live on" in the bishops to whom they have transmitted the core of their function. This guarantees Christ's active presence in the Church as her head.[39]

Monarchical Episcopate

Closely related to the question of apostolic succession is that of the origin of the monarchical episcopate. When was the tradition of a single bishop heading a Christian community firmly established in the Church?

In the New Testament period, when a community lacked the presence of an apostle, it cannot be proved that everywhere a single person, whether elder or bishop, held the fullness of apostolic ministry in his hands. Bouyer notes that "to state that the 'monarchical' episcopate was everywhere established from the outset, following the apostles and at their command, would seem to go beyond what reasonable proof can support."[40] Rahner also admits that "at one time the monarchic episcopate existed side by side with other community structures in the apostolic age."[41] The New Testament provides no undisputed evidence that the apostles or their co-workers appointed in every community one man as a "bishop" with authority over its elders. Local leadership at this point was, at least in some places, shared more collegially.[42] No doubt, while the apostles and their immediate co-workers were alive, communities perceived no need for a single pastoral leader. The apostle who founded them, or his close collaborator, met their requirements. At this stage of development a single "residential bishop" in every local church was not yet the norm. The need for a single leader came to the fore when this original apostolic authority was unavailable to a local community.

Though apostolic authority was necessary for the life of every local church, leadership seems to have been shared by assorted elders, bishops, and others, whose precise prerogatives and obligations varied from place to place. Especially in the Judeo-Christian communities, this collegial type of ministry coexisted, in the Greek world, with an apostolic ministry centered on a single figure.[43] Even so, it is reasonable, though not provable, to believe that where many bishops-elders worked together, "one of them was probably responsible for unity amongst his colleagues and within the congregation as a whole."[44] The example of Peter reporting to James as head of the elders in Jerusalem (cf. Acts 12:17), and the later uncontested passage to a single bishop heading every community, point in the direction of a monarchical episcopate already within the apostolic generation.

Perhaps with slight exaggeration, Ignatius had earlier claimed that the pattern of monarchical episcopacy had been established "unto the ends of the earth."[45] Most scholars conclude that Ignatius' strong statements on the monarchical episcopate were, as patrologist Robert Eno says, "a sort of campaign to promote what he thought the churches needed, namely, the prestige and authority of a single leader in the local community."[46] By the mid-second century, however, the pattern of a single leader, claiming full apostolic ministry and assisted by a council of presbyters, was everywhere established in the Church.[47] These principal leaders were now called "overseers" to distinguish them from the "elders": a terminological and theological precision that became normative. Bishops

Origins, Development, and Mission of the Papacy

with their twofold ministry of pastoral leadership and teaching were recognized as successors to the apostles.[48]

A theological note is in order. While admitting that the monarchical episcopate came about as the result of historical choices, Catholic doctrine holds that its emergence was guided by the Spirit. As such, the episcopal structure belongs to the permanent and irreversible constitution of the Church as divinely willed.[49] The authority of the bishop is of divine origin. The extant texts of the second and third century all agree that the bishop did not receive his authority either from a collegial body of presbyters or from the people of God as a whole.[50]

Petrine Succession

Now let us examine whether Peter, as the "first" among the Twelve, had a personal successor to his particular ministry in the apostolic college. Just as Scripture furnishes no explicit testimony regarding apostolic succession, neither does it provide explicit proof of Petrine succession. In the Church's teaching, the pope's succession to Peter was officially defined at Vatican I, before that of the bishops' succession to the apostles at Vatican II. Petrine succession, however, should be included as a special instance within apostolic succession.

Was Peter the Bishop of Rome?

By means of their tradition which considers Peter as the first bishop of Rome, Catholics have secured the line of papal succession. Still, it is necessary to examine this affirmation more carefully in the light of history and doctrine.

Is it anachronistic to think of Peter as the first monarchical bishop of Rome? Many today think so. First, it is not at all clear to them, as I shall later explain, that the monarchical episcopacy was established at Rome in the first decades following Peter's death. Second, the earliest catalog of Roman bishops considers him, together with Paul, as the "founder" of the Church, not its first bishop. To regard Peter as "the first link in a chain of bishops, in a purely juridical conception of the transmission of powers is," says Tillard, "to devalue his proper function."[51]

The earliest extant list of Roman bishops distinguishes between Peter's function as the founder of the local church and Linus's function as bishop. Irenaeus writes: "The blessed apostles [Peter and Paul], having founded and built up the church [of Rome], they handed over the office of the episcopate to Linus. . . . To him succeeded Anacletus; and after him, in third place from the apostles, Clement was chosen for the episcopate."[52] Here the first bishop is Linus. Peter and Paul are assigned the more prestigious work of founding the Roman church. Their foundational significance rests upon a priority other than that of heading a local community. They are the beginning of the episcopacy in the Roman see, founding this church on their martyrdom, thereby giving it, as Tillard says, "the most powerful and greatest apostolic authenticity."[53]

Later, when other episcopal registers were drawn up, they began their lists of Roman bishops with Peter. The Liberian Catalog, drawn up in the mid-fourth century, considered

Peter as the first bishop of Rome. It was an appropriate, if anachronistic, way to explain the prominent role which Peter had held in the Roman community. As Brown points out, "since the task of the bishop was to administer a small congregation and live among them, I would say that the importance of Peter ranged far above all: as first of the Twelve he represented the wholeness of the renewed Israel and the role of judging all the Christian people of God."[54] Although correct from one point of view, calling Peter the first bishop of Rome can obscure his distinctive foundational role as "founder" of the Roman church.

When Peter came to Rome he did so bearing his unique ministry as rock and shepherd. That office belonged to him personally, no matter where he was. After arriving in Rome, it is likely that the presbyters/bishops, who held apostolic authority in the community, "did not lose their office on Peter's arrival, but now they were subject to Peter, as those had been in Antioch or Corinth when he paid his visits of whatever duration to those places."[55] Peter's contemporaries might well have failed to designate him "bishop" of Rome, not because they rejected his authority, but because this title inadequately emphasized his unique role as pastor of the whole of Christ's flock.

Questioning the fact that Peter was the first local head or bishop of the Roman community presents no dogmatic difficulty. As head of the apostles, his ministry was not locally limited or specified. His role as pastor of all Christians was independent of having any local function in the Roman church.[56] The link between Peter and Rome was established only after his martyrdom there.

Monarchical Episcopacy at Rome

Since the monarchical episcopacy was not a universal and normative ecclesial structure before the mid-second century, the question inevitably arises when monarchical bishops can be identified at Rome. Did a single bishop succeed to Peter's function? On the one hand, if the episcopal lists which catalog the names of individual successors to Peter are historically accurate, then no problem arises. On the other hand, if there were not monarchical bishops in the first years after Peter, which is a hypothesis now frequently proposed, can this absence be reconciled with a Catholic understanding of the papacy's origins?

In recent years, many scholars have suggested that the original form of pastoral government in Rome following Peter's martyrdom was more collegial than monarchical. After examining the available documentation, Eno concludes that it "points us in the direction of assuming that in the first century and into the second, there was no bishop of Rome in the usual sense given to that title."[57] The evidence he adduces comes from the letters of Clement and Ignatius, and the writings of Hermas. In his *Letter to the Romans*, Ignatius fails to greet or even mention the bishop of the community. Nor does he offer any instruction concerning the role of the bishop. Both omissions are singular, departing from the style and content of his other correspondence. Similarly, Clement's *First Letter to the Corinthians* does not mention a chief bishop at Rome. Besides, its description of leadership appears to be no different from that exercised by the group of presbyters who governed the church in Corinth. Later, in the mid-century, Hermas makes some incidental remarks about pastoral leadership in Rome. Significantly, all his references to "leaders,"

Origins, Development, and Mission of the Papacy

"elders," or "bishops" are in the plural. Eno therefore concludes that in the earliest decades after Peter's death, the church in Rome did not have a single chief bishop.[58]

How then was the local church governed? Before the monarchical episcopacy took hold in Rome, ecclesial matters there might have been in the hands of a group of presbyters/bishops. As Brown comments, however, "inevitably in that group an individual stood out as a natural and implicitly recognized leader for a specific purpose."[59] Clement, for example, would have been one such leader, though not a monarchical bishop in the later sense of the term. Lists of the bishops of Rome preserved the names of outstanding individuals such as Clement in the community. Because they thought that the more developed structure they knew had been present from the beginning, the compilers of episcopal lists called them bishops.

Episcopal authority (*episkope*) was, however, present in the church at Rome. Indeed, presbyters/bishops led the community, though in this very early period succession to Peter's personal primacy might have been held collegially. There might have been a time when no single bishop presided over the Roman church. Even so, the ministry of Peter would still have been "present" in the unique apostolic authority held by its presbyters/bishops. Petrine authority was present in whoever the legitimate officeholders were. When the need arose, in Rome, as in other local churches, one man emerged as the chief pastor. Such a development, which corresponded to Christ's will, had already begun during the apostolic Church and continued afterward under the guidance of the Holy Spirit.

Petrine Succession Within Apostolic Succession

Once the principle of apostolic succession to the ministry is accepted, it is reasonable to maintain, in similar fashion, succession to the apostolic ministry of Peter. As the Anglican-Roman Catholic International Commission (ARCIC) remarks in its joint ecumenical statement: "what is true of the transmissibility of the mission of the apostolic group is true of Peter as a member of it."[60]

If the original structure of apostolic ministry continues in the Church in the succession of bishops, then it follows that someone should succeed to Peter's role within the episcopal body. In other words, you can't have one without the other. Since Peter alone was singled out as the rock, keybearer, and shepherd of the flock, he has his own successor. Within succession to the apostolic ministry, the Petrine office has its own line of succession.

As with the other apostles, not everything about Peter's "firstness" could be transmitted. No successor would ever be picked directly by Jesus himself, profess the Lord's messiahship directly to his face, or witness his risen life. These functions were once-for-all; other roles included a mission and responsibilities which last forever.

Jesus' Will for Successors to Peter

When Jesus made Peter his vicar as shepherd of the Church, the apostle did not immediately fulfill this role. Christ commissioned him with an eye to the future. Such a function would come into play only after the ascension. Because Jesus was concerned with the community's future, his interest in safeguarding his flock was not limited to Peter's lifetime. The Lord provided for his Church by promising, even if implicitly, that her original Petrine form, with which he emphatically connected her solidity, would endure.

Peter's office as "rock" must last so that "every successive generation of disciples will have, like the first generation, its living Peter, its rock, which will enable it to triumph over all the assaults of the gates of hell."[61] As long as the power of evil is menacing, and it will be until all things are subjected to Christ (cf. 1 Cor 15:28), then the means to overcome the power of darkness will also remain. That means is Peter, the Church's rock-foundation. To meet all assaults a "living rock of resistance must be there — a living rock, not the memory of one long dead."[62] Because the Church is to endure for all ages, then "the functions and services assigned to Peter, including the function of the rock of the Church of Jesus, cannot be restricted to the person of Peter."[63] In the promises Jesus made to Peter, he implicitly willed that others would succeed to the apostle's ministry.

The Church's preservation of Peter's office corresponds, therefore, to God's providential plan. At the beginning, Petrine succession takes place quietly, without any detailed theoretical claims or sophisticated justifications. That is exactly what one would expect in an institution which the Church calmly integrated into her life.[64]

The Bishop of Rome as Successor to Peter

Having established that fidelity to Christ's will requires the Church to preserve the ministry of Peter, we must now identify *who* that successor is. We have already seen that Peter most probably lived and died in the capital of the Empire. Even so, his martyrdom there does not of itself prove succession to his ministry. What, then, is the justification for identifying the bishop of Rome as the successor of Peter?

Why Rome?

Even though Peter had preached at Jerusalem and Antioch, playing an important role in both places, no Jerusalem or Antiochene tradition grew up which held that its bishop succeeded to Peter's ministry. At Rome, however, the story is different. From the oldest evidence available, this church alone claimed that its bishop succeeded to Peter's office in the Church universal, a prerogative recognized by the other churches.

Peter himself left no record of why he went to Rome to preach. What we can piece together are reasons which make that choice remarkably fitting. In the ancient world, "all roads led to Rome." Peter probably went there because it was the capital of the Empire: cosmopolitan, rich, and fertile ground for missionary activity. It was simply *the* city, the *Urbs*, the "eternal Rome" of pagan legend. As the center of the known civilized world, Rome symbolized "the end of the earth" (Acts 1:8), the heart of paganism which was to be converted to the gospel. Moreover, Rome hosted one of the principal Jewish communities of the diaspora. Having adapted well to life in a pagan milieu, it had a large number of proselytes. Consequently, in Rome the transition could easily be made from

Jewish Christianity to one bringing Jews and Gentiles together.[65] Not surprisingly, then, the chief fisherman, who had been the first to admit pagans into the Church, made Rome the final goal of his missionary journeys.

The Eastern tradition of Christianity emphasized that Peter's going to Rome expressed God's plan for the Church. Eusebius recounts that Peter went to Rome to confound the errors of Simon the Magician (cf. Acts 8:18-23), whom he believed to have gone there: "the all-gracious and kindly providence of the universe brought to Rome to deal with this terrible threat to the world, the strong and great apostle, chosen for his merits to be spokesman for all the others, Peter himself."[66] Others, like Athanasius (†373), also believed that Peter's coming to Rome was the necessary fulfillment of God's plan.[67] Leo the Great (440-461) begins one of his sermons on the feast of Sts. Peter and Paul by apostrophizing Rome in these words: "It was through these men, O Rome, that the light of Christ's gospel shone upon you. . . . It was they who promoted you to such glory, making you . . . the capital of the world through Peter's holy See."[68]

Another influential factor which contributed to Rome's prominence was the fact that its Christians were extraordinarily generous in sharing their wealth and extending their hospitality to the other churches. From very early on, the Roman church "developed something like a sense of obligation to the oppressed all over Christendom."[69] Furthermore, as the only apostolic see in the West, it could assume a leadership role there over other churches.

Some scholars argue that the Roman church later emerged as the principal one in the *koinonia* or universal communion of churches only because it was located in the capital of the Empire. In that way it shared by association in the city's imperial prestige. German historian Ludwig Hertling points out that, if the special position of Rome had developed due to the fact that Rome was the capital city, its preeminence would have been of a different kind. "In this hypothesis," he says, "the bishop of Rome would have become a miniature emperor and the administrative element would have been prominent in his government of the Church. But in Christian antiquity there is no trace of a central administration conducting ecclesiastical affairs."[70]

Furthermore, the bishops of Rome never attributed to the city's civil and political importance the reason for their primacy. At the Council of Constantinople (381), the Fathers granted to the bishop of Constantinople, the new capital of the Eastern Empire, "privileges of honour after the bishop of Rome, because it is New Rome."[71] Rome agreed that Constantinople's "honor" could be acknowledged on political grounds, but it refused to accept the same justification for itself. If Rome's ecclesiastical prominence were to be divorced from any connection with Peter, then the role of the Roman church and its bishops would be reduced to a matter of practical human expediency. In that case, it could no longer be held to be divinely instituted as proposed by Catholic doctrine. Even so, historical-human factors contributed to, though they were not the legitimizing reason for, the early authority of the Roman see.

First Successors to Peter

Available documentation, as we have seen, does not tell us conclusively who held Petrine authority at Rome after Peter's death. In the mid-second century Hegesippus wrote that when he visited Rome he made a list of the bishops, but his list does not go back to the first century.[72] The oldest extant record, from Irenaeus, undoubtedly reflects the tradition, by then universal, of the monarchical episcopacy. It gives the names of individual bishops going back to the see's founding: Peter and Paul "committed unto Linus the office of the episcopate."[73] Irenaeus and Eusebius identify this Linus as a companion of Paul (cf. 2 Tim 4:21). While Linus's leading position in the church at Rome need not be doubted, his precise role and functions remain unclear. While Peter was alive, Linus would not, however, have exercised Petrine authority. That could only have been assumed, either personally or collegially, after the apostle's death. After Linus (67-76), ancient testimony preserves the names of Anacletus (76-88), Clement (88-97), and Evaristus (97-105) as the successors of Peter.

Dual Apostolicity

Another argument explaining why the bishops of Rome assumed the role of successors to Peter links the Roman church with its foundation by the two greatest apostles, Peter and Paul, the true "founders" of the church at Rome. According to first- and second-century evidence, the "prominence and leadership role of Rome in the universal Church," writes Cistercian theologian Roch Kereszty, "derives from the fact of having been jointly founded by these two martyr apostles."[74] They received the title "founders" because they confirmed the Roman church with their apostolic teaching and ratified their teaching by their martyrdom. Peter and Paul were not founders in the sense that they were the first to bring the gospel to Rome; the Christian community was established there before their arrival. Paul explicitly denied that he was the first to preach the gospel in Rome (cf. Rom 15:19-22; Acts 28:15). Nor is there a sound tradition for Peter doing so. Nonetheless, because Peter and Paul taught, gave witness, and were martyred there, the Church regarded them as the preeminent founders of the see in a moral and spiritual, if not historical, sense.

For the early Church, the fact that the chief apostles were martyrs was intrinsic to their apostolic mission, "and their martyrdom at Rome is constitutive of the leadership role of Rome."[75] This witness — for that is the root of the word "martyr" — is the supreme guarantee of the fruitfulness of the apostles' fidelity to the gospel. Christ testifies in and through them. As founders, Peter and Paul remain mystically present in the community of their martyrdom.

According to the testimony of the Church's liturgy and doctrine, her saints intercede for the faithful. This intercessory influence of Peter and Paul was thought to be especially strong at Rome, the city where they consummated their witness, were buried, and where their relics rested.[76] Their apostolic ministry continued in Rome, governing the church by means of their intercessory prayer. The presence there of these two great martyrs' tombs favored the rise of the see's preeminence in the universal Church. When eulogizing the city of Rome, St. John Chrysostom (†407) wrote that "like a great, strong body it has the bodies of these two saints like two glistening eyes."[77] No less flattering were the remarks of Theodoret of Cyr (†466), who wrote to Leo the Great, praising the Roman church for its faith and for keeping "the tombs . . . of our common fathers and teachers, Peter and Paul. . . . They have rendered your see most glorious; this is the crowning achievement of your blessings."[78]

Though Paul's connection with Peter is always mentioned in this context, and this link supported the development of Roman primacy, the bishops at Rome, as we shall see in chapter four, became increasingly aware of their special relation to Peter. Although popes have occasionally called themselves successors of Peter and Paul, this title has never taken firm hold.[79] Indeed, Innocent X (1644-1655) censured the view of their juridical equality (cf. DS 1999), a condemnation which Pius X (1903-1914) reaffirmed (cf. DS 3555). Because of Paul's very special position among the apostles and the uniqueness of his vocation, no one can, in the juridical sense, "succeed" to his role.[80] While it is readily understandable why the bishop of Rome could succeed to Peter as the authoritative head of a group, "it is less easy to think of a man taking the place of a charismatic whose particular gift was to go from town to town preaching the gospel with startling freedom. . . . There is certainly no succession (in the usual sense of the word) to a prophet."[81]

Nonetheless, a Pauline heritage remains in Rome. The bishop of Rome "can also be called the heir of Paul," writes John Paul II, "the greatest representative of the early Church's missionary efforts and of the wealth of her charisms."[82] While succession suggests that the successor continues the office of his predecessor, the heir receives a heritage to protect, guard, and fructify. Among the responsibilities that the pope, as the heir of Paul, should carry out are preaching the power of the risen Christ who rules the Church in the Spirit, encouraging and testing charisms, and evangelizing all nations.[83] This Pauline heritage of the Roman see, though underdeveloped in comparison with its Petrine nature, has not been totally forgotten. In their solemn acts throughout the centuries, the popes have convened councils, canonized saints, and defined dogmas by appealing to "the authority of the apostles Peter and Paul." The common celebration of their martyrdom on June 29, a tradition dating from the mid-third century, remains the great feast of the church in Rome and of its bishop.

◆

In forming the apostolic group of the Twelve, "Jesus established the Church as a visible society organized to serve the gospel and the coming of God's kingdom."[84] They shared in Christ's mission as disciples, friends, confidants. Although their functions included a foundational role reserved to them alone, which others could not inherit, the apostles understood that it was Christ's will that they provide successors to their ministry. As heirs and representatives of the apostles, these successors continued their mission, remaining in communion with each other.

Jesus intended that the apostolic ministry which he established should remain forever at the service of reconciliation, drawing all into his Body through baptism, celebrating his presence in the Eucharist and other sacraments, teaching the saving truth, and governing the people with a shepherd's care. Christ himself willed for his Church a ministerial structure formed by the apostles, their collaborators and, upon their death, by their successors to the apostolic ministry. These successors continue the work of evangelization through their mission of authoritative teaching and pastoral leadership.

Among the apostles commissioned was Peter, the one apostle to whom Jesus delegated additional obligations. These tasks were later to be carried out by personal successors who would assume the function of providing stability to the community. The ministry of Peter, though in some ways personal and unique, is intrinsic to Christ's saving plan for humanity, a plan which was to last "to the close of the age" (Mt 28:20). The office that Christ had conferred on Peter was inherited by his successors; the bishops of Rome were included in the promises made "in Peter." The keys of the kingdom were not buried with the chief apostle. Just as in the body a vital function cannot cease if the body is to stay alive, so in the Church, herself living and life-giving, the office of Peter continues in the papal ministry entrusted to Peter's successors. In willing that the Church maintain her apostolic identity, Christ implicitly willed the means necessary for its preservation, the episcopacy and the papacy. From the second century onward, the Roman church possessed an authority which no other had.

Christ himself did not choose Rome as the see of Peter. He entrusted the choice of deciding the concrete conditions of Peter's succession, and working out the implications of his ministry, to divine providence. Whatever the weight of the varying reasons for Peter's succession being linked with Rome, what emerges unmistakably from the mists of history is that no other see ever made a similar claim. The special role of the Roman church is primarily based on its unique relationship with Peter.

Notes for Chapter three

1. Avery Dulles, *The Resilient Church* (Garden City: Doubleday & Company, 1977), 116-117.
2. Raymond E. Brown and John P. Meier, *Antioch and Rome* (New York: Paulist Press, 1982), 98.
3. In the fourth century, Eusebius attributed this letter to Clement. See *The History of the Church*, rev. ed. and introduction Andrew Louth, trans. G. A. Williamson (London: Penguin Books, 1989), 3.16, p. 80.
4. Clement, *First Letter to the Corinthians*, 5.
5. Ignatius of Antioch, *Letter to the Romans*, 4.3.
6. Eusebius, *History of the Church*, 2.25, p. 63.
7. Tertullian, *The Prescription of Heretics*, 36.
8. Karl Baus, "From the Apostolic Community to Constantine," in *Handbook of Church History*, ed. Hubert Jedin and John Dolan, vol. 1 (Montreal: Palm Publishers, 1964), 114-115.
9. James T. Shotwell and Louise Ropes Loomis, *The See of Peter* (New York: Columbia University Press, 1991), 120-127.
10. Eusebius, *History of the Church*, 2.25, p. 63.
11. Jose Ruysschaert, "The Memorial of the Apostle and the Constantinian Basilica," in *The*

Vatican and Christian Rome, ed. Gabriel-Marie Garrone (Vatican City: Polyglot Press, 1975), 34.
12. Margherita Guarducci, "Vatican," *Encyclopedia of the Early Church*, ed. Angelo Di Berardino, trans. Adrian Walford, vol. 2 (Cambridge: James Clarke & Co., 1992), 862.
13. Cited in John Evangelist Walsh, *The Bones of St. Peter* (Garden City: Doubleday & Company, 1982), 74.
14. Cited in Walsh, *Bones of St. Peter*, 2.
15. Stephan Otto Horn, "The Petrine Mission of the Church of Rome: Some Biblical and Patristic Views," *Communio*, 18:4 (1991), 315.
16. Louis Bouyer, *The Church of God*, trans. Charles Underhill Quinn (Chicago: Franciscan Herald Press, 1982), 381.
17. Leo Scheffczyk, *Il ministero di Pietro*, trans. Franco Ardusso (Turin: Marietti, 1975), 34.
18. Bouyer, *Church of God*, 381.
19. Raymond E. Brown, *Biblical Reflections on Crises Facing the Church* (New York: Paulist Press, 1975), 70.
20. Otto Karrer, *Peter and the Church*, trans. Ronald Walls (New York: Herder and Herder, 1970), 33.
21. International Theological Commission, "The Priestly Ministry," in *International Theological Commission: Texts and Documents 1969-1985*, ed. Michael Sharkey (San Francisco: Ignatius Press, 1989), 40.
22. Bouyer, *Church of God*, 316.
23. Francis A. Sullivan, *Magisterium: Teaching Authority in the Catholic Church* (New York: Paulist Press, 1983), 42.
24. Joseph Ratzinger, *La Chiesa: Una comunità sempre in cammino*, trans. Luigi Frattini, 2nd ed. (Turin: Edizioni Paoline, 1992), 87.
25. Karrer, *Peter and the Church*, 108.
26. International Theological Commission, "Catholic Teaching on Apostolic Succession," in *International Theological Commission: Texts and Documents 1969-1985*, ed. Michael Sharkey (San Francisco: Ignatius Press, 1989), 98.
27. International Theological Commission, "Priestly Ministry," in *Texts and Documents*, 45.
28. Francis A. Sullivan, *The Church We Believe In: One, Holy, Catholic and Apostolic* (New York: Paulist Press, 1988), 167.
29. International Theological Commission, "Catholic Teaching on Apostolic Succession," in *Texts and Documents*, 98.
30. Robert B. Eno, *The Rise of the Papacy* (Wilmington: Michael Glazier, 1990), 21.
31. Bouyer, *Church of God*, 391.
32. Karl Rahner, "The Hierarchical Structure of the Church, with Special Reference to the Episcopate," in *Commentary on the Documents of Vatican II*, ed. Herbert Vorgrimler, vol. 1 (New York: Herder and Herder, 1967), 190.
33. Bouyer, *Church of God*, 321.
34. Clement, *First Letter to the Corinthians*, 44.
35. Irenaeus, *Against Heresies*, 3.3.3.
36. Yves Congar, *"La Chiesa è apostolica," in L'evento salvifico nella comunità di Gesù Cristo*, Mysterium Salutis, ed. Johannes Feiner and Magnus Löhrer, trans. Giovanni Moretto, Dino Pezzetta, and Gino Stefani. vol. 7 (Brescia: Queriniana, 1972), 643, n. 12.

37. Charles Journet, "Collegiality," *L'Osservatore Romano*, 35 (August 28, 1969), 5.
38. Congar, "La Chiesa è apostolica," 651-653.
39. Bouyer, *Church of God*, 319.
40. Bouyer, *Church of God*, 322.
41. Karl Rahner, "Aspects of the Episcopal Office," in *Theological Investigations*, trans. David Bourke, vol. 14 (London: Darton, Longman & Todd, 1976), 189.
42. Sullivan, *The Church We Believe In*, 167.
43. J. M. R. Tillard, *Church of Churches: The Ecclesiology of Communion*, trans. R. C. De Peaux (Collegeville: Liturgical Press, 1992), 182.
44. Karrer, *Peter and the Church*, 110.
45. Ignatius of Antioch, *Letter to the Ephesians*, 3.2.
46. Eco, *Rise of the Papacy*, 23.
47. Bouyer, *Church of God*, 373.
48. Sullivan, *Magisterium*, 49.
49. Rahner, "Aspects of the Episcopal Office," 189-190.
50. Charles Munier, "Authority in the Church," *Encyclopedia of the Early Church*, ed. Angelo Di Berardino, trans. Adrian Walford, vol. 1 (Cambridge: James Clarke & Co., 1992), 103.
51. J. M. R. Tillard, *The Bishop of Rome*, trans. John de Satgé (Wilmington: Michael Glazier, 1983), 84.
52. Irenaeus, *Against Heresies*, 3.3.3.
53. Tillard, *Church of Churches*, 286.
54. Raymond E. Brown, *Responses to 101 Questions on the Bible* (New York: Paulist Press, 1990), 133.
55. Karrer, *Peter and the Church*, 109.
56. Karl Rahner, "The Episcopal Office," in *Theological Investigations*, trans., Karl-H. and Boniface Kruger, vol. 6 (Baltimore: Helicon Press, 1969), 323-324.
57. Eno, *Rise of the Papacy*, 29.
58. Eno, *Rise of the Papacy*, 26-29.
59. Brown, *Responses to 101 Questions on the Bible*, 132.
60. Anglican-Roman Catholic International Commission (ARCIC), *Authority in the Church II*, #8.
61. Karl Adam, *The Spirit of Catholicism*, rev. ed., trans. Justin McCann (Garden City: Doubleday & Company, 1954), 97-98.
62. Karrer, *Peter and the Church*, 95.
63. Heinrich Fries and Karl Rahner, *Unity of the Churches: An Actual Possibility*, trans. Ruth C. L. Gritsch and Eric Gritsch (Philadelphia: Fortress Press, 1985), 64.
64. Hans Urs von Balthasar, *The Office of Peter and the Structure of the Church*, trans. Andrée Emery (San Francisco: Ignatius Press, 1986), 245.
65. Bouyer, *Church of God*, 383.
66. Eusebius, *History of the Church*, 2.14, p. 49.
67. J. M. R. Tillard, "The Presence of Peter in the Ministry of the Bishop of Rome," *One in Christ*, 27:2 (1991), 112-113.
68. Leo the Great, *Sermon*, 82.1.
69. Shotwell and Loomis, *See of Peter*, 217.
70. Ludwig Hertling, *"Communio": Church and Papacy in Early Christianity*, trans. Jared Wicks

70 ✦ SUCCESSION TO PETER'S MINISTRY

(Chicago: Loyola University Press, 1972), 65.
71. Norman P. Tanner, ed., *Decrees of the Ecumenical Councils*, vol. 1 (Washington, D.C.: Georgetown University Press, 1990), 32.
72. See Eusebius, *History of the Church*, 4.22, p. 129.
73. Irenaeus, *Against Heresies*, 3.3.3.
74. Roch Kereszty, "Peter and Paul and the Founding of the Church of Rome: Some Forgotten Perspectives," *Communio*, 15 (1988), 217.
75. Kereszty, "Peter and Paul and the Founding of the Church of Rome," 223.
76. William R. Farmer and Roch Kereszty, *Peter and Paul in the Church of Rome* (New York: Paulist Press, 1990), 92.
77. John Chrysostom, *Homilies on Romans*, 32; translation in Thomas Halton, *The Church*, Message of the Fathers of the Church, vol. 4 (Wilmington: Michael Glazier, 1985), 109.
78. Translation in Halton, *The Church*, 109.
79. Tillard, *Bishop of Rome*, 93.
80. Kereszty, "Peter and Paul and the Founding of the Church of Rome," 220.
81. Tillard, "Presence of Peter," 120.
82. John Paul II, Discourse, January 27, 1993, *L'Osservatore Romano*, 5 (February 3, 1993), 11.
83. Kereszty "Peter and Paul and the Founding of the Church of Rome," 221-222.
84. John Paul II, Discourse, July 1, 1992, *L'Osservatore Romano*, 27 (July 8, 1992), 11.

Chapter four
EARLY DEVELOPMENT OF ROMAN PRIMACY

Nonscriptural evidence dating from the end of the first century already testifies to the special position of the Roman see and its bishop in the universal Church. From the close of the second century onward, witnesses multiply in support of Roman primacy, and their interpretation becomes easier. Increasingly aware that it had a solicitude for the universal Church, the church at Rome intervened in the affairs of other churches. At the same time, the first explanations of why Rome and its bishop assumed the duty of preserving the apostolic faith and fostering ecclesial communion were formulated. Pope Leo drew together the threads on the theory and practice of Roman primacy that had been forming for more than two centuries. Leo is called "the Great" precisely because of his contribution to the development of the primacy of the Roman see. By the end of the fifth century, the Petrine office had achieved its basic shape and had been given its fundamental theological justification.

After some theological remarks on the development of doctrine with regard to the papacy, I will trace the evolution of Roman primacy from Clement of Rome (88-97) to Leo the Great (440-461). Three fundamental questions dictate the choice of material. Is there evidence that the Roman church played a unique role in the universal Church? If so, how did the other churches react to this ministry? What reasons were advanced to justify the special function in the universal *koinonia* which the Roman see and its bishop assumed?

To answer these questions I shall examine the early interventions of Popes Clement and Victor, and the recognition of the Roman church's uniqueness recorded by Ignatius, Irenaeus, and others. Then I shall look at the arguments put forward to justify Roman primacy, especially those concerning its Petrine foundation. Lastly, I discuss the important contribution of Leo the Great. From the historical and doctrinal point of view, he is the founder of the modern papacy as we know it.[1]

Papal Primacy and the Development of Doctrine

According to Catholic teaching, because Jesus bestowed unique responsibilities on Peter, the papacy is a permanent element in the Church. The early Christians, however, could not, and did not, think about the principal realities of faith in the same way we do.[2] In the first generations, the full meaning, authority, and importance of the Petrine office were not immediately evident. It appears that the church at Rome and the other churches in the *koinonia* understood little about the import of the ministry of Peter or how it would function. Under God's providence, the passage of time was needed for its seeds to take root and flourish.

While the Petrine ministry originated in Jesus' will, as a historical institution embodying his plan, the papacy developed gradually. This slow unfolding, however, should not surprise us. As the Second Vatican Council teaches: "The Tradition that comes from the apostles makes progress in the Church, with the help of the Holy Spirit. There is a growth in insight into the realities and words that are being passed on" (DV 8). To allow for development in the Church's practice and doctrine of the papacy is in keeping with her nature as a historical institution.

The evolution from Peter's original ministry to the pope's full claim to, and exercise of, primacy was slow. It took several centuries, after all, before the scriptural canon was officially determined as such, even though it was "present" in the Church from the apostolic age. As early as the end of the first century, some Church writings began to be recognized as sacred Scripture. The process of gathering them all together to form the New Testament, however, reached its conclusion only two centuries later. By comparison, the Roman church's role as the standard of the true apostolic faith is more ancient than the Church's recognizing the New Testament canon as sacred Scripture.[3] Other truths of faith were also implicitly present in the Church's consciousness before they were explicitly professed. The christological and trinitarian definitions of the early ecumenical councils, sacramental doctrine, and the Marian dogmas of the Immaculate Conception and the Assumption likewise point to doctrinal development. It took time for the Church to arrive at an adequate understanding of what Christ instituted and of what was contained in the deposit of faith.

As far as the Petrine ministry is concerned, the pope's role evolved within a set of complex historical factors. It appears that he did not use full primatial authority from the beginning. Without anachronism, we cannot say that the first popes *exercised* their jurisdiction in the sense solemnly defined at the First Vatican Council in 1870. Only in the process of discharging her mission did the Church recognize the fuller implications of Peter's office. At the outset, the Petrine ministry was at least partially "dormant." To be sure, the function was there, but only as the germ of the form which it later acquired.

The popes first acted in "primatial" ways before explaining why, or on what grounds, they did so. This initial period of the papacy is marked by what Jesuit theologian Cardinal Henri de Lubac calls an "early sobriety." Simple practice, not theoretical expositions, claims, and "an arsenal of proofs," was sufficient for the early Christians.[4] Only slowly did the bishops of Rome explicitly articulate their unique role in the *koinonia*. The Church grasped gradually what Jesus had intended. His will for Peter's successors was always embedded in human factors of personality, politics, and social and Church life. Very frequently these factors played a significant role in shaping the development of the papacy as an institution.

The classical texts from the patristic tradition provide a valuable witness to the rise of the papacy: from the exercise of particular authority evident in the *First Letter to the Corinthians*, to its recognition by Ignatius, to the first reason justifying it in Irenaeus, to its mature development in Leo. Before examining these testimonies, two caveats, however, are in order.

On the one hand, although this early documentary evidence is valuable, by itself it does not confirm everything that the Church has come to believe about the papal ministry.

The Shepherd and the Rock

The earliest texts, especially, are fragmentary. Moreover, particular details of interpretation are widely disputed. Nonetheless, when taken together, this ancient testimony furnishes a convincing argument for accepting papal primacy as the historical embodiment of the Petrine office willed by Christ. On the other hand, not every papal claim made at this time can be equated with Church teaching. When the doctrine of certain witnesses is judged in light of later dogmatic developments, it must sometimes be regarded as incomplete, inadequate, or exaggerated.

Early Interventions of the Roman Church

Rome's Letter to Corinth

The *First Letter to the Corinthians* provides the earliest example of a Roman intervention in the life of another local church. This Roman action testifies to an exercise of Petrine authority, even though it is not explicitly claimed as such.

A revolt had taken place in the church at Corinth, where some of its duly selected presbyters had been deposed. Rome's letter to the Christian community there judged this deposition of clerics to be "sedition, so alien and out of place in God's elect."[5] The letter urged the Corinthians to restore peace and fervor in their church. After setting out the principle of apostolic succession by tracing it back to Christ's will, the letter called for the reinstatement of the expelled presbyters.

It is not entirely certain whether the Roman church intervened on its own authority, the more usual Catholic interpretation,[6] or because the Corinthians had invited Rome to resolve the dispute.[7] All commentators, however, draw attention to the unusual nature of this Roman intervention in another church's affairs. For at least four reasons this step was atypical. First, the early churches did not routinely write to one another using the imperious tone evident in the letter. Second, the church at Rome vigorously combated pagan "Babylon" and would not likely have ridden on the shirttails of civil authority as a pretext to interfere. Third, Corinth was the older church, founded by Paul. Why would the Roman church be meddling in its internal affairs, unless it sensed a right to do so? Fourth, when the letter was written the apostle John was probably still alive and lived closer to Corinth. If the Corinthians needed fraternal support, why did they not ask him, or any other apostolic church in the area, to help them resolve their internal strife?

The tone of the Roman intervention in as vital a matter of Church order as the nature and source of ecclesial office is authoritarian. Though cleverly and diplomatically written, the letter calls for obedience "to the things which we have written through the Holy Spirit."[8] American patristic scholar Agnes Cunningham comments that it contains signs "of prophetic awareness, of what seems to be a charism of universality and of personal conviction that what the author does is right, in admonishing the rebellious Corinthians."[9] The Roman church took action because it felt a sense of obligation for the welfare of other communities, even those geographically distant.[10]

After giving many reasons why the Corinthian troublemakers should feel remorse, the epistle clinches its argument by invoking the authority of the Roman church: "But if any disobey the words spoken by Him [Christ] through us, let them know they will involve themselves in transgression and no small danger."[11] Echoing the decree of the council at Jerusalem (cf. Acts 15:28), the letter then adds an admonition: "For you will give us joy and gladness if, obedient to what we have written through the Holy Spirit, you root out the lawless anger of your jealousy."[12] Though not a formal intervention which would legally bind the Corinthians, the epistle betrays a tone that is more than merely admonitory. It expects the church at Corinth to obey its directives.

While betraying the Roman church's awareness of its obligation and authority, the letter furnishes no reasons which would sanction its right to intervene. In order to justify this step, the epistle neither invokes the biblical Petrine texts nor mentions the fact of Rome as Peter's church. All that history has preserved is the bare fact of the intervention. At very least, however, this action reveals the Roman community's intuitive sense of a right to help settle the affairs of other churches, a right received by the Corinthians with a similar awareness.

This epistle could not be used to support an argument for the early exercise of the primacy if its recipients had contested or repelled the intervention as presumptuous. While it is uncertain whether the Corinthians obeyed the Roman injunctions, the document was well received at Corinth. They did not consider the gesture as an improper intrusion into their affairs. Indeed, the Corinthians held the letter in such high regard that for many years afterward they read it at their liturgical services, almost on a par with sacred Scripture itself.[13]

Who wrote this letter? Nowhere does it explicitly mention the bishop of Rome as its author. Many scholars propose that it was more a communal effort: a message from one church to another. Eusebius, however, records the name of its author: "Clement has left us one recognized epistle, long and wonderful, which he composed in the name of the church at Rome and sent to the church at Corinth."[14] At least by the early fourth century, the preeminence of the local church at Rome was identified with its bishop. It is possible that Clement was not the monarchical bishop of Rome, but a presbyter/bishop who handled relations with other churches, writing to them on behalf of the Roman church.[15] If this is true, while the letter would not prove that the bishop of Rome personally exercised Petrine authority, it would still provide an argument for an early use of Petrine prerogatives by the Roman church.

Excommunication by Pope Victor

Within less than a century after Clement's letter, the historical sources furnish yet another instance of a decisive Roman intervention in another local church. Among the most forceful of second-century popes, Victor (189-199) displayed remarkable authority in his attempt to resolve the Quatrodeciman controversy. In many churches of Asia, which guarded the memory of the apostle John, Easter was celebrated on the feast of Passover. Because this was always the fourteenth day of the Jewish month Nisan, it did not usually fall on Sunday. Although his predecessors had tolerated this Eastern custom, Victor sought to get all the churches to agree to the same date. He wanted Easter celebrated throughout the Church on the first Sunday following the Passover, not on the fourteenth of Nisan. This would keep it on the original day of the resurrection. At Victor's prompting, synods of bishops were held all over the Mediterranean world to discuss his proposal. Strengthened by the votes of the majority who sided with him, Victor threatened with excommunication any bishop who did not accept his ruling. The churches of Asia Minor, however, did not yield in face of his threat.[16] In response, Victor excommunicated those dissident churches. Eusebius records his reaction: "Thereupon Victor, head of the Roman church, attempted at one stroke to cut off from the common unity all the Asian dioceses, together with the neighboring churches, on the ground of heterodoxy, and pilloried them in letters in which he announced the total excommunication of all his fellow-Christians there."[17]

Irenaeus of Lyons (†200), for one, opposed Victor's action, begging that he allow the Eastern tradition of dating Easter to stand. Significantly, however, he did not question Victor's right to intervene. "By the very fact that he adjured Pope Victor not to excommunicate the Asians, Irenaeus recognized his power to take such a measure."[18] We do not know whether the bishop of Lyons, himself from Asia Minor, was successful in restraining the Pope from actually imposing excommunication. In any case, even after Victor's forceful intervention, the Quatrodeciman practice continued in some churches of the East. It was only at the Council of Nicaea in 325 that the Quatrodecimans were definitively excommunicated from the whole Church.

Before Victor's pontificate, bishops acting together in assemblies had expelled heretics from their own churches. Individual bishops had done likewise. Victor, however, maintained that his action severed communion not just with the local church at Rome, but also with all the other churches of the *koinonia*. His action was novel because he singlehandedly excommunicated the whole church of another province.

Contemporary sources tell us nothing about the reasons which Victor gave to justify his action. While it cannot be proven, it is reasonable to conclude that Victor legitimated his authority by using arguments similar to those invoked by his contemporary Irenaeus. The principal reasons for Roman preeminence at this time were "the full and well-authenticated, apostolic tradition of Rome, which could not be in error, confirmed as it had been, by members of other apostolic communions over the Empire."[19] Victor's assertion of his right to break off communion with another church — an excommunication with effects for the universal Church — marks a significant step in the consolidation of Roman primacy.

Recognition of Roman Primacy

From the beginning of the second century, written documents testify that local churches outside Rome recognized its special role in the *koinonia*. Although they sometimes argued that the Roman bishop had acted imprudently or ill-advisedly, none, either in the East or in the West, disputed his right to provide pastoral care for churches other than his own.[20]

Ignatius' Letter to the Church at Rome

A distinctive feature of the *Letter to the Romans* of St. Ignatius (†107), written very early in the second century, is its unconventional salutation. When compared with the sober prefaces of the other six letters which he sent to churches in Asia Minor, the originality of its enthusiastic introduction stands out. He heaps praise upon praise in his greeting: "To the church ... which has the chief seat in the place of the district of the Romans, worthy of God, worthy of honor, worthy of congratulation, worthy of praise, worthy of success, worthy in purity, having the chief place in love."[21] Ignatius addresses no other church with such accolades.

His letter begins by referring to the principal church "in the place of the district of the Romans"; that is, in the environs of Rome or central Italy. The last phrase, "having the chief place in love" or "presiding in love," has caused extensive comment. Though probably not intending to signify any legal precedence for the Roman community, it could mean that the Roman church presides over the "whole Church." The term "in love" is *agape*, which elsewhere refers to the universal Church.[22] A good argument can therefore be made, and John Paul II makes it, that the phrase "having the chief place in love" expresses "the primacy in that communion of charity which is the Church, and necessarily the service of authority, the *ministerium Petrinum*."[23]

The bishop of Antioch gave no specific explanation why the Roman church enjoyed its preeminence. However, two reasons for Rome's prominence are suggested in his letter. Very free in offering advice to the other communities to which he wrote, Ignatius, nonetheless, refrained from admonishing the church at Rome. According to him, while the Roman community could instruct other churches, it was not itself taught. This teaching function might explain why its authority extended beyond Rome: "You have never envied anyone; you have taught others, but I wish that what you enjoin in your teaching may endure."[24] Ignatius implies that the Roman church enjoyed some kind of teaching authority, a fact which probably accounts for the letter's flattering salutation.

Second, Ignatius mentioned Sts. Peter and Paul as apostles and preachers connected with Rome.[25] This could be a further reason for acknowledging the church's prominence. In any case, Ignatius' testimony furnishes a solid foundation for holding that early Christians recognized Rome as having a "presiding" role in the universal Church. This charge included its right to teach others.

Appeals to the Roman See

During the second century, Rome's tenacious confession of orthodox faith was a point of reference for the entire Church. Communion with Rome, the focal point of the *koinonia*, was a particular church's guarantee of belonging to the true Church. When Bishop Cyprian of Carthage (†258) wrote to Pope Cornelius (251-253) in 252 that the Roman see was "the chair of Peter and ... the principal church in which sacerdotal unity has its source,"[26] he recognized that Rome was more than the geographical center of the *koinonia*. As Church historian Ludwig Hertling concluded, Rome was "the center of its [a church's] power and legitimacy."[27] In early Christianity, a community's membership in the universal Church depended on communion with the see of Peter. Her bishops were bound together by sharing the same faith and by the tie of a sacramental-juridical *communio* whose center was the bishop of Rome.[28]

Consequently, when questions about faith or discipline arose in the various churches throughout the world, the disputants went to Rome to gain a favorable hearing for their ideas.[29] Rome was both the standard of reference in doctrine and the judge of other churches' orthodoxy.[30] In the third century, recognition of Rome's juridical preeminence was added to that of acknowledging its doctrinal authority. From the very outset, Hans Urs von Balthasar observes, "whenever the activity of the Roman bishop went beyond the boundaries of his diocese, it was linked to the task of arbitrating disputes."[31] This took the form of appealing to the Roman see so that it would settle all manner of disputes between churches. Since officials in the Roman Empire were accustomed to seek rescripts from Rome when dealing with difficult questions, it was normal that ecclesiastics sought the same help from the bishop of Rome. When matters could not be resolved within a local church or province, Rome's judgment was sought.

The Synod of Sardica (343-344), held near present-day Sofia, decreed in its disciplinary canons that the Roman bishop was the legal court of appeal and recourse in disputes between churches (cf. DS 133-135). According to subsequent Western interpretations, this synod, with its approximately equal number of participants from the East and the West, expressly confirmed that Rome was the see of appellate jurisdiction for the universal Church. Rome's further claim to have the right to review all major questions was undoubtedly an outgrowth of this appellate jurisdiction recognized by the Synod of Sardica.[32] The synod participants' recognition of this right no doubt depended, at least in part, on the model provided by the imperial system. The pope's right of appellate jurisdiction was patterned procedurally on that of the emperor.[33]

The authority of the Roman bishop to issue definitive judgments was not limited to disciplinary matters. As doctrinal controversies became more intense, judging matters of faith became increasingly important. Rome was more and more consulted on many different questions regarding the faith.

St. Jerome (†420), for example, appealed to Rome for an authoritative pronouncement on the meaning of the term "three *hypostases*." The Greek-speaking Cappadocian Fathers used this terminology in their trinitarian doctrine to describe the Father, Son, and Holy Spirit as distinct persons. Because Jerome translated the Greek *hypostasis* with the Latin word *essentia* or "essence," this sounded to him as if the Cappadocians were tritheists. In desperation he appealed to Pope Damasus in 376: "Since the East, rent asunder by feuds of long standing, is tearing to shreds the seamless robe of the Lord . . . , I think it my duty to consult the Chair of Peter. . . . As I follow no leader save Christ, so I communicate with none save your Beatitude; that is, with the Chair of Peter. For this, I know, is the Rock on which the Church is built. This is Noah's ark, and he who is not found in it shall perish when the flood overwhelms all."[34] Jerome is just one witness among the many who recognized that the bishop of Rome could resolve disputes threatening to compromise the Church's unity of faith.

Pope Innocent I (401-417) enhanced Rome's juridical role even further. He asserted Rome's right to judge all major cases (*causae maiores*) within the universal Church. No case could be considered definitively resolved until the Roman see had adjudicated it. In

417, the bishops of North Africa sent Innocent the decrees of their recent council in Carthage, which had been called to settle controversies on original sin, infant baptism, and grace. In his reply, the Pope expressed his satisfaction for the content of the synodal decrees and for their sending them for his convalidation. To the African bishops, he wrote: "In your pursuit of the things of God, . . . following the examples of ancient tradition, . . . you have made manifest by your proper course of action the vitality of our religion . . . when you agreed to have recourse to our judgment, knowing what is due to the apostolic See, since all of us placed in this position wish to follow the apostle (Peter), from whom have come this episcopate and all the authority belonging to this dignity" (DS 217).

The Roman see assumed the task of guaranteeing the orthodoxy of the faith and seeing that it was promoted in the *koinonia*. Other churches throughout the world were to learn from Rome what teachings they were to correct and which they were to avoid, even if Rome itself had not judged the particular cases.[35] Popes Zosimus (417-418) and Boniface (418-422) reinforced the rule laid down by Innocent, holding that it was unlawful to reconsider a decision previously rendered by the Roman see.

Testimony of Irenaeus

Beginning in the mid-second century, the Church was threatened by gnosticism. This heresy claimed to have access to a tradition of apostolic "secrets" which gave the sect's adherents privileged knowledge (*gnosis*) of Christ's message. Bishop Irenaeus of Lyons was very anxious to preserve, without any false accretions, the original teaching of Jesus and the apostles. In order to vindicate Catholic truth against error, he was unable to use Scripture, since the gnostics appealed to their own "enlightened" interpretations channeled through their own tradition. The question therefore became the identification of the true tradition.

Irenaeus replied that the apostles, entrusted with the gospel, passed on its full truth to their successors, the bishops who inherited their authority in the churches where they presided. He argued against the gnostic claims to secret knowledge in two ways. First, all true bishops and their predecessors taught doctrines opposed to gnosticism. Second, present-day bishops, he said, can trace their appointment to office in a line of legitimate succession from apostolic times — something the gnostics could not do. This discussion led to his invaluable testimony to Roman primacy.

Confident that the apostolic teaching publicly proclaimed by bishops is the standard of truth, Irenaeus then proposed that those looking for the authentically transmitted gospel should turn to the bishops of the apostolic sees. If this succession exists in one church, which is united to the others, then it exists in all of them. To avoid giving a list of bishops for every church in the *koinonia*, he took the Roman church as his example: "But . . . by pointing out the apostolic tradition and faith announced to mankind, which has been brought down to our time by successions of bishops, in the greatest, most ancient, and well-known church, founded and established by the two most glorious apostles, Peter and Paul, at Rome, we can confound all who in any other way, either for self-pleasing or vainglory, or by blindness or perversity, gather more than they ought."[36] Although

Irenaeus' selection of Rome appears to be arbitrary, this is unlikely. From his description of Rome as "the greatest, most ancient, and well-known church," he implied that it is the foremost community which preserved the authentic tradition.

Among all the apostolic sees, Irenaeus argued that Rome stands alone. He then drew a very important conclusion: "For with this church, because of its superior origin [*propter potentiorem principalitatem*: 'more powerful preeminence'], all churches must agree; that is, all the faithful in the whole world; for in her the apostolic tradition has always been preserved for the benefit of the faithful everywhere."[37] Because the original Greek manuscript has been lost, only a literal Latin translation of this famous passage is extant. Its ambiguity has led to the following questions: What is "this church" to which Irenaeus refers? Why does it have a "superior origin" or "more powerful preeminence"? What are "all [the] churches" which must "agree" with this church? What justification does Irenaeus offer for demanding agreement with the Roman church?

Though some have argued that "this church" refers to the universal Church, the context of the passage seems to preclude this on textual, if not syntactical, grounds. The disputed sentence is preceded by a reference to Peter and Paul and followed by a list of Peter's successors. Doubtlessly, Irenaeus is alluding here to the local church at Rome.

The "superior origin" or "more powerful preeminence" of the Roman church is due to its previously mentioned "foundation" by "the glorious martyrs, Peter and Paul." Irenaeus believed that this dual apostolicity, authenticated by the seal of martyrdom, was reason enough to single out Rome among all the churches. This preeminence (*principalitas*) of the Roman church was widely recognized in the first centuries.

The fact that "all churches must agree" with the Roman church is, for Irenaeus, essential to the nature of the Church. The gospel, entrusted to the apostles and faithfully handed down to their successors, cannot contradict itself. Dissension regarding the rule of faith was heterodox. According to theologian Roch Kereszty, by "all churches" Irenaeus "means every local church everywhere in the world."[38] As "the greatest, most ancient, and well known" church, Rome is the criterion for orthodoxy.[39] All other churches must therefore agree with the Roman church. Commenting on this text of Irenaeus, John Paul II has said this agreement "entails unity of faith, teaching and discipline — precisely what is contained in the apostolic tradition."[40] For Irenaeus, the church at Rome, having guarded the rule of faith, is the standard of the apostolic authenticity of the other churches.

What reason does Irenaeus give for presenting Rome as the universal norm of orthodoxy? He does not justify Roman primacy by appealing to Jesus' promises to Peter or to the bishop of Rome as the apostle's successor. In Kereszty's judgment, "the joint activity of the two 'most glorious apostles' Peter and Paul in Rome, their preaching to, founding and building up the church of Rome, is the most obvious ground for Rome's special position."[41] For Irenaeus, martyrdom brought apostleship to perfection, confirming the truth of the apostolic preaching. Through their witness at Rome, Peter and Paul guaranteed that the gospel is taught there in all its purity. Irenaeus is the first writer to provide a justification for Rome's position of leadership:

the martyrdom of Sts. Peter and Paul. For this reason, the apostolic tradition in Rome is preserved undefiled.

Primacy of the Roman Bishop

The earliest witnesses imply that during the Church's first two centuries, it was the Roman *church* which enjoyed primacy in the universal communion. Until the end of the second century, Rome's religious prestige "seems to have attached to the church as a whole and to have been based upon its primitive connection with both Paul and Peter and its legacy of a double apostolic tradition."[42] Only in the third, and especially in the fourth, century did justifications for the primacy shift from the privileges of the Roman church to those of its bishop.

As we have seen, the motives for attributing preeminence to the church over the bishop included Ignatius' effusive salutation in his *Letter to the Romans:* "to the church . . . which has the chief seat in the place of the district of the Romans." He linked primacy to the church at Rome rather than explicitly to its bishop. Irenaeus, too, accorded the Roman church a primacy due to its *potentior principalitas*, the "more powerful preeminence" of its apostolic foundation by Peter and Paul.[43] Rome was the first church in the *koinonia*. Its authority was legitimated by the claim to dual apostolicity. The bishops of Rome assumed a leadership role based on the prerogatives of their see before they invoked arguments based on their personal succession to Peter.

In the initial stages of the papacy's development, those who recognized the primacy of the Roman church also accepted, at least implicitly, the primacy of its bishop. Apostolic *episkope* is essential to the nature of every church. Though the primacy was sometimes attributed to the Roman church ignoring its bishop, and arguments were occasionally articulated in this way, this was not, in fact, the case.

When the monarchical episcopacy was firmly in place, the bishop came to personify his local church. Whatever primacy was associated with the church belonged to him as head of the community. Ecclesial preeminence focused on the church's bishop. Irenaeus argued, for example, that the preservation of authentic apostolic teaching depends on the personal succession of bishops in apostolic sees, not the mere historical existence of any see. While not yet explicitly expressed in the earliest documents, it appears that papal primacy was included within Roman primacy. It was the presence in Rome of Peter's successors that gave the church there its special role.[44]

Even when Catholics accept the later Petrine justification for Roman primacy, they need not cast aside its previously formulated legitimation as irrelevant. Instead, when joined to the argument based on Petrine succession, the earlier reason enriches the theological justifications for the foundation of papal primacy. Attuned to possible ecumenical openings, Kereszty maintains that "the theological importance of the church of Rome is not based only upon the fact that its bishop is the vicar of Peter; the earlier ground for the primacy is not simply more primitive and less valid than the latter. The theological content of the first has not been adequately explicated by the second."[45] Without denying the value of the later justifications for papal primacy, which appealed to the Petrine texts, the full riches of tradition are best served by integrating the earlier explanation of the primacy of the Roman *church* into the later dogmatic development of the primacy of its *bishop*.

Petrinitas

By the mid-third century, the explicit legitimation for Roman primacy was increasingly based on its *petrinitas*; that is, Rome had a preeminent role in the worldwide *koinonia* because it was the church of Peter's successors. At this point, the popes began to apply the Petrine texts of the gospels directly to themselves and their ministry. The commission Jesus had confided to Peter, they believed, was renewed personally to the apostle's successors in the Roman see. Popes justified their authority because of their unique link with Peter.

An articulated justification for papal primacy based on *petrinitas* took time to develop. Toward the end of the second century, this Petrine argument first emerged, possibly due to the increasing role of the New Testament canon in Church life. As we have seen, the Scriptures set out clearly the importance which all strands of the apostolic tradition give to Peter. Once the connection between Peter and the pope came to explicit consciousness, this became the conventional argument used to justify Rome's decisive position in the universal Church.

Early Use of the Petrine Texts

Tertullian (†225) is the earliest ecclesiastical writer known to have cited Matthew 16:18-19 to make a theological point. The casual and abbreviated way in which he refers to this Petrine text implies that it was already familiar to his audience. Arguing against heretics, he wrote in favor of the apostolic tradition publicly preserved by the bishops: "Was anything withheld from Peter, who was called 'the rock on which the Church should be built,' who also obtained the 'keys of the kingdom of heaven' with the power of loosing and binding in heaven and on earth?"[46] However, Tertullian does not infer from the gospel text anything more than a special privilege bestowed on the individual apostle Peter. He says nothing about Matthew's passage as the foundation for justifying a continuing role for a successor. Similarly, the ecclesiastical writers who immediately followed Tertullian in citing this Petrine text failed to use it to justify any particular authority held by the pope.

The explicit association of the bishop of Rome with Peter's primacy, as recounted in the New Testament, took shape in the third century. Pope Callistus (217-222) is the first recorded pope who invoked the power to bind and loose (cf. Mt 16:19) as his right — one sarcastically contested by Tertullian.[47] By the mid-third century, however, the Petrine text of Matthew exercised an enormous influence on the maturing theology of the papacy.

Cyprian of Carthage, despite his controversies with the Roman church about the validity of baptism administered by heretics and his ambiguous position regarding its juridical preeminence, referred to Rome as "the chair of Peter" and "the principal church."[48] Pope Stephen (254-257), the first exponent of a developed theory of the primacy, borrowed Cyprian's phrase "the chair of Peter" (*cathedra Petri*); he applied it exclusively to the Roman see in a way unintended by Cyprian. Stephen was also the first bishop of Rome to cite the Matthew text to justify his authority. Rome possessed a superior authority, according to Stephen, because its bishop was heir to the unique prerogatives Jesus gave to Peter. When Stephen excommunicated heretics, he demanded that other churches accept his decision, appealing specifically to Peter's authority. Just as Christ had granted to Peter a primacy among the apostles, so, he claimed, the Roman bishop was assigned leadership among the bishops.[49]

In reply, Bishop Firmilian of Caesarea in Cappadocia (†268) wrote bitingly to Cyprian concerning what he thought about Stephen's Petrine pretensions. He complained that "[Stephen] glories in the place of his episcopate and claims to hold the succession of Peter, on whom are placed the foundations of the Church."[50] Because of Firmilian's remarks, we have proof that Pope Stephen believed he possessed the chair of Peter through succession. This inheritance warranted, Stephen thought, his interventions in other churches' doctrinal and disciplinary affairs.

Because Peter's supremacy continued in Rome, its bishop exercised his authority from "the chair of Peter" which he inherited. Among the many witnesses to this *petrinitas* is that of Optatus of Milevis (†370): "the episcopal seat was established first in the city of Rome by Peter and . . . in it sat Peter, the head of all the apostles."[51] Peter was the chief, the head of the apostles. According to St. Ambrose (†397), Peter was personally the rock upon which Christ built the Church.[52] The bishop of Milan, convinced that the responsibility given to Peter was transmitted to his successors on the *cathedra* at Rome, was also the first to draw together coherently the three Petrine texts of Matthew, Luke, and John.[53] By the middle of the fourth century, the see of Peter became more simply "the apostolic see" without comparison — as if no others worth mentioning existed.

"Petrinitas" and the Fourth-Century Papacy

After the Edict of Milan in 313, which granted toleration to the Church, the bishop of Rome increasingly assumed special prerogatives. Remaining in Rome, he sent legates to settle affairs if matters outside the city needed his attention. Furthermore, bishops more and more sought guidelines from Rome, a factor which led to increased centralization and, at least in the West, greater uniformity of ecclesiastical discipline. The Roman bishop, however, did not bypass the other bishops by seeking to establish direct relations with either the lower clergy or the laity.[54]

From the pontificate of Damasus (366-384) onward, documentary evidence is plentiful that the "tone of papal correspondence is one of command, of supreme authority and undisputed primacy, unclouded by hesitation or shadow of self-doubt."[55] Damasus composed letters in a formal, chancery style, modeled on imperial rescripts. In his public statements, he adopted the plural of majesty using "we" rather than "I" and addressed his fellow bishops as "sons" instead of "brothers."[56]

Pope Damasus also vigorously defended his belief that Rome owed its privileged place in the Church to its connection with Peter. When canon 3 of the Council of Constantinople (381) insinuated that Rome's primacy could be justified because it was the capital of the Empire, Damasus contested that interpretation. In 382, he called a synod

The Shepherd and the Rock

which declared that "the holy Roman Church has been set before the rest by no conciliar decrees, but has obtained the primacy by the voice of our Lord and Savior in the gospel" (DS 350). The same Roman Synod confirmed the privileges of Alexandria and Antioch, although not Constantinople, because the former two also shared, by association, in *petrinitas*: "The first see, therefore, is that of Peter the Apostle, that of the Roman Church, which has neither stain nor anything like it. The second see, however, is that at Alexandria, consecrated in behalf of blessed Peter by Mark, his disciple and an evangelist, who was sent to Egypt by the Apostle Peter, where he preached the word of truth and finished his glorious martyrdom. The third honorable see, indeed, is that at Antioch, which belonged to the most blessed Apostle Peter, where first he dwelt before he came to Rome, and where the name *Christians* was first applied as a new people."[57]

Pope Damasus relied on Matthew 16:18-19 to bolster papal authority, but he also leaned heavily on the authority of Peter and Paul who were venerated at Rome as the princes of the apostles. According to patristic scholar Basilio Studer, Damasus "founded a theory of Roman primacy which his successors needed only to extend."[58] Once the Church had discerned the extent of the power handed over to Peter, any authority exercised beyond the confines of a local church looked to the first of the apostles in order to legitimate its use. Justifications for possessing ecclesial authority over other churches, such as that which Antioch and Alexandria enjoyed, relied on establishing a bond with Peter.

Successor and Vicar of Peter

The theory of Rome's *petrinitas* brought into clearer focus that the pope was both the successor and vicar of Peter. Initially, the term "successor" had a linear, chronological meaning. Popes used it in reference to popes before them. Callistus (217-222), for example, succeeded Zephyrinus (199-217), who succeeded Victor (180-199). Despite occasional earlier use, it was not until the end of the fourth century that the title "successor" of Peter entered official papal terminology.[59] Referring to the pope in this way became common by the eighth century, gradually replacing the earlier title "vicar" of Peter.

In the late patristic and early medieval Church, the title "vicar of Peter" was frequently used. Early Christians had a lively sense that, from heaven, the apostles continue to preside over and guide the Church's destiny. After the death of the apostles, they believed, successors in their ministry continued their apostolic mission, though without assuming their irreplaceable foundational functions. Just as the first "apostolic men" represented the original Twelve, so also did the bishops now take the place of the apostles in glory. In order to maintain this representative structure after the model of the original apostolate, writers emphasized Peter's unique role among the bishops.

The presence of the apostle's tomb in Rome likewise provided a visible symbol of Peter's lasting presence and enduring authority in the pope. Peter's original primacy among the apostles was perpetuated or "sacramentalized" in those succeeding to the Roman bishop's *cathedra*. "The once-for-all nature of his office," writes Tillard, "remains present through the vicars who successively occupy his seat."[60] Each bishop of Rome is the vicar of the apostle Peter, and not of his immediate predecessor. In his own ministry, the pope carried out the same mission Jesus confided to Peter.

The decretal of Damasus, dispatched by Pope Siricius (384-399) to the bishop of Tarragona in 385, illustrates this idea: Peter continues to govern the Church through the pope, who is his heir. "We carry the burden of all who are burdened," he wrote. "In fact, the blessed apostle Peter carries these burdens in us, he who, we trust, protects and defends us in everything as the heirs to his office" (DS 181). Siricius was the first pope to apply Paul's "care for all the churches" (*sollicitudo omnium ecclesiarum*) to the apostolic ministry of the bishop of Rome. In theory, if not yet in practice, the popes claimed a jurisdiction extending to all the churches of the Roman Empire.

Among the most well-known testimonies to the bishop of Rome as the vicar of Peter is the text read by the papal legate, Philip, at the Council of Ephesus in 431. Referring to Pope Celestine (422-432), he said: "There is no doubt, and in fact it has been known in all ages, that the holy and most blessed Peter, prince and head of the apostles, pillar of the faith, and foundation of the Catholic Church, received the keys of the kingdom from our Lord Jesus Christ . . . : who, even to this time and always, lives and judges in his successors. Our holy and most blessed Pope Celestine the bishop is according to due order his successor and holds his place."[61] This straightforward declaration of the pope as both successor and vicar of Peter, similar though not identical designations, was later cited by Vatican I (cf. DS 3056).

Leo the Great

In the first four centuries, no systematic theology of the papacy was formulated, even though individual elements which are the foundations of the later structure were already in place. While Leo the Great's understanding of the papacy was in continuity with his immediate predecessors, he developed a more explicit theology, bequeathing to posterity a carefully articulated understanding of the authority, purpose, and justification for papal primacy. In Leo's idea of the papal office, "all the separate strands of papal tradition coalesce to form a single cord."[62] His well-developed theory, formulated in his letters and sermons, can be summed up in three words: Christ-Peter-Pope. According to Leo, the primatial role of the Roman see was founded on two facts: the intimate union of Christ and Peter, and the legacy of Peter's ministry that survives in his vicars, the bishops of Rome.[63]

Jesus and Peter

In many sermons, especially those preached on the anniversary of his election as bishop of Rome, Leo the Great solidified the Roman and Western interpretation of Matthew 16:18-19. For the Pope, this text proved that Christ gave to Peter personally, and to him alone, a primatial role in the apostolic college. Without any human mediation, Jesus bestowed on the apostle an authority to be exercised for the good of the whole Church.[64] Basing himself on gospel testimony, Leo taught that Peter was the "chief of the whole Church."[65]

The Petrine texts revealed the reason for Peter's preeminence: an intimate relation or *consortium* between him and Jesus. Peter, Leo believed, "indefectibly obtains a consortium with the eternal priest."[66] In one of his sermons, he said: "By this appointment, God conferred on this man [Peter] a great and wonderful share in his power."[67] Christ himself shared with Peter his own functions as rock and shepherd of the Church. Leo aptly paraphrased Jesus' words to Peter recorded in Matthew 16:18, leaving no doubt that the disciple depended upon the Master: "I am the foundation and no one can lay any other. And yet, you Simon, you also are a Rock because I am going to give you my strength, in such a way that, by this sharing, the power which is only mine will be common to you and to me."[68] With more clarity and rigor than any of his predecessors, Leo the Great asserted that Peter "continues as the foundation rock in the strength which he received and does not abandon the control of the Church which he has undertaken."[69]

Pope = Peter

The pope was, for Leo, both the legal and sacramental embodiment of the apostle Peter. In the judgment of historian Walter Ullmann, Leo's "supreme mastery of Roman law enabled him to construct the thesis of Peter's function, and therefore that of the pope, in so satisfactory a way that it stood the test of time."[70] He translated papal claims into the language of law and public policy.

Leo did this by teaching that a close bond existed between Peter and his successors in the Roman see. Papal primacy was nothing more than Petrine primacy transferred to the present. The pope's exercise of his ministry was totally conditioned by reference to Peter. In a sermon preached on the anniversary of his episcopal consecration, this lively awareness of Peter's continuing power in his successors is very evident: "He [Peter] continues to carry out with full effect the work which has been entrusted to him; he discharges every duty, every task of his office in Christ and with Christ, and through him he is glorified. So whatever I [Leo] may achieve, whatever effective steps I may take . . . is done through his work and his merits; his power is still living in his see and his authority is supreme."[71] Whenever Leo was called upon to intervene in other churches, he always referred to Peter.

By using the Roman legal concept of the heir (*haeres*), Leo explained the way in which the pope was linked to Peter. Roman law accorded the *haeres* the same authority, rights, and obligations as the one whom he replaced. The power of the keys which Peter had received from Christ passed undiminished, therefore, to those who succeeded the apostle in the Roman *cathedra*. As the apostle's heir, the pope enjoyed the same office as Peter, fulfilling his mission in his absence.[72] "What Peter believed in Christ endures," wrote Leo, "so too what Christ instituted in Peter."[73]

According to the Pope, Peter continues his ministry in the Church through his visible vicar, who is his sacramental instrument. Unlike a successor, who receives juridical power from a predecessor, the vicar continues the presence of the one whom he represents. He takes the place of the living Peter in heaven, who enjoys a special relationship with Christ. Because of this bond, the pope can exercise the Petrine ministry: "Peter, who was united to Christ, the true founder and pastor of the Church, in a singular way, continues even now to exercise his primacy over all the churches; the bishop of Rome, the heir and successor of Peter, renders this primacy visible in the community of all Christians. Just as Christ transmitted his mission to the apostles *per Petrum* so are the faith and the ecclesiastical order guaranteed by the See of Peter."[74] In theological shorthand we can say that the pope is Peter himself (*Papa = Petrus ipse*).

Leo the Great did not mean, however, that the pope was indistinguishable from Peter or that he assumed his non-transmissible role as a witness to the foundational revelation. Not "reincarnating" Peter, the bishop of Rome served as the apostle's visible instrument, similar to a priest who acts "in the person of Christ" at the Eucharist. The successor of Peter acts, as it were, "in the person of Peter." In his theology of papal primacy, Leo fused a strongly juridical understanding of the bishop of Rome as the holder of an undiminished fullness of power with a sacramental vision in which the pope is the living instrument of Peter in governing the Church.

Fullness of Authority

Leo believed he was responsible for the universal Church, vigorously upholding his predecessors' conviction that the bishop of Rome has an "anxiety [care] for all the churches" (2 Cor 11:28): "all parts of the Church are ruled by his care and enriched by his help."[75] While recognizing that each bishop has authority over his local church, he also held that "Peter especially rules all whom Christ has also ruled originally."[76] The Roman church was, for him, "the head of the world."[77] Its bishop was responsible for providing "that love of the whole Church entrusted to him by the Lord."[78] What distinguished Peter's authority from that of the other apostles was its universality. This universal authority was inherited by the bishop of Rome. Leo is also the first to claim to possess the fullness of authority (*plenitudo potestatis*) to teach as well as to govern and make laws in the Church.[79]

Leo's right to teach authoritatively is nowhere more evident than when he sent his *Tome to Flavian*, a long treatise summarizing orthodox Christology, to the Fathers gathered at Chalcedon in 451 for the fourth ecumenical council. He was convinced that his letter would definitively settle the christological controversy. According to Leo, the pope had the determinative voice at an ecumenical council. The council was to ratify his decisions. Furthermore, once a council's decisions had been confirmed by the Roman see, they were no longer open to revision, let alone reversal.[80]

Because of his strong sense of responsibility, Leo formulated the specific purpose of Roman primacy: it was to serve the *koinonia* by fostering unity and communion. The pope was to defend the apostolic tradition, supporting the churches in their confession of faith: "We have received from Peter, the Prince of the Apostles, the certainty of possessing the right to defend the truth which brings our peace."[81] The Lord's special prayer upholding Peter's faith (cf. Lk 22:31-32) enabled his vicars to pass on that same strength and firmness to others.[82] By guaranteeing the faith's stability, certainty, and accuracy, the pope showed his care for the Church. As guardian of the *koinonia*'s faith, the successor of Peter was to call another church to account if he thought that it had in any way compromised orthodoxy.

While aware of the possible misinterpretations involved in using terminology derived from secular models, we can nonetheless conclude that Leo regarded the papacy as a monarchical institution. Insofar as the Church was a society — though she was far more than that — her full power and juridical authority were concentrated in the hands of the pope, from whom it passed to others. Leo claimed absolute spiritual sovereignty for the papacy.[83]

The Pope and the Other Bishops

Whereas the pope had his authority from Christ, the other bishops, Leo believed, had only a share in his *plenitudo potestatis*. Bishops accordingly came from the whole world seeking his judgment. The bishop of Rome served as a kind of "umpire" in the *koinonia*, exercising a judging role for all those who sought recourse at the see of Peter.[84] Papal stewardship required that the pope be on the lookout for abuses in the universal *koinonia*. Leo also expected that local or regional episcopal decisions should be forwarded to Rome for papal confirmation.[85] Not only did appeals and requests come *to* Rome, the pope, on his own initiative, sent out decretals *from* Rome. Leo continued the practice begun by Siricius of dispatching these papal letters giving authoritative decisions to the other churches. These directives, he claimed, had the same binding force as the decrees of synods.

While recognizing the value of uniform practice as a support for the unity of faith, Leo refrained from imposing Roman views and ecclesiastical traditions on the other churches. He always aimed "at a communion in the faith of the Roman church, not in her customs."[86] Insisting resolutely on the need for harmony with the Roman see, Leo nonetheless intervened in other churches only as a last resort. He encouraged the bishops to act on their initiative, a right which he defended for his "brothers and fellow bishops."[87]

Although the bishops were equal "in honor" with the successor of Peter, there was a certain distinction of power among them. More precisely, Leo believed that the other apostles received their power *through* Peter, thereby participating in his stability: "So then in Peter the strength of all is fortified, and the help of divine grace is so ordered that the stability which through Christ is given to Peter, through Peter is conveyed to the apostles."[88] In another sermon, Leo wrote in praise of Peter: "the one who was so flooded with grace from the very fount of all grace that whereas he had so many gifts which he alone received, no one had any that did not pass through his hands."[89]

Not all of Leo's views on papal-episcopal relations were accepted. When his legates at the Council of Chalcedon suggested that the pope was the "bishop of all the churches" or the "bishop of the universal Church," a kind of "universal bishop," the Fathers rejected this. Later, Gregory the Great (590-604) explicitly repudiated all titles which could easily have led to infringing the rights of the bishops.[90] After the example of Christ, he preferred the title "servant of the servants of God" (*servus servorum Dei*), understanding that all authority in the Church, especially that of the pope, is essentially a service.[91] Leo also went further than the dogmatic teaching of Vatican I when he claimed that episcopal authority is entirely contained in Christ's bestowal of authority on Peter.

◆

The early centuries testify to an unmistakable development in the practice and doctrine of papal primacy. Founded by Jesus and guided by the Spirit, this office took shape as the result of an extended and intricate historical process. Only gradually did the Church become aware of the enduring ministry Christ had assigned to Peter.

In the first two centuries the evidence, taken as a whole, provides an argument in favor of Rome's exceptional role in the *koinonia*. The cumulative witness of both the church at Rome and other churches testifies to the primacy of the Roman see. The church at Rome took initiatives in order to maintain harmony in other communities or to restore the unity of faith. On the one hand, because of its dual apostolic origins, Irenaeus sees in the Roman church the supreme example of a church which preserved the apostolic faith. On the other hand, Clement, Ignatius, and Victor assign to the Roman see some kind of responsibility for the other churches. The fact of Roman primacy emerged before its nature was explained and justified. Moreover, Rome never needed to demand recognition for its prerogatives; rather, it was peacefully accepted.

Already in the third century, when the universal structures of ecclesial communion were being more definitely shaped, the Roman church became more conscious of its duties to the other churches. Increasingly it sought ways to fulfill its mandate effectively. Yet it was not until the fourth century that Rome's jurisdictional authority — the right to govern and enforce obedience to its disciplinary laws and teaching — became the subject of reflective thought. By the mid-fifth century, Leo the Great, with his supreme mastery of Roman law, translated papal claims into a theology which articulated a justification for a monarchical papacy according to which the fullness of Church authority was in the hands of the pope.[92] It is also true, however, that in practice Leo's theory of papal primacy was limited by a variety of factors.

As heirs to Peter's promises and responsibilities, the bishops of Rome came to believe that they had a unifying ministry in the *koinonia*. They were to define doctrine and defend the orthodox faith. As a corollary of this prerogative, they also claimed the right to exclude from communion those who disagreed about essential matters of faith or practice. Using Peter's power to bind and loose, the popes also set the terms of receiving other bishops into communion. It also became the common practice for bishops to seek protection from Rome when their rights were challenged. Likewise, they appealed to the pope for final decisions in legal and doctrinal matters. Despite the bishops' occasional grumbling, they wanted to obtain, at any price, Roman sanction for what they thought to be vital matters in the life of the Church. In this way, they repeatedly verified the tension between Peter and Paul at Antioch, all the while recognizing the singular authority of Peter's successor.[93]

Even though no sustained theological justification for Roman leadership was advanced until the third century, the popes never regarded their office merely as a matter of practical ecclesial organization subject to adjustment and compromise. At Rome, and with varying degrees of agreement elsewhere, the ministry of the vicar of Peter was held to be in conformity with God's will for his Church.

By the fifth century, the papacy claimed and exercised a primacy of teaching and of government in the universal Church. Both in theory and in practice, Leo the Great perfected the doctrine of papal primacy. He systematically applied to the bishop of Rome the responsibilities and authority that Peter had enjoyed among the apostles. Thanks to his clear exposition, the papacy could be defended with a well-formulated theology, grounded in both Scripture and Roman law. Giving the papacy a decidedly universal function, Leo established the foundation for the theory of papal monarchy which shaped the institution for more than a millennium.

Notes for Chapter four

1. Walter Ullmann, "Leo I and the Theme of Papal Primacy," *Journal of Theological Studies*, 11 (1960), 25.
2. Throughout this chapter and the following one, I am much indebted to Father Janusz A. Ihnatowicz, Scanlon Professor of Theology at the University of St. Thomas, Houston.
3. Joseph Ratzinger, "The Primacy of Peter," *L'Osservatore Romano*, 27 (July 8, 1991), 8.
4. Henri de Lubac, *The Motherhood of the Church*, trans. Sergia Englund (San Francisco: Ignatius Press, 1982), 288.
5. Clement, *First Letter to the Corinthians*, 1.
6. Michael Schmaus, *The Church: Its Origin and Structure*, Dogma 4, trans. Mary Ledderer (New York: Sheed & Ward, 1972), 181.
7. John de Satgé, *Peter and the Single Church* (London: SPCK, 1981), 38.
8. Clement, *First Letter to the Corinthians*, 63.2.
9. Agnes Cunningham, "The Power of the Keys: The Patristic Tradition," in *The Papacy and the Church in the United States*, ed. Bernard Cooke (New York: Paulist Press, 1989), 149.
10. Robert B. Eno, *The Rise of the Papacy* (Wilmington: Michael Glazier, 1990), 37.
11. Clement, *First Letter to the Corinthians*, 59.
12. Clement, *First Letter to the Corinthians*, 63.
13. Eusebius, *The History of the Church*, rev. ed. and introduction Andrew Louth, trans. G. A. Williamson (London: Penguin Books, 1989), 4.23, p. 131.
14. Eusebius, *History of the Church*, 3.16, p. 80.
15. Charles Pietri, "Rome," *Encyclopedia of the Early Church*, ed. Angelo Di Berardino, trans. Adrian Walford, vol. 2 (Cambridge: James Clarke & Co., 1992), 740.
16. J. N. D. Kelly, *The Oxford Dictionary of Popes* (London: Oxford University Press, 1986), 12.
17. Eusebius, *History of the Church*, 5.24, p. 172.
18. De Lubac, *Motherhood of the Church*, 290-291.
19. James T. Shotwell and Louise Ropes Loomis, *The See of Peter* (New York: Columbia University Press, 1991), 277.
20. Aidan Nichols, *Rome and the Eastern Churches* (Collegeville: Liturgical Press, 1992), 156.
21. Ignatius, *Letter to the Romans*, intro.
22. Arialdo Beni, *La nostra Chiesa*, 5th ed. (Florence: Fiorentina, 1982), 497. This is the meaning given by Johannes Quasten, as cited in Eno, *Rise of the Papacy*, 35.

23. John Paul II, Discourse, January 27, 1993. *L'Osservatore Romano*, 5 (February 3, 1993).
24. Ignatius, *Letter to the Romans*, 3.
25. Ignatius, *Letter to the Romans*, 4.
26. Cyprian, *Letter*, 59.14.
27. Ludwig Hertling, *"Communio" : Church and Papacy in Early Christianity*, trans. Jared Wicks (Chicago: Loyola University Press, 1972), 59.
28. Hertling, *"Communio" : Church and Papacy in Early Christianity*, 71.
29. James F. McCue, "Roman Primacy in the First Three Centuries," *Concilium*, 64 (1971), 39.
30. James Provost, "The Papacy: Power, Authority, Leadership," in *The Papacy and the Church in the United States*, ed. Bernard Cooke (New York: Paulist Press, 1989), 204.
31. Hans Urs von Balthasar, *The Office of Peter and the Structure of the Church*, trans. Andrée Emery (San Francisco: Ignatius Press, 1986), 167.
32. John E. Lynch "The History of Centralization: Papal Reservations," in *The Once and Future Church: A Communion of Freedom*, ed. James A. Coriden (New York: Alba House, 1971), 66-67.
33. Nichols, *Rome and the Eastern Churches*, 162.
34. Jerome, *Letter*, 15.1-2; translated in *Documents Illustrating Papal Authority A.D. 96-454*, ed. E. Giles (London: SPCK, 1952), #117.
35. Jared Wicks, *Introduction to Theological Method*, Introduction to the Theological Disciplines, vol. 1 (Casale Monferrato: Piemme, 1994), 103.
36. Irenaeus, *Against Heresies*, 3.3.
37. Irenaeus, *Against Heresies*, 3.3.
38. William R. Farmer and Roch Kereszty, *Peter and Paul in the Church of Rome* (New York: Paulist Press, 1990), 58.
39. Terry J. Tekippe, ed., *Papal Infallibility: An Application of Lonergan's Theological Method* (Washington, D.C.: University Press of America, 1983), 341, n. 11.
40. John Paul II, Discourse, January 27, 1993, *L'Osservatore Romano*, 5 (February 3, 1993), 11.
41. Farmer and Kereszty, *Peter and Paul in the Church of Rome*, 62.
42. Shotwell and Loomis, *See of Peter*, 222.
43. Irenaeus, *Against Heresies*, 3.3.
44. Here I part company with J. M. R. Tillard, who affirms: "He [the bishop of Rome] has no personal authority apart from the prerogatives (*presbeia*) of his local church" (*The Bishop of Rome*, trans. John de Satgé [Wilmington: Michael Glazier, 1983], 86-87).
45. Farmer and Kereszty, *Peter and Paul in the Church of Rome*, 84-85.
46. Tertullian, *The Prescription against the Heretics*, 22.
47. Tertullian, *On Modesty*, 21.9-10.
48. Cyprian, *Letter*, 59.14.
49. Shotwell and Loomis, *See of Peter*, 224.
50. Firmilian, *Letter to Cyprian*, 75.17.
51. Optatus of Milevis, *The Schism of the Donatists*, 2.2.
52. Ambrose, *The Faith*, 4.56.
53. Bernard Dupuy, "Le fondement biblique de la primauté romaine en Orient et en Occident," in *La primauté romaine dans la communion des églises*, ed. André Quélen (Paris: Cerf, 1991), 24-25.
54. Shotwell and Loomis, *See of Peter*, 228-231.
55. Eno, *Rise of the Papacy*, 132.

56. Nichols, *Rome and the Eastern Churches*, 163.
57. Translation in William A. Jurgens, ed., *The Faith of the Early Fathers*, vol. 1 (Collegeville: Liturgical Press, 1970), 406-407.
58. Basilio Studer, "Papacy," *Encyclopedia of the Early Church*, ed. Angelo Di Berardino, trans. Adrian Walford, vol. 2 (Cambridge: James Clarke & Co., 1992), 641.
59. Michele Maccarrone, " '*Sedes Apostolica — Vicarius Petri*': La perpetuità del primato di Pietro nella sede e nel vescovo di Roma (Secoli III-VIII)," in *Il Primato del Vescovo di Roma nel Primo Millennio: Ricerche e Testimonianze*, ed. Michele Maccarrone (Vatican City: Polyglot Press, 1991), 308.
60. Tillard, *Bishop of Rome*, 97.
61. Translation in Giles, ed., *Documents Illustrating Papal Authority*, #220.
62. Trevor Gervase Jalland, *Church and Papacy* (London, 1944), 302.
63. Studer, "Papacy," 641.
64. J. Michael Miller, *The Divine Right of the Papacy in Recent Ecumenical Theology*, Analecta Gregoriana, vol. 218 (Rome: Gregorian University Press, 1980), 8-9.
65. Leo the Great, *Sermon*, 4.4; translation in Giles, ed., *Documents Illustrating Papal Authority*, #238.
66. Leo the Great, *Sermon*, 5.
67. Leo the Great, *Sermon*, 4.
68. Leo the Great, *Sermon*, 3.
69. Leo the Great, *Sermon*, 3.
70. Walter Ullmann, "Papacy: 1 — Early Period," *New Catholic Encyclopedia*, vol. 10 (New York: McGraw-Hill Book Company, 1967), 952.
71. Leo the Great, *Sermon*, 3.3.
72. Leo the Great, *Sermon*, 94.4.
73. Leo the Great, *Sermon*, 3.2.
74. Leo the Great, *Letter*, 10.9.
75. Leo the Great, *Sermon*, 5.4; translation in Giles, ed., *Documents Illustrating Papal Authority*, #239.
76. Leo the Great, *Sermon*, 4.2.
77. Leo the Great, *Sermon*, 82.1.
78. Leo the Great, *Sermon*, 5.2
79. Leo the Great, *Letter*, 14; translation in Jalland, *Church and Papacy*, 303.
80. Eno, *Rise of the Papacy*, 110.
81. Leo the Great, *Letter*, 43; translation in Tillard, *Bishop of Rome*, 123.
82. Leo the Great, *Sermon*, 83.3.
83. Ullmann, "Papacy," 953.
84. Leo the Great, *Sermon*, 5.
85. Leo the Great, *Letter*, 12.13
86. Tillard, *Bishop of Rome*, 185.
87. Leo the Great, *Letter*, 114.
88. Leo the Great, *Letter*, 14.11.
89. Leo the Great, *Sermon*, 4.2.
90. Wilhelm de Vries, "Theoretical and Practical Renewals of the Primacy of Rome: The Development after Constantine," *Concilium*, 64 (1971), 47.

91. John Paul II, "Letter for the Fourteenth Centenary of the Elevation of St. Gregory the Great to the Papacy (590-1990)," *L'Osservatore Romano*, 28 (July 9, 1990), 3.
92. Ullmann, "Papacy," 952-953.
93. Louis Bouyer, *The Church of God*, trans. Charles Underhill Quinn (Chicago: Franciscan Herald Press, 1982), 384.

Chapter five
FROM THE EARLY MIDDLE AGES TO THE CATHOLIC REFORM

Leo the Great (440-461), together with Popes Gelasius (492-496) and Gregory (590-604), shaped the fundamental doctrine of the papacy as we know it. Although considerably less than during the first five centuries, further dogmatic development did occur over the next millennium. What is most significant about this period is the way the pope carried out his ministry, especially in the West. Owing to practical exigencies, new ideas about the papacy were formulated. From the staggering amount of historical material, I have selected five themes which most affected the West's *theological* understanding of papal primacy as it developed in the Western Church after Pope Leo's death: the role of the papacy in temporal affairs, the consolidation of its monarchical vision during the Middle Ages, the challenge of conciliarism, the rejection of Roman authority by the Protestant reformers, and the defense of the papacy by the theologians of the Catholic Reform. Each of these has contributed significantly to Catholic practice or teaching on the Petrine ministry.

The Pope's Role in Temporal Affairs

Beginning in the fourth century, and picking up momentum in the following centuries, the role of the pope in secular affairs expanded dramatically. Without precedent in the New Testament and in the earliest tradition, the papacy drew increasingly on the model of the Roman Empire and developed in this light.

Pope and Emperor

Because of the Edict of Milan in 313, the moving of the new imperial capital to Constantinople between 324 and 330, and the declaration of Christianity as the Empire's state religion in 380 by Theodosius (†395), the Church underwent a profound change. The papacy developed in the shadow of the Church's newly acquired rights in the secular arena. There were two principal consequences of this evolution. First, in the West, as imperial power waned, the papacy became stronger, eventually culminating in what came to be known as the monarchical papacy of the Middle Ages. When the emperor's authority became ineffective, the bishop of Rome assumed many of his functions. The pope asserted that he inherited the functions of both Constantine and St. Peter,[1] becoming the center of unity and stability in Western Europe. Second, in the East, the emperor appropriated a custodial role regarding the Church, a responsibility that led to conflicts with papal claims. As heir to Constantine, who was considered an equal of the apostles, the emperor believed that he was responsible for administering Christendom. I shall leave to the following chapter these Eastern developments, but it is important to note how differently the pope's role evolved in different regions of the Empire.

Like their pagan predecessors, the Christian emperors initially assumed the role of guaranteeing the Empire's unity by promoting religious harmony. Although the emperor was not supposed to interfere in doctrinal questions, he was responsible for enforcing Church law. When he shouldered this duty, it became more urgent for the pope to articulate specific *ecclesial* principles which would guarantee Church unity. By the end of the fifth century, the popes had formulated a position to which they adhered throughout the following centuries: "the overall direction, the final authority in matters that affected the vital interests and the structural fabric of the Church — in short the *auctoritas sacrata* — belonged by virtue of his function solely to the pope."[2] This vision involves asserting, against the traditional power of the emperor, the pope's distinctive authority. First articulated by Popes Leo and Gelasius, the theory recognized that God gave the emperor authority in temporal affairs, while he was subject to the pope in spiritual matters. At the same time, the popes assimilated theories and practices from imperial institutions, developing a stronger and more centralized papacy.

Without either approving or rejecting the imperial theory of ecclesial oversight, the popes accepted this *de facto* situation. Meanwhile, they directed their attention to the West and to areas outside the emperor's immediate control. In the newly-evangelized lands of eastern and northern Europe, their own theory of papal primacy took hold.[3] Unlike the East, the West underwent dramatic social and economic changes with the advent of what historians have called "the barbarian invasions." In time, despite their desire to be independent from imperial control, the Church and papacy in the West fell under the dominating influence of newly emerging secular rulers, a situation which lasted until the Gregorian Reform of the eleventh century.

Two Swords Theory

From the fifth century onward, the popes asserted that they had the obligation of moderating the temporal affairs of Western society. In theory, this duty arose from their spiritual supremacy in the Church. When the idea of Christendom emerged — one society, a religious-temporal organism united by one faith — the popes claimed that their authority, because it concerned humanity's spiritual end, was superior to any secular power.

In his letter to the Emperor Anastasius in 494, Pope Gelasius expounded the classical theory of the two powers governing the world: "There are two . . . by which the world is chiefly ruled: the sacred authority (*auctoritas*) of bishops and the royal power (*potestas*). Of those the responsibility of bishops is more weighty insofar as they will answer also for the kings of men themselves at divine judgment" (DS 347). Each was a divine trust, but spiritual authority was inherently superior. Having Christ as its source, it was exercised by bishops as vicars of Christ, and by the pope as vicar of Peter. The popes did not claim to wield the temporal sword but to direct its proper use.[4] Like Leo the Great, Gelasius emphasized that ecclesial office included a power to govern. To the Roman church's authority founded on the faith of Sts. Peter and Paul, it added the more juridical notion of "power." Gelasius conceived Church governance as analogous to that exercised by temporal rulers. This juridical understanding of the papacy guided papal theory and practice in subsequent centuries.

The two swords theory maintained that secular leaders were subject to the pope's spiritual authority. Not necessarily aspiring to political power as such, the popes could intervene in temporal questions insofar as they had a moral dimension. Later, in the Middle Ages, some papal theorists held that the Church herself had received both swords, with the pope delegating the secular sword to the state. For them, nothing, even in the temporal order, was beyond the pope's authority: *whatever* he bound or loosed on earth was bound or loosed in heaven (cf. Mt 16:19). Boniface VIII (1294-1303), taking this view to its extreme, believed that because the Church's spiritual power was superior to the temporal power of civil rulers, the pope could instruct and sit in judgment of them. I shall return to this theoretical understanding of the papacy, but first some of the historical factors that affected this development should be noted.

Papal States

For more than a thousand years, the pope was both a religious and a temporal ruler. From the eighth century onward, the pope was the civil governing authority of central Italy, "a sort of petty Italian duke as well as head of the Church."[5] In 754, Pepin (†768), king of the Franks, responded to an appeal of Pope Stephen II (752-757), who asked that the lands stolen by the invading Lombards be restored to the Church, since they belonged to him by right of previous grants. Stephen wanted the pope to rule central Italy.

Pepin agreed to Stephen's plea and deeded some captured cities to "St. Peter and the Roman church," promising to guarantee these and other possessions as belonging to the bishop of Rome. These lands came to be known as the Patrimony of Peter. From these territories the Papal States were formed in central Italy. Because of this temporal responsibility, the pope involved himself in secular affairs as a sovereign in his own right. This situation lasted until the Kingdom of Italy occupied the Papal States through a process culminating in the seizure of Rome itself in 1870. For more than half of the papacy's life to date, the pope was a temporal ruler, with all the difficulties associated with that role.

Carolingian Revolution

When Pope Leo III (795-816) crowned Charlemagne (†814) as emperor in Rome on Christmas Day 800, it was a dramatic moment filled with symbolic significance. The Pope probably intended to show that he had the right to delegate imperial authority to whomever he willed. Charlemagne, however, seems to have understood this gesture differently. He regarded himself as the head of a new reality, Christendom (*respublica christiana*), with himself as the vicar of Christ on earth. In the Church, the bishop of Rome was the first among the bishops.[6] Charlemagne rejected the pope's claim to temporal supremacy. By crowning him, Leo, in fact, created a rival power to the papacy that lasted for centuries. After 800, the pope had to contend with powerful secular leaders in the West who were themselves ready to lay claim to both the spiritual and the temporal swords.

In the early Middle Ages, because land was held on feudal terms, the Church's properties and offices often became subject to secular power. Although, at first, secular lords had authority only over Church lands, eventually they extended their authority over the holder of the properties, the bishops. Thus began lay investiture. Through this practice, non-clerical lords installed their chosen bishops in office by investing them with its symbols, the pastoral staff and ring. Unlike other bishops, however, the popes controlled the Papal States; consequently, they were not directly subject to lay investiture. Nonetheless, powerful secular leaders tended to regard the pope in the same way that they did other bishops. In effect, the papacy became beholden to secular powers.

At the beginning of the eighth century, a famous document, the so-called Donation of Constantine, was widely circulated to justify papal rights vis-à-vis human authority. Although the document purported to be a letter from the Emperor Constantine (†337) written to Pope Silvester I (314-335), in fact it reflected Rome's view of its primacy during the Carolingian Renaissance. This forgery represented Constantine as entrusting the pope with temporal dominion over the city of Rome and much of Italy. It also recognized the popes as "vicars of the prince of the apostles," gave them a primacy over the four patriarchal sees of Constantinople, Antioch, Alexandria, and Jerusalem, and acknowledged the Roman bishop's superiority over all other bishops.[7] The Donation exalted the pope as the universal bishop. He was the teacher, defender, and godfather of the emperor, the vicar through whom St. Peter displayed his power, and the supreme temporal authority in the West.[8] Until exposed as a forgery in the fifteenth century, clerics, theologians, and princes, even those who contested the rights of the papacy, accepted this document as authentic. Its doctrine greatly influenced the development of the monarchical papacy.

Another document which served to expand papal claims was the False Decretals, a collection of texts of Frankish origin. Although they were drawn up in the mid-ninth century, at the time they were attributed to Isidore of Seville (†636). A mixture of authentic and spurious texts from early popes and councils, the Decretals defended the rights of diocesan bishops and asserted the pope's authority over metropolitan bishops and synods. According to the Decretals, the pope owed his primacy to "the Lord and Savior himself" (PL 130, 77) and enjoyed true juridical power in the Church.

Monarchical Vision of the Papacy

After the year 1000, the papacy increasingly assumed the institutional form and trappings and of a monarchy. The pope was regarded as the supreme ruler, governing the Church alone. With the decadence of the tenth-century papacy behind them, and buttressed both by the pro-papal sentiment of the newly evangelized peoples and by the Cluniac reform movement which was reversing lay investiture, the popes and their fellow reformers sought to restore the papacy as the major directing force in ecclesial life and European society.

Freedom for the Church

A reforming pope, Gregory VII (1073-1085) zealously pursued his vision of freedom for the Church (*libertas ecclesiae*), that is, the freedom of the clergy from the control of lay rulers. To further the kingdom of God on earth, he sought to establish a universal papal sovereignty which would guarantee justice and peace throughout Christendom. Reformers believed that the supreme spiritual authority of the successors of Peter could secure this unified world order.[9]

Some provisions of the Donation of Constantine were incorporated into the first collections of canon law that were being drawn up. It contained the legend that the Emperor Constantine gave Pope Silvester authority over other churches and offered him the imperial crown, an honor which he refused. To the reformers this account suggested an unacceptable papal subservience to secular authority. According to Gregory VII and his successors, papal authority over kings and emperors came from God alone.[10] This was the principal governing idea of the sweeping Gregorian Reform.

From the mid-eleventh century onwards, the popes saw that needed ecclesial reform could be successful only if the Church was freed from the interference of secular lords. They thought it was intolerable for spiritual authority to be subordinate to temporal power. As the spirit should dominate the flesh, so should ecclesiastical power dominate the world.[11] To root out secular meddling in Church affairs, the popes of the Gregorian Reform waged a frontal attack on lay investiture, working to remove the episcopacy from the control of temporal rulers.

In Gregory's view of the relationship between the two swords, the sacred authority (*auctoritas*) of the Church was superior to the secular power (*potestas*) of princes, including the emperor. He went beyond the principles of Gelasius by concluding that the temporal was therefore subject to the spiritual. According to the Gregorian reformers, because God had instituted the state to eradicate evil, temporal power was subject to ecclesial oversight. Insofar as the Church was concerned with humanity's final end, only the pope had the means available to provide for this.[12] Canonists began to teach that the two swords were placed in the hands of the pope. He directly wielded the spiritual sword, confiding the temporal one to the king.

The coronation rite of the pope, first introduced in 1059 for Nicholas II (1059-1061), illustrates this high doctrine of papal authority. Its liturgy contained the following texts: "See, I have set you this day over nations and over kingdoms, to pluck up and to break down, to destroy and to overthrow, to build and to plant" (Jer 1:10); "The spiritual man judges all things, but is himself to be judged by no one" (1 Cor 2:15); and "Do you not know that we are to judge angels? How much more, matters pertaining to this life" (1 Cor 6:3).[13]

Church Reform

Besides their efforts to abolish lay investiture, the popes also sought to curtail the clerical abuses of simony and co-habitation, to exact episcopal oaths of obedience to the apostolic see, and to enforce periodic visits of bishops to Rome. As a way of justifying these measures, the reformers defined the Church as a perfect society, enjoying her own autonomy and law. They also fostered centralized papal authority, the spiritual equivalent of a powerful imperial state. Centralization in this instance, writes American theologian

Kilian McDonnell, "was an instrument of reform not a will-to-power."[14] At the same time, other reform movements in the Church buttressed renewal efforts by appealing to Rome to assist them, thereby swelling administrative centralization.

The pope's increasing role in episcopal elections was a further important factor in expanding papal authority. The Gregorian reformers mandated that the canons of cathedral churches, not temporal lords, had the right to elect their own bishops. All irregularities in elections were to be adjudicated by Rome. The popes justified this interventionist role in episcopal appointments by invoking Leo the Great's theory that the successor of Peter enjoyed the fullness of ecclesial power. While bishops were still usually chosen by local secular or religious authorities, before entering office they needed papal approval. It was not until the fourteenth century, however, that the pope directly controlled episcopal appointments, though not in the present way.[15]

"Dictatus Papae"

Among the most significant contributions of the Gregorian Reform to the development of Roman primacy was its formulation of a juridical ecclesiology. The reformers' writings described the Church as dominated by the papacy, conceived as a power divinely equipped to confront other religious and secular powers. Yves Congar holds that this new juridical emphasis, which focused on the papacy, marked a revolutionary turning point in Catholic ecclesiology. Everything in the Church was said to depend on the successor of Peter: he was the rock, source, hinge, and head from which all other churches received life and direction. When bishops governed their own churches, they shared in the pope's fullness of power.[16] With Gregory, the theoretical principles of papal authority previously formulated in the tradition were tested in practice. As a result, an innovative style of papal leadership evolved. The pope emerged not only as the undisputed head of the Church but also as the unifying force in medieval Europe.[17]

As the key document of the Gregorian Reform, the *Dictatus papae* expresses the theoretical basis which Gregory relied on to justify his movement of renewal. It contains guidelines designed to foster a vigilant and vigorous papal authority capable of dealing with both religious and temporal abuses. The *Dictatus papae* summarizes the monarchical conception of the papacy. Its theses describe the superiority of the Roman church and its bishop, the relationship of the pope both to other bishops and ecumenical councils, the papacy's legal claims, and the pope's secular authority. Likely headings from a canonical treatise which is no longer extant, these propositions might have been formulated in light of the schism with Constantinople in 1054.

Among the most significant propositions of the *Dictatus papae* are the following:

> The Roman church was founded by the Lord alone.
> Only the Roman bishop deserves to be called universal.
> His name [*papa*] is unique in the world.
> The Roman Church has never erred and, as Scripture shows, can never err.
> Only he can depose or absolve bishops.
> He may, should the need arise, translate a bishop from one see to another.

In a Council, his legate can give orders to all bishops even if he is himself of
lower rank and he alone is empowered to pronounce a sentence of deposition.
No canonical text exists outside his authority.
Important cases from every church must be referred to him.
He may not be judged by anyone.
No one may repeal a decision of the Holy See.
He may depose emperors.
He alone may use the imperial insignia.
The Roman pontiff, if canonically ordained, undoubtedly becomes holy by the merits of St. Peter (PL 148, 407-408).[18]

The twenty-seven propositions of the *Dictatus papae* condense and organize the Gregorian Reform's understanding of papal primacy. The adjective "only," used to highlight the uniqueness of the pope's prerogatives, predominates. Indeed, the key to Gregory's theology of the papacy was his view that *only* the Roman church was founded by Christ *alone*.[19] Taken together, these statements provided a program for action in which papal sovereignty dominated the affairs of the Christian community. Except for the last thesis on the holiness of the popes, the West accepted all of them as legitimate expressions of papal authority.

Canonists and the Papacy

In the eleventh century, the West produced a systematic juridical theology of papal primacy which supported the pope's effective rule by means of law. From 1150 to 1250, canonists and canonist popes reinforced the view of the Gregorian reformers, defining the papacy as a power of jurisdiction distinct from the sacramental power of orders. With the mid-twelfth century publication of the *Decretum Gratiani* — a collection of nearly four thousand patristic texts, conciliar decrees, and papal pronouncements touching all areas of Church life — papal authority was described as a primacy of jurisdiction. This primacy was justified as deriving from Christ's institution, and not from conciliar or human decisions.[20]

For Gregory, Church reform was linked to the divine origin of pontifical authority, and he drew consequences from this position which his predecessors had not.[21] Canonical collections, such as that of Anselm of Lucca (†1086), which were inspired by the Gregorian Reform, upheld the divine authority of the Roman see (PL 149, 485-490). For the canonists and Gregory VII, the successors to Peter in the Roman episcopacy had universal jurisdiction *ex iure divino*: it came to them owing to divine institution.[22] The papacy "was derived, as the popes loudly, insistently and constantly proclaimed, from the Bible and was held by them and by contemporary Europe to be nothing less than the practical realization of biblical doctrine," writes Walter Ullmann. "The link with divinity was a most potent element that supplied — in the contemporary environs — the firmest possible base."[23]

The papacy's claim to supremacy was justified by the argument that papal authority came immediately from God. "There is no statement or action by any medieval pope," says Ullmann, "that justified papal jurisdiction solely on grounds that were or could be considered purely temporal."[24] At the apex of the hierarchical pyramid, the pope held his position *iure divino*: because God himself willed it. Consequently, he had the right to exercise his authority directly over every bishop and member of the faithful.

Gregory insisted on the superiority of the pope's spiritual authority. In a letter addressed to his brother bishops, the Pope elaborated on his own understanding of the papacy: "So now, my dearly beloved brothers, listen carefully to what I say to you. All who in the whole world bear the name of Christian and truly understand the Christian faith know and believe that Saint Peter, the prince of the apostles, is the father of all Christians and their first shepherd after Christ, and that the holy Roman church is the mother and mistress of all the churches. If, then, you believe and unshakably hold this, such as I am, your brother and unworthy master, I ask and command you by Almighty God to help and succour your father and mother."[25] According to Gregory, believing that Peter was the first shepherd after Christ meant accepting that the Roman church had primacy over the other churches.

Until Marsilius of Padua (†1342), all Western medieval theorists taught that papal primacy was divinely revealed in the New Testament.[26] In *Defensor pacis* (1324), however, Marsilius explicitly denied the divine institution of papal primacy. Influenced by the political ideas of Aristotle and the revival in the study of Roman law, Marsilius subordinated the Church to the State, where he believed that the people were sovereign. He maintained that Peter had no jurisdictional primacy over the other apostles. Moreover, the bishop of Rome was not the successor to Peter, since the apostle probably never went there. The historical primacy of Rome was due, he held, merely to the memory of the apostles and the early prestige of its leaders rather than to God's will.[27] Marsilius also rejected the pope's *plenitudo potestatis*, insisting that Christ alone was the head of the Church.[28] Pope John XXII (1316-1334) condemned these opinions in 1327 (cf. DS 942-944).

"Papa"

The ancient title "pope" comes from the Greek word *pappas*, an affectionate and venerable term for "father." In the East, with its strong sense of clerical spiritual paternity, bishops, especially the bishop of Alexandria, were referred to as "popes." So, too, were abbots and ordinary priests.

Beginning in the early third century in the West, *papa* (the Latin form of *pappas*) was used for bishops. Pope Marcellinus (296-304) was the first bishop of Rome referred to as *papa*. By the end of the fourth century, *papa* was well on its way to becoming the bishop of Rome's most common title of honor. In the fifth century, he was called *Papa Urbis Romae*, Pope of the City of Rome. When the popes dropped the reference to Rome in the eighth century, they were simply called *papa*.

Other Western bishops, however, continued to call themselves "popes" until nearly the end of the first millennium. At the Synod of Pavia in 998, the bishop of Milan was rebuked for calling himself "pope." Later, in the *Dictatus papae*, Gregory VII forbade anyone other than the bishop of Rome to use *papa*: "his name is unique in the world." Today's title "Holy Father," which dates from the twelfth century, corresponds to the original affectionate connotation of *papa*.[29]

Vicar of Christ

As a title referring to the pope, "Vicar of Peter" came into common use in the second half of the first millennium. Peter Lombard (†1160) preserved "Vicar of Peter" in his *Book of Sentences*, the first theology text of the Middle Ages, as did Gratian in his systematic collection of canon law. From the eighth to eleventh centuries, other churches, especially in the West, frequently appealed to the power of the apostle Peter which continued to be active in the bishop of Rome — a notion already developed in the fourth century. Though not altogether ignoring the current successor of Peter, writes medieval historian R. W. Southern, "they quite simply looked through him to the first occupant of his throne."[30]

The first pope known to have been saluted as "vicar of Christ" was Gelasius I at the Roman Synod in 495. The synod Fathers regarded him as an image of Christ, faithful in his ministry to the Lord. This early usage primarily conveyed a "sacramental" vision: in the Church the pope made present the transcendent power of Christ.[31] Down through the twelfth century, kings, bishops, and sometimes even priests were designated vicars of Christ. St. Bernard of Clairvaux (†1153), for example, referred to the pope as the "one vicar of Christ" who had charge of the entire flock; the other vicars of Christ were responsible for only a portion of God's people.[32]

With Innocent III (1198-1216), the Gregorian Reform came to fruition. The medieval papacy reached its pinnacle, supervising the West's religious, social, and political life. It acquired all the trappings of a monarchy, with its tiara, ceremonies, and vesture.[33] Styling himself "vicar of Christ," Innocent rejected the more traditional title, "vicar of Peter." "Although successor to the prince of the apostles," Innocent wrote, "we are not his vicar nor that of any man or apostle, but we are the vicar of Jesus Christ himself" (PL 214, 292). No longer merely heirs of Peter, the popes were "deputies of Christ in all the fullness of His power."[34] Unlike the title "vicar of Peter," which situated the pope *in* the Church, the more direct christological reference of "vicar of Christ" tended to place the pope *above* the Church. Dependence on the apostle's mystical presence in the bishop of Rome had been popular when the popes had little power of practical direction. When the situation changed, the title "vicar of Peter" fell into disuse. The canonists preferred "vicar of Christ," a title which bolstered their theories that the pope held a supreme authority which he could exercise broadly.

Holding a lofty view of his position in a worldwide papal theocracy, Innocent III attributed his authority to being Christ's vicar, the recipient of authority from him alone. To the title's original sacramental meaning, he added a juridical one. The latter soon came to take precedence: the pope received a mandate from Christ to be his visible substitute, making use of the powers given him for that purpose.[35] No longer was the "vicar of Christ" understood primarily as his representative. Now it was associated with being Christ's earthly replacement.[36] As a title, *vicarius Christi* made a claim to universal sovereignty, implying an authority which extended over both spiritual and temporal realms. The emperor, consequently, was regarded as the vicar of the pope.[37]

The canonists backed up this papal theory concerning the Roman bishop's fullness of power. Some held that the pope was the only person who received any power of Church government directly from God. Medieval canonists distinguished two powers *within* the Church: the power of orders coming from sacramental ordination; and the power of jurisdiction coming from the pope. As vicar of Christ, the pope held the fullness of jurisdictional power. In his celebrated maxim, Agostino Trionfo (†1328) captured the spirit of this view: "the title 'pope' designates jurisdiction" (*papa est nomen iurisdictionis*).[38] All other jurisdictional authority in the Church, namely that of the bishops, was held to derive exclusively from the vicar of Christ.[39]

Later, the Council of Florence (1431-1445) officially endorsed the title *vicarius Christi*, adding the modifier "true": the pope is the "true vicar of Christ" (DS 1307). Vatican I (1869-1870) incorporated this text into its definition of papal primacy (cf. DS 3059). Moreover, Vatican II (1962-1965) kept the title. *Lumen gentium* refers to the bishop of Rome as the "Vicar of Christ" and "pastor of the entire Church" (LG 22).

Thomas and Bonaventure

Founded in the thirteenth century, the Franciscans and the Dominicans both enjoyed special papal protection. Because residential bishops often hindered the new mendicant orders in their apostolic work, the great theologians among them, especially St. Bonaventure (†1274) and St. Thomas Aquinas (†1274), argued in favor of strong papal authority. The growth of these new religious orders gave a forceful impulse to the notion that the pope, not the local bishop, had "immediate" jurisdiction over them.[40]

Drawing on the canonical idea of jurisdiction, Bonaventure affirmed that all ecclesial authority derived from the pope.[41] The Franciscan theologian maintained that the pope's *plenitudo potestatis* meant that all power to govern in the Church came from him, just as "in heaven all the glory of the saints flows from Christ."[42] More specifically than the earlier canonists, Bonaventure asserted that the power of the keys, held by all bishops and priests, originated with the power of jurisdiction. Only the pope enjoyed this power in virtue of his election to office. Not relying on arguments from Scripture or tradition, Bonaventure drew upon neo-Platonic thought. According to him, in every realm there is a first and supreme principle. Within the Church, the pope is the summit of her hierarchical structure. All authority, therefore, stems from him.[43] In effect, he held that the bishops were vicars of the pope with respect to their authority to pastor their churches.

Thomas Aquinas, too, used philosophical rather than scriptural arguments to justify papal primacy as the perfect form of ecclesial government: a monarchy. Nonetheless, he situated the pope's *plenitudo potestatis* within the Church and not in the temporal order.[44] In his *Summa contra Gentiles*,[45] Thomas invoked arguments taken from philosophy and political theory. American Jesuit theologian Avery Dulles has summarized Thomas's arguments for papal monarchy in four points. First, just as one bishop represents and assures the unity of his diocese, so does the pope guarantee the unity of the universal Church. Second, only a single head can settle disagreements about doctrinal questions which arise among bishops. Third, monarchy is the highest form of government, since one ruler can best promote peace and unity among his subjects. Fourth, since in the heavenly Church there is one shepherd and one fold, so also the earthly Church requires a single visible head.[46] Like Bonaventure, Thomas upheld the pope's jurisdictional primacy over the whole Church. He, too, argued that the bishops derived their episcopal power from the pope and that the most suitable form of Church government was a papal monarchy. At the same time, Aquinas also defended the autonomy of the state in pursuing its own goals, provided that it avoided interfering with the higher goals of spiritual authority.[47]

Boniface VIII

For the thirteenth-century popes, the fullness of power given them by Christ was supreme even outside the ecclesiastical order. Their *plenitudo potestatis* included power over kings and emperors, giving them the right to intervene directly in temporal affairs. At this time, writes Tillard, "the Church and indeed the whole design of God is riveted to the papacy, dependent upon it, concentrated on it. Apart from God himself, nothing can escape the *plenitudo potestatis* of Christ's vicar . . . [it] allows no exceptions and no concessions."[48]

According to papal theory, the successor of Peter exercised his full power as holder of the two swords which Christ had entrusted to Peter. Because the pope did not exercise political power in person, but through his deputies, primarily the emperor, he struggled to control the selection of the West's highest temporal sovereign. To make this indirect authority effective, the popes often had to back their political maneuvers with threats of force. In doing so, they compromised the spiritual authority which legitimated their entry into the temporal realm.

The highest, even extreme, claim for the papacy as a spiritual and temporal power was undoubtedly formulated by Boniface VIII (1294-1303) in *Unam sanctam* (1302). At the time, Philip the Fair of France (†1314) wanted to separate spiritual from temporal authority, thus rupturing the unity of Christendom guided by the pope. In his bull, Boniface attempted to stem this tide by reasserting the principle that the king should exercise temporal power within and for the Church, at the discretion of the pope.[49] The Pope regarded the temporal as ordered to the spiritual, which was superior to it and able to judge it.

This understanding led Boniface to unite temporal and spiritual claims in a desire for a theocratic world order under the pope. Except in the Papal States, he avoided making any claim to control temporal dominions. In the bull, Boniface VIII proclaimed: "Both are in the power of the Church, the spiritual sword and the material. But the latter is to be used for the Church, the former by her; the former by the priest, the latter by kings and captains but at the will and by the permission of the priest. The one sword, then, should be under the other, and temporal authority subject to the spiritual" (DS 873).

Enthralled by the ideal of unity, Boniface thought that one body should have one head.[50] Just as Christ was head of his own body, so also was the pope head of the mystical body. The Church, he said, "has only one body and one head — not two heads, like a monster — namely Christ, and Christ's vicar is Peter, and Peter's successor" (DS 872).

Boniface's theory of a papal monarchy failed in practice almost as soon as it was formulated. With the death of Boniface VIII in 1303, "the grandiose idea of a theocratic world order with all power, temporal and spiritual, emanating from the Pope"[51] was laid to rest. Even so, the theory reinforced the pope's control over the ecclesiastical hierarchy.

Conciliarism: Council Over Pope?

Captive to the interests of the French kings in the fourteenth century, the popes took up residence in Avignon, while remaining bishops of Rome. From 1309-1377, they lived in France during what is called the Babylonian Captivity. When this exile ended, the Great Western Schism (1378-1417) began. For forty years there were two, then three, rival claimants to the papacy. After a generation of bickering, "it became widely accepted," writes historian Brian Tierney, "that only a general council, exercising authority over all the claimants, could bring the schism to an end."[52]

With their theories of absolute papal power, the theologians and canonists of the late Middle Ages recognized the pope's right to resolve all ecclesiastical affairs. When the papacy itself was in straits, however, other solutions had to be proposed. As a way out of this structural crisis, churchmen, especially canonists, drew upon ideas that had begun to circulate in the twelfth and thirteenth centuries. Proponents of these new opinions were called "conciliarists," because they thought that holding an ecumenical council was the way to assure Church reform. According to them, only a general council, which constituted the supreme authority in the Church, could restore her unity.

Moderate and Radical Conciliarists

Conciliarist ideas, developed by Marsilius of Padua (†1342), William of Occam (†1347), Pierre d'Ailly (†1420), and John Gerson (†1429), reached their theoretical and practical zenith in the fifteenth century. Conciliar theory provided a doctrinal foundation for extricating the Church from the schism caused by rival papal claimants. Discussion of this crisis was limited by the way in which the debate was framed: the alternative presented was the supremacy of either the council or the pope.

On the one hand, moderate conciliarists, centered at the University of Paris and headed by Pierre d'Ailly and John Gerson, contended that the pope was not in principle subordinate to an ecumenical council. They maintained that the successor of Peter held the fullness of Church power and that a council could not limit it. Even so, according to Frederick Cwiekowski, "it was generally agreed that the authority of pope and bishops acting in a general council was greater than the authority of the pope acting alone."[53] Only in emergency situations, such as in the case of a heretical pope or the uncertainty caused by rival claimants to the papacy, could a general council act without the pope as a "kind of constitutional supreme court of the Church."[54] Their interest was to find a way out of an anomalous predicament which was compromising the general welfare of the Church

The Shepherd and the Rock

and the institution of the papacy. Faced with the historical situation of division, the moderate conciliarists defined the unity of the Church more in terms of her bond with her one head, Christ, than her union with the pope as the vicar of Christ.[55] They refrained, however, from drawing the conclusion that a council is essentially superior to the pope.

On the other hand, more radical conciliarists argued in favor of the principle that an ecumenical council holds supreme authority in the Church. They regarded the pope as the Church's chief elected representative, who could be deposed for abuse of his functions. Moreover, against him an appeal to a general council could be made. These conciliarists also proposed that, if a pope were to refuse to obey the council, he should be subject to ecclesiastical and civil penalties. They were not solely interested in providing a justification for a council which could legitimately choose a new pope. Radical conciliarists taught the theory that the pope was accountable to the bishops gathered in council. Rejecting the monarchical papacy, they believed that the pope, however divinely-instituted his office, was in some sense a constitutional ruler. He possessed a merely ministerial authority delegated to him by the faithful for the good of the Church. Radical conciliarists believed that the authority of the universal Church resided in an ecumenical council, as a kind of ecclesiastical parliament distinct from, and superior to, the pope.

Ending the Schism

In order to end the division caused by having two or more "popes," all parties finally agreed that a general council should be summoned to restore ecclesial unity. In 1414, the sixteenth ecumenical council was called to reform the Church and resolve the question of rival papal claimants. The following year at Constance the council published the decree *Haec sancta*, which stated: "constituting a general council and representing the entire Catholic Church militant, it [the holy synod of Constance] has power immediately from Christ; and that everyone of whatever state or dignity, even papal, is bound to obey it in those matters which pertain to the faith, the eradication of the said schism and the general reform of the said Church of God in head and members."[56]

The signers of the decree maintained that the council held its power directly from Christ and that the pope was obliged to obey it in matters of faith and discipline. A subsequent decree, *Frequens* (1417), provided that every five, then every seven and ten years, a general council should be held and that the pope, in some measure, should furnish it with an account of his stewardship.

Historians and theologians have disputed at length the interpretation of *Haec sancta*. Some, like Tierney, think that the decree did not define conciliar supremacy as an abiding element in Church, but limited itself to dealing with a specific emergency situation. In other words, the Council of Constance adopted the moderate conciliarist position of providing a solution for the Church when she was unable to determine who the legitimate pope was. If there had been a universally recognized pope, then his approval would have been necessary before promulgating any conciliar decision.[57] For these scholars, the council's decisions were aimed at solving an exceptional case rather than defining the Church's permanent constitution. Only later, say these historians and theologians, did radical conciliarists claim that the Council of Constance sanctioned their conviction that every pope was, in principle, subordinate to a council.[58]

Other scholars, however, maintain that the council itself endorsed the radicals' position that an ecumenical council had a "control function" with respect to the pope, a function which was not limited to emergency situations.[59] Without resolving this difference of historical interpretation, we can say that some participants and theologians at the council held moderate conciliarist views, while others proposed more radical opinions.

The schism ended in 1417, when Martin V (1417-1431) was elected pope. Agreeing to promote Church reform "in head and members," which he later did halfheartedly, Martin also decisively reasserted papal authority by denouncing radical conciliarism. His successors were equally determined to uproot the radical conciliarist opinions. In 1460, Pius II (1458-1464), convinced that the papacy's decline in influence was due to the inflated authority attributed to general councils, published a decree that forbade appeals to a council against the pope (cf. DS 1375).[60] Conciliarist theories then went underground. In modified form, they later resurfaced in seventeenth-century Gallicanism in France, and eighteenth-century Febronianism in Germany and Josephinism in the Hapsburg Empire. The death-blow to radical conciliarism was definitely struck with Vatican I's teaching on papal primacy.

The Reformation: Church Without a Pope

The Reformation formulated the principle that the Church could, indeed should, abolish the papal office. The Reformers attacked the pope as the antichrist of biblical prophecy. Unanimously contesting the papacy's origins as divinely willed, the first Protestants developed an ecclesiology with no role for the pope.[61]

Lutheran Rejection of the Papacy

Only two years after publishing his Ninety-Five Theses (1517) in Wittenberg, Martin Luther (†1546) denied that the papacy had a scriptural foundation, thereby denying it as an institution of divine right. Nevertheless, Luther was willing to acknowledge that the papacy was a historical institution which, if reformed, could be retained as a useful ministry serving the universal Church.

In his 1519 dispute at Leipzig with Catholic theologian John Eck (†1593), an ardent upholder of papal primacy, Luther repudiated its divine institution. Aware of the importance of Matthew 16:18-19 to the Roman claim, Luther proposed that the "rock" of verse 18 referred to the apostle's "faith" rather than to Peter or his successors. Christ had promised, he maintained, to build his Church upon such faith, the model of faith for all Christians.

Furthermore, because Jesus had assured the apostles that the gates of hell would not prevail against what was built on rock, that edifice could not be the papacy. Why? "The gates of hell have frequently contained the papacy," wrote Luther. "God would never have permitted this to happen if, in Christ's words, the rock meant this same papacy. For then his promise would not be true, and he would not fulfill his own words."[62] The power of the "keys," he went on to assert, was given "neither to Peter nor to a successor, nor to any one church, but to all the churches."[63] By means of this exegesis, Luther felled the two theological pillars buttressing papal theory: Petrine primacy and Petrine succession. According to him, Christ assigned primacy in the Church neither to Peter nor to anyone claiming to be his successor.

In his *Resolution Concerning the Power of the Pope*, Luther attributed the origin of papal primacy entirely to historical factors, which were later enshrined in ecclesiastical law. The papacy was without a divine warrant attested to by biblical witness. The Roman church acquired preeminence, he said, on account of papal decrees which contradicted the teaching of Scripture. Conciliar decisions also served to bolster Rome's position as the principal church in the West.[64]

The great Reform theologian Philip Melanchthon († 1560) agreed with Luther that the New Testament furnished no evidence that Christ intended a primatial office. Like his mentor, he attributed the papacy's origin to ecclesiastical law. Citing a series of patristic and conciliar texts, Melanchthon asserted that the bishop of Rome neither exercised a primacy nor did the early Church recognize one. Consequently, the papacy "was not instituted by Christ and does not come from divine right."[65]

Lutherans and a Papacy of Human Right

Despite their firm denial that the papacy could be justified as an institution of divine right, some early Reformers expressed a willingness to accept the papacy as a historical institution. According to Luther, within the visible Church the bishop of Rome was above others. Even so, God did not mandate the papacy; its origin was due entirely to human factors. Luther proposed that the pope should renounce his claim that salvation required submission to the bishop of Rome. If the pope would do this, then Luther said he could accept the papacy as a human institution.[66]

A few years later, however, Luther abandoned this appeasing view. When he realized that Catholics insisted that the papacy was instituted by Christ, he hardened his anti-papal stance. In the *Smalcald Articles* of 1537, he wrote: "Manifestly (to repeat what has already been said often) the papacy is a human invention, and it is not commanded, it is unnecessary, and it is useless."[67] As long as the pope maintained that the papacy was divinely instituted, Luther continued to label him as the antichrist.

Near the end of his life, Luther reproached himself severely for his earlier willingness to concede that the papacy had some legitimacy as a purely historical institution. Convinced of the papacy's blasphemous nature, he wrote *Against the Roman Papacy, an Institution of the Devil* (1546), leaving as his testament "hatred of the Roman Pontiff." In this tract Luther popularized the idea that the pope is the antichrist: "I believe that the Pope is the masked and incarnate devil because he is the antichrist. As Christ is God incarnate, so the antichrist is the devil incarnate."[68]

The younger and more conciliatory Melanchthon retained his hope for a reformed papacy: one that Catholics would be willing to justify as an institution of human right. In his subscript to the *Smalcald Articles*, Melanchthon wrote: "Concerning the Pope I hold that, if he would allow the gospel, we, too, may concede him that superiority over the bishops which he possesses by human right, making this concession for the sake of peace and general unity among Christians who are now under him and who may be in the future."[69] Even though this note was included in the Lutheran *Book of Concord* (1580), subsequent Lutheran theology followed Luther's later views, not his earlier ones or those of Melanchthon.

Anglicans and the Antichrist

With the Act of Supremacy in 1534, the church in England separated itself from Roman obedience. As on the continent, polemical writers frequently looked upon the pope as the antichrist. In the English Litany of 1544, Anglicans offered prayers which begged God to deliver his people "from the tyranny of the bishop of Rome and his detestable enormities." Article 37 of the Thirty-Nine Articles (1563), the doctrinal formulae accepted by the Church of England, summarized the Anglican position on the papacy: "The Bishop of Rome hath no jurisdiction in this Realm of England." This implies, however, as Anglican historian Henry Chadwick points out, "that the bishop of Rome has jurisdiction elsewhere — in short, he is the Catholic bishop of Rome."[70]

Although at first the Anglicans attacked abuses in the papacy, soon they lambasted the legitimacy of the papacy itself. A well-known apologist for early Anglicanism, John Jewel, bishop of Salisbury (†1571), tried to undo the papal claims by interpreting Matthew 16:18-19 in such a way that it supported an Anglican ecclesiology. Like the Reformers, he relied on two principal arguments: first, the papacy had no biblical foundation; and second, Rome's preeminence in the Church was the result of purely historical factors.

According to Jewel, Jesus assigned Peter no special authority or role in the Church. The "rock" was Jesus himself: "The old Catholic Fathers have written and pronounced not any mortal man, as Peter was, but Christ himself, the Son of God, to be this rock."[71] Jewel accepted what he thought to be Origen's interpretation of the passage: "These words (Mt 16:18-19), saith he, are not spoken directly or only unto Peter, but as unto Peter. And the other apostles have the keys and are the rock, as well as Peter."[72]

Nothing in Scripture, therefore, could justify the papacy as an institution rooted in Christ's will. Faced with the fact of papal primacy, Anglican writers insisted that the papacy developed just like any other historical institution — from purely secular factors. Acknowledging that the bishop of Rome had enjoyed, as Jewel wrote, "an estimation and a credit, and a prerogative before all others,"[73] Anglicans interpreted this as only a historical fact. The antiquity of the Roman church, its dual apostolicity, its position as the only apostolic see in the West, its numerous martyrs, the generosity of its members, its stalwart preservation of the orthodox faith, and its imperial and political significance as the "Old Rome" furnished, so Anglicans believed, sufficient reasons to account for the pope's leading role in the Church.

Anglicans and a Primacy of Honor

A century after the separation of Canterbury from Rome, some Anglican churchmen and theologians, known as the "Caroline divines," reexamined the anti-papal polemics of early Anglicanism. They willingly accepted that Peter had enjoyed certain privileges among the apostles. Even so, like William Laud, archbishop of Canterbury (†1645), they limited any primacy he enjoyed to his own person.[74] No one admitted that Peter had successors to his primacy, let alone that the bishop of Rome could legitimately claim that role. Notwithstanding their willingness to recognize that Christ bestowed some unique privileges upon Peter, these Anglican scholars rejected Petrine succession.

Nevertheless, because of their historical studies, the Caroline divines adopted a more favorable view of the papacy as a historical and ecclesiastical institution. They willingly recognized the prominent role it had played in the early Church. In *A Relation of the Conference Between William Laud and Mr. Fisher the Jesuit*, Archbishop Laud admitted that "the Roman patriarch, by ecclesiastical constitutions, might perhaps have a primacy of order — but for the principality of power, the patriarchs were as even, as equal, as the apostles were before them."[75] Accordingly, the church of Rome could legitimately claim to be the principal church within Christendom, holding a primacy of honor. The Caroline divines acknowledged only that the bishop of Rome held an ecclesiastically bestowed primacy of honor in the universal Church. All Anglicans were united in resolutely denying the divine institution of papal primacy.

The Catholic Reform

The Council of Trent (1545-1563) initiated the official phase of the Catholic Reform out of which Counter-Reformation Catholicism emerged. The council, however, did not develop a theology of the papacy in its official documents. The suggestions of some Roman theologians that the decree on the sacrament of orders also affirm papal primacy along the lines of the Council of Florence were rejected.[76] German historian Herbert Jedin suggested that Trent refrained from defining papal primacy because "Catholic theology had not yet reached that agreement and clarity which are the premise of a conciliar definition."[77]

Even so, the council sparked vigorous papal leadership after it was concluded. The Fathers made the pope responsible for implementing Trent's decrees, thereby enabling him to intervene in almost every aspect of Church life. Following the Fathers' recommendations, Pius IV (1560-1565) drew up a profession of faith, which all prelates were to take. Summing up the Church's faith in face of the Reform errors, it mentioned papal primacy: "I acknowledge the holy, catholic and apostolic, Roman church as the mother and teacher of all the churches, and I promise and swear obedience to the Roman pontiff, successor of blessed Peter, chief of the apostles, and vicar of Christ" (DS 1868).

Imitating the newly emerging absolutist states, the central government of the Church strengthened itself. In addition, theologians wrote many tracts on ecclesiology. Contrary to the Protestant Reformers' emphasis on the invisible Church as a communion of saints, Catholic treatises, which were frequently polemical, stressed her visible hierarchical structure.

In the ecclesiology of the Catholic Reform, the Church was presented after the analogy of a secular state. She was a "perfect society"; that is, the Church was independent of every other society, lacking nothing to achieve her own ends. The well-known Jesuit controversial theologian St. Robert Bellarmine (†1621) affirmed that the Church was a society "as visible and palpable as the community of the Roman people, or the Kingdom of France, or the Republic of Venice."[78] Essential to the society of the Church was government by legitimate pastors, "especially the one vicar of Christ on earth, the Roman pontiff."[79] Submission to papal authority was held to be the ultimate criterion for defining membership in the visible society of the Church. For the next three centuries, especially in the theological institutions at Rome, the role of the pope was increasingly stressed in the polemical theology which pitted Catholics against Protestants. This ecclesiology strengthened the Church in her battles against Protestantism, royal absolutism, and the encroachment of the liberal State.

When discussing which form of government best describes the Church, Counter-Reformation theologians followed the medieval tradition. They, too, distinguished three principal forms of government: democracy, aristocracy, and monarchy. Canonists and theologians rejected the first two as inappropriate to the Church. Authority resides neither in the people nor in the successors to the apostles as a whole, they held, but in the pope as the vicar of Christ. Hence, Catholic theologians proposed that the Church best resembles a monarchy in which the pope holds universal sovereignty. In his *De controversiis*, Bellarmine defended the papacy as a monarchy, since this was the most suitable form of government for the Church. The Jesuit theologian outlined four advantages to monarchical rule which he believed was established by Christ. First, because of the clear distinction between ruler and ruled, it best preserves ecclesial order. Second, a monarchy creates a strong bond of unity because all depend on one head, thus minimizing conflicts among the faithful. Third, as an individual the pope can harness the energies of the people to help them reach their end. Fourth, monarchical rule provides the Church with stability since it is less subject to the divisions caused by factions and ambition.

Because Bellarmine recognized that this ideal form of government could not be realized perfectly in any human society, he also admitted aristocratic and democratic elements in the Church's structure. Counter-reformation views left a significant mark on the Catholic theology of the papacy. Between the Council of Trent and Vatican I, the Church was routinely described as a monarchy, although theorists admitted that such designations applied only analogously. For three centuries, the predominant model in ecclesiology was that of the Church as a perfect society headed by the pope as a spiritual monarch.[80]

◆

In the late fifth century, Pope Gelasius' two swords theory outlined the distinction between spiritual authority and temporal power. Until the turn of the millennium, nonetheless, the emperors and other rulers involved themselves in the Church's internal affairs, assuming a responsibility for safeguarding ecclesial unity. During this time, Pope Stephen II became the first pope to be a temporal ruler in the territories which Pepin deeded to the papacy in 757. The tension between the holders of the "swords" became intense as the Church increasingly fell under the temporal power, especially through the practice of lay investiture. Only at the beginning of the second millennium, with the Gregorian Reform's call for *libertas ecclesiae*, did the tables turn. Whereas earlier the "two swords" represented a division of power, gradually the popes claimed superiority, albeit indirect, even over temporal rulers. Both swords were ultimately in papal hands, so the new theory maintained, and the pope entrusted the temporal one to kings and emperors who were to use it for the service of the Church.

The canonists produced a justification for a genuine papal monarchy: the pope was head of both the Church and Christendom. The use of philosophical, theological, and legal concepts solidified this description of the papacy as a monarchy. From the Middle Ages onward, the papacy more and more appeared as a juridical institution justified by an ecclesiology which took its models from political society. The popes claimed to be the source, root, and head of all power, asserting their right to be the absolute sovereigns of Christendom. Innocent III further developed the notion of the emperor-pope, which culminated in the claims of Boniface VIII to be the one and only head of Christendom, the center of unity in the worldwide community. Within the Church, this monarchical vision led to regarding the bishops merely as sharers in the pope's universal jurisdiction.

As an institution, the papacy played an essential role in the development of Western civilization. Even so, papal primacy is an ecclesial, not a temporal, ministry. The papacy's direct involvement in temporal affairs was a detour in the development of dogma on the papacy.

During the fourteenth century, the first full-scale canonical treatises on the Church were written. Although most canonists defended the theory of papal monarchy, some dealt with ways of limiting the pope's authority. A few even raised theoretical objections against the papacy itself. In light of the crisis of multiple contenders for the papacy, conciliarist thought appeared. Radical theorists held that an ecumenical council is the supreme authority in the Church, and that the pope possesses his authority as the representative either of the whole Church or of her bishops. After the end of the Western Schism, both of their positions were judged to be incompatible with Catholic teaching.

The Reformation churches and ecclesial communities all defended the thesis that the Church exists in her divinely given integrity without the papal ministry. Lutherans and Anglicans both rejected the theological justification that the papacy is divinely instituted. At the same time, both traditions contain the seeds for a more positive evaluation of the papacy than their antichrist polemics first suggest. The twentieth-century ecumenical movement has been able to exploit this opening to considerable advantage.

The theology of the Catholic Reform stressed the Church's visible, hierarchical dimensions. Its controlling image of the Church was that of a pyramid crowned by a centralized papacy. These developments take us up to the First Vatican Council in the West. Before examining the council's dogmatic constitution on papal primacy and infallibility, however, we now turn to the views of the papacy which evloved in the Christian East.

Notes for Chapter five

1. Steven Runciman, *The Eastern Schism* (London: Oxford University Press, 1970), 22.
2. Walter Ullmann, "Papacy: 1 — Early Period," *New Catholic Encyclopedia*, vol. 10 (New York: McGraw-Hill Book Company, 1967), 954.
3. Ullmann, "Papacy," 954.

Origins, Development, and Mission of the Papacy

4. Louis Bouyer, *The Church of God*, trans. Charles Underhill Quinn (Chicago: Franciscan Herald Press, 1982), 30.
5. Brian Tierney, "Pope and Bishops Before Trent: An Historical Survey," in *The Papacy and the Church in the United States*, ed. Bernard Cooke (New York: Paulist Press, 1989), 14.
6. Heinrich Fries, "Mutamenti dell'immagine della Chiesa ed evoluzione storico-dogmatica," in *L'evento salvifico nella comunità di Gesù Cristo*, Mysterium Salutis, ed. Johannes Feiner and Magnus Löhrer, trans. Giovanni Moretto, Dino Pezzetta, and Gino Stefani, vol. 7 (Brescia: Queriniana, 1972), 288.
7. Giuseppe Alberigo, "Papa," *Nuovo Dizionario di Teologia*, ed. Giuseppe Barbaglio and Severino Dianich, 6th ed. (Milan: Edizioni Paoline, 1991), 1080.
8. Richard William Southern, *Western Society and the Church in the Middle Ages* (Harmondsworth: Penguin Books, 1970), 93.
9. Leo Scheffczyk, *Il ministero di Pietro*, trans. Franco Ardusso (Turin: Marietti, 1975), 65.
10. Southern, *Western Society and Church*, 100-101.
11. Brian Tierney, "Modelli storici del papato," *Concilium*, 11:8 (1975), 96.
12. Ullmann, "Papacy," 956.
13. Fries, "Mutamenti dell'immagine della Chiesa," 291.
14. Kilian McDonnell, "Papal Primacy: Development, Centralization, and Changing Styles," in *Papal Primacy and the Universal Church*, Lutherans and Catholics in Dialogue V, ed. Paul C. Empie and T. Austin Murphy (Minneapolis: Augsburg Publishing House, 1974), 180.
15. Southern, *Western Society and Church*, 158.
16. Congar, *L'Eglise de saint Augustin à l'époque moderne* (Paris: Cerf, 1970), 96-97, 103.
17. Patrick Granfield, *The Papacy in Transition* (Garden City: Doubleday & Company, 1980), 7.
18. Translation in J. M. R. Tillard, *The Bishop of Rome*, trans. John de Satgé (Wilmington: Michael Glazier, 1983), 53-54.
19. Karl Hofman, *Der "Dictatus Papae" Gregors VII: Eine rechtsgeshichtliche Erklärung* (Paderborn: Schöningh, 1933), 25-27.
20. Aemilius Friedberg, ed., *Decretum Magistri Gratiani*, vol. 1 (Graz, 1955), col. 69, 70, 73.
21. Austin Fliche and Victor Martin, *La réforme grégorienne et la Reconquête chrétienne (1057-1125)*, Histoire de l'Eglise, vol. 8 (Paris: Bloud & Gay, 1946), 63.
22. Renato Montanari, *La "Collectio Canonum" di S. Anselmo di Lucca e la riforma gregoriana* (Mantua: Industriale, 1941), 99.
23. Walter Ullmann, *The Growth of Papal Government in the Middle Ages*, 2nd ed. (London: Methuen, 1970), x.
24. Ullmann, "Papacy," 956.
25. Gregory VII, *Letter*, 64.
26. Brian Tierney, *Origins of Papal Infallibility: 1150-1350* (Leiden: Brill, 1972), 22.
27. G. Glez, "Primauté du Pape," *Dictionnaire de Théologie Catholique*, vol. 13 (Paris: Letouzey et Ané, 1936), col. 309.
28. Congar, *L'Eglise de saint Augustin à l'époque moderne*, 289.
29. Yves Congar, "Titoli dati al papa," *Concilium*, 11:8 (1975), 76-77.
30. Southern, *Western Society and Church*, 96.
31. Congar, "Titoli dati al papa," 82.
32. Bernard of Clairvaux, *De consideratione*, 2.8.
33. Granfield, *Papacy in Transition*, 44-46.

34. Southern, *Western Society and Church*, 105.
35. Congar, *L'Eglise de saint Augustin à l'époque moderne*, 188.
36. Giuseppe Alberigo, "Autorità e potere," *Nuovo Dizionario di Teologia*, ed. Giuseppe Barbaglio and Severino Dianich, 6th ed. (Milan: Edizioni Paoline, 1991), 84.
37. Alberigo, "Papa," 1084.
38. Congar, *L'Eglise de saint Augustin à l'époque moderne*, 279; cf. Tillard, *Bishop of Rome*, 60.
39. James H. Provost, "The Hierarchical Constitution of the Church," in *The Code of Canon Law: A Text and Commentary*, ed. James A. Coriden, Thomas J. Green, and Donald E. Heintschel (New York: Paulist Press, 1985), 261.
40. Klaus Schatz, *La primauté du Pape*, trans. Joseph Hoffmann (Paris: Cerf, 1992), 130.
41. Bonaventure, *Opera Omnia*, vol. 8 (Quaracchi, 1882-1902), 376.
42. Cited in Tierney, "Pope and Bishops Before Trent," 19.
43. Georg Schwaiger, "Pope," *Encyclopedia of Theology: A Concise Sacramentum Mundi*, ed. Karl Rahner, trans. John Griffiths, Francis McDonagh, and David Smith (London: Burns & Oates, 1975), 1246.
44. Congar, *L'Eglise de saint Augustin à l'époque moderne*, 237.
45. Thomas Aquinas, *Summa contra Gentiles*, 4.76.
46. Avery Dulles, *A Church to Believe In* (New York: Crossroad Publishing Company, 1982), 162.
47. Dulles, *A Church to Believe In*, 163-164.
48. Tillard, *Bishop of Rome*, 57.
49. George H. Tavard, "The Bull *Unam Sanctam* of Boniface VIII," in *Papal Primacy and the Universal Church*, Lutherans and Catholics in Dialogue V, ed. Paul C. Empie and T. Austin Murphy (Minneapolis: Augsburg Publishing House, 1974), 110-111.
50. Congar, *L'Eglise de saint Augustin à l'èpoque moderne*, 277.
51. Granfield, *Papacy in Transition*, 46.
52. Tierney, "Pope and Bishops Before Trent," 21.
53. Frederick J. Cwiekowski "Conciliarism," *The New Dictionary of Theology*, ed. Joseph A. Komonchak, Mary Collins, and Dermot A. Lane (Wilmington: Michael Glazier, 1987), 219.
54. Schatz, *Primauté du Pape*, 160.
55. Jaroslav Pelikan, *Reformation of Church and Dogma (1300-1700)*, The Christian Tradition: A History of the Development of Doctrine, vol. 4 (Chicago: University of Chicago Press, 1983), 73.
56. Translation in Norman P. Tanner, ed., *Decrees of the Ecumenical Councils*, vol. 1 (Washington, D.C.: Georgetown University Press, 1990), 409.
57. Tierney, "Popes and Bishops Before Trent," 23.
58. Odilio Engels, "Council," *The Encyclopedia of Theology: A Concise Sacramentum Mundi*, ed. Karl Rahner, trans. John Griffiths, Francis McDonagh, and David Smith (London: Burns & Oates, 1975), 305.
59. Hans Küng, *Structures of the Church*, trans. Salvator Attanasio (New York: Thomas Nelson & Sons, 1964), 285.
60. J. N. D. Kelly, *The Oxford Dictionary of Popes* (Oxford: Oxford University Press, 1986), 248.
61. In this section I draw on my two earlier works: *The Divine Right of the Papacy in Recent Ecumenical Theology*, Analecta Gregoriana, vol. 218 (Rome: Gregorian University Press, 1980), 83-97, 119-134; and *What Are They Saying about Papal Primacy?* (New York: Paulist Press, 1983), 10-17.

62. Martin Luther, "On the Papacy in Rome, Against the Most Celebrated Romanist in Leipzig," in *Luther's Works*, ed. Eric W. Gritsch, vol. 39 (Philadelphia: Fortress Press, 1958), 93-94.
63. Martin Luther, "Resolutio Lutheriana super propositione sua decima tertia de potestate papae," in *D. Martin Luthers Werke: Kritische Gesamtausgabe*, vol. 2 (Weimar: Hermann Böhlau, 1883ff), 191.
64. J. Michael Miller, *The Divine Right of the Papacy in Recent Ecumenical Theology*, Analecta Gregoriana, vol. 218 (Rome: Gregorian University Press, 1980), 87.
65. Philip Melanchthon, "Treatise on the Power and Primacy of the Pope" (1537), in *The Book of Concord: The Confessions of the Evangelical Lutheran Church*, ed. Theodore G. Tappert (Philadelphia: Fortress Press, 1959), 322-323.
66. Luther, "On the Papacy in Rome," 101-102.
67. *Book of Concord*, 299.
68. *Luther's Works*, ed. and trans. Theodore G. Tappert, vol. 57 (Philadelphia: Fortress Press, 1967), #4487, p. 346.
69. *Book of Concord*, 316-317.
70. Henry Chadwick, "Local and Universal: An Anglican Perspective," *The Jurist*, 52:1 (1992), 510.
71. *The Works of John Jewel*, ed. John Ayre, vol. 1 (Cambridge: Cambridge University Press, 1845), 340.
72. "A Defence of the Apology of the Church of England," in *The Works of John Jewel*, vol. 3, 289.
73. *The Works of John Jewel*, vol. 1, 375.
74. *The Works of William Laud*, ed. William Scott, 6th ed., vol. 2 (Oxford, 1849), 205.
75. *The Works of William Laud*, vol. 2, 186.
76. Giuseppe Alberigo, "L'unité de l'Eglise dans le service de l'Eglise romaine et de la papauté (XIe-XXe siécle," *Irénikon*, 51 (1978), 58-61.
77. Herbert Jedin, "Il significato del Concilio di Trento nella storia della Chiesa," *Gregorianum*, 26 (1945), 124.
78. From *De Controversiis*; translation in Avery Dulles, *Models of the Church* (Garden City: Doubleday & Company, 1974), 31.
79. From *De Controversiis*; translation in Dulles, *Models of the Church*, 14.
80. Granfield, *Papacy in Transition*, 9-10, 55-56.

Chapter six
THE PAPACY AND THE EAST

Among the crucial questions which still divide the Catholic Church from the Orthodox Church of the East is the Petrine ministry held by the bishop of Rome. From the outset, the East both experienced and theologized about the papacy differently from the West. Easterners disputed the nature of the pope's authority, how he exercised it, and how he could justify it. Despite these divergences, and the periodic schisms which temporarily divided them, East and West managed to remain in communion until the fateful rupture of 1054. Each "lung" of the Church nourished "its own theological, disciplinary, and liturgical traditions, with even notable differences," writes John Paul II, "but there existed full communion with reciprocal relations between the East and West, between Constantinople and Rome."[1]

The roots of the present-day disagreement about the papacy have their origin in the different ecclesiologies which developed in the early Church. This chapter will first examine the East's understanding of the papacy in the first millennium: the role it attributed to Peter, the place of the pope in its ecclesiology, and the kind of "primacy" it accorded to the bishop of Rome. It will then discuss the schism of 1054, the East's view of papal primacy after its separation from Rome, and the unsuccessful attempts at reunion proposed by the Second Council of Lyons and the Council of Florence.

Owing to the polemical character of so many writings, it is necessary to use carefully both Catholic and Orthodox sources, avoiding the extreme positions of each tradition. On the one hand, some Catholics have overemphasized that the East's willingness to accept a primatial role for the Roman see in the first millennium implied full recognition of papal claims as they were advanced in the West. On the other hand, as Orthodox theologian Alexander Schmemann notes, "Orthodox theology is still awaiting a truly Orthodox evaluation of universal primacy in the first millennium of Church history — an evaluation free from polemical or apologetic exaggerations."[2] Against the background of the Western tradition already outlined, this chapter examines the Eastern view of the papal ministry from the early Greek Fathers to the Council of Florence.

Peter and the Bishop of Rome

Eastern theologians nurtured the tradition that many of their churches originated with the apostles or disciples close to them. Jerusalem, for example, was believed to have been founded by James, the brother of the Lord; Antioch, by Peter; Athens, Thessalonica, and Corinth, by Paul; and Alexandria, by Mark, Peter's companion. Because so many Eastern churches traced their origins to an apostle, no see was granted prerogatives for this reason alone. In the West, where Rome was the only apostolic see, the founding role of Peter was evaluated differently.[3] For Latin Christians, the Roman church was their only direct link with the New Testament community. Consequently, they accorded it a particular prestige.[4] This argument made little impression in the East. Its understanding both of Peter's original leadership in the apostolic college and of succession to his ministry diverged from the theology of the papacy which was developing in the West.

Petrine Primacy

From the third century on, the West drew from the words of Christ, recorded in the three Petrine texts of the gospels, divine authorization for Rome's unique authority in the universal Church. In the East, however, a different standard of interpretation grew up regarding Peter's role in the New Testament and the identity of successors to his mission.

For the most part, the Greek Fathers acknowledged Peter's distinctive function in the apostolic college. He had a personal role as the "rock" upon whom Christ promised to build his Church.[5] Byzantine writers frequently praised Peter as the head of the apostles, recognizing the importance of his faith as the Church's foundation. St. Ephraim (†373), the classic author of the Syrian church, regarded Peter's confession as the archetype of all later professions of faith. "Our Lord chose Simon Peter and appointed him chief of the apostles, foundation of the holy Church and guardian of his establishment," Ephraim wrote. "He appointed him [Peter] head of the apostles and commanded him to feed his flock and teach it laws for preserving the purity of its beliefs."[6]

A later example, typical of the kind of Eastern tribute paid to the apostle Peter, is the witness of Photius (†895), the patriarch of Constantinople. Despite Peter's betrayal of Christ, the apostle was not, he wrote, "deprived of being the chief of the apostolic choir, and has been established as the rock of the Church and is proclaimed by the Truth to be keybearer of the Kingdom of heaven."[7] It is worth noting that Photius wrote this accolade while he was embroiled in controversy with the Roman see over its claim to be the center of unity for the universal Church.

The East, therefore, widely accepted Peter as the *coryphaeus* (head) of the apostolic college, the first of the disciples who confessed the true faith on behalf of all. However, as Orthodox theologian John Meyendorff explains, the Orientals "simply did not consider this praise and recognition as relevant in any way to the papal claims."[8] While the Greek Fathers acknowledged Peter's leadership in the early community, they denied that he had a directing role which involved exercising power over the other apostles. By divine institution Peter enjoyed a preeminence and a dignity above the others but no jurisdiction over them.[9] Praised though he was in the East, Peter held only a primacy of honor and preeminence. The Orientals respected Peter for his witness to the apostolic faith rather than for his power of jurisdiction.

Petrine Succession

From Peter's prominence among the apostles, Easterners drew different conclusions than Westerners did. Some Orientals held that all believers were successors of Peter. Others limited Petrine succession only to bishops. Very few conceded that the bishop of Rome was the successor to Peter in a unique sense.

The ecclesiastical writer Origen (†254) was the primary source for the East's interpretation of Matthew 16:18-19. In his commentary, Origen was unconcerned whether a connection existed between Rome's claim to primacy and Peter's office among the apostles.[10] According to Origen, Simon was called "Rock" because of his confession of faith: "If we also say 'You are the Christ, the Son of the living God,' then we also become Peter . . . for whoever assimilates to Christ, becomes rock." He then added: "Does Christ give the keys of the kingdom to Peter alone, whereas other blessed people cannot receive them?"[11] Primacy belonged to Peter because he confessed his faith in Jesus as the Christ. For Origen, the apostle deserved to be lauded as the first believer. The "keys" Peter received in response to his confession opened for him alone the gates of heaven. If others want to follow Christ, then they, too, will have to imitate Peter, confessing Jesus as the Son of the living God. When they do so, they will receive the same keys to the kingdom and the same surname "Rock."[12] According to Origen, all believers are successors of Peter and beneficiaries of the promise that the gates of hell will not prevail against the Church. Many Byzantines followed Origen's interpretation of Matthew's Petrine text. Whoever believed as Peter did, they maintained, would not go astray.[13]

A second Eastern interpretation of Petrine succession focused on the bishops as successors to Peter. Each bishop in his own church, they asserted, sits on the *cathedra Petri*,[14] a fact also true for the bishop of Rome. Just as Peter was to strengthen the faith of his brethren (cf. Lk 22:32), so were bishops to foster the faith of their flocks. Every bishop fulfilled the office of Peter, the first true believer, by preserving and teaching the faith he had professed.

Consequently, most Easterners disavowed that the pope was the *only* successor to Peter. Sts. Basil (†379), John Chrysostom (†407), and John Damascene (†749) wrote glowingly about Peter without concluding that the Petrine texts applied in a particular way to the Roman bishop. Among the Orientals, the pope's claim to be Peter's successor was insufficient reason for accepting his claim to universal primacy. The Western argument in favor of papal primacy based on Petrine succession at Rome was unconvincing. Easterners preferred to invoke the decrees of ecumenical councils as the reason for Rome's privileged position in the *koinonia*.[15]

While the West increasingly justified Roman primacy because it believed in the presence of Peter in its bishop, the East had no expression for the term "vicar."[16] The idea that the pope is the vicar of Peter (*Papa = Petrus ipse*), so influential for the Latin understanding of the papal ministry, was at first rare, and then later rejected in the East. For the most part, Greek theologians refrained from applying the Petrine texts directly to the bishop of Rome in the way that their Latin counterparts did.[17]

Some few testimonies do exist, however, in which Eastern ecclesiastical writers, perhaps currying favor with the pope, conceded that the bishop of Rome was the heir of Jesus' promises to Peter in a singular way.[18] Among these is the witness of Theodore of Studios (†826). While struggling against the heresy of the iconoclasts, Theodore appealed to Rome. In his letter, he spoke explicitly of Rome as the see of Peter, the criterion of the Church's faith and unity. The Roman church could claim this privilege because of the words of Christ to the apostles (cf. PG 99, 1017). Due to the existence of such statements,

Origins, Development, and Mission of the Papacy

we can say that at least occasionally the East referred to the bishop of Rome as *the* successor of Peter.

Eastern Ecclesiology and the Pope

In the first millennium, divergent views on the papacy between East and West grew out of their respective ecclesiologies. Eastern theologians concentrated their attention on the local church, the eucharistic community headed by its bishop. He, in turn, was in communion with other bishops, including the bishop of Rome, all of whom held the same apostolic faith. As a complete manifestation of the universal Church, each local church, centered on the Eucharist, made Christ fully present. Consequently, Orientals attributed less significance to the Church's visible structure than did the Latins. The Byzantines considered her outward organization as secondary when compared to her inner, sacramental life of grace. As a result, they were much more willing than Westerners to let the Church's external structure be regulated by conciliar decrees and cared for by the emperor.

The West, on the other hand, fixed its attention more on the Church as a visible reality throughout the world. The bishop of Rome was uniquely responsible for preserving the unity of the whole Church's faith. Furthermore, Latin ecclesiology was more analytical than the East's, tending to view the local churches as parts of the universal Church. More at home with juridical categories, the West regarded Rome as the center of a great society, responsible for directing the worldwide community. For its part, the East described the Church less juridically.[19] Its ecclesiology first considered the concrete local community; only afterward did it treat the unity of all the churches. Episcopal letters, hospitality, and mutual service maintained relations among the churches at the personal level. At the institutional level, relations were fostered by means of synods and synodal letters. Oriental ecclesiology never attributed to the bishop of Rome power *over* the Church; it always limited it to authority *within* the communion of churches. Byzantine theology excluded a monarchical vision of the papacy.[20]

Ecclesiastical law regulating Church life also took different forms in East and West. Whereas the East insisted that conciliar canons determined ecclesial organization and discipline, the West increasingly recognized the pope as a source of law independent of, even superior to, the councils. The letters and rescripts of the popes were among the most important sources for Western canon law, but they were almost totally absent from Eastern collections.[21] Latin theologians and canonists had a source at their disposal from which they could draw conclusions on Roman primacy, a resource unavailable in the East.

Order of the Ancient Sees

The hierarchical ordering of the great sees of Christianity, which later gave rise to the theory of the pentarchy, played a key role in Eastern ecclesiology. To a great extent this ranking conditioned the Oriental perception of Roman primacy. For the East, the Councils of Nicaea, Constantinople, and Chalcedon all contributed significantly to the determination of the Church's hierarchical structure.

Basing themselves on "ancient customs," the Fathers at the Council of Nicaea (325) recognized the special privileges (*presbeia*) of the churches of Rome, Alexandria, and Antioch. Canon 6 stated: "The ancient customs of Egypt, Libya and Pentapolis shall be maintained, according to which the bishop of Alexandria has authority over all these places, since a similar custom exists with reference to the bishop of Rome. Similarly in Antioch and the other provinces the prerogatives of the churches are to be preserved."[22] The bishops of these three sees enjoyed a degree of jurisdiction which was greater than that of the other bishops in their region.[23] The usual Eastern interpretation of canon 6 rejects the common Western explanation, which holds that the Fathers recognized that a true, if limited, jurisdictional "power" existed in the three sees.[24] Besides, according to the Byzantines, among themselves the three sees of Rome, Alexandria, and Antioch were equal. Each one had the same kind of authority within its own sphere of influence. In any case, they point out, the council attributed no special preeminence in the universal Church to the Roman see.

At the Council of Constantinople in 381, the Fathers added Constantinople to the group of three privileged sees, placing it ahead of Alexandria, the former second city of the Empire. Canon 3 declared that "because it is New Rome, the bishop of Constantinople is to enjoy the privileges of honour after the bishop of Rome."[25] The council maintained that the reason for Constantinople's new privileges was political. While ratifying Rome's first-place "privileges of honor," the Fathers neither recognized nor granted it any superior juridical rights. Rome contested the council's right to re-order the sees and the reasons it gave for doing so. Invoking canon 6 of Nicaea, Rome argued that the "Petrine" sees of Alexandria and Antioch had the right to precedence over the New Rome, since Constantinople's privileges rested on a human foundation.

Canon 28 of the Council of Chalcedon (451) put forward the same argument as Constantinople for ordering sees according to their political importance: "The fathers [at the Council of Constantinople] rightly accorded prerogatives to the see of older Rome, since that is an imperial city; and moved by the same purpose the 150 most devout bishops apportioned equal prerogatives to the most holy see of new Rome, reasonably judging that the city which is honoured by the imperial power and senate and enjoying privileges equalling older imperial Rome, should also be elevated to her level in ecclesiastical affairs and take second place after her."[26]

While acknowledging Rome's "primacy" in rank, canon 28 articulated the Eastern principle that ecclesiastical organization followed the administrative structure of the Empire as ratified by conciliar decree. The East endorsed the principle of accommodation, granting ecclesial primacy in light of a see's position within the Empire's political framework. Without explicitly denying that Rome's primacy was due to Peter's succession in the *cathedra* of the see, the council justified its special position in another way: because it was the church located in the capital of the Empire. According to Meyendorff, canon 28 expressed "the logical development of ecclesiastical organisms in the Byzantine period which, since the era of Constantine, had admitted the principle that ecclesiastical organization coincided with the secular structure of the Empire."[27]

Origins, Development, and Mission of the Papacy

Although the Eastern majority at Chalcedon espoused this canon, the papal legates opposed it. The council Fathers ignored their attempted veto. Despite the East's later persistent attempts to get Western approval, Pope Leo the Great refused to ratify canon 28. To him, it undermined the prerogatives of other more ancient churches which the Fathers at Nicaea had recognized. Furthermore, he judged that it failed to recognize that "the ordering of temporal matters is one thing; that of divine matters, another."[28] As a consequence, the West never received canon 28 as an authentic conciliar decree. Notwithstanding the East's own original hesitation about including it among the council's official decrees, it soon exploited this canon to justify Constantinople's "equal prerogatives" with Rome's. Within less than a century, both imperial and Eastern ecclesial legislation accepted it as a genuine conciliar canon.[29] From an Oriental viewpoint, Rome's rejection of canon 28 and its claim to legitimate primacy on a basis other than that of political accommodation appeared both arrogant and disparaging of conciliar authority.

Regional Primacies

The East maintained ordered communion among the churches by the two interdependent principles of episcopal collegiality and episcopal primacy. Apostolic Canon 34, found in a late fourth-century collection of canon law, probably from Syria, describes the Eastern view of relations between a bishop and the particular primate in his ecclesiastical province: "The bishops of every nation must acknowledge him who is first among them and account him as their head, and do nothing of consequence without his consent. . . . But neither let him who is the first do anything without the consent of all."[30] Byzantines accepted the "primacy" of a metropolitan bishop or patriarch with respect to the bishops of a region. They held, however, that the primate had no power or jurisdiction over them. He could act only with the consent of all the bishops of his region. The primate represented and expressed their collegial unity.

All primacy, including that of the bishop of Rome, was to manifest the unity of faith shared by all the bishops. In contrast to the West's stress on the monarchical principle, which assigned power over the other bishops to the pope, the East emphasized the sacramental equality of the bishops, each of whom was the head of a local church. For Byzantines, primacy never entailed the idea of a "supreme power" over the other churches.[31] Given their ecclesiology, it was extremely difficult for them to understand, let alone accept, the Western conviction that the pope enjoyed a teaching and jurisdictional power in the Church superior to that of the other bishops.[32]

Pentarchy

Byzantine ecclesiology, therefore, developed a theory of Church organization based on the conciliar canons which recognized the privileges of certain churches. From the fifth century onward, five sees were held in particular honor and arranged in order of precedence. Rome headed the list, followed by Constantinople, Alexandria, Antioch, and Jerusalem. Together they formed the pentarchy or "rule of five." These sees divided into spheres of jurisdiction the whole known world, except Cyprus, which the Council of

Ephesus had recognized as outside the pentarchy.[33] The five patriarchs were to handle all major issues affecting the universal Church. According to Eastern theologians, the Church preserved her apostolic faith by means of the joint witness of these five sees.

By the sixth century, the heads of these churches, and only these churches, were called "patriarchs."[34] Patriarchal privileges were conceded by conciliar authority and as such were a matter of ecclesiastical arrangement.[35] First by custom, and then by conciliar decision, each patriarchal church was to confine its evangelizing and sacramental activity within a well-defined ecclesiastical jurisdiction. No church or patriarch was to intervene, therefore, in the internal affairs of another patriarchate. The Orientals maintained that by divine right all bishops were equal as successors to the apostles. Nonetheless, among the five patriarchs, the East recognized a special place for the bishop of Rome. The Emperor Justinian (†565) believed that the "elder Rome" was "head of all the most holy priests of God."[36]

The West insisted that the bishop of Rome was superior in kind, and not only in degree, to the other patriarchs.[37] Even so, the Roman church recognized the unique privileges of the five patriarchs. From St. Gregory the Great (590-604) onward, Rome accepted the *de facto* privileges of the patriarch of Constantinople as first among the patriarchs of the East. Nonetheless, when Rome ordered the sees, it always preferred one which privileged the Petrine connection of certain churches.

Reluctantly, the East also admitted the importance of *petrinitas* as a determining reason which established a church's preeminence. Jerusalem, Antioch, and Rome were all explicitly Petrine sees, while Alexandria was linked through Mark, believed to be Peter's disciple. In the sixth and seventh centuries, in order to consolidate its second place within the pentarchy, Constantinople fostered the legend of its own apostolic foundation by Andrew, reputed to be Peter's elder brother. In this way, New Rome justified its preeminence on grounds that went beyond that of political accommodation to imperial structures.[38] Commenting on the pentarchy, Joseph Ratzinger says that "with this structure the East too has maintained the idea of a Petrine foundation of unity and of the concreteness of the unity and universality of the Church in the succession of St. Peter."[39] With the rise of Islam in the seventh century, Alexandria, Antioch, and Jerusalem fell into relative obscurity. This left Constantinople as the great patriarchate in the East and Rome in the West.

Throughout the first millennium, the popes resisted every attempt to attribute their primacy to a political rather than a Petrine principle. Rome continued to insist that its own primatial function, unlike that of the other patriarchates, was divinely instituted. The pope, Westerners maintained, enjoyed a double primacy. He was patriarch of the Latin West and, as successor to Peter, he also had the mission of caring for the universal Church.

Ecumenical Councils and the Pope

Another major ecclesiological difference between East and West was the way in which each tradition evaluated the pope's role at an ecumenical council. When the bishops were gathered in council, they represented the highest expression of ecclesial authority.[40]

"In the Eastern tradition," writes Jesuit theologian Wilhelm de Vries, "decisions concerning faith and discipline which affected the whole Church could, normally at least, only be made by the whole college of bishops with the pope as its head."[41] In significant matters, bishops were to reach a consensus analogous to that achieved by the apostles at the original council of Jerusalem (cf. Acts 15:6-29). For a council to be ecumenical, the bishops' mutual agreement was essential.[42]

From the seventh century onward, Eastern theologians maintained that the ecumenicity of a council depended on the participation of each of the five patriarchs.[43] Nonetheless, Orientals attributed to the bishop of Rome a particular function at an ecumenical council. Beginning at Ephesus, the East attached a singular importance to both the pope's doctrinal interventions and his confirmation of the council's decisions. The Byzantines did not give the same significance to the contributions or endorsements of the other patriarchs.[44] They denied, however, that Rome's judgment on an issue was determinative by itself, a conviction upheld by the popes. For the most part, this papal claim was not openly contested at the councils. More often than not, it was quietly ignored.[45]

Oriental ecclesiology regarded the Church as a communion of local churches, where no single bishop could impose his will on the rest. As a result, when Easterners received papal interventions at a council, they considered it their prerogative to debate what the pope had written.[46] At the Council of Ephesus, Pope Celestine's legate, Philip, made known the papal claim that the council was obliged to accept Rome's negative judgment regarding the teachings of Nestorius. It is unclear, however, whether the Fathers condemned Nestorius because of Celestine's intervention or because of their own decision to do so. The Eastern Fathers always wanted to get the pope's assent to the conciliar deliberations. With his approval, their decisions would be those of the entire Church, including the churches under Rome's patriarchal jurisdiction.[47] Ephesus set the pattern that emerged in the five subsequent councils: the pope insisted on his personal right to render definitive judgments, but the council Fathers still discussed his declarations before acknowledging that they conformed to the apostolic faith.

At the Council of Chalcedon, Leo the Great repeated the claim made by his predecessor at Ephesus. He demanded that the papal delegates should preside over the council and that all doctrinal questions should be avoided. To his mind, the christological controversy was closed. He had already settled it in his *Tome to Flavian*. Leo thought that the council should ratify, not debate, his judgment. As at the Council of Ephesus, however, the Fathers bypassed this papal command. "For the East, the council took into account the Roman decision but debated the issues on its own judgment," observes Robert Eno. "The decision of the council was the definitive one."[48] The Roman view held that a council should accept papal decisions because the pope had received from Christ the authority to judge questions for the universal Church. Easterners, however, agreed to papal teaching only "when they were satisfied that it was consonant with Scripture and tradition."[49]

In writing about Nicaea II (787), Patriarch Nicephorus of Constantinople (†829) summed up the Oriental view of the pope's role at an ecumenical council. "If ever there

The Shepherd and the Rock

was a council assembled rightly and with guarantees of legality, it is this one [Nicaea II]. For the church which has the greatest weight of importance in the Western part, that of ancient Rome, has indeed played her part in directing and presiding, in accordance with the divine norms formulated from the beginning. Without them [the Romans], a dogma held in the Church, based from the beginning on canonical norms and sacred customs, could still not be approved and commended for circulation"(PG 100, 597).[50] Even so, the East did not understand that the pope's confirmation was that of a higher authority. Instead, a council's ecumenicity was guaranteed because the West adhered to its decisions. Papal confirmation was necessary to insure the unanimous agreement of all the patriarchs.[51] While recognizing a unique position for the bishop of Rome at councils, Easterners disagreed with the Western interpretation of his role. They routinely ignored the pope's assertions that his teaching was determinative because he spoke with the formal authority of Peter's successor.

What Kind of Roman Primacy?

During the first centuries of the Church, the pope exercised his governing function differently in three geographical regions. Most of Italy was organized into one ecclesiastical province, where he ordained bishops and regularly intervened in the life of the churches. In the rest of the West, the pope maintained communion between the churches and unified discipline by communicating decisions of local councils to other provinces, exercising moral authority, and fostering the apostolic faith. For the most part, he intervened directly in a local church only in matters where a bishop was involved (*causae maiores*). In the third zone, the East, Rome intervened to safeguard the observance of major disciplinary regulations, preserve doctrinal orthodoxy, and ensure communion between the two parts of the Church.

The churches of the East were always geographically distant from Rome. Beginning in the early fourth century, this remoteness was exacerbated. When the capital of the Empire was transferred to Constantinople in 330, the bishop of Rome became even more remote. Secure in the structures of the new Christian Empire, Eastern Christians discovered, writes English theologian Aidan Nichols, that they "could do without Rome."[52] Nonetheless, when they found themselves in difficulty, the Orientals clamored for Rome's attention and approval.

Papal Jurisdiction

The pope intervened in the East's affairs differently from the way he did in the West. Of the more than 4300 extant papal documents from the first millennium, only 300 refer to the East; most of these touch dogmatic questions. When the bishop of Rome had reason to, and was conceded the right, he adjudicated disciplinary and doctrinal questions as a higher moderator, leaving intact the East's administrative and canonical autonomy.[53] Yet, despite these periodic interventions, Congar concludes that the East "never accepted the regular jurisdiction of Rome."[54]

For the Byzantines, it was erroneous to interpret Roman primacy as a "supreme" or "full" juridical power over the Church. When evaluating Roman claims to universal jurisdiction, the East judged that this governing authority could not be a power *over* other bishops. For them, the ministry of ecclesial government was a charism, received in episcopal ordination. Schmemann affirms that "no sacramental order of primacy" and "no charism of primacy" exist in the Orthodox Church.[55] Consequently, Western affirmations were in some sense incomprehensible, insofar as they appeared to base papal primacy on a non-sacramental foundation.

No evidence exists that the Eastern tradition as a whole ever admitted papal primacy as it was formulated in the West. A few Byzantine ecclesiastical writers did, on occasion, come close to according Rome the kind of primacy it claimed for itself. For example, St. Maximus the Confessor (†662), the leading seventh-century Byzantine theologian, wrote: "The Apostolic See . . . from the very Incarnate Word of God and from all the holy synods of all the churches throughout the world in their sacred canons and definitions has received and possesses, in and for everything, dominion, authority, and power to bind and to loose. With it the Word, set at the head of heavenly powers, binds and looses in heaven."[56] During the first millennium, a few Eastern bishops and theologians subscribed to the universal jurisdictional primacy of the bishop of Rome. Even so, they always carefully pointed out that the exercise of papal primacy was limited by the decrees of ecumenical councils.

Only in matters of appellate jurisdiction were the Orientals willing to submit, on a regular basis, to Roman decisions. In the first millennium, the East recognized that the bishop of Rome had the right to hear appeals from other churches that came to him for judgment. Agreeable to allowing appeals to Rome, the Byzantines nonetheless did so under the specific conditions laid down by their interpretation of the canons of the Synod of Sardica (343-344). To "honor the memory of Peter, the apostle," a bishop could appeal to Rome, and the pope, if he saw fit, could order a retrial. If, on the other hand, he refused to re-open the case, then the pope had to confirm the original judgment. Whereas the Latin text of canon 3 did not specify which bishops were to retry a case, the Greek version said that they were to come from the neighboring provinces.[57] While consenting to this appellate jurisdiction by Rome, the East denied that this was a primacy which involved power over the individual church making the appeal.

Byzantine writers advanced four reasons for recognizing Rome's right to hear appeals. First, they esteemed Rome as the city where Peter and Paul were martyred for the faith, a historical fact which granted it a certain preeminence owing to its dual apostolicity. Second, Easterners believed that the Roman church enjoyed a superior rank because of its location in the capital of the Empire. Third, the Fathers at the earliest ecumenical councils had granted Rome its unique privileges. Fourth, the Orientals revered the Roman see for its preservation of orthodox doctrine and its steadfast loyalty to the gospel when confronted by heresies and persecutions.[58]

Witness to the Faith

By the end of the fourth century, many Byzantines admitted that the Roman bishop received from God the grace to uphold and pass on undefiled the truth of the gospel.

Rome, therefore, enjoyed authority, "a weight of faith more than of powers," comments Tillard, "of example in witness more than of jurisdiction."[59] The East recognized that the Roman church had been spared, compared to itself, from the inroads of heresy. This nearly spotless record of doctrinal orthodoxy provided Easterners with a reason for accepting Rome's special role within the *koinonia*.

The Roman bishop's steadfast support of christological and trinitarian orthodoxy in the fourth and fifth centuries "contrasted sharply," writes Eno, "with the constant bickering, infighting and dubious theological positions held by some of the Eastern bishops, including those of the principal sees."[60] Due to this dissension in the East, the leaders of both orthodox and heterodox factions sought the support and approbation of the Roman see. According to Shotwell and Loomis, during these crises, the Orientals were ready to admit that Rome "had received from God through Peter the priceless gift which the Eastern prelates as a body seemed to lack, namely, the power to hold fast to the truth and to transmit it undefiled to posterity."[61]

The advance of Arianism in the fourth century led many Eastern theologians to take refuge in Roman orthodoxy. In desperation, bishops like Sts. Basil (†379) and Gregory of Nazianzus (†389) sent letters to Pope Damasus (366-384), acknowledging that God had given him an unswerving steadfastness in protecting the truth. They pleaded that he send envoys who would help them to restore orthodoxy and peace in the East.[62] In 378, Damasus replied to them, commending that they had rendered "to the Apostolic See the reverence which is its due" (PG 82, 1219). He did not, however, respond effectively to their appeals. Eventually the Eastern bishops solved their difficulties without his help. Later, Theodoret of Cyr (†466) appealed to Pope Leo: "If Paul, the herald of truth, the trumpet of the Holy Spirit, had recourse to the great Peter in order to obtain a decision from him concerning those at Antioch (Acts 15:1-35), much more do we, small, humble folk, run to the apostolic throne to get healing from you for the woes of the churches."[63]

The doctrinal contributions made by Leo the Great to the decisions of the Council of Chalcedon, where the Fathers had recognized him as a pillar of orthodoxy, left an unforgettable impression in the East. Oriental writers repeatedly cited his decisive intervention: "Peter has spoken through Leo!" The Latins interpreted the Fathers' declaration in keeping with their theology that the pope was the visible vicar of Peter who had a superior authority in doctrinal matters. The Orientals, however, interpreted the Fathers' response differently. According to them, it meant that Leo's letter agreed with the authentic doctrine of the apostles which he had articulated. Papal authority inherently depended on the witness the pope gave to Peter's faith. Easterners did not accept Leo's teaching on Christ's two natures by reason of his formal authority, because *he* said it, but because of *what* he said. They acclaimed the bishop of Rome insofar as he, like Peter, held firmly to the apostolic faith. In this regard, American Lutheran theologian Jaroslav Pelikan recalls how Latins and Greeks diversely interpreted Roman authority: "to the East the pope was chief bishop because he was orthodox, while to the West he was and always would be orthodox because he was chief bishop."[64]

Another case in point is the testimony of the *Libellus Hormisdae*, signed by the

Eastern bishops to end the Acacian schism in 519. This document affirmed that the Roman church was the one guarantor of true Christianity, the pillar of doctrinal authority: "We cannot pass over in silence the affirmations of our Lord Jesus Christ, 'You are Peter, and upon this Rock I will build my Church'. . . . These words are verified by the facts. It is in the apostolic see that the Catholic religion has always been preserved without blemish. . . . This is why I hope that I shall remain in communion with the apostolic see in which is found the whole, true and perfect stability of the Christian religion" (PG 63, 460).[65] This formula of Pope Hormisdas (514-523) entered Western ecclesiastical law as a foundational text supporting the development of papal primacy.

For nearly a millennium Easterners identified Rome as a bulwark of orthodoxy, despite what they regarded as occasional lapses, as in the case of Pope Vigilius (537-555), whose defense of Chalcedonian orthodoxy appears to have wavered. In their struggles against heretical doctrine, they confidently turned to the Roman bishop. When appealing to the pope, they did so because the Roman church had preserved the faith of Peter. Sts. Maximus the Confessor, John Damascene, and Theodore of Studios sought out Rome in times of crisis: the former in the monothelite controversy, and the latter two in their struggles against the iconoclasts.

In his dispute with the Monothelites, who held that Christ had only a divine will, Maximus the Confessor looked for help to the power of the keys held by the bishop of Rome. Maximus believed that the pope could judge questions of orthodoxy, opening the gates of the Church to true believers and closing them to heretics (cf. PG 63, 460). Battling against the iconoclasts, Theodore of Studios urged the emperor to consult the pope to ascertain what was true apostolic doctrine: "If there is anything in the patriarch's reply about which you feel doubt or disbelief . . . you may ask the chief elder in Rome for clarification, as has been the practice from the beginning according to inherited tradition."[66] When writing to the bishop of Rome, Theodore said: "Because you are the first in rank of all, you have strength from God, who has graced you into this rank" (PG 99, 1153).[67] Later he declared that the Roman see had been, "from the beginning until now, by the very providence of God, the one and only help in recurrent crises . . . , the pure and genuine source of orthodoxy . . . , the distinct calm harbor for the whole church from every heretical storm" (PG 99, 1159).[68] As Congar notes, nearly all the clearest Byzantine declarations in favor of papal primacy were written when the Greek protagonists of orthodoxy were looking for the support of the Roman see against those seeking to impose error.[69]

The Latins, however, frequently interpreted these acclamations and accolades from the East as if the Orientals accepted the Western understanding of universal papal jurisdiction. About these pro-Roman statements, Meyendorff observes that "the Christian East for a long time did not realize that in Rome this primacy of authority and influence was being progressively transformed into a more precise claim."[70] Only later, when the quarrel over the *filioque* and other issues erupted, did Easterners appreciate the extent to which different views about the papacy had contributed to the separation of East and West.

The Shepherd and the Rock

Primacy by Ecclesiastical Right

While accepting the idea of the primacy of one bishop over others in a region, the East regarded such leadership as a matter regulated by conciliar legislation. Consequently, when Byzantines considered the Roman claim to a primacy by divine right, they interpreted it using their own ecclesiological principles. For them, the papacy was an institution legitimated by human and ecclesiastical law. Because Roman primacy had never been defined by a council, the Byzantines moved back and forth between declaring in its favor and ignoring, even contesting, it.

"The authority of Rome is an authority of first rank," wrote French historian Pierre Battifol, "but there is nothing to suggest that the East has ever regarded it as being of divine right."[71] While accepting the pope as the "first among equals" (*primus inter pares*), Byzantines justified Roman primacy in the same way they did all patriarchal primacies. It was an institution of ecclesiastical right whose preeminence was confirmed by the sacred canons of the ecumenical councils.

Separation of East and West

The Second Vatican Council endorsed the common judgment of historians that East and West eventually parted ways through a progressive estrangement. The council noted that the schism between the Orthodox churches and the Catholic Church was not the result of a single action. Rather, it was the outcome of a gradual dissolution of ecclesiastical communion between the Eastern and Western patriarchates (cf. UR 13). Even if the mutual excommunications of 1054 did not effect the definitive institutional break between them, still "it was in 1054 that all the elements of disunity which had come to light over the centuries were first concentrated into a single event."[72]

Early Schisms

In the complicated history of the various schisms between Rome and Constantinople after the Council of Chalcedon, papal primacy was frequently the central issue. The Acacian schism (482-519) brought to the fore whether the bishop of Rome by himself, without either a council or the agreement of the other patriarchs, could depose the patriarch of Constantinople. In order to defend orthodox teaching, the Roman see steadfastly maintained its right and duty to do so. In this case it eventually prevailed.[73]

More serious crises affecting communion between East and West arose later, when for various reasons the West decided forcefully to assert papal authority. Two notable confrontations erupted before the schism. Popes Nicholas I (858-867) and John VIII (872-882) challenged Photius, patriarch of Constantinople;[74] and the popes of the Gregorian Reform crossed swords with Patriarch Michael Cerularius.

By the ninth century, the West described the pope as the bishop whom God had entrusted with directing the affairs of the universal Church. Pope Nicholas I vigorously asserted papal jurisdiction in the East, insisting on his right to intervene in problems affecting every church, including the patriarchate of Constantinople. Writing to Photius, Nicholas declared that "the entire company of believers looks for its doctrine to this holy

Roman church, which is the head of all the churches."[75] It was the pope's responsibility, Nicholas maintained, to be solicitous for the doctrinal orthodoxy and general welfare of every other church. Rome was the Church's final authority and the decisive center of ecclesial communion. Consequently, when Constantinople fell into heresy, breaking with the church at Rome, the pope declared that it was outside the true Church of Christ.[76] On the other hand, according to Easterners, when Nicholas demanded a retrial of Photius in Rome, he was violating the tradition established at the Synod of Sardica. The pope had the right only to hear appeals made to him, they held, not to intervene on his own initiative.[77] After a series of tangled events and temporary schism, communion was eventually restored. Nonetheless, the Roman assertions of papal authority during the crisis caused great offence at Constantinople, preparing the way for the events of 1054.

Precisely in these critical years of conflict, however, witnesses emerged in the East who worked strenuously to preserve the Church's unity. The apostles to the Slavs, Sts. Cyril (†869) and Methodius (†885), were evangelizing while controversy raged between the patriarch and the pope. Belonging to the ecclesiastical tradition of the Christian East, the two brothers were subject to the patriarch of Constantinople under whose aegis they had begun their mission. Even so, they considered it their duty to give an account of their missionary labor to the pope, asking him to confirm their work. The two brothers submitted to the pope's judgment "in order to obtain his approval for the doctrine which they professed and taught, the liturgical books which they had written in the Slavonic language and the methods which they were using in evangelizing those peoples."[78] Their witness is yet another example of the complex relations between East and West in the first millennium.

Reasons for Estrangement

Besides the differing ecclesiologies of Latins and Greeks, each with their own view of papal primacy, other causes led to increasing separation. For many reasons — political, cultural, disciplinary, and jurisdictional, but primarily theological — the churches in the East and West became strangers to each other.

Latins and Greeks lived and judged differently the role of the emperor in the Church. For the East, Church and Empire "formed a single organism," explains Orthodox bishop and theologian Timothy Ware, "yet within this one organism there were two distinct elements, the priesthood (*sacerdotium*) and the imperial power (*imperium*)."[79] Both civil and ecclesial life belonged to the earthly kingdom, at the head of which was the emperor. Although each was supposed to be autonomous in its own sphere, this ideal was frequently violated in practice. Beyond his civil responsibilities, the emperor helped local churches to preserve their bonds of communion. He also intervened in Church affairs by calling councils, appointing patriarchs, personally intruding in doctrinal questions, and promulgating conciliar definitions and canons as imperial laws. The emperor was responsible for legally guaranteeing the unity of faith, the most fundamental principle underlying the unity of the Empire.

Until the eighth century, the popes tolerated this state of affairs. They denied, however, the principle that the emperor could regulate the Church's internal life.[80] In fact, the emperor's interventions in ecclesial life were regarded as encroaching upon papal claims. This led the popes to define their primacy more sharply against any insinuation that the privileges of the Roman see depended on an imperial concession.

With the barbarian invasions and collapse of order in the West, the pope increasingly assumed responsibility for providing stability in both its spiritual and social life. His authority over the Church, not to mention society, developed according to a monarchical model unfamiliar to the Orientals. Easterners were unhappy with the West's theory of the "two swords," with its emphasis on the juridical relations between the two "powers." To them the principle appeared to endorse a secular understanding of both the Church and the papacy.[81]

Another cause of estrangement was provoked by Easterners, who vaunted their cultural superiority. Proud of being heirs to the authentic Roman Empire, they frequently disdained those who had assumed control of the Empire in the West. Both Latins and Greeks, moreover, had developed some different ecclesiastical customs. The East, for example, allowed married men to become deacons and priests, and it had always used leavened bread in its celebration of the Eucharist. The West, on the other hand, was increasingly mandating and enforcing priestly celibacy and, by the eleventh century, had settled on offering Mass with unleavened bread. While these issues are theologically secondary, they fed a climate of suspicion, even of hostility.

In the last resort, it was two theological questions, the *filioque* and the papacy, which furnished the most serious grounds for the break.[82] The issues are closely linked. According to the Orientals, the Roman bishop unjustifiably added the *filioque* to the Nicene-Constantinopolitan creed without consulting them. By the turn of the millennium, the West had everywhere added to the ancient creed that the Holy Spirit proceeds "from the Father *and the Son*" (*filioque*). The Byzantines regarded the insertion of this formula into an ecumenical creed as a grave scandal, even apart from the question of its theological orthodoxy.

Another serious theological problem was the papacy itself. The bishop of Rome claimed universal jurisdiction and justified his primacy "by divine institution." The Byzantines were indifferent to the fact that the Western Church was centralized under the pope's jurisdiction because, according to them, that concerned his patriarchate alone. However, when he tried to enforce the same jurisdictional power over the East, they objected. As long as the popes were subject to the emperor, they refrained from insisting on exercising in practice the primatial rights which they claimed in theory. To a limited extent, Rome accepted the need for harmonious cooperation between the Eastern Empire and the Western papacy. Without ever yielding to any principle which would curtail his jurisdiction in the East, Pope Gregory the Great (590-604), for example, did not try to enforce it.[83] Ware comments that "up to 850, Rome and the east avoided an open conflict over the Papal claims, but the divergence of views was not the less serious for being partially concealed."[84] Even if the pope was unable to exercise jurisdictional primacy *de facto* in the East, he still assumed the right *de iure* to do so. Nonetheless, as Schmemann

Origins, Development, and Mission of the Papacy

notes, "the rejection of Roman claims at the time of the Western Schism was due to an Orthodox 'instinct' more than to a positive ecclesiological doctrine."[85]

Schism of 1054

Yet another cause of alienation in the years immediately preceding 1054 was the West's "latinizing" of conquered lands in southern Italy. The patriarch of Constantinople, Michael Cerularius, responded in kind by forcing Greek practices on Latins under his jurisdiction. To resolve this difficulty, Pope Leo IX (1049-1054), the first of the reforming popes of the Gregorian Reform, sent Cardinal Humbert of Silva Candida (†1061) to Constantinople. Frustrated because the Patriarch refused to receive them, the papal delegation went to the church of Hagia Sophia. During the Divine Liturgy on July 16, 1054, they placed a bull of excommunication on the main altar. In response, Cerularius anathematized the contents of the document and its authors.

Though subsequent history has anchored the Great Schism in 1054, at the time neither the East nor the West thought that a definitive separation had taken place.[86] At first, this gesture provoked only a break between the patriarchal sees of Old Rome and New Rome. Other churches of the East, however, gradually followed suit, similarly separating themselves from communion with the bishop of Rome.

One of the goals of the Crusades was to restore good relations between Rome and the East. However, when French and Venetian soldiers, who were officially the allies of the Constantinopolitans, sacked their city, the separation between East and West was solidified. Christians slaughtered other Christians, and Latins took over Byzantine churches. The *coup de grâce* was the installation of a Latin patriarch at Constantinople in 1204. Easterners interpreted the pope's action as a sign that the West rejected the patriarch's jurisdiction. By these appointments in the East, Rome had altered the traditional procedure for episcopal election, extending its direct jurisdiction beyond the confines of the West. Because of the measures taken against the ancient tradition and decrees of ecumenical councils, Easterners considered that the bishop of Rome had fallen into heresy.

Orthodoxy and Papal Primacy

Devotion to Peter

Even after the schism, the East did not waver in its devotion to St. Peter. It regarded the apostle as the origin and model of all episcopal ministry in the Church. According to Meyendorff, Orthodox writers were "never ashamed of praising the 'coryphaeus' and of recognizing his preeminent function in the very foundation of the Church."[87] Gregory Palamas (†1359), archbishop of Thessalonica, for example, distinguished Peter from the other apostles. "Peter belongs to the choir of apostles, and yet is distinct from the others," Gregory wrote, "because he bears a higher title."[88] For all their praise of Peter, however, Orthodox writers disavowed that their esteem meant the endorsement of Rome's juridical claims over them.

In their writings on the papacy, Easterners turned their attention to the succession to

Peter as the central issue. Typical is the statement of the mystical writer Nicholas Cabasilas (†1363), successor to Gregory Palamas as archbishop of Thessalonica: "I do not find it necessary to investigate the authority of the blessed Peter in order to know whether he was the head of the apostles and in which measure the holy apostles had to obey him. There can be here a freedom of opinion. But I affirm that it is not from Peter that the Pope got his primacy over the other bishops. The Pope has indeed two privileges: he is the Bishop of Rome . . . and he is the first among the bishops. From Peter he has received the Roman episcopacy; as to the primacy, he received it much later from the blessed Fathers and the pious Emperors, for it was just that ecclesiastical affairs be accomplished in order" (PG 149, 701).[89] To ensure ecclesiastical order, at least some in the East were still willing to accept among the bishops a primate who fulfilled a role analogous to that of Peter among the apostles.

After 1054, the Orientals uniformly rejected the notion of a papal monarchy, a theory which proposed that all authority in the Church flowed from Peter and his successors. Byzantine writers in the Middle Ages formulated an ecclesiology in which Christ gave all the apostles the same power, sending them to evangelize the whole world. No apostle was tied to any one place. The bishop of Rome, therefore, could not succeed personally to Peter. He was a successor to the whole body of apostles, just as all other bishops were.

Anti-Papal Polemics

While recognizing the pope as patriarch of the West and the first among the bishops, the Orthodox came to believe that the Latin doctrine of papal primacy was heretical. They maintained that it vitiated the principle of the equality of the patriarchal churches. In each one, succession to the faith of Peter was preserved. Writing to Anselm of Havelberg in 1136, Nicetas, archbishop of Nicomedia, exemplifies this view: "My dearest brother, we do not deny to the Roman church the primacy among the five sister patriarchates; and we recognize her right to the most honorable seat at an ecumenical council. But she has separated herself from us by her own deeds, when through pride she assumed a monarchy which does not belong to her office."[90] In a similar vein, Cabasilas wrote: "We have never contested the primacy with the Roman church. . . . We know the ancient customs and decrees of the Fathers which declare the Roman church to be the most ancient of all the churches."[91] Most Orthodox still conceded that Rome was the first among equal sisters in the pentarchy. Only in a few anti-Roman polemical writings did some controversialists place Constantinople ahead of Rome in the pentarchy. They justified their position on the grounds that Andrew was Peter's elder brother and the first one whom Jesus called (cf. Jn 1:40-42).[92]

Backed by the Gregorian reforms, the popes continued to press their prerogatives. Innocent III, for instance, claimed that the Roman church was the "mother and teacher" of all the faithful (DS 774). His declarations met resistance in the East. Patriarch John X Camateros (†1206) answered him: "Where do you find in the holy Gospels that Christ said that the Church of the Romans is the head and universal mother and the most catholic of all the churches at the four points of the compass; or by what ecumenical council was

Origins, Development, and Mission of the Papacy

what you say about your church decided? . . . It is not, then, for these reasons that Rome is the mother of the other churches, but, as there are five great churches adorned with patriarchal dignity, that of Rome is the first among equal sisters. . . . So the church of the Romans has the first rank, it is the first of the other churches which, as sisters equal in honor, are born of the same heavenly father."[93] When faced by the "mother," "teacher," and "head" claims advanced by the West, the Byzantines rejected them. They vigorously affirmed that all churches were "sisters" and that Christ was the only head of the Church.[94]

After separation from the East, Western theological and canonical developments confirmed the view that the church at Rome was the mistress of the other churches of the pentarchy. At Lateran IV in 1215, the Roman church called itself the "mother and teacher of all Christian faithful." Only after asserting this primacy did the council then list the other four patriarchates in their traditional order (cf. DS 811). On the other hand, true to their ecclesiology of communion, the Byzantines held that all authority in the universal Church was to be exercised by the five patriarchs acting in collegial agreement. Nothing could be imposed on any church which all had not freely discussed and assented to.[95] Drawing on its understanding of the Church as a divine mystery, the East judged very critically the development of the theology of papal monarchy. In its eyes, Roman ecclesiology was legalistic, concentrating on the Church's external organization instead of on her internal life.

Councils of Reunion

Notwithstanding their mutual anathemas, even after 1054 both Rome and Constantinople continued to hope for the restoration of communion. Popes, patriarchs, and emperors yearned for reunion. Two attempts at healing the schism were made: the first, in the thirteenth century, at the Second Council of Lyons; and the second, in the fifteenth century, at the Council of Florence. At these reunion councils the dominant ecclesiology was Western and universalist, describing the Church as a worldwide society unified by the pope.[96] Both endeavors ended in failure.

Second Council of Lyons

In 1272, Pope Gregory X (1271-1276) issued invitations to a general council with a threefold agenda: clerical reform, a crusade to the Holy Land, and reunion with the Greek churches. Especially important was his desire to reunite East and West. Pope Clement IV (1265-1268) had previously sent a formula to Emperor Michael Palaeologus outlining his doctrine on the papacy. The Emperor sent this profession of faith back to the Council of Lyons, where it was read for the Fathers' approval. The text expressed the common theological and canonical understanding of papal primacy developed by the West in the mid-thirteenth century. At the council itself the Greek representatives accepted this profession. It is the first decree promulgated by an ecumenical council which dealt explicitly with the papacy.

The section on papal primacy assented to by the Greek representatives reads as follows:

> The Holy Roman Church possesses also the highest and full primacy and authority over the universal Catholic Church, which she recognizes in truth and humility to have received with fulness of power from the Lord Himself in the person of Blessed Peter, the chief or head of the apostles, of whom the Roman Pontiff is the successor. And, as she is bound above all to defend the truth of the faith, so too, if any questions should arise regarding the faith, they must be decided by her judgment. Anyone accused in matters pertaining to the forum of the Church may appeal to her; and in all causes within the purview of ecclesiastical enquiry, recourse may be had to her judgment. To her all the Churches are subject; their prelates give obedience and reverence to her. Her fulness of power, moreover, is so firm that she admits the other churches to a share in her solicitude. The same Roman Church has honoured many of those Churches, and chiefly the Patriarchal Churches, with various privileges, its own prerogative being, however, always observed and safeguarded both in general Councils and in some other matters (DS 861).

Because the Emperor appears to have imposed the union on his subjects for political reasons, the Eastern churches did not back the proposed reunion, and its effects were short-lived. Paul VI (1963-1978) commented on the reasons why reconciliation failed. "The Latins chose texts and formulae expressing an ecclesiology that had been conceived and developed in the West," he wrote. "These were proposed to the Emperor and the Greek Church to be accepted simply without discussion. It is understandable then that, no matter what may have been the sincerity of its authors, a unity achieved in this way could not be accepted completely by the mentality of eastern Christians."[97]

Council of Florence

Nearly two centuries later, there was another attempt to reunite East and West. Greek theologians and bishops, along with the Emperor John VIII and the patriarch of Constantinople, arrived in Ferrara, Italy, in 1438 to take part in a second reunion council. Both sides made serious attempts to restore full ecclesial communion. While respecting diversity in the rites and traditions peculiar to each, they recognized the need for unanimity in doctrine. In the bull *Laetentur coeli* (1439), promulgated at Florence, where the council had been relocated, the Fathers declared that "the wall that divided the Western and Eastern church has been removed, peace and harmony have returned, since the cornerstone, Christ, who made both one [Eph 2:20, 2:24], has joined both sides with a very strong bond of love and peace, uniting and holding them together in a covenant of everlasting unity."[98]

The Greek delegation agreed to a definition of papal authority couched, as at Lyons, in thoroughly Latin terms: "We define that the holy apostolic See and the Roman Pontiff have the primacy over the whole world, and that the same Roman Pontiff is the successor of St. Peter, the prince of the apostles, and the true vicar of Christ, the head of the whole Church, the father and teacher of all Christians; and that to him, in the person of St. Peter, was given by our Lord Jesus Christ the full power of feeding, ruling, and governing the whole Church as is also contained in the acts of the ecumenical councils and in the sacred canons" (DS 1307). With an eye to the East, the decree also reconfirmed the order of the patriarchates "as transmitted in the canons... all of whose privileges and rights evidently remain intact" (DS 1308).

At Florence, the Orientals did not, in fact, consider papal primacy as the greatest theological difference dividing East from West. That was reserved for the *filioque*. They "looked on the whole question of the Western patriarchate's relationship to other patriarchates as a canonical one," affirms British historian Joseph Gill, "and not as a dogmatic one."[99] Although the Greek delegates might have failed to appreciate the full import of the Latin formulas, they must have understood that the decree proposed, writes Gill, that the Roman church "was, not the equal, but the head of the other churches, because founded on St. Peter, the Christ-appointed head of the Apostles; that it had the right of governing the rest, and that with authority; that it had a universal jurisdiction and was therefore a court of appeal from all the world."[100] Unfortunately, when the delegates returned home, the agreement which they had reached was almost unanimously rejected. With the decree's formal repeal in 1484, the schism between East and West was cemented.

◆

Beginning in the mid-fifth century, the West's view of the papacy became increasingly monarchical. Such a theory was at odds with the Byzantine doctrine of the Church's fundamental collegial structure. The East, therefore, resisted this Western theological development. It resolutely taught that the universal Church was composed of a multiplicity of local churches, with patriarchs as the heads of the most important ones.

It is also true, however, that the East did grant a *certain* primacy to the Roman church and its bishop. Easterners acknowledged this primacy on the grounds that it had been granted by conciliar decrees, which had been formulated in light of the Empire's political structure. In the pentarchy, Rome held the first place. Furthermore, the pope's role at ecumenical councils was unique. As a witness to the faith of Peter, he had a singular doctrinal authority. Consequently, the East recognized that the Roman see enjoyed certain rights of appellate jurisdiction which extended to all the churches.

Did the East, then, accept Roman primacy in the first millennium? If we are asking whether the Byzantines acknowledged papal primacy as claimed by Rome after Leo the Great, then the answer is no. While the Orientals recognized the pope's jurisdictional primacy over the Western Church, where he was patriarch, they denied that he held the same kind of primacy over the Eastern churches. Easterners rejected the West's claim that Rome could unilaterally formulate legal norms or doctrine for the whole Church. Notwithstanding their admiration for the apostle Peter, they attributed no special Petrine succession to the bishop of Rome.

Besides disagreements about Rome's jurisdictional claims, East and West also had different theories regarding the theological justification which could be attributed to papal primacy. Even when the Orientals recognized a primacy, they qualified their acceptance. As an institution of ecclesiastical right, it was not essential to the Church's structure. Pragmatic in their approach to primacy, they were willing to adapt ecclesial structures to the demands of the Empire. Whereas Latins insisted on the special prerogatives of the "apostolic see of Peter," the only one in the West, Easterners ignored arguments for primacy based solely on a see's apostolic origins. Instead, they based their recognition of Roman primacy on a mixture of religious, political, and ecclesiastical factors. They accepted Rome neither as the "mother," "teacher," and "head" of all churches nor as the unique Petrine see; rather, she was a "sister" which was "the first among equals." For the Byzantines, canon 28 of the Council of Chalcedon, which attributed ecclesial rank according to political prominence, was axiomatic.

In its Decree on Ecumenism, the Second Vatican Council summarized the kind of primacy acknowledged by Latins and Greeks during this first millennium: "For many centuries the churches of the East and of the West followed their separate ways though linked in a union of faith and sacramental life; the Roman see by common consent acted as guide when disagreements arose between them over matters of faith and discipline" (UR 14). For a thousand years, the Eastern churches, while jealously protecting their freedom, regarded communion with Rome as a primary, if not the only, safeguard for ecclesial unity. From very early on, Rome articulated its claims and pressed them. Nonetheless, it refrained from insisting on them in the East as it did in the West. In theory, the popes maintained their right to universal jurisdiction, even if political and ecclesiological factors often limited its practical application. Throughout the first millennium, East and West, despite periodic ruptures in communion, accepted that their different theologies of papal primacy were compatible with the apostolic faith.

After the turn of the millennium, the growing estrangement between East and West led to schism, one of whose causes was doubtlessly the Roman claim regarding papal primacy. In the East, this led to increasing polemics against the West's monarchical understanding of the papacy. Nevertheless, most Byzantine writers in some fashion still acknowledged the preeminent place which the early councils and Fathers had accorded the Roman see. Like the West, the East kept alive the hope of restoring full communion with Rome. Sadly, the attempts to do so at the Councils of Lyons and Florence both failed.

Notes for Chapter six

1. John Paul II, *Euntes in Mundum* (1988), #4.
2. Alexander Schmemann, "The Idea of Primacy in Orthodox Ecclesiology," in *The Primacy of Peter*, ed. John Meyendorff et al., 2nd ed. (Leighton Buzzard: Faith Press, 1973), 49.
3. John Meyendorff, "Rome and Orthodoxy: Authority or Truth?" in *A Pope for All Christians?* ed. Peter J. McCord (New York: Paulist Press, 1976), 132.
4. James T. Shotwell and Louise Ropes Loomis, *The See of Peter* (New York: Columbia University Press, 1991), 220-221.
5. John Meyendorff, *Byzantine Theology* (New York: Fordham University Press, 1974), 97-98.
6. Ephraim, *Homilies*, 4; translation in Shotwell and Loomis, *See of Peter*, 665-666.
7. Cited in John Meyendorff, "St. Peter in Byzantine Theology," in *The Primacy of Peter*, ed. John Meyendorff et al., 2nd ed. (Leighton Buzzard: Faith Press, 1973), 7.
8. Meyendorff, "St. Peter in Byzantine Theology," 11.

9. Bernard Dupuy, "Le fondement biblique de la primauté romaine en Orient et en Occident," in *La primauté romaine dan la communion des églises*, ed. Comité mixte catholique-orthodoxe en France (Paris: Cerf, 1991), 20.
10. Robert B. Eno, *The Rise of the Papacy* (Wilmington: Michael Glazier, 1990), 43. This contrasts with the opinion of Shotwell and Loomis, who think that Origen was emphatically rejecting "the Roman legalistic theory of the keys bestowed upon Peter" (*See of Peter*, 317).
11. Origen, *Commentaries on Matthew*, 12.10. In *Antidote against the Scorpion*, 10, Tertullian had previously written (*circa* 211-212) that Christ had left the "keys" to Peter, and through him to the Church, especially those who confessed the faith when facing persecution.
12. Origen, *Commentaries on Matthew*, 12.11.
13. Jaroslav Pelikan, *The Spirit of Eastern Christendom (600-1700)*, The Christian Tradition: A History of the Development of Doctrine, vol. 2 (Chicago: Chicago University Press, 1974), 161.
14. Meyendorff, *Byzantine Theology*, 98.
15. Meyendorff, "St. Peter in Byzantine Theology," 8.
16. Yves Congar, *L'Eglise de saint Augustin à l'époque moderne* (Paris: Cerf, 1970), 85; cf. Yves Congar, *L'ecclésiologie du haut Moyen-Age* (Paris: Cerf, 1968), 367-369.
17. Pelikan, *Spirit of Eastern Christendom*, 160.
18. Daniel Stiernon, "Interprétations, résistances et oppositions en Orient," in *Il primato del vescovo di Roma nel Primo Millennio: Ricerche e Testimonianze*, ed. Michele Maccarrone (Vatican City: Polyglot Press, 1991), 663.
19. Congar, *L'ecclésiologie du haut Moyen-Age*, 342-343.
20. Eugenio Corecco, "The Bishop as Head of the Local Church and Its Discipline," in *Readings, Cases, Materials in Canon Law*, ed. Jordan P. Hite, Gennaro J. Sesto, and Daniel J. Ward (Collegeville: Liturgical Press, 1980), 141-142.
21. Congar, *L'ecclésiologie du haut Moyen-Age*, 375.
22. Translation in Norman P. Tanner, ed., *Decrees of the Ecumenical Councils*, vol. 1 (Washington, D.C.: Georgetown University Press, 1990), 8-9.
23. Vittorio Peri, "Local Churches and Catholicity in the First Millennium of the Roman Tradition," *The Jurist*, 52:1 (1992), 94.
24. Schmemann, "Idea of Primacy in Orthodox Ecclesiology," 47.
25. Translation in *Decrees of the Ecumenical Councils*, vol. 1, 32.
26. Council of Chalcedon, canon 28; translation in *Decrees of the Ecumenical Councils*, vol. 1, 99-100.
27. John Meyendorff, *Orthodoxy and Catholicity* (New York: Sheed & Ward, 1956), 74.
28. Leo the Great, *Letter*, 104.
29. Wilhelm de Vries, *Orient et Occident* (Paris: Cerf, 1974), 148-149.
30. Translation in John H. Erickson, "The Local Churches and Catholicity: An Orthodox Perspective," *The Jurist*, 52:1 (1992), 497.
31. Emmanuel Clapsis, "The Papal Primacy," *Greek Orthodox Theological Review*, 37 (1987), 128.
32. Congar, *L'ecclésiologie du haut Moyen-Age*, 387.
33. Timothy Ware, *The Orthodox Church* (Harmondsworth: Penguin Books, 1980), 34.
34. Peri, "Local Churches and Catholicity, 92.
35. J. M. R. Tillard, "The 'Horizon' of the Primacy of the Bishop of Rome," *One in Christ*, 12 (1976), 16.

36. *Codex Justiniani*, I.1.7; cited in Aidan Nichols, *Rome and the Eastern Churches* (Collegeville: Liturgical Press, 1992), 173.
37. Pelikan, *Spirit of Eastern Christendom*, 166.
38. Francis Dvornik, *The Idea of Apostolicity in Byzantium and the Legend of the Apostle Andrew*, Dumbarton Oaks Studies, vol. 4 (Cambridge: Harvard University Press, 1958).
39. Joseph Ratzinger, "Theological Notes," attached to the statement of the Congregation for Bishops, "Directory for the *ad Limina* Visit," *L'Osservatore Romano*, 28 (July 11, 1988), 7.
40. Meyendorff, "Rome and Orthodoxy: Authority or Truth?" 133.
41. Wilhelm de Vries "Theoretical and Practical Renewals of the Primacy of Rome: The Development after Constantine," *Concilium*, 64 (1971), 52.
42. J. M. R. Tillard, *The Bishop of Rome*, trans. John de Satgé (Wilmington: Michael Glazier, 1983), 185; cf. de Vries, *Orient et Occident*, 243.
43. Yves Congar, "The Pope as Patriarch of the West," *Theology Digest*, 38:1 (1991), 3; cf. Congar, *L'ecclésiologie du haut Moyen-Age*, 379.
44. De Vries, *Orient et Occident*, 279.
45. Luis M. Bermejo, "Jurisdictional Authority by Divine Right: A Moot Question," *Bijdragen*, 40 (1979), 281.
46. Congar, *L'ecclésiologie du haut Moyen-Age*, 387; cf. de Vries, *Orient et Occident*, 248, 254.
47. De Vries, *Orient et Occident*, 64-65.
48. Eno, *Rise of the Papacy*, 115.
49. Francis A. Sullivan, *Magisterium: Teaching Authority in the Catholic Church* (New York: Paulist Press, 1983), 68.
50. Nicephorus, *Great Apology*; translation in Tillard, *Bishop of Rome*, 187.
51. De Vries, *Orient et Occident*, 80.
52. Nichols, *Rome and the Eastern Churches*, 163.
53. Congar, *L'ecclésiologie du haut Moyen-Age*, 359.
54. Yves Congar, *Diversity and Communion* (Mystic: Twenty-Third Publications, 1985), 26.
55. Schmemann, "Idea of Primacy in Orthodox Ecclesiology," 33.
56. *St. Maximus the Confessor: Ancient Christian Writers Series*, ed. Polycarp Sherwood (Westminster: Newman, 1955), 76.
57. Nichols, *Rome and the Eastern Churches*, 161-162.
58. Ware, *The Orthodox Church*, 35-36.
59. Tillard, *Bishop of Rome*, 84.
60. Eno, *Rise of the Papacy*, 148.
61. Shotwell and Loomis, *See of Peter*, 226.
62. See, for example, Basil, *Letter*, 70: PG 32, 433-436; Basil et al., *Letter*, 92: PG 32, 477-484; Basil, *Letter*, 242: PG 32, 900-901.
63. Translation in Thomas Halton, *The Church*, Message of the Fathers of the Church, vol. 4 (Wilmington: Michael Glazier, 1985), 109.
64. Pelikan, *Spirit of Eastern Christendom*, 161.
65. Cited in Nichols, *Rome and the Eastern Churches*, 171.
66. Theodore of Studios, *Letter*, 2; *Letter*, 86; cited in Clapsis, "Papal Primacy," 130.
67. Translation in Pelikan, *Spirit of Eastern Christendom*, 155.
68. Translation in Pelikan, *Spirit of Eastern Christendom*, 155.
69. Congar, *L'ecclésiologie du haut Moyen-Age*, 363.

Origins, Development, and Mission of the Papacy

70. Meyendorff, "St. Peter in Byzantine Theology," 8-9.
71. Pierre Batiffol, *Cathedra Petri: Etudes d'histoire ancienne de l'Eglise* (Paris: Cerf, 1938), 75.
72. Richard William Southern, *Western Society and the Church in the Middle Ages* (Harmondsworth: Penguin Books, 1970), 67-68.
73. Eno, *Rise of the Papacy*, 119-121.
74. See Francis Dvornik, *The Photian Schism: History and Legend* (Cambridge: Cambridge University Press, 1959).
75. Cited in Pelikan, *Spirit of Eastern Christendom*, 159.
76. De Vries, *Orient et Occident*, 198, 229, 240, 272-273.
77. Ware, *The Orthodox Church*, 62.
78. John Paul II, *Slavorum Apostoli* (1985), #13.
79. Ware, *The Orthodox Church*, 49.
80. Congar, *L'ecclésiologie du haut Moyen-Age*, 345-346.
81. Congar, *L'ecclésiologie du haut Moyen-Age*, 355.
82. Ware, *The Orthodox Church*, 51-52.
83. Walter Ullmann, "Papacy: 1 — Early Period," *New Catholic Encyclopedia*, vol. 10 (New York: McGraw-Hill Book Company, 1967), 954.
84. Ware, *The Orthodox Church*, 58.
85. Schmemann, "Idea of Primacy in Orthodox Ecclesiology," 37.
86. John D. Farris, *The Eastern Catholic Churches: Constitution and Governance* (New York: Saint Maron Publications, 1992), 22-23.
87. Meyendorff, "St. Peter in Byzantine Theology, 11.
88. Gregory Palamas, *Triads*, I.1.38; translation in Meyendorff, "St. Peter in Byzantine Theology," 13.
89. Translation in Meyendorff, "St. Peter in Byzantine Theology," 28.
90. Cited in Ware, *The Orthodox Church*, 58.
91. Nicholas Cabasilas, *On the Causes of the Dogmatic Differences in the Church*; translation in Nichols, *Rome and the Eastern Churches*, 155, n. 6.
92. Pelikan, *Spirit of Eastern Christendom*, 169.
93. Cited in Congar, *Diversity and Communion*, 87.
94. Congar, *L'Eglise de saint Augustin à l'époque moderne*, 100.
95. Congar, *L'Eglise de saint Augustin à l'époque moderne*, 264-266.
96. Nichols, *Rome and the Eastern Churches*, 275.
97. Paul VI, "Letter to Cardinal Willebrands for the Seventh Centenary of the Council of Lyons," *L'Osservatore Romano*, 44 (October 31, 1974), 14.
98. Council of Florence, *Laetentur coeli* (1439); translation in *Decrees of the Ecumenical Councils*, vol. 1, 524.
99. Joseph Gill, "The Definition of the Primacy of the Pope in the Council of Florence," *Heythrop Journal*, 2 (1961), 28.
100. Gill, "Definition of the Primacy," 29.

Chapter seven
PRIMACY OF JURISDICTION

"Papal authority, either directly or through the Curia," writes theologian Patrick Granfield, "touches the lives of every Catholic — bishops, clerics, religious and laity. No one is exempt and no aspect of Catholic life is unaffected."[1] Canonist James Coriden observes that "the Christian lives of ordinary Catholics all over the world are influenced much more by the pope than by their own bishop."[2] Why is this so?

In 1870, the First Vatican Council solemnly defined the Church's teaching on papal primacy and papal infallibility. In its dogmatic constitution *Pastor aeternus*, the Fathers proposed to all the faithful what they are to believe and hold "with regard to the establishment, the perpetuity and the nature of this sacred apostolic primacy" (DS 3052). While the focus in this chapter is on the primacy of pastoral government, the council's teaching on the institution, permanence, and purpose of the papacy provides the necessary context for the definition of the pope's authority.

The interpretation I give to the teaching of Vatican I will be guided by the understanding expressed by the bishops themselves. By their express intention, the Fathers' definitions are to be understood "according to the ancient and constant belief of the universal Church" (DS 3052), expressed in the testimony of "the proceedings of the ecumenical Councils and in the sacred canons" (DS 3059), and lived according to the "perpetual practice of the Church" (DS 3065).

The First Vatican Council's treatment of papal primacy provides the framework and sets the parameters within which Catholic discussion on the pope's primacy of jurisdiction still takes place. *Pastor aeternus* is not, however, the last word on the subject. A century of theological development, which culminated in the Second Vatican Council, has broadened the context of discussion, correcting the particular vision of Vatican I. Furthermore, despite the emphasis given here to the pope's primacy of government in the Church, it is important that this way of looking at the papacy should not "mislead one into a view of the Petrine and papal office that places the emphasis too much on legislation, jurisdiction, and administration in the various areas of the Church's life."[3]

After providing some background to the First Vatican Council, I take up this council's treatment of the institution of Petrine primacy by Christ (*petrinitas*), succession to Peter's ministry (*perpetuitas*), and the identification of Peter's successor as the bishop of Rome (*romanitas*). The chapter then discusses the purpose and nature of papal jurisdiction in light of its definition in *Pastor aeternus*, the subsequent teaching of Vatican II, the 1983 Code of Canon Law, and the reflection of contemporary theologians. A presentation of the limits to papal jurisdiction rounds out the present discussion.

First Vatican Council

With nearly seven hundred bishops present, Vatican I opened on December 8, 1869. Pius IX (1846-1878) had a broad agenda in mind. The council's opening discussion focused on errors regarding the meaning of faith and the nature of revelation, which subsequently resulted in the promulgation of the dogmatic constitution *Dei Filius* (April 24, 1870). The council's Preparatory Commission had also drafted a document on the Church, *De ecclesia Christi*. Of its sixteen chapters, only chapter eleven dealt with the primacy. When it became clear that Italian forces would occupy Rome and the council would be suspended, debate went ahead only on the section dedicated to papal primacy. Later, a chapter on papal infallibility was added to that on the primacy.[4] Both primacy and infallibility were therefore discussed apart from the fuller ecclesiological context that Pius IX and the council had originally intended. The result was the dogmatic constitution *Pastor aeternus*, passed on July 18, 1870.

Why Was Papal Primacy Defined?

In the eighteenth and early nineteenth centuries, certain conciliarist tendencies survived in France (Gallicanism), Germany (Febronianism), and Austria (Josephinism). Common to all these views, often referred to as "Gallican" because they were influenced by strong nationalistic feelings, was the defense of the autonomy of national churches, a desire for a strong episcopacy, and the toleration of state interference in Church affairs.[5] Advocates of a Gallican ecclesiology maintained the right to qualify papal decisions by appealing to a general council, the episcopate, or the people. In this way, they followed the radical conciliarist interpretation given to the decrees *Haec sancta* (1415) and *Frequens* (1417) of the Council of Constance[6] — a point discussed in chapter five.

By the mid-nineteenth century, however, neither Gallican nor radical conciliarist ideas posed a threat to Church unity. Even so, Pius IX wanted to eliminate any remaining hints of conciliarism. When faced with the loss of the remaining portion of the Papal States, he decided to strengthen the Church's internal life by emphasizing papal authority. Rome's long memory of anti-papal tendencies, more than any imminent danger, meant that the conciliar formulations were framed to combat the minimalist view of papal primacy proposed in Gallican ecclesiologies.[7]

Other reasons for calling Vatican I depended on socio-political considerations, especially in Western Europe, where many were reacting against the excesses of the Enlightenment and French Revolution. The nineteenth-century political climate left many Catholics feeling bewildered, and they looked to Pius IX as a source of strength. He was "a point of stability and hope at the moment when so many civil societies were breaking up."[8] The opinion of the French ultramontanist writer Joseph de Maistre (†1821) summarizes why strong papal authority was often promoted for reasons which were social and political: "No public morals or national character without religion, no European religion without Christianity, no Christianity without Catholicism, no Catholicism without the pope, no pope without the supremacy which belongs to him."[9] Many looked to the papacy to restore the dignity of Christianity, revive the principle of authority, and prevent ambitious political leaders from fragmenting the power of the Church.[10]

As the Church's influence in Europe declined, bishops from Catholic countries, but from others as well, wanted a forceful papacy: to bolster ecclesial authority; to help combat state interference in France, Germany, and Austria; to resist nationalism in Italy and Spain; to support "minorities" in the United States, Holland, Ireland, and England; to combat liberalism, materialism, and other modern errors; and to give a clear identity to the expanding missions. National episcopates often relied upon Rome to defend their interests against new, often liberal, governments. Many believed that only a vigorous papacy could both save the Church from splitting into different national churches and preserve her freedom against state encroachment.

Two developments in the nineteenth century favored the development of an energetic papacy: ultramontanism and centralization. With their focus on Rome and the importance of its bishop, both influenced the doctrine defined in *Pastor aeternus*.

Ultramontanism was a movement which originated in a certain nostalgia for the old pre-revolutionary order. Ultramontanists — so called because they looked to Rome, "beyond the mountains" — argued for a strong, unified Church government, concentrating all ecclesial power in the pope. Opposed to Gallicanism, they favored the centralization of ecclesiastical authority in Rome, the "center of the Church." Standing up for the independence of the Church from the State, ultramontanists believed that all major Church initiatives and judgments must come from the pope.[11] They advocated unified liturgy, discipline, customs, and devotion according to the Roman pattern. Ultramontanists also fostered sympathy for the persecuted "martyr popes," Pius VI (1775-1799) and Pius VII (1800-1823), who had been humiliated by various French regimes.[12]

Faced with the papacy's weakening temporal authority, the ultramontanists worked to strengthen its spiritual power. Their efforts were spread by the Catholic press's adulation for the charming Pius IX. When coupled with a Romantic enthusiasm for the pope, extreme ultramontanism often fell into devotional and theological excess. While at Vatican I the ultramontanists' wings were clipped, *Pastor aeternus* nonetheless reflects their ecclesiology.

In the nineteenth century, the Church's pastoral life was becoming more centralized. It became increasingly commonplace to refer all matters to Rome, a trend enthusiastically endorsed by the ultramontanists. Canonists and theologians similarly abetted a reinforcement of Roman authority. To serve that end they had available the strongly juridical ecclesiology of Robert Bellarmine (†1621), who situated the papacy within the realm of the constitutional law of the Church.[13] Modern means of transportation also made it possible for pilgrims to go to Rome. Easier travel also allowed Pius IX to enforce the requirement that bishops from all over the world had to report to him every five years.

In a climate marked by political reaction, popular adulation, and theological ultramontanism, Pius IX announced in 1867 that an ecumenical council would be convened so that "the necessary antidotes might be found for the so numerous evils oppressing the Church."[14]

Institution of Petrine Primacy

In its dogmatic constitution *Pastor aeternus*, the First Vatican Council defined the following with regard to the jurisdictional primacy of the apostle Peter.

Chapter One: We, therefore, teach and declare, according to the testimony of the Gospel, that the primacy of jurisdiction over the whole Church was immediately and directly promised and conferred upon the blessed apostle Peter by Christ the Lord (DS 3053).

Canon: Therefore, if anyone says that the blessed apostle Peter was not constituted by Christ the Lord as the Prince of all the apostles and the visible head of the whole Church militant, or that he received immediately and directly from Jesus Christ our Lord only a primacy of honour and not a true and proper primacy of jurisdiction, *anathema sit* (DS 3055).

In the draft *De ecclesia Christi* submitted to the bishops on January 21, 1870, the Deputation of the Faith, or Theological Commission, summarized the three principal errors on Peter's primacy which they wished to exclude: the Protestant denial of its divine institution; the Orthodox affirmation of the jurisdictional quality of all the apostles; and the Gallican opinion that Peter received his primacy through the mediation of the Church (cf. M 51, 598).

The final text, *Pastor aeternus*, subsequently condemned two errors. First, it censured those who denied that "Peter alone in preference to the other apostles, either singly or as a group, was endowed by Christ with the true and proper primacy of jurisdiction" (DS 3054). Second, it rejected the view that papal jurisdiction was given to "the Church and through the Church to Peter as a minister of the Church" (DS 3054). The dogmatic constitution insisted that Christ was responsible for directly conferring this ministry on Peter. Invoking John 1:42, Matthew 16:18-19, and John 21:15-17, the Fathers held that Jesus himself made Peter visible head of the Church.

The council accepted the standard interpretation of the Petrine texts which had prevailed in the West since the Middle Ages. It read these texts in light of the received tradition and according to the standards of biblical scholarship known at the time. Typical of the Fathers' exegesis is that of Bishop D'Avanzo, who spoke for the Deputation of the Faith: "Since the Church is to be built upon Peter as the foundation stone, it follows that in this text the relation between Peter and the apostles is the same as that between the foundation and the building. . . . Therefore the relation of the apostles to Peter is in itself a relation of absolute dependence" (M 52, 1204). While not intending to give a definitive exegesis to the Petrine texts cited, the bishops declared that Petrine primacy was revealed in the "very clear teaching of the Holy Scripture, as it has always been understood by the Catholic Church" (DS 3054). As we saw in chapters one and two, modern scholars are more reserved in the conclusions they draw from their exegesis of these texts.

Permanence of the Primacy

Chapter two of *Pastor aeternus* treats two related, but distinct, questions: first, succession to Peter's original primacy (*perpetuitas*); and second, the identification of who succeeds to the primacy of Peter (*romanitas*). The chapter and attached canon read as follows.

Chapter Two: Now, what Christ, the Lord, the Prince of Shepherds and the great Shepherd of the flock, established in the person of the blessed apostle Peter for the perpetual safety and everlasting good of the Church must, by the will of the same, endure without interruption in the Church which was founded on the rock and which will remain firm until the end of the world. Therefore, whoever succeeds Peter in this Chair, according to the institution of Christ Himself, holds Peter's primacy over the whole Church (DS 3056-3057).

Canon: Therefore, if anyone says that it is not according to the institution of Christ our Lord Himself, that is, by divine law, that St Peter should have perpetual successors in the primacy over the whole Church; or if anyone says that the Roman Pontiff is not the successor of St Peter in the same primacy, *anathema sit* (DS 3058).

The theological consultants who prepared the draft of chapter two had in mind to refute those who denied either that Peter had successors to his ministry after his death or that Petrine succession was of divine institution.[15] The official explanatory note distributed to the Fathers stated that the canon was directed "against heretics and schismatics who generally deny that Peter, by the institution of Christ the Lord himself, has perpetual successors in the primacy over the whole Church" (M 51, 627).

According to *Pastor aeternus*, whatever role Christ assigned to Peter continued in his successors, who were included, so to speak, "in the person of the blessed apostle Peter" (DS 3056). The theological argument which the Fathers used to teach that Petrine succession was of divine right differed from the one they used to make the same point for Petrine primacy. While they were unable to appeal to any explicit gospel texts in which Christ had revealed his intention for the permanence of Peter's ministry, the bishops invoked implicit arguments from Scripture to justify their teaching. Because Jesus intended the Church to last, they reasoned, he likewise must have willed that the papacy should endure as well. The chapter contains allusions to the New Testament when it refers to "the Church, which was founded on the rock and which will remain firm until the end of the world" (DS 3056). Matthew 16:18 and 28:20 are the references here.[16]

Petrine succession is perpetual because it belongs to Jesus' design for his Church. Christ willed, the council taught, that Peter was to have successors to his ministry, and that whoever succeeded to Peter's office succeeded, by divine right, to his primacy of jurisdiction. "Divine right" is to be understood here in contrast to what can be regarded as simply a human development.

The First Vatican Council clearly proposed that succession to the Petrine ministry is essential to the Church of every age. It did not, however, explain how this succession came about and refrained from directly affirming that there was an unbroken succession of personal successors to Peter in the Roman church from the beginning. That is a historical, not a dogmatic, judgment. While no conclusive historical evidence is available for the earliest period, the Fathers at Vatican I assumed, but did not define, that there was a continuous line of personal successors to Peter.

Successor of Peter and Bishop of Rome

At the time of Vatican I, the question whether the successor of Peter had to be the bishop of Rome, rather than the bishop of any other see, was disputed. This classical theological problem influenced the council's deliberations and judgment on the matter.

Then, as now, two major positions were in the air. Some argued that the bishop *of Rome* enjoys a primacy of jurisdiction only as a matter of Church law, and not by the will of Christ. They did not believe that the successor of Peter necessarily had to be the Roman bishop. For good reasons the see of Peter could be transferred from the city of Rome. Others defended the view that the connection between the primacy and the Roman see derived from divine institution, making the two inseparable. For them, the successor of Peter would always be bishop of Rome, whether he resided there or not.

The council simply affirmed that whoever succeeds to Peter's role acquires primacy over the whole Church, "according to the institution of Christ himself." The bishops agreed *not* to define that succession to Peter's primacy was tied by divine right to being the bishop of Rome. They rejected the draft which had proposed this necessary connection. The council accepted the distinction between the need for Petrine succession, which is willed by Christ, and where that succession takes place, which is governed by God's providential plan for the Church (cf. M 52, 31). The canon, therefore, deliberately did not define that the link between the papacy and Rome (*romanitas*) was of divine institution (cf. M 52, 1308). The Fathers left open the possibility that the see of the successor of Peter could be permanently transferred from Rome and established elsewhere.

Rome: The Eternal City

The writings of many early authors, as well as those of modern popes, have praised the fittingness of Rome as the church of Peter's successor. They combine a long, quasi-mystical tradition exalting the greatness of Rome with the panegyrics of believers describing it as the most noble city in Christendom. The Carolingian hymn attributed to Paulinus of Aquileia (†802) and appointed for the feast of Sts. Peter and Paul apostrophizes Rome:

> Rejoice, O Rome, this day; thy walls they once did sign
> With princely blood, who now their glory share with thee.
> What city's vesture glows with crimson deep as thine?
> What beauty else has earth that may compare with thee?

Through the centuries the specific vocation of Rome has been repeatedly recalled. A Roman himself, Pius XII (1939-1958) once said: "No city anywhere in the world can surpass the destiny of Rome.... Rome remains the city of God, the city of wisdom incarnate, the city that has the *magisterium* of truth and holiness." Years later, Pius again praised Rome's special character, a uniqueness it enjoyed "because its supernatural mission places it outside time and above distinctions of nationality. Rome is the homeland (*patria*) of all Catholics wherever they are."[17]

In much the same vein, Pope Paul VI (1963-1978) commented on the way in which the pagan heritage of the ancient capital flowed into Christian Rome. "We cannot but feel a thrill of emotion when we think of this historical continuity, this universalistic, ecumenical mission, handed down through the centuries in conformity with a mysterious and elevated providential plan," he said. "Continuity, let us say, of pacification, teaching, balance, contained in that *pax Romana* which was the ideal condition to accept the joyful evangelical message and to assure its irradiation in the world."[18] On another occasion, the same Pope wrote: "Upon the remains of Rome's first greatness arose the great monuments of Christian civilization, and all these together have earned for her the title of City par excellence, simply 'the City,' *Urbs*. Rome has long been, and is still today, in a 'prophetic' rather than in an exaggerated or 'triumphal' sense, *caput mundi* and *lux orbis terrarum*, *arx omnium gentium* as Cicero called her."[19] Through the centuries, Rome has been revered as the chosen city and the bearer of a sublime destiny.

Rome's unique place in the universal Church — and not just in human civilization — is due, of course, to the consecration it received in Peter. The church at Rome is the church of Peter. Pope Paul VI spoke of divine providence linking the pope to Rome, the "prophetic city" with its "religious mission with which are bound up the spiritual and transcendent destinies of mankind."[20] Rome is unique in the world "because, by divine dispensation, it contains the tomb of the prince of the apostles and the living magisterium of his chair of truth."[21] At the end of his pontificate, the Pope wrote that Peter's tomb and relics were living proof of his presence in Rome, "of the transplantation of the new-born Church from Jerusalem and Antioch to the principal city of the Roman Empire; as if inheriting and replacing its idea of civil and political unity with the unity characteristic of the Christian religion, which is universal and perennial, the spiritual capital of the world."[22] These considerations suggest the fittingness of Rome as the see where the Petrine ministry continues to be exercised.

Purpose of Jurisdiction

In order to understand Vatican I's definition of the primacy of jurisdiction, it is necessary to keep in mind the distinction between the pope's function (*munus*) and his power (*potestas*). Jesus entrusted Peter both with an office (*munus*) in the Church and with the necessary power (*potestas*) to carry out that mission.

Vatican I concentrated more on the pope's power than on his Petrine mission. Nonetheless, before describing the nature and extent of papal authority, the bishops described the purpose of primatial authority. They found the ultimate source of the papacy's mission in Christ's will that all might be one as he is one with the Father (cf. Jn 17:20-21), "united together in the bond of one faith and one love" (DS 3050).

In the introduction to *Pastor aeternus*, the Fathers stated that the Petrine ministry was given "in order that the episcopate itself might be one and undivided, and in order that the entire multitude of believers might be maintained in unity of faith and of communion" (DS 3051). To guarantee this unity, Jesus selected Peter and "established in him the perpetual principle and the visible foundation of this twofold unity" (DS 3052). According to *Pastor aeternus*, the ultimate reason for the primacy is safeguarding the unity "both of communion and of profession of the same faith" so that the Church of Christ may be "one flock under one supreme shepherd" (DS 3060). In order for the

Origins, Development, and Mission of the Papacy

successor of Peter to carry out his responsibilities, God has provided him with the necessary authority to discharge his ministry.

Power and Jurisdiction

Pastor aeternus speaks of the pope's power or *potestas* in terms of the authority which he exercises in order to fulfill his primatial mission. The Fathers refer to the pope's governing power as "jurisdiction," using a canonical term derived from the Roman juridical tradition. Nevertheless, "jurisdiction" can be applied to the Church only by way of analogy.[23]

Papal jurisdiction refers to the pope's power to teach and govern the universal Church and to call for obedience from believers.[24] This power of jurisdiction is necessary so that he can carry out his mission of serving the entire Church. Because the pope is *head* of the college of bishops, his power of jurisdiction is also a *primacy* of jurisdiction.

Vatican I reflected Western ecclesiology from the Middle Ages onward, which increasingly separated the power of jurisdiction from the power of orders. The bishop received from the sacrament of orders the fullness of sanctifying power. However, his power of jurisdiction, the right to teach and govern his flock, was held to come from the pope. While the power of orders was linked to the Eucharist, that of jurisdiction was understood in relation to the Church as an institution. Given this separation, it was inevitable that jurisdiction was often conceived "chiefly as a power of external administration and government," writes Seamus Ryan. "It is not surprising, then, that jurisdiction differed little in its definition or manner of exercise from profane governing power, and, like the latter, tended to become more and more centralized."[25] All too easily the pope's unique *potestas* was understood in secular legal terms.

The First Vatican Council mixed theological and juridical categories. For at least two reasons the Fathers considered legal language appropriate in their dogmatic constitution. First, the term "jurisdiction" describes the pope's power in the same language used to portray the Church as a perfect society. A society is characterized as "perfect" because it has at its disposal all the means needed to achieve its end, including the power of government. In the nineteenth century, referring to the Church as a perfect society was common. The first draft of *De ecclesia Christi* presented at Vatican I affirmed that "the Church has all the marks of a true society,"[26] though the document was never put to a vote. Second, the heavily juridical cast of the definition of *Pastor aeternus* can also be explained as a response to the legal language in which Gallican propositions were formulated.[27] In contesting these ideas, the Fathers used the same language as their opponents.

Many contemporary scholars question whether jurisdiction is a felicitous expression, since it seems unduly to juridicize Petrine authority.[28] Already at Vatican I, some Fathers recognized the term's limitations. Bishop Krementz of Ermland, Prussia, cautioned that "the notion of *plenitudo potestatis* is not to be sought from the analogy of worldly powers ... but is to be derived from the constitution that Christ the Lord gave to his Church" (M 52, 693). While aware of this objection, Vatican I nonetheless referred to the leadership role of Peter as one of "true and proper jurisdiction" (DS 3055), and it later described papal authority in the same terms. Even so, as Dominican theologian Fergus Kerr notes, "it seems unfortunate, to say the least, that the gospel figure of the shepherd, and hence the vicar of St Peter too, should become so predominantly focussed in *jurisdiction*."[29] In the same vein, Pope John Paul II has cautioned that "terms proper to the world of civil law . . . must be given their correct ecclesial meaning."[30] By recalling the idea of authority as ministry, Vatican II enlarged the framework for discussing the pope's primacy of jurisdiction.

Vatican II: Authority as Service

While the bishops at Vatican I chose scholastic and canonical language to describe papal authority, leaving the impression that the pope was a ruler who dominated the Church, Vatican II emphasized the diaconal dimension of the papal office. It provided a scriptural foundation for hierarchical ministry in the Church.

According to the New Testament, Christ has been given "all authority in heaven and on earth" (Mt 28:18). Jesus' authority allowed him to forgive sins, perform miracles, cast out demons, teach, judge, and subject the powers of the universe. This authority was directed to serving others, ultimately giving his life for them.

As the privileged circle among Christ's disciples, the Twelve lived with him, sharing his mind, readiness to suffer, spirit of service, and his divine authority in healing and preaching (cf. Lk 9:1-2). He gave them the right to be obeyed (cf. Lk 10:16) and effectively empowered them to help those whom they were to judge (cf. Mt 19:28; Lk 22:30). The apostles received a "supreme power given for service,"[31] not a worldly sovereignty. Office in the Church can be exercised because the individual has received authority from Christ. There are no privileges from birth or from intellectual formation, "but vocation, mission and endowment with grace from on high are alone decisive."[32]

According to the New Testament witness, authority exists for service. Jesus forbade his disciples to "lord it over" anyone (cf. Mt 20:25-28). As successors to the apostles, bishops serve the Church by exercising sacred power. They are servants who exercise in Christ's name *his* authority for the good of all.[33] The people of God benefit from this power because divine authority is effectively present in their work of proclaiming the word and celebrating the sacraments.[34] The authority of the risen Christ becomes present in the Church through all pastors who act "in the person of Christ." Therefore, bishops are rightly called "vicars of Christ" (LG 27).

The Fathers at the Second Vatican Council defined the bishop's office as, "in the strict sense of the term, a service, which is called very expressively in sacred Scripture a ministry or *diakonia* (cf. Acts 1:17, 25; Rom 11:13; 1 Tim 1:12)" (LG 24). Power in the Church is to be exercised as a ministry; "before anything else it is the authority of a shepherd" (PB 1). As a pastoral office, the papacy is similarly a ministry. The ancient papal title "servant of the servants of God," first used by Gregory the Great (590-604) and still frequently invoked today, captures this ministerial aspect of the papacy.

In the teaching of Vatican II, the power of order and of jurisdiction was reunited. This allows us to appreciate that the Church's visible structure flows from, and is determined by, its inner sacramental nature. In this light, the pope's role within the Church is increasingly described as an ecclesial service. Consequently, the term "Petrine ministry" is often used today to refer to the pope's mission in the Church. As Tillard says, "it is not a question formally of a power of *dominium* but of a 'power' which is pastoral and oriented toward service."[35]

After the promulgation of *Lumen gentium*, Paul VI described the papacy as a unique kind of ministry: "What service is asked of the one clothed with functions of guidance and direction? A service that is supposed to make him subject to those being served and that is supposed to answer to them? No — a service for the benefit of the brethren, but without being subject to them; a service to which Christ entrusted not a servant's insignia but a sign of mastery, the keys, which is to say, powers over the kingdom of heaven."[36] A papacy of service is not, therefore, a papacy without authority and its obligations. "And how could a shepherd, if he is not provided with authority," writes von Balthasar, "lead a flock and defend it against 'savage wolves' attacking from without and, 'from among you', men who will distort the truth and lead astray any who follow them (Acts 20:29-30)?"[37]

Nature of Papal Authority

In describing papal authority as "supreme, full, episcopal, immediate, ordinary, and universal," the bishops intended to propose traditional doctrine as it was already taught and believed in the Church. These six descriptive attributes of papal jurisdiction provide the framework for our presentation of its nature. The distinctions between them are not always sharp, but together they convey the Church's teaching on what is involved in the pope's primacy of jurisdiction as defined in *Pastor aeternus*.

> *Chapter Three:* And so we teach and declare that, in the disposition of God, the Roman Church holds the pre-eminence of ordinary power over all the other Churches; and that this power of jurisdiction of the Roman Pontiff, which is truly episcopal, is immediate (DS 3060).
>
> *Canon:* And so, if anyone says that the Roman Pontiff has only the office of inspection and direction, but not the full and supreme power of jurisdiction over the whole Church, not only in matters that pertain to faith and morals, but also in matters that pertain to the discipline and government of the Church throughout the world; or if anyone says that he has only a more important part and not the complete fulness of this supreme power; or if anyone says that this power is not ordinary and immediate either over each and every Church or over each and every shepherd and faithful, *anathema sit* (DS 3064).

Supreme Jurisdiction

Papal jurisdiction is "supreme" because no ecclesial authority is above it, not even an ecumenical council. Down through the centuries, variants of conciliarism and Gallicanism have advanced arguments in favor of stipulating conditions which would regulate the exercise of papal authority. In response, Vatican I taught that "those who say that it is permitted to appeal to an ecumenical Council from decisions of the Roman Pontiffs or to authority superior to the Roman Pontiff, are far from the straight path of truth" (DS 3063).

The papacy does not claim, as it had in the Middle Ages, to be a superior jurisdiction to civil authorities in the secular domain.[38] In purely worldly matters, the bishop of Rome has no political power. In Church affairs, however, the pope's primacy of governance includes supreme executive, legislative, and judicial power. Because the pope holds in his own hands these three powers, there is no balance or "separation" of powers. They are firmly joined and held by the bishop of Rome.[39] However, we can distinguish these powers, and even analogously speak of him as the chief executive in the Church. Today he conducts the affairs of the universal Church using the Roman curia and his representatives in the various countries. This role will be discussed in chapter fourteen.

We can also speak of the pope as the highest legislator in the Church, because it belongs to him personally to promulgate laws for the universal Church. As far back as the fifth century, the popes issued decretals, or law-giving decrees, which had wide authority, even though they were addressed to one bishop or region. These letters were the first display of the pope's legislative power.[40] From this practice developed the tradition that the pope can change, suspend, or abrogate Church laws which are of human origin. By his own authority, the pope alone promulgated the 1983 Code of Canon Law for the Western church and the 1990 Code for the Eastern churches. If he chooses to do so, he can delegate his legislative power. The Roman curia, which acts in the name of, and by the authority of the pope, can enact laws, though only with his specific approval (cf. PB 18).

The supremacy of papal authority in juridical affairs includes two prerogatives: he can judge all cases and can be judged by no one. As "the supreme judge of the faithful," affirms *Pastor aeternus*, "one can have recourse to his judgment in all cases pertaining to ecclesiastical jurisdiction" (DS 3063). Because nothing is beyond his canonical competence, any member of the faithful, despite his or her rank, can take a case to Rome, if justice has not been carried out at the local level (cf. CIC 1417.1). The pope is the final court of appeal for all canonical cases. He enjoys universal appellate jurisdiction. In ordinary circumstances, the Roman bishop exercises this power through the tribunals of the Apostolic See: the Rota and the Apostolic Signatura. The current Code of Canon Law repeats the ancient maxim: "The First See is judged by no one" (CIC 1404). No tribunal, either in the Church or in civil society — contrary, for example, to the claim made by Henry VIII — can be used to appeal the pope's decisions in Church matters: "There is no appeal or recourse against a decision or decree of the Roman Pontiff" (CIC 333.3).

Full Jurisdiction

The Fathers incorporated into *Pastor aeternus* the Council of Florence's designation that the pope has "full power" in the Church (DS 1307; cf. DS 3059). There is no ecclesial authority greater than his, whether in matters of faith and morals, or discipline and government. The bishop of Rome has the fullness of authority in teaching (cf. CIC 749.1), in regulating the sacramental life of the Church (cf. CIC 838.1-2), and in governing.

In the Church, no "reserve" power exists that is anchored outside papal primacy. The pope's authority would not be full if some aspect of episcopal jurisdiction escaped him; for example, if a bishop could exercise an authority which the pope could not. As far as ecclesial authority extends, so does the pope's. *Pastor aeternus* definitively buried any remaining conciliarist ideas which attributed to the episcopacy a power independent of, or greater than, the papacy. Full power in the Church is not parceled out but, like Christ's, is indivisible. While the Fathers at the First Vatican Council located this indivisible power in the papacy alone, those at the Second Vatican Council, as we shall see in chapter ten, situated it in the broader context of the episcopal college headed by the pope.

Pastor aeternus also excluded the opinion that the primacy of jurisdiction was merely "an office of inspection and direction" (DS 3064). Understanding the papacy in this way would have made the office comparable to that of a supreme magistrate whose competency was limited to safeguarding a pre-established order and managing lower-level officials. It would have denied the pope the power to make laws for the Church.[41] The papal ministry does not come into play only as an arbiter of last resort. Nor does the pope merely give general direction with his counsel and exhortation to the autonomous activities of the particular churches. Commenting on this text of Vatican I, John Paul II said that such limitations "did not conform to the mission Christ conferred on Peter."[42] Therefore, the council proposed that the pope's jurisdiction was full, and not just "a more important part" of supreme power (cf. DS 3064).

In addition, the bishops at Vatican I rejected the opinion, maintained especially by many in the East, that the pope held only a "primacy of honor" (DS 3055). As an idea which originated in the culture and ideology of the Byzantine Empire,[43] an "honorary" primacy, the Fathers maintained, was foreign to the gospel. Any attempt to weaken the primacy of jurisdiction by equating it with one of ceremonial honor was declared to be contrary to Church teaching.

The fullness of the pope's jurisdiction does not mean that the Roman bishop is the only holder of Church authority nor that all authority derives from him. Though these interpretations were common in the years after the promulgation of *Pastor aeternus*, the Second Vatican Council, as we shall see, ruled them out.

Episcopal Jurisdiction

In *Pastor aeternus*, the bishops affirmed that the pope's authority is "truly episcopal" (DS 3061). As distinct from an authority which is "political" or "monarchical," the adjective "episcopal" describes the kind of authority enjoyed by the pope. It is the pastoral authority inherent in the office of a bishop. What Vatican I calls episcopal power is the effective authority necessary for the pope to carry out his unique episcopal mission.

The first draft of the constitution omitted the term "episcopal" to describe the pope's jurisdiction, probably because its framers thought that it was already included in the terms "ordinary" and "immediate." Numerous objections were raised when the Deputation of the Faith later introduced it. Some regarded it as superfluous or unfounded in the tradition. Others thought it would compromise the teaching on the episcopacy in a future conciliar constitution. And yet another group contended that it was contradictory to speak of two jurisdictions, papal and episcopal, over the same faithful.[44]

In reply to those who preferred to designate the pope's authority as "primatial" rather than "episcopal," Bishop Zinelli of Treviso, spokesman for the Deputation of the Faith, explained: "It must be admitted that the power of the sovereign pontiff is in reality of the same kind as that of the bishops. Why not, then, use the same word to indicate the quality of jurisdiction exercised by the popes and by the bishops, and why not speak of episcopal power in the bishops and of supreme episcopal power in the sovereign pontiff?" (M 52, 1104). Zinelli also added that the term "episcopal" should stand because it helped to clarify that the pope's jurisdiction is that of a shepherd responsible for pastoring his flock. The spokesman's arguments won the day.

Papal jurisdiction is a pastoral charge, which goes beyond the office of a lawgiver or judge. The pope's primacy, comments Tillard, "is to be understood within the nature of the episcopal *officium* as such, which is identical in kind for him and for every other bishop."[45] As the bishop of Rome, the pope, like all other bishops, has received the highest degree of holy orders. He receives the grace proper to fulfill his ministry with regard to both the church at Rome and the universal *koinonia*.[46]

What bishops are responsible for in their own dioceses — their duties of teaching, sanctifying, and governing — the bishop of Rome is responsible for in his diocese and in the universal Church. The pope's ministry is therefore both an episcopal office, and also a primatial one, a combination which gives it a particular specificity. This means that primatial authority is more than simply an administrative authority. In this sense it is different from that which patriarchs or archbishops exercise over other churches as a matter of ecclesiastical law.[47]

Although the pope's jurisdiction is episcopal, this does not mean that he is *the* bishop of the universal Church or a "bishop of bishops." He cannot suppress episcopal authority or reduce it to a simple delegation of his own.[48] The frequently used title "Bishop of the Catholic Church," already known in the fourth century and used by Paul VI to sign the documents of Vatican II, can easily be misinterpreted. In its more ancient expression the precision "of the City of Rome" was usually added to this title. The pope is a bishop *in* the Catholic Church.[49] When properly understood, "Bishop of the Catholic Church" denotes that the pope is the bishop of the particular church at Rome rather than a "superbishop" over the universal Church.[50]

According to the medieval canonical tradition, the papacy was a jurisdictional office independent of episcopal ordination. It held that the man chosen, even if he was not yet a bishop, received universal jurisdiction in its fullness at the time of accepting election. For many centuries, popes exercised their primacy of jurisdiction before receiving episcopal orders.[51] The 1917 Code of Canon Law incorporated this traditional opinion in its legislation: "The Roman Pontiff, legitimately elected, obtains by divine right full power of supreme jurisdiction as soon as he has accepted election" (canon 219). By invoking this medieval principle, the Code fell short of reflecting the more profound significance of describing the pope's jurisdiction as "truly episcopal."

Recent ecclesiology and Church teaching have moved steadily in the direction of linking papal jurisdiction more closely with episcopal ordination. In this view, only a bishop can exercise papal authority. The pope's mission is rooted within the sacramentality of the episcopacy. Like all other bishops, he becomes a member of the college of bishops only with episcopal ordination. But the pope cannot be head of the episcopal college without himself being a bishop. While not resolving the theological question whether episcopal ordination is an indispensable condition for exercising papal jurisdiction, the Code of Canon Law (1983) reflects the emerging theological consensus: "The Roman Pontiff obtains full and supreme power in the Church by means of legitimate election accepted by him together with episcopal consecration; therefore, one who is already a bishop obtains this same power from the moment he accepts his election to the pontificate, but if the one elected lacks the episcopal character, he is to be ordained a bishop immediately" (CIC 332.1; cf. RPE 88). If a man without episcopal orders is elected pope, he is legally bound to accept episcopal ordination in order to become the head of the college of bishops.

While the pope must be a bishop, there is no sacrament of papal primacy. Almost alone among theologians, Karl Rahner raised the question "why it is taken so much for granted that the act of transmitting the supreme pastoral power resident in the pope is not a grade of the Sacrament of Orders."[52] He argued that the appointment to the highest office in the Church was accompanied by God's promise of grace for carrying out the Petrine ministry. Consequently, he thought that it was possible for theologians to consider the papacy as the highest degree of the sacrament of orders. His suggestion met with little endorsement. Bouyer called such a theory "fantastic" and without any solid basis in tradition.[53] In truth, with regard to the power of orders, the pope is the same as all other bishops. For this reason, the man elected bishop of Rome is not ordained to the papacy but is installed at a public ceremony as the Church's supreme pastor .

Immediate Jurisdiction

Pastor aeternus gives two meanings to its description of the pope's jurisdiction as "immediate." He neither receives his authority from others nor does he exercise it through others.

Papal jurisdiction is not delegated by the college of cardinals, who elect the pope, nor by the college of bishops, of which he is the head, nor by the body of the faithful, of whom he is the supreme pastor. Papal authority comes directly from Christ, bestowed by him alone at the moment of accepting election. The pope's primacy of jurisdiction is not, therefore, mediated through any other body in the Church.

The pope's power is also described as "immediate" because he can exercise it directly, without the consent of either ecclesial or secular authorities. He is not a third party between a bishop and his particular church. In his final report, Bishop Zinelli explained to the Fathers the meaning of the term: "That power is called immediate which may be exercised without having to pass through an intermediary. But is not the pope able by himself to perform episcopal acts in every diocese, without passing through the mediation of the local bishop?" (M 52, 1105) The pope, therefore, can relate directly to bishops, religious, clerics, and faithful. This way of describing the primacy of jurisdiction rules out any theory which proposes that the pope must first consult or seek the permission of the local bishop before exercising his jurisdiction outside the diocese of Rome. Unlike other bishops who can take responsibility for matters outside their own dioceses only with and through others, the pope is free to intervene when he chooses. Moreover, unlike the bishops who can only offer advice, the pope can prescribe solutions which are to be carried out.[54]

Before using his primatial authority, the pope need not seek the permission of secular authorities. During the nineteenth century, some civil governments claimed that their approval was needed before papal decrees could be promulgated among their citizens. Vatican I rejected such a view of state interference, maintaining instead that spiritual power transcends all national boundaries. No government has the right to control the pope's direct access to all Catholics. According to *Pastor aeternus*, the pope's supreme power of governing means that he "has the right of freely communicating with the shepherds and flocks of the whole Church in the exercise of his office so that they can be instructed and guided by him in the way of salvation" (DS 3062). This statement assures the pope — and, indirectly, the entire Church — that civil authorities have no right to define the limits within which pastoral ministry can be exercised.

Ordinary Jurisdiction

Closely linked to immediate jurisdiction is the pope's "ordinary" jurisdiction, so called because it is attached to the Petrine office itself (cf. M 52, 1105). In its definition, *Pastor aeternus* used the conventional canonical distinction between ordinary power and delegated power. The latter is exercised in the name of another person who enjoys it "ordinarily." The pope's power resides in him by virtue of his divinely given charge; he does not receive it by delegation from any earthly authority. According to John Paul II, the pope's ordinary jurisdiction "means only to exclude the possibility of imposing norms on him to limit the exercise of the primacy."[55]

In order to carry out his mission to the universal Church, the successor of Peter has all the necessary ecclesial power. By qualifying papal authority as "ordinary," the First Vatican Council rejected the opinion of those few bishops who thought that papal jurisdiction outside Rome was valid only in emergency or extraordinary situations.[56] Nonetheless, Vatican I assigned the bishop of Rome neither the responsibility nor the authority to intervene daily in the particular churches in a way which would call into question the authority of the local bishop. It rejected the view that "the Petrine commission was to manage every detail of diocesan life as far as the mental and physical stamina allowed, leaving to bishops only what was left over after he had gone exhausted to bed," writes Garrett Sweeney.[57] In a certain sense, the pope's jurisdiction is "extraordinary," because it is not exercised habitually or day-to-day in every diocese. But it is *not* "extraordinary" in that its use is restricted only to specific unusual cases.[58]

The ordinary and immediate jurisdiction of the Roman bishop is less concerned with the internal life of the particular churches than with their communion with the universal Church. Only local bishops have "the permanent and daily care of the sheep" (LG 27). The pope's ministry is to bring pastors the help they need to keep their people in the fullness of faith, communion, and charity.[59]

Universal Jurisdiction

As "universal," papal jurisdiction extends to all areas of Church life. The pope's authority is directed to all the faithful, individually or collectively, of whatever rank. Although the successor of Peter is also bishop of the particular church at Rome, primate of Italy, and patriarch of the West — areas for which he has specific responsibility under these titles — as pope, he has a primatial function concerning the whole Church.

According to Vatican I, this universal power means that "the shepherds of whatever rite or jurisdiction and the faithful, individually and collectively, are bound by a duty of hierarchical subjection and of sincere obedience" (DS 3060). The pope's jurisdiction extends to bishops, whom he can appoint, whose election he confirms (cf. CIC 377.1), or whose authority he can limit (cf. CIC 381.1). The proper, ordinary, and immediate jurisdiction which bishops exercise in Christ's name is "ultimately controlled by the supreme authority in the Church and can be confined within certain limits should the usefulness of the Church and the faithful require that" (LG 27). As head of the college of bishops, the bishop of Rome is pastor of the pastors, with the duty of seeing that each bishop faithfully discharges his duties.

Unlike the charism of infallibility, which is restricted to questions of faith and morals, papal jurisdiction is not so limited. Universal jurisdiction entails obedience "not only in matters that pertain to faith and morals, but also in matters that pertain to the discipline and government of the Church throughout the world" (DS 3060, cf. 3064). The many prerogatives which the Code of Canon Law gives to the pope as expressions of his supreme and universal jurisdiction include the following: to dispense from religious vows, the law of celibacy, and a ratified but non-consummated marriage; to approve the constitutions of religious institutes and confirm the dismissal of their members; to review the decrees of episcopal conferences before they can be promulgated; to send legates to particular churches and sovereign nations; to regulate the liturgy of the sacraments and oversee the publication of liturgical books; and to administer and steward ecclesiastical goods.

Limits to Papal Authority

Whereas the council meticulously set out the conditions for the exercise of papal infallibility, it did not do likewise for papal jurisdiction. Even so, the bishops recognized that the pope's authority was subject to definite limits in its exercise. "It was a common view-point of the Fathers that primatial power was not all-embracing, unlimited and able to do what it liked, but subject to definite limits in its exercise," writes Sweeney. "Whether those limits were not only definite but definable was another matter — and the ultimate decision was that they not be defined."[60] The council, accordingly, produced no juridical or canonical norms limiting papal jurisdiction.

Papal jurisdiction is conditioned by God's will for the Church. Responding to concerns from some bishops about a jurisdictional authority unrestricted by canonical regulations, Zinelli answered that the full and supreme power of Peter and his successors was not "limited by any human power superior to it, but only by natural and divine right" (M 52, 1109). The Majority resisted all attempts to include in the council's definition of papal primacy anything that even appeared to restrict the pope's fullness of power.

Most of the bishops did not fear a reckless or unrestrained use of papal jurisdiction. While unwilling to express any juridical limiting principles, they were conscious of the non-juridical restrictions on the papacy. Bishop Salas of Concepción, Chile, summarized the attitude of the Majority: "The power of the supreme pontiff is limited by natural and divine law. It is limited by the commandments and teachings of Jesus Christ our Lord. It is limited by the common good of the Church. It is limited by the voice of conscience. It is limited by right reason and by common sense. It is limited by the rule of faith and discipline, and so on. . . . But it cannot be limited or restricted by the bishops, either individually or corporately, either in council or out of council" (M 52, 579-580).

During the Second Vatican Council, Paul VI requested the Theological Commission to affirm that in his actions the pope is "answerable to the Lord alone." The Commission responded that the request was superfluous and an oversimplification, since "the Roman Pontiff is also bound to revelation itself, to the fundamental structure of the Church, to the sacraments, to the definitions of earlier councils, and other obligations too numerous to mention."[61] Like the Fathers at Vatican I, the members of the Theological Commission assumed that the exercise of papal primacy was restricted by the nature of the Church and of the pope's office as established by Christ. In the words of Patrick Granfield, "papal authority has its specific mission or purpose that, in an overarching sense, determines and delineates all its action."[62] The pope is therefore obliged to observe the natural law; that is, he is to be reasonable, prudent, diligent, and just. He must also submit to everything that has been revealed by God, and so cannot act contrary to the divine commandments, sacraments, mission of the Church, or her divinely instituted structures, including the episcopacy.[63] In the absence of human safeguards against a possible abuse of papal power, the Church remains dependent upon the protection of the Holy Spirit who will not allow misuse to destroy anything essential in her structure.[64]

The greatest fear expressed by some bishops at Vatican I, as well as some commentators after the council, was that a juridically unrestricted papacy would overpower the episcopacy. The similar terms which *Pastor aeternus* uses to describe the jurisdiction of both the pope and the bishops could possibly create such a misunderstanding. Does each diocese have two heads, the local bishop and the bishop of Rome, since each can exercise immediate, ordinary, episcopal jurisdiction in the particular church over the same faithful?

One council Father intervened to say that "the assertion of episcopal jurisdiction, ordinary and immediate over the whole Church, sounds very like that other thing: . . . the pope is the immediate, ordinary bishop of every diocese, as much that of Gubbio as that of Rome" (M 52, 338). If this were true, then the other "bishops appear only . . . as vicars of the Roman pontiff" (M 52, 678), remarked another Father. The council, however, did not intend to weaken the episcopacy but to preserve its structure. The Fathers approved the final text, expressing their conviction that the bishops were not vicars of the pope (cf. M 52, 338, 678).

In response to an amendment suggesting that the respective jurisdictions of pope and bishop be delimited because of possible undue papal interference in diocesan administration, Zinelli rhetorically replied: "Certainly, if the sovereign pontiff, having the right to perform any properly episcopal act in whatever diocese, were, so to speak, to multiply himself every day without any regard for the bishop, abolishing what had been wisely laid down, he would be using his power *non in aedificationem sed in destructionem*, and confusion in spiritual leadership would follow. But who could imagine such an absurd hypothesis? I would beg all of you therefore to keep quiet, put your trust in the self-restraint of the Holy See, and express no doubt that the authority of the Holy See will be a source of strength to the powers of the bishops and not harmful to them" (M 52, 1105). Accordingly, Vatican I left it to the pope's judgment to take the necessary measures to defend the episcopacy.

Primatial Ordinary Jurisdiction

Whereas the pope's "ordinary and immediate" jurisdiction secures for him the right to intervene in a particular church when necessary and without asking permission, the bishops' ordinary and immediate jurisdiction in their dioceses is everyday or habitual. When the pope intervenes, he is acting as pastor of the universal Church. Though both the local bishop and the Roman bishop exercise jurisdiction over the same subjects, as "primatial" the pope's is a particular kind of jurisdiction. His immediate and ordinary power in the universal Church does not mean that he exercises day-to-day authority in every diocese. Such authority is proper to the local bishop. When the successor of Peter does intervene, he does so in order to exercises his *own* ministry, not replace that of the bishop.

Only in the local church at Rome does the pope have a power which is ordinary and immediate in the same way as that of other bishops in their dioceses. In the churches outside Rome, the pope exercises a primatial power of ordinary jurisdiction. If the pope tried to perform all episcopal acts in a diocese on an everyday basis, he would be usurping the proper ordinary authority of the bishop. That would go beyond the exercise of power belonging to the papal office (cf. M 52, 1105).

As ordinary power, papal jurisdiction is limited to what pertains to the pope's office of building up the Church. He is morally obliged to intervene directly in a local situation only to support a particular church, for its edification. His power to intervene directly is for sustaining the proper and immediate authority of the bishop and his church. To intervene unnecessarily would be to use a power contrary to its purpose.[65] Papal interventions should uphold and strengthen ecclesial unity. "To do so," writes Bouyer, "the pope can, and when necessary must, intervene with an authority that no one can question, which is why the pope . . . can do everything that each bishop or all the bishops together can do, always and everywhere."[66]

The pope's ministry to the universal Church, therefore, serves the episcopacy, which likewise exists as an institution of divine right. The designation of papal power as "truly episcopal" does not mean that the pope is the *only* true or real episcopal authority in the Church. To meet the objections of the Fathers who feared that defining papal jurisdiction as immediate and ordinary power would undermine the bishops' authority, a paragraph on the episcopacy was added to the final text. According to *Pastor aeternus*: "The power of the Supreme Pontiff is far from standing in the way of the power of ordinary and immediate episcopal jurisdiction by which the bishops, who, under the appointment of the Holy Spirit (cf. Acts 20:28), succeeded in the place of the apostles, feed and rule individually, as true shepherds, the particular flock assigned to them" (DS 3061).

The First Vatican Council refrained from repeating the age-old opinion that all authority in the Church, including that of the bishops, had its origin in the pope. It also imposed on the pope the duty of aiding the bishops to exercise their authority effectively by asserting, confirming, and vindicating their rights (cf. DS 3061; LG 27; CIC 333.1). In the constitution, the Fathers inserted the words of Gregory the Great (590-604) to buttress their argument: "My honour is the honour of the whole Church. My honour is the firm strength of my brothers. I am truly honoured when due honour is paid to each and every one" (DS 3061). To distort the episcopal function would be to falsify the nature of the Church herself. The pope's *potestas* is to serve the bishops by asserting and confirming their own authority, and to bind the bishops together in communion.

Official Interpretation

In 1872, the German Chancellor Bismarck sent a directive to his diplomatic personnel, ordering them to bypass local bishops and deal directly with the pope in religious affairs. He took this step because he thought that Vatican I had lessened the authority of the bishops, turning them into papal officials. In response to Bismarck, after his circular letter became public, the German bishops issued a declaration in 1875. In this statement, the German hierarchy asserted that the First Vatican Council left unchanged the fundamental constitution of the Church; it did not abolish episcopal authority. Pius IX solemnly approved the bishops' declaration, saying that they expounded "the true meaning of the Vatican Council" (DS 3117).

The bishops' statement corrected the German Chancellor's false interpretations of the relations between the episcopacy and the papacy. Among the errors which the bishops noted were Bismarck's statements that "episcopal jurisdiction has been absorbed into the papal"; that the pope has "in principle taken the place of each individual bishop"; and that the bishops are now "no more than tools of the Pope, his officials, without responsibility of their own" (DS 3115). The German hierarchy also affirmed that "the Pope has to watch over each bishop in the fulfillment of the whole range of his episcopal charge. If a bishop is hindered, or if some need has made itself felt, the Pope has the right and the duty, in his capacity as Pope and not as bishop of the diocese, to order whatever is necessary for the administration of that diocese" (DS 3113). The bishops also affirmed that "it is in virtue of the same divine institution upon which the papacy rests that the episcopate also exists" (DS 3115), officially clarifying the relation between papal and episcopal authority as taught by Vatican I.

◆

Despite the great changes in the historical forms of the papacy and some exaggerated theories proposed to buttress it between the early Middle Ages and the nineteenth century, there is no substantive difference between the vision articulated by Leo the Great and that defined by the bishops at the First Vatican Council. Both claimed a universal jurisdictional primacy for the pope and justified it as an institution of divine right.

At Vatican I, the Fathers solemnly proposed, using canonical language, the Western Church's common teaching on the institution, permanence, and nature of papal primacy. Although the council's juridical terminology might not be the only way to explain the nature of the papal ministry, the truth of what the bishops intended to define must be safeguarded. First, they affirmed that Peter's primacy of jurisdiction over the Church was directly instituted by Christ. By citing biblical passages, the council professed its conviction that Petrine primacy expresses a revealed truth testified to in sacred Scripture. Second, the Fathers taught that Christ willed that there should be successors to Peter's primacy as long as the Church endures. Third, they recognized that the bishop of Rome is, in fact, the successor of Peter, though without defining that the primacy is linked to the Roman see by divine right.

In describing the nature of the pope's primacy of jurisdiction, the council summarized it as supreme, full, episcopal, immediate, ordinary, and universal. Papal authority belongs inherently to the Petrine ministry. The pope has all the necessary pastoral power to carry out the mission first confided to Peter. He has the fullness of the apostolic office to sanctify as a priest, to proclaim as a teacher, and to lead as a shepherd. It is universal because it enables the successor of Peter to serve the Church as a whole and each of the particular churches. Unlike his brother bishops, the pope always has ordinary and immediate jurisdiction over the whole Church. This permanent responsibility is what distinguishes his ministry of caring for all the churches (cf. 2 Cor 11:28).

Because the description of papal jurisdiction at the First Vatican Council has raised some questions about its seeming absoluteness, a faithful interpretation of *Pastor aeternus* must keep two principles in mind. First, papal authority is to be interpreted in light of the purposes for which Jesus gave it to the Church: to build up her unity of faith, communion, and charity; and to proclaim the gospel to the whole world. Second, papal primacy is circumscribed by everything in the Church that comes from God: divine law, the gospel, tradition, the solemn teaching of ecumenical councils and previous popes, and so on. Since papal jurisdiction is to strengthen and protect episcopal power, the primacy is limited, even if these norms are not expressed in juridical terms. Vatican I had no intention of replacing a bishop's pastoral role in his diocese with that of the pope. Nonetheless, because the Fathers were unable to complete their planned statement on ecclesiology, the council shows a certain "ecclesiological disequilibrium."[67] *Pastor aeternus* left many questions unanswered, including how the relationship between the papacy and episcopacy should be worked out in practice. This is the subject of later chapters.

Notes for Chapter seven

1. Patrick Granfield, *The Limits of the Papacy* (New York: Crossroad Publishing Company, 1987), 50.
2. James A. Coriden, *An Introduction to Canon Law* (New York: Paulist Press, 1991), 68.
3. Johann Auer, *The Church: The Universal Sacrament of Salvation*, Dogmatic Theology, trans. Michael Waldstein, vol. 8 (Washington, D.C.: Catholic University of America Press, 1993), 288.
4. Edmund Hill, *Ministry and Authority in the Catholic Church* (London: Geoffrey Chapman, 1988), 90-91.
5. Patrick Granfield, *The Papacy in Transition* (Garden City: Doubleday & Company, 1980), 49.
6. William L. Portier, "Church Unity and National Traditions: The Challenge to the Modern Papacy, 1682-1870," in *The Papacy and the Church in the United States*, ed. Bernard Cooke (New York: Paulist Press, 1989), 30.
7. Hill, *Ministry and Authority in the Catholic Church*, 90-91.
8. J. M. R. Tillard, *The Bishop of Rome*, trans. John de Satgé (Wilmington: Michael Glazier, 1983), 19.
9. Cited in Tillard, *Bishop of Rome*, 21.
10. Avery Dulles, "Papal Authority in Roman Catholicism," in *A Pope for All Christians?* ed. Peter J. McCord (New York: Paulist Press, 1976), 49-50.
11. Tillard, *Bishop of Rome*, 20.
12. Portier, "Church Unity and National Traditions," 33-34.
13. Yves Congar, *Ministères et communion ecclésiale* (Paris: Cerf, 1971), 172.
14. Cited in Karl-Heinz Ohlig, *Why We Need the Pope* (St. Meinrad: Abbey Press, 1975), 83.
15. J. Michael Miller, *The Divine Right of the Papacy in Recent Ecumenical Theology*, Analecta Gregoriana, vol. 218 (Rome: Gregorian University Press, 1980), 42-43.
16. Miller, *Divine Right of the Papacy*, 45.
17. Cited in Peter Hebblethwaite, *In the Vatican* (Bethesda: Adler & Adler, 1986), 15-16.
18. Paul VI, Discourse, January 14, 1974, *L'Osservatore Romano*, 5 (January 31, 1974), 3.
19. Paul VI, Discourse, June 12, 1969, *L'Osservatore Romano*, 26 (June 26, 1969), 12.
20. Paul VI, Angelus, November 19, 1972, *L'Osservatore Romano*, 47 (November 23, 1972), 12.
21. Paul VI, Discourse, January 31, 1974, *L'Osservatore Romano*, 7 (February 14, 1974), 2.
22. Paul VI, Homily, June 29, 1978, *L'Osservatore Romano*, 27 (July 6, 1978), 1.
23. Dulles, "Papal Authority in Roman Catholicism," 57.
24. Jean-Marie Tillard, "The Jurisdiction of the Bishop of Rome," *Theological Studies*, 40:1 (1979), 5.
25. Seamus Ryan, "The Hierarchical Structure of the Church," in *The Church: A Theological and Pastoral Commentary on the Constitution on the Church*, ed. Kevin McNamara (Dublin: Veritas Publications, 1983), 181.

26. Cited in J. Neuner and H. Roos, eds., *The Teaching of the Catholic Church* (New York: Alba House, 1967), 213.
27. Portier, "Church Unity and National Traditions," 27.
28. Avery Dulles, *The Resilient Church* (Garden City: Doubleday & Company, 1977), 122.
29. Fergus Kerr, "Vatican I and the Papacy — 1: A Proud Appellation," *New Blackfriars*, 60 (1979), 172.
30. John Paul II, Discourse, February 24, 1993, *L'Osservatore Romano*, 9 (March 3, 1993), 11.
31. Hans Urs von Balthasar, *The Office of Peter and the Structure of the Church*, trans. Andrée Emery (San Francisco: Ignatius Press, 1986), 23.
32. Rudolf Schnackenburg, *The Church in the New Testament*, trans. W. J. O'Hara (London: Burns & Oates, 1974), 126.
33. Louis Bouyer, *The Church of God*, trans. Charles Underhill Quinn (Chicago: Franciscan Herald Press, 1982), 389.
34. Von Balthasar, *Office of Peter*, 126.
35. J. M. R. Tillard, *Church of Churches: The Ecclesiology of Communion*, trans. R. C. De Peaux (Collegeville: Liturgical Press, 1992), 273.
36. Paul VI, Discourse, July 7, 1965, *The Pope Speaks*, 10:4 (1965), 349.
37. Von Balthasar, *Office of Peter*, 31.
38. James H. Provost, "The Hierarchical Constitution of the Church," in *The Code of Canon Law: A Text and Commentary*, ed. James A. Coriden, Thomas J. Green, and Donald E. Heintschel (New York: Paulist Press, 1985), 291.
39. James A. Coriden, "A Canonical Reflection," in *The Papal Office in the Life of the Church* (Silver Springs: Washington Theological Union, 1987), 9-10.
40. Coriden, *Introduction to Canon Law*, 13.
41. Umberto Betti, "Dottrina della costituzione dommatica *Pastor aeternus*," in *De doctrina Concilii Vaticani Primi* (Vatican City: Polyglot Press, 1969), 325.
42. John Paul II, Discourse, February 24, 1993, *L'Osservatore Romano*, 9 (March 3, 1993), 11.
43. Von Balthasar, *Office of Peter*, 31.
44. Wilfrid F. Dewan, "*Potestas vere episcopalis* au premier Concile du Vatican," in *De doctrina Concilii Vaticani Primi* (Vatican City: Polyglot Press, 1969), 369-372.
45. Tillard, "Jurisdiction of the Bishop of Rome," 11.
46. Tillard, *Church of Churches*, 265.
47. Dulles, "Papal Authority in Roman Catholicism," 59.
48. Bouyer, *Church of God*, 388.
49. Hervé-Marie Legrand, "Ministero romano e ministero universale del papa: il problema della sua elezione," *Concilium*, 11:8 (1975), 68, n. 12.
50. Yves Congar, "Titoli dati al papa," *Concilium* 11:8 (1975), 75-76.
51. While he was still a deacon, Hadrian V was elected pope on July 11, 1276 and died on August 18, 1276. Though he was never ordained priest or bishop, he has always been considered as a legitimate pope.
52. Karl Rahner, "The Episcopal Office," in *Theological Investigations*, trans. Karl-H. and Boniface Kruger, vol. 6 (Baltimore: Helicon Press, 1969), 347, n. 16.
53. Bouyer, *Church of God*, 402, n. 32.
54. Cuthbert Rand, "The Universal Pastoral Ministry of the Bishop of Rome: A Roman Catholic Approach," *One in Christ*, 22:1 (1986), 13.

55. John Paul II, Discourse, February 24, 1993, *L'Osservatore Romano*, 9 (March 3, 1993), 11.
56. Dewan, "*Potestas vere episcopalis*," 378.
57. Garrett Sweeney, "The Primacy: The Small Print of Vatican I," *Clergy Review*, 54:2 (1974), 111.
58. Bonaventure Kloppenburg, *The Ecclesiology of Vatican II*, trans. Matthew J. O'Connell (Chicago: Franciscan Herald Press, 1974), 172.
59. Tillard, "Jurisdiction of the Bishop of Rome," 20.
60. Sweeney, "The Primacy," 108-109.
61. *Acta synodalia sacrosancti concilii oecumenici Vaticani II*, vol. 3, pt. 1 (Vatican City: Polyglot Press, 1973), 247; cited by Karl Rahner, "The Hierarchical Structure of the Church, with Special Reference to the Episcopate," in *Commentary on the Documents of Vatican II*, ed. Herbert Vorgrimler, vol. 1 (New York: Herder and Herder, 1967), 202.
62. Granfield, *Limits of the Papacy*, 59.
63. John E. Linnan, "Subsidiarity, Collegiality, Catholic Diversity, and Their Relevance to Apostolic Visitations," *The Jurist*, 49:2 (1989), 437-438.
64. Ryan, "Hierarchical Structure of the Church," 186
65. Pedro Rodriguez, "The Primacy of the Pope in the Church," in *On Being Catholics*, ed. Charles Connolly (Houston: Lumen Christi Press, 1983), 59.
66. Bouyer, *Church of God*, 388.
67. Gustave Thils, "The Theology of the Papacy: Towards a Revision," *One in Christ*, 10 (1974), 19.

Chapter eight
ORDINARY PAPAL TEACHING

From the outset, the development of the papacy as an office having a primacy of jurisdiction was coupled with that of unique responsibilities of teaching. To his task as pastor, the bishop of Rome added that of being a special, indeed the supreme, teacher in the Church.

If the pope's teaching ministry were limited to those extraordinary occasions when he speaks *ex cathedra* (to be discussed in chapter nine), then since 1950 the papal magisterium would have been in abeyance. We know, however, that this is not so. In the Church's day-to-day life, the pope and the other bishops, individually and collectively, teach the faith "authoritatively" but without exercising the charism of infallibility. Besides exercising an extraordinary magisterium, the pope also teaches through what is called his "ordinary" magisterium.

This chapter deals specifically with the everyday magisterium of the bishop of Rome. Much of what is said, of course, also applies to the magisterium of individual bishops and the universal ordinary magisterium, although they are not treated here. After a brief look at the historical origins of the pope's teaching role, I will examine the characteristics of his ordinary magisterium: the reasons why he teaches in this everyday way, the different degrees in which he engages it, the various documents he uses, and the response Catholics are expected to give to his ordinary teaching.

Because he is the successor of Peter, the pope has an ordinary magisterium which belongs to his ministry as universal teacher. Embodying an essential feature of his Petrine office, the Roman bishop's ordinary magisterium enjoys its own specific charism and is universal in its scope. The pope has the "grace of office" corresponding to this ministry as the Church's preeminent teacher.[1] As the principal guardian of the deposit of faith and the guarantor of the Church's obedience to revelation, the successor of Peter enjoys a "supreme teaching authority" (LG 25), even when he is not speaking *ex cathedra*.

From Testimony to Teaching

Beginning in the early Middle Ages, the churches of the East and the West recognized the bishop of Rome as a primary witness to the gospel. Soon after the turn of the first millennium, however, the way in which he confirmed his brethren in their faith shifted in emphasis. In the early centuries, his teaching was held to be binding because it conformed to the confession of the apostolic faith. In the second millennium, the binding nature of a teaching depended more on the fact that the successor of Peter proposed the doctrine to be held.

First Millennium: Witness

From the outset, the bishop of Rome carried out his ministry to the truth through his witness to the deposit of faith. When doctrinal contention arose, he was a point of reference, a model of fidelity. The successor of Peter guarded and defended the Christian memory of the foundational event of the new covenant. Unlike the more speculative East, Rome was renowned for its conservatism, for sticking to the tradition handed down from the apostles. As early as Irenaeus (†200), the reason for the unique role of the Roman church was its steadfast vigilance for the gospel: "For with this church, because of its superior origin all churches must agree; that is, all the faithful in the whole world; for in her the apostolic tradition has always been preserved for the benefit of the faithful everywhere."[2] The church of Rome was the standard of reference for doctrine, representing and expressing the mind of the whole Church in questions of belief. As the primary witness to the apostolic tradition transmitted in the Roman church, the pope assumed the role of being the spokesman for doctrinal orthodoxy. The other churches acknowledged that right. What Rome rejected as repugnant to its apostolic standards, the whole Church came to reject.[3] When faced with controversy, the bishop of Rome reasserted the apostolic tradition, and other churches recognized in his voice the faith of Peter.

The fact that it was the pope who was teaching a particular doctrine was less important than that he was confirming the tradition. The church of Rome called to mind the confession of the apostolic faith spoken to it by Sts. Peter and Paul.[4] Rome was the touchstone of orthodoxy, and for that reason the pope could arbitrate disputes about the faith which arose anywhere in the *koinonia*. He taught by witnessing.

As the living memorial of the apostolic faith, its sentinel and guardian, the pope discharged his teaching ministry. The Roman bishop exercised vigilance by sounding the alarm when the integrity of the faith was threatened. This was essentially an episcopal task, belonging to the sacrament of orders through which he was linked to the original witness of Christian revelation. The pope directed his concern to the universal Church in the same way that a bishop showed doctrinal oversight in his local church. To "preside in love" expressed itself, writes Tillard, "in the fact of telling out the faith, of guiding the understanding and practice of it."[5]

Supporting the churches in their confession of the true faith was the particular service which the successor of Peter rendered to the worldwide community. His magisterium was to recall, restate, and reaffirm what had been entrusted to the entire Church. He kept the whole body of Christ in the communion of one faith. In this sense, his responsibility was primarily that of a guardian. Under normal circumstances, the pope did not take the initiative in teaching. As a watchman, he did not usually declare or define doctrine. The pope fulfilled his ministry of strengthening his brothers simply by being for them a mirror of the purity of the apostolic tradition. The successor of Peter was a model of faithful obedience, guarding the holy origin of the deposit of faith. This way of witnessing to the truth predominated until the pontificate of Leo the Great (440-461).

After Leo, however, the way in which the Roman bishops safeguarded the revelation by confessing the faith of the Church's origins changed course. Gradually the pope became more an arbiter and judge of orthodoxy in his own right rather than a touchstone against which others measured their faith. This movement corresponded to a general shift in emphasis concerning the exercise of the primacy. With the Christianization of the

Empire, many of the attributes characteristic of secular Rome — its juridical cast of mind, its charism of government, its arbitration of disputes, and its practical realism — were assumed by the local Roman church. The Rome of ecclesial tradition became the Rome of legislation, extending as well to matters of teaching.[6] Nonetheless, it was still the pope's charism of witnessing to the apostolic deposit which grounded his expanding teaching ministry.

According to Yves Congar, before the turn of the first millennium, the pope's doctrinal authority rested principally on the special religious quality which Rome owed to Sts. Peter and Paul. The city was the place of their martyrdom and the custodian of their tombs. Rome was also the privileged church of Peter, who was the first to confess faith in Christ's divinity. For the first thousand years, the true teaching authority in the Church was tradition: the deposit of faith, the dogmas and canons of the councils, and the doctrine of the Church Fathers. This tradition was preserved by all the bishops, but especially by the bishop of Rome.[7]

In the first millennium, the pope's magisterial interventions were of two kinds. Principally he exhorted the churches, reaffirming the traditional expressions of faith. When necessary, he also decided an issue about which the Church was divided. Leo the Great did this in his *Tome to Flavian*, where he taught the existence of two natures in Christ.[8] This witnessing function began to change significantly with the Gregorian Reform of the early second millennium.

Second Millennium: Teacher

From the mid-eleventh century onward, the Roman Church increasingly asserted itself as the head of the universal Church. No longer just the principal witness to the authentic apostolic tradition, the pope intervened more frequently in the affairs of local churches. The theology of papal monarchy attributed to the pope an ever more active role both in government and in teaching. Less the foremost spokesman and guarantor of the apostolic ancient tradition, he extended his teaching ministry by increasing his doctrinal interventions directed to the universal Church.[9]

During the pontificate of Alexander III (1159-1181), the first of the medieval popes who were skilled canonists, the range of papal teaching was broadened. Canonists and theologians repeatedly stressed that the Roman church was the "head and *teacher* of all the churches." Between the twelfth and fourteenth centuries, they underscored the pope's own magisterium, emphasizing that he was more than a witness to the tradition. According to them, he could actively define the tradition of faith. Faced by the inability of bishops to deal effectively with heresies, especially the Albigensians and the Catharists, the popes took up the fight to defend orthodox teaching. With Lucius III (1181-1185), the pope assumed the responsibility for judging all questions of faith, and he had procedures drawn up for the repression of heretics.[10]

Accompanying the birth of medieval universities in the twelfth century, another teaching authority came on the scene: that of the masters of theology, who were not bishops. These men, licensed to teach in the name of the Church, were officially recognized as qualified to discourse on doctrinal matters. Once a question had been disputed, they could make a determination which carried considerable authority.[11] These masters were regarded as having a true teaching function, the so-called magisterium of the teaching chair (*magisterium cathedrae magistralis*). This was different from the pastoral teaching chair of bishops and the pope (*magisterium cathedrae pastoralis*). Gratian (†1159), the father of canon law, distinguished between the roles of theologians and bishops, leaving to the bishops the right to make the final determination in disputed questions of faith.[12] Despite the ultimate episcopal limitation on their authority, the doctors of theology acquired great prestige. Faculties of theology became arbiters of orthodoxy, initiating proceedings and passing sentence on those judged guilty of heresy. In the late Middle Ages, especially in conciliarist circles, the masters' authority reached its apogee.[13] Right up through the Reformation and afterward, the doctors of theology, preeminently at the Sorbonne in Paris, remained influential in judging whether a particular doctrine could be considered orthodox.

One effect of this division of labor in teaching was that the pope became more involved in theological and doctrinal matters. Like a prince who had the responsibility for promoting the overall welfare of society, so also the pope took a dynamic role in the Church, especially through his teaching ministry.[14] He frequently took a stand on disputed questions, reserving the right to make final determinations regarding the orthodoxy of different positions. When the Council of Florence (1439) declared that the pope was "the father and teacher of all Christians" (DS 1307), it articulated the importance which the Western Church attributed to the papal magisterium on the brink of the modern era.

The decline of the medieval universities, the rise of controversial theology after the Council of Trent, and the need to resist nationalistic and secularist movements within the Church solidified the increased role assigned to the successor of Peter's teaching ministry. Beginning in the sixteenth century, ecclesiology concentrated on papal jurisdiction and teaching as signs of a specifically Catholic theology. The views of the English controversialist theologian Thomas Stapleton (†1598) were typical of this trend. He influenced St. Robert Bellarmine (†1621) and many other writers up to Vatican I. These theologians assigned to the pope's teaching authority a major place in their theology. When arguing against Protestants, they invoked the principle of ecclesial authority, especially that of the pope, in presenting their case. At the same time, the bishop of Rome increasingly practiced doctrinal vigilance. In 1542, he established the Roman Inquisition, later called the Holy Office, to oversee orthodoxy in the Church directly.

A major consequence of this Counter-Reformation theology was that the person *who* formulated the faith became a crucial factor in determining orthodox doctrine.[15] Certitude, which rested on the authority of the lawgiver, rather than the truth was the focus. This was the fruit of nominalism which flourished after the Reformation. Whereas Protestants claimed that they had the truth because "it said so in the Bible" (*sola scriptura*), Catholics claimed the same because "the pope said so" (*sola papa*). Both were seeking grounds of certainty. The Catholic approach frequently led to calling upon the pope's formal teaching authority, even when not finally determinative, as a way of being assured of the Catholic faith. "To gage the truth of a proposition," writes Tillard, "you looked first of all at who said it, not, as in the days of Leo the Great, at what it said."[16] As visible head of the Church, what the pope taught came to enjoy a unique authority precisely because *he* proposed it. The Church's magisterium, especially that of the pope, was more and more regarded as the proximate norm for revealed truth.[17]

In the nineteenth century, ultramontanism fostered this emphasis on the pope as an active teacher. In the ultramontanist view, when the pope exercised his teaching office, he was using his power of jurisdiction. He taught authoritatively by acts of legislation which demanded the faithful's obedience.[18] Beginning under Pius IX (1846-1878), when improved communications made travel to Rome much easier, a cult of the person of the pope developed. Whereas in earlier times pilgrims went to Rome to pray at the tombs of the apostles, in the nineteenth century they went to see the pope. Because of the faithful's desire to hear his words, this popular movement, encouraged by ultramontanists, further enhanced a more active teaching role for the pope.[19]

Neo-scholastic theologians at the time of Vatican I emphasized that the Church carries on Christ's mission as priest, prophet, and king in her tasks of sanctifying, teaching, and governing.[20] The pope acted not only as a judge of the faith when controversies arose, but he also had the duty of actively and authoritatively preaching it. The neo-scholastic threefold division was intended to stress that teaching authority was not primarily an act of jurisdiction which emanated in legislation. This distinction between jurisdiction and teaching was not, however, often made. After Vatican I, adherence to papal teaching was still frequently presented in terms of obedience to the pope's supreme legislative authority rather than as adherence to the truth.

At Vatican I itself, the Fathers devoted little attention to the ordinary papal magisterium. They seem to have overlooked that this was the normal way in which the bishop of Rome could teach on matters of faith and morals. Despite Vatican I's lack of attention, the pope's role as the principal teacher in the Church became more and more manifest after the council. Even when not teaching infallibly, all the popes from Pius IX onward exercised vigorous doctrinal leadership through their frequent teaching on all matters touching upon Christian doctrine and life.[21] The technological and media revolutions abetted this development, making papal teaching widely known throughout the Church.

Characteristics of the Everyday Magisterium

In order to describe the ordinary papal magisterium, I would now like to address four critical questions. Is the ordinary papal magisterium divinely guided? Does it teach the gospel with certainty? Is it open to revision? Does it propose doctrine with varying degrees of authority?

Divine Assistance

The pope exercises his ordinary magisterium in the name, and with the authority, of Christ, that is, "at the divine command and with the help of the Holy Spirit" (DV 10).

Owing to his episcopal ordination and valid election as bishop of Rome, the pope is assured a charism of teaching which accompanies his ministry as successor of Peter. Due to this office, he is equipped with a gift of grace which assists him in preserving the truth of the gospel entrusted to the Church. Independently of his personal merits, the bishop of Rome enjoys this special assistance of the Spirit, promised by Christ, in discharging his teaching role.

This divine help is afforded the pope whenever he exercises his teaching mission. All papal teaching derives from Christ as its source and is upheld by the Holy Spirit. The Spirit of Truth does not sustain the successor of Peter only on some occasions and withhold it on others, according to whether the pope's teaching is more or less important. Following the promise of Christ, the Spirit is ever present to the pope's prophetic ministry, though in varying degrees of intensity. The Spirit guides papal teaching according to the pope's intention, the circumstances of the moment, and the needs of the Church.[22] A pope's personal opinions, off-the-cuff remarks, and observations on issues not relating to faith and morals are extrinsic to his ordinary magisterium. The same is true regarding the views John Paul II expressed in his book *Crossing the Threshold of Hope* (1994). In these instances, the pope is not fulfilling his ministry as supreme teacher.

Certainty and Truth

Ordinary papal teaching does not share in, nor is it enhanced by, the charism to teach infallibly. Because of the Spirit's perpetual guidance of the Church, the ordinary papal magisterium is authoritative in its own right. Whenever the successor of Peter is teaching, he advances what he says as certain and true, even if not in a definitive way.[23] The pope formulates doctrinal statements as conscientiously as possible, making every effort to guarantee that what he says is true. This care comes from his awareness that it is not certainty but truth which sets man free (cf. Jn 8:32). The bishop of Rome speaks out only if he is convinced that the doctrine to be put forward is without error. Before engaging his ordinary magisterium, the pope should be morally certain that the Spirit wishes to speak to the Church in this way. This conviction is not lessened by the pope's simultaneous awareness that such teaching is capable of later revision.

What the pope proposes firmly and authoritatively, even if not definitively, he regards as true. The pope's official teaching is a sure guide to know what Christ thinks about a particular matter. Furthermore, such teaching echoes what has been revealed, even if this has not yet been conclusively determined.[24] Consequently, American canonist Ladislas Örsy remarks that "we must handle the beliefs that have not been infallibly defined cautiously; some of it (perhaps a great deal of it) may be part of God's revelation."[25]

Through his ordinary magisterium the bishop of Rome frequently reaffirms truths which the Church holds to be irrevocable. They belong to the permanent patrimony of faith for one of two reasons: either because they have already been defined by a pope or an ecumenical council, or because they are taught by the Church's universal ordinary magisterium in a definitive way. When the pope teaches, for example, that Jesus Christ rose bodily from the dead, such a teaching is already proposed infallibly by the universal ordinary magisterium.

Origins, Development, and Mission of the Papacy

Error and Revision

When the successor of Peter does not intend to propose a teaching definitively, theologians refer to his magisterium as "non-infallible," "non-irreformable," or "reformable." He proposes his teaching in a non-definitive way.[26] Is it possible that the non-definitive judgments of the pope's ordinary magisterium could be wrong and thus open to revision?

In a 1967 pastoral letter, the German bishops stated that "in the exercise of its official function this [papal] teaching authority of the Church can, and on occasion actually does, fall into errors."[27] Francis Sullivan, too, puts it plainly: "if the non-definitive teaching of the magisterium is not infallible, it can be erroneous; if it is not irreformable, it can stand in need of correction."[28] This is common Catholic teaching. Karl Rahner reminds us that this non-definitive teaching is not only in principle open to revision but has, on occasion, actually been revised. Catholics, he believes, have the right, even the duty, to recognize this fact. At the same time, Rahner adds, this does not imply that in a specific instance the teaching should be presumed to be "false, inadequate, or in need of revision."[29] Because permanent truth and historically conditioned statements are intermingled in the pope's non-definitive magisterium, the Congregation for the Doctrine of the Faith also admits that some magisterial teachings "might not be free from all deficiencies" (DVE 24). Hence, they might be in need of correction. Has this in fact ever happened?

History records that some authoritative papal teaching has, in time, proved to be an inadequate presentation of a particular truth or even actually wrong.[30] On occasion, the pope's concern for doctrinal integrity led to an excessively defensive reaction regarding developments in the physical and historical sciences. The condemnation of Galileo in the seventeenth century and the decrees of the Biblical Commission at the beginning of this century are good examples of this Roman caution. In discussing the Galileo case, John Paul II has called attention to the difficulty of "knowing how to judge a new scientific datum when it seems to contradict the truths of faith." The Roman magisterium made a judgment which later turned out to be incorrect. The same is true for Rome's initial reaction to using the historico-critical method in studying Scripture. Because of the rationalist context in which these methods were at first frequently presented, they seemed to be dangerous to Christian faith. John Paul II then added in this regard: "That was a hasty and unhappy decision."[31] In light of later reappraisal, the ordinary papal magisterium has thus showed itself to be reformable.

Because when they appeared it seemed that the "new" theories were incompatible with Catholic teaching, the bishop of Rome acted to protect the faith. Perhaps by the pope's conservatism in these matters, the bishop of Rome shielded the faith of many Catholics who would have been shaken by the new advances.[32] Joseph Ratzinger remarks that the papal decisions concerning Galileo and biblical criticism were "a warning cry against hasty and superficial adaptations. . . . But the details of the determinations of their contents were later superseded once they had carried out their pastoral duty at a particular moment."[33] In such cases the pope's interventions contained, along with solid principles, a "certain contingent and conjectural element." Only the passage of time allowed the

Church more precisely "to distinguish between what is necessary and what is contingent" (DVE 24) in her teaching. To filter out what is provisional, imperfect, and in need of greater precision requires patience, study, and time.[34] With changing circumstances, a specific teaching can later be seen from a fresh perspective. New discoveries in theology and the other sciences can, moreover, furnish greater insight and a more profound grasp of the truth.

The Second Vatican Council refrained from expressly treating the possibility of error in the ordinary papal magisterium. Its own teaching, however, "corrected" earlier papal statements. *Lumen gentium*, for instance, failed to identify the mystical body of Christ exclusively with the Catholic Church, as Pius XII's *Mystici corporis Christi* (1943) had done.[35] Moreover, the council abandoned the teaching, reaffirmed on several occasions by Pius XII, that the power of episcopal jurisdiction derives directly from the pope. Instead, the Fathers asserted that God conferred it directly through episcopal ordination (cf. LG 21). Similarly, Vatican II's *Dignitatis humanae* marks true progress on the right to religious liberty for heretics over the views expressed from Augustine up through the mid-twentieth century.[36]

Development in papal teaching is no more surprising than the fact that doctrine itself "makes progress in the Church, with the help of the Holy Spirit" (DV 8). This openness to change in the pope's ordinary teaching is due to the limitations which the socio-cultural situation imposes on all non-definitive doctrinal statements. For this reason, the gospel has to be constantly re-stated in different contexts, with all the risks and benefits attending to that effort. The papal ministry is one of the self-corrective means the Church has at her disposal for dealing with this challenge. If there is further maturation in some non-definitive papal teaching, Catholics trust that the Spirit guides the magisterium in this continual process of discernment. According to the needs of the Church, prayer and theological reflection will lead to a fuller understanding of her teaching.[37]

Consequently, the ordinary papal magisterium is open to change. It would be erroneous, however, to conclude that it "can be habitually mistaken in its prudential judgments, or that it does not enjoy divine assistance in the integral exercise of its mission" (DVE 24). Moreover, this openness to revision does not necessarily involve the correcting of an error. More frequently the revision takes the form of furnishing greater clarity in proposing a doctrine. The possibility of error notwithstanding, ordinary papal teaching is more than merely provisional or high-level ecclesiastical opinion. Such teaching cannot be brushed aside as merely "non-infallible," or worse, as "probably fallible." To interpret the ordinary papal magisterium in this way would mistakenly limit the pope's effective teaching only to *ex cathedra* definitions.

At a given moment in the Church's life, the pope has the duty of providing authoritative guidance on matters about which there might not be the kind of certitude provided by judgments of the extraordinary magisterium. To remain faithful to his ministry, the bishop of Rome must teach on these questions, even at the risk that they might some day require correction. He has available an alternative between proclaiming a dogma of faith and remaining silent. In order to present Catholic teaching in a way which corresponds to the world of his day, the pope issues non-definitive statements in his ordinary magisterium.[38] Since the theologians' search for truth can be off track or incomplete, authoritative guidance can be both needed and corrective. The Petrine ministry requires that the pope, who must listen devoutly to the word of God, should explain the faith in a vital way, applying it to the concrete circumstances of the times.

Purpose of the Pope's Ordinary Magisterium

Because the Church is to preach Christ's message convincingly in every age, the pope addresses issues that directly touch upon the truths of the gospel or how it is to be lived. Unlike the occasional nature of his *ex cathedra* statements, the ordinary papal magisterium is ongoing. As a service to the truth, ordinary papal teaching, though sharing the following functions in many ways with the episcopal magisterium, has a specificity corresponding to the Petrine office.

Custodian of the Deposit of Faith

As a listener and servant of the word of God, the pope is to guard the truth with dedication and expound it faithfully. More than anyone else, he is responsible for maintaining the integrity of the Church's deposit of faith. Fulfilling the trust first given to Peter, the bishop of Rome safeguards the original *kerygma*, assuring the Church's obedience to the will of Christ.[39] In the words of John Paul II, the mission of Peter's successor is "to establish and authoritatively confirm what the Church has received and believed from the beginning, what the apostles taught, what sacred Scripture and Christian tradition have determined as the object of faith and the Christian norm of life."[40] The bishop of Rome authoritatively passes on and interprets "the word of God, whether in its written form or in the form of tradition" (DV 10).

Faced by harmful opinions or errors, the pope watches over the Church's common profession and unity of faith. In the apostolic letter *Ordinatio sacerdotalis* (1994), John Paul II spoke out authoritatively on the question of women's ordination. He did so because widespread uncertainty had arisen about whether the Church could ordain women to the ministerial priesthood. Not issuing a new dogmatic formulation, the pope confirmed a certainty which the Church has constantly held and lived; that is, he rendered the judgment that reserving priestly ordination to men alone was not a prudential teaching, nor a more probable opinion, nor merely a matter of discipline.[41] The successor of Peter made this determination "in order that all doubt may be removed regarding a matter of great importance, a matter which pertains to the Church's divine constitution itself" (*Ordinatio sacerdotalis*, 4).

The pope's magisterium is more conservative than innovative. It stresses fidelity to the received tradition and the continuity of Church teaching through time. The pope is also charged with preaching the fullness of the faith, recalling and confirming those "hard sayings" of the gospel which are easily lost sight of.

Prophet

Like all bishops, the successor of Peter "should present the doctrine of Christ in a manner suited to the needs of the times," says Vatican II, "that is, so it may be relevant to those difficulties and questions which men find especially worrying and troublesome" (CD 13). The pope, moreover, has the obligation to contribute to the on-going inculturation of the Church's faith. It would be a betrayal of the gospel to suppose that no new questions, answers, or reformulations are possible.[42] Accordingly, popes now have a greater teaching responsibility than was evident in earlier epochs. Their everyday magisterium has proved to be a valuable instrument for responding to questions not explicitly treated in the deposit of faith. Papal teaching authority extends to all areas necessary for preaching and defending the truth of the gospel. The pope himself is the judge who decides whether a particular matter lies within his competency.[43]

Because the gospel "inspires and guides the whole sphere of human behavior" (DVE 16), particularly critical in the contemporary world is the pope's charge to teach on moral matters. Much of the Church's constantly developing tradition of social doctrine falls into this category.[44] Here it is easy to see why the pope's ordinary magisterium is open to revision. According to the *Catechism of the Catholic Church*, "the authority of the Magisterium extends also to the specific precepts of the *natural law*, because their observance, demanded by Christ, is necessary for salvation" (CCC 2036).[45] The Code of Canon Law similarly asserts that the hierarchy has the right "to make judgments on any human matter to the extent that they are required by the fundamental rights of the human person or the salvation of souls" (CIC 747.2; cf. CCC 2032). The successor of Peter can teach authoritatively, guiding the formation of the faithful's consciences, on moral issues, even those which, by their very nature, cannot be proposed infallibly.[46]

Guided by the deposit of revealed truth, the bishop of Rome applies the light of the gospel to difficult new problems, addressing questions in his ordinary magisterium not previously considered. In recent decades, contraception, *in vitro* fertilization, innumerable bio-ethical problems, massive poverty, and peace have all been treated at length by various popes in their ordinary magisterium.

Homilist

Through his magisterium the successor of Peter is to "guarantee that the salvific word of Christ will be really addressed to the concrete situation of a given age, in view of Christian life."[47] He fosters a more profound living of the gospel by Christians.

If the pope's magisterium is understood primarily as the commands of an authority exercising jurisdiction, it then follows that he need not furnish any reasons for his teaching. His duty would be to teach by making laws. In this view, the emphasis is on his formal authority as the successor of Peter. On the other hand, when the Roman bishop's magisterial function is associated more closely with Christ's teaching ministry, then he has another kind of authority: one which seeks to convince.

Since the nineteenth century, the pope has increasingly assumed an exhortative role, making efforts to explain how his teaching is consonant with the original deposit of faith.

Appeals to formal papal authority — that it is the successor of Peter who is teaching — are now routinely complemented by arguments directed to persuading the faithful. He teaches not only *what* is true but also in such a way that the people of God can see *why* it is true.[48]

Most papal teaching intends to enlighten and explain as well as to clarify the truth. The very length of recent papal documents, frequently running 150-200 pages in the pontificate of John Paul II, testifies to the pope's desire to present Church teaching with convincing reasons which help the faithful to understand it.[49] The arguments he puts forward to explain or back up a particular teaching are not propounded, however, with the same authority which belongs to the judgment he has reached. For example, Paul VI's teaching in *Humanae vitae* (1968) that "every act that intends to impede procreation must be repudiated . . . whether it is done in anticipation of marital intercourse, or during it, or while it is having its natural consequence" (*Humanae vitae*, 14) is the most authoritative judgment in his encyclical. The supporting reasons he gives for the Church's teaching do not express his magisterial charism in the same way.

Important as it is to furnish persuasive explanations, the authority of the pope's magisterium does not depend on the reasons he gives for his teaching. "If that were true," observes Francis Sullivan, "papal teaching would have no more claim on the assent of Catholics than it does on the assent of anyone else who might happen to read an encyclical."[50] In his everyday teaching the pope is not a theologian whose authority depends on the strength of the arguments he adduces to sustain his judgment; he is acting as an authoritative teacher endowed with a charism. It is due to the divine assistance promised to Peter and his successors that the pope's teaching has a validity beyond the force of argumentation (cf. DVE 34).

In the documents of his ordinary magisterium, the pope takes pains to avoid committing the Church to a particular school of philosophical or theological thought. Nonetheless, as Avery Dulles observes, the papal magisterium "takes over the terminology, thought-categories, and theories of theologians, insofar as these can be made to bear and convey the Christian faith."[51] In this sense, the popes engage in theology. It is apparent, for example, that John Paul II brings his own phenomenological method to bear on his magisterial documents.[52] To be sure, it would be impossible not to use theology, philosophy and, when necessary, other sciences, to help the faithful understand Church doctrine. Papal teaching is frequently convincing precisely because it conveys the insights and strength of its author's theological or philosophical orientation.

A close examination of the sources cited in papal documents shows that the pope only rarely quotes modern or living theologians. In his magisterium he relies heavily upon Scripture, the Fathers of the Church, St. Thomas Aquinas and other doctors, as well as previous statements of the papal and conciliar magisterium. The pope also uses a certain rhetorical style in his teaching in order to guarantee that it will remain above the fray of theological debate.

It is well known that the pope receives help from theologians and other experts in preparing his magisterial interventions. Though the individuals consulted are bound to secrecy, a close scrutiny of the documents provides some clues about which theologians had a hand in their preparation. For many years, the Jesuits at Roman institutions of higher learning were primary consultants to the popes. Pius XII's *Mystici corporis Christi* (1943) reflects the views of Sebastian Tromp, as *Divino afflante Spiritu* (1943) shows the influence of Augustin Bea.[53] Whatever the assistance he receives, when the pope publishes a document in his own name, it is his teaching and not that of those whom he may have consulted.

Judge

Papal teaching also has a judging role. When debate threatens the unity of faith, the bishop of Rome exercises his ordinary magisterium with the spiritual authority of a decision maker. In the words of the International Theological Commission, the pope's teaching gives believers a certainty about the faith when they are "faced with a baffling babel of voices and never-ending theological disputes."[54] On occasion, the successor of Peter intervenes to declare that certain views are contrary to the Church's faith. In doing so, the pope is "defending the right of the people of God to receive the message of the Church in its purity and integrity and not be disturbed by a particular dangerous opinion" (DVE 37).

Even when he does not use his charism to teach *ex cathedra*, the pope points out dangers and errors opposed to Catholic faith or morals. *Humanae vitae* (1968) and *Veritatis splendor* (1993) are recent examples of papal interventions which, while by no means capable of being seen only in this light, nonetheless made a judgment on vital matters. Both condemned positions judged to be incompatible with Catholic teaching: contraception in the first instance, and the denial of intrinsically evil acts in the second. Either directly, or, more often, through the Congregation for the Doctrine of the Faith acting for him, the bishop of Rome censures opinions which endanger the integral confession of the Church's faith and her teaching on moral matters.[55]

Documents and Degrees of Authoritative Teaching

The successor of Peter exercises his authoritative teaching ministry in a threefold way. First and most often, he teaches by means of the spoken word: in homilies, weekly catecheses, and discourses. Modern means of communication allow him to fulfill his teaching mission in a way never before possible. Similarly, widespread travel allows the pope to visit the most distant regions to speak directly to Catholics throughout the world. Second, he teaches by means of his writing: through documents which he issues in his own name or those published by the Roman curia under his mandate. The pope conveys his ordinary teaching by apostolic constitutions, encyclicals, exhortations, and letters. Third, he carries out his teaching responsibility by initiating, fostering, and authorizing institutions, such as seminaries, faculties of theology, and academies, which operate under his auspices.[56]

The pope's ordinary magisterium, expressed in its highest form on very rare occasions, is a solemn profession of faith. Paul VI's *Creed of the People of God* (1968), issued to mark the end of the Year of Faith, is a case in point.[57] Apostolic constitutions are a more common way in which the pope regularly engages his Petrine authority. They deal with major doctrinal, disciplinary, or administrative matters. While previously such constitutions enunciated legal norms, and they are still principally legislative documents, they now often have a strong doctrinal component.[58]

John Paul II, for example, promulgated the *Catechism of the Catholic Church*, a document whose publication he regarded as "one of the most significant events" of his Petrine ministry,[59] with the apostolic constitution *Fidei depositum* (1992). He also issued the current codes of canon law with an apostolic constitution: *Sacrae disciplinae leges* (1983) for the Latin church, and *Sacri canones* (1990) for the Eastern churches. *Pastor bonus* (1988), which deals with the ministry and organization of the Roman curia, and those promulgated to erect new dioceses, are examples of apostolic constitutions whose contents treat more administrative questions. For less weighty matters, more legislative than magisterial, the pope draws up a document in his own name (*motu proprio*).

Other major documents include encyclicals, which will be described in the next section, and apostolic exhortations, now issued after meetings of the synod of bishops or for matters of less import than what is treated in encyclicals. Recent post-synodal apostolic exhortations are: *Evangelii nuntiandi* (1975), on evangelization in the modern world; *Catechesi tradendae* (1979), on catechetics; *Familiaris consortio* (1981), on the role of the Christian family; *Reconciliatio et paenitentia* (1984), on reconciliation and penance in the mission of the Church; *Christifideles laici* (1988), on the vocation and mission of the laity; and *Pastores dabo vobis* (1992), on priestly formation. Non-synodal related apostolic exhortations include *Redemptionis donum* (1984), addressed to religious on their consecration in the light of the mystery of the redemption; and *Redemptoris custos* (1989), on the person and mission of St. Joseph in the life of Christ and the Church.

A distinction should be made between papal teaching directed to restricted audiences and that intended for the universal Church. Every so often, the pope writes letters to different groups of people: for example, the *Apostolic Letter to the Youth of the World* (1985), or the *Letter to Families* (1994). He also addresses certain topical issues, as he did in *Salvifici doloris* (1984), on the Christian meaning of human suffering; *Mulieris dignitatem* (1988), on the dignity and vocation of women; *Ordinatio sacerdotalis* (1994), on reserving priestly ordination to men alone; and *Tertio millennio adveniente*, (1994) on preparations for the jubilee year 2000. These letters, too, belong to the pope's ordinary magisterium.

From the sixth century onward, the papal chancery used a lead seal to authenticate its documents. Since Innocent IV (1243-1254), the most important papal documents have received the additional descriptive name of "bull," from the Latin *bulla* (capsule or disc) within which the papal seal was embedded. This gave rise to the inaccurate but common term for all documents stamped with a leaden seal.[60] The apostolic constitution *Munificentissimus Deus* (1950), promulgated by Pius XII when he defined the Assumption of Mary, is, for example, frequently referred to as a papal bull.

Only teaching directed to the whole Church expresses the ordinary papal magisterium in the fullest sense. This means that the pope's *ad limina* discourses given to bishops of a particular region and the speeches delivered during his pastoral visits to various countries do not belong to his ordinary magisterium in the same way as discourses or writings addressed directly to the universal Church.

The bishop of Rome often treats specific social, economic, and political questions with an eye to shedding on them the light of the gospel. Besides teaching certain moral principles, here his pronouncements more often than not also contain recommended courses of practical action. These latter proposals deserve respectful consideration, but, as practical suggestions for implementing fundamental moral principles, they do not call for the religious assent due to his ordinary teaching on faith and morals. John Paul II's support for financial compensation equal to other kinds of work for mothers who stay at home to take care of their children,[61] or his plea to cancel the debt of Third World nations as a way to alleviate massive poverty,[62] fall into this category. Catholics are free to disagree with these papal guidelines as ways in which to secure justice. They can submit to debate alternative practical solutions, provided that they accept the moral principles which the pope propounds in his teaching.

Statements of the Roman Curia

Routinely the pope uses the dicasteries or "ministries" of the Roman curia, the administrative bureaucracy which helps him in exercising his Petrine ministry of teaching. Especially since the Second Vatican Council, the various congregations, councils, and commissions of the Roman curia have published a stream of documents. Without authority in their own right, curial officials receive it by delegation from the pope in "innate dependence" on him (PB 8). Statements from the Roman curia can, therefore, never claim to share the pope's charism of infallibility, since he cannot delegate this gift to any person or any group.

Papal authority is to be attributed to the decrees and instructions issued by the Roman curia only when this is clearly indicated in a particular document. Curial statements which deal directly with Church teaching belong to the pope's ordinary magisterium when he explicitly approves them (*in forma communi*) and orders their publication.[63] In these instances, the pope lends his own authority to the document, though in a lesser way than to one he issues in his own name. A statement issued with papal approval remains an act of the particular congregation. It receives its authority from the fact that the pope exercises his primatial power through the congregation and from his approval.[64] At times, the bishop of Rome can also approve a document "in specific form" (*in forma specifica*), such as the acts of regional synods or of a Roman congregation. In this case, they become properly papal statements, enjoying the same authority as if he had issued them himself.

Within the Roman curia, the Congregation for the Doctrine of the Faith, formerly called the Holy Office, has a special link with the ordinary magisterium of the pope. This Congregation "is to promote and safeguard the doctrine on faith and morals in the whole Catholic world" (PB 48). When the pope expressly approves documents dealing with these matters, they "participate in the ordinary magisterium of the successor of Peter"

Origins, Development, and Mission of the Papacy

(DVE 18). Because the competence of this Congregation is to express the mind of the pope on important doctrinal and moral questions, its teachings "require the same adherence which is owed to the non-infallible magisterium of the Roman pontiff."[65]

Most often documents from the Congregation for the Doctrine of the Faith are issued to confirm Church doctrine. This holds true, for example, for the teaching of the *Declaration on Procured Abortion* (1974), the *Declaration on Euthanasia* (1980), or the *Instruction on Respect for Human Life in Its Origin and on the Dignity of Procreation* (1987). Though in these instances the formal authority of each statement is only that of an approved document, they enjoy magisterial weight to the extent that they reaffirm Catholic teaching. When it is clear that the Congregation for the Doctrine of the Faith is speaking in the name of the Church, indicated by expressions such as "the Church forbids," or "the Church remains opposed to," or "the Church teaches," it is expressing the ordinary magisterium of the successor of Peter.

Assessing the Degree of Authority

Unlike the pope's extraordinary magisterium, which admits of no degrees, the "intensity" of the Spirit's presence varies in his ordinary magisterium. The degree of divine assistance given to the different kinds of magisterial interventions varies.[66] The Fathers of the Second Vatican Council furnished criteria to be used for gauging the different degrees in which the pope exercises his authoritative magisterium. These criteria help theologians and the faithful to discern the pope's "manifest mind and intention." According to *Lumen gentium*, the force of an authoritative teaching can be recognized "by the character of the documents in question, or by the frequency with which a certain doctrine is proposed, or by the manner in which the doctrine is formulated" (LG 25; cf. DVE 24). The penalties imposed on those who dissent from a particular teaching provide yet another criterion.

• KIND OF DOCUMENT   Statements which bear the direct papal stamp, especially apostolic constitutions, encyclicals, apostolic exhortations, and letters, are vehicles which the pope uses for his most decisive teaching. An instruction from a Roman congregation whose publication the pope approves does not enjoy the same degree of formal authority as an encyclical dealing with a similar question. If, for example, Paul VI (1963-1978) had made known his teaching on contraception only through lower-level documents rather than his encyclical *Humanae vitae* (1968), then it is unlikely that such controversy would have resulted from its publication.

• FREQUENCY   If the pope recalls the same teaching repeatedly, this repetition is a further indication that it properly belongs to his ordinary magisterium. This category includes John Paul II's constant teaching on the indissolubility of marriage, contraception, and the inviolable dignity of human life from the moment of conception until natural death.

• MANNER   The way in which the bishop of Rome teaches on an issue also reveals the weight of papal authority behind a doctrine. If the pope says, for example, that he is speaking on behalf of the Church, this tells us that the matter belongs to ordinary papal teaching. John Paul II's teaching on the inadmissibility of women to the ministerial priesthood can be put into this category. In *Ordinatio sacerdotalis* (1994), he appealed specifically to his "ministry of confirming the brethren" (cf. Lk 22:32), before rendering his judgment prefaced by the formal term "I declare" (*Ordinatio sacerdotalis*, 4).

• *PENALTIES* Lastly, the nature of any disciplinary action taken against those who reject a papal teaching provides a good measure for determining the degree of the pope's commitment to what he is teaching. The removal of canonical mission or an individual's right to be called a "Catholic" theologian because of dissent from a papal teaching confirms that such a teaching properly belongs to his ordinary magisterium.[67] For example, the measures taken against those who deny Church teaching on abortion indicate that the pope is authoritatively proposing the doctrine of its intrinsic evil.

When the successor of Peter engages his teaching ministry, he invokes his formal authority to varying degrees. These different levels can be discerned by taking into account the four factors mentioned above. It is always necessary to discover the mind of the bishop of Rome before asserting that a particular statement belongs to his ordinary magisterium. This investigation allows an individual to know the extent to which the pope is using his Petrine authority and, consequently, the kind of assent called for by a particular teaching.

Encyclicals

Beginning in the early Church, bishops frequently sent letters to other bishops to ensure unity in ecclesial doctrine and life. Benedict XIV (1740-1758) revived the custom of the pope sending out "circular letters" to the other bishops. These papal letters touch on doctrine, morals, or discipline affecting the whole Church. Paul VI defined an encyclical as "a document in the form of a letter sent by the Pope to the bishops of the entire world; *encyclical* means circular. It is a very ancient form of ecclesiastical correspondence that characteristically denotes the communion of faith and charity that exists among the various 'churches,' that is, among the various communities that make up the Church."[68]

With Gregory XVI (1831-1846), the term "encyclical" came into general use.[69] Leo XIII (1878-1903) wrote more than twice the number of encyclicals as his predecessor Pius IX (1846-1878), seventy-five in all. Leo also changed the emphasis of their tone, which had previously been chiefly condemnatory. He began to sketch out positively how the Church should respond to concrete problems, especially in the social-ethical order. Leo XIII's innovative approach popularized encyclicals as reference points not only for Catholic doctrine but also for many programs of action.[70] In the pontificates of the twentieth century, the number of encyclicals published has varied widely: sixteen for Pius X (1903-1914), twelve for Benedict XV (1914-1922), thirty for Pius XI (1922-1939), forty-one for Pius XII (1939-1958), eight for John XXIII (1958-1963), seven for Paul VI (1963-1978), and nine between 1978 and 1994 for John Paul II.

By definition, encyclical letters formally have the value of teaching directed to the universal Church. However, when they deal with social, economic, or political questions, they are commonly addressed not only to Catholics but also to all men and women of good will, a practice begun by John XXIII in *Pacem in terris* (1963). From time to time, as in *Veritatis splendor* (1993), the pope includes only bishops in his opening salutation, even though he intends the encyclical's doctrine for the instruction of all the faithful. Tillard maintains that addressing only his brother bishops would always be the wiser course of action for the pope to follow. The bishops, he holds, have the obligation to pass on the pope's message, with suitable explanation, to their particular churches.[71] During this century, however, the bishops of Rome have nearly always chosen to address personally all the faithful through an encyclical.

Kinds of Encyclicals

Pius XI introduced a clear distinction between encyclical "letters" and encyclical "epistles." The latter are exhortations either concerning a particular question or directed primarily to the bishops of a specific country or part of the Church.[72] Since they are not directed to the whole Church, encyclical epistles enjoy less formal authority than encyclical letters. To commemorate the eleven hundredth centenary of the evangelizing work of Sts. Cyril and Methodius, for instance, John Paul II wrote *Slavorum apostoli* (1985). Such encyclical epistles are rare. Common theological language uses the term "encyclical" to refer to both an encyclical epistle and an encyclical letter.

According to their subject matter, three major kinds of encyclical letters can be distinguished: doctrinal, exhortatory, and disciplinary.

• DOCTRINAL   This kind of encyclical develops at length the reasons for the teaching which the pope proposes. Many of these have significantly marked the life of the Church. Among the most important doctrinal encyclicals of recent pontificates are Pius XII's *Mystici corporis Christi* (1943), on the Church as the mystical body of Christ, *Divino afflante Spiritu* (1943), on promoting biblical studies, and *Mediator Dei* (1947), on the sacred liturgy; Paul VI's *Mysterium fidei* (1965), on the Eucharist; and the trinitarian cycle of John Paul II: *Redemptor hominis* (1979), on redemption and human dignity; *Dives in misericordia* (1980), on divine mercy; and *Dominum et vivificantem* (1986), on the Holy Spirit in the life of the Church and the world.

When faced by unsound theological opinions, the popes sometimes issue encyclicals to point out the dangers of certain views and to expound orthodox teaching. Pius XII's *Humani generis* (1950) dealt with false opinions threatening to undermine the foundations of Catholic doctrine. In *Humanae vitae* (1968), Paul VI reaffirmed the Church's teaching on contraception. An example of this type of encyclical is *Veritatis splendor* (1993). It deals with fundamental questions of moral theology, warning of the dangers posed by the moral theories of consequentialism and proportionalism. To combat these views, John Paul II reasserted the Church's tradition that some acts are in themselves "intrinsically evil."[73] *Evangelium vitae* (1995), on the defense and dignity of human life, is also a doctrinal encyclical.

Other documents of the papal ordinary magisterium which have had a great impact on the Church's life are the so-called "social encyclicals." Here the popes have very often led the way. Since the end of the nineteenth century, they have formulated a social doctrine which has enriched the Church's tradition. While articulated in different ways and applied to various problems, the heart of the popes' teaching has been the defense of the human person created in God's image and likeness. Primary among these social encyclicals are Leo XIII's *Rerum novarum* (1891), on the problems of capital and labor; Pius XI's *Quadragesimo anno* (1931), on the reconstruction of the social order; John XXIII's *Mater et magistra* (1961), on Christianity and social progress; Paul VI's *Populorum progressio* (1967), on the development of peoples; and John Paul II's *Laborem exercens* (1981), on human work; *Sollicitudo rei socialis* (1987), on the social concerns of the Church; and *Centesimus annus* (1991), on various questions of social doctrine.

• *EXHORTATORY* Some encyclicals deal specifically with more spiritual themes. Their primary purpose is to help Catholics in their sacramental and devotional life. Not framed in view of any particular doctrinal or theological controversy, exhortatory encyclicals expound a dimension of the Christian mystery as an aid to piety. Pius XII's *Haurietis aquas* (1956), on devotion to the Sacred Heart, and John Paul II's *Redemptoris mater* (1987), on Mary's role in the life of the pilgrim Church, are examples of exhortatory encyclicals.

• *DISCIPLINARY* Now and then an encyclical letter treats particular disciplinary or practical questions. Pius XII's *Fidei donum* (1957) set in motion the transfer of many priests to mission lands, and Paul VI's *Sacerdotalis caelibatus* (1967) reaffirmed the Latin tradition of priestly celibacy.

Creeping Infallibility

In the period after Vatican I, the exercise of the pope's ordinary magisterium, especially through encyclicals, expanded considerably. Two consequences followed from the increased number of papal documents. First, in line with the council's emphasis on the papacy, the papal magisterium overshadowed the universal ordinary magisterium of the bishops. Their voice often became merely an echo of papal teaching. Second, some theologians and faithful came to think that encyclicals somehow shared in the charism of infallibility.[74] Despite the restrictive nature of the conditions laid down in *Pastor aeternus*, a kind of nimbus of infallibility frequently surrounded papal encyclicals. In practice, encyclicals were sometimes given a theological weight almost indistinguishable from that of an *ex cathedra* statement. This attitude, typical of a "court mentality," promoted an exaggerated papalism which went far beyond the teaching of Vatican I.[75]

The principal argument these theologians put forward to justify their view that the ordinary papal magisterium could be infallible rested on a misinterpretation of *Pastor aeternus*.[76] The First Vatican Council, they held, did not intend to restrict papal infallibility only to solemn definitions. This position, however, is mistaken. A close examination of Bishop Gasser's report at Vatican I shows that the Fathers voted on the proposition that the pope enjoys infallibility "only when" he is speaking *ex cathedra* (M 52, 1213).[77] Vatican I set precise and restrictive conditions for the exercise of papal infallibility.

During the pontificate of Pius XII, the idea of extending the infallibility to the pope's ordinary magisterium reached its high point. Theological manuals of the period demanded an assent to ordinary papal teaching that was, in Sullivan's words, "hardly different from the response required by a solemn dogmatic definition."[78] Pius XII's remarks in *Humani generis* (1950) were interpreted as supporting that tendency. "Nor must it be thought," he wrote, "that what is expounded in encyclical letters does not of itself demand assent, since in writing such letters the popes do not exercise the supreme power of their teaching authority.... But if the supreme pontiffs in their official documents purposely pass judgment on a matter up to that time under dispute, it is obvious that that matter, according to the mind and will of the same pontiffs, cannot be any longer considered a question open to discussion among theologians."[79]

At least two repercussions followed from this tendency to lend to the ordinary papal magisterium a share in the charism of papal infallibility. First, many Catholics came to regard the pope not only as the Church's supreme teacher but also as her *only* reliable teacher. Second, papal teaching was understood in the restricted choice of a misleading alternative: infallible or non-infallible. Consequently, if a doctrine was proposed without exercising the charism of infallibility, it was thought to be non-obligatory or optional. Congar calls attention to this "inflation of the category of infallibility" which obscures the large area of partial truth, of probable certitude, of approximations, and of precious truth not guaranteed by the risks of human finiteness.[80] When the note of infallibility is the primary reason for accepting the pope's teaching, then, if this certitude is not present, a given doctrine can be easily ignored.

Assent to Ordinary Papal Teaching

According to Vatican II, "loyal [religious] submission of the will and intellect must be given, in a special way, to the authentic [authoritative] teaching of the Roman Pontiff, even when he does not speak *ex cathedra*" (LG 25; cf. CIC 752). The pope formulates such teaching either personally or through the doctrinal statements of the Congregation for the Doctrine of the Faith. The ordinary papal magisterium calls for an assent which is an act of human faith grounded "within the logic of faith and under the impulse of obedience to faith" (DVE 23). While remaining distinct from the act of faith, religious assent is "nonetheless an extension of it" (CCC 892). It is also the work of grace. Between the act of the pope as teacher and the reception of the hearer is the mystery of God's grace which stirs up in the believer the appropriate assent. The truth of faith is neither information nor orders from on high but the living and active word of God which confronts the believer's will and intellect.

The current profession of faith, which was issued in 1989, is taken by those assuming an official position in the Church.[81] It reflects conciliar teaching in its formula: "I adhere with religious submission of will and intellect to the teachings which either the Roman pontiff or the college of bishops enunciate when they exercise the authentic magisterium even if they proclaim those teachings in an act that is not definitive."[82] Religious assent is, therefore, neither the assent of divine and catholic faith owed to what is revealed nor the firm acceptance due to a doctrine that is definitively taught.

Religious Assent

The religious submission of will and intellect which Catholics are to give to the pope's ordinary teaching involves more than showing respect for his ministry or giving a merely exterior obedience. Religious assent means accepting such teachings, writes moral theologian Germain Grisez, "in the sense that one agrees with them, holds on to them, and acts in accord with them."[83] Such assent is called *religious* submission because it is rooted in the love of God and trust in the Church. This confidence includes the belief that the pope is a reliable guide in matters of faith and Christian living. Assent to ordinary papal teaching is based on the conviction that the Spirit guides the pope's doctrinal and moral teaching.[84] The assent given by the faithful to the ordinary papal magisterium is not, therefore, motivated by their personal evaluation of the truth of a particular teaching but by their trust in the divine gift of the Petrine ministry.

Religious *submission* also involves adopting an attitude of docility to papal teaching. It calls for an open attitude, always giving it a fair hearing and attempting to understand the reasons for it.[85] Authoritative papal teaching engages both the mind and the will, calling for an assent, which is an act of judgment.[86] This docility is related to the Catholic's desire to be one with the Church.[87] Recognizing that dissension is a cause of scandal which impedes evangelization, is a further reason why Catholics give religious submission to the pope's ordinary magisterium.

Reasonable Assent

A reasonable person follows the best teacher available at a given time. Since Christ entrusted Peter with the care of his flock, the authoritative teaching of his successors commends itself as reasonable. Catholics believe that the pope, as Peter's successor, is heir to the apostle's mandate and the promised assistance of the Holy Spirit. Divine guidance furnishes a motive for confidence, making it reasonable for a person to accept the pope's ordinary teaching.[88]

Furthermore, it is less reasonable to follow the possibly erroneous judgments of other authorities, such as theologians, religious education teachers, or clerics. Common experience confirms the value of such docile prudence. In everyday life, people constantly act with less than absolute certainty about whether a given decision is right. Doctors, for example, must routinely make diagnoses without absolute certainty. Nonetheless, individuals follow their recommendations, knowing that there is a possibility that physicians might be mistaken. Because of their expertise, they are the best judges of the medical situation at a particular time.[89] Even more so, Catholics accept that it is reasonable and prudent to give their religious submission of will and intellect to the pope's ordinary teaching.

Respectful Obedience

Religious assent is owed only to some papal statements. The pope can speak as a private theologian; he can offer teaching in a tentative way; and he can issue disciplinary statements, including those which concern what should be taught and how to teach it. In these instances, respectful obedience, not the religious submission of intellect and will, is required.[90]

Through the Congregation for the Doctrine of the Faith, the papal magisterium sometimes judges the orthodoxy of theological opinions. If an opinion is censured, the loyal response is to refrain from teaching what has been condemned.[91] Nonetheless, such obedience does not oblige the individual's mind either to approve the decision or judge it correct. The Catholic's response to acts of papal legislation is an obedience of the will, not of the judgment. Similarly, the pope's decisions in matters of discipline, such as those regulating liturgical practice, call for obedience rather than religious submission.

Withholding Interior Assent

As an inner disposition of intellect and will, religious submission to the ordinary papal magisterium normally results in accepting what the successor of Peter teaches. This is not the place to discuss the possibility and limits of dissent from the pope's ordinary teaching. It can be said, however, that if a Catholic, for serious reasons, is unable to give sincere internal assent to a particular non-definitive teaching, such an individual does not on that account jeopardize his or her communion with the Church (cf. DVE 28-31). When withholding interior assent to a particular doctrine, however, it must be clearly evident that the Church is not teaching it infallibly.[92] In fact, much of what the pope teaches through his ordinary magisterium already belongs to the universal ordinary magisterium of the episcopal college and is proposed "to be held definitively and absolutely" (LG 25).

The withholding of interior assent is different from dissent. The latter either rejects the pope's non-definitive teaching as irrelevant to the individual case or judges it to be false. Respectful questioning of authoritative but non-definitive papal teaching can, on the other hand, be compatible with the religious submission of intellect and will.[93] The distinction between the religious assent due to non-definitive papal teaching and the absolute assent due to *ex cathedra* pronouncements and definitively proposed teaching must, however, always be retained. To be sure, "the willingness to submit loyally to the teaching of the magisterium on matters *per se* not irreformable must be the rule" (DVE 24). According to the Code of Canon Law, when faced with non-definitive teaching, "the Christian faithful are to take care to avoid whatever is not in harmony with that teaching" (CIC 752).

◆

Among the primary pastoral tasks of the Petrine ministry is to ensure that all "come to the knowledge of the truth" (1 Tim 2:4). As the successor of Peter, the pope is "the first herald of the faith"[94] and the chief teacher in the Church. He fulfills his doctrinal mission by a continual series of oral and written interventions which form his ordinary magisterium.

In the first millennium, the pope was regarded above all as a privileged witness to the apostolic faith. The other churches of the *koinonia* recognized the harmony between the words of Peter and those of the pope. Beginning with the eleventh-century Gregorian

Reform, however, the bishop of Rome assumed increasing responsibility for actively applying the truths of faith to new situations. This development, rooted in Christ's commission to Peter, was guided by the Holy Spirit and belongs to God's design for his Church.

As the principal, though not sole, teacher in the Church, the pope is to preach the apostolic faith throughout the world. To him, "in a special way, the noble task of propagating the Christian name" has been entrusted (LG 23). He does so as the Church's supreme guide in the truth, endowed with the authority of Christ and a charism of the Spirit. To teach effectively, the pope must be personally well-informed about the faith of the people of God, contemplate the Church's tradition, consult others, and study. Nevertheless, the authority of papal teaching stems from the divinely instituted Petrine ministry which he discharges.

According to historical circumstances and the effective means available to him, the pope has exercised his teaching ministry in many different ways. Recent popes have usually used apostolic constitutions and encyclicals when engaging the highest level of their everyday magisterium. The documents of the Congregation for the Doctrine of the Faith, which are expressly approved by the pope, are also proving to be increasingly significant vehicles of papal teaching.

Not every papal utterance on a matter concerning faith and morals belongs to the pope's ordinary magisterium. Nor is all his teaching authoritative to the same degree. Catholics are expected to give the religious submission of will and intellect to his magisterium to the degree in which it expresses his desire to teach with Petrine authority. It is also true that, despite the Spirit's assistance to the papal magisterium, it still admits the possibility that some of his statements might fall short of the full truth of the gospel. If this is so in a particular instance, such a statement is open to future revision.

Catholics show a fundamental openness to accept the pope's teaching, animated by their love for God and the Church. With a moral certitude which excludes any prudent doubts, they give the religious submission of will and intellect to his teaching. In the believer's response the mystery of grace is at work, seeking to effect a change in the individual. This is so even when a particular teaching is less than definitively certain. After much prayer, study, and a willingness to examine both the pope's reasons for his teaching and one's own motives in finding difficulty with it, an individual may still be unable to accept a particular papal teaching. Withholding assent is, in this case, compatible with living in communion with the Church.

The pope's ordinary magisterium is an integral part of the universal ministry of the successor of Peter. In fulfilling his mission, the bishop of Rome must be ever attentive to Paul's words to Timothy: "Preach the word, be urgent in season and out of season, convince, rebuke, and exhort, be unfailing in patience and in teaching" (2 Tim 4:2).

Notes for Chapter eight

1. Avery Dulles, *A Church to Believe In* (New York: Crossroad Publishing Company, 1982), 120.
2. Irenaeus, *Against Heresies*, 3.3.

3. Gregory Dix, *Jurisdiction in the Early Church*, reprinted with introduction by T. M. Parker (London: Faith House, 1975), 120.
4. J. M. R. Tillard, *The Bishop of Rome*, trans. John de Satgé (Wilmington: Michael Glazier, 1983), 85.
5. Tillard, *Bishop of Rome*, 92.
6. Klaus Schatz, *La primauté du Pape*, trans. Joseph Hoffmann (Paris: Cerf, 1992), 59.
7. Yves Congar, *L'ecclésiologie du haut Moyen-Age* (Paris: Cerf, 1968), 159-161.
8. Ladislas Örsy, *The Church: Learning and Teaching* (Wilmington: Michael Glazier, 1987), 48.
9. Schatz, *Primauté du Pape*, 123.
10. Congar, *L'Eglise de saint Augustin à l'époque moderne*, 191-192.
11. Marie-Dominique Chenu, *Toward Understanding St. Thomas* (Chicago: Regnery, 1964), 20.
12. Congar, *L'Eglise de saint Augustin à l'époque moderne*, 241.
13. Francis A. Sullivan, *Magisterium: Teaching Authority in the Catholic Church* (New York: Paulist Press, 1983), 182.
14. Schatz, *Primauté du Pape*, 181.
15. Congar, *L'Eglise de saint Augustin à l'époque moderne*, 371.
16. Tillard, *Bishop of Rome*, 168.
17. Hermann J. Pottmeyer, "Reception and Submission," *The Jurist*, 51:2 (1991), 272.
18. Pottmeyer, "Reception and Submission," 277.
19. Schatz, *Primauté du Pape*, 224, 241.
20. Richard R. Gaillardetz, *Witnesses to the Faith: Community, Infallibility and the Ordinary Magisterium of Bishops* (New York: Paulist Press, 1992), 15-16.
21. Dulles, *A Church to Believe In*, 113-114.
22. Réal Tremblay, "Document Provides Food for Thought," *L'Osservatore Romano*, 45 (November 11, 1992), 9.
23. William E. May, *An Introduction to Moral Theology* (Huntington: Our Sunday Visitor, 1991), 205-207.
24. Germain Grisez, *Christian Moral Principles*, The Way of the Lord Jesus, vol. 1 (Chicago: Franciscan Herald Press, 1983), 851-853.
25. Örsy, *The Church: Learning and Teaching*, 58.
26. Umberto Betti, "The Profession of Faith and Oath of Fidelity: Doctrinal Considerations," *L'Osservatore Romano*, 11 (March 13, 1989), 3.
27. Cited in Karl Rahner, "The Dispute concerning the Church's Teaching Office," in *Theological Investigations*, trans. David Bourke, vol. 14 (London: Darton, Longman & Todd, 1976), 85.
28. Sullivan, *Magisterium*, 157.
29. Karl Rahner, "On the Encyclical *Humanae Vitae*," in *Theological Investigations*, trans. David Bourke, vol. 11 (New York: Seabury Press, 1974), 271-272.
30. James T. O'Connor, *The Gift of Infallibility* (Boston: St. Paul Editions, 1986), 115-116.
31. John Paul II, Address to the Pontifical Academy of Sciences, October 31, 1993, *Origins*, 22:22 (November 12, 1993), 372.
32. Avery Dulles, *The Reshaping of Catholicism* (San Francisco: Harper & Row Publishers, 1988), 101.
33. Joseph Ratzinger, June 26, 1990, *L'Osservatore Romano*, 27 (July 2, 1990), 5.
34. Avery Dulles, *The Craft of Theology* (New York: Crossroad Publishing Company, 1992), 113-114.

35. Compare the statements of Pius XII's *Mystici corporis Christi* (#14, #40-41) and *Humani generis* (#27), which identify the mystical body of Christ exclusively with the Catholic Church, and Vatican II's *Lumen gentium*, which does not (#8). See Francis A. Sullivan, *The Church We Believe In: One, Holy, Catholic and Apostolic* (New York: Paulist Press, 1988), 3-33.
36. John T. Noonan, "Development in Moral Doctrine," *Theological Studies*, 54:4 (1993), 667-668.
37. American Bishops, *The Teaching Ministry of the Diocesan Bishop: A Pastoral Reflection* (Washington, D.C.: National Conference of Catholic Bishops, 1992), 15.
38. Karl Rahner, "Magisterium and Theology," in *Theological Investigations*, trans. Edward Quinn, vol. 18 (New York: Crossroad Publishing Company, 1983), 57.
39. Joseph Ratzinger, "The Limits of Church Authority," *L'Osservatore Romano*, 26 (June 29, 1994), 6-7.
40. John Paul II, Discourse, March 10, 1993, *L'Osservatore Romano*, 11 (March 17, 1993), 11.
41. "Presentation of Letter," *L'Osservatore Romano*, 22 (June 1, 1994), 2.
42. Karl Rahner, *Theology of Pastoral Action* (New York: Herder and Herder, 1968), 116.
43. Karl Rahner, "Magisterium," in *Sacramentum Mundi*, ed. Karl Rahner, vol. 3 (New York: Herder and Herder, 1969), 354.
44. Germain Grisez and Russell Shaw, *Fulfillment in Christ* (Notre Dame: University of Notre Dame Press, 1991), 417.
45. Cf. DVE 16; DH 14; Paul VI, *Humanae vitae* (1968), #4.
46. Francis A. Sullivan, "The 'Secondary Object' of Infallibility," *Theological Studies*, 54:3 (1993), 544.
47. Rahner, "Magisterium," 353.
48. Karl Rahner, "*Mysterium ecclesiae*," in *Theological Investigations*, trans. Margaret Kohl, vol. 17 (New York: Crossroad Publishing Company, 1981), 146.
49. In the official Vatican versions, the number of pages of text in a sampling of recent papal documents: *Familiaris consortio* (167), *Dominum et vivificantem* (141), *Redemptoris missio* (153), *Centesimus annus* (114), *Pastores dabo vobis* (224), *Veritatis splendor* (179).
50. Sullivan, *Magisterium*, 165-166.
51. Dulles, *A Church to Believe In*, 127.
52. See the various contributions in *The Thought of John Paul II: A Collection of Essays and Studies*, ed. John M. McDermott (Rome: Gregorian University Press, 1993).
53. Örsy, *The Church: Learning and Teaching*, 50.
54. International Theological Commission, "On the Interpretation of Dogmas," *Origins*, 20:1 (May 17, 1990), #C.III.6, p. 13.
55. International Theological Commission, *Theses on the Relationship between the Ecclesiastical Magisterium and Theology* (Washington, D.C.: United States Catholic Conference, 1977), #5.1, p. 4.
56. John Paul II, Discourse, March 10, 1992, *L'Osservatore Romano*, 11 (March 17, 1993), 11.
57. *Acta Apostolicae Sedis*, 60 (1968), 433-445. Translation in *The Christian Faith in the Doctrinal Documents of the Catholic Church*, ed. J. Neuner and J. Dupuis, rev. ed. (New York: Alba House, 1982), 22-29.
58. Francis G. Morrisey, "Papal and Curial Pronouncements: Their Canonical Significance in Light of the 1983 Code of Canon Law," *The Jurist*, 50:1 (1990), 108.

59. John Paul II, *Ad limina* Address to American Bishops, March 20, 1993, *L'Osservatore Romano*, 12 (March 24, 1993), 3.
60. J. T. Catoir, "Documents, Papal," *New Catholic Encyclopedia*, vol. 4 (New York: McGraw-Hill Publishing Company, 1967), 746-747; cf. W. M. Plöchl, "Diplomacy, Ecclesiastical," *New Catholic Encyclopedia*, vol. 4, 884-885; and A. H. Skeabeck, "Bulla," *New Catholic Encyclopedia*, vol. 2, 880-881.
61. John Paul II, *Letter to Families* (1994), #17.
62. John Paul II, *Centesimus annus* (1991), #35.
63. Francis A. Sullivan, "Magisterium," *The New Dictionary of Theology*, ed. Joseph A. Komonchak, Mary Collins, and Dermot A. Lane (Wilmington: Michael Glazier, 1987), 622.
64. Jerome Hamer, *To Preach the Gospel: The First Duty of the Bishop* (Washington, D.C.: United States Catholic Conference, 1979), 14.
65. Gianfranco Ghirlanda, *Il diritto nella Chiesa: mistero di comunione*, 2nd ed. (Turin: Edizioni San Paolo, 1993), 408.
66. Francis A. Sullivan, "The Theologian's Ecclesial Vocation and the 1990 CDF Instruction," *Theological Studies*, 52:1 (1991), 61.
67. J. Michael Miller, "The Pope: Religious Consultant or Chief Teacher?" *Homiletic and Pastoral Review*, 91:2 (November 1990), 14-15.
68. Paul VI, Discourse, August 5, 1964, *The Pope Speaks*, 10:3 (1965), 249.
69. Joaquín Salaverri, "Encyclicals," in *Sacramentum Mundi*, ed. Karl Rahner, vol. 2 (New York: Herder and Herder, 1969), 229.
70. Schatz, *Primauté du Pape*, 244-245.
71. Tillard, *Bishop of Rome*, 171.
72. Claudia Carlen, "Introduction," in *The Papal Encyclicals: 1740-1878*, ed. Claudia Carlen, vol. 1 (Raleigh: Pierian Press, 1990), xviii.
73. John Paul II, *Veritatis splendor* (1993), #75-82.
74. Congar, *L'Eglise de saint Augustin à l'époque moderne*, 455.
75. Editorial, "Il ministero del Papa dopo i due Concili Vaticani," *La Civiltà Cattolica*, 3249 (November 2, 1985), 217.
76. Schatz, *Primauté du Pape*, 244-245; cf. Joaquín Salaverri, *Sacrae Theologiae Summa*, 5th ed., vol. 1 (Madrid: Biblioteca de Autores Cristianos, 1962), #645-648; Paul Nau, "Le Magistère pontifical ordinaire, lieu théologique," *Revue Thomiste*, 56 (1956), 389-412; and Paul Nau, "Le Magistère pontifical ordinaire au premier concile du Vatican," *Revue Thomiste*, 62 (1962), 341-397.
77. Gustave Thils, *Primauté et infaillibilité du pontife romain à Vatican I* (Louvain: University Press, 1989), 305-307.
78. Sullivan, *Magisterium*, 155.
79. Pius XII, *Humani generis* (1950), #20.
80. Yves Congar, *Ministères et communion ecclésiale* (Paris: Cerf, 1971), 151.
81. For a list of those personally obliged to make the profession of faith, see CIC 833.
82. Congregation for the Doctrine of the Faith, *Origins*, 18:40 (March 16, 1989), 663; cf. CIC 752.
83. Germain Grisez, *Living a Christian Life*, The Way of the Lord Jesus, vol. 2 (Chicago: Franciscan Press, 1993), 46.
84. American Bishops, *Teaching Ministry of the Diocesan Bishop*, 14.

85. Sullivan, *Magisterium*, 164; cf. Sullivan, "Magisterium," 622; Örsy, *The Church: Learning and Teaching*, 88.
86. Sullivan, *Magisterium*, 162.
87. American Bishops, *Teaching Ministry of the Diocesan Bishop*, 15.
88. Sullivan, *Magisterium*, 34.
89. Rahner, "Dispute concerning the Church's Teaching Office," 96.
90. Grisez and Shaw, *Fulfillment in Christ*, 418-419.
91. Dulles, *Craft of Theology*, 111.
92. Örsy, *The Church: Learning and Teaching*, 96.
93. May, *Introduction to Moral Theology*, 216, 220-221; cf. DVE 24-41.
94. John Paul II, Discourse, March 10, 1993, *L'Osservatore Romano*, 11 (March 17, 1993), 11.

Chapter nine
PAPAL INFALLIBILITY

Having examined Catholic belief about the pope's ordinary teaching authority, this chapter analyzes his *extraordinary* magisterium, the *ex cathedra* pronouncements which he proposes infallibly. While much of what is said about infallibility also applies to the teaching of ecumenical councils and the universal ordinary magisterium of the episcopal college, this discussion deals specifically with papal infallibility.

After a brief look at indefectibility, the infallibility of the whole Church, and the origins of the doctrine of papal infallibility, a detailed analysis of chapter four of *Pastor aeternus* (1870), which defined papal infallibility, follows. In the light of Vatican I and II, official Church documents, and contemporary theology, I then treat the following questions in a systematic way. What is the object of papal infallibility? How are the faithful to respond to extraordinary papal teaching? Under what conditions can it be exercised? What role do consultation, consent, and reception play in an *ex cathedra* teaching?

Gift to the Church

Misunderstandings

Several common misunderstandings about infallibility should be cleared up at the outset. Not to be confused with impeccability, infallibility makes no claim regarding the personal sinlessness of the pope. Nor is papal infallibility equivalent to inspiration, which is the charism given to the biblical authors so that their writings contain without error that truth which God wished to confide to sacred Scripture (cf. DV 11). In addition, infallibility is not inerrancy, which is the *a posteriori* recognition that Scripture is free from error. On the contrary, when a doctrine is taught infallibly this gives certainty, from that time forward, that it is without error.[1]

Sometimes Catholic teaching on papal infallibility is misinterpreted as arrogance. To many, it suggests that the pope is somehow divinized by being deprived of the capacity to make mistakes which marks the human condition.[2] Non-Catholics frequently think that this doctrine shows a lack of confidence in the power of the Holy Spirit to maintain the Church in the truth. Instead of trust in God, they see Catholics as relying on the miraculous intervention of a *deus ex machina*, a pope who can propose doctrine infallibly. Catholics, however, see the matter differently. They understand that infallibility is "the supreme degree of participation in the authority of Christ" (CCC 2035), which is given to the Church so that the gospel will be preached in its integrity, a concern shared by all Christians.

To hold that a doctrine is taught infallibly does not mean that it is unchangeable in its formulation or that the timing of its definition was opportune. Like all statements of faith, *ex cathedra* teachings necessarily fall short of capturing fully the divine realities to which they refer. Changing historical and cultural contexts might well call for new formulations of the same truth. "It sometimes happens that some dogmatic truth is first expressed incompletely (but not falsely)," affirms the Congregation for the Doctrine of the Faith, "and at a later date, when considered in a broader context of faith or human knowledge, it receives a fuller and more perfect expression" (ME 5). Infallibility assures that no future doctrine, however, will ever contradict an *ex cathedra* definition. Whatever the Church has declared to be true remains part of her permanent witness to the gospel.

Ministry to the Truth

God wills that all people should be saved and "come to the knowledge of the truth" (1 Tim 2:4). The Church's magisterium has the function of preserving "the truth of the gospel" (Gal 2:5) for God's people. Speaking the truth in love to the Church (cf. Eph 4:15), the Spirit ensures that when the pope teaches infallibly he is free from error in his judgment. This allows believers to confront the truth which makes them free (cf. Jn 8:32).

When a doctrine is defined infallibly, it does not either "become" true or "more" true. Infallibility is concerned with the certitude it provides believers because of the way in which it is proposed to them. "Strictly speaking, therefore, it is the act of judgement which is infallible," writes the J. M. R. Tillard. "The proposition is true but it is guaranteed by the judgement of him who pronounces it."[3] A papal definition "from the chair of Peter" (*ex cathedra*) is not true because the pope teaches it. He teaches it because it is true. What changes when a teaching is proclaimed infallibly is the degree of certitude which the faithful have regarding it. When the pope teaches definitively, he gives the faithful full certitude that God's saving truth is being expressed. In this specific instance the pope professes the faith of the Church without error.[4] The exercise of papal infallibility therefore assures certainty about the truth which is taught. At the same time, this certainty is compatible with an imperfect knowledge of that truth.[5]

Indefectibility of the Church

Indefectibility is the belief that until the end of time the Church will remain in existence and preserve her fidelity to the truth of the gospel. The Church will never succumb to worldly or demonic hostility which would betray her essence or destroy her faith. She will endure until the *parousia*, even if as a small flock which has kept the apostolic faith. This indefectibility is based on Christ's promise and the Spirit's perpetual guidance of the Church (cf. Jn 14:16-17, 15:26, 16:13). Because "Jesus Christ is Lord" (Phil 2:11), he has won a decisive victory over the powers of hell, and no enemy will triumph over him.[6] The Holy Spirit guarantees "that in the Church there will always continue *the same truth* which the apostles heard from their Master."[7]

Christians believe that the Spirit abides in the Church to protect the integrity of the gospel through the ages. However, they do not agree on how he guarantees this indefectibility. To believe that, despite serious errors here and there in her dogma, she has nonetheless remained on the right road would compromise Catholic teaching. To hold that there can be error in infallibly proposed teaching is incompatible with the Church's faith (cf. ME 3). Catholics recognize that the successors to the apostles have the particular mission of guaranteeing the truthfulness of the original revelation. Moreover, among the bishops, the successor of Peter is entrusted with a personal charism of giving voice to the Church's infallibility.

Infallibility in Believing

Papal infallibility is rooted in the infallibility of the Church. All recent ecclesiastical documents dealing with the magisterium repeat that the entire Church shares in God's own infallibility (cf. LG 25; ME 2; DVE 13). Ecclesial infallibility is not found in the pope alone and then communicated from him to others in the Church. It is the reverse. As a whole body, the Church is the repository of this charism. The pope is its privileged bearer for building up the body of Christ.

The fundamental conviction underlying the doctrine of infallibility is that "the universal Church cannot err, since she is governed by the Holy Spirit who is the Spirit of truth."[8] At the Second Vatican Council, the Fathers declared that "the whole body of the faithful who have an anointing that comes from the holy one (cf. 1 Jn 2:20, 27) cannot err in matters of belief" (LG 12). As a divine gift bestowed on the whole Church, infallibility allows her members both to believe fully and to proclaim integrally divine revelation.[9] This "sense of the faith" (*sensus fidei*) enables all believers, from peasant to pope, to adhere personally to the Truth.

God fashions the Church as a believing community which has this supernatural sense of the truth of the faith. Before the truth can be infallibly proposed by official teachers, it is lived by the faithful. The corporate presence of this supernatural gift in the community is the "mind of the Church" or the *sensus fidelium*. Because of the Spirit's guidance, this profound agreement among those who profess and live the same faith is incapable of error. Theologians often refer to this unerring witness as the infallibility of the Church in believing.[10] An indissoluble bond exists between this "passive" infallibility of the faithful and the "active" infallibility of the Church's pastors. While the former safeguards the revealed truth in its belief, life, and worship, the latter authoritatively judges that truth with Christ's authority.

The Catholic faith belongs to the whole Church, not to any group within her. In her entirety she is "the trustee of the word of God."[11] To his Church, God, who alone is absolutely infallible, has given "a certain shared infallibility . . . which is present when the whole people of God unhesitatingly holds a point of doctrine pertaining to these matters [faith and morals]" (ME 2). This infallibility of the believing community is not, however, an ecclesiastical variant of majority rule. Jerome Hamer points out that the *sensus fidei* is not the same thing as public opinion. "A group, however numerous it may be in the Church," he says, "can never claim for itself the guarantee given by the *sensus fidei*, for a group can always be mistaken and the past gives us an example of this."[12] Not every idea which circulates among the people of God is compatible with the Church's faith (cf. DVE 35).

God has promised infallibility to believers, that is, to those who are open to Christ and his Spirit, and who are living in full communion with the Church. It is a gift of grace. Those who cling to private beliefs or who identify only partially with the Church cannot lay claim to this infallibility in believing.[13] Consequently, the bishops and the pope must discern to what extent the true sense of faith exists among the faithful at any given moment. The people of God participate in divine infallibility together with, and under the guidance of, the Church's pastors, who are the authoritative interpreters of revelation (cf. DV 10). The Church's teaching authority sometimes has to judge what is presented as Christian teaching. In rarer situations, and under strict conditions, the pope makes this judgment by teaching *ex cathedra*.

Origins of the Doctrine

In the early centuries, Christians did not neatly distinguish between the pope's primacy of jurisdiction and his primacy in teaching. Nevertheless, as was discussed in earlier chapters, the bishop of Rome's obligation to defend orthodox teaching was essential to the papal ministry. He frequently settled doctrinal controversies that arose in the churches. When appeals came to Rome to ask whether a certain doctrine conformed to the apostolic tradition, it was the pope, the community's official leader, who settled the doctrinal controversy. In examining the people and movements which sought his approbation for their views, the bishop of Rome did not act as a theologian, but as a judge of orthodoxy.[14]

The outstanding record of the Roman church in defending orthodoxy was well recognized. St. Paul praised the Romans because their "faith is proclaimed in all the world" (Rom 1:8). This text was often invoked to justify the witness of the Roman community's faith as the standard for the universal Church. Since Rome was *the* apostolic see, the conviction developed there, but elsewhere as well, that the Roman church had consistently defended the purity of the apostolic faith.

Besides the claim that the church at Rome had, in fact, never failed in its witness to the apostolic tradition, a bolder idea developed. Some churchmen began to teach that the Roman church, with divine assistance, *could not* err in its teaching. Pope Gelasius (492-496) believed that if the see of Peter were contaminated with error, "which we trust could not be," then heresy could not be resisted.[15] Rome was *the* pillar of orthodoxy.

The theory of conciliar infallibility — that ecumenical councils could pronounce definitively on matters of faith — also supported the idea that some judgments of the pope could be free from error. By the end of the first millennium, it was universally acknowledged that if a council was truly ecumenical, then its solemn teachings were to be affirmed as true.[16] In similar fashion, the pope's doctrinal interventions at ecumenical councils were to be accepted because they witnessed to the inerrancy of the apostolic tradition preserved by the Roman church.[17] In light of her conciliar experience, the Church recognized that in the pope's decisive determinations he enjoyed the same kind of protection from error that she attributed to councils.

Another catalyst for the doctrine of papal infallibility was the interpretation given to the legal maxim that "the first see is judged by no one." Although the proposition originally concerned jurisdictional matters, it eventually came to be used to support the pope's primacy of teaching as well.[18] From the twelfth century on, theologians and canonists increasingly emphasized the decisive role of the pope in settling disputed matters of faith. To bolster their arguments, they frequently referred to the *Decretum* of Gratian (†1159). One of the principles he recorded stated that "it belongs to the pope to decide questions in matters of faith."[19]

High Middle Ages

Because of the experience of papal primacy, and building on the theoretical foundations already laid, by the mid-thirteenth century the West had developed a well-defined understanding of the pope's supreme teaching ministry. Theologians accepted that the pope had the authority, as St. Thomas Aquinas (†1274) held, to "decide matters of faith finally so that they may be held by all with unshaken faith."[20] If the situation warranted it, Thomas contended, the pope could issue, on his own authority, a doctrinal decision which guaranteed for the whole Church one and the same faith. Normally, however, the pope would render definitive judgments in matters of faith together with an ecumenical council.[21] On the analogy of a medieval university professor, the bishop of Rome could settle a dispute, after having heard the arguments for and against a given thesis. As Jared Wicks comments: "This suggests a magisterium that is not creative, but instead discerning and discriminating of the views of others, as it adjudicates a controversy over what is conformed to God's word of revelation received in faith."[22]

While Thomas did not use the term "infallibility" or say that the pope could teach infallibly, his writings imply this idea. Just as ecumenical councils could teach without error, so also could the pope formulate doctrines belonging to divine revelation.[23] Yves Congar concludes that in Aquinas we have "a first statement of what would soon become the theological idea, and six centuries later, the dogma, of the infallibility of the pontifical magisterium."[24]

At the end of the thirteenth century, controversies among the Franciscans over the nature of Christ's poverty introduced the term "infallibility" into theological debates. Peter Olivi (†1298) defended a thesis on infallibility: the pope's teaching in matters of faith and morals could be irrevocable. He argued in this way in order to safeguard the teaching of previous popes against later reversals by their successors.[25] From this point on, "infallibility" became a technical theological term, and the schools of theology increasingly favored the doctrine of papal infallibility. When faced by radical conciliarist theories in the fourteenth and fifteenth centuries, the pro-papal theologians and canonists advanced the opinion that the pope could personally exercise the same infallibility attributed to councils. During the Catholic Reform, St. Robert Bellarmine (†1621) and Francisco Suarez (†1617) both taught that papal infallibility was a doctrine proximate to faith. It also became the official position of the theology faculty at Louvain in the seventeenth century.[26] At the same time, especially in France, many theologians contested this development. Foremost among these opponents of papal infallibility was Jacques

Bossuet (†1704), an ardent defender of the dignity and rights of the episcopacy. He held that the bishops' agreement was necessary before a doctrinal determination of the pope could be imposed on the universal Church. This third of his Four Articles of the Gallican Clergy (1682) set the stage for Vatican I's debate on papal infallibility.

Definition of Vatican I

By the mid-nineteenth century, many theologians and other Catholic scholars, especially the ultramontanists, were calling for the definition of papal infallibility. They hoped that a strong affirmation of the papacy's spiritual authority would provide a bulwark against the evils of a free-thinking liberalism which they regarded to be the fruit of Protestantism and the French Revolution. The definition of the prerogative of papal infallibility, the ultramontanists believed, would serve this end.[27]

Chapter four of *Pastor aeternus*, which the council Fathers promulgated as the dogmatic constitution on the Church of Christ, is entitled "The Infallible Teaching Authority of the Roman Pontiff." It extends the pope's primacy, defined in chapters one to three, to his teaching office: "the supreme power of teaching is also included in this apostolic primacy which the Roman Pontiff, as the successor of St Peter, the Prince of the apostles, holds over the whole Church" (DS 3065). The bishop of Rome is therefore the Church's principal pastor and teacher. Concerning the pope's extraordinary magisterium, the First Vatican Council defined the following:

> It is a divinely revealed dogma that the Roman Pontiff, when he speaks *ex cathedra*, that is, when, acting in the office of shepherd and teacher of all Christians, he defines, by virtue of his supreme apostolic authority, a doctrine concerning faith or morals to be held by the universal Church, possesses through the divine assistance promised to him in the person of Blessed Peter, that infallibility with which the divine Redeemer willed His Church to be endowed in defining doctrine concerning faith or morals; and that such definitions of the Roman Pontiff are therefore irreformable of themselves, not because of the consent of the Church (DS 3074).

Debate

Far more than the debates about jurisdictional primacy, those concerning infallibility were spirited and intense. Here the division between the Minority and the Majority of the Fathers was more keenly felt. The latter, who comprised about eighty percent of the bishops, were frequently called "infallibilists."[28] They were persuaded that a pope with infallible teaching authority would be a stabilizing force for both society and the Church. Pius IX (1846-1878) encouraged them in this conviction. He expressly asked the council to add a chapter on infallibility to its statement on the primacy of jurisdiction.

Some of the Minority, while convinced of the doctrine of papal infallibility, thought the timing of the definition to be inopportune. Only a small group of them was uncertain about the dogma itself. Most of the Minority believed that the infallible teaching office resided in the body of bishops united to the pope. Whether the pope could teach infallibly without consulting the episcopate was, they argued, an open question.[29] Furthermore, the

Minority objected to isolating papal infallibility from a wider discussion on the nature of the episcopacy and the Church. With determination, they opposed any theory of papal infallibility which described it as absolute, unconditioned, or independent from the rest of the Church.

On July 18, 1870, the final vote on *Pastor aeternus* registered 533 *placets* and two *non placets*. Eighty-eight Fathers left the day before the roll in order to avoid publicly opposing the constitution. The two bishops who cast negative ballots immediately endorsed the definition. As soon as the voting was over, they accepted it without hesitation on their knees.

Vincent Gasser, bishop of Brixen in the Tyrol, was a leading member of the Deputation of the Faith. This commission had the responsibility of preparing the document on papal infallibility. After the Fathers had studied the first draft, the Deputation entrusted Gasser with drawing up an official explanation (*relatio*) which outlined in great detail the proposed definition. His four-hour speech, the longest at the council, provided the Fathers with background and commentary so that they would know precisely what they would be voting on. It is a measured statement, in the camp neither of the Majority nor of the Minority. Because this *relatio* is the most authoritative document available for interpreting papal infallibility as defined in *Pastor aeternus*, the following sections refer to it frequently.

Purpose

According to Vatican I, the purpose of infallibility is to ensure the Church's unity of communion in the apostolic faith. It is a charism given so that the pope might "jealously guard and faithfully explain the revelation or deposit of faith handed down through the apostles" (DS 3070). Gasser was clear in his report: "the purpose of this prerogative is the preservation of truth in the Church," and it is normally to be exercised when "scandals against the faith" arise (M 52, 1213).

The principal reason for issuing a papal definition is to preserve the unity and integrity of the Church's faith. Accordingly, *ex cathedra* statements are rare occurrences in ecclesial life. The popes, however, can also promote the unity of faith by solemnly defining a doctrine which is already peacefully believed by the people of God. This was the situation when the Marian dogmas of the Immaculate Conception and the Assumption were proposed *ex cathedra*.

Source

Infallibility is not based on the human factors of intelligence, shrewdness, or political maneuvering. Gasser pointed out to the Fathers that papal infallibility "rests on a special promise of Christ and therefore on a special assistance of the Holy Spirit" (M 52, 1213). He went on to say that the "principal or efficacious cause of infallibility is the protection of Christ and the assistance of the Holy Spirit" (M 52, 1225). This Spirit guides the Church "into all the truth" (Jn 16:13), saving her from ever obliging Catholics to believe false doctrine. The root of infallibility is "the fidelity of the Spirit: he cannot abandon God's chosen ones to falsehood."[30]

The Shepherd and the Rock

Infallibility involves God's own faithfulness to his covenant with the Church. It is a divine gift for preaching the gospel with certitude. This charism of teaching infallibly is linked with the Church's episcopal office, especially with that of the bishop of Rome, heir to Jesus' special promise of prayer for Peter (cf. Lk 22:31-32). Although canonical strictures precisely regulate the exercise of papal infallibility, it nonetheless always remains "an event of grace, a calling from Christ through his Spirit; it is a gift and presence of the Spirit in the whole Church."[31]

Charism of Assistance

Papal infallibility is "personal" insofar as it is an individual pope who enjoys the charism. But "in saying this we do not separate the pontiff from his ordained union with the Church" (M 52, 1213). The successor of Peter can use this gift of grace only as a "public person, that is, as head of the Church" (M 52, 1213). Vatican II teaches the same: when the pope makes a definitive judgment he does so as the supreme teacher "in whom the Church's charism of infallibility is present in a singular way" (LG 25).

The charism of teaching definitively does not belong to the successor of Peter as a permanent possession. Scholastic theology refers to this gift as an actual grace.[32] Because it is a charism, papal infallibility comes into play only when circumstances warrant its exercise. Not always "in act," it is operative in certain judgments. When the pope teaches *ex cathedra*, but only then, he will neither err nor lead others into error. For this reason, Vatican I avoids saying that the pope *is* infallible. It is more accurate to say that he *possesses* the charism of infallibility while exercising his office as supreme teacher.[33]

Theologians emphasize that the charism granted to the pope is one of assistance and not of illumination.[34] Gasser stated that "the infallibility of the Roman pontiff does not come to him in the manner of inspiration or of revelation but through a divine assistance" (M 52, 1213). *Pastor aeternus* itself speaks of the "divine assistance" promised to the pope (DS 3074). In making a definitive judgment, the pope shares in God's own infallibility, which is communicated to him for that specific purpose. At such times the successor of Peter is assisted by the Holy Spirit who enlightens his mind to know the truth and strengthens his will to propose it. This charism, says Kilian McDonnell, is "a *lux transiens* (a passing light) directed to that extended moment which is the defining process."[35] The special divine assistance embraces all the steps involved in reaching a judgment: from the time of its preparation to its solemn proclamation.[36] The charism works through all the normal channels of human effort.

By choosing the word "assistance" to describe the Spirit's influence on the pope when making an *ex cathedra* statement, Vatican I affirmed that papal infallibility is not the ability to "disclose a new doctrine by His revelation" (DS 3070). God communicates to the pope no new truth about which he was ignorant prior to defining it. The bishop of Rome defines doctrine as a believer and not as a revealer of new teaching. Consequently, a definitive papal statement cannot be the word of God in the way that Scripture is.

Origins, Development, and Mission of the Papacy

Arguments From Scripture

All parties at the council recognized that in some way the Church's supreme magisterium, as the decisive organ for transmitting divine revelation, could teach infallibly.[37] *Pastor aeternus* relies on arguments from Scripture and sacred tradition to furnish the foundation for its doctrine of papal infallibility.

Chapter four of the dogmatic constitution builds on the texts which the Fathers had already used in their definition of jurisdictional primacy in chapters one to three. With one exception, *Pastor aeternus* adduces no additional scriptural arguments to support its teaching on papal infallibility. The Majority argued principally from the Church's present awareness of her faith. This faith, they believed, accepted papal infallibility, and so the Majority interpreted the biblical testimony in this light.

The only Petrine text cited explicitly and in its entirety is Luke 22:32. Beginning with Leo the Great, this text was frequently interpreted to justify the pope's unique teaching office.[38] Despite Peter's denials, Jesus' prayer that the apostle's faith would not "fail" was believed to be efficacious also in his successors in the Roman episcopate. For the council Fathers, this Lucan verse furnished biblical evidence for the assertion that "this See of St Peter always remains untainted by any error, according to the divine promise of our Lord and Saviour made to the Prince of His disciples" (DS 3070).

In addition, there are allusions to the two other Petrine texts. Matthew 16:18 is in the background when the constitution states that the Church's unity of faith rests on her "foundation" so that she "might stand firm against the gates of hell" (DS 3071). The conciliar text also points indirectly to John 21:15-17, when it refers to "the whole flock of Christ" which is to be "kept away from the poison of error" and "nourished by the food of heavenly doctrine" (DS 3071). Both allusions suggest that, according to the mind of the council, Peter needed to have the power to teach infallibly so that he could carry out his mission. While papal infallibility is without explicit support in the New Testament, Scripture nonetheless contains the necessary "seminal factors." These led to the conclusion that its later development is in continuity with Christ's promises to Peter.[39]

Arguments From Tradition

Pastor aeternus relies sparingly on the testimony of the Church Fathers to uphold its definition of the extraordinary papal magisterium. Gasser nonetheless referred to the support they provided for the council's teaching on papal infallibility (cf. M 52, 1207-1208). They are, so to speak, in the background of the definition. From the council Fathers' interventions in this regard, it seems that they believed that the pope's primacy of teaching had been accepted without contestation until the appearance of conciliarism in the fourteenth century.[40] The Majority held that the collective testimony of the Church Fathers confirmed not only the pope's primacy of jurisdiction but also his primacy of teaching. While contemporary scholars are more cautious about detecting irrefutable proofs in the patristic sources, these venerable texts still provide valuable testimony about Rome's early teaching authority. The writers of the ancient Church regarded communion with the see of Peter as a reliable guarantee for knowing the truth of the apostolic faith.

According to the council Fathers, the weightiest argument for their teaching on papal infallibility was the witness provided by ecumenical councils. These references were included in the final version of chapter four. As proofs for the Church's long-standing teaching on papal infallibility, *Pastor aeternus* selected statements from three councils: Constantinople IV (869-870), Lyons II (1274), and Florence (1439). Although the Orthodox no longer recognized them as truly ecumenical, churches from the East had participated in all three councils. For the drafters of *Pastor aeternus*, each one attests to the pope's infallible teaching authority.

As requested by the Roman delegates, the Fathers at Constantinople IV all signed the profession of faith drawn up by Pope Hormisdas (514-523). The Pope had sent the text to Constantinople in 515 in order to end the Acacian schism. This statement affirmed that "in the apostolic See the Catholic religion has been kept unsullied, and its teaching kept holy [DS 363]" (DS 3066). The First Vatican Council also invoked the confession of faith professed at the Second Council of Lyons, which attributed a primacy in teaching to the Roman church. Disputes about the faith, Lyons II asserted, had to be judged by Rome: "And, as she is bound above all to defend the truth of faith, so too, if any questions should arise regarding the faith, they must be decided by her judgment [DS 861]" (DS 3067). The Fathers at Vatican I interpreted this right of the pope to resolve disputes in such a way that it involved the irrevocability of his judgment. Lastly, they invoked evidence from the Council of Florence. Its statement that "the Roman Pontiff is the true vicar of Christ, the head of the whole Church, father and teacher of all Christians" (DS 3068) implicitly defined, they believed, the doctrine of papal infallibility. According to Vatican I, therefore, the teaching of these three ecumenical councils warranted the council's conviction that Rome had assumed and been granted a supreme magisterium in the Church.

Object of Papal Infallibility

What is the scope of the bishop of Rome's privilege to teach definitively? *Pastor aeternus* put it this way: The pope possesses "that infallibility with which the divine Redeemer willed his Church to be endowed in defining doctrine concerning faith and morals" (DS 3074). Whereas the primacy of jurisdiction extends to matters of discipline and government, as well as of faith and morals (cf. DS 3064), the charism of infallibility is limited to teaching truths which must be believed or held.

According to the Second Vatican Council, "this infallibility, however, with which the divine Redeemer willed his Church to be endowed in defining doctrine pertaining to faith and morals is co-extensive with the deposit of revelation, which must be religiously guarded and loyally and courageously expounded" (LG 25). Whatever the scope of the Church's infallibility, this is also true for that of the pope. He enjoys the same infallibility which Christ promised to his Church. By distinguishing the sources of a particular doctrine and the kind of response it is to be given, theologians have differentiated primary from secondary objects of *ex cathedra* teaching.

Primary Objects

Whatever has been *revealed* for our salvation, whether written in Scripture or handed on in tradition, the pope can propose infallibly. Only revealed truths, whether they pertain to matters of faith or of moral life, are primary objects of infallible teaching. While the entire deposit of faith was not explicitly affirmed by the Church from the beginning, it was there at least implicitly. All Catholic theologians agree that the pope can teach *ex cathedra* on matters contained in the revealed deposit of faith.

Secondary Objects

Teachings which are not revealed in the deposit of faith but are intimately tied to revelation and judged necessary for its preservation and explanation are called secondary objects of infallibility.[41] Concerning these secondary objects, Sullivan says that "it is common Catholic doctrine that the infallibility of the magisterium is engaged when it speaks in a definitive way about truths which, though not in themselves revealed, have a necessary connection with revealed truth."[42] Most, but not all, theologians would include the following as secondary objects. First, the pope could use his charism of infallibility to judge to be erroneous a proposition which is contrary to revealed truth. Second, some truths of their very nature are intimately tied to foundational revelation itself. Third, certain kinds of historical facts could also be the object of *ex cathedra* teaching. It might be necessary, for example, to determine which councils are truly ecumenical or to pronounce on the validity of a papal election.[43]

The First Vatican Council expressly refrained, however, from putting forward as a dogma of faith that the pope could propose such secondary teachings *ex cathedra*. According to the bishops, it was only "theologically certain" that the charism of papal infallibility extends to these secondary objects.[44] While officially the Fathers excluded as possible objects of papal infallibility matters not revealed in the deposit of faith, most believed that they could be infallibly proposed. According to Bishop Gasser, for example, the pope can teach such truths infallibly insofar as they are *"required* [my emphasis] in order to guard fully, explain properly, and define efficaciously the very deposit of faith" (M 52, 1226). Furthermore, in their definition the Fathers left unsettled the possibility for a future development along this line. Quite deliberately, *Pastor aeternus* says that a doctrine taught *ex cathedra* must be "held" (DS 3074). By avoiding the verb "believed," a term used only for the assent of faith given to divine revelation, the bishops did not rule out that secondary objects could be infallibly proposed.[45]

At the Second Vatican Council, the question of secondary objects of infallibility was again discussed. In its report on *Lumen gentium* 25, the Theological Commission affirmed that it excluded limiting the object of infallibility to what was directly revealed. The Commission's report explained that the object of infallibility "extends to all those things, and only to those, which pertain directly to the revealed deposit itself, or are required in order that the same deposit may be religiously safeguarded and faithfully expounded."[46] In the final formulation of *Lumen gentium* the object of infallibility was abbreviated to what "is co-extensive with the deposit of revelation, which must be religiously guarded and loyally and courageously expounded" (LG 25). Without formally defining it, the Second Vatican Council teaches that the object of infallibility includes truths necessary to safeguard the deposit of revelation, even if they are not themselves revealed either explicitly or implicitly.[47] Because the Fathers wanted to leave open the possibility of rejecting with certitude new errors opposed to revealed truth, they were deliberately less restrictive.

The conciliar position was later confirmed and clarified in the 1973 declaration *Mysterium ecclesiae* of the Congregation for the Doctrine of the Faith: "According to Catholic doctrine, the infallibility of the Church's magisterium extends not only to the deposit of faith but also to those matters without which that deposit cannot be rightly preserved and expounded" (ME 3). In its 1990 instruction *Donum veritatis*, the Congregation again took up the question of the secondary objects of infallibility. It appears to expand the secondary object of infallibility to what is "intimately connected" with revelation rather than to what is "necessary" to defend it. The instruction states: "By its nature, the task of religiously guarding and loyally expounding the deposit of divine revelation (in all its integrity and purity), *implies* [my emphasis] that the magisterium can make a pronouncement 'in a definitive way' on propositions which, even if not contained among the truths of faith, are nonetheless intimately connected with them, in such a way, that the definitive character of such affirmations derives in the final analysis from revelation itself" (DVE 16, cf. 23). The *Catechism of the Catholic Church* cites *Mysterium ecclesiae* when it states that infallibility "extends to all those elements of doctrine, including morals, without which the saving truths of the faith cannot be preserved, explained, or observed" (CCC 2035, cf. 2051).

Francis Sullivan summarizes what most theologians propose: secondary objects of infallibility are limited "to what is strictly required in order for the magisterium to be able to defend or explain some revealed truth."[48] It is, then, common teaching, though not itself defined, that the pope can teach *ex cathedra* on these secondary objects. He does so if they have a "necessary connection" (CCC 88) to the truths of revelation, in order to preserve, defend, or explain the integrity of the deposit of faith. Pope John Paul II has said that "the reason for *ex cathedra* definitions is almost always to give this certification to the truths that are to be believed as belonging to the 'deposit of faith'."[49] Consequently, papal interventions at the highest level which concern secondary matters of infallibility will be very rare.

Infallibility and Moral Teaching

At the Second Vatican Council, the Fathers stated that the Church could teach authoritatively on questions of the natural moral law. She can "declare and confirm by her authority the principles of the moral order which spring from human nature itself" (DH 14). The competence of the magisterium extends to questions not explicitly revealed but knowable by natural reason. The *Catechism of the Catholic Church* reaffirms the magisterium's right to teach on "specific precepts of the *natural law*" (CCC 2036). But can such matters be taught infallibly?

In *Pastor aeternus*, the First Vatican Council did not define what was included by the term "morals." The expression "faith and morals," Gasser noted, "is very well known, and every theologian knows what is to be understood by these words" (M 52, 1224). It seems that nineteenth-century theologians understood the term "morals" to include specific norms of natural morality.[50]

Insofar as the principles and some specific precepts of the natural moral law are revealed, as in the Decalogue, then they are primary objects of infallibility. *Donum veritatis* states that "it is a doctrine of faith that these moral norms [contained in revelation] can be infallibly taught by the magisterium" (DVE 16). If a specific norm of the natural law is contained in the deposit of faith, the pope could, therefore, teach it *ex cathedra*. Such questions include, for example, the prohibitions against adultery or fornication. Because these norms are revealed, they belong within the scope of papal infallibility.[51]

Because it is theologically certain that the object of infallibility extends to matters necessarily connected with revelation, some theologians argue that this might also include moral norms not found in divine revelation. Just as there are secondary objects of infallibility on questions of faith, they argue, so can there be on moral norms deriving from the non-revealed natural law.[52] This, however, is a theological position which has not been officially endorsed by the magisterium and remains a disputed question in contemporary theology.

Response to Extraordinary Papal Teaching

Catholics are required to give the pope's *ex cathedra* teaching a response commensurate with the object of the teaching.

• *PRIMARY OBJECTS* When the pope proposes a doctrine whose contents are a primary object of infallibility, then such an *ex cathedra* teaching pertains to what is revealed. Consequently, it calls for the believer's "obedience of faith" (Rom 16:26). By such an act of surrender, "man freely commits his entire self to God, making 'the full submission of his intellect and will to God who reveals' [DS 3008]" (DV 5). The act of faith is not directed to the pope who is now teaching but to God who has spoken: what is taught belongs to the deposit of faith.[53] In theological terminology, an *ex cathedra* judgment is "to be believed with divine and Catholic faith" (DS 3011). It requires from the faithful an assent which is irrevocable and unconditional (cf. CCC 88, 750). To dissent from an infallibly proposed judgment "knowingly, obstinately, and publicly is heresy and separates the dissenter from the Church."[54]

• *SECONDARY OBJECTS* Whereas the response of "divine faith" is accorded to what the pope teaches as belonging to the apostolic deposit, "firm acceptance" is given to what he proposes as a non-revealed *truth*. Recent magisterial documents scrupulously observe this distinction. A definitive judgment is proposed to "be firmly accepted and held" (DVE 23). It cannot, strictly speaking, be "believed," since the truth proposed does not belong to what has been revealed, though intimately connected to the deposit of faith and required for its defense or explanation.

The current profession of faith, taken by various persons with official functions in the Church, respects the distinction between the kinds of response given to revealed and non-revealed truths. Whatever has been divinely revealed, an individual is to "believe with firm faith." All that the Church proposes "definitively with regard to teaching concerning faith and morals," one is to "firmly accept and hold."[55] When the pope proposes a non-revealed truth "in a definitive way," it is irreformable of its nature and calls for the irrevocable assent of the faithful.[56] While not the irrevocable assent of faith given to God who has revealed a particular doctrine, a Catholic must give firm intellectual assent to the proposition as true. As far as its meaning is concerned, such a statement is not open to revision.[57]

Conditions for Exercising Papal Infallibility

The Minority at Vatican I worked zealously so that the definition of papal infallibility would specify strict conditions to be met for an *ex cathedra* judgment.[58] Many of the Majority, on the other hand, defended what they called "absolute" papal infallibility. Opposing the last remnants of a Gallican ecclesiology, these infallibilists were reluctant to place any restrictions on the exercise of papal infallibility. They had total confidence that the Holy Spirit and the pope's wisdom would prevent any arbitrary use of the prerogative.[59] Gasser, however, rejected the Majority's view. "In no sense is pontifical authority absolute; because absolute infallibility belongs to God alone, who is the first and essential truth and who is never able to deceive or be deceived. All other infallibility, which is communicated for a specific purpose, has its limits and its conditions. The same is valid in reference to the infallibility of the Roman pontiff" (M 52, 1214).

According both to *Pastor aeternus* and to later theologians who explained its teaching, the successor of Peter must meet precise conditions in order that a teaching be considered *ex cathedra*. Each of the following six stipulations must be fulfilled if the bishop of Rome is to propose a doctrine infallibly.

• *UNIVERSAL TEACHER*   When he is defining, the pope must be "acting in the office of shepherd and teacher of all Christians" (DS 3074). In rendering a solemn judgment, he is not exercising his authority as a private theologian. Nor is he acting as pastor of the local Roman church as when, for example, he decides a diocesan policy regarding the age of confirmation. Furthermore, he is not exercising his rights as patriarch of the West, as he does in regulating the Latin liturgy.

• *SUPREME APOSTOLIC AUTHORITY*   In his extraordinary magisterium, the bishop of Rome acts "by virtue of his supreme apostolic authority" (DS 3074), putting the whole weight of the Petrine ministry behind his assertion. Frequently the pope addresses the entire Church, but without using the full apostolic authority which only he can exercise. Whether he is invoking his supreme power as successor of Peter is evident in the document itself. Here he employs a formula such as "by the authority of our Lord Jesus Christ, of the blessed apostles Peter and Paul, and by our own authority." Pius XII used this form when he defined Mary's Assumption (cf. DS 3903).

• *PERSONAL*   An *ex cathedra* teaching must be the act of an individual pope who is acting in his public office as successor of Peter. In this sense, papal infallibility is personal.

Gallican theorists, who were well known to the Fathers at Vatican I, held that either the teaching of the Roman *church* or that of a sequence of popes over time could be infallible. Some theologians at the time of Vatican I defended the opinion that an individual pope could err, but a whole series of popes or the long-term doctrinal continuity of the Roman see could not. In this view an individual pope would not exercise the charism of infallibility. Vatican I expressly excluded the opinion which understood the subject of infallibility to be the Roman church as opposed to an individual bishop of Rome (cf. M 52, 1212).

While not defined in *Pastor aeternus*, the Fathers recognized that the pope had to be free from coercion in making an infallible judgment. This freedom guarantees the personal nature of his act. A decision taken while under physical coercion or in a state of mental duress or incompetency cannot be proposed *ex cathedra*. Furthermore, as a truly personal act, whatever the pope defines must follow from his own grasp of the doctrine. American theologian Peter Chirico comments that "one cannot get the pope to approve infallibly a statement that he has not understood or assimilated."[60] This is why it is imperative to discover the "mind of the pope" in order to interpret an *ex cathedra* teaching.

• INTENTION TO DEFINE   The bishop of Rome must intend to "define" a certain teaching for it to be definitive (cf. DS 3074). In other words, he must want to make a final judgment which forever binds the entire Church: a decision from which there is no appeal. In his *relatio*, Gasser explained that "there is required the manifest intention of defining doctrine, either of putting an end to a doubt about a certain doctrine or of defining a thing, giving a definitive judgement and proposing that doctrine as one which must be held by the universal Church" (M 52, 1225). More than a mere verbalization of a wish, a definition must proceed from the pope's will. His mere wanting to teach a truth of faith or morals is insufficient by itself. He must also engage his authority in such a way that he settles a question by pronouncing a definitive judgment. The pope must will to issue a binding definition which is "to be held by the universal Church" (DS 3074).

• MANIFEST   The successor of Peter is obliged to make his intention to define explicitly known to the faithful. Canon law guarantees that there can be no uncertainty about whether he is using the charism to define a doctrine infallibly: "No doctrine is understood to be infallibly defined unless this is manifestly demonstrated" (CIC 749.3). How the pope chooses to make his intention known is left to his discretion. No particular exterior form or specific document is required to signal his will. What is important is that the pope meet the conditions for making an *ex cathedra* statement, not that he use a particular kind of document for its promulgation.[61]

This criterion ensures that the members of the Church will always know when they are bound by an infallible judgment of the extraordinary magisterium. Consequently, any guessing whether the pope has definitively settled a particular question is ruled out. Concerning statements before 1870, except for the dogma of the Immaculate Conception, theologians disagree about which papal teachings have met the conditions set down by Vatican I.

• *FAITH AND MORALS* The bishop of Rome is also conditioned by what matters he can teach infallibly. As we have discussed above, he is limited to questions of faith and morals.

Consultation, Consent, and Reception

To the necessary conditions which must be met for the exercise of papal infallibility should be added the moral obligations which accompany its use. The questions of consultation, consent, and reception give a fuller picture of what is involved in an *ex cathedra* judgment.

Vatican I and Consultation

No dogmatic or canonical provision is imposed on the bishop of Rome which requires him to consult either his brother bishops or the wider Church before teaching infallibly. This lack of a formal juridical restraint has sometimes misled people into thinking that the pope's supreme teaching ministry is isolated from the faith of the Church.

At the First Vatican Council, the Minority expressed its fear that the proposed definition would leave the impression that the pope was severed from the Church's faith. They wanted to insert into the definition of papal infallibility that, in the act of defining, the pope was doing so not only as head of the Church but as the spokesman of her faith.[62] Consequently, many Fathers from the Minority spoke in favor of obliging the pope to seek consultation from the bishops before defining a doctrine (cf. M 52: 68, 742, 746, 926). Since the pope does not enjoy any special "illumination," they wanted the conciliar dogma to contain a specific condition: he must consult the faith of the Church, to which the bishops give witness, before rendering a definitive judgment.

The Majority refused to make consultation of the bishops a *sine qua non* condition for teaching infallibly. In his report, Gasser supported them, rejecting the Minority's proposal that some form of prior consultation be required. He begged the Fathers not to write a moral condition compelling consultation into the definition, elevating the provision to a matter of dogma. Like the Majority, Gasser believed that the successor of Peter should be free to make rapid decisions when the Church's faith is at stake. He also argued that there should be no doubt whether the necessary conditions were met for an *ex cathedra* teaching, holding that the demand for consultation would make such a determination more difficult.[63]

Nonetheless, the pope's *moral* obligation to consult the faith of the Church is, Gasser conceded, a serious matter. He maintained that "the pope, by reason of his office and the gravity of the matter, is held to use the means suitable for properly discerning and aptly enunciating the truth.... These means are councils, or the advice of the bishops, cardinals, theologians, etc." (M 52, 1213). Before making a definitive decision, the pope discerns what the Church believes. He explores the witness of the Church's faith by using the means divine providence gives to him.

While granting that "the consent of the present preaching of the whole magisterium of the Church, united with its head, is a rule of faith even for pontifical definitions," Gasser denied that it could be "deduced that there is a strict and absolute necessity of seeking that consent from the rulers of the churches or from the bishops" (M 52, 1216). The spokesman for the Deputation of the Faith supported the Majority, confident that it was unnecessary to impose on the pope the strict obligation to consult anyone before he engaged his charism of infallibility. "For the protection of Christ and the divine assistance promised to the successors of Peter is a cause so efficacious," he reminded the Fathers, "that the judgment of the supreme pontiff would be impeded if it were to be erroneous and destructive of the Church" (M 52, 1214).

Consequently, the bishop of Rome is free from a strict and absolute necessity to consult the bishops before issuing an *ex cathedra* judgment. How he arrives at a definition cannot be regulated beforehand by legal norms that would require either prior episcopal consultation or subsequent approval.[64] In no sense, however, did *Pastor aeternus* suggest that the pope was independent of the witness of tradition or the faith of the Church. The Majority understood that before defining a matter of faith, the pope is morally obliged to consult the rest of the Church.[65] In the end, the First Vatican Council left open how the pope should seek input before coming to a decision.

Marian Definitions

Ecclesial practice has verified the pope's moral obligation to consult the bishops before making an *ex cathedra* definition. Pius IX (1846-1878) and Pius XII (1939-1958) both took counsel with the worldwide episcopate before exercising their infallible teaching office. In 1849, Pius IX wrote to all bishops regarding the possibility and timeliness of the definition of Mary's Immaculate Conception: "We wish to know what you yourselves, in your wise judgment, think and desire on this matter."[66] Referring to this papal consultation in his report, Gasser commented that "such a case, however, is not able to be established as a rule" (M 52, 1217).

Even so, in 1946 Pius XII followed Pius IX's example by seeking input from the universal episcopate. Before defining the Assumption of Mary, he wrote to the bishops: "We wish to know if you, venerable brethren, with your learning and prudence consider that the bodily Assumption of the immaculate Blessed Virgin can be proposed as a dogma of faith, and whether in addition to your wishes this is desired by your clergy and people."[67] When he defined the dogma *ex cathedra* in 1950, Pius referred to the results of this massive consultation: "the bishops from all over the world ask almost unanimously that the truth of the bodily Assumption of the Blessed Virgin Mary into heaven be defined as a dogma of divine and catholic faith" (DS 3902).

Both popes engaged in broad consultation with bishops and, through them, with the faithful. In each case the dogma was an "echo" of the doctrine of the Council of Ephesus (431) that Mary is appropriately called the Mother of God. Popular teaching, piety, and devotion had already "received" each of these Marian dogmas before their formal proclamation.[68] Nonetheless, the authority of papal teaching stems from the unique charism of the successor of Peter rather than from the fact of consultation.

Agreement With the Church's Faith

The Fathers at Vatican II inserted a statement on the pope's need to take appropriate measures before exercising his charism of infallibility: "The Roman pontiff and the bishops, by reason of their office and the seriousness of the matter, apply themselves with zeal to the work of enquiring by every suitable means into this revelation and of giving apt expression to its contents" (LG 25). Later, *Mysterium ecclesiae* again mentioned the need for inquiry. Before teaching infallibly, it said, the pope must study "with appropriate means the treasure of divine revelation" (ME 3). The pope is to use whatever resources are available to make a judgment concerning the timeliness of defining a doctrine and how best to express it. Karl Rahner has provided a list of what he considers to be "appropriate means" for the pope to use: constant recourse to Scripture, the work of exegetes, historians, and dogmatic theologians, living contact with the *sensus fidelium*, and concern for the hierarchy of truths, the spiritual and theological heritage of the East.[69]

The moral obligation requiring that the pope discern the faith of the Church before teaching *ex cathedra* belongs to the very nature of his charism. If he did not have recourse to the faith of the Church, this would imply that an *ex cathedra* judgment was the proclamation of a new revelation. According to Chirico, because the pope receives divine assistance rather than inspiration or revelation, he has the moral obligation to consult, among others, the bishops who are witnesses to the Church's faith. At least in some implicit way, the object of a papal judgment must already be in the minds and religious life of the faithful. It is never an expression of the pope's private opinion or belief.[70] Pope John Paul II has commented that the bishop of Rome "feels the need, one could say even the duty, to explore the *sensus ecclesiae* before defining a truth of faith."[71] Thus, the pope can teach infallibly only what the Church believes, even if that doctrine is not yet appropriated by all her members. Nonetheless, the need for the pope to determine the Church's faith is not the same as merely ratifying what the whole Church has already explicitly accepted.[72] Room must also be left for seeing the extraordinary papal magisterium as a prophetic charism. How he judges what the Church believes is the pope's own decision.[73]

Many contemporary theologians stress that it would be desirable to mandate broad consultation "as part of the process by which the Church teaches, even when it teaches infallibly."[74] Like the Minority at Vatican I, these scholars wish to spell out some specific steps which the pope must take before making an *ex cathedra* judgment. Tillard, for example, proposes that *ex cathedra* decisions should be made only when the whole body of bishops agrees that the apostolic faith is in danger. Additionally, the pope should take into account "all available means" of consulting the sense of the faith and the state of theological discussion.[75] Rahner also held that moral norms concerning consultation should "be more clearly articulated and codified today, even though the observance of these norms would not be open to legal verification by an authority higher than that of the pope."[76] According to him, consultation of the episcopacy should be canonically codified as a necessary condition to be met before the pope proposes a doctrine infallibly. Rahner defended his position by noting that if the pope were to define a matter opposed by the great majority of bishops, "this would amount to asserting that he had received a fresh revelation," a possibility excluded by both Vatican councils.[77]

Francis Sullivan points out a serious disadvantage if a morally unanimous consent of the episcopate were required prior to a definition. Such a legal norm would eliminate, he says, the possibility of an *ex cathedra* decision which could resolve a dispute among the bishops themselves.[78] As the primary visible watchman of the Church's faith, there are occasions, writes Walter Kasper, bishop of Rottenburg-Stuttgart, when the pope "represents the sovereignty of the gospel over the Church."[79] Whatever the methods he uses to discern the Church's faith, the outcome of such endeavors is always the result of a divine gift. It is never merely a human activity.[80]

Consent of the Church

The First Vatican Council also rejected the theological opinion that the subsequent "consent" of the Church was a necessary condition for the pope to teach infallibly. Probably the most contested phrase of *Pastor aeternus* is that the pope's *ex cathedra* definitions are "irreformable of themselves, not because of the consent of the Church" (DS 3074). This expression comes from the third of the Articles of the Gallican Clergy (1682). Pope Alexander VIII (1689-1691) condemned the following Gallican proposition: "In questions of faith the Supreme Pontiff has a principal role, and his decrees pertain to each and every church, but his decision is not irreformable unless it obtains the consent of the Church" (DS 2284). While not denying the infallibility of the whole Church, the Gallicans maintained that the pope could exercise this prerogative only if the bishops gave their subsequent approval.

Edmund Hill believes that this sentence of Vatican I on the irreformability of *ex cathedra* judgments "might be called the final defiant flourish of ultramontane victory over Gallicanism."[81] Thinking primarily in juridical categories, the Majority was ever anxious to assert the independence of the pope with respect to the other bishops. They assumed that the successor of Peter was somehow "above" instead of "in" the Church.[82] Through Bishop Pie of Poitiers, the Deputation of the Faith replied to the Majority's seeming placement of the pope above the Church. The spokesman rejected any view which would separate the pope from the Church when defining a doctrine. He commented that such a "decapitation" of Peter's successor from the rest of the bishops was unthinkable (cf. M 52, 26-27). Gasser's *relatio* furnishes the official meaning of the phrase: the juridical consent of the Church is not a condition which is either antecedent or consequent to a papal definition (cf. M 52, 1214).

A statement of the extraordinary magisterium is irreformable in the sense that it does not depend for its validity on the *a posteriori* juridical "consent" either of the episcopal college or of the Church at large. Just as the pope's primacy of jurisdiction gives him the last word in canonical judgments, so his primacy of teaching accords him the final judgment in matters of doctrine. For the Fathers at Vatican I, the certitude about the truth of a doctrine relied on Christ's commission to Peter and his successors rather than on episcopal approval.

Vatican II emphasized this same point, adapting the wording of *Pastor aeternus*. The pope's definitions, it stated, "are rightly said to be irreformable by their very nature and not by reason of the assent of the Church, in as much as they were made with the assistance of the Holy Spirit promised to him in the person of blessed Peter himself; and as a consequence they are in no way in need of the approval of others, and do not admit of appeal to any other tribunal" (LG 25). No higher Church authority exists which could ratify the pope's *ex cathedra* judgment.

The certitude attaching to a definitive teaching excludes the possibility of error in expressing the Church's faith. However, to hold that a papal definition is irreformable does not necessarily mean accepting its opportuneness. A teaching can be free from error but untimely. According to Rahner, a definition "can be uttered too hastily, couched too harshly, be of too little use for the real life of Christians or formulated against certain backgrounds of thought which make the obedience of faith unjustifiably difficult."[83]

Reception

Official promulgation of an *ex cathedra* teaching opens the way to the faithful's appropriation of a papal definition. The Church "receives" a teaching when she embodies it in her prayer, liturgical celebrations, spiritual and moral life, and theological writings. This reception neither confers validity upon a doctrine nor legitimates the action of the pope who defined it. But it "does declare and give witness," writes Granfield, "that a doctrine is beneficial for the entire Church."[84] Reception is a sure "sign" that the definition is a true expression of the Church's faith. It confirms what the Fathers at the Council of Chalcedon (451) said about Leo the Great's teaching. "It is the faith of the Fathers! . . . It is the faith of the Apostles! . . . It is the true faith!"[85]

The Second Vatican Council taught that "the assent of the Church can never be lacking to such definitions on account of the same Holy Spirit's influence, through which Christ's whole flock is maintained in the unity of the faith and makes progress in it" (LG 25). Reception of an infallibly proposed doctrine follows from the fact that what the pope defines is already, in the deepest sense, the mind of the Church. History shows that sometimes not everyone gives this assent. At the outset, a doctrine might even be contested. Nor is reception always immediately apparent; it can be a process which takes a long time. Faulty communications, failure to preach the definition properly, ignorance, and bad will are among the factors which impede the manifestation of its reception.[86] As the "living assimilation" of the dogma into the Church's life, reception points to the fruitfulness of truth.

◆

In the Church's certain teaching there is a foretaste of Christ's definitive victory over the "father of lies" (Jn 8:44). As God's Word made flesh, Jesus taught the word with supreme confidence. He was not ambivalent or uncertain about what he taught. At the same time, he frequently used parables and metaphors in his manner of teaching. The listener's response of faith was always dependent on the mystery of grace, a complex and profound work of God in the hearer's heart and mind, a fact which is no less true today.

From the apostolic age onward, Christians have been convinced that Jesus is forever united to his Church, faithful to his promise to send the Spirit of Truth from the Father (cf. Jn 15:26, 14:16-17). Because Christ is the revealer of God, his word of truth abides indefectibly in his body, the Church. Truth is not lost or obscured with the passage of time. Knowing that human beings are fallible, Christ left the bishops, and above all the successor of Peter, with the gift of infallibility in order to guarantee the Church's fidelity to the gospel through the ages. Infallibility is a divine gift which enables the Church to believe faithfully and teach with certainty the truths of revelation.

Entailed in the pope's universal pastoral mission is a specific teaching responsibility. Because the unity of the Church is primarily a unity in faith, the Petrine ministry first and foremost serves that faith. It is a primacy of faith for teaching the gospel. As holder of the Petrine office, the pope has the unique apostolic charism of personifying Peter's doctrinal mission of preserving and interpreting the gospel for the Church, as circumstances may require. At crucial times and in situations of pastoral need, he can make a definitive judgment, an *ex cathedra* statement. Such a judgment becomes part of the Church's permanent witness to the truth.

Catholics believe that there is an implicit biblical and patristic foundation for the doctrine of papal infallibility. Rome's emergence as the principal church in the West, the notion that no appeal from its decisions was possible, and the tradition of its untainted orthodoxy all prepared the way for the medieval formulation of the doctrine of papal infallibility which was later defined at Vatican I. The definition of *Pastor aeternus* is carefully worded and lays down strict criteria which the pope must meet before making an *ex cathedra* judgment. Without exception, all the necessary conditions must be fulfilled in order for the faithful to have the assurance that the pope is defining a particular doctrine.

Even if pressing needs of the day conditioned the formulation of the definition of papal infallibility at the First Vatican Council, it remains a truth of the Catholic faith. Christ gives this charism to the pope to assure that the successor of Peter will confirm the faith of the Church, feeding her with true doctrine. To be sure, papal infallibility is not among the most central truths of faith, such as the mystery of the Trinity or the Incarnation. Nonetheless, the doctrine of papal infallibility is a specific gift by means of which the pope fulfills his Petrine ministry for the good of the Church, "the pillar and bulwark of the truth" (1 Tim 3:15).

Notes for Chapter nine

1. Hans Küng, *Structures of the Church*, trans. Salvator Attanasio (New York: Thomas Nelson & Sons, 1964), 380.
2. American Lutheran-Roman Catholic Dialogue, "Teaching Authority and Infallibility: Roman Catholic Reflections," in *Teaching Authority and Infallibility in the Church*, Lutherans and Catholics in Dialogue VI, ed. Paul C. Empie, T. Austin Murphy, and Joseph A. Burgess (Minneapolis: Augsburg Publishing House, 1980), #13, p. 42.
3. J. M. R. Tillard, *The Bishop of Rome*, trans. John de Satgé (Wilmington: Michael Glazier, 1983), 174; cf. J. M. R. Tillard, *Church of Churches: The Ecclesiology of Communion*, trans. R. C. De Peaux (Collegeville: Liturgical Press, 1992), 281.
4. Leo Scheffczyk, *Il ministero di Pietro*, trans. Franco Ardusso (Turin: Marietti, 1975), 90.

5. Pedro Rodriguez, "The Primacy of the Pope in the Church," in *On Being Catholics*, ed. Charles Connolly (Houston: Lumen Christi Press, 1983), 63.
6. Francis A. Sullivan, *Magisterium: Teaching Authority in the Catholic Church* (New York: Paulist Press, 1983), 4-5.
7. John Paul II, *Dominum et vivificantem* (1986), #4.
8. Thomas Aquinas, *Summa Theologiae*, II-II, q 1, a 9.
9. John T. Ford, "Infallibility," *The New Dictionary of Theology*, ed. Joseph A. Komonchak, Mary Collins, and Dermot A. Lane (Wilmington: Michael Glazier, 1987), 517.
10. Patrick Granfield, *The Limits of the Papacy* (New York: Crossroad Publishing Company, 1987), 136.
11. Ladislas Örsy, *The Church: Learning and Teaching* (Wilmington: Michael Glazier, 1987), 45.
12. Jerome Hamer, *To Preach the Gospel: The First Duty of the Bishop* (Washington, D.C.: United States Catholic Conference, 1979), 2.
13. Leo Scheffczyk, "*Sensus Fidelium* — Witness on the Part of the Community," *Communio*, 15 (1988), 196-197.
14. Ludwig Hertling, *"Communio": Church and Papacy in Early Christianity*, trans. Jared Wicks (Chicago: Loyola University Press, 1972), 74.
15. Gelasius, *Letter*, 1.27; cited in Robert B. Eno, "Some Elements in the Pre-History of Papal Infallibility," in *Teaching Authority and Infallibility in the Church*, Lutherans and Catholics in Dialogue VI, ed. Paul C. Empie, T. Austin Murphy, and Joseph A. Burgess (Minneapolis: Augsburg Publishing House, 1980), 244, n. 12.
16. Sullivan, *Magisterium*, 87.
17. Klaus Schatz, *La primauté du Pape*, trans. Joseph Hoffmann (Paris: Cerf, 1992), 83-84.
18. American Lutheran-Roman Catholic Dialogue, "Teaching Authority and Infallibility in the Church: Common Statement," in *Teaching Authority and Infallibility in the Church*, ed. Empie et al., #18-20, pp 21-23.
19. Cited in Schatz, *Primauté du Pape*, 181.
20. Thomas Aquinas, *Summa Theologiae*, II-II, q 1, a 10.
21. Sullivan, *Magisterium*, 73-74.
22. Jared Wicks, *Introduction to Theological Method*, Introduction to the Theological Disciplines, vol. 1 (Casale Monferrato: Piemme, 1994), 104, n. 12.
23. Avery Dulles, *A Church to Believe In* (New York: Crossroad Publishing Company, 1982), 162-163.
24. Yves Congar, "Saint Thomas Aquinas and the Infallibility of the Papal Magisterium," *The Thomist*, 38 (1974), 103.
25. See the study of Brian Tierney, *Origins of Papal Infallibility: 1150-1350* (Leiden: E. J. Brill, 1972).
26. Yves Congar, *L'Eglise de saint Augustin à l'époque moderne* (Paris: Cerf, 1970), 386-387.
27. Sullivan, *Magisterium*, 94.
28. Schatz, *Primauté du Pape*, 230.
29. William L. Portier, "Church Unity and National Traditions: The Challenge to the Modern Papacy, 1682-1870," in *The Papacy and the Church in the United States*, ed. Bernard Cooke (New York: Paulist Press, 1989), 42.
30. Örsy, *The Church: Learning and Teaching*, 55.
31. Rodriguez, "Primacy of the Pope," 70.

32. Kilian McDonnell, "Infallibility as Charism at Vatican I," in *Teaching Authority and Infallibility in the Church*, Lutherans and Catholics in Dialogue VI, ed. Paul C. Empie, T. Austin Murphy, and Joseph A. Burgess (Minneapolis: Augsburg Publishing House, 1980), 284.
33. Gustave Thils, *Primauté et infaillibilité du pontife romain à Vatican I* (Louvain: University Press, 1989), 174; cf. J. P. Torrell, "L'infaillibilité pontificale est-elle un privilège *personnel?* Une controverse au premier Concile du Vatican," in *De doctrina Concilii Vaticani Primi* (Vatican City: Polyglot Press, 1969), 500.
34. Yves Congar, *Ministères et communion ecclésiale* (Paris: Cerf, 1971), 144.
35. McDonnell, "Infallibility as Charism at Vatican I," 285.
36. Thils, *Primauté et infaillibilité du pontife romain à Vatican I*, 175.
37. Avery Dulles, *The Resilient Church* (Garden City: Doubleday & Company, 1977), 124.
38. Eno, "Some Elements in the Pre-History of Papal Infallibility," 251.
39. Sullivan, *Magisterium*, 83.
40. Schatz, *Primauté du Pape*, 232.
41. Giandomenico Mucci, "La competenza del magistero infallibile," *La Civiltà Cattolica*, 3318 (1988), 21.
42. Francis A. Sullivan, "The 'Secondary Object' of Infallibility," *Theological Studies*, 54:4 (1993), 536-537.
43. Sullivan, *Magisterium*, 135-136.
44. Stephen Duffy, "The Modern Period," in *Papal Infallibility: An Application of Lonergan's Theological Method*, ed. Terry J. Tekippe (Washington, D.C.: University Press of America, 1983), 72.
45. Karl Rahner, "The Hierarchical Structure of the Church, with Special Reference to the Episcopate," in *Commentary on the Documents of Vatican II*, ed. Herbert Vorgrimler, vol. 1 (New York: Herder and Herder, 1967), 210.
46. Cited in Sullivan, *Magisterium*, 132.
47. Rahner, "Hierarchical Structure of the Church," 212.
48. Francis A. Sullivan, "The Theologian's Ecclesial Vocation and the 1990 CDF Instruction," *Theological Studies*, 52 (1991), 56.
49. John Paul II, Discourse, March 17, 1993, *L'Osservatore Romano*, 12 (March 24, 1993), 11.
50. Germain Grisez, "Infallibility and Specific Moral Norms: A Review Discussion," *The Thomist*, 49:2 (1985), 268.
51. Grisez, "Infallibility and Specific Moral Norms," 248-287.
52. Mucci, "La competenza del magistero infallibile," 24-25.
53. Sullivan, *Magisterium*, 29.
54. Granfield, *Limits of the Papacy*, 155.
55. *Origins*, 18:40 (March 16, 1989), 663; cf. DVE 23.
56. Sullivan, "The Theologian's Ecclesial Vocation," 58.
57. Sullivan, "The 'Secondary Object' of Infallibility," 541-547.
58. Edmund Hill, *Authority and Ministry in the Catholic Church* (London: Geoffrey Chapman, 1988), 98-99.
59. Thils, *Primauté et infaillibilité du pontife romain à Vatican I*, 195-199.
60. Peter Chirico, *Infallibility: The Crossroads of Doctrine* (Wilmington: Michael Glazier, 1983), 145.
61. Umberto Betti, *La Costituzione dommatica 'Pastor aeternus' del Concilio Vaticano I* (Rome: Antonianum, 1961), 647.

62. Duffy, "The Modern Period," 64.
63. Schatz, *Primauté du Pape*, 235.
64. Chirico, *Infallibility*, 144.
65. J. Robert Dionne, *The Papacy and the Church: A Study of Praxis and Reception in Ecumenical Perspective* (New York: Philosophical Library, 1987), 340.
66. Pius IX, *Ubi primum* (1849), #6, in *The Papal Encyclicals: 1740-1878*, ed. Claudia Carlen, vol. 1 (Raleigh: Pierian Press, 1990), 292.
67. Pius XII, *Deiparae Virginis Mariae* (1946), #4; in *The Papal Encyclicals: 1939-1958*, ed. Claudia Carlen, vol. 4 (Raleigh: Pierian Press, 1990), 109-110.
68. Tillard, *Church of Churches*, 282-283.
69. Rahner, "Hierarchical Structure of the Church," 214.
70. Chirico, *Infallibility*, 243-244.
71. John Paul II, Discourse, March 24, 1993, *L'Osservatore Romano*, 13 (March 31, 1993), 11.
72. Dulles, *A Church to Believe In*, 139.
73. Sullivan, *Magisterium*, 104.
74. Granfield, *Limits of the Papacy*, 143.
75. Tillard, *Bishop of Rome*, 178; cf. Dulles, *A Church to Believe In*, 141-142.
76. Karl Rahner, "Pseudo-Problems in Ecumenical Discussion," in *Theological Investigations*, trans. Edward Quinn, vol. 18 (New York: Crossroad Publishing Company, 1983), 47.
77. Karl Rahner, "The Teaching Office of the Church in the Present-Day Crisis of Authority," in *Theological Investigations*, trans. David Bourke, vol. 12 (London: Darton, Longman & Todd, 1974), 15.
78. Sullivan, *Magisterium*, 105.
79. Walter Kasper, "Dienst an der Einheit and Freiheit der Kirche," in *Dienst an der Einheit*, ed. Joseph Ratzinger (Düsseldorf: Patmos, 1978), 99.
80. Johann Auer, *The Church: The Universal Sacrament of Salvation*, Dogmatic Theology, trans. Michael Waldstein, vol. 8 (Washington, D.C.: Catholic University of America Press, 1993), 293.
81. Hill, *Authority and Ministry*, 101.
82. Congar, *L'Eglise de saint Augustin à l'époque moderne*, 443-445.
83. Karl Rahner, "Magisterium," in *Sacramentum Mundi*, ed. Karl Rahner, vol. 3 (New York: Herder and Herder, 1969), 358.
84. Granfield, *Limits of the Papacy*, 149; cf. Tillard, *Church of Churches*, 282.
85. Tillard, *Bishop of Rome*, 177.
86. James T. O'Connor, *The Gift of Infallibility* (Boston: St. Paul Editions, 1986), 110.

Chapter ten
PAPACY AND EPISCOPACY AT VATICAN II

In the wake of the First Vatican Council, two trends in ecclesiology can be discerned. One interpreted *Pastor aeternus* in an ultramontanist way, frequently exaggerating the pope's role in the Church. Another delved into the sources of the faith by studying Scripture and the Church Fathers in order to recover the way in which the Petrine ministry was exercised and justified in the early tradition. This latter movement had a great deal of influence on the Second Vatican Council, providing the theological foundation for a renewed understanding of papal primacy. The doctrine on the papacy defined at Vatican I was subsequently incorporated into a broader vision at Vatican II, overcoming the legacy of a one-sided interpretation of the Petrine ministry.[1]

Among the principal ideas of the tradition retrieved by this "return to the sources" is the theology of episcopal collegiality. Collegiality expresses the unity and collaboration of the pope with the other bishops who together pastor the Church, both particular and universal. A second contribution of recent scholarship has been the development of an ecclesiology of communion. This, too, situates the primacy in a fresh perspective. Yet, as the debates and texts of Vatican II amply prove, a juridical presentation of papal primacy still has its place. The last council's attempt to reconcile the ecclesiological insights of the ancient tradition with those developed in the second millennium is the reason there are two different emphases in post-conciliar theology of the office of Peter.

This chapter looks at the papacy's mission in the Church as it was portrayed by the Fathers at Vatican II and has subsequently been explained by theologians and canonists. It focuses on how the council's teaching on the episcopal college has situated the pope's office in a new context. Among the topics I will address in order to describe this renewal are the complementarity of the teaching of Vatican II and Vatican I, the origins of collegiality, the characteristics of the episcopal college, and the subject of supreme authority in the Church.

Reception of Vatican I's Teaching on the Papacy

Although Vatican I defined the papacy in sober terms, after the council *Pastor aeternus* was frequently interpreted from an ultramontanist perspective. Tillard has coined a phrase which summarizes the vision of the papacy which theologians and others put forward: the bishop of Rome was presented as "more than a pope."[2] Without in any way compromising the doctrine of *Pastor aeternus*, Vatican II provided a broader framework within which it depicted the papacy in a fuller way.

Between the Councils

Because the First Vatican Council did not clearly delineate the rights and responsibilities of the episcopacy to balance those claimed by the pope, that council's teaching on the Church's hierarchical structure is incomplete.[3] By describing the pope's role in isolation from that of the bishops, the council made later misunderstanding inevitable. Among the factors which fostered an exaggerated view of papal primacy after Vatican I was the influence of Roman theologians, a "pyramid" ecclesiology, popular catechisms, and increasing administrative centralization.

The Roman schools of theology contributed to a maximalist interpretation of papal authority. With professors who were primarily Jesuits, Franciscans, and Dominicans — all of whom had long theological traditions of support for a strong papacy — the schools favored a lofty doctrine of papal primacy. The Roman theologians published widely, promoting an ecclesiology which stressed the pope's singular prerogatives in teaching and governing. Because many future bishops and seminary professors came to the various Roman institutions to study, the influence of these teachers spread throughout the world.

Theologians after Vatican I regularly compared the Church's hierarchy to a pyramid. All authority flowed from the top down, that is, from the pope to the bishops. They taught that episcopal consecration conferred the power of orders, with the office of sanctifying; but the power of jurisdiction, with the twofold office of teaching and pastoring, came from the pope. In other words, the bishop of Rome allowed the bishops to be associated with him in governing the Church; they did so as participants in his supreme jurisdictional authority. This view was expressed in the 1917 Code of Canon Law and by Pius XII (1939-1958) in *Mystici corporis Christi* (1943). In his encyclical, the Pope wrote: "Yet in exercising this office [feeding the local church] they [the bishops] are not altogether independent, but are duly subordinate to the authority of the Roman pontiff; and though their jurisdiction is inherent in their office, yet they receive it directly from the same supreme pontiff."[4] Insofar as the pope was the source of all power in the Church, says Seamus Ryan, "it is difficult to see how the bishops could be much more than subordinate functionaries."[5] A pastoral letter written in 1943 by the bishop of Strasbourg, France, provides a typical example of this pyramid ecclesiology concentrating on the papacy. The bishop referred to Pius XII as "the supreme head of the Church, first bishop of the diocese of Strasbourg."[6]

During the years between the Vatican Councils, theologians often described the relationship between pope and bishops in a way which minimized the episcopacy. Since the bishop was without "full," "supreme," and "universal" jurisdiction — attributes of papal power defined in *Pastor aeternus* — his inferior position was emphasized. While Vatican I provides no justification for this view, it nonetheless took hold. At its worst, a papalist ecclesiology created the impression that the pope was the only real bishop in the Church. A practical consequence of this attitude was the custom of looking only to Rome for spiritual guidance and authoritative teaching, by passing the bishop of the local church.

Hans Urs von Balthasar suggested that the majority of bishops at Vatican I might have intended to surrender some of their responsibilities into the hands of the pope. He regarded this abdication of authority as a "defective attitude," adding that the dogmatic formulation of *Pastor aeternus*, taken in such isolation, "totally lacks equilibrium."[7] A sign of this undue episcopal subordination to the pope was the practice of the Holy See to "grant" to the bishops numerous faculties and indults, even in very minor matters. Many privileges, having nothing to do with what is essential to the papal ministry, were reserved to Rome.

Popular teaching and catechisms of the late nineteenth and early twentieth century also frequently reflected a reading of Vatican I which separated the successor of Peter from the other bishops. These formative catechetical instruments placed a great deal of emphasis on the pope alone as *the* vicar of Christ. Innumerable catechisms stressed that he alone had the duty to carry out Christ's mission. The successor of Peter was regularly described as "taking the place of Jesus," thereby separating him from the other bishops. For many, the pope had the same role in the Church which Jesus had with respect to the original apostles. Such simplistic readings of *Pastor aeternus* dominated much catechesis and sermonizing after Vatican I.[8] It was also during this time that the pope emerged more markedly as a religious cult figure, a symbol of Catholic identity. This view reinforced the juridical centralization of the papal office. As the so-called "prisoner of the Vatican," who never left the tiny state in the heart of Rome between 1870 and 1929, the pope was both isolated and highly revered.

A strongly universalist trend in the world further served to emphasize the dominant role of the papacy in the Church. In the 1950s, the Jesuit canonist Jean Beyer wrote: "If in a world which is becoming one, the Church wishes to remain one, the papacy must speak, must speak often and must direct everything.... And as the national states disappear, the bishoprics will lose their sovereignty, leaving to Peter and his successors the general management of the whole Catholic movement, of all Catholic activity, of all apostolic work."[9] If the pope could, even should, do everything, what was left for the bishops? The same inflation of the papal office also occurred, as was discussed in chapter nine, with respect to its teaching ministry.

Vatican I at Vatican II

When the Franco-Prussian war led to suspending the First Vatican Council, a draft on the episcopacy had already been prepared to complement its doctrine on papal jurisdiction and infallibility. Because the document drawn up on the episcopacy could not be discussed, an ecclesiology lacking balance was the result.[10] The Second Vatican Council was able to complete the unfinished work of 1870, describing the Petrine ministry in a more comprehensive context.

With the renewal in biblical, patristic, and ecumenical studies, the Fathers at Vatican II had in hand the necessary tools to forge an updated theology of the papacy. This pre-conciliar scholarship unlocked the door for the Fathers to restore equilibrium to ecclesiology.[11] Furthermore, the influence of theologians who were not from the Roman schools, the increased awareness of Eastern theology, and the pastoral and ecumenical concerns which were surfacing left their mark on the conciliar documents.[12]

In light of the historical data known to the Fathers, the First Vatican Council defined certain essentials of the papal office. Vatican I's teaching on the primacy, which reflected how the nineteenth-century popes exercised their office, describes a fully legitimate way in which the Petrine ministry can serve the Church. Nonetheless, it is also important to recall, as Hermann Pottmeyer does, that *Pastor aeternus* refrained from defining that its teaching on papal primacy was the *only* justifiable way to describe the Petrine office instituted by Christ. It could not have made that claim "without disparaging the venerable tradition of the ancient Church to which it, in fact, appeals."[13] Consequently, the bishops at Vatican I did not intend to foreclose future developments in the theological understanding of the Petrine ministry.

Vatican I began its presentation of the Church's hierarchy with the papacy — and ended there. Papal prerogatives were portrayed "in terms of sovereign authority, the most urgent issue in a Church quite literally under siege."[14] Describing the pope's privileges primarily in legal-canonical terms inevitably reinforced the pyramidal view of the Church's hierarchical constitution. Vatican II, on the other hand, focused its discussion of ecclesiastical authority on the episcopal college. A major item on its agenda was the desire to enunciate clearly the doctrine concerning bishops as the successors of the apostles (cf. LG 18). Its discussion of the primacy takes place within the framework of the Church as the people of God and of the episcopacy. This point of departure differs from that of Vatican I because of its emphasis on the episcopacy and its ecclesiology of communion.

Chapter three of *Lumen gentium*, which describes the hierarchical structure of the Church, recaptured a traditional ecclesiology in which the episcopacy is central.[15] In portraying the Church's structure, Vatican II took its starting point from the bishops rather than from Peter alone. It replaced the conception of the ecclesiastical hierarchy as a pyramid with that of a circle or an ellipsis. Invoking this imagery, Pope Paul VI addressed the 1969 Synod of Bishops: "Collegiality inserts each of us into the circle of the apostolic structure destined for the edification of the Church in the world."[16] Papal-episcopal relations are no longer a one-way street where there is movement only from the pope to the bishops. Now there is also movement from the bishops to the pope. At the Second Vatican Council, the Church was presented "in its 'apostolic' origin and nature," writes Tillard, "with the bishop of Rome's function placed within that apostolicity which guarantees it but at the same time limits it."[17]

For the Fathers of the First Vatican Council the primary ecclesial reality was the universal Church, which was then divided into dioceses governed by bishops. According to the common interpretation of *Pastor aeternus*, the pope alone was responsible for the whole flock, exercising that office as the vicar of Christ and the pastor of the universal Church.

While remaining primarily within the universalist ecclesiology long dominant in the West, Vatican II took the first steps to reclaim the importance of the local church for a richer Catholic ecclesiology. The council described the Church as a communion of particular churches, a theme to be treated at greater length in chapter twelve. It also revived an ecclesiology of communion which brings together, as Granfield says, "two essential qualities of the Church — its locality and universality — as coherent aspects of

Origins, Development, and Mission of the Papacy

one and the same reality."[18] The Final Report of the 1985 Synod of Bishops stated that "the ecclesiology of communion is the central and fundamental idea of the Council's documents."[19] This ecclesiology lies "at the heart of the Church's self-understanding" (CN 3) and is key in describing the hierarchical structure of the Church. In similar fashion, when John Paul II promulgated the Code of Canon Law in 1983, he wrote: "the doctrine in which the Church is seen as a *communion* . . . therefore determines the relations which are to exist between the particular churches and the universal Church, and between collegiality and primacy."[20] Despite these post-conciliar views which attribute pride of place to the ecclesiology of communion at Vatican II, it must be admitted that in the sections where the Fathers of Vatican II dealt explicitly with the primacy, they only partially integrated the ecclesiology of the local church and of communion. With regard to the presentation of the Petrine ministry, *Lumen gentium* is still primarily dependent on a traditional universalist ecclesiology.[21]

These theological developments concerning the episcopacy, the local church, and the ecclesiology of communion furnish the context for Vatican II's reaffirmation of the teaching of *Pastor aeternus*:

> This sacred synod, following in the steps of the First Vatican Council, teaches and declares with it that Jesus Christ, the eternal pastor, set up the holy Church by entrusting the apostles with their mission as he himself had been sent by the Father (cf. Jn 20:21). He willed that their successors, the bishops namely, should be the shepherds in his Church until the end of the world. In order that the episcopate itself, however, might be one and undivided, he put Peter at the head of the other apostles, and in him he set up a lasting and visible source and foundation of the unity both of faith and of communion. This teaching concerning the institution, the permanence, the nature and import of the sacred primacy of the Roman Pontiff and his infallible teaching office, the sacred synod proposes anew to be firmly believed by all the faithful, and, proceeding undeviatingly with this same undertaking, it proposes to proclaim publicly and enunciate clearly the doctrine concerning bishops, successors of the apostles, who together with Peter's successor, the Vicar of Christ and the visible head of the whole Church, direct the house of the living God (LG 18; cf. CD 2).

The council Fathers could not have reasserted papal primacy more unequivocally. Chapter three of *Lumen gentium*, for example, mentions the primacy forty times, fourteen in paragraph twenty-two alone. Even so, the council left the door open to an innovative explanation of the papal ministry in the Church.

Papal Titles at Vatican II and Afterward

In the decrees of Vatican II and in post-conciliar magisterial documents, there is an evident shift in the titles used to describe the pope and his office. They are more biblical and less triumphalistic. At the same time, the titles relate the pope more closely both to the episcopal college and to the local church of Rome. While far from exhaustive, the following observations suggest the extent of this change in emphasis.

The conciliar documents continue to use the title "vicar of Christ," though very sparingly.[22] Without implying the monarchical theory of the Middle Ages, this usage highlights the singular responsibilities proper to the pope. In a certain way *Lumen gentium* relativizes it, by also applying the title, according to ancient usage, to the bishops, who are "vicars and legates of Christ" (LG 27). With conciliar teaching in mind, John Paul II once confided to the students of the Roman Seminary his views on this title: "The Pope is the Vicar of Christ for the Church of Rome and because of the vocation, because of the characteristic of this Roman Church, he is also Vicar of Christ for the universal Church. . . . I must tell you that I prefer not to abuse this title, and to use it rarely. I prefer to say 'Successor of Peter,' yes; but better still, I prefer to say 'Bishop of Rome'. That other title must be reserved for most solemn moments."[23]

Among the titles used for the pope in the documents of the Second Vatican Council are the following: "visible head of the whole Church" (LG 18); "pastor of the entire Church" (LG 22), "supreme pastor and teacher of all the faithful" (LG 25), "supreme pastor of the Church" (CD 5; AG 5), and the new title, "head of the college of bishops" (LG 22, 25; CD 4). Among the most common designations is "successor of Peter."[24] "Pope," on the other hand, appears only twice (LG 22, 23).

The designation most frequently given to the pope in the Vatican II documents is "Roman pontiff."[25] The Code of Canon Law follows suit. As early as the fourth century, the term "pontiff" was used synonymously with "bishop." Hence, the title "Roman pontiff" is equivalent to "bishop of Rome." It is, however, different from *pontifex maximus*, a pagan title which popes in the early Church sometimes used. With the demise of paganism in Rome, the title continued to be attributed to the highest religious authority, and the popes assumed it in the fifth century.[26] Only in the Renaissance, however, did *pontifex maximus* come into common use on monuments, coins, and in discourses addressed to the pope.[27]

The title "supreme pontiff" also frequently appears in the conciliar documents.[28] It translates the Latin *summus pontifex*, and was used from the fifth through the eleventh century to designate bishops. Even during this time, however, it was applied primarily to the bishop of Rome.[29] Today canonists, among whom it enjoys a long tradition, still often use this designation in their writings. "Supreme pontiff" also appears in the titles of encyclicals, in magisterial texts, and in certain discourses.

In the council's decrees, the title "bishop of Rome" is all but overlooked (cf. LG 22). This is probably because the Fathers identified the pope's role almost exclusively with the whole Church, even though he is never called "universal bishop."[30] While in the Code of Canon Law "bishop of Rome" is the first designation given to him (cf. CIC 331), it is then abandoned. The *Catechism of the Catholic Church*, on the other hand, uses it often.[31] However, unless citing other documents, the *Catechism* prefers the simple designations "pope" and "successor of Peter."

Origins of Collegiality

In the deliberations of the Second Vatican Council, some Fathers opposed the idea of episcopal collegiality, contending that it would jeopardize papal primacy by making the bishops independent of the pope.[32] The statements the council approved, however, provide no basis for the worry that collegiality would weaken the pope's doctrinal or governing authority. The majority of the Fathers were convinced that collegiality had a solid foundation both in Scripture and in Church tradition. Thus they declared: "Indeed, the very ancient discipline whereby the bishops installed throughout the whole world lived in communion with one another and with the Roman Pontiff in a bond of unity, charity and peace; likewise the holding of councils in order to settle conjointly, in a decision rendered balanced and equitable by the advice of many, all questions of major importance; all this points clearly to the collegiate character and structure of the episcopal order, and the holding of ecumenical councils in the course of the centuries bears this out unmistakably" (LG 22). Episcopal collegiality, therefore, rests on the foundation of the collegial nature of the original apostolic body and the subsequent practice of the ancient Church.

Collegial Traditions in the Early Church

Before the Council of Nicaea (325), bishops expressed their fellowship with one another in various ways in order to protect and verify ecclesial communion. Very early, what would only much later be called "collegiality" manifested itself in liturgical traditions. A particularly vivid embodiment of episcopal fraternity was the custom of the bishop sending a fragment of the Eucharist to neighboring bishops as a sign of the unity of his church with theirs. Another ancient liturgical-sacramental practice also showed the bonds of episcopal communion: the tradition of having at least three bishops from surrounding sees take part in episcopal ordinations, a custom mandated by canon 4 at Nicaea.

Other signs of brotherhood were more institutional. The practice of holding local synods or councils of bishops was already at work in the second century. Held with increasing frequency in later centuries, these regional assemblies, which regulated matters of faith and discipline, fostered unity and cooperation among local churches and their pastors. After the end of the age of persecution in the early fourth century, bishops from the whole world were free to gather in one place. At these ecumenical or worldwide assemblies, the whole episcopal college expressed itself as a corporate body, assuming doctrinal and disciplinary responsibility for the universal Church.

A further institutional support to cooperative activity among the churches was the establishment of metropolitan sees and patriarchates. Even before the Council of Nicaea, some local churches began to exercise influence over other churches. Reasons for this ranking of churches include the association of a church with a founding apostle, the number of a church's martyrs, the clarity of its learning and teaching, its generosity and wealth, and its political importance in the Roman Empire. Principal churches emerged which enjoyed certain privileges that allowed them to regulate the life of other churches in their sphere of influence. This, too, was a way of guaranteeing harmony in the universal Church.[33] The relations which developed among bishops within these new ecclesiastical provinces provide the clearest evidence in the ancient Church of episcopal collegiality at work.[34]

Another way of fostering communion in early Christianity was the custom of exchanging various kinds of letters among bishops. These letters contained information about liturgical calendars, celebrations, and doctrinal positions. Other letters were used to provide the faithful with a kind of passport which vouched for their good standing when they visited another Christian community.[35]

Through these and other ways of expressing their unity and cooperation, the bishops of the first centuries showed an awareness of their responsibilities not only to their own churches but also to the Church throughout the world. St. Cyprian (†258) summed up the sentiment which guided episcopal interaction. "All together we must look after the body of the whole Church," he wrote, "whose numerous members are scattered in the various regions."[36] At the center of this sophisticated network of communication was Rome. These early liturgical, institutional, and letter-writing practices all involved the church of Rome, the hub of ecclesial communion and episcopal collegiality. Its bishop received innumerable letters and, in turn, circulated them among the other churches. Commenting on this practice, Optatus of Milevis (†370) wrote: "Thanks to an exchange of official letters, the entire universe agrees and becomes one with the bishop of Rome in a society of communion."[37] The Roman see was the center to which the churches dispersed throughout the world looked for guidance and received assistance. Communion with the church of Peter and Paul was essential to ecclesial life.

Weakening of Collegial Bonds in the Middle Ages

For at least five reasons the collegial spirit which was so alive among bishops in the Church of the Fathers declined during the Middle Ages. First, with the rise of feudalism, bishops became more divided from one another, each one a lord in his own fief.[38] Second, beginning with the Gregorian Reform, the college of cardinals assumed an increasingly active role in the church at Rome; they shared with the pope some governing responsibilities for the universal Church. The solidarity of bishops among themselves remained very much in the background. Third, due to the development of a universalist ecclesiology and a monarchical vision of the papacy, the fraternal ties of bishops with one another and with the bishop of Rome took a back seat. Not *communio* but *plenitudo potestatis* was the controlling paradigm which dominated the thought of canonists and theologians.[39] They emphasized the individual bishop's direct and subordinate relation to the successor of Peter. Fourth, theology and canon law minimized collegiality by attributing no sacramental value to the episcopacy and by maintaining that the bishops were dependent on the pope for their jurisdiction. Both ideas eclipsed the more ancient sense of ecclesial communion and episcopal collegiality.[40] Lastly, although conciliarist writers in the thirteenth century resurrected the notion of corporate episcopal authority when they stressed that the bishops in council were superior to the pope, they sowed the seeds of their own undoing. With the defeat of conciliarism, the idea and practice of collegiality suffered a similar setback.[41] After the Reformation, Gallicanism had the same dampening effect on the development of a theology of episcopal collegiality. Some indications at Vatican I notwithstanding, it was only at Vatican II that the traditional idea once again took its rightful place in ecclesiology.

Origins, Development, and Mission of the Papacy

Characteristics of the Episcopal College

In its discussion of the Church's hierarchical constitution, the Second Vatican Council took the apostolic college as its point of departure. The Fathers taught in *Lumen gentium*: "Just as, in accordance with the Lord's decree, St Peter and the rest of the apostles constitute a unique apostolic college, so in like fashion, the Roman Pontiff, Peter's successor, and the bishops, the successors of the apostles, are related with and united to one another" (LG 22; cf. CIC 330; CCC 880). In its summary of the teaching of Vatican II, the *Catechism of the Catholic Church* says that "it belongs to the nature of ecclesial ministry that it have a *collegial character*.... Chosen together, they [the Twelve] were also sent out together, and their fraternal unity would be at the service of the fraternal communion of all the faithful: they would reflect and witness to the communion of the divine persons" (CCC 877). The collegiality of the episcopal college provides the framework within which the papal ministry is now to be situated.

The council applied the term "college" to both the original group of apostles and the body of bishops. Describing the order of bishops as a college is a usage dating from at least the third century.[42] Coming from Roman law, the term applies analogously to ecclesial structures. In the New Testament, the college of apostles is not "a group of equals who transfer their powers to their chairman." Rather, it is "a permanent body whose form and authority is to be ascertained from revelation" (NEP 1). The collegiality which exists among bishops is therefore a spiritual solidarity which derives from God's design for the Church.

How the Fathers understood collegiality can be clarified by comparing five characteristics of the episcopal college with those of the apostolic college: the college of bishops is one body, willed by Christ, primatially structured, and exists as a permanent group holding corporate authority in the Church. Each of these descriptive terms merits our attention.

One Body

Christ established the Twelve as a body. He did not simply select individuals who later decided on their own to group together; he founded them as a "college." Jesus "appointed" or "instituted" some of his disciples as the Twelve (cf. Mk 3:14). Peter and the other apostles thus formed one body in which all were members.

Like the apostolic college, the episcopal college is a permanent and single "collegial subject."[43] Between the apostolic and episcopal college there is a parallelism which implies not identity, but continuity, between them. On the one hand, the non-transmissible powers of the apostles, those proper to the Church's foundation in the age of revelation, are not found in the episcopal college. On the other hand, the same kind of relationship which existed between Peter and the other apostles now exists between the pope and the other bishops.

Willed by Christ

Not the result of either mere chance or practical arrangement, the apostolic college was established "in accordance with the Lord's decree" (LG 22). Christ willed that his apostles form a group. In point of fact, he brought them into being precisely as a single body.

The origin of the episcopal college lies in the same divine decision which established the apostolic college. Bishops do not form a natural community or become a body by their own choice to associate freely. Johann Auer calls the body of bishops "a supernatural community founded ... upon the very person of Christ."[44] The collegiality of the episcopacy, says John Paul II, "fulfills the will of Christ, as it comes to us in Tradition."[45] Because of this act of divine institution, the collegial nature of the universal episcopate belongs permanently and irreversibly to the nature of the Church. By divine right, therefore, the Church's essential ministerial structure is not only primatial, as defined by Vatican I, but also collegial, as taught by Vatican II.

Primatial Structure

Jesus founded the college of apostles with Peter as its head. The chosen leader was called, writes Louis Bouyer, "to express, guide, and foment their unity of action from within."[46] Peter was the chief shepherd united to the other apostles, all of whom were together subject to Christ.

Because it succeeds to the apostolic college, the episcopal college, too, is primatially structured. Like all other bishops, the bishop of Rome is a successor of the apostles. At the same time, he is also the successor of the particular apostle Peter, with tasks analogous to those of Peter among the apostles.[47] As the successor of the Rock, the pope is within the episcopal college, not outside or above it. The bond which links the pope to the episcopal college is the same as the bond which linked Peter to the apostolic college.[48] While the bishop of Rome is called the vicar of Christ, he does not succeed to the position which Christ held with respect to the apostles.[49] He succeeds only to the charge which Christ entrusted to Peter. The pope can do as much as, but no more than, what Peter could.

Like the original apostolic college, the episcopal college exists only if it has the successor of Peter as its head. Without at least the implicit approval of the pope, no decision of the bishops is a collegial act in the strict sense. While the college cannot exist without its head, it is also true that the head cannot exist without the college.[50]

Permanent Group

When Christ chose the apostles, "he constituted [them] in the form of a college or permanent assembly" (LG 19). The apostolic college was a stable group. Though only rarely coming together as a body, each apostle always acted as a member of the group to which Christ had called him. In the early Church, apostolic communion was more an awareness of this solidarity than the carrying out of acts in common.[51]

Right from the outset, writes Bouyer, the bishops also "consciously strove to form a college, as the apostles did before them."[52] Today's members of the episcopal college similarly succeed to the apostles as a permanent group. The college does not come into existence only when the bishops are engaged in strictly collegial activity, but continues independently of their meeting together. Even when its members are dispersed throughout

Origins, Development, and Mission of the Papacy

the world, the college of bishops never ceases to exist.[53] All exercise of episcopal ministry, even that of a bishop in his own diocese, is essentially collegial. The bishops are the collective "we" of those who succeed to the apostles.[54]

Corporate Authority

In the post-Pentecost community, the apostolic college, precisely as a body, was the corporate holder of ecclesial authority. Jesus confided his power and mission to the apostles as a group (cf. Mt 18:18, 28:18-20; Jn 20:21-23; Lk 22:19). Each apostle received his authority from Christ insofar as he was a member of the apostolic body. Thomas, who was absent when the risen Christ conferred the power to forgive sins on the apostles (cf. Jn 20:21-23), did not need, for example, a later private commission. Nor did Matthias when he was chosen to replace Judas. He received full apostolic authority from the mere fact that "he was added to the eleven apostles" (Acts 1:26).[55] Integration into the college of apostles allowed a member to share personally in its collective authority.

Tillard remarks that the original collegiality of the apostles is unlike a democracy where the group makes a decision to which each member then adheres. On the contrary, the New Testament indicates that the apostles enjoyed considerable powers of initiative in their preaching and missionary efforts. Nothing suggests that the Spirit guided the individual apostles because they had drawn up a strategic pastoral plan. The collegial dimension of making decisions, clearly manifested in the meeting at Jerusalem (cf. Acts 15:1-29), came into play only when fundamental questions of faith and Christian life were at stake. In this case, no apostle was free to decide as he pleased, but was bound to the apostolic witness of all.[56]

The episcopal college, too, is the corporate holder of authority in the Church. "Apostolic authority, therefore, is not a personal possession of the Pope who then dispenses it to the other bishops," writes Granfield. "It is a common possession of the College of Bishops who are united with the Pope."[57] Papal authority is exercised from within, for, and on behalf of the whole college. While the pope must either call the college to act in a strictly collegial way or approve any initiatives coming from the other bishops, he does not create the authority of the college. Rather, he decides when it is to be exercised.[58]

The college of bishops is the subject of powers and duties which are intrinsically superior to those which result from adding up the powers of every bishop.[59] It has some functions which no individual bishop, except the pope, possesses on his own. For example, it is only as a corporate body that the bishops possess the "sure charism of truth"[60] which enables them to teach infallibly. The pope is the only bishop who can make definitive judgments on his own authority. Furthermore, the threefold power of the individual bishop comes to him insofar as he is a member of the college.

Co-responsibility for the Universal Church

Bishops who are heads of particular churches individually exercise ordinary jurisdiction only over the portion of the people of God assigned to them (cf. CD 11; CIC 381.1;

CCC 886). However, they also share the mandate, with the pope, of teaching and caring for the universal Church. As successors to the apostles and members of the episcopal college, bishops are closely united to one another "and should be solicitous for all the churches. By divine institution and by virtue of their apostolic office," Vatican II teaches, "all of them jointly are responsible for the Church" (CD 6). This solicitude for all the churches (cf. 2 Cor 11:28) is an episcopal responsibility which should lead to concrete action. Bishops are to extend their care "especially to the poor, to those persecuted for the faith, as well as to missionaries who are working throughout the world" (CCC 886).

Concern for all the churches arises from the nature of collegiality. It still remains true, however, that the bishops show their co-responsibility for the universal Church primarily by effectively pastoring their own churches. While in their dioceses, "all the bishops have the obligation of fostering and safeguarding the unity of the faith and of upholding the discipline which is common to the whole Church." In this way they contribute "to the welfare of the whole Mystical Body, which, from another point of view, is a corporate body of Churches" (LG 23).

Hierarchical Communion

The council Fathers at Vatican II established that two conditions had to be fulfilled for membership in the college of bishops: episcopal ordination and hierarchical communion. On the one hand, sacramental ordination to the episcopacy is the cause of incorporation in the college of bishops (cf. LG 21). It establishes a bond of sacramental and spiritual communion among all bishops, and of each one personally with the bishop of Rome. On the other hand, hierarchical communion is the necessary condition for incorporation into the episcopal college.[61]

Ordination to the episcopacy grants a share in the fullness of apostolic ministry by introducing the bishop into the apostolic succession. This succession ensures a vertical communion which guarantees the identity of the particular church entrusted to the bishop with the Church of the apostles.[62] Through episcopal consecration the bishop receives the three essential functions (*munera*) of the apostolic ministry: teaching, governing, and sanctifying (cf. LG 21).

Unlike Church documents from the Middle Ages onward, the Second Vatican Council refrains from mentioning the classical distinction between the power of orders, conferred by ordination, and the power of jurisdiction, conferred by the pope. The council avoided repeating the classical teaching that a bishop's power of jurisdiction derives from the successor of Peter. Instead, it stressed that each bishop in his own right has all the ordinary power necessary to carry out his apostolic functions (cf. CD 8).[63] Vatican II teaches that within his diocese the bishop possesses all the "proper, ordinary and immediate" power which is required for the exercise of his pastoral office (cf. LG 27; CD 8; CIC 381). A bishop's authority, then, has its origin in episcopal ordination, not in delegation from the pope.

Nonetheless, an essential role belongs to the pope before a bishop can exercise his authority in the college of bishops. The horizontal guarantee that a particular church is fully Catholic is communion with the successor of Peter. "The lawful ordination of a bishop," states the *Catechism of the Catholic Church*, "requires a special intervention of the Bishop of Rome, because he is the supreme visible bond of the communion of particular Churches in the one Church and the guarantor of their freedom" (CCC 1559). Due to the pope's singular ministry, a relationship of hierarchical subordination exists between him and the other bishops. Already in very early times, the bishop of Rome set the conditions for communion with his church and, consequently, with the Catholic Church throughout the world. He does this because the successor of Peter, alone among the bishops, derives his primatial authority directly from Christ, not from being granted communion by others. The Roman church is the primary source of communion among the churches.[64]

Today the pope guarantees the integrity of the universal communion by means of canonical mission. He must receive a bishop into communion if he is to exercise jurisdiction in his own diocese or in the universal Church. Although ordination gives bishops their threefold mission, the power to exercise these functions is determined by the pope. "Of their very nature [these functions] can be exercised only in hierarchical communion with the head and members of the college" (LG 21; cf. CIC 375.2). As the explanatory note appended to *Lumen gentium*, says: "*A canonical* or *juridical determination* through hierarchical authority is required for such power ordered to action" (NEP 2). Through some gesture by which the pope either initiates or confirms episcopal ordinations, he receives other bishops into ecclesial communion (cf. CIC 377.1). This papal action brings about the individual bishop's sharing in the fullness of collegial power which belongs to the episcopal college.[65]

The successor of Peter is the bishop who "situates" the episcopal office of a bishop to serve the *koinonia*. He assigns him either to a particular church, where the bishop has ordinary jurisdiction, or to a titular church. When the pope receives a bishop into communion, he exercises his supreme jurisdiction. By means of canonical mission, he guarantees that a bishop is assigned pastoral duties not only for the benefit of the local community over which he presides but also for the welfare of the whole Church.[66] This canonical mission establishes a condition for the valid exercise of jurisdiction, though it does not confer it. A particular church would cease to be fully Catholic if its bishop failed to be in hierarchical communion with the bishop of Rome and other members of the episcopal college. Lacking communion with the Roman see, a bishop, though validly ordained, is in imperfect communion with the college of bishops and its head.

Every individual bishop is subordinate both to the pope and to the college. Each successor of the apostles, as well as the episcopal college as a whole, is united "with Peter, and subject to Peter" (AG 38). Consequently, all bishops are united to each other because they share the same relationship with the bishop of Rome.[67] By being received into communion with Rome, a bishop is automatically in communion with the whole college. The conferral of canonical mission by the pope does not reduce bishops to being "vicars of the Roman Pontiff." Rather, they are "vicars and legates of Christ, [who] govern the particular Churches assigned to them" (LG 27). The Church's good order and unity require that all episcopal authority be exercised only in communion with the successor of Peter.

Subject of Supreme Authority in the Church

Vatican II teaches that the pope enjoys "full, supreme and universal power over the whole Church" and that he is "always free to exercise this power" (LG 22). The Fathers complement this reaffirmation of papal primacy with another assertion regarding the subject of supreme authority in the Church: "The order of bishops is the successor to the college of the apostles in their role as teachers and pastors, and in it the apostolic college is perpetuated. Together with their head, the Supreme Pontiff, and never apart from him, they have supreme and full authority over the universal Church; but this power cannot be exercised without the agreement of the Roman Pontiff" (LG 22). Repeating *Lumen gentium*, the Code of Canon Law states that the bishop of Rome "enjoys supreme, full, immediate and universal ordinary power in the Church" (CIC 331). It later adds that the college of bishops "is also the subject of supreme and full power over the universal Church" (CIC 336; cf. CCC 883). In both council and Code the language is primarily juridical, suggesting that the relationship between the primacy and the episcopacy can be worked out, at least in part, within a legal framework.

These two affirmations immediately present a problem. How can the pope and the episcopal college both be "supreme" authorities in the same Church? The precise relation between the body of bishops and the pope, each of which is the subject of supreme authority in the Church, remains a disputed question. While the affirmations of the Fathers at Vatican II set the parameters for the discussion, they deliberately left the theological explanation unresolved. Nonetheless, the way in which the council dealt with this issue sheds further light on its conception of the Petrine ministry.

On the one hand, in the history of theology three ways of discussing the connection between the papacy and episcopacy fail to do justice to defined teaching. First, there are the positions of the radical conciliarist and Gallican theologians. Minimizing the fullness of papal authority, they subordinate the pope either to an ecumenical council or to a national episcopate. The teaching of *Pastor aeternus* excludes both positions. Others have proposed that the subject of the Church's highest pastoral office is the college of bishops, which the pope must represent in such a way that he remains subservient to its will.[68] This position, as we shall see, contradicts the explicit teaching of *Lumen gentium*. A third group of theologians suggests that parliamentary democracies are the appropriate model for the Church's ministerial structure. All three of these theories contradict the affirmations of either or both Vatican Councils concerning the hierarchical nature of ecclesial ministry.

On the other hand, contemporary theologians and canonists defend three different interpretations of the relationship between the pope and the episcopal college. They argue that the subject of supreme authority is the pope as the vicar of Christ, the pope and the episcopal college as two inadequately distinct subjects, or the episcopal college as one collegial subject. All three can be harmonized with official Catholic teaching.

Origins, Development, and Mission of the Papacy

Pope as Vicar of Christ

One long-standing theological tradition resolves the question of supreme Church authority by stressing the pope's unique prerogatives as the vicar of Christ. The bishop of Rome *alone*, they hold, is the Church's supreme authority. Defenders of this position seek to defend the singular privileges of the successor of Peter, maintaining that the pope is the single visible source of ecclesial authority. To do so, they place all Church power in the pope's hands. In the classical theory of papal monarchy, the pope communicates his power to the bishops. He gives them a share in his supreme pastoral power, even when they are gathered at an ecumenical council,[69] which therefore derives its authority from the pope. Well articulated by anti-conciliarist and anti-Gallican theologians, this view continued to be widely held after Vatican I, though it is proposed much less so after Vatican II. While rejecting theories of papal monarchy as theologically incomplete, it we must admit that this explanation, regardless of its weakness, explicitly contradicts no defined teaching.

In point of fact, few theologians today defend this kind of papal monarchy. In light of Vatican II and the 1983 Code of Canon Law, two more common solutions to the question of the unity of the Church's supreme authority are put forward.

Two Inadequately Distinct Subjects

Many canonists, such as Gianfranco Ghirlanda, Jesuit professor at the Gregorian University in Rome, argue that "within the Church there are two subjects holding the supreme and full power of governance and authentic magisterium in the universal Church: the Supreme Pontiff and the college of bishops, although they are not completely distinct from one another."[70] First proposed by some Fathers at Vatican I (cf. M 52, 1109-1110), numerous theologians and canonists held this view in the years after the council. According to its contemporary advocates, the conciliar texts of Vatican II, reinforced by the preliminary explanatory note affixed to *Lumen gentium*, and the Code of Canon Law support the theory that there are two inadequately distinct subjects of supreme authority: a primatial subject (the pope alone) and a collegial subject (the episcopal college with the pope).

Proponents of this opinion point out that the pope is free to act alone as the vicar of Christ and the head of the Church. He need not expressly involve the episcopal college when exercising his primacy of jurisdiction or of teaching. The successor of Peter may exercise his power "at any time, as he sees fit, by reason of the demands of his office" (NEP 4). Not only is he able to function on his own, the bishop of Rome can also perform certain actions, such as convoking an ecumenical council, which the episcopal college cannot. Consequently, they believe, the doctrinal and canonical sources justify referring to the bishop of Rome as a primatial subject of supreme authority.

According to the theory's advocates, the pope can also exercise the Church's supreme authority together with the bishops in a collegial act. In this case, as at an ecumenical council, the primatially structured body of bishops is the subject of supreme authority. Unlike the proponents of the first theory, they hold that the episcopal college, as the collegial subject of supreme authority, does not receive its power from the pope. There are then two subjects of supreme authority, though they are distinct (pope and college). They add, however, that the distinction between these two subjects is inadequate or incomplete. While the pope is personally involved in "the two conjoined subjects,"[71] the two remain distinct. As supreme in both instances, the power does not pass from one to another.[72] Swiss theologian Charles Journet suggested a reason why Christ willed such a twofold subject of supreme power in the Church. On the one hand, the pope exercises it personally as a single subject, as a sign and instrument of the Church's visible unity. On the other hand, when supreme power is collegially exercised, it is a sign and instrument of her catholicity.[73]

Karl Rahner, Yves Congar, and many other theologians contest this theory of two inadequately distinct subjects of supreme ecclesial authority. According to them, it presents logical problems and is difficult to reconcile with the Second Vatican Council's teaching on collegiality. Rahner finds this proposal to be "obscure and imprecise in the extreme." After a lengthy analysis, he concludes his critique by suggesting that the axiom of two inadequately distinct subjects of supreme authority is really proposing something else. In the light of Vatican II, Rahner thinks that this theory describes the two ways (primatial and collegial) in which supreme authority in the Church is, in practice, exercised. However, he maintains that this view does not provide a compelling theological explanation of the magisterial data.[74]

One Collegial Subject

The more common theological opinion today is that there is one collegial subject of supreme Church authority. According to its proponents, the need to preserve ecclesial unity excludes the possibility that there are two distinct subjects. It is "quite impossible," wrote Rahner, "for two subjects to be vested with supreme power in one and the same single society precisely considered as single."[75] He thinks that it is contradictory to hold that there are two different possessors of the same full and supreme power in the Church. For Rahner, such a view leads almost inevitably to denying the supreme power either of the pope or of the college of bishops.

More in line with Vatican II is the theological opinion that the Church has only one subject of supreme authority: the episcopal college with its head, the successor of Peter. Rahner summarized this position as follows: "The bearer of the highest and supreme power in the Church is the united episcopate with and under the pope as its head. . . . But there are two modes in which this supreme college may act: a 'collegiate act' properly so-called, and the act of the pope as head of the college."[76] The episcopal college cannot exercise its supreme power except in union with the pope, but neither does the pope exercise his supreme power except in union with the college.[77] When the pope appears to act alone, he still always does so, Rahner and others maintain, as head of the college.

Although such personal papal actions are not collegial in the juridical sense of the word, nonetheless, they are related to the college. Supporters of this view expand the meaning of "collegial" acts to include not only those of the college as such but also those

Origins, Development, and Mission of the Papacy

which in some way pertain to it.[78] The pope alone can carry out these latter actions. As head of the Church, the successor of Peter is, at one and the same time, head of the episcopal college. It could not be otherwise, they maintain. The primatially structured college of bishops belongs to the very nature of the Church. At all times, so runs their argument, whenever the pope exercises his authority, even when he appears to be acting alone, he does so, says Rahner, as "integrated into the body of bishops."[79] Using the classical principle that "action follows being," it follows that the pope cannot act except as head of the episcopal college.[80]

The college of bishops is, therefore, the one bearer of supreme authority in the Church. Since the power it exercises comes from Christ, it is always vicarious. Because he is one, the power exercised in his name also ought to manifest that same unity.[81] Consequently, the explanation of one collegial subject of supreme ecclesial authority safeguards the Church's unity and catholicity taught by Vatican II: "This college, in so far as it is composed of many members, is the expression of the multifariousness and universality of the people of God; and of the unity of the flock of Christ, in so far as it is assembled under one head" (LG 22).

Pope as Head of the Episcopal College

One question still remains. Does the proposal that the episcopal college is the bearer of supreme authority in any way compromise defined teaching on papal primacy? The supreme power of the college is, as we have seen, primatially structured. In keeping with its intrinsic structure, the college of bishops has two modes of action: through the pope acting personally as head of the college, and through a strictly collegial action, as at an ecumenical council. Vatican II teaches that the pope himself is empowered to choose the way in which the primatial-collegial authority of the college is to be exercised. According to the needs of the Church, he always has the right "to determine the manner, either personal or collegial, of exercising this function" (CIC 333.2, cf. 337.3). While the bearer of supreme authority is the episcopal college headed by the pope, its essentially collegial authority can be exercised in two different ways, though not by two distinct subjects.

Because of his primacy within the college, the pope can exercise the fullness of ecclesial authority "*seorsim*"; that is, by an act of his own as distinct from a strictly collegial one (cf. LG 22; cf. CIC 331). Precisely as head of the college, the pope "is qualified to perform certain actions in which the bishops have no competence whatsoever" (NEP 3).

The successor of Peter is not bound by juridical norms regulating the situations in which he must use the college's authority in either a personal or a collegial way. There are, for example, no canonical restraints on the pope which require that he invite the bishops to full collegial activity in particular cases. He is not the representative of the college either in receiving his power from them or in being tied to their will as their spokesman. Upon election he receives his authority directly from Christ.[82] If he wishes, the bishop of Rome can also call other institutions, such as the synod of bishops, the college of cardinals, and the Roman curia to share in the exercise of his primatial ministry (cf. CIC 334).

The Shepherd and the Rock

While the pope can exercise supreme power "by himself," he does so in virtue of his office of headship. In doing so, he remains united to his brother bishops in the episcopal college. As Congar points out, the pope can exercise supreme authority alone because Peter was the first to receive it within the apostolic college. The one collegial power is always structured, since it was initially given individually to Peter, and then to Peter with the other apostles.[83]

This "personal" dimension of the papacy is irreplaceable. Henri de Lubac recalls that "to want to compel the bishop of Rome, by whatever means possible, to turn towards the other bishops in order to learn from them the path of fidelity would be to go contrary to the constitution of the Church and to her traditional practice."[84] The fact that the pope can act on his own initiative reminds us that the Church's hierarchy is a communion of persons. "Peter *has* to step forward as an individual, over against the others, be they the people with whom he is in *communion* or the bishops with whom he forms a *collegium*," explained von Balthasar, "not by 'domineering' (1 Pt 5:3), but as a servant who does not detach himself from *communio* or *collegium* but rather 'strengthens' them (Lk 22:32), frees them to be themselves in true liberty."[85] Christ did not give the Church a structure of bureaucratic and anonymous leadership. Like Peter, the pope has personal responsibilities belonging to his mission. These can be neither delegated to, nor absorbed by, any other ecclesial body or institution.[86]

In carrying out his pastoral office, the pope "is always united with the other bishops" (CIC 333.2). When the bishop of Rome acts personally, he invariably does so as pastor of the entire Church, which also means as head of the episcopal college. Even the pope's personal acts as the successor of Peter are intimately related to the episcopal college which is the one subject acting through its head. Rahner says that "the act of the pope, which he exercises in virtue of the commission given to him directly by Christ, is *ipso facto and in itself* an act of the college (*not* a collegiate act), because this power conferred on him by Christ of itself makes him the 'mandatory' of the college."[87]

Fidelity to the Church's divine constitution demands that the pope's personal right to exercise supreme authority not eclipse the role of the episcopacy. The pastoral co-responsibility of the episcopal college for the whole Church belongs to her constitution. Although the concrete forms of juridical collegiality are tied to historical circumstances, to deny all forms of collegiality in practice would betray the Church's nature as a communion.[88]

◆

One of the greatest contributions of the Second Vatican Council was to situate the papacy within the Church's fundamental episcopal structure. Consequently, in the words of John Paul II, the teaching on the primacy at Vatican II deserves to be called "full, balanced and serene."[89] Indeed, this council rejected any number of erroneous interpretations of *Pastor aeternus*, by harmonizing the Church's teaching on the Petrine ministry with that on episcopal collegiality. The documents of Vatican I and Vatican II should therefore be read together in order to grasp the Church's full doctrine of papal primacy.

Origins, Development, and Mission of the Papacy

The council Fathers at Vatican II received the teachings of Vatican I in such a way that they restored the episcopacy to the role it had in the Church of the first millennium. To this end, the Second Vatican Council marshaled the ecclesiological doctrines of the local church, the Church as a *communio*, and episcopal collegiality. When taken together, the two Vatican Councils hold in balance the unity and the tension between the primacy and the episcopacy. Christ endowed the Church with a structure that is simultaneously primatial and collegial. The apostles' collegial mission continues in the body of bishops which succeeds to this original group. Like the apostolic college, the episcopal college is primatially structured in such a way that its existence as a stable group depends upon the pope's presence within it. The bishop of Rome fulfills his primatial mission within the framework of collegiality.

While Vatican II's ecclesiology of communion revives the importance given to the bishop as head of a local church, it also situates the Petrine ministry at the heart of the universal *koinonia*. The visible bearer of supreme authority in the Church is one: the episcopal college, which always includes the pope. In keeping with this intrinsic structure, the college has two ways of exercising the supreme authority which it possesses: through the pope as its head or through a strictly collegial action of the whole college as such. Given that collegiality derives from divine institution, it belongs to the nature of the Church that the pope and the episcopal college work together harmoniously. The active collaboration of all bishops with the Petrine ministry supports papal authority, just as the bishops' recognition of the pope's right to act personally confirms the authority of the college of bishops. As head of the college of bishops, the pope fosters unity without thwarting diversity and promotes diversity without compromising unity. The bishop of Rome is the permanent and visible source of Church unity, but this unity is given its fullest expression through the collegial communion of the college of bishops.

Notes for Chapter ten

1. Johann Auer, *The Church: The Universal Sacrament of Salvation*, Dogmatic Theology, trans. Michael Waldstein, vol. 8 (Washington, D.C.: Catholic University of America Press, 1993), 286.
2. J. M. R. Tillard, *The Bishop of Rome*, trans. John de Satgé (Wilmington: Michael Glazier, 1983), 19.
3. James L. Heft, "From the Pope to the Bishops: Episcopal Authority from Vatican I to Vatican II," in *The Papacy and the Church in the United States*, ed. Bernard Cooke (New York: Paulist Press, 1989), 61.
4. Pius XII, *Mystici corporis Christi* (1943), #52.
5. Seamus Ryan, "The Hierarchical Structure of the Church," in *The Church: A Theological and Pastoral Commentary on the Constitution on the Church*, ed. Kevin McNamara (Dublin: Veritas Publications, 1983), 165.
6. Cited in Edmund Hill, *Authority and Ministry in the Catholic Church* (London: Geoffrey Chapman, 1988), 96.
7. Hans Urs von Balthasar, *Elucidations*, trans. John Riches (London: SPCK, 1975), 101.

8. Tillard, *Bishop of Rome*, 29-31.
9. Cited in Tillard, *Bishop of Rome*, 32
10. Gerard Philips, *L'Eglise et son mystère au deuxième Concile du Vatican*, vol. 2 (Paris: Desclée, 1967), 226.
11. Yves Congar, *Ministères et communion ecclésiale* (Paris: Cerf, 1971), 168.
12. Olegario González de Cardenal, "Development of a Theology of the Local Church from the First to the Second Vatican Council," *The Jurist*, 52:1 (1992), 11-43.
13. Hermann Pottmeyer, "Il Vaticano I nel Vaticano II: vie per un'intesa cattolica ed ecumenica," in *Papato e istanze ecumeniche*, ed. Giuseppe Ghiberti, et al. (Bologna: Dehoniane, 1984), 127.
14. John de Satgé, *Peter and the Single Church* (London: SPCK, 1981), 124.
15. J. M. R. Tillard, "The Jurisdiction of the Bishop of Rome," *Theological Studies*, 40:1 (1979), 6.
16. Paul VI, Homily, October 11, 1969, *L'Osservatore Romano*, 42 (October 16, 1969), 12.
17. Tillard, "Jurisdiction of the Bishop of Rome," 15.
18. Patrick Granfield, "The Church Local and Universal: Realization of Communion," *The Jurist*, 49:2 (1989), 450.
19. Synod of Bishops (1985), "The Final Report," *Origins*, 15:27 (December 19, 1985), #II.C.1, p. 448.
20. John Paul II, *Sacrae disciplinae leges* (1983).
21. Hervé Legrand, "La Iglesia local," in *Iniciación a la práctica de la Teología*, Dogmática 2, ed. Bernard Lauret and François Refoulé, trans. Rufino Godoy (Madrid: Ediciones Cristiandad, 1985), 289.
22. See LG 18, 22; OT 9.
23. John Paul II, Discourse, March 3, 1984, *L'Osservatore Romano*, 15 (April 9, 1984), 9; cf. John Paul II, *Crossing the Threshold of Hope* (New York: Alfred A. Knopf, 1994), 12-13.
24. See the following texts: LG 8, 15, 18, 22 (twice), 23 (three times), 24, 25 (twice); UR 2; CD 2; AG 5, 6.
25. See the following texts: LG 18, 22 (6 times), 23, 25 (7 times), 27, 29, 45; OE 3 (twice), 7, 9, 11; UR 18; CD 2, 4 (twice), 5, 8, 9 (3 times), 10, 38; AG 29, 42; PO 19.
26. Barbara Aland, "Pontifex Maximus," *Encyclopedia of the Early Church*, ed. Angelo Di Berardino, trans. Adrian Walford, vol. 2 (Cambridge: James Clarke & Co., 1992), 702.
27. Yves Congar, "Titoli dati al papa," *Concilium*, 11:8 (1975), 86.
28. See the following texts: IM 2, 19; LG 14, 45; CD 2, 3, 10, 11, 35 (twice); DH 1; AA 20; AG 29; PO 15; GS 43, 80.
29. Congar, "Titoli dati al papa," 85-87.
30. Roland Minnerath, *Le Pape: évêque universel ou premier des évêques?* (Paris: Beauchesne, 1978), 118.
31. See the following texts: CCC 887, 882, 892, 1559.
32. See the interventions of Ottaviani, Browne, and de Castro Mayer in *Acta synodalis sacrosancti concilii oecumenici Vaticani Secundi*, vol. 2, part 4 (Vatican City: Polyglot Press, 1972), 625, 627, and 631.
33. Legrand, "La Iglesia local," 272.
34. Klaus Schatz, *La primauté du Pape*, trans. Joseph Hoffmann (Paris: Cerf, 1992), 45.
35. Michael A. Fahey, "The Catholicity of the Church in the New Testament and in the Early

Patristic Period," *The Jurist*, 52:1 (1992), 65-68.
36. Cyprian, *Letter*, 36.4; translation in Henri de Lubac, *The Motherhood of the Church*, trans. Sergia Englund (San Francisco: Ignatius Press, 1982), 251.
37. Cited in de Lubac, *Motherhood of the Church*, 292.
38. De Lubac, *Motherhood of the Church*, 253.
39. Patrick J. Burns, "Communion, Councils, and Collegiality: Some Catholic Reflections," in *Papal Primacy and the Universal Church*, Lutherans and Catholics in Dialogue V, ed. Paul C. Empie and T. Austin Murphy (Minneapolis: Augsburg Publishing House, 1974), 155.
40. Legrand, "La Iglesia local," 294.
41. Congar, *Ministères et communion ecclésiale*, 110-117.
42. Philips, *L'Eglise et son mystère*, vol. 2, 284-286.
43. John Paul II, *Redemptoris missio* (1990), #61.
44. Auer, *The Church*, 221.
45. John Paul II, Discourse, October 7, 1992, *L'Osservatore Romano*, 41 (October 14, 1992), 11.
46. Louis Bouyer, *The Church of God*, trans. Charles Underhill Quinn (Chicago: Franciscan Herald Press, 1982), 386.
47. Bouyer, *Church of God*, 386.
48. Ryan, "Hierarchical Structure of the Church," 178.
49. Yves Congar, "La Chiesa è apostolica," in *L'evento salvifico nella comunità di Gesù Cristo*, Mysterium Salutis, ed. Johannes Feiner and Magnus Löhrer, trans. Giovanni Moretto, Dino Pezzetta, and Gino Stefani, vol. 7 (Brescia: Queriniana, 1972), 702; cf. Congar, *Ministères et communion ecclésiale*, 112-113.
50. Gianfranco Ghirlanda, *Il diritto nella Chiesa: mistero di comunione*, 2nd ed. (Milan: Edizioni San Paolo, 1993), 505.
51. Arialdo Beni, *La nostra Chiesa*, 5th ed. (Florence: Fiorentina, 1982), 584.
52. Bouyer, *Church of God*, 377.
53. De Lubac, *Motherhood of the Church*, 245-246.
54. Joseph Ratzinger, *La Chiesa: Una comunità sempre in cammino*, trans. Luigi Frattini, 2nd ed. (Turin: Edizioni Paoline, 1992), 70.
55. Congar, "La Chiesa è apostolica," 680.
56. J. M. R. Tillard, *Church of Churches: The Ecclesiology of Communion*, trans. R. C. De Peaux (Collegeville: Liturgical Press, 1992), 198-199.
57. Patrick Granfield, *The Limits of the Papacy*, (Garden City: Doubleday & Company, 1980), 84.
58. Julio Manzanares, "Il romano pontefice e la collegialità dei vescovi," in *Collegialità e primato*, ed. Velasio De Paolis (Bologna: Dehoniane, 1993), 36.
59. Karl Rahner, "The Hierarchical Structure of the Church, with Special Reference to the Episcopate," in *Commentary on the Documents of Vatican II*, ed. Herbert Vorgrimler, vol. 1 (New York: Herder and Herder, 1967), 198.
60. Irenaeus, *Against Heresies*, 4.26.
61. Donato Valentini, "An Overview of Theologians' Positions: A Review of Major Writings and the State of the Question Today," *Concilium*, 4 (1990), 36.
62. J. M. R. Tillard, "The Horizon of the 'Primacy' of the Bishop of Rome," *One in Christ*, 12 (1976), 23.
63. Eugenio Corecco, "The Bishop as Head of the Local Church and its Discipline," in *Readings,*

Cases, Materials in Canon Law, ed. Jordan P. Hite, Gennaro J. Sesto, and Daniel J. Ward (Collegeville: Liturgical Press, 1980), 150.

64. Ludwig Hertling, *"Communio" : Church and Papacy in Early Christianity*, trans. Jared Wicks (Chicago: Loyola University Press, 1972), 71-72.
65. Tillard, "Jurisdiction of the Bishop of Rome," 18.
66. John Paul II, Discourse, October 28, 1992, *L'Osservatore Romano*, 44 (November 4, 1992), 11.
67. Ghirlanda, *Il diritto nella Chiesa*, 512.
68. Auer, *The Church*, 319.
69. Congar, *Ministères et communion ecclésiale*, 179, 191-193; cf. Manzanares, "Il romano pontefice e la collegialità dei vescovi," 37.
70. Gianfranco Ghirlanda, "Universal Church, Particular Church, and Local Church at the Second Vatican Council and in the New Code of Canon Law," in *Vatican II: Assessments and Perspectives Twenty-five Years After (1962-1987)*, ed. René Latourelle (New York: Paulist Press, 1988), 249. This also appears to have been the view expressed by the Majority at Vatican I (cf. Jerome Hamer, *The Church Is a Communion* [New York: Sheed & Ward, 1964], 220-233).
71. Alexandre Ganoczy, "How Can One Evaluate Collegiality vis-à-vis Papal Primacy?" *Concilium*, 64 (1971), 90.
72. Manzanares, "Il romano pontefice e la collegialità dei vescovi," 39.
73. Charles Journet, "Collegiality," *L'Osservatore Romano*, 35 (August 28, 1969), 5-6.
74. Karl Rahner, "On the Relationship between the Pope and the College of Bishops," in *Theological Investigations*, trans. David Bourke, vol. 10 (London: Darton, Longman & Todd, 1973), 61; cf. Rahner, "Hierarchical Structure of the Church," 202.
75. Rahner, "On the Relationship between the Pope and the College of Bishops," 61.
76. Rahner, "On the Relationship between the Pope and the College of Bishops," 55.
77. Burns, "Communion, Councils, and Collegiality," 168.
78. Granfield, *Limits of the Papacy*, 85.
79. Karl Rahner, "Forgotten Dogmatic Initiatives of the Second Vatican Council," in *Theological Investigations*, trans. Joseph Donceel, vol. 22 (New York: Crossroad Publishing Company, 1991), 101.
80. Francis A. Sullivan, "Per un rinnovamento del ministero del Vescovo di Roma: principio di legittima diversità, collegialità, sussidiarietà," *Nicolaus*, 19 (1992), 48.
81. Beni, *La nostra Chiesa*, 592.
82. Rahner, "Hierarchical Structure of the Church," 203-204; cf. Rahner, "On the Relationship between the Pope and the College of Bishops," 55.
83. Congar, *Ministères et communion ecclésiale*, 180-182.
84. De Lubac, *Motherhood of the Church*, 330.
85. Hans Urs von Balthasar, *The Office of Peter and the Structure of the Church*, trans. Andrée Emery (San Francisco: Ignatius Press, 1986), 211.
86. Joseph Ratzinger, "Der Primat des Papstes und die Einheit des Gottesvolkes," in *Dienst an der Einheit*, ed. Joseph Ratzinger (Düsseldorf: Patmos, 1978), 168-171.
87. Rahner, "On the Relationship between the Pope and the College of Bishops," 58.
88. Congar, *Ministères et communion ecclésiale*, 202.
89. John Paul II, Discourse, February 24, 1993, *L'Osservatore Romano*, 9 (March 3, 1993), 11.

Chapter eleven
COLLEGIALITY AND THE PAPAL OFFICE

According to the Second Vatican Council, episcopal collegiality belongs to the nature of the Church. As a reality with its origins in Christ's will, it manifests the Church as a communion at the level of pastors. Episcopal collegiality unites the pope and the bishops in ways which include a juridical dimension, but more often extend beyond it. Though the episcopal college is a permanent body, it only occasionally engages in strictly collegiate activity. Consequently, Vatican II left open many other possibilities for the pope and the body of bishops to express their co-responsibility for the universal Church. The council's teaching on collegiality allowed for various institutional expressions of the "collegial spirit."

Within the Church's hierarchical structure collegial activity is manifested in different degrees. This chapter examines seven current embodiments of collegiality. Ecumenical councils and the dispersed episcopate can perform strictly collegial acts. But there are, as well, other forms of collegiality: the synod of bishops, the college of cardinals, episcopal conferences, the *ad limina* visits of bishops, and the pastoral visits of the pope. My primary interest is the light which each of these structures sheds on the Petrine ministry. When taken together, these collegial institutions give concrete expression to the doctrine of papal primacy taught by the Second Vatican Council and developed in its wake.

As Patrick Granfield says, collegial activity provides a "conditioning environment which helps define the nature of the papal role."[1] Despite the concerns voiced by some Fathers at Vatican II, the doctrine of collegiality does not imply the existence of competing institutional authorities which could weaken the Petrine ministry. Nor is collegiality an external control on the primacy, functioning as a system of checks and balances. The distinction between the college of bishops and the pope involves no structural antagonism. According to the preliminary explanatory note attached to *Lumen gentium*, in the episcopal college there "is not a distinction between the Roman Pontiff and the bishops taken together but between the Roman Pontiff by himself and the Roman Pontiff along with the bishops" (NEP 3). The body of bishops always needs the bishop of Rome in order to function as a college. According to Vatican II, the episcopal college has no authority as a body unless it is united to Peter's successor as its head (cf. LG 22).

Effective and Affective Collegiality

Theologians and official post-conciliar documents draw a distinction between two kinds of collegiality: effective and affective. The council Fathers distinguished between a "truly collegiate act" (LG 22) or effective collegiality, and "the collegiate spirit" (LG 23) or affective collegiality. A truly collegiate act engages the whole college either when it is gathered at an ecumenical council or dispersed throughout the world. Affective collegiality is the spirit of cooperation, fraternal interchange, and apostolic solidarity of bishops among themselves and with the successor of Peter, and of him with them.

In collegial actions it is not a case of all or nothing. While effective collegiality is manifested by actions which are specified with theological and canonical rigor, affective collegiality is a looser reality, admitting various degrees of expression. According to John Paul II, these affective or "partial" forms of collegiality are "very necessary, useful, and sometimes absolutely indispensable."[2] Recent developments in the practice of collegiality make it abundantly clear that these partial realizations are vitally important to Church life. They reveal a great deal about how the pope exercises his Petrine ministry.

Ecumenical Councils

Although the episcopal college is a permanent body, it is rarely engaged in strictly collegial activity. "The supreme power in the universal Church, which the college enjoys, is exercised in a solemn way in an ecumenical council" (LG 22; cf. CIC 337.1). Councils are the clearest expressions of effective collegiality. In these assemblies the whole episcopal body, in union with the pope, fulfills in the highest degree its mission to teach and guide the universal Church.[3] Since no specific embodiment of collegiality is essential to the Church's constitution, ecumenical councils are institutions of ecclesiastical right. They embody, however, a venerable structure of the ancient tradition wherein episcopal collegiality, which is of divine right, is most fully operative.

Through the centuries, general councils have been held infrequently: only twenty-one, from Nicaea (325) to Vatican II (1962-1965). As assemblies guided by the Spirit, they have dealt with questions of doctrine, liturgy, ecclesiastical discipline, pastoral practice, and political and social life. Until the Second Vatican Council, the definition of truths of faith was, however, the primary business of councils. Catholics and Orthodox both accept the special place of the first seven councils, held between 325 and 787, because of their role in defining the Church's fundamental christological and trinitarian doctrines. In the course of history, the recognition of a gathering of bishops as an "ecumenical" council depended on many different factors: the intention of the one who convoked the gathering, the number and representative nature of those assembled, and the reception and approval of its decisions by the whole Church. Moreover, in Western ecclesiology, the pope's role in determining the ecumenical nature of a synod became increasingly more precise.

Membership at ecumenical councils is now regulated by canon law. All bishops have the right and duty to take part in a council with deliberative vote (cf. CIC 339.2). In addition, the Church's supreme authority can invite others to participate in a council's deliberations and can decide the degree of their involvement, including granting them voting privileges (cf. CIC 339.2). While a general council is primarily an assembly of bishops with the pope, it is not necessarily only an episcopal gathering. Certainly the bishops participate in function of their episcopal office,[4] but there is no reason to exclude non-bishops from taking an active part in an ecumenical council. History is replete with examples of laity and religious who have shaped conciliar debate and voted on its proposals.

Origins, Development, and Mission of the Papacy

Role of the Pope

In general councils, the bishops exercise the supreme authority of the Church as members of the episcopal college. They are not the pope's counselors who make decisions in virtue of delegated authority. Corresponding to his ministry in the college of bishops, the bishop of Rome has a unique role to play in ecumenical councils. History shows that his functions, as currently prescribed by canonical norms, are the result of a long period of development. According to current teaching and discipline, one essential factor which determines the ecumenicity of a council is participation by the bishop of Rome. If a pope dies while a council is in session, it is automatically and immediately suspended. The next pope can either order it to be continued or dissolve it (cf. CIC 340). This happened when Pope John XXIII (1958-1963) died after the first session of the Second Vatican Council. The council went ahead only because Paul VI (1963-1978) reconvened it. Ecclesiastical law describes three different moments when the pope exercises his primacy with regard to an ecumenical council: convocation, celebration, and approval.

• *CONVOCATION* The right to convoke an ecumenical council is now reserved exclusively to the pope (cf. CIC 338.1). This was not always the case. For the first seven ecumenical councils, which were all held in the East, the emperors assumed this prerogative. Frequently they exercised this right on the advice or encouragement of bishops who looked to them as guarantors of the Church's unity and peace. Sometimes councils were called with the misgivings of the pope. Leo the Great (440-461), for instance, was initially opposed to the calling the Council of Chalcedon.

• *CELEBRATION* The pope has the right to preside at all sessions of the council (cf. CIC 338.1). While Pope Silvester I (314-335) did not participate in the deliberations at Nicaea, setting a precedent for the councils in the East, he did assume the singular prerogative of sending legates. Whereas the bishop of Rome presided personally at many of the councils later held in the West, the practice of sending papal legates was revived at Trent, Vatican I, and Vatican II. Both John XXIII and Paul VI attended sessions of Vatican II only on ceremonial occasions, assigning to others the presidency of the council during the times of active debate. Acting in the pope's place at the Second Vatican Council were various bishops who chaired the sessions under papal authority. As head of the episcopal college, the pope also sets the council's agenda, either alone or with the assistance of the Fathers (cf. CIC 338.2). At Vatican II, for example, Paul VI reserved to himself the questions of celibacy and contraception, removing them from discussion by the Fathers. The pope can also transfer the council, suspend it temporarily, or dissolve it permanently (cf. CIC 338.1).

• *APPROVAL* So that the decrees of a council can have binding force, they must be "approved by the Roman Pontiff together with the Fathers of the council and are confirmed by the Roman Pontiff and promulgated at his order" (CIC 341.1). In other words, the pope cannot be outvoted on any matter by a majority of his brother bishops. His approval is essential before conciliar authority can be attributed to any decree. While the pope refrains from voting on resolutions, when he gives his approval he does so as head of the episcopal college. In approving a conciliar decision, the Roman bishop's action is not "superimposed on the act of the college from outside," says Rahner. "It is a special intrinsic moment of this act itself."[5] This approval is then followed by separate personal acts of papal confirmation and of promulgation, thereby making the council's decrees obligatory.

Unlike the medieval councils, where resolutions often took the form of papal decrees which the bishops approved, at Vatican II the Fathers had a greater awareness that its decrees were decisions of the council as such. The formula used to approve the documents of the Second Vatican Council makes this clear: "Each and every one of the things set forth in this dogmatic constitution [or constitution, decree, declaration] has won the consent of the Fathers of this most sacred council. We, too, by the apostolic authority conferred on us by Christ, join with the venerable Fathers in approving, decreeing, and establishing these things in the Holy Spirit, and we direct that what has thus been enacted in synod be published to God's glory. — Rome, at Saint Peter's, [date]. I Paul, bishop of the Catholic Church. [There follow the signatures of the Fathers.]"[6]

Collegial Action of the Dispersed Episcopate

Besides exercising its supreme power during an ecumenical council, the episcopal college can also express this authority "while living in different parts of the world" (LG 22). A collegial action of the dispersed episcopate must be either initiated or freely accepted by the pope (cf. LG 22; CIC 337.2). He must also confirm and promulgate any such actions of the body of bishops (cf. CIC 341.2). It would be possible, for example, to have a "council by correspondence" from which a truly collegiate act would result.[7]

The role of the successor of Peter is decisive in determining whether the college is exercising its supreme authority. Even if all the bishops hold a common view on a particular question of faith or morals, it does not for that reason alone constitute a fully collegial act. "The intervention of the head of the college provides a juridically verifiable element for the action to be clearly collegial," writes canonist James Provost, "and determines when that action binds the Church universal."[8] The dispersed episcopate can act in a strictly collegial manner only in communion with its head.

As a permanent body which is primatially structured, there is, however, one way in which the dispersed episcopate is always operative: when it is collegially witnessing to the faith which Catholics are to believe and hold.[9] In this regard, Henri de Lubac recalls that "the most essential action of the college is normally carried on from day to day by the simple fact that each head of church teaches in his own church the same faith as the others do in theirs."[10] Nonetheless, this teaching is not one of ceaselessly engaging in fully collegial acts but of recalling previous decisions of the college. It shows affective rather than effective collegiality.

Little progress has been made in establishing methods of effective collegial activity outside an ecumenical council. Ways in which the episcopal college, dispersed throughout the world, could, at least on occasion, manifest its joint responsibility are yet to be found.[11]

Origins, Development, and Mission of the Papacy

Synod of Bishops

In order to prolong the experience of collegiality which animated the sessions of the Second Vatican Council, many Fathers recommended that a permanent body be established which would express the bishops' co-responsibility for the universal Church. In response to their request, Paul VI instituted the synod of bishops with the publication of *Apostolica sollicitudo* in 1965.

As subsequently expressed by Vatican II, the synod was to "bear testimony to the participation of all the bishops in hierarchical communion in the care of the universal Church" (CD 5). In his first encyclical, *Redemptor hominis* (1979), John Paul II called this institution established during the council "a permanent organ of collegiality."[12] He has also referred to the synod as "an instrument of collegiality and a powerful factor in communion . . . [which] expresses collegiality in a highly intense way, even if it does not equal that achieved by the Council."[13] De Lubac comments that the synod of bishops is "the most outstanding expression" of collegiality in today's Church.[14] The synod, then, is a true, though partial, embodiment of collegiality.

The synod of bishops meets at stated times with bishops representing different regions of the world. Three kinds of synods are held: ordinary, extraordinary, and special assemblies (cf. CIC 345). Ordinary synods now meet regularly every three years; nine of them took place between 1967 and 1994. The topics they have dealt with are priesthood, justice in the world, evangelization, catechetics, the family, penance and reconciliation, the laity, priestly formation, and the consecrated life.

Outside the regularly scheduled synods, the pope can convoke extraordinary synods to address matters of major importance to the whole Church. Between 1969-1995 there were two such gatherings. In 1969, the synod discussed ways and means of putting into practice the collegiality of the bishops with the pope. In 1985, John Paul II convened an extraordinary synod to evaluate the implementation of the decrees of the Second Vatican Council on the twentieth anniversary of its closing.

Special assemblies deal with questions which affect a specific local church or regions of the universal Church. From 1980 to 1994 there were three: one to discuss the pastoral life of Holland in 1980; one for Europe in 1991; and another for Africa in 1994.

Synods touch upon the relations of the college of bishops to the pope, of the pope to the universal Church, and of the Church to the world.[15] According to the Code of Canon Law, the synod of bishops has three purposes. First, it fosters a closer unity between the successor of Peter and the bishops, manifesting affective collegiality in a vivid way through the bishop's common solicitude for issues affecting the universal Church. Second, synods assist the pope in his primatial ministry. Bishops from throughout the world offer him their counsel on how best to defend and develop matters of faith and morals, and to strengthen ecclesiastical discipline. Third, synods consider questions pertaining to the Church's activity in the world (cf. CIC 342), a pastoral duty which has become increasingly significant since the Second Vatican Council.

The synod of bishops is meant "to realize concretely the participation of the episcopal college in the universal government of the Church."[16] It secures the fraternal bonds of solidarity between the bishops and the pope, and among the bishops themselves. Episcopal synods enjoy a different kind of authority and have a more limited membership than ecumenical councils. They are composed of bishops elected by their episcopal conferences, members of the Roman curia, appointees of the pope, and representatives of clerical religious institutes.

As a collegial structure, a fundamental responsibility of every synod, regardless of its kind, is to provide a forum for exchanging information about pastoral problems affecting the Church. It furthers knowledge on all sides and, when there is a lack of understanding, can help to promote agreement. A synod provides the occasion for what Joseph Ratzinger calls "mutual self-correction." It allows the bishops and the pope a unique opportunity to engage in fraternal reprimand. More than merely fostering reciprocal correction, continues Ratzinger, synods are meant to encourage and strengthen "the positive forces inside and outside the Church."[17]

Role of the Pope

In *Apostolica sollicitudo*, Paul VI stated that the synod of bishops was to be closely associated with the papal office. It is, he wrote, "directly and immediately subject to our power" (intro.). The Code of Canon Law adopted the same view, describing the synod as a collegial body at the service of the pope: "It is the role of the synod of bishops to discuss the questions on their agenda and to express their desires about them but not to resolve them or to issue decrees about them, unless the Roman Pontiff in certain cases has endowed the synod with deliberative power, and in this event, it is his role to ratify its decisions" (CIC 343). In many ways, the role of the pope in the synod of bishops is similar to that in an ecumenical council: he convokes it, ratifies the election of its members, determines the topics for discussion, sets the agenda, presides at its sessions, and can conclude, transfer, suspend, or dissolve it (cf. CIC 344). It is now customary for the pope to attend all sessions of the synod. His presence guarantees the unity of the assembly. The bishops' synod, then, is an institution through which the pope exercises *his* primatial office, but in a collegial way.[18] John Paul II draws a straight line between episcopal collegiality and the synod of bishops. "Episcopal Synods, established after Vatican II, are meant," he says, "to realize concretely the participation of the Episcopal College in the universal government of the Church."[19]

According to the Code of Canon Law, the function of the synod is preeminently advisory. Members give their opinions to the pope on matters he submits for their discussion. Because the synod is a consultative body, the pope is free to accept or reject its advice. It is also possible for him to grant the synod true deliberative power. In this case he would still have to ratify its decisions before they had the effect of law (cf. CIC 343). To date, no pope has delegated such power to a synod.

Since 1974, at its conclusion each synod has submitted a summary of its deliberations and recommendations to the pope. Sometimes it has also issued a concluding message on its own authority. While the bishop of Rome is not bound by a synod's decisions, they enjoy a large measure of moral authority. John Paul II has said that the vote of the synod

Origins, Development, and Mission of the Papacy

Fathers, "if morally unanimous, has a qualitative ecclesial weight which surpasses the merely formal aspect of the consultative vote."[20] In recent years, the usual practice has been that after an ordinary synod the pope has issued an apostolic exhortation in his own name. Even though prepared by the pope, John Paul II regards such documents as "a fruit of collegiality."[21] While the synod of bishops serves the pope, it does so as an organ which manifests the spirit of collegial cooperation between him and the other bishops.

Proposals for Remodeling the Synod

Due to the initial papal and conciliar documents which described and set up the synod, and to its later canonical codification, questions have arisen concerning its collegial nature. On the one hand, many of its elements link the synod closely to episcopal collegiality. On the other hand, some descriptions relate it more narrowly to being a collegial way for the pope to carry out the Petrine ministry. Because of this theological ambiguity, the current synodal structure, which is still in its infancy, remains open to further development. Consequently, many theologians offer suggestions about how the present synod of bishops could be modified. Some propose that it should become an organ of effective, not just affective, collegiality. Others recommend that the synod should be more genuinely consultative rather than merely advisory.

A first group of theologians suggests that the synod should be recognized as an instance of a truly collegial action of the dispersed episcopate, a possibility provided for by Vatican II and canon law (cf. LG 22; CIC 337.2). Their proposal rests on the fact that the bishops who participate in a synod do so as representatives of the episcopal college which elected them, and not as delegates of the pope.[22] James Provost, for example, believes that "there is nothing to preclude a strictly collegial act from being conducted in a representative manner."[23] If this is true, then the current legislation which gives synod members only consultative voice would have to be rethought. In effect, the implementation of this suggestion would turn the synod of bishops into a miniature ecumenical council, where the decisions are taken by a body having supreme authority in the Church.

More in keeping with current canon law and post-conciliar practice, however, is the view that the synod helps the pope "in exercising his office" (CIC 334). Synods of bishops are collective gatherings "which are authentically sign and instrument of the collegial spirit,"[24] says the Final Report of the 1985 synod. This affective collegiality is bi-directional. It allows the bishops a say in the pastoral government of the universal Church, and it gives the pope the chance to carry out his ministry in a collegial way.

Two reasons can be offered to explain why the synod cannot be an organ of effective collegiality. First, acts of ecumenical councils or of the dispersed episcopate are fully collegial insofar as they are actions of the subject of supreme authority in the Church. Bishops, however, can exercise this supreme power only as a corporate body. They cannot delegate their right to constitute the organ of supreme authority to representatives who attend a synod. Only the whole college of bishops can engage in fully collegiate acts. Second, even if the pope were regularly to give the synod of bishops deliberative power, its decisions would still not be strictly collegial acts. Effective collegiality depends on the corporate authority inherent in the episcopal college; it is not delegated to it by the successor of Peter. Without a radical reinterpretation of traditional teaching on the meaning of episcopal collegiality and a revision of current canon law, the synod of bishops will remain an ecclesial institution which manifests affective, but not effective, collegiality.

Less radical is the proposal of those who recommend that the synod become a more collaborative policy-making body with the pope. They liken it to a large "cabinet" or to the "senate of the Roman Pontiff," as the college of cardinals was called in the 1917 Code of Canon Law (canon 230). Unlike the previous group of writers, these theologians and canonists are unconcerned with whether the synod can perform strictly collegial acts. What they argue for is emphasizing the synod's collegiality more from the side of the bishops rather than from that of the pope. Hence, they stress that the bishops who participate in a synod do so in virtue of their own episcopal office, an office which is collegial by its very nature. While conceding that the synod is unable to act in a strictly collegial way, they maintain that it should represent the college of bishops which works *with* the pope rather than merely *under* him. In other words, they believe that the synod should function more "with Peter" rather than "subject to Peter" (AG 38).

Consequently, these writers propose that the synod should normally enjoy deliberative governing power. Even if ultimately granted to it by the successor of Peter, his concession would be to a body which already embodies episcopal collegiality. In this way, their argument runs, synodal decisions would result from a more genuine dialogue between the pope and the synod. Under the present arrangement, they regard the final decisions as stemming more from the collaboration between the pope, who receives the synod's recommendations, and the Roman curia, which shapes them.[25] Granfield thinks that if the synod were a truly deliberative body, "it would strengthen the collegial nature of the assembly and contribute to its effectiveness and credibility."[26] Insofar as this recommendation falls within current canonical norms, it could be implemented without any legislative changes.

Joseph Ratzinger sounds a warning note, however, about the expectations that some bishops and theologians have expressed regarding the synod as a collegial organ. He reminds the bishops that they share in caring for the universal Church principally by shepherding their own flocks and "not by being represented in some central organ.... The idea that it is only by being represented at the centre that they will have significance for the whole represents a fundamental misjudgment of the nature of the Church; it is the expression of a centralism which the Second Vatican Council in fact wanted to overcome."[27] Bishops pastor the universal Church in and through their care for the particular churches entrusted to them. This pastoral care at the local level embodies the principles of ecclesial communion and affective collegiality.

College of Cardinals

Another collegial instrument, which is more ancient than the synod of bishops, is the college of cardinals. It, too, is a partial realization of collegiality which helps the pope to fulfill his universal ministry. The cardinalate is intimately associated with the papal ministry for two reasons. First, in the history of the papacy, the college of cardinals has a long tradition of collaboration with the bishop of Rome. Second, the recent revival and implementation of the doctrine of collegiality has given new vigor to this body.

As an ecclesial institution, the college of cardinals should be differentiated from the episcopal college, and therefore from episcopal collegiality in the strict sense of the term. For centuries membership in the college of cardinals was not restricted to bishops. Unlike the episcopacy, presbyterate, and diaconate, the cardinalate does not belong to the essential elements which Christ willed for his Church. Through the ages, cardinals have been non-ordained laymen, as well as deacons, priests, and bishops. In 1962, John XXIII reversed this age-old tradition by requiring all cardinals to receive episcopal ordination, a provision incorporated into the current Code of Canon Law (cf. CIC 351.1). Nonetheless, the pope can dispense from this requirement, as John Paul II has done on occasion. Therefore, the college of cardinals is not essentially an episcopal body and so cannot engage in strictly collegial acts. Consequently, it "does not obscure the collegial character of the service of the episcopate but brings it even more clearly to light."[28]

Origin

During the first millennium, the college of cardinals gradually took shape, with priests, deacons, and bishops each having a role. Already in the eighth century, the senior priests of Rome's principal parishes, known as "titular churches," were sometimes asked to preside at certain liturgical functions at the martyrs' shrines or the major Roman basilicas. They were called cardinal priests. In the early Middle Ages, deacons in charge of charitable work and of administering the seven districts of Rome were also known as cardinals.[29] At the same time, the pope asked bishops from the seven surrounding or "suburbicarian" sees of Rome to take care of some celebrations in the Basilica of St. John Lateran, his cathedral church. Because they presided at services there, these seven cardinal bishops were designated "vicars of the pope."[30] Together these bishops, senior priests, and deacons formed a loosely knit but privileged body at the service of the Roman bishop.

During the eleventh-century Gregorian Reform, the pope gave these men, all commonly known as "cardinals" (from the Latin *cardo*, meaning "hinge"), greater administrative as well as liturgical functions.[31] As an educated cadre of papal assistants, they became major agents in the renewal of pastoral life at Rome and, as papal electors, in the universal Church. Increasingly the cardinals became aides and advisors to the pope, the "hinges" or pivots on whom he depended for various tasks. They frequently served as papal envoys and ambassadors, helping the bishop of Rome to carry out his responsibilities as pastor of the universal Church. From the eleventh century on, the pope named to the college men who did not reside in or near Rome.[32] Today he selects as cardinals both his close advisors in Rome, who serve as prefects and heads of the various dicasteries and offices of the Roman curia, which is the administrative arm of the pope, major archbishops from around the world, and other distinguished churchmen.

Upon his elevation to office, every cardinal, except the cardinal bishops from the suburbicarian sees and the patriarchs of the Oriental Catholic churches, is assigned a "titular" church in Rome (cf. CIC 350.2). Cardinals of the Latin rite are thus regarded as belonging to the Roman clergy. Just as every bishop shares with his priests the ministry of pastoring the church entrusted to his care, so, too, does the bishop of Rome. The welfare of every particular church demands that its bishop seek assistance in carrying out his ministry. As members of the Roman clergy, the cardinals are associated with the pope as brothers in his presbyterate. They help their bishop to fulfill his pastoral responsibilities, especially those directed to the worldwide Church. John Paul II has said that the cardinals "form in a special way the presbyterium of the Roman church as direct collaborators of the pope."[33] The bishop of Rome is their head, not just as pastor of the universal Church, but as presider of the Roman presbyteral college to which they belong.

Collegial Assistance to the Roman Bishop

Cardinals are best known for their role in electing the pope, a function to be discussed in chapter thirteen. Equally important, however, is their duty to "assist the Roman Pontiff collegially when they are called together to deal with questions of major importance" (CIC 349). This collegial function has its roots in the Gregorian Reform. At that time, they formed a college around the pope, an institution commonly held to be in continuity with both the apostolic body and the senate of ancient Rome.

Medieval theologians and canonists defended the divine institution of this special college. Wanting to legitimate the cardinalate as a necessary element in the Church's structure, they justified it by using the same arguments which they invoked for the papacy: it originated in the will of Christ, not that of a human legislator. Consequently, the pope could not abolish the college of cardinals at will. Its members, the scholars held, succeeded to the collegiate dimension of Church government established by the apostles. Consequently, from the thirteenth century on, the cardinals were often referred to as "parts of the body of the pope," and eventually even as successors of the apostles.[34] In the fourteenth century, belief in the divine right of the cardinalate was increasingly called into question. Even so, this opinion was not definitively rejected until the sixteenth century.[35]

Closely linked to this lofty doctrine of the college of cardinals was the attribution of divine institution to the Roman *church* as such. From the eleventh century onward, the term "the Roman church" (*Ecclesia romana*) designated both the pope and the cardinals who together governed the universal Church. St. Peter Damian († 1072) believed that the college of cardinals was like the Roman senate, which had shared sovereignty with the emperor.[36] Accordingly, he concluded that the cardinals partook in the power belonging to the bishop of Rome.[37] This led some later medieval authors to affirm that the college of cardinals participated in the pope's *plenitudo potestatis*.

Because of the theory of the divine institution of the cardinalate, many canonists and theologians argued that primatial authority was to be exercised with others' help. This was true even at a time when the theology of papal monarchy was at its height. The practice of the Roman church confirmed the theory. At first, cardinals gave their advice to the pope in synods which bishops also attended. Soon, however, collegial assistance was offered in meetings or consistories whose membership was restricted to cardinals and the bishop of Rome. Medieval canonists and theologians taught that the successor of Peter should seek the counsel of either the cardinals in consistory or of the bishops in council, especially in matters of faith. They disagreed, however, about the extent to which the pope was obliged to follow their guidance. During the Gregorian Reform, the pope issued decrees "with the advice of our brothers." But it was unclear precisely what juridical weight the counsel of cardinals and bishops had. When meeting in synods, which included bishops who were not cardinals, the pope appears to have given more weight to the body's advice. In consistories, on the other hand, the pope personally made the decisions.[38] Very early on, then, the bishop of Rome regarded the college of cardinals as a consultative body with a collegial function different from that provided by bishops assembled in synod.

Today the cardinals form a body which "through their collegial activity" counsels the pope. They give this advice either in ordinary consistories, which carry out more routine tasks, or in extraordinary consistories (cf. CIC 353.1). A consistory is a formal gathering of the college of cardinals, chaired by the pope. By the end of the Middle Ages, consistories had become highly formalized affairs. For this reason, the new Code of Canon Law included the possibility of convoking an extraordinary consistory, "which is celebrated when the special needs of the Church or the conducting of more serious affairs suggests that it should be held" (CIC 353.3).[39] Such extraordinary gatherings are means designed to help the pope in *his* task as universal pastor. John Paul II has shown considerable interest in revitalizing the college of cardinals as a collegial body whose wisdom and experience can assist him in his ministry. On several occasions, he has called extraordinary consistories, asking for the cardinals' advice on crucial matters affecting the Church: from finances, to the threats posed by the proselytism of sects, the defense of human life, and preparations for the holy year of 2000.

Episcopal Conferences

Consultation about common pastoral affairs among neighboring bishops is a traditional practice already known in the patristic Church. The prehistory of episcopal conferences is found in the ancient ecclesial structures which mediated between a particular church and the Holy See. This prehistory is almost identical with "the significance and effectiveness of metropolitans, patriarchs, primates, and with the effectiveness of provincial synods, plenary and national Councils," wrote Karl Rahner.[40] The manifestations of collegiality in the ancient Church, which were described in chapter ten, can also be considered as the remote foundation of today's episcopal conferences.

The real history of bishops' conferences began, however, in the last century. Between 1830 and 1950, it was customary in Western Europe and North America for national or regional hierarchies to meet about once a year. The bishops consulted with one another and planned some common pastoral initiatives. In 1919, the National Catholic Welfare

Council, the forerunner of the National Conference of Catholic Bishops, was established in Washington.

The Second Vatican Council endorsed the practice of bishops from the same region coming together to further their pastoral effectiveness. *Lumen gentium* praised the synodal form of government practiced by the local churches of the Eastern tradition. This ancient system of grouping churches, which shared the same rite and discipline, for consultation and the regulation of regional ecclesial life could serve, the Fathers taught, as a model for national bishops' conferences: "in a like fashion the episcopal conferences at the present time are in a position to contribute in many and fruitful ways to the concrete realization of the collegiate spirit" (LG 23; cf. CD 38). Here the Fathers compare episcopal conferences to the ancient patriarchates. However different they are from these traditional structures, the council proposed that conferences could also be instruments manifesting affective collegiality. The Fathers, however, deliberately left the powers and theological status of these bishops' conferences nebulous.

In 1966, Paul VI mandated that each nation or region was to establish a permanent conference of bishops, if one did not already exist. The 1983 Code of Canon Law confirmed their existence and drew up canons to regulate their functions (cf. CIC 447-459). National conferences also come together in continental groupings. CELAM (Council of Latin American Episcopal Conferences), CCEE (Council for European Episcopal Conferences), and the continental structures for Africa, Asia, and Oceania are organizations which link different national and regional conferences of bishops. They, too, must be counted among the expressions of affective collegiality which correspond to the requirements of the present age.[41] Such councils of bishops' conferences are innovative collegial structures through which the Church responds to current pastoral problems.[42] While no continental structure has any juridical power over other conferences or particular churches, they are proving to be valuable instruments of the collegial spirit, favoring the common study of problems and the coordination of pastoral activity.

Collegial Spirit

The episcopal college and the primacy can alone claim divine institution, because only they were established by Christ through the Holy Spirit. While all canonists and theologians recognize that episcopal conferences are structures of ecclesiastical right, they draw at least two different conclusions from this teaching. Some think that bishops' conferences are primarily administrative and functional structures, minimizing them as expressions of collegiality. Ratzinger, for example, maintains that episcopal conferences "do not belong to the structure of the Church, as willed by Christ, that cannot be eliminated; they have only a practical, concrete function."[43] In a similar vein is the position expressed by the International Theological Commission: "To describe them [episcopal conferences] by such terms as 'college', 'collegiality' and 'collegial' is to use language in an analogical and theologically 'improper' way."[44] Other writers, however, point out that bishops' conferences are significant collegial bodies which have a theological value, even though they are not rooted in divine institution.

In a true but limited way, episcopal conferences do embody the principle of collegiality, showing and nurturing the "collegial spirit." They are genuine realizations of the collegiality which has its origins in the nature of the episcopacy and of the Church.[45] According to Rahner, conferences are "today perhaps even an absolutely necessary expression of an essential element of the Church."[46] Bonaventure Kloppenburg also insists on the ecclesiological significance of conferences of bishops. They are "not simply an expression of charity or camaraderie," he wrote, "but an ontological and juridical requirement of the specifically episcopal status."[47] National conferences furnish a concrete way for individual bishops to express their solicitude for the universal Church, a care which is integral to the collegial nature of their office.

Bishops' conferences are not, however, instances of effective collegiality. When gathered in national bodies the bishops fall short of representing the whole college throughout the world. By definition, they include only a limited number of bishops in their membership. The actions carried out by conferences "have a certain partial character of collegiality" but fail to embody the universality necessary for a strictly collegial act.[48] Unquestionably, the fullest expressions of collegiality are actions of the universal episcopacy with the pope. While it is inexact to speak of strictly collegial acts in the case of the bishops' conferences, the alternative is not to dismiss them as merely bureaucratic structures. Conferences of bishops are a specific, though limited, expression and concrete instrument of episcopal collegiality. When bishops are gathered in national conferences they act as members of the college, though not in its most complete manifestation.[49]

The development of bishops' conferences is a forceful reminder that episcopal individualism is contrary to the teaching of the Second Vatican Council. Because of their solidarity, which is rooted in episcopal ordination and hierarchical communion, bishops fittingly offer one another mutual help and cooperation at all levels. In a real but limited way, a conference of bishops embodies episcopal collegiality, insofar as it helps its member bishops to fulfill their responsibilities to other churches in the *koinonia*.[50]

Relations With the Holy See

While episcopal conferences are primarily expressions of horizontal cooperation among the bishops of a particular region, they also have a vertical dimension uniting them with the successor of Peter. As partial embodiments of collegiality, national conferences must in some way manifest their communion with the pope. In theory, the existence of bishops' conferences confirms papal primacy.

The development of strong conferences of bishops has been criticized by those who think that in practice they might undermine the Petrine ministry. Some are convinced that a national conference places itself as an intermediate structure between a diocesan bishop and the pope. In this way, it indirectly limits papal prerogatives and "the inviolable right and duty" of each bishop "to approach the successor of Peter" (PB 10). These individuals are worried that episcopal conferences could detract from the authority of a bishop both as head of his particular church and in his direct relationship with the successor of Peter. The bishop's personal pastoral governance, these writers point out, cannot be absorbed, substituted, or suppressed by the conference.[51] Both de Lubac and Ratzinger, for example, insist that the often impersonal and bureaucratic style of bishops' conferences could cripple the efforts of a local bishop in fulfilling his pastoral duties to his flock.[52] The framers of the Code of Canon Law took these concerns into account, explicitly defending the powers of the individual bishop in his diocese (cf. CIC 455).

It is helpful in this regard to recall the record of past practice. In the ancient Church, regional primatial structures had real authority over each bishop. Yet these institutions existed in harmony with the Roman bishop's function as the center of ecclesial communion.[53] History teaches that intermediate ecclesial structures between the local bishop and the pope strengthen the bonds of their mutual communion. While today some fear that episcopal conferences could compromise an individual bishop's hierarchical communion with the see of Peter by introducing another body which calls for loyalty, in the past the situation was reversed. In the West, there is evidence that the primacy of the bishop of Rome sometimes overpowered the dignity and rights of the local bishop.[54]

According to John Paul II, bishops' conferences strengthen the bond of unity "which is the point of contact between the 'collegial' character of the bishops and the 'primatial' one of Peter in the exercise of their respective pastoral ministries in the Church."[55] As collegial instruments of the episcopal college, conferences serve a mediating function between the Roman see and the particular churches, inculturating the Church's faith in the various regions.

Episcopal conferences are valuable instruments through which the magisterium, whether of the pope or the entire episcopal college, comes to life in local situations. Whether a conference has the authority to teach on matters not already explicit in the papal or universal ordinary magisterium is disputed. Some writers stress that the conference is unable to teach on such questions. Truly doctrinal questions, they maintain, fall under the competence of the entire episcopal college.[56] Others, however, argue that the conference has a mandate to teach. They cite the Code of Canon Law in their favor: the bishops "either as individuals or gathered in conferences of bishops or in particular councils, are authentic [authoritative] teachers and instructors of the faith for the faithful entrusted to their care" (CIC 753).

Again, the solution is to be found by recalling that collegiality can be partially realized. A conference's teaching function, therefore, is also true but limited. In this regard, Avery Dulles refers to the teaching of the national bishops' conference as a "pastoral" magisterium. This pastoral teaching, he writes, is "to put the riches of the Gospel within reach of the faithful in a manner that will incline them to partake of and live by the word of salvation."[57] In the United States, for example, the National Conference of Catholic Bishops addresses in its pastoral letters issues pertinent to the particular challenges facing American Catholics. Foremost among these recent letters have been *The Challenge of Peace* (1983) and *Economic Justice for All* (1986). It is true, however, that the formal teaching authority of these conference documents is an open theological question.

Bishops' conferences also perform an intermediary role between the Holy See and the bishops of a particular nation or region. Roman authorities often call upon the national conferences to express their opinion on questions affecting the universal Church. In recent years, it has become a common practice for the pope and the Roman curia to seek input from the episcopal conferences before issuing significant documents. For example, before publishing the *Catechism of the Catholic Church* (1992), or the apostolic constitution *Ex corde ecclesiae* (1990) on Catholic universities, and before meetings of the triennial synod of bishops, draft documents were circulated to the bishops, and their responses were coordinated by the national conferences. In this way, episcopal conferences have provided curial authorities with valuable advice which has significantly shaped the final version of Roman documents.

Owing to the possible repercussions of the decisions of episcopal conferences, the Code of Canon Law requires that the Holy See review any decrees which they propose as binding (cf. CIC 455.2). The Petrine ministry guarantees "the coordination of the conferences' activities with the life and teaching of the universal Church" says John Paul II.[58] As Dulles warns, "the exercise of a totally independent magisterium by the conferences could lead to divisions in the church and to a species of ecclesiastical nationalism detrimental to catholicity."[59] No conference should infringe on the teaching function which pertains to the whole college. It is the pope's responsibility to oversee that the bishops' teaching is in harmony with that of the universal Church. He ensures that the bishops of one conference substantially agree with their brothers throughout the world.[60] This vigilance of the Roman see is a necessary service to the unity of the churches, not "an unwarranted intrusion upon their spiritual sovereignty."[61] At the same time, the pope must avoid replacing a legitimate diversity in approach with uniform directives which would compromise authentic catholicity.

Consequently, the bishop of Rome coordinates the efforts of bishops' conferences, reconciles significant differences between them, and encourages their efforts at mutual support.[62] On occasion, this involves arranging meetings between representatives of various conferences which are dealing with the same pastoral problems. The Holy See serves as a kind of central "clearing house" for the worldwide episcopate. As the *centrum unitatis*, the successor of Peter not only initiates communication with local churches, he also hands on the teaching of other bishops to the universal Church. In the words of Tillard, it pertains to the pope "to receive and pass on to all the churches those major decisions, of interest to all though taken by some of their number . . . to exert himself in putting the churches in touch with each other over their own particular decisions. . . . The Spirit speaks to the churches — to all the churches — by other channels than by the 'primate' only, and the responsibility of the 'primate' is to relay the Spirit's voice, not to absorb it into his own word."[63]

Ad Limina Visits of Bishops

Collegiality is also shown in the visits, at five-year intervals, which each diocesan bishop makes to Rome. These visits and the quinquennial reports prepared for them provide the opportunity for regular and structured contact between every diocesan bishop and the successor of Peter.

Origin

Paul's journeys to Jerusalem furnish the first recorded evidence of a special visit "to see Peter" (cf. Gal 1:18-19, 2:1-10). In the early centuries, many pilgrims, including bishops, imitated this apostolic model, going to Rome to venerate the tombs of Sts. Peter and Paul. According to the writings of Gregory the Great (590-604), the bishops went to Rome not only to pray but also to meet with the successor of Peter (cf. PL 77, 875). In the mid-eighth century, the Roman synod mandated that bishops from the surrounding dioceses were to go annually to Rome. This ruling, however, was not an innovation, since the synod's canons refer to the practice as an ancient tradition.[64] With the Gregorian Reform, the duty of bishops to visit the tombs of the apostles (*visitatio ad limina apostolorum*) took firm root. The reforming popes used the practice as a means of consolidating their primatial authority. The rationale they gave for requiring these visits was straightforward. Since the successor of Peter could not personally visit all the churches, the churches, in the person of their bishop, were to visit him. Gregory VII (1073-1085) ruled that all bishops whom he had ordained and all metropolitans were to visit Rome every year; those at a distance could fulfill their obligation through an accredited representative. Later these visits included the opportunity for the bishops to confer with members of the papal curia concerning the state of their dioceses.[65]

Though the tradition of *ad limina* visits waned during the late Middle Ages, the popes of the Catholic Reform restored it. Pope Sixtus V (1585-1590) revived the ancient practice, giving it a normative character. In his decree *Romanus pontifex* (1585), he outlined the procedures to be followed in planning for and carrying out the visit. While various details were altered in the following centuries, the constitution gave the *ad limina* visit the form which has survived to the present.[66] Depending on a church's distance from Rome, its bishop was expected to submit a complete report to the Holy See on the temporal and spiritual condition of his diocese every three, four, five, or ten years. The visit itself included three distinct phases: prayer at the tombs of Sts. Peter and Paul, a personal meeting of the bishop with the pope, and the presentation of the report both orally and in writing to the relevant congregations of the Roman curia. This visit and report became in fact, if not in law, equivalent to a regular canonical visitation of each diocese by the Holy See.[67]

Purpose

Bishops are answerable to their brothers in the episcopal college and, in a particular way, to the successor of Peter. Current legislation prescribes that every five years the diocesan bishop is to present a report to the pope "concerning the state of the diocese committed to him" (CIC 399.1). During the year when he draws up this quinquennial report, he "is to come to Rome to venerate the tombs of the blessed apostles Peter and Paul and is to appear before the Roman Pontiff" (CIC 400.1). The quinquennial report and visit provide a regular structure for episcopal accountability, enabling the bishop to assess the fidelity of his diocese to the gospel.[68] They are also the ordinary means which allow the pope to fulfill his duty of overseeing the bishop's stewardship of his particular church. The whole process of *ad limina* visits is an exercise of the executive discretion proper to primatial authority of the bishop of Rome.[69]

Meeting With Peter's Successor

The *ad limina* visits "constitute, as it were, the center of the highest ministry committed to the supreme pontiff" (PB 10). They foster collegiality in two directions: from the pope with the bishops, and from the bishops with the pope.

As the primary guardian of the deposit of truth, the pope uses *ad limina* visits to consolidate the unity and catholicity of the episcopal college, ensuring that the bishops have not run "in vain" (Gal 2:2). The bishop of Rome regards these periodic visits as an opportunity to sharpen the awareness of the bishop's responsibilities as a successor of the apostles. Indeed, to keep abreast with the affairs of all the churches, the pope needs to meet personally with his brother bishops who embody the Church's catholicity: "each part contributes its own gifts to other parts and to the whole Church, so that the whole and each of the parts are strengthened by the common sharing of all things and by the common effort to attain to fullness in unity" (LG 13). Requiring the quinquennial visit to Rome enables the pope to carry out his own charge to enrich the catholicity of the Church.

In addition, when the bishops meet with the successor of Peter they reaffirm their belief that the *koinonia* has an apostolic center. Not only does the pope assist the bishops, they, in turn, help him in his ministry to the universal Church. The bishops provide him with reliable and authoritative information on the life of the particular churches which they shepherd. According to the norms established for *ad limina* visits, the bishops bring their "richness of experience to the Petrine ministry and its service of illuminating the serious problems of the Church and the world as these problems are perceived in their various features within different places, times and cultures."[70] Carried out in the spirit of collegiality, the visit is meant to strengthen the bishops in fulfilling their office and to solidify their hierarchical communion with the successor of Peter.

During the *ad limina* visit there is always a personal meeting between the diocesan bishop and the pope. Because God has entrusted ministry to persons, these meetings are "a visible realization," writes Ratzinger, "of that mutual indwelling of the universal Church and the particular churches."[71] The radically personal structure of the Church's hierarchical constitution demands such a face-to-face encounter between brother bishops. There is also a group meeting with bishops from a region who go to Rome together. At this time the pope gives a talk which is designed to encourage the bishops, to praise their pastoral initiatives, and, if need be, to draw their attention to specific areas of concern in the local churches. Outside his pastoral visits, these discourses provide the pope with an occasion to address particular churches in the personal and direct way that corresponds to his universal ministry.

Pastoral Visits of the Pope

Another sign and instrument of the collegial spirit are the pastoral visits which the bishop of Rome makes to churches throughout the world. Traveling popes are an age-old phenomenon. Often they were missions of peace. Leo the Great (440-461) went to northern Italy to convince Attila the Hun to spare Rome. And Pius VI (1775-1799) set out for Vienna, hoping to persuade Emperor Joseph II to restore the Church's freedom. On occasion, the popes left Rome to promote the cause of Church reform. At the outset of the Gregorian Reform, Leo IX (1049-1054) traveled extensively throughout Europe to preside at councils which furthered his policies. Other forays were for war. Julius II (1503-1513) earned the title of "warrior pope" for his campaigns to regain territory lost to the Papal States. From the loss of these States in 1870 until 1934, no pope left the Vatican. John XXIII's visits to Assisi and Loreto in 1962 were the first papal trips outside Rome and the papal residence at Castel Gandolfo in nearly a century.[72]

Modern means of travel give the pope opportunities to be present as the chief shepherd within local churches in a way never before possible.[73] Since the pontificate of Paul VI (1963-1978), papal visits to particular churches have become yet another ordinary way through which to express affective collegiality between the successor of Peter and the successors of the apostles. Paul VI made nine visits outside Italy, carefully chosen as symbolic statements as head of the Catholic Church: to Jerusalem, Geneva, Fatima, the United Nations, Africa, Latin America, Asia, the Far East, and Oceania. John Paul II has undertaken more than one hundred visits within Italy, and sixty outside it. These international pilgrimages average about four per year and are an integral dimension of John Paul II's papal ministry. At the beginning of his pontificate, he said that the "pope cannot accomplish his service in any other way but by going towards man, therefore towards peoples and nations."[74] This means that the pope should travel a great deal. In the first fifteen years of his pontificate, John Paul II covered more than 110 different countries, and many times that number of local churches. In a hitherto unprecedented way, the hopes of the Church are focused on the pope, not only as her supreme authority but as her most charismatic figure. Unquestionably, these trips add a new dimension to the way in which the bishop of Rome carries out the Petrine ministry.

In some ways, papal trips are the reverse of *ad limina* visits. Consonant with a theology of communion, the centripetal movement of the bishops to Rome is complemented by the centrifugal movement of the pope to the local churches. There he meets with bishops and faithful. Pope Paul VI considered his pastoral visits to be expressions of collegiality: "Our mission [in making the journey to the Far East] will be in the spirit of communion and of collegiality with the bishops of those regions which are so extensive in area and so dense in population. We trust that the unity of the Catholic Church will thereby be reinforced, that the bond of collegiality will be still more strengthened, that missionary activity will be stimulated and that there will be a larger measure of understanding with other religions."[75] John Paul II refers to his meetings with bishops in their own countries "as special and unique moments of episcopal collegiality — in the 'primatial' framework . . . these visits really offer the possibility of a personal talk with every single pastor of the various particular churches, and of collegial meetings."[76]

Pastoral visits emphasize the significance of the local churches in the universal Church. They also give the pope the chance to manifest "the charism of Peter's daily

Origins, Development, and Mission of the Papacy

ministry in the streets of the world." Furthermore, adds John Paul II, these visits allow the bishop of Rome "to proclaim the gospel, to 'strengthen the brothers' in the faith, to console the Church, to meet man."[77] The pope visits the other churches in order to counteract by his presence any centrifugal tendencies which would distance them from one another and from the Church's center of unity.[78] Pastoral pilgrimages are signs both of episcopal collegiality and, perhaps even more, of the communion of the one people of God.

◆

The Second Vatican Council teaches that Peter's primatial mission is to be carried out within the framework of collegiality. As one of the major innovations of conciliar teaching, collegiality has contributed in many ways to the renewal of Church life. First, it has remedied the one-sided emphasis on papal prerogatives which dominated ecclesiology after Vatican I. Second, by its emphasis on the episcopacy, collegiality has strengthened the development of particular churches. Third, it has led to the formation of new ecclesial institutions, such as the synod of bishops, or strengthened ones already in existence, such as the college of cardinals and episcopal conferences. Fourth, because the principle of collegiality embodies a model of pastoral organization familiar to the Church of the first millennium, it has facilitated ecumenical discussion on papal primacy, especially with the Orthodox and Anglicans.[79]

Hierarchical communion calls for the collegial spirit to be embodied in concrete ecclesial structures. Through them, the bishops and the successor of Peter can manifest their fraternal bonds, solidarity, and mutual cooperation in pastoring the universal Church. Collegiality is expressed in various forms, whether in the strictly collegial activity of ecumenical councils and the dispersed episcopate or through the affective collegiality which animates the synod of bishops, college of cardinals, episcopal conferences, *ad limina* visits, and pastoral pilgrimages.

The coming together of Christians, especially pastors, to discuss and sometimes make determinations about major questions affecting the Church is a custom as ancient as the apostolic assembly in Jerusalem (cf. Acts 15:1-29). In various ways, this practice continues today in ecumenical councils, the synod of bishops, the college of cardinals, and episcopal conferences. While no particular form of collegiality can lay claim to being of divine right, each one is an apt way either for the college of bishops to express its union with its head, or for the pope to show his need for collegial assistance in fulfilling the Petrine ministry.

It is the "spirit" of collegiality, the mode of collaboration among those serving the kingdom of God, which has left the greatest imprint on post-conciliar Church life. The synod of bishops, for example, is designed to involve pastors in the formation of policy on major doctrinal and disciplinary questions facing the Church. It is not a small-scale ecumenical council; its primary purpose is to advise the pope. The episcopal synod is an institutionalized form of affective collegiality of the bishops among themselves and with the chief pastor. The synod is therefore a true but partial expression and instrument of episcopal collegiality. So, too, are episcopal conferences. By their very nature, these conferences can neither replace the rights of a bishop as head of his church nor undermine papal authority. Because their decisions have repercussions which reach beyond their regional confines, the bishop of Rome has the responsibility of guaranteeing the coordination of the conferences' activities with the life and teaching of the universal Church.

Less intense forms of collegiality are the college of cardinals, *ad limina* visits of the bishops to Rome, and papal pilgrimages to local churches. In its own way each one fosters the bonds of hierarchical communion and manifests the Church's unity in catholicity. As we shall see in the next chapter, the teaching of the Second Vatican Council on collegiality has opened yet other possibilities for understanding the function of the papal ministry in both the particular and universal Church.

Notes for Chapter eleven

1. Patrick Granfield, *The Limits of the Papacy* (Garden City: Doubleday & Company, 1980), 78.
2. John Paul II, Discourse, February 7, 1979, *L'Osservatore Romano*, 7 (February 12, 1979), 12.
3. International Theological Commission, "Select Themes of Ecclesiology on the Occasion of the Twentieth Anniversary of the Closing of the Second Vatican Council," in *International Theological Commission: Texts and Documents, 1969-1985*, ed. Michael Sharkey (San Francisco: Ignatius Press, 1989), #V.3, p. 285.
4. Remigiusz Sobanski, "Il concilio ecumenico, il sinodo dei vescovi, il collegio cardinalizio," in *Collegialità e primato*, ed. Velasio De Paolis (Bologna: Dehoniane, 1993), 80.
5. Karl Rahner, "The Hierarchical Structure of the Church, with Special Reference to the Episcopate," in *Commentary on the Documents of Vatican II*, ed. Herbert Vorgrimler, vol. 1 (New York: Herder and Herder, 1967), 200.
6. Cited in *Code of Canon Law Annotated*, ed. E. Caparros, M. Thériault, and J. Thorn (Montreal: Wilson & Lafleur Limitée, 1993), 270.
7. Rahner, "Hierarchical Structure of the Church," 201.
8. James H. Provost, "The Hierarchical Constitution of the Church," in *The Code of Canon Law: A Text and Commentary*, ed. James A. Coriden, Thomas J. Green, and Donald E. Heintschel (New York: Paulist Press, 1985), 278.
9. Julio Manzanares, "Il romano pontefice e la collegialità dei vescovi," in *Collegialità e primato*, ed. Velasio De Paolis (Bologna: Dehoniane, 1993), 43.
10. Henri de Lubac, *The Motherhood of the Church*, trans. Sergia Englund (San Francisco: Ignatius Press, 1982), 247-248.
11. Frederick R. McManus, "Local, Regional and Universal Church Law," in *The Papacy and the Church in the United States*, ed. Bernard Cooke (New York: Paulist Press, 1989), 184.
12. John Paul II, *Redemptor hominis* (1979), #5.
13. John Paul II, Address to the Council of the General Secretariat of the Synod of Bishops, April 30, 1983, *L'Osservatore Romano*, 21 (May 23, 1983), 9.
14. De Lubac, *Motherhood of the Church*, 315.
15. Joseph Ratzinger, *Church, Ecumenism and Politics*, trans. Robert Nowell (New York: Crossroad Publishing Company, 1988), 49.
16. John Paul II, Discourse, October 7, 1992, *L'Osservatore Romano*, 41 (October 14, 1992), 11.

254 ✦ COLLEGIALITY AND THE PAPAL OFFICE

17. Ratzinger, *Church, Ecumenism and Politics*, 61-62.
18. Gianfranco Ghirlanda, *Il diritto nella Chiesa: mistero di comunione*, 2nd ed. (Milan: Edizioni San Paolo, 1992), 518.
19. John Paul II, Discourse, October 7, 1992, *L'Osservatore Romano*, 41 (October 14, 1992), 11.
20. John Paul II, Discourse to the Council of the General Secretariat of the Synod of Bishops, April 30, 1983, *L'Osservatore Romano*, 21 (May 23, 1983), 9.
21. John Paul II, *Christifideles laici* (1988), #2.
22. Patrick R. Granfield, "The Uncertain Future of Collegiality," *Proceedings of the Catholic Theological Association of America*, 40 (1985), 100-101; cf. Granfield, *Limits of the Papacy*, 91-92.
23. Provost, "Hierarchical Constitution of the Church," 282.
24. Synod of Bishops (1985), "The Final Report," *Origins*, 15:27 (December 19, 1985), #II.C.4, p. 448.
25. Giuseppe Alberigo, "Per un papato rinnovato a servizio della chiesa," *Concilium*, 11:8 (1975), 33.
26. Granfield, *Limits of the Papacy*, 95.
27. Ratzinger, *Church, Ecumenism and Politics*, 51-52.
28. Remigiusz Sobanski, "Implications for Church Law in the Use of the Term 'Collegiality' in the Theological Context of Official Church Statements," *Concilium*, 4 (1990), 46.
29. Alfons M. Stickler, "The Roman Church and Cardinals," *L'Osservatore Romano*, 3 (January 15, 1976), 9.
30. Michele Maccarrone, "The Church of Rome Is the Church of Peter," *L'Osservatore Romano*, 3 (January 15, 1976), 8.
31. K. F. Morrison, "Cardinal, I (History of)," *New Catholic Encyclopedia*, vol. 3 (New York: McGraw-Hill Book Company, 1967), 104.
32. Provost, "Hierarchical Constitution of the Church," 286-287.
33. John Paul II, Address to the Roman Curia, June 28, 1980, *L'Osservatore Romano*, 28 (July 14, 1980), 13.
34. Yves Congar, *Ministères et communion ecclésiale* (Paris: Cerf, 1971), 110-111.
35. J. Michael Miller, *The Divine Right of the Papacy in Recent Ecumenical Theology*, Analecta Gregoriana, vol. 218 (Rome: Gregorian University Press, 1980), 21-22; cf. Giuseppe Alberigo, *Cardinalato et Collegialità: Studi sull'ecclesiologia tra l'XI e il XIV secolo* (Florence: Vallechi, 1969).
36. Yves Congar, *L'Eglise de saint Augustin à l'époque moderne* (Paris: Cerf, 1970), 115.
37. Joseph Lécuyer, "Posizione teologica della Curia romana," *Concilium*, 15:7 (1979), 30.
38. Giuseppe Alberigo, "Servire la comunione delle chiese," *Concilium*, 15:7 (1979), 41-42.
39. Provost, "Hierarchical Constitution of the Church," 290.
40. Karl Rahner, "On Bishops' Conferences," in *Theological Investigations*, trans. Karl-H. and Boniface Kruger, vol. 6 (Baltimore: Helicon Press, 1969), 371; cf. Louis Bouyer, *The Church of God*, trans. Charles Underhill Quinn (Chicago: Franciscan Herald Press, 1982), 445.
41. John Paul II, Discourse, February 7, 1979, *L'Osservatore Romano*, 7 (February 12, 1979), 12.
42. John Paul II, Discourse, October 7, 1992, *L'Osservatore Romano*, 41 (October 14, 1992), 11.
43. Joseph Ratzinger with Vittorio Messori, *The Ratzinger Report*, trans. Salvator Attanasio and Graham Harrison (San Francisco: Ignatius Press, 1985), 59; cf. Jerome Hamer, *To Preach the Gospel: The First Duty of the Bishop* (Washington, D.C.: United States Catholic Conference, 1979), 15.

44. International Theological Commission, "Select Themes of Ecclesiology," in *Texts and Documents*, #V.3, p. 286; cf. Congregation for Bishops, "Draft Statement on Episcopal Conferences," *Origins*, 17:43 (April 7, 1988), #A.IV.1, p. 734.
45. Frederick R. McManus, "The Scope of Authority of Episcopal Conferences," in *The Once and Future Church: A Communion of Freedom*, ed. James A. Coriden (New York: Alba House, 1971), 139.
46. Karl Rahner, "On Bishops' Conferences," 377.
47. Bonaventure Kloppenburg, *The Ecclesiology of Vatican II*, trans. Matthew J. O'Connell (Chicago: Franciscan Herald Press, 1974), 230.
48. Congregation for Bishops, "Draft Statement on Episcopal Conferences," #A.III.2, p. 734.
49. J. M. R. Tillard, *Church of Churches: The Ecclesiology of Communion*, trans. R. C. De Peaux (Collegeville: Liturgical Press, 1992), 206-207.
50. Avery Dulles, *The Reshaping of Catholicism* (San Francisco: Harper & Row, 1988), 212-213.
51. Giorgio Feliciani, "Le conferenze episcopali," in *Collegialità e primato*, ed. Velasio De Paolis (Bologna: Dehoniane, 1993), 215.
52. Ratzinger with Messori, *The Ratzinger Report*, 59-61; cf. de Lubac, *Motherhood of the Church*, 267-268.
53. Klaus Schatz, *La primauté du Pape*, trans. Joseph Hoffmann (Paris: Cerf, 1992), 259.
54. Gisbert Greshake, " 'Zwischeninstanzen' zwischen Papst und Ortsbischofen," in *Die Bischofskonferenz: Theologischer und juridischer Status*, ed. Hubert Müller and Hermann J. Pottmeyer (Düsseldorf: Patmos, 1989), 105.
55. John Paul II, Address to the Roman Curia, June 28, 1980, *L'Osservatore Romano*, 28 (July 14, 1980), 13.
56. Dulles, *Reshaping of Catholicism*, 203.
57. Avery Dulles, "What is the Role of a Bishops' Conference?" *Origins*, 17:46 (April 28, 1988), 791.
58. John Paul II, Discourse, October 7, 1992, *L'Osservatore Romano*, 41 (October 14, 1992), 11.
59. Avery Dulles, "The Mandate to Teach," *America*, 158:11 (March 19, 1988), 294.
60. Avery Dulles, "The Teaching Authority of Bishops' Conferences," *America*, 148 (June 11, 1983), 454.
61. Dulles, *Reshaping of Catholicism*, 224.
62. Granfield, *Limits of the Papacy*, 103.
63. J. M. R. Tillard, *The Bishop of Rome*, trans. John de Satgé (Wilmington: Michael Glazier, 1983), 172.
64. Ghirlanda, *Il diritto nella Chiesa*, 546.
65. John P. Beal, "The Apostolic Visitation of a Diocese: A Canonico-Historical Investigation," *The Jurist*, 49:2 (1989), 377-378.
66. Vicente Cárcel Ortí, "Historico-Juridical Consideration," attached to the statement of the Congregation for Bishops, "Directory for the *ad limina* Visit," *L'Osservatore Romano*, 28 (July 11, 1988), 9.
67. Beal, "Apostolic Visitation of a Diocese," 389-391.
68. Thomas J. Green, "The Pastoral Governance Role of the Diocesan Bishop: Foundations, Scope, and Limitations," *The Jurist*, 49:2 (1989), 496.
69. James H. Provost, "Toward Some Operative Principles for Apostolic Visitations," *The Jurist*, 49:2 (1989), 555.

70. Congregation for Bishops, "Directory for the *ad limina* Visit," *L'Osservatore Romano*, 28 (July 11, 1988), foreword, p. 5.
71. Joseph Ratzinger, "Theological Notes," attached to the statement of the Congregation for Bishops, "Directory for the *ad Limina* Visit," *L'Osservatore Romano*, 28 (July 11, 1988), 7.
72. Patrick Granfield, *The Papacy in Transition* (Garden City: Doubleday & Company, 1980), 93-94.
73. Dominic V. Monti, "Historical Reflections," in *The Role of the Papal Office in the Life of the Church* (Silver Spring: Washington Theological Union, 1987), 1.
74. John Paul II, Discourse, May 21, 1980, *L'Osservatore Romano*, 21 (May 26, 1980), 1.
75. Paul VI, Address at Fiumicino Airport, November 26, 1970, *L'Osservatore Romano*, 49 (December 3, 1970), 1.
76. John Paul II, Address to the Roman Curia, June 28, 1980, *L'Osservatore Romano*, 28 (July 14, 1980), 13.
77. John Paul II, Address to the Roman Curia, June 28, 1980, *L'Osservatore Romano*, 28 (July 14, 1980), 14; cited in *Redemptoris missio* (1990), #63.
78. Luigi Accattoli, "The Journeys of the Pope as Instruments of the 'Mission to the Nations'," *Communio*, 18:3 (1991), 481.
79. Granfield, *Limits of the Papacy*, 105.

Chapter twelve
PETRINE MINISTRY AND PARTICULAR CHURCHES

The word *communio* describes the inner nature of the Church as a mystery, as a transcendent and saving reality which is visibly manifested in this world. Because the Church is "the icon of the trinitarian fellowship of Father, Son and Holy Spirit,"[1] her members participate in divine life. The Trinity sustains ecclesial communion. In a secondary way, an ecclesiology of communion also touches upon matters of Church structure. During the first millennium, the idea of *communio* was often used to describe the hierarchy. When this concept is linked to the universalist ecclesiology of the second millennium, a more developed theology of the papal ministry emerges: the pope's mission as an instrument of unity and communion comes more clearly to light.

This chapter builds on the previous study of *Pastor aeternus*, *Lumen gentium*, and the Code of Canon Law, in order to describe more completely the relation of the Petrine ministry to both the particular church and the universal communion of churches. First, I clarify some terms applied to the Church: "local," "particular" and "universal." I then examine the Petrine ministry as a constitutive element of every particular church. Consequently, the papacy can be described as a ministry at the service of the local church "from within" and of the universal Church as the center of the *koinonia*. Lastly, I will take up the purposes, principles, and practice of papal interventions in local churches.

Universal and Particular Church

Along with the idea of communion, the Fathers at the Second Vatican Council drew on the increasingly influential ecclesiology of the local church when they drafted *Lumen gentium*. Just as collegiality widens the horizon for discussing papal-episcopal relations, so also does the theology of the local church situate papal primacy in a fresh perspective. Admittedly, the council Fathers took only the initial steps in breaking the monopoly of a universalist ecclesiology. They still approached the Church primarily as a universal reality. When *Lumen gentium* refers to "the Church," it nearly always means the universal Church. In following this convention, the council mirrored the ecclesiology prevalent in the West since the Middle Ages.[2]

Terminology

The texts of both the Second Vatican Council and theological writings use imprecise terms when describing the non-universal manifestations of the Church.[3] Frequently they apply the term "particular" church to a diocese. On occasion, however, they call a diocese a "local" church. A consistent terminology is lacking in the canonical, theological, and magisterial sources.

Henri de Lubac suggested a clarification in terminology which has met with some success. He concluded that the documents of Vatican II usually refer to a diocese as a "particular" church, and to a grouping of particular churches in the same region which belong to the same rite, as a "local" church.[4] The Code of Canon Law incorporated de Lubac's distinction; it calls a diocese a "particular" church (cf. CIC 369) and avoids any references to "local" churches. The *Catechism of the Catholic Church* adopts the same usage (cf. 833). For the most part, recent documents and statements of the Holy See have adopted this canonical usage.

Even so, this distinction is not universally accepted. Orthodox theologians and many of their Catholic colleagues, especially those involved in ecumenical dialogue, continue to refer to a diocese as a "local" church. Due to this traditional usage, the Code's more fixed terminology has not succeeded in becoming normative, replacing the more traditional designation.[5] Depending on the context, therefore, I will use either "particular" or "local," treating them both as synonymous terms indicating the diocesan church.

Questions also arise about the meaning of the term "church" in the New Testament. On the one hand, St. Paul uses "church" (*ekklesia*) to describe different *local* communities of Christians. In the plural, he refers to the "churches" existing in a province (cf. 1 Cor 16:19; Gal 1:1), in a city (cf. 1 Cor 1:2; Col 4:15; 1 Thess 1:1), or in the house of a family (cf. 1 Cor 16:19). The Second Vatican Council follows this usage which attributes ecclesial reality to local communities: the "Church of Christ is really present in all legitimately organized local groups of the faithful, which, in so far as they are united to their pastors, are also quite appropriately called Churches in the New Testament" (LG 26). On the other hand, Paul also uses "church" in a more *universal* sense: it designates all believers throughout the world united in the one body of Christ (cf. Eph 5:24; Col 1:18, 24).

For many years, it was conventional wisdom that in the New Testament *ekklesia* originally and primarily referred to the local community. Only in the later writings was it also applied to the universal reality. Raymond Brown, however, cautions that the biblical evidence indicates "*a far more complex situation.*"[6] There is, in truth, no clear progression from designating the *ekklesia* first as local to afterward as universal. In fact, it is more in keeping with the scriptural witness to describe the Church as simultaneously particular and universal. An individual enters the one Church of Christ only through a local church, where he or she is baptized. Every Christian, including the pope, belongs to a particular church.[7] Whoever is a member of a local church, however, also belongs to the worldwide communion of churches.[8] The universal Church is not an abstraction which exists without local churches. As Louis Bouyer comments, "the universal Church appears, and even exists, only in the local churches."[9] The full realization of the one Church of Christ requires both local and universal manifestations.

Priority of the Universal Church?

While there is a consensus concerning the Church's constitution as universal and local, the theological question regarding the priority of one over the other is the subject of considerable debate. In the background of this controversy are differing views of papal primacy. When the Petrine ministry is described in traditional ecclesiology, the Church's universal dimension is favored over the particular. Universalist ecclesiology is very vigilant lest the pope's primacy be weakened in any way. In recent ecclesiastical documents, the concern to uphold some kind of priority for the universal Church can be discerned. John Paul II has expressed the need to avoid "those unilateral and baseless theses according to which the Church is originally and primarily the local church."[10] He has also said that "each particular church lives the life of the universal Church, which is the fundamental reality of the Church."[11] Defenders of a universalist ecclesiology argue that the universal Church enjoys a certain ontological or historical priority with respect to the *individual particular church, giving the following reasons for their position.*

Manifested on Pentecost, the universal Church is temporally prior to every particular church. The Church, which was first brought to life in the local community at Jerusalem, was inherently universal. This original church, they hold, was not a particular church in the sense that it was restricted to a specific territory or group of people as are modern dioceses. Instead, it was, at that time, the people of God of the new covenant, the universal Church. While gathered in one place, it was open to other embodiments.[12]

Within a short time, due to missionary activity and the dispersion of Christians owing to persecution, the church of Jerusalem gave birth to particular churches. This original community, moreover, normatively embodied the way in which the Church was to be realized in every future particular community: presided over by Peter's successor and the successors of the apostles with him.[13] All other churches in some way derive from the mother church of Jerusalem, which was originally both local and universal. But these churches are not, as de Lubac insists, "the result of the division of the universal Church alleged to be anterior to them.... An anterior universal Church, or one alleged to be existing on her own, apart from all others, is only a creation of the mind."[14] The priority of the universal Church is, then, neither an abstraction floating above historical embodiments in time and place nor a reality originating from particular churches.

Joseph Ratzinger recalls that just as the unity of an organism precedes and sustains the individual organs, "so also the unity of the Catholic Church precedes the plurality of particular churches which are born from this unity and receive their ecclesial character from it."[15] Others argue in favor of the priority of the universal Church by noting that not all of her attributes are applicable to the local church. The Church's indefectibility, for example, is proper to her only as the universal *koinonia* and does not belong to any particular church by itself.[16] By defending this kind of priority for the Church universal, theologians and Roman documents assure that the ministry of the successor of Peter belongs to every fully authentic realization of the "Church." Right from the beginning, therefore, the Church is the body of Christ, the universal sacrament of salvation, and the flock committed to Peter's care.[17]

The Pope and the Local Church

Visible ecclesial communion is rooted in the bonds of the profession of the same faith, common celebration of the sacraments, and acceptance of the apostolic ministry (cf. CCC 815). Theologies of the local church assume the profession of the apostolic faith, turning most of their attention to the Eucharist and the episcopacy as constitutive elements of every particular church. Both are principles of a church's interior unity and express its openness to the other churches of the *koinonia*. The unity of a community around its bishop at the celebration of the Eucharist signifies its unity with every other church which celebrates the same Eucharist with its bishop.[18]

Primacy and the Particular Church

Integral to the episcopal office is hierarchical communion with the whole college of bishops, including the successor of Peter. Every bishop ensures the ecclesial reality of his particular church, which can exist only if he is its head. He is the linchpin of both a church's apostolicity, verified through episcopal succession, and its catholicity, guaranteed through communion with his brother bishops and the pope.

Some theologians, especially those in the Orthodox tradition, have drawn certain conclusions regarding the Petrine ministry from this Eucharistic-episcopal structure of the local Church. They hold that where Christ is present in the Eucharist, there is found the entire mystery of the Church. Nothing more than this can be added to the ecclesial fullness of a local church. In Byzantine theology, writes Orthodox scholar John Meyendorff, the Eucharist serves as "the ultimate theological norm for ecclesiastical structure." The local church which offers the Eucharistic sacrifice is, he says, "not merely a 'part' of a universal organization, but the *whole* Body of Christ."[19] Because of their belief in the centrality of the Eucharist to Church life and in the episcopacy as the fullness of apostolic ministry, Eastern theologians have no place for any ecclesial authority which would claim to be superior to the bishop by divine right.[20] The universal Church and local churches exist together as Eucharistic communities, with no priority of one over the other.[21]

From these principles follows the East's understanding of Roman primacy. Nicolas Afanassieff sums up the common view of Orthodox theologians: "eucharistic ecclesiology excludes the idea of primacy by its very nature."[22] Consequently, because the Petrine ministry does not belong to the Eucharistic ordering of any community, except for the local church at Rome, it is unnecessary to the universal *koinonia*. At best, it is harmless and superfluous. At worst, the claim that the Petrine ministry is of divine institution contradicts the Church's constitution, introducing a structure contrary to the gospel. This latter situation would be the case, they contend, if the bishop of Rome tried to impose a kind of Church unity based on worldly conceptions of power rather than on sacramental realities. The acceptance of a papal ministry enjoying an authority by divine right over the other churches is not, therefore, constitutive of the one Church.[23]

Unlike Orthodox eucharistic ecclesiology, which insists on the presence of a bishop for a community to be considered a local church, Protestants usually concentrate on the congregation as the reality which constitutes ecclesial fullness. In these congregations, where the power of the Word gathers two or more in Christ's name, there is the Church (cf. Mt 18:20). Such a Protestant ecclesiology also excludes the primacy of any individual church or of its pastor. It, therefore, bars any divinely mandated role for the pope in the worldwide community of Christians.

Mutual Indwelling

How the relationship between the universal Church and particular churches is explained sheds a great deal of light on the papal ministry. In order to describe their connection, it is helpful first to exclude two inadequate explanations of the way in which they are connected. Neither one provides a satisfactory interpretation of their reciprocal interiority.

First, local churches do not come together as a federation to form the universal Church. The universal Church is not a " 'federative unity'," says de Lubac, "as if particular churches were at first able to establish themselves, each one separately, and then were free to join together: she is the Spouse of Christ."[24] If each individual church first enjoyed an independent existence, then the bishop of Rome would have only whatever supervisory function they conceded to him. In this view, the pope would be the moderator of the agreement among the churches rather than their visible principle of unity.

Second, the relationship between the local and universal Church is unlike "that which exists between the whole and the parts in a purely human group or society" (CN 9). Particular churches are not components of a larger reality in which one completes the other, "substations of the church universal or branch offices of a world-wide organization."[25] The universal Church is unlike a mosaic in which each separate piece is needed to make up the whole. This view of their relationship implies that local churches remain exterior one to the other. Local churches, however, are not separate administrative units of the universal Church. Instead, they are, as Ratzinger says, "living cells, each of which contains the whole living mystery of the one body of the Church."[26]

A more theologically satisfactory way to address the question of the relationship which exists among the particular churches and between them and the universal Church is the category of mutual indwelling taken from trinitarian theology. The life of the Church is a reflection of the inner life of the triune God, a communion of three mutually-indwelling persons. In the relations between Father, Son, and Holy Spirit the one divine nature exists. The real distinction of persons leaves the single divine nature undivided. These fundamental truths of trinitarian doctrine reveal that true differences can exist in unity.

Like the Trinity, the Church is one and many. Because particular churches "form part of the one Church of Christ" (CD 6), they, too, have a relationship of reciprocal interiority or indwelling with one another, that is, with the universal Church. According to *Lumen gentium*, "it is in these [particular churches] and formed out of them that the one and unique Catholic Church exists" (LG 23). In each local church "the one, holy, catholic and apostolic Church of Christ is truly present and active" (CD 11). The International Theological Commission compares this close association between the particular churches and the universal Church to "a kind of osmosis."[27] Consequently, no local church can ever be autonomous but is always open to all its sister churches, and all together form the universal *koinonia*.

Origins, Development, and Mission of the Papacy

The particular and universal embodiments of the Church exist, therefore, in a reciprocal and constant relationship. They are mutually interdependent. Hence, every particular church, precisely as a realization of the unique Church, is in some way present in all other churches.[28] Furthermore, the one Church is present in each particular church, which must recognize itself as identical to every other church in the *koinonia*. Local churches exist therefore in a network of communion, maintaining ties with the other churches. French theologian Hervé Legrand comments that "if the local church is *fully* the Church of God, it is not the *entire* Church of God."[29] The fullness of the Church is found where there is a mutual recognition of the ecclesial fullness of each particular church which together constitute the universal *koinonia*. The Church is the universal sacrament of salvation that is embodied in multiple communities, each of which is gathered around its bishop in a local church.

Every local Church has its roots in a particular place and culture where it embodies the one Church. An individual church, writes Johann Auer, recognizes itself "as an image of this universal Church, as responsible to it, and, in its innermost nature, supported and determined by it."[30] Thus, if a particular church is to image and embody the full reality of the universal Church, it must itself have ecclesial integrity. To be sure, a local church is truly complete only "to the degree in which it *interiorly* possesses all the bonds of universal communion."[31] These essential ecclesial elements of communion are faith, sacraments, and the apostolic ministry. Individual particular churches and the universal Church dwell within one another. For this reason, Walter Kasper points out, "it is part of the essential structure of the church to have two focuses, like the two focuses of an ellipse: *iure divino*, it is both papal and episcopal."[32]

Petrine Ministry Within Every Church

Beginning with the mother church in Jerusalem there arose "different local churches as particular expressions of the one unique Church of Jesus Christ. Arising within and out of the universal Church, they have their ecclesiality in her and from her" (CN 9). While each one is shepherded by its own bishop, particular churches never were, and cannot now be, independent of the bonds of communion with the universal Church. The college of bishops, "with Peter, and subject to Peter" (AG 38), is one of the Church's essential structural elements. If a particular church is to be a full ecclesial expression of the universal Church and in perfect communion with her, then the apostolic ministry of the episcopal college must also be found in it.

This presence of the universal Church in the local church brings with it, "as a proper element, the supreme authority of the Church" (CN 13): the episcopal college. Speaking to a group of American bishops during their 1993 *ad limina* visit, John Paul II said: "My pastoral ministry on behalf of your particular churches is intrinsic to their fullness of communion in the one, holy, catholic and apostolic Church."[33] For a particular church to be constituted "after the model of the universal Church" (LG 23), its bishop must be in hierarchical communion with the other members and head of the episcopal college.[34] The Petrine ministry is, therefore, a "necessary expression of that fundamental *mutual interiority* between the universal Church and particular church" (CN 13). More than merely an external sign of communion among the churches, the papal office is an internal principle of unity necessary to the ecclesial wholeness of every particular church.

The Petrine ministry "belongs to the essence of every particular church 'from within'," says Pope John Paul II. It is "a requirement of the [particular] church's very constitution, and not . . . something added on from without for historical, sociological or practical reasons."[35] As a ministry interior to every particular church, the primacy of the bishop of Rome helps its pastor and faithful to preserve their bonds of communion with all the other churches of the *koinonia*.

On a practical level, this interiority of the papal ministry to a particular church illumines several questions. When the pope makes a pastoral visit to a local church, for example, he does not do so as an outsider. Instead, he goes to strengthen the flock which Christ has confided to him. It also clarifies why the bishop of Rome has the right, and sometimes the duty, to intervene in a local church. His full, supreme, and universal power necessarily includes ordinary and immediate jurisdiction in the local churches of the *koinonia*, since he has a direct pastoral responsibility for them.[36] In addition, this indwelling of the particular and universal Church explains the significance of mentioning the pope's name in every Eucharistic celebration. From the third century onward, the practice of praying for the pope during the Eucharistic prayer of the Mass can be documented. In its most sacred action, the Eucharist, a particular church expresses its communion with the whole Church by praying for both the local bishop and the pope. This prayer expresses the Catholic consciousness that the ministry of the bishop of Rome is intimately associated with the ecclesial identity of the local church.[37]

Visible communion in the Church is manifested and built up through an external principle: the episcopal college. This visibility of the *koinonia* belongs, by Christ's will, to the fullness of "the sole Church of Christ . . . [that] subsists in the Catholic Church, which is governed by the successor of Peter and by the bishops in communion with him" (LG 8). Among the constitutive elements of this full visible unity is the ministry assigned to Peter and his successors. The episcopal college with its head is therefore present in every local church which manifests ecclesial wholeness. Particular churches are "fully catholic" only if their bishop is in communion with the church of Rome (cf. CCC 834). Without the Petrine ministry, a particular church is, in some sense, "wounded" in its existence. It lacks an *interior* element essential to both the local and universal Church (cf. CN 17). If the head of a local community is not in hierarchical communion with the pope, then its fullness as a church is compromised. In this situation, characteristic of all non-Catholic churches and ecclesial communities, the bonds of communion with the one Church of Christ are, in varying degrees, imperfect (cf. UR 3).

Guardian of Unity and Advocate of Catholicity

Even though the pope is the "perpetual and visible source [principle] and foundation" of the Church's unity (LG 23; cf. DS 3051), he does not create such unity. Unity is a gift of the Spirit (cf. LG 7; UR 2). The successor of Peter, however, is the external instrument through which the Spirit exercises his power to "guard, defend, and promote the visible communion of believers."[38] According to Leo Scheffczyk, "it cannot be doubted that the papacy always understood its role as a service for the unity of the Church."[39] This is confirmed by John Paul II who has said that the mission of unity is "the specific office and . . . the charism of Peter and his successors."[40]

As far back as St. Cyprian of Carthage (†258), the role of the papacy in fostering Church unity has been recognized. Cyprian wrote: "the rest of the apostles were that which Peter was, endowed with an equal partnership of office and of power, but the beginning [in Peter] proceeds from unity, that the Church of Christ may be shown to be one."[41] St. Thomas Aquinas (†1274) argued that "the unity of the Church demands that there be one who presides as the head of the entire Church."[42] In these and innumerable other testimonies, writers through the centuries have borne witness that the bishop of Rome personifies the unity of the visible body of Christ.

The Church's duty to preserve her unity has a deeper foundation than the need for a united front in her mission of evangelizing the world. The reason for a ministry of unity derives from Christ's will. It is essentially linked to the command of Christ who prayed for her unity (cf. Jn 17:11, 21-23). Within the apostolic college, Peter was specially entrusted with defending, promoting, and representing this unity. Proper to the pope's ministry, perhaps even his primary task, is his care for the unity in faith and love in the *koinonia*.

In order to carry out his function, the pope must support the churches in their confession of the apostolic faith. First, as the chief guardian and protector of the sacred deposit of revelation, he safeguards the unity of faith. He also watches over the unity of the Church's general discipline, shapes her ordered structure, and preserves the means of salvation and their correct administration (cf. PB 11). The bishop of Rome shares this supervision of doctrine and discipline essential to ecclesial unity with the whole episcopal college. Nonetheless, as successor of the "first" of the apostles, the pope has the "first" responsibility in this regard. Both unity and catholicity are attributes proper to the Church. Because it is usually more difficult to create unity rather than diversity, theologians and the magisterium have traditionally emphasized the Petrine function more as a ministry of unity than as a ministry of catholicity.[43]

The gifts of each local church must be lived in harmony with those of the other churches. Among the principal functions of the pope is the mediating role he plays between the various churches of the *koinonia*. John Paul II has said that the pope's duty of watchful care ensures that these local charisms "flow toward the center of the Church and that these same gifts, enriched by the mutual encounter, flow out to the various members of the Mystical Body of Christ, bringing them new impulses of fervor and of life."[44] In coordinating these multiple charisms for the good of all the churches, the bishop of Rome acts as the *centrum unitatis*. He enables the multiplicity of churches "to recognize in themselves and in one another the apostolic Tradition on which every particular church must be built."[45]

By warding off attempts which would lead local churches to become watertight

The Shepherd and the Rock

compartments divided from one another, the pope promotes unity within catholicity. From his position at the center of ecclesial communion, he encourages the particular churches to interact with each other as well as with the see of Peter. In this way he fulfills his task as a "pontiff" (from the Latin word *pontifex* meaning "bridge-builder"): the pope links together the various churches. Originally this title was given to all bishops; later, during the Gregorian Reform, it was reserved to the bishop of Rome.[46] Through his ministry of coordination, the bishop of Rome watches lest a particular church isolate itself.

The successor of Peter is "the supreme visible bond of the communion of particular Churches in the one Church and the guarantor of their freedom" (CCC 1559). At the same time, this obligation to represent and preserve ecclesial unity requires that the pope not impose undue uniformity. Concerning the particular churches, "the Chair of Peter which presides over the whole assembly of charity," says Vatican II, "protects their legitimate variety while at the same time taking care that these differences do not hinder unity, but rather contribute to it" (LG 13). In the relations of local churches with one another, the Roman bishop prevents any one church from absorbing, minimizing, or threatening legitimate expressions of Christian life.[47] It follows, comments Ratzinger, that "the successor of Peter ought to exercise his ministry in such a way that it does not suffocate the gifts of the individual particular churches or force them into a false uniformity."[48]

Just as union with the pope symbolizes the Church's unity, the multiplicity of particular churches symbolizes her catholicity. When the bishops preach the faith with a vigor adapted to their churches, they are signs and instruments of the inculturation of the gospel. The diversity of popular religious expressions, liturgical rites, theologies, and discipline manifests an essential attribute of the Church and enriches her. In the Catholic Church there are several rites, two codes of canon law, and innumerable ecclesiastical traditions. As far as this catholicity is concerned, the charism of the successor of Peter is threefold. First, as head of the episcopal college, he fosters the inculturation of the gospel in all the churches. Second, the pope sees to it that bishops maintain and strengthen the bonds of communion among themselves and their churches. Third, he discerns, evaluates, and judges the extent to which diversity is a truly Catholic instance of incarnating the gospel in a specific time and place.[49]

The Roman bishop promotes unity and catholicity in the *koinonia*, guaranteeing that the local churches constitute the genuine communion which is the universal Church. Tillard understands the church of Rome to be "the guardian of communion, a communion which is realized in and by the local churches themselves, not imposed by some authority that transcends them. For communion is not realized around Rome, but thanks to Rome."[50]

"Sacrament" of Unity

In the early Church, the pope's presence as the fundamental point of ecclesial unity counted more than his juridical intervention in a community. "Paradoxical as it may seem," wrote Ludwig Hertling, "the basic function of the pope in the Church is not his performance of certain official actions, but simply that he be present."[51] It remains the bishop of Rome's duty to symbolize the Church's visible unity through his person.

Origins, Development, and Mission of the Papacy

Taking seriously the role of Peter's successor to signify unity, some recent theologians have applied traditional sacramental language, used in an analogous sense, to the papal ministry. As with all spiritual realities, this office can be understood only by faith. According to the classical definition, sacraments are objective "signs" which are efficacious in themselves, independent of the holiness of their minister and recipient. Similarly, the pope is a sign or sacrament of the Church's unity. Describing the papacy from a sacramental perspective saves it from being interpreted as a purely functional reality which likens the pope to the president of a nation or the chairman of a board.[52]

All ordained ministers represent Christ and make him present as head of the Church. Acting as Christ's instruments, bishops in the apostolic succession concretely incarnate his authority and mission. This is also true for the successor of Peter. Owing to its universal outreach, the pope's apostolic ministry is the highest ecclesial ministry. In a unique way, the pope, precisely as a single individual, symbolizes Christ in his role as head of the Church.[53]

Like the Church as a whole, the papacy is "a sacramental reality in which the external historical sign (successor on the chair of Peter) must be seen as united with the inner reality (vicar of Christ), which can only be grasped by faith."[54] The papal office is a visible sign of the ministry of Christ who is *the* Rock, Shepherd, and Teacher. As his representative, the pope makes Christ present in the fullness of his priestly, prophetic, and kingly functions. In his official capacity, the bishop of Rome acts *in persona Christi*, as an effective sign of Christ's presence in the Church and in the world. In the "function and charism of representing Christ on earth," wrote Paul VI, the pope is a "visible prolongation" of this mission until the end of time.[55]

Through his "sacramental" presence the pope is the focal point of the Church's unity, both symbolizing and fostering it. Merely by his presence, the successor of Peter recalls Christ's headship of the one Church. "The body of the Church is guided by a 'head' who is above her and is 'supernatural' in relation to her," writes Hans Urs von Balthasar. "The function of the Church's leadership, particularly that of the papacy, is unceasingly to focus attention on this transcendence and even to represent it."[56] At an audience early in his pontificate, Paul VI said that the pope was "the representative of Christ; he is a sign, a tangible and living link between this natural world of ours and the invisible supernatural world." He then added that "if the pope is so united to Christ as to be called his vicar, then you can look upon the pope as a symbol that first transfers the thought of the one who contemplates him to Christ and then to God."[57] Accordingly, the pope is an effective symbol of the unity and universality of the Church. He fulfills this function both by receiving bishops into communion with him and by maintaining communion among them and with the Roman see.

Papal Intervention in the Particular Church

Because of the indwelling of the universal Church and the particular churches, the pope can act in local situations as a pastor dealing with matters "from the inside." When the bishop of Rome intervenes in a particular church, he does so differently from the way in which the president of a company deals with lower-level executives. The pope acts from "within," since he possesses a special charism through which he is incorporated into the local community. Even so, this interior presence of the pope in a particular church does not mean that he is constantly exercising his jurisdictional primacy there.

All Roman interventions are directed by the pope's "anxiety [solicitude] for all the churches" (2 Cor 11:28): to protect and foster the unity of the Church's faith and communion. Their purpose is to build up the body of Christ (cf. 2 Cor 10:8) by contributing to the spiritual welfare of a particular church. Besides the organs of collegiality examined in chapter eleven, the pope uses other practices in order to discharge his ministry on behalf of local churches: apostolic visitations, canonical reservations, and *recognitio*. Interventions must never be used to exert authority, or to promote political advantage, or to serve any worldly purpose.

Apostolic Visitations

During the eleventh century, some local bishops lacked sympathy for the Gregorian Reform spearheaded by Rome. As a way of promoting his reforms measures, Gregory VII (1073-1085) and his successors empowered legates to visit local dioceses and to report their findings to Rome. Fortified by his claim to universal primacy, Gregory established the practice that the pope could order an investigation of a particular church's affairs and demand an account of the stewardship of its bishop. Armed with papal authority, legates were sent to various dioceses to regulate ecclesiastical discipline according to reformist principles. The canonist John Beal notes that because these legates "became the point men of ecclesiastical reform in provinces and dioceses, traditional intermediate structures of accountability were regularly by-passed and gradually atrophied."[58] These papal legates played a leading role in consolidating papal authority over the Church in the West. Through them the pope gained information about particular churches and insured that they implemented his decrees.

In a bull of 1075, Gregory expressed how he understood his legates' role: "Since it is impossible for Us to come to regulate by Ourselves matters so numerous and diverse, we have sent you our dear sons of the Holy Roman Church . . . who will represent Our authority among you and who will, with God's aid, regulate as procurators all that concerns your church."[59] Usually sent for a brief period, papal legates enjoyed extensive powers which they used to rectify irregular situations. Apostolic visitations were exercises of primatial authority. Indeed, the legates shared in the pope's primatial jurisdictional authority "to pluck up and to pull down, to destroy and to overthrow, to build and to plant" (Jer 1:10) — a biblical text which the bishop of Rome frequently invoked when naming his legates.

After the Council of Trent, papal legates again served as the agents of a reform-minded papacy. Permanent nunciatures and delegations, whose development accompanied the rise of emerging nation states, were established as the "long arm" of the pope in various countries and local churches. These nuncios and delegates sent regular reports to Rome on all matters affecting the life of the Church in the countries to which they were

Origins, Development, and Mission of the Papacy

assigned. Even so, this bureaucratization of the legates' responsibilities failed to bring an end to the need for direct papal interventions in order to deal with particular problems on an *ad hoc* basis.[60] The practice of apostolic visitations continues down to the present day.

Through these apostolic visitations the pope exercises his ordinary, immediate, and episcopal authority in a particular church. He uses this canonical institution "to call bishops to a more effective and faithful ministry in their particular churches entrusted to their care by salutary correctives, rebukes and decrees."[61] Apostolic visitations are an instrument designed to foster ecclesial accountability.

Using his primatial authority, the pope orders an apostolic visitation to remedy a situation which jeopardizes the welfare of a particular church or group of churches. While no legal norms set out specific criteria to be met before authorizing a visitation, and the pope is always free to initiate one, respect for the principles of collegiality and subsidiarity imposes the moral obligation that all other means of remedying an aberrant situation should have been tried and failed.[62]

In recent years in the United States, Roman authorities have made apostolic visitations of several dioceses and of the seminaries. The most well-known case was the investigation of the archdiocese of Seattle, which the Holy See undertook "so that it may evaluate the criticisms and support the archbishop [Hunthausen] in his ministry."[63] In the letter to Hunthausen which ended the investigation, the pro-nuncio explained that the reason for the visitation was "to evaluate certain allegations and also to explore in a wider and more positive fashion your pastoral service to the archdiocese." Cardinal Pio Laghi, then pro-nuncio to the United States, offered him certain "observations" designed "to support you in your efforts toward church renewal and to offer, where necessary, certain guidance and advice." The areas of concern touched "certain teachings of the church and their implications for the pastoral practice of the archdiocese."[64] The carrying out of this apostolic visitation was an instance of the use of papal authority whose primary purpose was, according to Laghi, "to promote the building up of the church in Seattle with the universal Church."[65] While some applauded this intervention as a necessary and timely exercise of the Petrine ministry, others viewed it, as Granfield records, "as unjustified, ill-timed, and detrimental to the vitality of Catholic life."[66]

Reservations and "Recognitio"

The practices of papal reservations and of *recognitio* are expressions of the primacy which have developed in canon law over centuries. A particular action is reserved to the pope when he retains for himself, or for those who act in his name, a power which local bishops could, in principle, exercise. Among the matters which are currently reserved to the Holy See are the direction and promotion of the ecumenical movement (cf. CIC 755), the approval of national catechisms published by episcopal conferences (cf. CIC 775.2), the approval of the normative edition of liturgical books and their translation into the vernacular (cf. CIC 838.2), the definition of what is required for valid sacramental celebrations (cf. CIC 841), dispensation from specified marriage impediments (cf. CIC 1078.2, 1079.1, 1080.1), the creation of new dioceses (cf. CIC 373), the naming of bishops or the confirmation of those legitimately elected (cf. CIC 377.1), the acceptance of a bishop's resignation (cf. CIC 401.1), and a host of other questions. In response to the desires of the Fathers at the Second Vatican Council, the number of reservations has been drastically diminished. When the successor of Peter reserves certain matters to the Apostolic See, he exercises his primatial authority in the universal Church.[67]

Recognitio is the canonical process by which the pope reviews and confirms a law issued by others, before it can be authoritatively promulgated. Unlike reserved matters, the obligatory force of what the pope confirms comes from the original lawgiver rather than from him. *Recognitio* is a kind of "second look" at legislation. It is used to determine whether the proposal submitted to the Holy See contravenes general Church law, exceeds the authority of the lawgiver, contains anything contrary to Catholic doctrine, or could harm another particular church. In addition, the bishop of Rome can also modify any proposed law or decree presented for his approval.[68]

When the pope makes use of his power of *recognitio*, he reinforces particular legislation with his own authority.[69] His approval provides greater security that a law or decree will be helpful to the universal Church. *Recognitio*, moreover, involves a practical acknowledgment of papal primacy by those who submit their decisions to the Holy See. It also stimulates a greater care in preparing texts, and facilitates reception by the faithful.[70] According to current legislation, papal *recognitio* applies primarily to the decrees of an episcopal conference (cf. CIC 455.2, 456). In this regard, American canonist Frederick McManus has expressed his concern that this practice of Roman review could be used to curtail the legitimate responsibility of episcopal conferences or to replace legitimate diversity with centralized uniformity.[71] As always, the pope must walk the narrow line between too much and too little intervention, holding both unity and catholicity in balance.

Strengthening the Bishops

In *Pastor aeternus*, the Fathers of the First Vatican Council avoided specifying any canonical norms which would regulate papal interventions in a particular church. The Second Vatican Council and the Code of Canon Law similarly refrain from setting down conditions which the pope would have to meet before taking action. While Vatican II defended the rights of the bishops in their dioceses, it also acknowledged that their authority "is ultimately controlled by the supreme authority of the Church and can be confined within certain limits should the usefulness of the Church and the faithful require that" (LG 27). It is an arduous undertaking for theologians to recommend norms applicable to such an eventuality, since neither ecumenical councils nor canon law furnish official criteria. In their proposals, however, they must consider at least the following two principles: respect for episcopal authority and regard for subsidiarity.

Both Vatican Councils taught that episcopal authority, "far from being damaged by the [pope's] supreme and universal power, is much rather defended, upheld and strengthened by it" (LG 27; cf. DS 3061; CIC 333.1). Any papal intervention in a particular church should foster the collegial spirit among bishops of the diocese or of the region concerned. Not seeking to replace episcopal authority, the pope recalls the duties which oblige the bishops. As pastor of the pastors, the pope sees to it that bishops carry out their responsibilities. For this reason, he can regulate episcopal authority, directing the other bishops to care for both their own churches and the universal Church.

In virtue of his primatial authority, the pope intervenes directly in a particular church, writes Tillard, if the local bishop "is unable to control a situation where some problem has put in peril the apostolic faith and the communion of the churches."[72] The bishop of Rome acts when he perceives that a particular church "has run out of resources and is allowing itself to deteriorate in a way that seriously threatens its identity (and thereby the universal *koinonia*), or is neglecting, in grave situations, to make decisions that are called for."[73] When serious reasons within a local church demand it, the pope "cannot fail to intervene in order to protect unity in faith, in charity, or in discipline" (PB 11). All share the conviction that, at least in theory, papal and episcopal authority are complementary in the service they provide to the Church. Papal interventions in local churches are aimed at building them up. In this regard the *Catechism of the Catholic Church* points out: the pope's "ordinary and immediate authority over the whole Church does not annul, but on the contrary confirms and defends that of the bishops" (CCC 895).

Not infrequently, the bishops of particular churches which are weak and struggling, especially in face of hostile political or social situations, are grateful for direct papal interventions. Down the centuries, close ties with the bishop of Rome have supported many churches, protecting their independence and saving them from falling victim to totalitarian pressures of all kinds. The churches of the eastern Europe of yesterday, as well as the young churches of today, look to a strong and active papacy as an effective instrument which safeguards their own identity.[74]

Concrete local situations always require that the pope must make a prudential judgment concerning at what point an intervention will foster the ecclesial life of a particular community. While canonically the pope is always free to intervene in a local church, nonetheless, he is morally obliged to refrain from doing so arbitrarily. In a certain sense the pope is on a tightrope. He could fail to intervene when necessary, or he could intervene too soon, thereby threatening to absorb episcopal responsibilities. Bouyer concludes that a pope who would intervene in every difficulty which arises in a local church "would prove that he understands nothing about his function."[75] Still, when all is said and done, the successor of Peter has the final responsibility of deciding when and how he should use his primatial authority in a local church.

Subsidiarity

Subsidiarity is a principle which regulates the relations between higher and lower levels of authority in an institution. The principle has consequences for social action in two directions. First, it favors finding solutions to problems at the lowest possible organizational level, without interference from above. For their part, higher authorities should seek as far as possible to restrict their interference, respecting the sphere of competence of lower authorities. Second, higher authorities should offer assistance (*subsidium*) to smaller groups when, for any number of reasons, they are unable to carry out their responsibilities.[76]

As a principle of social philosophy, subsidiarity was developed by German Catholics in the early twentieth century. In *Quadragesimo anno* (1931), Pius XI (1922-1939) was the first pope to apply the principle to social-political questions. His encyclical extolled subsidiarity as necessary for the effective exercise of social, political, and economic authority. A higher unit should play a subsidiary role with respect to lower ones; it should come into play only when the lower unit is unable to meet its obligations to the common good.

In 1946, Pius XII (1939-1958) stated that the principle of subsidiarity could be applied "to social life at all of its levels and also for the life of the Church, without prejudice to her hierarchical structure."[77] Although the debates at the Second Vatican Council addressed the application of subsidiarity with reference to the Church, no document of Vatican II explicitly invokes the principle.[78] Despite this silence, after the council theologians frequently described papal-episcopal relations using the principle of subsidiarity. The 1985 Extraordinary Synod, however, seems to have called into question the value of this approach, even though its application to ecclesial life relied upon Pius XII's encouragement. The synod recommended "that a study be made to examine whether the principle of subsidiarity in use in human societies can be applied to the Church and to what degree and in what sense such an application can and should be made."[79] This new reserve about subsidiarity might express the bishops' awareness that the recent ecclesiology of the local church is disinclined to describe the universal Church as a "higher" instance with respect to the particular church.

The principle of subsidiarity does not describe the bond between the pope and the bishops in a way which would confuse the spiritual fraternity of hierarchical communion with the relation that exists between a central state authority and its smaller administrative units.[80] Insofar as the Church is a visible society, however, the principle can be a help in describing her external organization and functioning. Subsidiarity provides an appropriate way of structuring the theological realities of communion and collegiality. On the one hand, attention to subsidiarity recalls that the pope, under normal conditions, accepts the decisions taken by particular churches.[81] On the other hand, the principle of subsidiarity allows for papal interventions in local churches. If, for example, a bishop is too weak to fulfill his duties, then the successor of Peter intervenes for the good of the people of God. In normal circumstances, other means of accountability should have failed before the bishop of Rome directly takes action. Papal intervention is a last step, not a first one.[82] The pope also intervenes in cases where the episcopacy is internally divided. Likewise, the Roman bishop acts to safeguard particular churches from either falling into excessive particularism or using their freedom to the detriment of another ecclesial community.[83]

As a principle, subsidiarity implies the acceptance of decentralized authority and a measure of diversity in unity. When applied to relations between the primacy and the episcopacy, it means that the Holy See should use its authority only when a particular

Origins, Development, and Mission of the Papacy

church fails to meet its obligations to itself or the other churches. Decentralization, therefore, calls for recognizing the proper authority and competence which belong to both individual bishops and episcopal conferences. Rome must carefully avoid reserving to itself responsibilities and decisions which either divine institution or ecclesial tradition allow lower levels of authority to discharge. Some theologians and bishops are now invoking the principle of subsidiarity to temper what they regard as undue centralizing tendencies which would monopolize activities and responsibilities properly belonging to the particular churches. To use subsidiarity as a way of distancing a particular church from the Roman see would, however, be an abuse. De Lubac notes that such a unilateral view would lead to the "sterilization" instead of the fruitful activity of a local church.[84] At Vatican II, the Fathers had no intention of eliminating the practical use of primatial authority. Lastly, subsidiarity also requires that the local bishops assume responsibility for their own flocks and for the entire Church. These duties should not simply be shifted onto the shoulders of the pope.

Could the Pope Intervene Less?

A worthwhile distinction is made between what is essential to the Petrine ministry and what is conditioned by the changing social, cultural, geographic, and political factors which have influenced the development of the historical papacy. The specific responsibilities which belong to the Petrine office in virtue of divine mandate are, however, sometimes difficult to discern. While recognizing that the doctrine of papal primacy belongs to the divine constitution of the Church, we must also acknowledge that the pope has exercised his authority in various ways in the course of history.

The concrete manner in which the bishop of Rome uses his jurisdiction is always embodied in human structures of ecclesiastical right. What properly belongs to the pope's primacy of jurisdiction cannot simply be identified with the way in which he now exercises it. The line between what essentially belongs to the supreme jurisdiction of the successor of Peter and what he has reserved to himself is difficult to draw. Much of what the pope now does is not, as Rahner says, "a matter of divine law, but has come to existence historically and is therefore changeable."[85] It is the task of theologians to examine the different ways in which the pope has exercised his ministry in the past as a help in discerning which elements must be preserved in the future.

Some powers retained by the bishop of Rome are "pontifical" only by human or ecclesiastical law. The pope's right to nominate bishops, for example, is not intrinsic to his primatial office, whereas his mission to assure hierarchical communion is. In fact, the direct nomination of bishops by the pope first came about in order to curtail abuses in local elections. When the pope wanted to free episcopal appointments from the meddling of secular authorities, he took this right to himself. By the mid-thirteenth century, Rome justified the practice of the papal appointment of bishops on the grounds that the pope granted jurisdiction as an expression of his *plenitudo potestatis*.[86]

As events unfolded, what the pope *could* do sometimes became what he *should* do. Once the danger of undue secular intrusion in episcopal appointments passed, for example, the bishop of Rome maintained his right to name bishops. Such a practice has served, and can continue to serve, the good of the Church. Nonetheless, because the present procedure does not belong to the essence of the Petrine office, it is legitimate to raise the question whether another practice for the nomination, election, and appointment of bishops might better meet the needs of the Church.[87]

In the judgment of Hermann Pottmeyer, the present way in which the pope exercises his primacy of jurisdiction and teaching "is totally overwhelming both for the pope himself and for his governing body, the Curia. . . . Today's profusion of papal responsibilities . . . [is] the greatest since the Church's beginning."[88] While many responsibilities were legitimately added to the Petrine office, great prudence is needed before considering them either as constitutive of the papal ministry or as merely optional accretions. The present juridical and organizational form of the office of Peter "is neither the best imaginable nor the only possible realization."[89] In the third millennium, the number and manner of papal interventions in the local churches could, therefore, be modified.

✦

The papacy and the episcopacy are the twin pillars of the Church's ministerial structure willed by Christ. Notwithstanding some open questions in theory and occasional problems in practice, the two Vatican Councils have defined the fundamental doctrines concerning the Church's hierarchical constitution. In the last forty years, the ecclesiology of communion, episcopal collegiality, and the theology of the local church have each contributed to the renewal of the papal office.

The universal Church is embodied in particular churches which are united to one another by bonds of communion. Because of the mutual interiority of the local church and the universal Church, the ministry of Peter entrusted to the bishop of Rome touches the life of particular churches as an office interior to them. It is present and active in the local churches from within. Thus, only those churches which accept this ministry are in full communion with one another in the Catholic Church. Communion with the successor of Peter is a constitutive element of every particular church in the *koinonia*. When this relationship is missing in a local church, even if the episcopacy and Eucharist are present, the bonds of communion with the whole Church are necessarily imperfect.

Bishops are to promote in their own churches, and throughout the *koinonia*, the communion of faith and charity. The successor of Peter, who is uniquely responsible for the universal communion, points out and corrects actions which would sow confusion or harm the unity of the universal Church. In this way the pope helps the bishops to carry out their duties locally and in the whole Church. As the center of unity, the bishop of Rome watches over the *koinonia*, protecting the unity of its faith and the complementarity of its catholicity.

In writing to the American bishops in 1986, John Paul II summarized his understanding of the papal ministry, furnishing a kind of job description: "To promote the universality of the Church, to protect her legitimate variety, to guarantee her Catholic unity, to confirm the bishops in their apostolic faith and ministry, to preside in love — all this is what the successor of Peter is called by Christ to do. This Petrine service by the will of Christ is directed to the good of the universal Church and all the ecclesial communities that compose her."[90]

Origins, Development, and Mission of the Papacy

Helpful as papal interventions can be, the role of the successor of Peter extends far beyond his ability to resolve the problems of other churches. Often even he is unable to redress difficult situations. This limitation, however, does not lessen a Catholic's appreciation for his ministry and the veneration of his person. The pope is more than an effective administrator; he is an indispensable sign and instrument of the Church's visible unity and the point of reference for the apostolic tradition of Peter and Paul.[91] His sacramental role as the vicar of Christ, who is the invisible head of the Church, contributes significantly to the spiritual welfare of the *koinonia*.

Notes for Chapter twelve

1. Walter Kasper, *Theology and Church*, trans. Margaret Kohl (New York: Crossroad Publishing Company, 1989), 152.
2. Seamus Ryan, "The Hierarchical Structure of the Church," in *The Church: A Theological and Pastoral Commentary on the Constitution on the Church* (Dublin: Veritas Publications, 1983), 212.
3. Joseph A. Komonchak, "The Local Church and the Church Catholic: The Contemporary Theological Problematic," *The Jurist*, 52:1 (1992), 416-417; cf. Henri de Lubac, *The Motherhood of the Church*, trans. Sergia Englund (San Francisco: Ignatius Press, 1982), 180-185.
4. De Lubac, *Motherhood of the Church*, 189-190.
5. Hervé Legrand, " 'One Bishop per City': Tensions Around the Expression of the Catholicity of the Local Church since Vatican II," *The Jurist*, 52:1 (1992), 372, n.4.
6. Raymond E. Brown, *Biblical Exegesis and Church Doctrine* (New York: Paulist Press, 1985), 115.
7. Patrick Granfield, *The Limits of the Papacy* (New York: Crossroad Publishing Company, 1987), 112.
8. Joseph Ratzinger, *La Chiesa: Una comunità sempre in cammino*, trans. Luigi Frattini, 2nd ed. (Turin: Edizioni Paoline, 1992), 63.
9. Louis Bouyer, *The Church of God*, trans. Charles Underhill Quinn (Chicago: Franciscan Herald Press, 1982), 390, 396.
10. John Paul II, Discourse, December 11, 1986, *L'Osservatore Romano*, 2 (January 12, 1987), 5.
11. John Paul II, Discourse, October 28, 1992, *L'Osservatore Romano*, 44 (November 4, 1992), 11.
12. [Unnamed authority], "Church Unity Rooted in Eucharist," *L'Osservatore Romano*, 27 (July 7, 1993), 4.
13. [Unnamed authority], "Church Unity Rooted in Eucharist," 4.
14. De Lubac, *Motherhood of the Church*, 207-208.
15. Discourse to the College of Cardinals in 1985; cited in Komonchak, "Local Church and the Church Catholic," 429, n. 31.
16. Patrick Granfield, "The Church Local and Universal: Realization of Communion," *The Jurist*, 49:2 (1989), 459.
17. Congregation for Bishops, "Draft Statement on Episcopal Conferences," *Origins*, 17:43 (April 7, 1988), #A.IV.2, p. 735.
18. De Lubac, *Motherhood of the Church*, 206.

19. John Meyendorff, *Byzantine Theology* (New York: Fordham University Press, 1974), 209.
20. Meyendorff, *Byzantine Theology*, 210.
21. Olivier Clément, "The Church as a Communion: An Orthodox Response," *Catholic International*, 3:16 (1992), 768.
22. Nicolas Afanassieff, "The Church which Presides in Love," in *The Primacy of Peter*, ed. John Meyendorff et al., 2nd ed. (Leighton Buzzard: Faith Press, 1973), 81.
23. Joseph Ratzinger, *Church, Ecumenism and Politics*, trans. Robert Nowell (New York: Crossroad Publishing Company, 1988), 9.
24. De Lubac, *Motherhood of the Church*, 203.
25. Patrick J. Burns, "Communion, Councils, and Collegiality: Some Catholic Reflections," in *Papal Primacy and the Universal Church*, Lutherans and Catholics in Dialogue V, ed. Paul C. Empie and T. Austin Murphy (Minneapolis: Augsburg Publishing House, 1974), 152.
26. Joseph Ratzinger, "The Pastoral Implications of Collegiality," *Concilium*, 1:1 (1965), 44.
27. International Theological Commission, "Select Themes of Ecclesiology on the Occasion of the Twentieth Anniversary of the Closing of the Second Vatican Council," in *International Theological Commission: Texts and Documents 1969-1985*, ed. Michael Sharkey (San Francisco: Ignatius Press, 1989), #V.2, p. 284.
28. John Paul II, Address to the Roman Curia, December 21, 1984, *L'Osservatore Romano*, 3 (January 21, 1985), 7.
29. Legrand, " 'One Bishop per City'," 371; cf. [Unnamed authority], "Church Unity Rooted in Eucharist," 4; and the statement of Jean-Jacques von Allmen: "the local church is wholly Church but it is not the whole Church" ("L'Eglise locale parmi les autres églises locales," *Irénikon*, 43 [1970], 512).
30. Johann Auer, *The Church: The Universal Sacrament of Salvation*, Dogmatic Theology, trans. Michael Waldstein, vol. 8 (Washington, D.C.: Catholic University of America Press, 1993), 112.
31. [Unnamed authority],"Church Unity Rooted in Eucharist," 4.
32. Kasper, *Theology and Church*, 160.
33. John Paul II, Ad limina Address to American Bishops, June 5, 1993, *Origins*, 23:8 (July 15, 1993), 127.
34. Gianfranco Ghirlanda, "Universal Church, Particular Church, and Local Church at the Second Vatican Council and in the New Code of Canon Law," in *Vatican II: Assessments and Perspectives Twenty-five Years After (1962-1987)*, ed. René Latourelle (New York: Paulist Press, 1989), 251.
35. John Paul II, Discourse, November 18, 1992, *L'Osservatore Romano*, 47 (November 25, 1992), 11; cf. CN 13.
36. Ghirlanda, "Universal Church, Particular Church, and Local Church," 251.
37. Joseph Ratzinger, "Theological Notes," attached to the statement of the Congregation for Bishops, "Directory for the *ad Limina* Visit," *L'Osservatore Romano*, 28 (July 11, 1988), 7.
38. J. M. R. Tillard, *The Bishop of Rome*, trans. John de Satgé (Wilmington: Michael Glazier, 1983), 125.
39. Leo Scheffczyk, *Il ministero di Pietro*, trans. Franco Ardusso (Turin: Marietti, 1975), 82.
40. John Paul II, Address to the Roman Curia, December 21, 1984, *L'Osservatore Romano*, 3 (January 21, 1985), 7.
41. Cyprian of Carthage, *The Unity of the Catholic Church*, 4; translation in Thomas Halton, *The*

Church, Message of the Fathers of the Church, vol. 4 (Wilmington: Michael Glazier, 1985), 96.

42. Thomas Aquinas, *Summa contra Gentiles*, 4.76.
43. Cormac Burke, *Authority and Freedom in the Church* (San Francisco: Ignatius Press, 1988), 206-207.
44. John Paul II, Address to the Roman Curia, December 21, 1984, *L'Osservatore Romano*, 3, (January 21, 1985), 7.
45. John E. Linnan, "Subsidiarity, Collegiality, Catholic Diversity, and Their Relevance to Apostolic Visitations," *The Jurist*, 49:2 (1989), 432.
46. Yves Congar, "Titoli dati al papa," *Concilium*, 11:8 (1975), 86-87.
47. Wolfgang Beinert, "Das Petrusamt und die Ortskirche," in *Petrus und Papst*, ed. Albert Brandenburg and Hans Jörg Urban (Münster: Aschendorff, 1977), 113.
48. Ratzinger, *La Chiesa*, 72.
49. Granfield, *Limits of Papal Primacy*, 122-123.
50. J. M. R. Tillard, "The Local Church Within Catholicity," *The Jurist*, 52:1 (1992), 454.
51. Ludwig Hertling, *"Communio": Church and Papacy in Early Christianity*, trans. Jared Wicks (Chicago: Loyola University Press, 1972), 71.
52. Leo Scheffczyk, "Das 'Amt der Einheit': Symbol oder Wirkmacht der Einheit?" in *Petrus und Papst*, ed. Albert Brandenburg and Hans Jörg Urban (Münster: Aschendorff, 1977), 131-135; cf. J. Michael Miller, "Paul VI on the Papacy," *America*, 149:4 (August 13, 1983), 65-66.
53. Scheffczyk, *Ministero di Pietro*, 74-81.
54. Auer, *The Church*, 287.
55. Paul VI, Discourse, December 22, 1974, *L'Osservatore Romano*, 2 (January 9, 1975), 5.
56. Hans Urs von Balthasar, *The Office of Peter and the Structure of the Church*, trans. Andrée Emery (San Francisco: Ignatius Press, 1986), 15.
57. Paul VI, Discourse, July 22, 1964, *Insegnamenti di Paolo VI*, vol. 2 (Vatican City: Polyglot Press, 1965), 923.
58. John P. Beal, "The Apostolic Visitation of a Diocese: A Canonico-Historical Investigation," *The Jurist*, 49:2 (1989), 375.
59. Gregory VII, *Registrum*, 2.40; translation in Beal, "Apostolic Visitation of a Diocese," 367-368.
60. Beal, "Apostolic Visitation of a Diocese," 379-380.
61. Beal, "Apostolic Visitation of a Diocese," 395.
62. Thomas J. Green, "The Pastoral Governance Role of the Diocesan Bishop: Foundation, Scope, and Limitations," *The Jurist*, 49:2 (1989), 496.
63. *Origins*, 13:22 (November 10, 1983), 379.
64. *Origins*, 15:28 (December 26, 1985), 457,459.
65. *Origins*, 16:11 (November 6, 1986), 363.
66. Granfield, *Limits of the Papacy*, 31.
67. Julio Manzanares, "Papal Reservations and *Recognitio*: Considerations and Proposals," *The Jurist*, 52:1 (1992), 231, 240-241, 247.
68. Frederick R. McManus, "Local, Regional and Universal Church Law," in *The Papacy and the Church in the United States*, ed. Bernard Cooke (New York: Paulist Press, 1989), 183.
69. Manzanares, "Papal Reservations and *Recognitio*," 235.
70. Manzanares, "Papal Reservations and *Recognitio*," 250.
71. McManus, "Local, Regional and Universal Church Law," 183.

72. Tillard, *Bishop of Rome*, 169.
73. J. M. R. Tillard, "The Horizon of the 'Primacy' of the Bishop of Rome," *One in Christ*, 12:1 (1976), 31-32.
74. De Lubac, *Motherhood of the Church*, 300-303.
75. Bouyer, *Church of God*, 387.
76. Linnan, "Subsidiarity, Collegiality, Catholic Diversity," 416.
77. Pius XII, Discourse, February 20, 1946, *The Catholic Mind*, 44 (April 1946), 196.
78. Joseph Komonchak, "Subsidiarity in the Church: The State of the Question," *The Jurist*, 48:2 (1988), 326.
79. Synod of Bishops (1985), "The Final Report," *Origins*, 15:27 (December 19, 1985), #II.C.8, p. 44. Peter Huizing notes, however, that this recommendation was not in line with the synod participants who felt no need to call the principle into question ("Subsidiarity," *Concilium*, 188 [1986], 121).
80. Granfield, *Limits of Papal Primacy*, 131.
81. Tillard, "Horizon of the 'Primacy' of the Bishop of Rome," 27.
82. Granfield, "The Church Local and Universal," 468-469.
83. Alexandre Ganoczy, "How Can One Evaluate Collegiality vis-à-vis Papal Primacy?" *Concilium*, 64 (1971), 92.
84. De Lubac, *Motherhood of the Church*, 297-299.
85. Karl Rahner, "Structural Change in the Church of the Future," in *Theological Investigations*, trans. Edward Quinn, vol. 20 (New York: Crossroad Publishing Company, 1981), 119.
86. Klaus Schatz, *La primauté du Pape*, trans. Joseph Hoffmann (Paris: Cerf, 1992), 151-155.
87. Karl Rahner, "The Election of Bishops Today," in *Karl Rahner in Dialogue: Conversations and Interviews*, ed. Paul Imhof and Hubert Biallowons, trans. Richard W. Rolfs (New York: Crossroad Publishing Company, 1986), 321-323.
88. Hermann J. Pottmeyer, "Why Does the Church Need a Pope?" *Communio*, 18:3 (1991), 305.
89. Pottmeyer, "Why Does the Church Need a Pope?" 312.
90. John Paul II, Letter to the American Bishops, November 4, 1986, *Origins*, 16:23 (November 20, 1986), 399.
91. Schatz, *Primauté du Pape*, 258.

Chapter thirteen
THE POPE'S TENURE OF OFFICE

Unlike a hereditary monarchy, there is no automatic right of succession to the papacy. On her own authority the Church has decided how the pope is to be selected. "Down through the centuries the supreme pontiffs have considered it their prerogative, and their right and duty," wrote Paul VI, "to determine in the manner considered best the election of their successors, opposing all tendencies that sought, through alterations of ecclesiastical institutions, to take away their exclusive right to decide upon the composition of the body of electors and the latter's manner of exercising its functions" (RPE, intro.). Each pope has the freedom to abrogate any previous regulations and to establish the norms by which his successor is to be chosen.

This chapter first explores how the pope has been appointed, from the earliest practice of designation, to the choice by the clergy and people of Rome, and, finally, to the establishment of the college of cardinals as the sole electoral body. After examining the historical models of papal elections, it then describes contemporary legislation regulating the electoral procedure: the role of the cardinals, the conclave, and the different methods of election for the bishop of Rome. The final sections deal with questions regarding how a pope's tenure of office can end through resignation, irreversible illness, or heresy.

Historical Models of Papal Election

The way in which papal elections are regulated was not divinely instituted. As a process which has varied greatly through the centuries, it is a matter of changeable ecclesiastical law. Chapter three concluded that Christ willed that there always be a successor of Peter whose ministry is directed to the whole Church. Even so, the Scriptures give no hint regarding how he is to be chosen.

Designation of a Successor

At the outset, the first bishops of Rome were probably named by the incumbent who designated a successor to take his place after his death. Without remarking on anything unusual in this action, Irenaeus (†200) records that "the blessed Apostles [Peter and Paul], having founded and built up the Church [of Rome] handed over the office of the episcopate to Linus."[1] Such a custom corresponds to the apostolic practice of appointing elders in the early communities (cf. Titus 1:5). Clement's *First Letter to the Corinthians* recounts that "illustrious men" were chosen to succeed the apostles "with the consent of the whole Church."[2] Appointment by the current head of the community who designated his successor was likely the case for the three bishops of Rome who followed Linus (67-76): Anacletus (76-88), Clement (88-97), and Evaristus (97-105).[3] By the early second century, however, this practice was replaced by another, except for the following two exceptions.

Four hundred years later, Pope Felix IV (526-530) tried to revive the procedure of naming his own successor to the Roman episcopate as a way of curtailing secular interference in the election. On his deathbed, he handed his pallium to his archdeacon Boniface, formally designating him as his successor. The senate was outraged by Felix's action, which it regarded as contrary to tradition. It subsequently published an edict which forbade both discussion of succession during a reigning pope's lifetime and the acceptance of such a nomination. Most of the Roman clergy disregarded Felix's choice of Boniface II (530-532) and proceeded to elect Dioscorus. Only after the sudden death of the antipope Dioscorus, within less than a month, did the clergy finally recognize Boniface as their bishop.[4] His own unfortunate experience notwithstanding, Boniface also tried to designate his successor. Before his death, however, he rescinded his nomination. The practice of designation was then definitively laid to rest.

Because of the ancient testimony to this tradition, such a method of choosing the successor of Peter was doubtlessly legitimate. Nothing in divine law forbids it. Theologians have disputed whether the pope's designation of his successor itself constituted legal election. It might be that the clergy and people, in their act of accepting such a designation, actually "chose" the pope. Many scholars, however, deny that the pope can impose his will in choosing his own successor. Regardless of the way in which these past cases are judged, present legislation does not provide for this method of selecting the pope.[5]

Role of the Roman Community

From the first few centuries, there is little documentation concerning the precise details about how papal elections were conducted. It is reasonable to assume that the local church at Rome named its bishop in the same way other communities did at the time: with the participation of the faithful and their leaders. According to Italian Vaticanologist Giancarlo Zizola, Alexander I (105-115) was the first pope elected "by means of a consultation of the entire Christian community" of Rome.[6]

This practice of consulting clergy and laity replaced the earlier method of designation and became the normal way of naming the bishop of Rome. When Novatian, a Roman presbyter and theologian, contested the election of Pope Cornelius (251-253), Cyprian of Carthage (†258) wrote to a fellow bishop defending the legitimacy of Cornelius' election. In his letter, St. Cyprian describes the electoral procedure used at Rome: "Cornelius was made bishop by the decision of God and of His Christ, by the testimony of almost all the clergy, by the applause [vote] of the people then present, by the college of venerable priests and good men."[7] By the mid-third century, a well-defined pattern is evident. Episcopal elections, including that of the bishop of Rome, involved the whole community: laity, clergy, and neighboring bishops.[8] Two centuries later, the same basic procedure was still in place.

For the most part, the Roman church, like the other Christian communities, attempted to put into practice the principle of Leo the Great (440-461) for selecting bishops: "He [the bishop] who is in charge of all, should be chosen by all" (PL 54, 634). The community proposed names of candidates thought to be suitable. Respected laity and clerics then examined these names and gave their own evaluation of the candidates. Finally, the clergy and bishops made the final determination, choosing who would succeed to the chair of Peter. The process, however, was not always carried out in this orderly way. It was occasionally shortened when the community chose a man to be pope by popular acclaim.

Political Interference

Changes, even very significant ones, were gradually introduced into the electoral process. In the sixth and seventh centuries, the clergy and bishops from the neighboring sees began to play a more prominent role in selecting the Roman bishop. While lay involvement in suggesting the names of desirable popes remained the rule, it was increasingly limited to the more influential faithful: imperial functionaries, magistrates, and military officials. They alone came to represent the voice of the people.[9] The growing interest of the emperor in the choice of the pope brought about a second change. By the sixth century, the popes grudgingly accepted that imperial approval (*placet*) was necessary before the newly-elected man assumed office. This often meant that many months passed before the new pope could take up his full pastoral responsibilities. Even more meddlesome was the practice of civil authorities who nominated candidates for the papacy, as they did for the election of all bishops, exerting considerable pressure on the electors to secure their acceptance.[10]

In order to minimize this intrusion of secular rulers, a Roman synod in 769 reserved the election of the pope to clerics.[11] Within fifty years, however, this decree had fallen into abeyance. Lay participation, especially that of the political, social, and economic elites continued unabated, reaching its greatest level in the tenth century. This darkest century in the papacy's history records twenty-three popes. Powerful individuals, Roman families, and other interest groups intervened directly in elections which were poorly regulated by ecclesiastical authorities. Gross political intrigue, especially toward the end of the millennium, was rampant.[12] Public rioting and disorder often accompanied the period of transition from one pope to the next. In a world where political, economic, and religious power were mingled within the feudal structure, the procedure for electing the bishop of Rome had been brought almost totally under the control of lay magnates.

Throughout the first millennium, however, one fact remains constant. Insofar as the election of the pope was an ecclesiastical affair, it was always the exclusive competence of the church at Rome. Except for the dioceses surrounding Rome, no other church or patriarchal see ever put forward the slightest claim to interfere with this election.[13] Despite the theory of papal monarchy which emphasized the pope's role as head of the universal Church, his election remained the responsibility of the local church at Rome.

Gregorian Reform

Intent upon freeing the Church from subservience to secular authorities and restoring her liberty, the Gregorian reformers recognized the need to revise papal elections. In 1059, Pope Nicholas II (1059-1061) promulgated *In nomine Domini*, the initial juridical document of the Gregorian Reform. Nicholas wanted to eliminate all secular and imperial interference in papal elections, thereby placing the proceedings exclusively in the hands of the Church. By giving the right to select the pope primarily to the cardinal bishops, this decree took the first step to reestablishing ecclesial control. It revived the ancient practice of the pope's free election by the local church at Rome.

Nicholas' legislation further specified that the cardinal bishops of the six neighboring sees should first look for a worthy successor among their own number and nominate him as their candidate for pope. With this nomination in hand, they were then to admit the cardinal priests to their deliberations, asking them to approve their choice. Finally, the cardinal bishops were to take counsel with the rest of the Roman clergy and laity, who were to ratify the election.[14] St. Peter Damian (†1072), one of the decree's drafters, summarized this reformed procedure: "The cardinal bishops make the principal judgment; second, the clergy give assent; third, the people give applause" (PL 144, 243).[15]

Although the laity were mentioned as integral to the electoral process, their function was now entirely passive. Neither the faithful nor the lower clergy played a determinative role. The decree reserved the real choice of the pope to the cardinal bishops. Nicholas regarded this restrictive practice as the only way in which to guarantee the electors' independence from secular encroachment. He also reversed the custom of limiting the roster of eligible candidates for the papacy to Romans, stipulating that it should include worthy contenders from elsewhere. Another major proviso specified that the newly-elected pope had the right to exercise pontifical jurisdiction immediately. It was no longer necessary that he wait for imperial confirmation before assuming his pastoral duties.[16]

Medieval Legislation

More changes followed. The rules concerning papal election continued to be refined. At the Third Lateran Council in 1179, the Fathers, anxious, as they said, "to avoid dissension in the choice of a sovereign pontiff," modified the previous legislation. In the first canon of the constitution *Licet de vitanda*, they decreed that a two-thirds majority of the votes cast by the cardinals was needed for electing the pope.[17] The Fathers introduced this provision in order to reduce the possibility of schisms following the election. They hoped that the small losing faction, which might contest the legitimacy of an election, would be discouraged from choosing an antipope. Furthermore, the conciliar decree gave all cardinals, not just cardinal bishops, the right to vote. It mentioned no role for either the lower clergy or the laity during the proceedings.[18] The election of the Roman bishop was exclusively reserved to the college of cardinals, now composed of bishops, priests, and deacons, which represented the Roman church. After the decree of Lateran III, wrote Paul VI, "all further dispositions have merely applied or adapted this fundamental ordering of the election of the Roman pontiff" (RPE, intro.).

Still, one serious problem concerning papal elections remained unresolved. All too frequently, the cardinal electors let a very long time pass before selecting a new pope. To remedy this situation, the Second Council of Lyons (1274) ruled in *Ubi periculum* that "if the pope dies in a city where he was residing with his curia, the cardinals present in that city are obliged to await the absent cardinals, but for ten days only."[19] Long delays were forbidden.

Additionally, the Fathers at Lyons legislated the practice of strictly secluding the electors, anticipating that under difficult living conditions the cardinals would come to a swift agreement. *Ubi periculum* reinforced this hope by mandating certain practical measures. It restricted the electors' diet and income while they were secluded for voting: "If, which, God forbid, within three days after the cardinals have entered the said conclave, the Church has not been provided with a shepherd, they are to be content for the next five days, every day both at dinner and supper, with one dish only. If these days also pass without the election of a pope, henceforth only bread, wine and water are to be served to the cardinals until they do provide a pope. While the election is in process, the cardinals are to receive nothing from the papal treasury, nor any other revenue coming from whatever source to the Church while the see is vacant."[20]

This decree also forbade the conclave participants to make any pacts or "deals" which would in any way limit the freedom of the newly-elected pope. Though strictly outlawed and repeatedly condemned, such pre-electoral agreements continued to be made. Electors were also reminded: "They are electing the vicar of Jesus Christ, the successor of Peter, the ruler of the universal Church, the guide of the Lord's flock. . . . Their one aim is to provide, by their service and speedily, what is so useful and necessary for the whole world, a fitting spouse for the Church."[21]

The Veto

Although *In nomine Domini* had limited the emperor's role merely to being informed of the election results, Nicholas' decree did not end all political interference. With the rise of absolute monarchies in the sixteenth century, Europe's Catholic kings insisted on their right to influence the cardinals from their countries. These monarchs frequently told them which politically undesirable candidates they should veto in the conclave. For their co-nationals the monarchs also prepared lists of desirable prospects from among whom they wished the pope to be chosen.[22] Despite papal opposition, the sovereigns of Spain, France, and Austria came to regard this veto or *exclusiva* as an inalienable right.

They exercised this right, often with success, right up to the twentieth century. In the election of 1903, Emperor Franz Joseph of Austria-Hungary instructed Cardinal Puzyna of Krakow to pronounce the veto against Cardinal Rampolla. The cardinals resisted this outside intervention in the conclave, and it appears to have had no bearing on the outcome.[23] To end this practice once and for all, Pope Pius X (1903-1914) forbade any political intervention in papal elections in *Commissum nobis* (1904). He admonished civil rulers that the privilege of the veto was abolished and that they had no right to make their desires known to the conclavists. A cardinal who dared to communicate the veto in any way was automatically excommunicated.

In *Vacantis apostolicae sedis*, Pius XII (1939-1958) extended the penalty of excommunication to those who abetted any kind of outside interference. Paul VI later reaffirmed these prohibitions of secular intrusion in papal elections. Under pain of excommunication, the electors are forbidden "to accept under whatsoever pretext, from whatsoever civil authority, the task of proposing the *veto* or *exclusiva*, even in the form of a simple wish, or to reveal such either to the entire electoral body assembled together or to individual electors, in writing or by word of mouth, directly and personally or indirectly through others, both before and during the conclave" (RPE 81). All opposition or requested preference of civil authorities is to have no bearing on the choice of the bishop of Rome. The apostolic constitution is clear about its purpose in this regard: "We intend this prohibition to include every possible interference, opposition and desire whereby the secular authorities of whatever order and degree or whatever group or individual persons would wish to interfere in the election of the pontiff" (RPE 81).

Cardinal Electors

In 1975, Pope Paul VI issued the apostolic constitution *Romano pontifici eligendo*. In minute detail it regulates every facet of what happens between the death of the pope and the election of his successor. To guarantee certainty about the legitimacy of the election and to assure its total freedom from outside pressures, Paul VI specified every aspect of the electoral process. This legislation remains in force, without modification, at the present time.

Representing the "kernel" of the Roman presbyterate, the college of cardinals is fittingly entrusted with electing its bishop.[24] Canon law confirms this ancient practice, stating that the first and specific prerogative of cardinals "is to provide for the election of the Roman Pontiff" (CIC 349). At the same time, the international character of this college guarantees that representatives from other churches also take part in this election which is of singular importance for the universal Church. Today the cardinals come from more than fifty countries, providing a diversity which gives to the papal election a truly "catholic" dimension.

The present law states that a maximum of 120 cardinals can enter the conclave which elects the pope. Any cardinal over eighty years of age at the conclave's beginning is excluded from participating in the election with active voice (cf. RPE 33).[25]

Modifying the Electoral Body

Beginning in the 1960s, some theologians proposed that bishops should take a more active role in selecting the pope. Karl Rahner, for example, emphasized that the pope's principal function is to be head of the Church and the episcopal college. For Rahner, the pope's role as bishop of Rome "only indicates who the head of the whole Church is, it is not the reason for his headship."[26] Consequently, he maintained that papal elections were not primarily concerned with choosing the bishop of Rome. "*Because* someone is elected as supreme pastor of the Church (and accepts *this*)," Rahner wrote, "he is Bishop of Rome."[27] At least in theory, he maintained, the papal ministry is relatively independent of the pope's ministry as head of the local Roman church.

Due to this independence, Rahner concluded that it would be more in keeping with the Church's constitution if the college of bishops were to participate in naming the

Origins, Development, and Mission of the Papacy

successor of Peter. Because of the universal nature of his primacy, Rahner argued, the pope is most fittingly chosen by representatives of the whole Church. Only the primacy and the episcopacy, not the cardinalate, exist by divine right. Given the pope's greater importance to the universal Church than to the local church at Rome, the former function should be highlighted in choosing him. Consequently, Rahner proposed that the college of cardinals should be reconstituted as "a practical representation of the college of bishops."[28] In later years, when writing about the papal ministry in a more ecumenical context, he defended the same principle: the pope is primarily the supreme pastor of the universal Church, and future election procedures should, in various ways, be modified with this in mind.[29] Other theologians, like Hans Küng, go further than Rahner. They advocate a return to the practice of the early Church, when the laity participated in the choice of their pastors. That custom, they propose, should also be revived in selecting the bishop of Rome.[30]

While he was preparing the current legislation, Paul VI took seriously these proposals, as well as Vatican II's teaching on collegiality. Publicly, he raised the question whether patriarchs of the Eastern churches, even if not cardinals, should take part in papal elections. The Pope also mentioned "the possibility of associating with the sacred college of cardinals for so important a task those whom the Synod of Bishops — a group deriving from the episcopate of the entire world — elect as its representatives and who constitute the Council of the General Secretariat of the Synod, including also those designated by the Roman Pontiff himself."[31] Adding the fifteen members of the synod, twelve of whom were elected by their colleagues, would have, he explained, "the double advantage of uniting with the sacred college itself, for the election of the Pope, highly qualified representatives of the Synod of Bishops, and admitting to the election a group that is frequently renewed."[32] By not limiting papal electors to the college of cardinals, Paul VI thought that an expanded electoral body would be more representative of the world's bishops and a concrete application of episcopal collegiality.

Electing the Bishop of Rome

Nonetheless, when Paul VI promulgated *Romano pontifici eligendo*, he upheld the nine-hundred-year-old tradition of restricting the choice of papal electors to the cardinals. "We reaffirm the principle," he wrote, "whereby the election of the Roman pontiff is by ancient tradition the competence of the church of Rome, that is, of the sacred college of cardinals which represents her" (RPE, intro.). The apostolic constitution explicitly denies that either the episcopal college or the synod of bishops is competent in this matter (cf. RPE 34). Why did the Pope decide to preserve this custom?

Both theological and ecumenical reasons seem to have played a part. The method of election by the clergy of the Roman church expresses that the pope is the pastor of the universal Church precisely *because* he is the bishop of Rome. If the episcopacy or its delegates were to select the pope, such a procedure could possibly lead to a misinterpretation of the Petrine ministry. The successor of Peter would be regarded, above all, as the "bishop of bishops" rather than as the bishop of a particular church. Concerning the proposal that a delegated body of the universal episcopate should choose the pope, Henri de Lubac wrote: "Would that not, whether we like it or not, make the pope a kind of super-bishop with neither local nor temporal roots, a constitutional monarch of a Church conceived and, as it were, remolded in imitation of some modern State?"[33]

At the press conference presenting the apostolic constitution to the public, Roberto Tucci drew the same conclusion. "The hypothesis of an expansion of the electoral body beyond the college of cardinals would have threatened to leave somewhat in the shadow," he said, "the fact that it is a question of electing the bishop of the Roman church, the Roman Pontiff, and would have changed a tradition that goes back to the very beginning of the Church."[34] To have the bishops, as representatives of the universal Church, elect the pope would have called into question the theology of the local church expressed at Vatican II. It would also have weakened the ecclesial tradition which links papal primacy to the primacy of the church which Peter and Paul "founded" by their martyrdom.

The pope, moreover, is not a delegate of the episcopacy any more than Peter was of the Twelve. The apostles did not elect their leader. Nor did Peter choose the disciples. In like manner, the bishop of Rome receives his power immediately from Christ, and not from his electors or from the Church.[35] Catholic theology has always been careful to avoid portraying the pope as the representative of those who elected him. Instead, the juridical act of election "consists merely in indicating the person who is to receive from the Spirit his full authority as pope."[36]

Ecumenical reasons also played a part in preserving the age-old tradition of cardinal electors. The Orthodox and the other Oriental churches not yet in full communion with the Roman see attentively watch any changes in Catholic practice which might eventually affect them. In a special way, they protect very jealously the traditions which existed before the separation of the East from the West. De Lubac recalled that the Orthodox, who always tie the primacy of a bishop to a specific local see, would undoubtedly "refuse to accept the primacy of a super-bishop installed by a representation of the Western churches alone (or nearly so)."[37] Insofar as the East's ecclesiology of communion has any place for a Petrine ministry, this is true only if the pope is bishop of the local church at Rome, which gives him the title by which he exercises his primacy in the *koinonia*. To include Catholic patriarchs from the East in a papal election would therefore weaken, not strengthen, Catholic-Orthodox relations.[38] Any move suggesting that the pope could separate his primacy from that of the Roman church would have imperiled ecumenical dialogue. This ecumenical argument was very influential in persuading Paul VI to maintain the ancient practice of papal electors being representatives of the Roman church.

From the Protestant perspective, Jean-Jacques von Allmen pointed out that the pope must resist all attempts to "secularize" the sacramental nature of his office. Its non-bureaucratic nature is best preserved by stressing his role as bishop of Rome. The essentially episcopal character of the papacy would be endangered, he said, by any change which could foster the impression that the pope is a kind of general secretary of the universal Church.[39]

While Paul VI did not expand the electoral body, he took pains to accentuate the representative character of the college of cardinals. First, it truly represents the Roman clergy to which each cardinal belongs in virtue of the vital bond established by his being given "title" to a church in the city. Second, because of its increasingly international nature, the college also represents the particular churches of the *koinonia* to the church at Rome, emphasizing their mutual indwelling. Lastly, since cardinals are now normally bishops, they are representative, in a certain way, of the episcopal college. Nonetheless, what specifically qualifies the cardinals to be papal electors is their intimate relationship to the clergy of the local Roman church.[40] The college of cardinals continues the tradition of the early Church, where the election of the bishop of a particular church was in the hands of the local presbyterate, under the leadership and with the approval of the neighboring bishops, who then consecrated the man elected.[41]

It is therefore entirely in keeping with the principles of collegiality and ecumenism to have representatives of the Roman church choose their own bishop. By maintaining this manner of election, the Church clarifies that during a conclave she does not directly elect the head of the episcopal college. Instead, the particular church of Rome selects its bishop who is, *ipso facto,* head of the college of bishops. For true collegiality to be realized, the pope must remain *within* the body of bishops. He is their head because representatives of his own diocese elect him. Election by the college of cardinals ensures that the pope is sacramentally rooted as bishop of a local church and, for that very reason, the Church's chief pastor. These two functions cannot be separated; one derives from the other. Because the successor of Peter is the bishop of Rome, he is also the supreme pastor of the universal Church.[42]

Although choosing the Roman bishop is now exclusively in the hands of the cardinals, *Romano pontifici eligendo* contains an allusion to the ancient practice of lay participation in papal elections. The election is not to be "something unconnected with the people of God" but is to "be in a certain sense an act of the whole Church." To achieve this end, the Church is invited to pray with the cardinals that God "may enlighten the electors and make them so like-minded in their task that a speedy, unanimous and fruitful election may take place, as is required by the salvation of souls and the good of the whole Catholic world" (RPE 85).

Electoral Procedures

Any Catholic who can be validly and licitly ordained to the episcopacy may be elected the bishop of Rome. There is no restriction on his race, age, nationality, or status in the Church. If the man chosen has not yet received episcopal orders, he must be ordained bishop immediately so that he can assume jurisdiction as pastor of the Roman church and head of the universal Church (cf. RPE 88; CIC 332.1).

The Conclave

The word "conclave" comes from the Latin words *cum clave,* to shut "with a key." It refers to the place where the cardinals gather to choose the pope. Sealed from any contact with the outside world, the electors remain there "night and day until the election has taken place, without having any dealings with extraneous persons or things." This seclusion is designed to provide the "character of a sacred retreat" so that the cardinals can deliberate in prayer and freedom (cf. RPE 42).

After the pope's death, the conclave must begin no sooner than fifteen days and no later than twenty days (cf. RPE 37). The ban on discussing the election of a successor to the bishop of Rome, which is in force during the pope's lifetime, is now lifted (cf. RPE 80). While condemning all pre-election promises, the law does not "have the intention of forbidding the exchange of views concerning the election during the period in which the see is vacant" (RPE 82). If any elector makes a pact requiring anyone to vote for or against someone, such commitments are declared null and void. Furthermore, those who enter into such agreements are excommunicated (cf. RPE 82-83). All who enter the conclave are also obliged to the strictest secrecy. Under oath they swear never to reveal anything regarding the papal election, promising "to observe with the greatest fidelity and with all persons, including any conclavists, the secret concerning everything that in any way relates to the election of the Roman pontiff and concerning what takes place in the conclave or place of the election, directly or indirectly concerning the scrutinies" (RPE 49). The results of each ballot are kept in the secret archives (cf. RPE 73).

Methods of Election

Romano pontifici eligendo outlines three methods of election: acclamation or inspiration, by delegation or compromise, and by scrutiny or balloting.

• *ACCLAMATION* A remnant of ancient tradition and, at least once, of recorded practice, is election by acclamation. Eusebius (†340) tells the story, perhaps legendary, of the election of 236: "When the brethren had all assembled with the intention of electing a successor to the bishopric, a large number of eminent and distinguished men were in the thoughts of most, Fabian, who was present, came into no one's mind. But suddenly out of the blue a dove fluttered down and perched on his head (the story goes on), plainly following the example of the descent upon the Saviour of the Holy Spirit in the form of a dove."[43] More soberly, current law states that election by acclamation occurs when the electors "as it were through the inspiration of the Holy Spirit, freely and spontaneously, unanimously and aloud, proclaim one individual as supreme pontiff" (RPE 63). For this procedure to be valid, every elector must assent to the "inspired" choice either orally or in writing.

• *DELEGATION* In the method of delegation the cardinals unanimously agree to entrust to a small group of their number the power to elect the pope on behalf of them all. In this case, they choose as their representatives an uneven number of cardinals, from nine to fifteen. The electors must also clearly instruct their delegates regarding all the details about the way in which they are to proceed and what is required for a valid election. The delegates, for example, could propose a name to the others for ratification or they could themselves choose the bishop of Rome in the name of all (cf. RPE 64). This method of compromise is foreseen in the situation in which prolonged balloting has failed to produce a candidate who can obtain the number of votes required for election (cf. RPE 76).

• *SCRUTINY* The ordinary form of election and the procedure described by the law in the greatest detail is balloting (cf. RPE 65-76). In this case written ballots are used, a practice first resorted to in 1198 for the election of Innocent III.[44] A two-thirds plus one majority is required for a valid election. If no one is elected within three days, with four daily ballots (cf. RPE 74), a day of rest and prayer follows. After this, seven more ballots are taken; and then, after another rest day, seven more. At that time, if all the electors unanimously agree, the requirement for a two-thirds plus one majority may be abandoned. The cardinals are then free to accept either a majority plus one as sufficient for election or a run-off between the two candidates in the preceding session who received the highest number of votes (cf. RPE 76).

Acceptance and Naming

When the required number of votes is attained, the one elected is asked: "Do you accept your canonical election as supreme pontiff?" No one chosen is forced to accept. After freely giving his consent, the new pope is next asked, "By what name do you wish to be called?" (RPE 87).

The 140 popes of the first millennium used about 80 different names, nearly always the ones they had received at baptism. The custom of name-changing first appeared in the sixth century. In 533, a priest with the name of a pagan god, Mercury, was elected. Thinking such a name to be unfitting, he called himself John II (533-535), after a saintly predecessor. For the next four centuries, however, popes simply kept their own names. John XII (955-964), who had been baptized Octavian, a name of the pagan emperor, is credited with beginning in earnest the custom of name-changing.[45]

After the year 1000, the practice of taking a new name became standard and has persisted up to the present. The only exceptions to this tradition are the three Renaissance popes, Julius II (1503-1513), Hadrian VI (1522-1523), and Marcellus II (1555); each of them kept his baptismal name after his election.

Why did the popes begin to change their names? Both negative and positive reasons can be offered. First, some names, such as Mercury or Octavian, were associated with paganism and therefore deemed inappropriate. Second, some names would have sounded outlandish or ridiculous to Roman ears. Name-changing was a way for a newly-elected pope who was not from the City to Romanize himself. Third, a taboo surrounded the name Peter. Those so called at the time of their election chose not to use it out of respect for the apostle.

Among the more positive reasons for name-changing is the example offered by Sts. Peter and Paul. When divinely commissioned, both Simon and Saul received new names. Additionally, the name-change served to emphasize that the man elected assumed a new function in the Church. Leaving his former life behind, the new successor of Peter was to dedicate himself completely to his office. This custom reflected the much earlier tradition of name-changing which accompanied the profession of religious vows. Among the popes of the late tenth and eleventh centuries, some of whom were former monks, the change of name signified this new identity. It also highlighted the transcendent nature of the papal office, its superiority to secular authorities.[46]

In recent centuries, most popes have chosen names that have honored a recent predecessor. Some, however, have chosen a name in order to associate themselves with earlier popes or to suggest an ideal or quality evident in the name. Pius, Clement, Innocent, and Benedict are adjectives that suggest the virtues of piety, mercy, innocence, and blessedness. The first innovation in centuries was John Paul I's (1978) choice of a double name, a designation also adopted by his successor.

End of a Pope's Tenure: Resignation and Illness

Death is certainly the usual reason which leads to the vacancy of the Roman see and the election of a new pope. There are, however, other situations which could bring about the end of a pope's mandate. Besides his voluntary resignation, canonists and theologians have discussed irreversible mental illness as a condition which might involve the end of a pope's tenure of office.

Resignation

Traditionally, popes have held the Petrine ministry for life. As an office freely accepted, it can, however, also be surrendered freely. Impressing no sacramental character, the papacy is not necessarily the permanent possession of the one who assumes the office. A pope who has resigned remains a bishop, but he is no longer head of the episcopal college.

Although the historical record is obscure, it appears that the first pope to have abdicated was Pontian (230-235), who was deported to Sardinia during a persecution. He resigned on September 28, 235, the first precisely recorded date in papal history, to allow a replacement to be chosen. Ironically, Pontian outlived his successor.[47] The most famous pope to have resigned his office was St. Celestine V in 1294. Having consulted the college of cardinals and declared that the Roman pontiff could freely relinquish his proper functions, he did just that. Overpowered by the papacy's demands after just five months as pope, he returned to his hermetical life. Though not without opposition, his declaration on the legitimacy of papal resignation was received into the subsequent canonical tradition.[48]

Current canon law specifies the procedure for giving up the papal office: "If it should happen that the Roman Pontiff resigns his office, it is required for validity that he make the resignation freely and that it be duly manifested, but not that it be accepted by anyone" (CIC 332.2).[49] The three conditions set out for his resignation to be valid are straightforward. First, the pope must renounce his office of his own free will, without being subjected to physical force or undue moral pressure. He must be in full possession of his mental faculties to resign. Second, since resignation is not merely a private act, he must make it publicly known. As is true for any resignation from ecclesiastical office, the pope must submit it orally or in writing before at least two witnesses. The college of cardinals merely acknowledges the fact and proceeds to fill the vacancy. Third, the pope needs no one's consent, permission, or acceptance to resign. Just as no human authority confirms his election, similarly no one accepts his resignation.[50] He simply announces his abdication and when it will take effect.

Origins, Development, and Mission of the Papacy

It could happen that the good of the Church would be served if a pope were freely to offer his resignation. In no situation, however, is the pope under any legal obligation to give up his office. Any "obligation" would be strictly moral. During the Second Vatican Council, Hans Küng addressed the circumstances under which he thought the bishop of Rome should offer his resignation. "If a pope sees that his person — guilty or not — is no longer able to fulfill this fundamental function of the Petrine office [to serve the Church]," wrote Küng, "he is morally obliged to give up his office for the sake of the unity and peace of the Church, as well as for the sake of a more credible presentation of the Petrine office, and voluntarily make way for another pope who can more properly perform this fundamental function of the Petrine office."[51] Patrick Granfield also advocates this view. "Whenever a Pope becomes unable to function adequately as the leader of the Christian community and whenever his continuance in office becomes seriously harmful to the Church," Granfield maintains, "he would seem to be morally obliged to resign."[52]

Other theologians have argued that, like his brother bishops, the pope should offer his resignation at a certain age. They suggest that he should do this either at seventy-five, when other bishops do, or at eighty, when cardinals lose their right to elect the pope. Still, the fact that only one pope in a millennium has resigned and that impeding illnesses have been rare has created a tradition that resignation is an unlikely, even undesirable, procedure. While many rumored that Paul VI would resign at eighty, he did not do so — no doubt because he felt in conscience still able to fulfill his ministry. He is reported to have said that just as a father cannot cease to be a father, neither can the pope cease to be pope.[53]

As a variant on resignation, some contemporary writers have pointed out the advantages of limiting the pope to a fixed term of office or establishing an age for retirement. Above all, this limitation would de-emphasize even more a monarchical view of the papacy. Furthermore, there are, so they maintain, advantages to a limited term: "Such a practice would facilitate the regular circulation of fresh ideas, energy, and talent within the papacy; introduce a greater sense of urgency in the direction of the Church; and prevent an ineffective Pope from causing spiritual harm to the Church."[54] Moreover, a fixed term would underscore the papacy as a charism of service, enabling the Church to distinguish more clearly between the person of the pope and the Petrine ministry. Against such proposals, it can be pointed out that compulsory retirement or fixing the terms of office would lend credence to thinking of the papacy as a bureaucratic or functional ministry, compromising its symbolic role in the Church.

Irreversible Mental Illness

A *vacancy* in the Roman see arises either through death or resignation. The see is *impeded* when the pope is unable to exercise his office, a possibility mentioned in canon law (cf. CIC 335). While it addresses at great length the question of vacancy, *Romano pontifici eligendo* says nothing about the Roman see being impeded. This possibility should therefore be treated as parallel to the situation which arises in the case of a diocesan bishop. The Roman see would be impeded if the pope was truly incapable of exercising his office, whether because of mental illness, imprisonment, or exile. In all circumstances, as long as the Roman see is impeded, no properly primatial authority can be exercised in the Church (cf. CIC 335).

The early twentieth-century canonist F. X. Wernz held that "through mental illness, if it is certain and permanent, the Roman pontiff *ipso facto* loses the pontifical jurisdiction."[55] Some compare permanent mental illness to "spiritual death," which renders the pope incapable of exercising his jurisdiction. In other words, the fact of such an illness renders the Roman see "vacant" and requires the election of a new pope.

Recent commentators on the Code of Canon Law have described some situations in which the Roman see would be impeded. It is possible that a pope "either because of illness, an accident, or an attempt on his life, could be in a prolonged coma or in any other state of health totally impeding him from discharging his office."[56] No legal provisions are public regarding the way in which the Church should proceed if a pope were to be irreversibly incapacitated and therefore unable to exercise his office. According to current public legislation, no individual or group has the authority to certify that the pope is impeded from exercising the Petrine office. It seems reasonable to hold that if such a situation were to become irrefutably manifest to the Church, the college of cardinals could proceed to elect a new pope. As the electoral body for the bishop of Rome, the college of cardinals would be the qualified body to declare the fact of the pope's incompetency. An ecumenical council would not be called, because current canon law explicitly forbids holding a council without the pope (cf. CIC 338). To raise the specter of conciliarism at such a delicate moment would be imprudent.

Loss of the Papal Office Through Heresy

Given the vital importance of the papacy to Church life, theologians for at least a millennium have raised the question of what can be done should a pope fall into heresy. Although this situation is unlikely to arise, theologians and canonists have dealt with its possibility. Does a heretical pope lose the Petrine ministry?

From the Middle Ages onward, two axioms have governed the theological and canonical discussion of the problem of a heretical pope. The first principle is that "the first see is judged by no one," a proposition which set the parameters for all debates on the subject. A second principle originally appeared in the ninth century: the papacy could be lost through heresy. Without denying the first principle, this second axiom conditions it in practice.[57] In other words, the bishop of Rome, in the case of a heretical pope, can be judged.

The theology of the *Ecclesia romana* developed during the Gregorian Reform distinguished between the person of the pope and the local *church* of Rome. The latter reality included the college of cardinals united to the pope. This distinction allowed theologians to hold, for example, that the Roman church itself was indefectible in its faith, while the pope could fall into heresy.[58] The local church at Rome, a designation which included the college of cardinals, had always preserved intact, they maintained, the

Origins, Development, and Mission of the Papacy

deposit of faith.[59] It was the standard opinion of medieval theologians, says Francis Sullivan, that "a pope could fall into heresy in his private opinions."[60] Furthermore, most canonists believed that the pope lost his office because of heresy.[61] This remains the common teaching today.

Classical theologians proposed two main solutions to deal with the problem of a heretical pope. One group held that he was automatically deposed by God himself. Another group maintained that some ecclesiastical body must judge and declare the pope to be heretical, before proceeding to an election.

Without developing the point, the twelfth-century canonist Gratian reproduced a statement from the previous century in his *Decretum*: "No mortal shall presume to rebuke his [the pope's] faults, for he who is to judge all is to be judged by no one, unless he is found straying from the faith."[62] Even Innocent III (1198-1216), during whose pontificate the papacy reached its zenith as a spiritual-temporal institution, believed that "only on account of a sin committed against the faith can I be judged by the church" (PL 217, 656).[63] The *plenitudo potestatis* resided in the vicar of Christ, but only as long as he himself professed the faith of the Church.

Throughout the Middle Ages it was commonly, though not universally, held that in questions of faith an ecumenical council could judge the pope.[64] In the *Summa de Ecclesia*, one of the earliest and most influential ecclesiological treatises of the late Middle Ages, John of Torquemada (†1468), for example, admitted that a heretical pope could, in a certain sense, be "judged" by a council. Even so, the council would not be judging a true pope. Precisely because he was heretical, he would already have ceased, by that very fact, to hold the papal office.[65] Jesus' words, "He who does not believe is condemned already" (Jn 3:18), provided a biblical proof text which justified the automatic loss of office if a pope fell into heresy.

After the Council of Trent, Robert Bellarmine (†1621) and others took up the theory of John of Torquemada: a pope who falls into heresy forfeits his office. No formal deposition is required since divine law already put the pope outside the Church. A kind of direct divine deposition took place, stripping the pope of his primacy.[66] Whatever juridical body "judged" the pope would simply declare the fact of the pope's heresy, making public that he was no longer in communion with the Church. Theologians frequently compared such a declaration to a death certificate, which publicly makes the death known but does not cause it. With regard to heresy, this judgment would, however, have legal consequences. The Church would be free to elect a new pope.[67] Because these theologians did not give an ecumenical council the right to depose a pope, their theory avoids the pitfalls of conciliarism.

On the other hand, writers such as Cajetan (†1534), John of St. Thomas (†1644), and Francisco Súarez (†1617), argued that heresy does not automatically depose the pope. They held that some body, whether an ecumenical council or the college of cardinals, must first establish his guilt and then declare him to be a heretic. Only after the rendering of a negative judgment would an accused pope cease to hold the Petrine office. Súarez affirmed that "if the pope becomes an unrepentant heretic, after having passed on him the declaratory sentence of his crime, by legitimate ecclesiastical jurisdiction, he ceases to be pope."[68] What an ecumenical council or other juridical body does in such a case is to dissolve the bond existing between the person of the pope and the papal ministry.

At present, the Church has no canonical norms for dealing with a heretical pope. On the one hand, the pope is obviously in the Church, belonging to the community of faith. Like any Catholic who publicly professes heresy, a pope would place himself outside her communion and by that very fact loses his ministry. Even though this is not a pressing problem for the Church, as Yves Congar says, the idea of a possibly heretical pope is significant to ecclesiology. As a hypothesis, it clarifies that the pope is within the Church and not over or outside her.[69] Even if it is not a problem in practice, the question reminds us that "the loss of the authentic truth of the apostles means the loss of apostolic authority."[70]

It is difficult to imagine what specific juridical procedures could be drawn up to deal with the situation should it arise. Speaking for the Deputation of the Faith at Vatican I, Bishop Zinelli recognized the tradition which admitted the possibility of a heretical pope. The solution he proposed avoided the mention of anything which would lessen papal authority. If a pope were to fall into heresy, he said, God would provide the means of handling it (cf. M 52, 1109). Karl Rahner held the same opinion. No one, he maintained, can ever depose a pope for heresy. Bishops or cardinals can only ascertain that the pope is no longer the legitimate successor of Peter. Because it concerns a question of fact rather than law, there can be no set legal procedure for this process.[71] Following the same line of thought, Patrick Burns believes that "Catholicism relies primarily on Christian prophetic protest to compensate for the lack of juridical limitations on the exercise of papal primacy."[72]

"Bad" Popes

History confirms that the Church cannot always depend on saintly popes as helmsmen of the bark of Peter. Not only anti-Roman polemics, but also the writings of scholars and saints are replete with tales of the corruption, vice, and wickedness in the lives of some popes. Here a very sensitive problem surfaces. What can the Church do when faced with a pope who is morally reprehensible in a prolonged and serious way?

Christ's promise that the "the powers of death shall not prevail against it" (Mt 16:18) still leaves the Church and the papacy vulnerable to attacks from all sides. As an institution embodied in history, the Church has leaders, including the pope, who can falter. If the Church of God is both sinful and holy, it can also happen that the papacy will reflect the image of her sin.[73] Scandal reaches the Church even in her highest ministry. Peter was only the first in a long line of shepherds who stumbled and fell. The somber biblical accounts of the apostle's failures foreshadow the mingling of sinfulness and greatness which marks the history of the popes. Hans Urs von Balthasar observed that there has been "a large number of popes who, from a Christian point of view, are highly questionable and under whose rule the function of the office did indeed shrink to the guaranteed minimum explicitly adumbrated by Vatican I."[74] What remains certain is that the pope's sins, no matter how serious, can never destroy the Church. "All that we are assured of," says Bouyer, "is that no act of treason, by the watchful grace of Christ, the conquering power of his Spirit, can ruin the building that the incarnate Son of God founded, nor ever estrange it from the presence of the Spirit of life."[75]

G. K. Chesterton, that great lover of paradoxes, contrasted the indestructibility of the Church, divinely founded on the weak man Peter, to the failed kingdoms of this world founded by the strong.[76] As St. Paul so starkly stated, divine election is paradoxical: "God chose what is weak in the world to shame the strong" (1 Cor 1:27). He manifests the power of his love in human weakness. And this is nowhere more evident than in Christ's commission to Peter. It was to the Peter who failed that Christ entrusted his flock, "so that no human being might boast in the presence of God" (1 Cor 1:29). Through the tension between the office and the office-holder, between God's fidelity and human infidelity, the example of Peter and the popes remains a "scandal," indeed the central scandal of Catholicism.[77]

The problem posed by a pope's immorality is best grasped in the light of a crucial distinction advanced by Leo the Great. His understanding of Roman law led him to distinguish between the transferable powers Jesus gave to Peter, his office, and the pope's personal qualifications and merits. Heir to Peter's fullness of power in his office, the person of the pope counted for little. Leo repeatedly proclaimed he was Peter's "unworthy heir" who assumed the onerous burden of the papacy. Orderly ecclesial life depends on the office, not the individual pope, saint or sinner that he might be. Though there have been many exemplary popes who were personally holy, their distinctive charism is not to be models of personal holiness. Leo the Great clarified theoretically what history has confirmed. Even though a pope might be personally unworthy of leading the Church, he does not for that reason lose his office.

The theological underpinnings of this Leonine view, universally accepted by Catholics, rest on the Church's condemnation of the Donatist heresy. In the early Church, the Donatists held that the validity of a sacrament depended on the holiness of its minister. Von Balthasar affirms that "letting the credibility of the office depend on the personal holiness of its bearer is the most disastrous of the heresies combatted by Augustine."[78] When applied to the papacy, a theoretical variant of this heresy links the right to hold office to the virtue of the officeholder. However, just as it is not Paul or Apollos who baptizes, but Christ, so it is not Pius, Boniface, or John Paul who really holds the keys of the kingdom, but Peter associated with Christ. Whenever anyone has proposed that the pope's right to his office depends on his personal holiness, fitting as that sanctity is, the Church has opposed such an opinion. Defenders of the papacy have held firm against any traces of a resurgent Donatism.

In the sixteenth century, Cajetan made the same point against those Reformers who held that "ecclesiastical authority does not reside in wicked ministers."[79] Whether an admired saint or a scandalous sinner, the bishop of Rome is always "absorbed" by the witness to the gospel provided by his church, the holy see of Sts. Peter and Paul.[80] The Church teaches that by itself a pope's personal immorality is insufficient reason for losing the papal office.

Canonists and theologians deny that the pope can be deposed for immorality. Since forced removal from office is impossible, what can be done? If a wicked pope is governing the Church, the faithful must first of all pray for his conversion. Furthermore, those most closely associated with him, especially the college of cardinals, should make every effort to persuade him that the good of the Church would be served by his resignation. If this also fails, some theologians have called for resisting the pope. Cajetan advised that Catholics should "oppose the abuse of power which destroys by suitable remedies such as not obeying, not being servile in the face of evil actions, not keeping silence, by arguing and by urging leaders to follow the example of Paul and his precept found at the end of the Epistle to the Colossians [4:17]: 'Tell Archippus, "See that you fulfill the ministry which you have received in the Lord." ' [Do this] and there will be little or no abuse of power."[81]

◆

The procedure for electing the pope has evolved significantly in the course of the Church's history. Assuming the right to regulate the way in which their successors were chosen, the popes have shown great care to guarantee the lawfulness, regularity, and freedom of papal elections. Throughout most of the first millennium, surrounding bishops, as well as the clergy and people of Rome, took part in the election of their bishop. After the Edict of Milan (313), secular authorities increasingly exerted pressure on the electoral process of all bishops, including the bishop of Rome, a practice which the popes consistently tried to bring under control. The most crucial step in freeing the Church from worldly interventions was taken at the outset of the Gregorian Reform. Beginning in the eleventh century, various papal and conciliar decrees established that the cardinals, as representatives of the Roman church, were the pope's exclusive electors. Even so, the Church was not totally free from undue intrusions until the early twentieth century.

Modern proposals that the electoral college should be widened to include delegates of the world's bishops have been rejected. In his apostolic constitution *Romano pontifici eligendo* (1975), Paul VI reaffirmed the tradition that the right to elect the pope belongs to the college of cardinals. Due to the influence of the ecclesiology of communion, it is more desirable than ever that choosing the pastor of the universal Church be clearly perceived as the election of the bishop of Rome. Consequently, the college of cardinals, which perpetuates the ancient model of a local church choosing its bishop, is the appropriate electoral body for the successor of Peter. Moreover, it is owing to his election as bishop of the particular church of Rome that the pope receives from Christ his supreme power of jurisdiction in the universal Church.

The sensitive theological-canonical question of the conditions under which the papacy can be lost shows the importance of distinguishing clearly between the person of the pope and the Petrine ministry which he exercises. Besides death, current canonical norms foresee the possibility of a pope freely resigning from his office. Neither canon law nor the regulations governing papal elections, however, deal with the thornier topics of irreversible mental incapacitation or intractable heresy. These questions await further canonical and theological development.

Notes for Chapter thirteen

1. Irenaeus, *Against Heresies*, 3.3.3.
2. Clement, *First Letter to the Corinthians*, 44.1.
3. Giancarlo Zizola, *Il conclave: Storia e segreti* (Rome: Newton Compton, 1993), 21-22.
4. J. N. D. Kelly, *The Oxford Dictionary of Popes* (New York: Oxford University Press, 1986), 57.
5. Patrick Granfield, *The Papacy in Transition* (Garden City: Doubleday & Company, 1980), 138-139.
6. Zizola, *Il conclave*, 22.
7. Cyprian, *Letter*, 55.8.
8. Granfield, *Papacy in Transition*, 126.
9. Granfield, *Papacy in Transition*, 127.
10. A. Swift, "Popes, Election of," *New Catholic Encyclopedia*, vol. 11 (New York: McGraw-Hill Book Company, 1967), 572.
11. Zizola, *Il conclave*, 32.
12. Granfield, *Papacy in Transition*, 127-129.
13. Roberto Tucci, "A Juridical and Pastoral Document," *L'Osservatore Romano*, 50 (December 11, 1975), 9.
14. K. F. Morrison, "Papal Election Decree (1059)," *New Catholic Encyclopedia*, vol. 10 (New York: McGraw-Hill Book Company, 1967), 974.
15. Translation in Granfield, *Papacy in Transition*, 130.
16. Zizola, *Il conclave*, 38-39.
17. Lateran III, canon 1; translation in Norman P. Tanner, ed., *Decrees of the Ecumenical Councils*, vol. 1 (Washington, D.C.: Georgetown University Press, 1990), 211.
18. Granfield, *Papacy in Transition*, 130.
19. Lyons II, *Ubi periculum*; translation in *Decrees of the Ecumenical Councils*, vol. 1, 314-315.
20. Lyons II, *Ubi periculum*; translation in *Decrees of the Ecumenical Councils*, vol. 1, 315.
21. Lyons II, *Ubi periculum*; translation in *Decrees of the Ecumenical Councils*, vol. 1, 317.
22. Zizola, *Il conclave*, 122-123.
23. Zizola, *Il conclave*, 176-185.
24. Louis Bouyer, *The Church of God*, trans. Charles Underhill Quinn (Chicago: Franciscan Herald Press, 1982), 394-399.
25. This restriction was already decreed by Paul VI in *Ingravescentem aetatem* (1971), #62.
26. Karl Rahner and Joseph Ratzinger, *The Episcopate and the Primacy*, trans. Kenneth Barker, Patrick Kerans, Robert Ochs, and Richard Strachan (New York: Herder and Herder, 1962), 128.
27. Karl Rahner, "The Episcopal Office," in *Theological Investigations*, trans. Karl-H. and Boniface Kruger, vol. 6 (Baltimore: Helicon Press, 1969), 322.
28. Rahner, "Episcopal Office," 326.
29. Heinrich Fries and Karl Rahner, *Unity of the Churches*, trans. Ruth C. L. Gritsch and Eric W. Gritsch (Philadelphia: Fortress Press, 1985), 92; cf. Karl Rahner, *Faith in a Wintry Season*, ed. Paul Imhof and Hubert Biallowons, trans. Harvey D. Egan (New York: Crossroad Publishing Company, 1990), 171.
30. Hans Küng, *Truthfulness: The Future of the Church* (New York: Sheed & Ward, 1968), 172-173.

31. Paul VI, Discourse, March 5, 1973, *L'Osservatore Romano*, 11 (March 15, 1973), 1.
32. Paul VI, Address to the Council of the General Secretariat of the Synod of Bishops, March 24, 1973, *L'Osservatore Romano*, 14 (April 5, 1973), 4.
33. Henri de Lubac, *The Motherhood of the Church*, trans. Sergia Englund (San Francisco: Ignatius Press, 1982), 316-317.
34. Tucci, "Juridical and Pastoral Document," 9.
35. Hervé-Marie Legrand, "Ministero romano e ministero universale del papa: Il problema della sua elezione," *Concilium*, 11:8 (1975), 62.
36. Rahner, "Episcopal Office," 349.
37. De Lubac, *Motherhood of the Church*, 323.
38. Legrand, "Ministero romano," 66-67, 70.
39. Jean-Jacques von Allmen, "Ministero papale, ministero di unità," *Concilium*, 11:8 (1975), 135.
40. Michele Maccarrone, "The Church of Rome Is the Church of Peter," *L'Osservatore Romano*, 3 (January 15, 1976), 9.
41. Bouyer, *Church of God*, 398-399.
42. Roberto Tucci, "Foundations and Reasons for the Regulations for the Election of the Roman Pontiff," *L'Osservatore Romano*, 48 (November 27, 1975), 9.
43. Eusebius, *The History of the Church*, rev ed. and introduction Andrew Louth, trans. G. A. Williamson (London: Penguin Books, 1989), #VI.29, p. 204.
44. Zizola, *Il conclave*, 47.
45. Tim Nau, "The Names of the Popes," *Onomastica Canadiana*, 75:2 (December 1993), 62.
46. Nau, "Names of the Popes," 60-62.
47. Kelly, *Dictionary of Popes*, 16.
48. Zizola, *Il conclave*, 264, n. 15.
49. Paul VI had foreseen the possibility that the Roman see could "become vacant as a result of the resignation of the supreme pontiff" (RPE 78).
50. Gianfranco Ghirlanda, *Il diritto nella Chiesa: mistero di comunione*, 2nd ed. (Milan: Edizioni San Paolo, 1993), 506.
51. Hans Küng, *Structures of the Church*, trans. Salvator Attanasio (New York: Thomas Nelson & Sons, 1964), 258.
52. Granfield, *Papacy in Transition*, 165.
53. Peter Hebblethwaite, *Paul VI: The First Modern Pope* (New York: Paulist Press, 1993), 564.
54. Granfield, *Papacy in Transition*, 149.
55. F. X. Wernz and P. Vidal, *Ius Canonicum*, 3rd ed., vol. 2 (Rome, 1943), 516.
56. E. Caparros, M. Thériault, and J. Thorn, eds., *Code of Canon Law Annotated* (Montreal: Wilson & Lafleur Limitée, 1993), 267.
57. Klaus Schatz, *La primauté du Pape*, trans. Joseph Hoffmann (Paris: Cerf, 1992), 118, 147.
58. Yves Congar, *L'Eglise de saint Augustin à l'époque moderne* (Paris: Cerf, 1970), 96.
59. Schatz, *Primauté du Pape*, 181.
60. Francis A. Sullivan, *Magisterium: Teaching Authority in the Catholic Church* (New York: Paulist Press, 1983), 92.
61. Jaroslav Pelikan, *Reformation of Church and Dogma (1300-1700)*, The Christian Tradition: A History of the Development of Doctrine, vol. 4 (Chicago: University of Chicago Press, 1984), 108.
62. *Decretum Gratiani*, Dist. 40, c. 6; translation in Patrick Granfield, *The Limits of the Papacy*

(New York: Crossroad Publishing Company, 1987), 71.
63. Translation in Pelikan, *Reformation of Church and Dogma*, 107.
64. Congar, *L'Eglise de saint Augustin à l'époque moderne*, 306, 309-310.
65. Congar, *L'Eglise de saint Augustin à l'époque moderne*, 342-343.
66. Granfield, *Papacy in Transition*, 171.
67. Küng, *Structures of the Church*, 267.
68. Francisco Súarez, *Opera Omnia*, vol. 12 (Paris: L. Vivès, 1858), tract. 1, disp. 10: *De summo pontifice*, sect. 6, 317; translation in Küng, *Structures of the Church*, 261-262.
69. Yves Congar, *Ministères et communion ecclésiale* (Paris: Cerf, 1971), 198.
70. Congar, *Ministères et communion ecclésiale*, 80.
71. *Karl Rahner in Dialogue*, ed. Paul Imhof and Hubert Biallowons, trans. Harvey D. Egan (New York: Crossroad Publishing Company, 1986), 97-98.
72. Patrick J. Burns, "Communion, Councils, and Collegiality: Some Catholic Reflections," in *Papal Primacy and the Universal Church*, Lutherans and Catholics in Dialogue V, Paul C. Empie and T. Austin Murphy, eds. (Minneapolis: Augsburg Publishing House, 1974), 170.
73. J. M. R. Tillard, *The Bishop of Rome*, trans. John de Satgé (Wilmington: Michael Glazier, 1983), 166.
74. Hans Urs von Balthasar, *The Office of Peter and the Structure of the Church*, trans. Andrée Emery (San Francisco: Ignatius Press, 1986), 242-243.
75. Bouyer, *Church of God*, 501.
76. G. K. Chesterton, *Heretics* (London, 1950), 60-61.
77. Hermann J. Pottmeyer, "Why Does the Church Need a Pope?" *Communio*, 18:3 (1991), 312.
78. Hans Urs von Balthasar, *A Short Primer for Unsettled Laymen*, trans. Mary Theresilde Skerry (San Francisco: Ignatius Press, 1985), 105.
79. Cajetan, *De divina institutione pontificatus Romani Pontifici (1521)*, 2; translation in Pelikan, *Reformation of Church and Dogma*, 273.
80. Tillard, *Bishop of Rome*, 166.
81. Cajetan, *De comparatione auctoritatis papae at concilii*, Scripta Theologica, ed. Vincent M. Pollet, vol. 1 (Rome: Angelicum, 1936), 180; translation in Harry McSorley, "Some Forgotten Truths about the Petrine Ministry," *Journal of Ecumenical Studies*, 11 (1974), 216.

Chapter fourteen
THE ROMAN CURIA AND THE PETRINE MINISTRY

Those who hold responsible offices are generally unable to carry out personally all the functions expected of them. They require the help of others. In most institutions, the welfare of the community being served requires that this assistance be stable and regulated. Because the Church is, in some respects, an institution, it is not surprising that the mission entrusted to Peter and his successors should also require collaboration. In this regard, Paul VI commented in the introduction to his 1967 apostolic constitution *Regimini ecclesiae universae* that "there can be no doubt about the need for the Roman curia. How could the supreme pontiff, weighed down by so many great labors of matters involving the care of all the churches, possibly carry on alone without aides and advisors?"

As "the circle of the closest collaborators of the Pope,"[1] the Roman curia is the administrative apparatus at his service. Similar to the bureaucracy of a secular state, it assists the pope in his duties to the communion of churches, "a function that has been growing and expanding from day to day" (PB 3). The curia helps the pope with his primatial ministry in the universal Church. It has no authority either for the pastoral life of the diocese of Rome or for the welfare of Vatican City State. Through the curia's collaboration, the pope has yet another way of fulfilling his service to the *koinonia*.

Basing itself on the teaching of the Second Vatican Council, the Code of Canon Law succinctly describes the role of the papal bureaucracy: "The Supreme Pontiff usually conducts the business of the universal Church by means of the Roman Curia, which fulfills its duty in his name and by his authority for the good and the service of the churches" (CIC 360; cf. CD 9). The curia is made up of the offices and people which the pope uses to support his care for all the churches (cf. 2 Cor 11:28). According to John Paul II's apostolic constitution *Pastor bonus* (1988), it also "promotes the mission proper to the Church in the world" (PB art. 1).

In this chapter, I examine the administrative machinery which helps the pope, seeing what further light it sheds on the Petrine ministry. I will first look at the origin, authority, and organization of the Roman curia, and then discuss papal representatives as instruments which the pope uses in his service to the communion of churches. I close the chapter with a brief discussion of some proposals regarding curial reform.

Origin

The root of the word "curia" is traced to the term for "assembly" in ancient Rome. The word was later applied to the hall in which people gathered and, in particular, to the building where the senate met. The Latin *curare* means "to take care of." The curia, then,

300 ✦ THE ROMAN CURIA AND THE PETRINE MINISTRY

refers to the persons or the place which take care of certain business. Adapted for ecclesiastical usage, a "curia" is composed of officials who assist the bishop. The "Roman" curia refers to the people and offices providing the support which helps the pope to meet the obligations of his universal ministry.[2]

Almost from the outset, the bishops of Rome have engaged the help of others in carrying out their duties to the worldwide *koinonia*. Like all bishops, the pope was assisted by the priests of Rome, his presbyterate, in formulating his teaching and in enforcing ecclesiastical discipline. This presbyterate dealt with much ordinary business in council, easing the pope's burden. Meanwhile, subordinate officials carried out the more routine administrative work at the pope's Lateran palace. This latter group was uninvolved in decision-making and had little pastoral interest or experience.[3] During the eleventh century, the body of presbyters, deacons, and lower-order clergy which had formerly assisted the bishop of Rome, was restricted to only the leading priests and deacons. At the same time, the Roman presbyterate was broadened to include the bishops near Rome, thus forming the college of cardinals.

Another significant advisory group to the pope was the synod, which met at least once a year, usually during Lent.[4] Bishops from surrounding sees and others who were invited to these meetings examined serious matters of doctrine and discipline which the pope submitted for their deliberation. The Roman synod also acted as a tribunal, judging cases referred to the pope. This synodal structure of the Roman church corresponded to the pattern found at the time in the patriarchate of Constantinople.

Beginning with the Gregorian Reform in the eleventh century, the papacy became increasingly centralized. This came about both by limiting the powers of diocesan bishops and by developing administrative controls from Rome over them.[5] After the thirteenth century, consistories of the college of cardinals gradually replaced the meetings of the Roman presbyterate and synods. These consistories became the principal instrument of collegial advice for the bishop of Rome. At the same time, permanent offices were established to handle the growing business which accompanied a more active papacy. Stable administrative bodies with specific competencies developed to meet the expansion of papal responsibilities. Royal courts provided the model for this growing bureaucratic apparatus. Because the pope also governed the Papal States in central Italy, a sector of his curia handled temporal affairs. By the end of the Middle Ages, however, the administrative system was overburdened and needed a more efficient organization.

Sixtus V and the Modern Curia

The modern curial structure is rooted in the sixteenth-century Catholic Reform, when the popes took forceful measures to foster the implementation of the Council of Trent. Until then, the pope had delegated ordinary administrative affairs to commissions of cardinals, each of which handled whatever matters he assigned to them. In 1588, Sixtus V (1585-1590) restructured the papal administration in an orderly way. Sixtus' apostolic constitution *Immensae aeterni Dei* (1588) laid out the classic reason why the pope needs a curia: "[he] calls and rallies unto himself many collaborators . . . so that he, the holder of the key of all this power, may share the huge mass of business and responsibilities among them — that is, the cardinals — and the other authorities of the Roman curia, and by God's helping grace avoid breaking under the strain" (*Immensae aeterni Dei*, 1; cf. PB 3).

In his decree, Sixtus diminished the power of the consistories of the college of cardinals. Until then, they had met regularly with the pope to deliberate on crucial matters affecting the Church. This change effectively ended any notion that the cardinals co-ruled with the pope as a single corporate body. Instead, Sixtus designed the curia as an instrument to help the successor of Peter by providing him with advice and executing his commands. In place of regular consistories, he established fifteen permanent "congregations" or administrative committees of cardinals to advise him in specific areas of government: five to oversee the temporal administration of the Papal States, and ten to manage the religious affairs of the universal Church.[6] These agencies were also called "dicasteries," the term used for the law courts in ancient Athens. Every congregation had the same structure: each was headed by a prefect, who was joined by other cardinals for the principal meetings of the "congregations." Together they dealt with matters within the dicastery's particular competence, reporting through the prefect directly to the pope, who was at the peak of the administrative pyramid. It was his responsibility to assure a global vision in the approach to Church problems and to coordinate the curia's activity.[7] Because the congregations needed regular personnel to help them with their duties, the Vatican bureaucracy mushroomed.[8] At the same time, the curia's competence extended to more matters. It abandoned the earlier principle that it handled only major cases (*causae maiores*).

By the early twentieth century, the curia suffered from several serious problems. Because the competencies of the different congregations were no longer clearly distinguished, the curia was a bewildering tangle of administrative and judicial bodies. Temporal questions were not precisely demarcated from spiritual ones, and executive powers were inadequately differentiated from judicial ones. Furthermore, owing largely to the loss of the Papal States, the work of the congregations was inequitably distributed. Financial problems abounded as well. This administrative chaos provoked the reforms of Pius X (1903-1914), which he promulgated in *Sapienti consilio* (1908). Pius distinguished more explicitly the competencies of the congregations, tribunals, and offices. He also restricted curial business to purely ecclesiastical matters.[9] With few changes, the 1917 Code of Canon Law incorporated these reforms into Church legislation (cf. canons 242-264).

Reforms After Vatican II

At the Second Vatican Council, the call for curial reform was voiced once again. The Fathers expressed "the earnest desire" that the various departments of the Roman curia "should be reorganized and modernized." They were also to be "more in keeping with the different regions and rites, especially in regard to their number, their names, their competence, their procedures and methods of coordination" (CD 9). Furthermore, the bishops requested that the central agencies of the Church should have "a truly universal spirit." Their members, officials, and consultors were to be chosen, "as far as possible, on a more representative basis" (CD 10).

These recommendations were formulated against the background of the criticism raised by some bishops. Among their complaints were the following: the Italian chauvinism and careerism in the curia, the lack of pastoral experience often shown by Vatican officials, the need for frequent recourse to Rome for what was ordinarily needed to govern a diocese, and the curia's alleged independence from the pope and diocesan bishops. Other reasons for reform included the managerial difficulties presented by the open-ended appointments of major officials, the irregular meetings of the congregations, and the poorly delineated responsibilities of the various dicasteries. It was, however, primarily the doctrine of episcopal collegiality which provoked the desire for curial reform. The council brought to light the need to situate the curia in a fresh ecclesiological framework. Cardinal Bernard Alfrink of the Netherlands, for example, insisted that the future reform should guarantee that the curia was to be at the service of the episcopal college. It was not to place itself as a screen between the pope and the bishops.[10]

Motivated by his own long experience in the Roman curia and by the complaints voiced against it at Vatican II, Paul VI restructured the papacy's administrative apparatus. He forged it into an instrument to carry out the reforms of the Second Vatican Council. In 1967, he promulgated *Regimini ecclesiae universae* to streamline the papal bureaucracy according to the council's wishes. In this apostolic constitution, Pope Paul took into account the ecclesiology of Vatican II, especially episcopal collegiality and the nature of ecclesial authority as service.

So that the curia would reflect the teaching on collegiality, Paul VI included a provision that diocesan bishops should play a role in the Church's central government. He appointed many of them to the various "congregations" which met regularly in Rome. In this way the curia was to reflect better the nature of papal authority, which is simultaneously primatial and collegial.[11] The Pope stimulated a pronounced internationalization of the curia, allowed modern languages to be used in official letters and documents, limited the appointments of major officials to five years, ordered the tendering of resignations at seventy-five, and ruled that all principal offices lapse on the death of the pope. The constitution also restructured many dicasteries, added new ones to support post-conciliar pastoral initiatives, defined competencies more explicitly, and assigned the Secretariat of State and the Council for the Public Affairs of the Church the task of coordinating the various dicasteries. This major overhaul of the Holy See's administrative machinery earned for Paul VI the title "second founder of the curia."[12] The reform, however, was not without its shortcomings. It was criticized for concentrating on improving the curia's efficiency without sufficiently incorporating Vatican II's ecclesiology of communion.[13]

Within twenty years there was yet another reform. To mark the four-hundredth anniversary of Sixtus V's *Immensae aeterni Dei* in 1988, John Paul II published the apostolic constitution *Pastor bonus* on the Roman curia. In the Pope's words, its purpose was "to make sure that the structure and working methods of the Roman curia increasingly correspond to the ecclesiology spelled out by the Second Vatican Council" (PB 13). Consequently the Pope emphasized, even more than did Paul VI, the dignity of the episcopacy, the principle of collegiality, and the service dimension of ecclesial ministry. By entitling his apostolic constitution "The Good Shepherd," John Paul II wanted to stress the pastoral nature of the Petrine office, a ministry whose burden the curia helps him to carry. *Pastor bonus* filled out the meager two canons dedicated to the Roman curia in the 1983 Code of Canon Law (cf. CIC 360-361). First, it changed the nomenclature of many congregations and rearranged some of their competencies. Second, it gave juridical parity to the "new" conciliar and post-conciliar offices, including them as dicasteries. Third, the constitution recommended greater mutual collaboration among the dicasteries. Fourth, the Pope encouraged the curia to be more pastoral both in its purposes and in the spirit animating its work.

Participation in the Petrine Charism

The curia is a contingent historical structure without any claim to be of divine right. It is, nonetheless, "a venerable institution, so necessary to the government of the Church" (PB 14). John Paul II has called it "an indispensable instrument for the Pope in carrying out the enormous burden of this ministry."[14] A key notion in *Pastor bonus* is its description of the papal office as the "Petrine ministry." This idea furnishes the context for presenting the Roman curia as an extension of the pope's unique service. The curia has a distinctive ecclesial character "because it draws its existence and competence from the pastor of the universal Church. For the curia exists and operates only insofar as it has a relation to the Petrine ministry and is based on it" (PB 7). Acting on the pope's behalf, his administrative arm labors "to lend its help to the Petrine ministry" (PB 3).

The Roman curia participates in the pope's primatial service. As we have discussed in chapter ten, the Petrine ministry is always carried out by the head of the episcopal college "who is always united in communion with the other bishops and with the universal Church" (CIC 333.2). Just as the Petrine ministry serves both the universal Church and each particular church, "similarly, the Roman curia, as the servant of Peter's successor, looks only to help the whole Church and its bishops" (PB 7). The curia is at the service of the Church's primatial-episcopal structure. According to John Paul II, "the Curia by its very nature is linked to the Petrine ministry, and as such it is directed to the service both of the universal Church and of the local Churches, of the College of Bishops and of the episcopal conferences. Its purpose is, therefore, to strengthen the unity and communion of the People of God and to promote the Church's own mission in the world."[15] Because it assists the charism of Peter's successors, the curia is likewise bound to serve the episcopal college. The bishops are "the first and principal beneficiaries of the work of the dicasteries" (PB 9). Consequently, the papal curia is not "a barrier or screen blocking personal communications and dealings between bishops and the Roman pontiff, or restricting them with conditions, but, on the contrary, it is itself the facilitator for communion and the sharing of concerns" (PB 8).

Origins, Development, and Mission of the Papacy

Since the members of the episcopal college have a solicitude for the whole Church, the Roman dicasteries help them to meet this responsibility. For their part, the pastors of particular churches "must take steps to communicate with the Roman curia, so that, dealing thus with each other in all trust, they and the successor of Peter may come to be bound together ever so strongly" (PB 12). This bilateral communication, which expresses the mutual indwelling of the universal Church and the particular churches, promotes communion between the bishops and the pope. Due to this collegiality, mediated in part by the Roman curia, the Petrine ministry is present within every particular church.[16] For its part, the curia acts as the administrative arm of the pope who serves the pastors and faithful of local churches. It, too, is "strongly imbued with a certain note of collegiality" (PB 10). By promoting the spirit of collegiality between the bishops and the pope, the curia helps the Roman bishop to exercise his office in a collegial manner.[17]

Vicarious Authority

According to the Code of Canon Law, the terms "Apostolic See" and "Holy See" apply to the pope together with his curia. This is true "unless the nature of the matter or the context of the words makes the contrary evident" (CIC 361). Insofar as the Holy See is identified with the pope's primatial office, it has "the nature of a moral person by divine law itself" (CIC 113.1). However, a theological distinction must always be made between the Petrine ministry, which belongs personally to the pope, and the curia which acts for him. Accordingly, whenever the Holy See is said to be of "divine institution" or "divine law," these qualifications are attributed directly to the pope, and only indirectly to the Roman curia. Usually, however, the "Holy See" or the "Apostolic See" refers to the interventions within the competence of the Roman curia acting with delegated papal authority.[18]

Even though the pope is unable to delegate his charism to teach infallibly, he can invite others to share his primacy of jurisdiction. Whereas bishops enjoy their authority as "vicars of Christ" (LG 27), curia officials act as "vicars of the pope." The authority exercised by the Roman curia is always vicarious and is strictly subject to the pope. He imparts a share in his fullness of power to the dicasteries, "according to the competence and scope of each one" (PB 8). The vicarious powers enjoyed by the curial agencies are "ordinary"; that is, each department has its faculties defined within an area of competence where it can exercise its delegated authority.[19] According to Ladislas Örsy, "the curia has no more power than what the pope gives to it."[20] It does not function by its own right or on its own initiative. On the contrary, "it must display a faithful and harmonious interpretation of his [the pope's] will and manifest, as it were, an identity with that will, for the good of the churches and service to the bishops" (PB 8).

As head of the episcopal college, the pope remains the one who is ultimately responsible for the action of his curia.[21] Although its decisions are enacted in the pope's name and with his authority, they nonetheless remain acts of the dicastery which issues them. Only if the pope approves them *in forma specifica*, making them his own, do they cease to be curial acts. The principle is clear: "It is of the utmost importance that nothing grave or extraordinary be transacted unless the supreme pontiff be previously informed by the moderators of the dicasteries" (PB art. 18). In other words, no major curial decision is to surprise or embarrass the pope. Furthermore, the dicasteries are generally unable to issue or, except for the appropriate bodies, to interpret laws. Their authority extends only to administrative matters.

Organizational Structure

The well-known management theorist Peter Drucker once quipped that the Holy See is one of the three most efficiently run administrations in history, an honor shared with General Motors and the Prussian army.[22] Besides the cardinals and bishops who hold important positions, the pope calls priests, religious, and lay men and women from around the world to assist him. "By this coalition of many forces," wrote John Paul II, "all ranks within the Church come to join in the ministry of the supreme pontiff" (PB 9). With fewer than 2,500 employees, there is about one worker for every 400,000 Catholics. At present, non-Italians outnumber Italians in the curia by about two to one.

It is impossible here to describe in detail the structure and responsibilities of the various dicasteries and other offices. The following sections, however, give an idea of the universal responsibilities which the pope, through his curia, carries out for the Church. Every department, John Paul II has said, "corresponds to a definite field of the life and activity of the universal Church." Each one facilitates "the carrying out of Peter's ministry before the Church, sharing in a deep and competent way the magisterial and pastoral concern of each Successor of St. Peter."[23]

Secretariat of State

By law, all the dicasteries, whether congregations, councils, tribunals, or offices, are juridically equal. None has general authority over the others. Each one is directly responsible to the pope. Nevertheless, the Secretariat of State enjoys a "coordinating role" within the Roman curia. According to current norms, it is to foster relations with the various dicasteries and "coordinate their work, without prejudice to their autonomy" (PB art. 41.1). The English journalist Peter Hebblethwaite has remarked that this "coordinating" role is not much different from a "controlling" one.[24] Velasio De Paolis, a canonist at Gregorian University in Rome, has also noted the unofficial priority of the Papal Secretariat in the curial flowchart. "One cannot ignore, however, that frequently the Holy Father acts through the Secretariat of State," he wrote. "Often the different dicasteries are, in fact, in the position of having to render account to this dicastery. While not in theory, it does in practice assume and exercise an authority over the other dicasteries."[25] James Provost forthrightly refers to the Papal Secretariat as "the chief middle manager in the Curia."[26] At some point, all questions or decisions of major importance are funneled through it to the pope.

The Secretariat of State is not the oldest dicastery. Nor has it always been the weightiest. Its position as the curia's main executive and coordinating body is a modern development, consolidated by Paul VI's reforms.[27] From then on, the *Annuario Pontificio* has listed it first in the section on the Roman curia. As Cardinal Paul Poupard, head of the Pontifical Council for Culture, remarked, the Secretariat's task is to be the "eye, the heart and the arm of the pope."[28]

The Cardinal Secretary of State, as the chief curial official in rank and status, presides over the Secretariat. He is the pope's right-hand man, functioning as a kind of prime minister. Both internal Church affairs and the Holy See's relations with states and international organizations fall under his supervision.

Canonist Alfons Stickler describes the Secretariat as "the direct instrument of the Pope in all the activity of the government of the universal Church, particularly in relations with other departments which are competent in specified areas, with the bishops, the cardinals, and the various papal representatives throughout the world."[29] Providing "close assistance to the supreme pontiff in the exercise of his supreme function" (PB art. 39), the Secretariat of State is divided into two sections.

The First Section, or that for General Affairs, is under the immediate direction of a titular archbishop, who is called "the Substitute." After the Cardinal Secretary of State, he is generally regarded as holding the most significant curial post. Especially in matters affecting the Church's internal life, this Section's task is "in a special way to expedite the daily service of the supreme pontiff " (PB art. 41.1). It is "to draw up and dispatch apostolic constitutions, decretal letters, apostolic letters, epistles, and other documents entrusted to it by the supreme pontiff " (PB art. 42). The First Section also supervises pontifical representatives in nunciatures and delegations throughout the world, to the extent that their work concerns specifically ecclesial matters. To expedite its duties, the Section divides its work on a linguistic basis. At present, there are eight language departments or "desks": English, French, German, Italian, Latin, Polish, Portuguese, and Spanish.

Formerly called the Council for the Public Affairs of the Church, the Second Section, or that for Relations with States, is directed by a Secretary. A titular archbishop, he is commonly known as the Vatican's "foreign minister." The Second Section is "to foster relations, especially of the diplomatic kind, with state and other subjects of public international law, and to deal with matters of common interest, promoting the good of the Church and of civil society" (PB art. 46.1). Diplomatic relations, political matters, and contacts with international organizations are in its domain. In particular situations, which require delicate negotiations with civil authorities, it also oversees the nomination of bishops and the erection of dioceses.[30] Unlike the First Section, it draws most of its principal collaborators from the Holy See's professional diplomatic corps.

Congregations

Originally a Roman "congregation" was a gathering of cardinals and bishops who met together to discuss topics submitted to it by the pope. It is also the name given to the nine dicasteries located near the Vatican. These congregations express concretely the pope's primatial ministry to the universal Church, dealing with major areas for which he is now responsible. The congregations handle those matters which are reserved to the Apostolic See, those which exceed the competence of individual bishops and their conferences, and those which are entrusted to them by the pope. Questions are always to be dealt with according to law, "yet with pastoral means and judgments, attentive both to justice and the good of the Church and especially to the salvation of souls" (PB art. 15). The congregations also study major problems within their domain and promote some pastoral initiatives.

At the head of each congregation is a cardinal prefect. He is assisted by a secretary, who is a titular archbishop, and a professional staff. Matters of major importance are submitted to the full "congregation" (*plenarium*), which is usually held annually. At these meetings policy decisions are either made or approved. Louis Bouyer contends that these "congregations" illustrate the principle of collegiality; they "receive from the pope a share in his decision-making power on matters that touch more or less closely on the unity of the Catholic church, though their decisions are submitted to later confirmation."[31] Members of the full "congregation" include other curial cardinals as well as members of the episcopal college from around the world. All dicasteries, including the congregations, make use of consultors, many of whom are on the faculty at the Roman universities.

The nine congregations currently in place are the following. In parenthesis the date of original approval of the same or a similar congregation is given. The order is that given in the *Annuario Pontificio*.

• *DOCTRINE OF THE FAITH* (1542) Formerly called the "Holy Office" and regarded as the Supreme Congregation whose prefect was the pope himself, this dicastery is most intimately connected with the pope's teaching ministry. It is "to promote and safeguard the doctrine on faith and morals in the whole Catholic world; so it has competence in things that touch this matter in any way" (PB art. 48). In keeping with the Petrine ministry which it supports, the Congregation also "helps the bishops, individually or in groups, in carrying out their function as authentic teachers and doctors of the faith" (PB art. 50). One way it meets this responsibility is by publishing decrees and declarations on topical theological and pastoral problems. In recent years these have dealt with such questions as abortion (1974), sexual ethics (1975), the admission of women to the ministerial priesthood (1976), euthanasia (1980), infant baptism (1980), eschatology (1983), bio-ethics (1987), the pastoral care of homosexuals (1987), liberation theology (1987), the ecclesial vocation of the theologian (1990), the Church as a communion (1993), and the reception of Holy Communion by divorced persons (1994).

Current norms reaffirm the Congregation's pivotal role in the curia. All documents published by the other dicasteries, "insofar as they touch on the doctrine of faith or morals, are to be subjected to its prior judgment" (PB art. 54). The Doctrine of the Faith is the pope's instrument for carrying out his role as chief guardian of the faith. As a result, "it searches out writings and opinions that seem to be contrary or dangerous to true faith" (PB art. 51.2). If sufficient investigation shows it to be necessary, the Congregation reproves them. This dicastery also supervises the work of the Pontifical Biblical Commission and the International Theological Commission.[32]

• *ORIENTAL CHURCHES* (1862) This Congregation takes care of most matters for the twenty-one Eastern Catholic churches in communion with the pope. Questions which touch faith and morals or the canonization of saints, however, are excluded from its competency. Its jurisdiction extends to all non-Latin Catholics, wherever they may live.

Origins, Development, and Mission of the Papacy

- *DIVINE WORSHIP AND THE DISCIPLINE OF THE SACRAMENTS* (1908) The pope's concern for the "regulation and promotion of the sacred liturgy, primarily of the sacraments," falls within this Congregation's competence (PB art. 62). It watches over the valid and licit celebration of all the sacraments and sees to the drawing up and revision of liturgical texts. The dicastery also "grants the *recognitio* to translations of liturgical books and adaptations of them that have been lawfully prepared by conferences of bishops" (PB art 64.3).
- *CAUSES OF SAINTS* (1588) Since the Middle Ages, it has been the prerogative of the bishop of Rome to propose men and women to the faithful for imitation, veneration, and invocation by declaring them to be saints in the solemn act of canonization. This Congregation handles everything which leads to the canonization of a servant of God, submitting its recommendations to the pope. It also examines granting the title "doctor" to certain saints and has competence concerning the authentication and preservation of relics.
- *BISHOPS* (1588) This dicastery assists the pope in his ministry to the pastors and people of particular churches. Primarily it handles the erection and suppression of dioceses, as well as everything concerning the appointment of bishops, excluding those areas under the jurisdiction of Oriental Churches or Evangelization of Peoples. The Congregation also oversees "the correct exercise of the pastoral function of the bishops, by offering them every kind of assistance" (PB art. 79).
- *EVANGELIZATION OF PEOPLES* (1622) Formerly called *Propaganda Fide*, its name was changed because of the modern connotation of "propaganda" and the renewed awareness of the missionary nature of the whole Church. This Congregation has wide authority over the "young churches" found in former mission territories. It plays an important role in the ecclesial life of almost all of Africa, the Far East, and much of Oceania. In areas under its jurisdiction, Evangelization of Peoples sees to the education of secular clergy and catechists, supervises religious men and women working in missionary lands, erects dioceses, and provides for the appointment of bishops. In his encyclical *Redemptoris missio* (1990), John Paul II confirmed the need for this dicastery: "In order to re-launch the mission *ad gentes*, a center of outreach, direction and coordination is needed, namely, the Congregation for the Evangelization of Peoples" (*Redemptoris missio*, 75).
- *CLERGY* (1564) Without prejudice to episcopal authority, this Congregation expresses papal concern for "the life, conduct, rights, and obligations of clergy" (PB art. 95.1). In collaboration with the Doctrine of the Faith, it grants the Holy See's approval for catechisms and writings on catechetical instruction.
- *INSTITUTES OF CONSECRATED LIFE AND SOCIETIES OF APOSTOLIC LIFE* (1586) Institutes of consecrated life and apostolic societies "are subject to the supreme authority of this same [universal] Church in a special manner" (CIC 590.1). In return, the pope has a special responsibility for their members. The principal function of this dicastery is "to promote and supervise in the whole Latin church the practice of the evangelical counsels . . . [and] the work of societies of apostolic life" (PB art. 105). About

one million men and women are under its purview. The Congregation approves or suppresses religious institutes and societies, and is concerned especially with their constitutions, formation, dispensation from vows, and dismissal of members. It also establishes conferences of major superiors, approves their statutes, and oversees their activity.

• *CATHOLIC EDUCATION* (1588)   This Congregation gives practical expression to the pope's concern for the formation of seminarians and the promotion of Catholic education at all levels. It supervises seminaries and erects and approves ecclesiastical universities and institutions.

Tribunals

Unlike the congregations and councils, whose activities are in some way coordinated by the Secretariat of State, the three major tribunals of the Holy See are immediately subject to the pope. These tribunals are the major arm through which the pope oversees and administers justice in the Church. They help him to carry out his ministry as the Church's supreme judge.

• *APOSTOLIC PENITENTIARY*   While not a tribunal in the usual sense, the Apostolic Penitentiary deals with all matters touching the internal forum of conscience and the granting and use of indulgences.

• *SUPREME TRIBUNAL OF THE APOSTOLIC SIGNATURA*   This dicastery "functions as the supreme tribunal and also ensures that justice in the Church is correctly administered" (PB art. 121). It serves as a kind of supreme court in the external forum, although the pope, as the highest judge in all matters, still has the final say in any decision.

• *ROMAN ROTA*   This tribunal "is a court of higher instance at the Apostolic See, usually at the appellate stage, with the purpose of safeguarding rights within the Church; it fosters unity of jurisprudence, and, by virtue of its own decisions, provides assistance to lower tribunals" (PB art. 126). The Rota is the ordinary tribunal established by the pope to hear appeals which come to him (cf. CIC 1443). Most of its cases have to do with marriage annulments.

Pontifical Councils

Among the current councils, only the offices dealing with the interpretation of canonical legislative texts, social communications, and ecumenism were in place before Vatican II. In the last thirty years, many other departments have been added to the curia. The pontifical councils handle the additional tasks of the Petrine ministry which have emerged in light of Vatican II. As dicasteries of the Roman curia, their primary purpose is "supporting special pastoral activity and research in the Church which, at an ever accelerating pace, are filling pastors with concern and which with the same urgency demand timely and well thought out answers" (PB 13). Since 1988, these newer departments of the Roman curia have been called pontifical councils. Formerly, they were secretariats, a non-traditional designation, or commissions, which are less prominent than dicasteries. Pontifical councils are usually described as "promotional agencies" rather than as true organs of government.[33] Compared to the congregations, the councils generally have less to do with problems concerning the Church's hierarchical and institutional structure. In some form, each one expresses the pope's care for "the mission proper to the Church in the world" (PB art. 1). At the head of every council is a president. He is often, but not necessarily, a cardinal. Unlike the nine congregations whose directive committee is composed only of cardinals and bishops, provision is made for laity to serve on the chief advisory boards of the Council for the Laity, the Family, *Cor Unum*, and Culture.

At present there are the following eleven councils. The date of their original founding is given in parenthesis, and the order is that of the *Annuario Pontificio*.

• *LAITY* (1976)   The promotional nature of the pontifical councils is evident in the competence assigned to this dicastery: "to urge and support lay people to participate in the life and mission of the Church in their own way, as individuals or in associations" (PB art. 133.1). The Council also erects and approves the statutes of lay associations having an international character.

• *PROMOTING CHRISTIAN UNITY* (1960)   Established by John XXIII as a preparatory organ for the Second Vatican Council, the original Secretariat then served as a consultative office which assisted in the preparation of council documents touching ecumenical questions. This dicastery now oversees the pope's solicitude for the restoration of full visible unity among Christians, a responsibility to which recent popes have paid increasing attention. It supervises the implementation of Vatican II's decrees pertaining to ecumenism. The fostering and coordination of national and international Catholic organizations promoting Christian unity are also under its purview. As well, the Council represents the Holy See in officially organized ecumenical dialogues, such as those between Catholics and Anglicans (ARCIC) and Catholics and the Lutheran World Federation. Before issuing any statement on a matter related to faith or morals, it must have the approval of the Congregation for the Doctrine of the Faith. Through the Commission for Religious Relations with Jews, the Council studies, from a religious perspective, matters which concern the Jewish people.

• *FAMILY* (1973)   This dicastery promotes the pastoral care of families, protecting their rights and dignity both in the Church and in society. It provides the pope with an instrument through which he defends the family. The Council also "supports and coordinates initiatives to protect human life from the first moment of conception and to encourage responsible procreation" (PB art. 141.3).

• *JUSTICE AND PEACE* (1967)   Another office set up by Paul VI, this dicastery reflects the papal ministry's increasing interest in questions of social justice, development, human rights, and peace. Its purpose is "that justice and peace in this world may be strengthened in accordance with the gospel and the social teaching of the Church" (PB art. 142). The Council also collects information and research on human development and the violation of human rights. When necessary, the pope sends its president as his representative to world trouble spots.

• *"COR UNUM"* (1971)   This dicastery shows the pope's effective solidarity with the needy. It was established "in order that human fraternity may be fostered and that the charity of Christ may be made manifest" (PB art. 145). First, the Council stimulates the faithful to be generous. Second, it coordinates the initiatives of Catholic institutions that assist those in urgent need, facilitating their relations with other international organizations.

• *PASTORAL CARE OF MIGRANTS AND ITINERANT PEOPLES* (1970)   This dicastery brings to bear the successor of Peter's concern for refugees, exiles, migrants, nomads, and others without a stable home. It is also to ensure that the faithful become more aware of the particular needs of these people.

• *PASTORAL ASSISTANCE TO HEALTH CARE WORKERS* (1985)   Founded by John Paul II, the Council reflects his awareness of the special role which the sick and suffering play in the work of redemption. It is "to spread the Church's teaching on the spiritual and moral aspects of illness as well as the meaning of human suffering" (PB art. 153.1). The dicastery also supports health care workers in their ministry of mercy to the sick and the afflicted.

• *INTERPRETATION OF LEGISLATIVE TEXTS* (1917)   First set up by Benedict XV to interpret authoritatively the 1917 Code of Canon Law, this dicastery later assumed the responsibility for revising the Code. Since the publication of the revised Code in 1983, the Council publishes "authentic interpretations of universal laws of the Church which are confirmed by pontifical authority" (PB art. 155).

• *INTERRELIGIOUS DIALOGUE* (1964)   Born as a fruit of the Second Vatican Council, which gave a new impulse to the Church's relations with non-Christians, this dicastery expresses a dimension of the pope's duty to all religious believers. It "fosters and supervises relations with members and groups of religions that do not carry the Christian name as well as those who are in any way endowed with religious feeling" (PB art. 159). The Council encourages dialogue, study, and other means "to develop mutual information and esteem, so that human dignity and the spiritual and moral riches of people may be advanced" (PB art. 160). Given the importance of Islam, the Council has a special commission which promotes religious relations with Moslems.

• *CULTURE* (1965)   So that the pope's teaching will be effective in the contemporary world, it must confront and dialogue with the wide variety of human cultures. As the advocate for catholicity, the pope encourages the attempts to inculturate Christianity among all peoples. This dicastery fosters relations between the Holy See and the world of culture, "especially by promoting discussion with various contemporary institutions of learning and teaching, so that secular culture may be more and more open to the gospel" (PB art. 166). In 1993, it assumed the responsibility for dialogue with non-believers, a task that *Pastor bonus* had assigned to a separate council.

• *SOCIAL COMMUNICATIONS* (1959)   This promotional agency reveals the pope's concern that the media appropriately assist the Church in her task of evangelization. The primary function of the Council is "to arouse the Church and the Christian faithful, in a timely and suitable way, to action in the many forms of social communication, and to sustain them in it" (PB art. 170).

Administrative Offices and Other Institutes

In the Roman curia there are three administrative offices which have the rank of dicastery. In some way each of them deals with financial matters. The Apostolic Camera exercises its responsibilities for the temporal affairs of the Holy See almost exclusively when the Roman episcopate is vacant. The Administration of the Patrimony of the Apostolic See administers the temporal goods of the Holy See on behalf of the pope. The Prefecture for the Economic Affairs of the Holy See establishes the annual budget and supervises the financial activities of the dicasteries.

The Prefecture of the Papal Household and the Office for the Liturgical Celebrations of the Supreme Pontiff are both agencies of the Roman curia, but they are not dicasteries. The former institute is responsible for the pope's private and public audiences as well as his trips. The latter handles all the liturgies at which the pope presides.

Institutions Connected to the Holy See

Besides the dicasteries and agencies, there are other institutions, some ancient and some recently established, which are closely connected to the Apostolic See. Strictly speaking, they do not belong to the Roman curia, but they provide useful or necessary services to the pope, the dicasteries, and the whole Church. Among these institutions are the Vatican Secret Archives, the Vatican Library, the publishing house, *L'Osservatore Romano*, Vatican Radio, and the Pontifical Academies of Sciences, Life, and the Social Sciences.

Papal Representatives

The practice of Church leaders sending emissaries to other communities began in the apostolic age (cf. Acts 11:22) and continued in the early Church. Besides circulating letters, the principal churches of antiquity frequently exchanged envoys with one other. The sending of representatives from one Christian community to another was "an outgrowth of the concept of communion that bonded together the early churches."[34]

Already in the fourth century, the Roman bishop commissioned legates to represent him at particular and ecumenical councils. Pope Silvester (314-335), for example, authorized two priests to be his envoys at the Council of Nicaea in 325. He was the only bishop accorded this privilege, and his two representatives signed the council's acts immediately after the president of the assembly. Leo the Great (440-461) extended the practice of representation. He appointed Bishop Julian of Cos as his personal resident agent at the court of Byzantium.[35] This gave birth to a stable structure of papal representation in Constantinople. Expediting the pope's relations with the emperor and the patriarch, this system of permanent ambassadors remained in place until the end of the seventh century.[36] The regular presence of envoys at Constantinople and the sending of emissaries on special missions foreshadow the later development of permanent missions of the Holy See.[37]

Beginning in the Carolingian renaissance, the popes began to send legates to the courts of the king of the Franks and other princes. During the medieval struggle for the freedom of the Church, the practice of papal representation expanded significantly. Some legates had permanent responsibilities, while others performed *ad hoc* tasks for the pope. Whatever the mission they fulfilled, papal emissaries took precedence over secular ambassadors at every court in Christendom. From the thirteenth century onward, canonists developed rules for the status, privileges, and conduct of papal envoys. Secular authorities later adapted these norms for their own use.[38]

By the mid-fourteenth century, the popes were receiving permanent ambassadors, first at Avignon and then later at Rome. Initially, however, they did not reciprocate by sending papal representatives on permanent missions to temporal powers. In 1500, at Venice, the Holy See established its first embassy or "nunciature" with a resident papal representative. Subsequently, in order to supervise the implementation of the decrees of the Council of Trent, Gregory XIII (1572-1585) institutionalized the practice of sending permanent legates to the various nations. Because the success of Church reform was, in part, dependent on rulers who held considerable authority in religious matters, the pope sent nuncios to states as well as to the local churches.[39] At the Catholic courts of Europe, the Holy See established a full-fledged network of papal ambassadors, known as apostolic nuncios. These envoys were charged with a dual responsibility. They were to oversee the spiritual interests of the Church in the nation concerned, and they were to defend the temporal interests of the Papal States. Increasingly, the nuncios' concerns concentrated on ecclesiastical affairs. In the seventeenth century, the system of permanent nunciatures was firmly consolidated. Though with many adaptations, this arrangement remains in place today.[40]

Right of Legation

In assigning his representatives to various countries and receiving their ambassadors, the pope today makes use of an age-old prerogative.[41] Active legation is the pope's right to send his representatives to churches and states. Passive legation is his right to receive ambassadors from nations on either temporary or permanent missions. Even between 1870-1929, when the pope possessed the temporal power neither of the Papal States nor of Vatican City State, this right continued to be exercised and acknowledged.

For centuries the Catholic states of Europe accepted that the pope had the right to send representatives to other nations and international bodies. The Congress of Vienna (1815) formally recognized the status of papal legates. It also granted them certain prerogatives, including the right to be dean of the diplomatic corps if the host country agreed. In 1961, the Convention of Vienna confirmed the Holy See's right to legation in accordance with international regulations. This agreement also allowed the custom to stand, where countries so wished, of ranking the papal representative as dean of the diplomatic corps. Many countries of Europe and Latin America have retained the tradition of recognizing this privilege of the papal nuncio.[42]

From the canonical perspective, it is the pope's religious authority which gives him the right of legation to nations and churches. It is totally independent of the temporal sovereignty which he exercises over Vatican City State. According to the Code of Canon Law, "the Roman Pontiff possesses the innate and independent right to nominate, send, transfer and recall his own legates to particular churches in various nations or regions, to states and to public authorities" (CIC 362; cf. SOE 3.1). This papal right derives from the Petrine ministry itself (cf. SOE intro.).

When sending his legates to particular churches, the bishop of Rome requires the permission neither of the local bishops nor of the civil authorities. This practice belongs to the pope's fundamental right to communicate with every particular church (cf. DS 3062). As Provost comments, canon 362 "is a clear affirmation of the Church's independence from civil authorities insofar as its inner life and structures are concerned, an affirmation that reflects years of struggle to keep civil authorities from attempting to control the naming of legates to the church in their countries."[43]

When dispatching representatives to states, the bishop of Rome is exercising a right belonging to the Church as a "perfect" society. He enjoys this right independently of any degree of temporal power he might have at a given period of history. The Holy See sends envoys to nations because both Church and State, each in its own domain, "act for the benefit of a common subject — man" (SOE intro.). Because some of their interests are complementary, dialogue and mutual understanding are advantageous to both parties. However, unlike the pope's total freedom regarding the sending of legates to particular churches, canon law recognizes his limits regarding envoys to nations: "the norms of international law are to be observed concerning the sending and the recalling of legates appointed to states" (CIC 362).

Kinds of Representatives

Papal legates represent the pope to local churches and, if they have the rank of nuncio, to the state as well. All papal representatives are titular archbishops, and most are trained at the Pontifical Ecclesiastical Academy in Rome. A distinction is made between nuncios and apostolic delegates, depending on their duties to governments.

Nuncios are "messengers" of the pope to local churches and the state. From the sixteenth century onward, the term "nuncio" has been applied exclusively to a papal representative with a permanent mission. They are described as such to differentiate them from secular ambassadors. This emphasizes both the unique status of the Holy See in the international community and the religious and temporal responsibilities of the nuncio. A nuncio has the rank of ambassador and, where acceptable to the host country, is automatically dean of the diplomatic corps. Formerly, where governments chose not to accept this provision of the Congress of Vienna, the papal legate to a nation and local church was called a "pro-nuncio." He still held, however, the diplomatic rank of ambassador. Until recently, this was the status of the papal representative in most countries. In 1993, the title of pro-nuncio was abolished for all future appointments. From then on, every papal representative to a state has been given the title of nuncio.

Apostolic delegates are papal representatives with a permanent mission to the local churches of a nation or region but not to a civil government; hence, they do not enjoy the diplomatic rank of ambassador. These envoys are, however, to maintain contact with public authorities in the countries to which they are posted. This had been the situation in the United States from 1893, where the first modern apostolic delegation was created, until formal diplomatic relations were established with the Holy See in 1984.[44]

The Shepherd and the Rock

Responsibilities

In the 1917 Code of Canon Law the first duty of a nuncio was to promote relations between the Holy See and the government to which he was accredited (cf. canon 267.1). At the Second Vatican Council, the Fathers expressed their desire that "the functions of the legates of the Roman Pontiff should be more precisely determined" (CD 9). Consequently, during the pontificate of Paul VI, a more pronounced ecclesial and pastoral role was assigned to the papal representative. So that he would no longer be regarded as "a stranger to the local Church,"[45] a complaint frequently voiced by the bishops at Vatican II, his activity was to be less administrative.

In his apostolic letter *Sollicitudo omnium ecclesiarum* (1969) on the role of papal representatives, Paul VI linked their role to his ministry of caring for all the churches (cf. 2 Cor 11:28). As vicar of Christ, Paul wrote, the pope "should be adequately present in all parts of the world and be informed about the state and condition of each church" (SOE intro.). Pope Paul described the legates' function as "spreading from the center to the periphery and carrying, so to speak, to each and all of the local churches, to each and all of the pastors and the faithful, the presence and the testimony of that treasure of truth and grace of which Christ has made us [the pope] the partaker, the depository and the dispenser" (SOE intro.). Omitting any explicit reference to collegiality, the document was firmly grounded in the ecclesiology of the primacy defined at Vatican I. Church historian James Hennesey commented that Paul VI chose in this apostolic letter "to take his stand firmly in the 'paternal' rather than in the 'fraternal' tradition of the Church."[46]

Later, however, the Pope corrected this oversight. In a speech to papal representatives in Manila the following year, he presented their duties in light of an ecclesiology emphasizing collegiality: "You, the representatives of the Pope, must be for the local hierarchies a living sign of collegiality, sharing as far as you can their pastoral preoccupations. Coming from the heart of Christianity, you are the witnesses of the catholicity, that is, the universality of the Christian message. Sharing as you do in the special charism of Peter, you represent in a privileged way the demands of unity in the desired diversity of expressions of the same faith."[47]

Drawing heavily on the reforms of Paul VI, the 1983 Code of Canon Law also affirms the primacy of the representatives' responsibilities with respect to the local churches. Their principal duty "is to work so that day by day the bonds of unity which exist between the Apostolic See and the particular churches become stronger and more efficacious" (CIC 364; cf. SOE 4.1). Papal legates are not to override local episcopal authority. In keeping with the Petrine ministry of unity, envoys foster communion between the bishops of particular churches and the bishop of Rome. As a way of fulfilling this task, they are to inform the Holy See about the conditions of the local churches, help the bishops with their advice, and promote relations between the Vatican and the national episcopal conference.

Probably the representatives' most time-consuming and significant duty is "to transmit or propose the names of candidates to the Apostolic See in reference to the naming of bishops" (CIC 364, cf. 377.3). Papal legates first assumed this responsibility after the Council of Trent. The popes charged them to oversee the process by which rulers chose candidates for episcopal sees.[48] Today, representatives are to ensure discretion and impartiality in the selection of a country's bishops. Furthermore, they are to safeguard the pope's freedom in these nominations, even when there are arrangements which concede special privileges to the state.[49] In carrying out this mandate, the representatives are also to indicate their own preference when submitting the names of the three episcopal candidates to the Holy See. The papal legates' other duties likewise reflect commitments of the Petrine ministry: the promotion of peace and development, and the fostering of ecumenism and interreligious dialogue (cf. CIC 364).

If the representative is a nuncio, he also discharges a diplomatic function before the civil authorities of the country where he is accredited. He is to promote cordial relations between the Holy See and State authorities, preventing or resolving discord. The nuncio also deals with Church-State questions, especially those concerning the drafting and implementation of concordats and other similar agreements (cf. CIC 365). While the bishops of a country are not directly involved in these negotiations, the representative is to seek their advice and keep them informed of the state of affairs.

Proposals for Reforming the Papal Bureaucracy

Both the curia in Rome and the network of nuncios and delegates throughout the world have often been the subject of adverse criticism. Some of this goes beyond merely carping about the "complexity and intransigence of the Church's central administration"[50] and touches ecclesiological questions relevant to the papal office itself.

Roman Curia

Many criticisms, such as the small number of laity and women in the papal curia, especially in higher administrative posts, the slowness of its internationalization, and its supposed pastoral insensitivity, have little theological significance. These could be remedied with no noticeable effect on the Petrine ministry. *Pastor bonus* encourages internationalization and leaves the door open to increasing the number of laity in the Church's central government.

Other suggestions, however, are more theologically substantive. Church historian Giuseppe Alberigo considers the curia to be "the historical and political result of the progressive affirmation of a monarchical ideology at the head of the Church."[51] French theologian Joseph Lécuyer similarly points out that authentic curial reform means moving away from the model of a monarchical papacy, in which the curia is a kind of papal court, to one that embodies the Second Vatican Council's ecclesiology of communion.[52] He maintains that any serious reform can only be effected by a significant renewal in the papal ministry itself.

Jan Kerkhofs is a theologian who thinks that the expansion of the curia's responsibilities after Vatican II has hindered the development of episcopal collegiality by favoring undue centralization. Consequently, he suggests that some of its tasks, such as the appointment of bishops and the granting of many dispensations, should be entrusted to the various episcopal conferences. He proposes, moreover, that following the example of the United Nations, some dicasteries could be relocated outside Rome. The Pontifical Council for Interreligious Dialogue, for example, might be moved to Asia or Africa, where non-Christian religions present a more immediate pastoral challenge to the local churches. Lastly, Kerkhofs suggests that the curia, besides forwarding communications from Rome to the particular churches, should also encourage the participation of the periphery with the center in a spirit of genuine reciprocity.[53] In this way, he believes, Rome would become a pulsating hub of exchange and catholicity.

In the same vein, others believe that the curia still does not sufficiently value the Second Vatican Council's teaching on the particular church and the episcopacy. They maintain that the curia pays inadequate attention to the principles of subsidiarity and diversity, favoring uniformity over catholicity. These writers have suggested, for example, that the annual meetings of congregations could be held in places outside Rome.[54] Alberigo asserts that more attention should be paid to reducing the instances for which curial interventions are required. Just as there is a "hierarchy of truths" in theology, the same principle, he thinks, should be applied to matters under curial jurisdiction. After the example of the Church of the first millennium, the pope and his curia should handle only those matters which touch major issues. Other concerns are better resolved, Alberigo contends, by local bishops or episcopal conferences.[55]

Papal Representatives

In recent years, numerous complaints have surfaced about the appropriateness of the pope having representatives to states and particular churches. First, some writers find nunciatures and their trappings a throwback to an "institutional" model of the Church. Hebblethwaite refers to them as "a ghostly relic of the defunct Papal States."[56] In fact, as we have seen, the reforms of Paul VI and John Paul II have endeavored to situate the ministry of the papal representative within an ecclesiology of communion.

Second, other commentators believe that the representatives meddle in Church-State affairs where local bishops are better equipped to handle them. This interference, they maintain, contradicts Vatican II's theology of the local church and minimizes the principle of subsidiarity which should govern relations between bishops and the pope. The critics regard the papal nuncio or delegate as superimposing his own "superior" authority on the particular churches, thereby compromising episcopal authority as spelled out by the Second Vatican Council.

The reality is different. Papal representatives are admonished to avoid creating the impression that they are above the bishops. Instead, they are to reinforce and sustain the authority and mission of the local episcopate. Through his legates, the successor of Peter's responsibility is to preserve the bond of communion between the particular churches and the Roman see. The representative watches lest civil authorities in any way attempt to subordinate a local hierarchy to state interests or curtail its free communication with the pope. In many countries, the papal representative is an effective force against those favoring the establishment of national churches.

Origins, Development, and Mission of the Papacy

Though they betray dissatisfaction with the Roman "system," other writings raise less serious theological objections. Primarily, they express a certain resentment about the pope's "overwhelming" presence through his representative to the church of a nation. The 1989 Cologne Declaration, signed by 163 European theologians, is an example of this sentiment: "In today's world the role of the nuncios becomes more and more questionable. While the means for sending news and for conducting personal consultations have been improved, the nunciature increasingly falls under the odium of being an intelligence agency, which through its one-sided selection of information is often responsible for creating the very deviations it is supposed to be looking for."[57] Despite the severity of this judgment, the declaration raises no theological objection to the principle of papal representation.

No theologian argues that papal representatives are absolutely necessary to the exercise of papal primacy. Instead, they are a contingent means of support for the pope's ministry of building up the particular churches and bringing to the world the light of the gospel. These are the two primary criteria by which to judge whether the practice of representation is appropriate to the Petrine ministry.

◆

The history of the papacy and of the Roman curia demonstrates a constant reformation in the structures which are at the service of Peter's successors. Over the centuries, many changes have taken place in the organization of the papal curia. Each change, however, has been aimed at making the pope's pastoral office more vital to a given age. Consequently, the curia, both in Rome and in missions throughout the world, has been constantly subject to reorganization. In 1988, John Paul II renewed the curia's structure so that it would conform more closely to the ecclesiology of the Second Vatican Council. Like the Petrine ministry to which it is linked, the papal curia serves the episcopacy, both as a college and in its individual members.

As the administrative arm helping the pope in his ministry to the universal *koinonia*, the Roman curia reveals the Church's structure as primatial, episcopal, and collegial. It shares in the charism of stewardship for the universal Church which belongs to the Petrine office. The curia nurtures the reciprocal communion between the successor of Peter and the successors of the apostles, promoting and defending the Church's unity of faith and discipline. To do this effectively, the bishop of Rome invites the curia to "act in his name and by his authority for the good of the churches and in the service of the sacred pastors" (CD 9). The Roman curia, therefore, is radically dependent upon the Petrine ministry. It is a "kind of agent in the hands of the pontiff" (PB 7), which is both instrumental and ministerial.

By carrying out the multiple activities assigned to it by the pope, the papal administration gives concrete shape to his ministry of unity and service to the faith. In the words of John Paul II, the responsibilities of the Roman curia represent the "entire panorama to which the See of Peter directs its concern."[58] The different curial departments, the Pope has said, "deal with the single tasks of Peter's ministry in the Church." Each one participates in the bishop of Rome's magisterial and pastoral concern for strengthening the brethren (cf. Lk 22:32).[59] By the pope's will, the Roman curia shares in the unique ministry which the successor of Peter offers to the Church, guarding and nourishing the life of ecclesial communion.

Notes for Chapter fourteen

1. John Paul II, Discourse, July 11, 1979, *L'Osservatore Romano*, 29 (July 16, 1979), 1.
2. James H. Provost, "The Hierarchical Constitution of the Church," in *The Code of Canon Law: A Text and Commentary*, ed. James A. Coriden, Thomas J. Green, and Donald E. Heintschel (New York: Paulist Press, 1985), 292.
3. Giuseppe Alberigo, "Servire la comunione delle chiese," *Concilium*, 15:7 (1979), 41.
4. Alfons M. Stickler, "The Pope and the Roman Curia," in *The Vatican and Christian Rome*, ed. Gabriel-Marie Garonne (Vatican City: Polyglot Press, 1975), 6-9.
5. Velasio De Paolis, "La curia romana secondo la costituzione apostolica *Pastor bonus*," in *Collegialità e primato*, ed. Velasio De Paolis et al. (Bologna: Dehoniane, 1993), 130.
6. Alfons M. Stickler, "Le riforme della Curia nella storia della Chiesa," in *La Curia Romana nella Cost. Ap. "Pastor Bonus"*, ed. Piero Antonio Bonnet and Carlo Gullo (Vatican City: Polyglot Press, 1990), 7-9.
7. Alberigo, "Servire la comunione delle chiese," 46.
8. Provost, "Hierarchical Constitution of the Church," 293.
9. Stickler, "Le riforme della Curia," 12.
10. James Hennesey, "Curia, Roman," *New Catholic Encyclopedia*, vol. 16 (New York: McGraw-Hill Book Company, 1974), 111.
11. De Paolis, "La curia romana," 132.
12. Peter Hebblethwaite, "The Curia," in *Modern Catholicism: Vatican II and After*, ed. Adrian Hastings (New York: Oxford University Press, 1991), 177.
13. Giovanni Cereti and Luigi Sartori, "La curia al servizio di un papato rinnovato," *Concilium*, 11:8 (1975), 168; cf. Alberigo, "Servire la comunione delle chiese," 59-60.
14. John Paul II, Address to the College of Cardinals and Roman Curia, June 28, 1984, *L'Osservatore Romano, 29 (July 16, 1984),* 6.
15. John Paul II, Address to the College of Cardinals and Roman Curia, December 22, 1988, *L'Osservatore Romano*, 3 (January 16, 1989), 9.
16. Jean Beyer, "Le linee fondamentali della Costituzione Apostolica *Pastor Bonus*," in *La Curia Romana nella Cost. Ap. "Pastor Bonus"*, ed. Piero Antonio Bonnet and Carlo Gullo (Vatican City: Polyglot Press, 1990), 22.
17. Piero Antonio Bonnet, "La natura del potere nella Curia Romana," in *La Curia Romana nella Cost. Ap. "Pastor Bonus"*, ed. Piero Antonio Bonnet and Carlo Gullo (Vatican City: Polyglot Press, 1990), 90.
18. Francesco Salerno, "Sede Apostolica o Santa Sede e Curia Romana," in *La Curia Romana nella Cost. Ap. "Pastor Bonus"*, ed. Piero Antonio Bonnet and Carlo Gullo (Vatican City: Polyglot Press, 1990), 48-50.
19. Gianfranco Ghirlanda, *Il diritto nella Chiesa: mistero di comunione*, 2nd ed. (Turin: Edizioni San Paolo, 1993), 524.
20. Ladislas Örsy, *The Church: Learning and Teaching* (Wilmington: Michael Glazier, 1987), 52, n.7.

21. Joseph Lécuyer, "Posizione teologica della Curia romana," *Concilium*, 15:7 (1979), 36.
22. Peter Hebblethwaite, *In the Vatican* (Bethesda: Adler & Adler, 1986), 54.
23. John Paul II, Discourse, July 11, 1979, *L'Osservatore Romano*, 29 (July 16, 1979), 1.
24. Hebblethwaite, *In the Vatican*, 61.
25. De Paolis, "La curia romana," 148.
26. Provost, "Hierarchical Constitution of the Church," 295.
27. Peter Nichols, *The Pope's Divisions: The Roman Catholic Church Today* (London: Faber and Faber, 1981), 154.
28. Cited in Hebblethwaite, *In the Vatican*, 66.
29. Stickler, "The Pope and the Roman Curia," 17.
30. Bruno Bertagna, "La Segreteria di Stato," in *La Curia Romana nella Cost. Ap. "Pastor Bonus"*, ed. Piero Antonio Bonnet and Carlo Gullo (Vatican City: Polyglot Press, 1990), 168.
31. Louis Bouyer, *The Church of God*, trans. Charles Underhill Quinn (Chicago: Franciscan Herald Press, 1982), 448.
32. Walter H. Principe, "The International Theological Commission," in *Modern Catholicism: Vatican II and After*, ed. Adrian Hastings (New York: Oxford University Press, 1991), 194-199.
33. T. Mauro, "I consigli: finalità, organizzazione e natura," in *La Curia Romana nella Cost. Ap. "Pastor Bonus"*, ed. Piero Antonio Bonnet and Carlo Gullo (Vatican City: Polyglot Press, 1990), 434.
34. Provost, "Hierarchical Constitution of the Church," 301.
35. Pierre Blet, *Histoire de la Représentation Diplomatique du Saint Siège* (Vatican City: Vatican Secret Archives, 1982), 27-31.
36. Blet, *Histoire de la Représentation Diplomatique*, 508-509.
37. Hyginus Eugene Cardinale, *The Holy See and the International Order* (Gerrards Cross: Colin Smythe, 1976), 64.
38. Sally Marks, "Diplomacy," *The New Encyclopaedia Britannica*, 15th ed., vol. 17 (Chicago: University of Chicago Press, 1993), 332.
39. Pierre Blet, "The Nunciatures in History," *L'Osservatore Romano*, 32 (August 7, 1969), 8.
40. Blet, *Histoire de la Représentation Diplomatique*, 515-521; cf. Cardinale, *The Holy See and the International Order*, 63-70.
41. Robert A. Graham, "Diplomacy, Papal," *New Catholic Encyclopedia*, vol. 4 (New York: McGraw-Hill Book Company, 1967), 881-882.
42. Donato Squicciarini, "The Role of Papal Representatives," *L'Osservatore Romano*, 12 (March 23, 1994), 7.
43. Provost, "Hierarchical Constitution of the Church," 302.
44. Robert A. Destro, "Nuncio, Apostolic," *New Catholic Encyclopedia*, vol. 18 (Washington, D.C.: Catholic University of America Press, 1989), 326-328.
45. Paul VI, Address to Papal Representatives, Manila, November 28, 1970, *L'Osservatore Romano*, 50 (December 10, 1970), 2.
46. James Hennesey, "Papal Diplomacy and the Contemporary Church," in *The Once and Future Church: A Communion of Freedom*, ed. James A. Coriden (New York: Alba House, 1971), 195.
47. Paul VI, Address to Papal Representatives, Manila, November 28, 1970, *L'Osservatore Romano*, 50 (December 10, 1970), 2.
48. Blet, "Nunciatures in History," 9.

49. Paolo Bertoli, "The Role of Apostolic Nuncios," *L'Osservatore Romano*, 32 (August 10, 1981), 6.
50. Patrick Granfield, *The Papacy in Transition* (Garden City: Doubleday & Company, 1980), 180.
51. Giuseppe Alberigo, "Per un papato rinnovato al servizio della chiesa," *Concilium*, 11:8 (1975), 37.
52. Lécuyer, "Posizione teologica della Curia romana," 36-37.
53. Jan Kerkhofs, "Ciò che i cristiani delle chiese non occidentali si aspettano dal ministero di Pietro negli anni '80," *Concilium*, 11:8 (1975), 162-165.
54. Cereti and Sartori, "La curia al servizio di un papato rinnovato," 171-176.
55. Alberigo, "Servire la comunione delle chiese," 64-66.
56. Hebblethwaite, *Inside the Vatican*, 75.
57. "The Cologne Declaration," *Origins*, 18:38 (March 2, 1989), #1, p. 633.
58. John Paul II, Address to the College of Cardinals and Roman Curia, June 28, 1984, *L'Osservatore Romano*, 29 (July 16, 1984), 6.
59. John Paul II, Discourse, July 11, 1979, *L'Osservatore Romano*, 29 (July 16, 1979), 1.

Chapter fifteen
THE HOLY SEE AND PAPAL POLITICS

From the beginning of the fourth century, the bishop of Rome has been a major actor in world affairs. While the Petrine ministry essentially serves the unity of the Church's faith and communion, the successor of Peter is also a force to be reckoned with in political and social life. This chapter examines a secondary dimension of the papal office, one which makes no claim to belong by divine right to the ministry that Christ confided to Peter. Just as the Church's primary role is evangelization,[1] so, too, is the pope's principal task building up the people of God. This fundamental responsibility, however, leaves room for another. In fact, the question is not whether the pope should be involved with the world, a principle clearly affirmed at Vatican II, but the reasons why he engages in political activity as the head of a sovereign entity guaranteed by international law. To what extent is the pope's role in the world community, a function he carries out largely through the activities of the Holy See, tied to his ministry as Peter's successor?

Vatican City State and the Holy See

Although ordinary discourse uses the "Vatican" and the "Holy See" interchangeably, they are distinct realities. The former refers to a territorial reality, while the latter to an ecclesial reality. Strictly speaking, the Vatican is the State of Vatican City, a political-territorial entity in the middle of Rome recognized as a subject of international law. Its 108.7 acres include St. Peter's Basilica, the apostolic palace, where the popes have lived since their return from Avignon in 1377, some offices, museums, residences, and gardens.

The statehood of Vatican City has its origins in the seizure of the Papal States in the nineteenth century, territory which since the mid-eighth century had made up the pope's temporal domain. Because they split Italy in two and foreign powers intervened to defend them, the Papal States were an obstacle to Italian national union. With the departure of the French forces from Rome in 1870, the Kingdom of Italy annexed the remaining papal territory. Pius IX (1846-1878) and his successors refused to concede this loss of their temporal power, preferring to remain "prisoners of the Vatican" for nearly sixty years. In 1871, the Italian government unilaterally promulgated the Law of Guarantees, which assured the extraterritoriality of the Vatican, the pope's freedom of communication with the outside world, and the Holy See's right to diplomatic missions. The popes, however, rejected the law. They said that it inadequately resolved the problems posed by the seizure of their domains.[2] In their view, the law failed to guarantee the pope's complete autonomy and freedom of action. It left him dependent on the benevolence of a national government, an Italian subject who was conceded certain rights and privileges.[3]

After endless disputes, this standoff, often described as the "Roman Question," was finally settled when, in 1929, Italy and the Holy See signed the Lateran Pacts. These comprise three distinct agreements: a political treaty acknowledging the Holy See as a sovereign entity in international law and creating the new State of Vatican City; a concordat regulating relations between the Catholic Church and Italy; and a financial convention remunerating the Holy See for the confiscation of its territories and properties.

Totally independent from Italy, Vatican City State is now under the pope's sovereignty, a jurisdiction he assumes immediately upon accepting the papal office. Its form of government is monarchical. Here the pope exercises direct temporal power as he once did in the Papal States. Without elections or a legislature, Vatican City statutes assign to the pope the fullness of legislative, executive, and juridical power. In practice, however, the pope delegates the administration of the City to others.

The Holy See, or the Apostolic See, refers either to the bishop of Rome by himself or to the pope together with the Roman curia (cf. CIC 361). According to canon law, the Holy See has "the nature of a moral person by divine law itself" (CIC 113.1). Independent of all secular authority, the Holy See represents the Catholic Church, which is an autonomous society in her own right. Besides addressing the religious and moral implications of world events, the bishop of Rome also influences international affairs in his capacity as head of the Catholic Church. Because in these instances the pope usually avails himself of the curia's help, his interventions in the international sphere are normally referred to as those of the Holy See. The pope assumes a responsibility for world affairs as the spiritual head of the Catholic Church.

In one of his yearly "state of the world" addresses to the diplomatic corps accredited to the Holy See, John Paul II formulated this principle very clearly. He affirmed that he was speaking to them "not in the name of a State, but in the name of the Holy See, in the name of the Catholic Church and in the name of Christian conscience."[4] Because of the nature and aims of the Apostolic See's spiritual mission, its participation in international life is very different from that of states. When the pope addresses world leaders and organizations, he does so as a spiritual leader. Today he keeps his temporal sovereignty well in the background. For example, even though, during his travels, the pope is received with the honors due to a head of state, he minimizes this role as much as possible. He regards such visits as pastoral in nature, primarily directed toward strengthening the local churches.

In international law, the Holy See enjoys the prerogative of a sovereignty which is distinct from that of Vatican City State. Over the years, the Apostolic See has consistently defended its right to be a subject of international law. Even when the popes still held the Papal States, they maintained that the Holy See existed as a juridical entity independent of any territorial possessions. In 1815, the Congress of Vienna recognized this claim. Its participants accepted the Holy See into the post-Napoleonic international community because of the papacy's spiritual and historical role. After the loss of the Papal States, this principle of independent sovereignty was demonstrated in practice. Between 1870-1929, some countries continued to send ambassadors to the pope as head of the Catholic Church. In article 2 of the 1929 Lateran Treaty, Italy recognized "the sovereignty of the Holy See in the international field as an inherent attribute of its nature, in conformity with its tradition and the exigencies of its mission in the world." Subsequently, many other nations explicitly or implicitly accepted this resolution, establishing diplomatic relations with the Holy See.

The Apostolic See did not become a sovereign legal personality as a result of the Lateran Pacts. Indeed, this status preceded it. It was a partner in signing the treaty with Italy. Moreover, if the agreement were ever to be abrogated, the Holy See would survive it. Almost universally, the international community now acknowledges the particular sovereignty of the Apostolic See. This recognition is confirmed by three factors: the right of active and passive legation; the right to conclude formal international agreements; and the participation in international conferences on the same footing as sovereign states.

Primacy and the Vatican

Vatican City State was created to enable the successor of Peter to carry out his mission more effectively. According to papal diplomat Luigi Barbarito, "the Holy See exercises sovereignty over Vatican City, not for the advantage of the state itself, but for the higher interest of the Church. The State was created with temporal sovereignty primarily to assure the juridical independence of the spiritual activity of the Holy See."[5] As a prerequisite for resolving the Roman Question, Pius XI (1922-1939) insisted that some degree of territorial sovereignty was necessary. Only in this way, he believed, could the pope freely exercise his jurisdictional primacy.[6] Its size was irrelevant. Indeed, the popes of the twentieth century have expressed satisfaction that their State is negligible as a territory. The same day that the Lateran Pacts were signed, Pius XI commented that he was pleased to see his "territorial realm reduced to such minute proportions." It was all that was needed to serve "the immense, sublime and truly divine spiritual power which it is destined to support."[7] Vatican City State is, therefore, a means to a higher end. It is an instrument of another pre-existing juridical subject, the Holy See, from which it cannot be separated.

The principal reason which justifies the statehood of Vatican City is the guarantee it furnishes that the pope will be free to pastor the universal Church. Agostino Casaroli, long-time "foreign minister" under Paul VI and Secretary of State under John Paul II, noted the value of this "minimum of territory." It establishes a condition for exercising the primacy which is "more psychological than juridical . . . [giving] the world almost visual certainty of the sovereign independence of the Pope with regard to any other State."[8] Because of the Vatican, the pope is subject to no earthly authority on whose goodwill he must depend to exercise his ministry. Referring to the Vatican as "an imperceptible point on the globe," Pius XII (1939-1958) concluded that "in the spiritual order it is a symbol of great value and of universal extension, for it is the guarantee of the absolute independence of the Holy See in the accomplishment of its worldwide mission."[9] Paul VI observed that the pope possessed "only a tiny and practically symbolic temporal sovereignty: the minimum needed in order to be free to exercise his spiritual mission and to assure those who deal with him that he is independent of any sovereignty of this world."[10] When John Paul II addressed the United Nations General Assembly in 1979, he declared that the sovereignty of the State of Vatican City is "warranted by the need of the papacy to exercise its mission in full freedom." Furthermore, he said, it enables the pope "to deal with any interlocutor, whether a government or international organization, without dependence on other sovereignties."[11] The pope's temporal dominion over the Vatican is, therefore, an expression of the autonomous sovereignty appropriate to the papal ministry.[12]

While the State of Vatican City is not constitutive of papal primacy, it is a valuable instrument which facilitates the Holy See's participation in the world community. In harmony with the popes' views, Arnold Toynbee once pointed out the function of the Vatican State. He observed that "it is a potential base of operations for conducting a spiritual campaign aiming at the objective of world-wide permanent peace."[13] Despite some voices of opposition, there is no indication that the popes will surrender the sovereignty of Vatican City State in the foreseeable future. Paul VI, for example, emphasized the continuing importance of the temporal rights of the Holy See in his apostolic constitution *Romano pontifici eligendo* (1975). Upon entering into the conclave, the cardinal electors take an oath, promising that whoever is elected pope "will not cease to affirm, defend and if necessary vindicate integrally and strenuously the spiritual and temporal rights and the liberty of the Holy See" (RPE 49).

World Politics and the Pope

The status of "the Vatican" in the world community depends on the dignity and prestige of the Petrine office. The pope's moral authority in international life is also contingent on his stature as an individual, the persuasiveness of his cause, and the enthusiasm he can generate. As a ministry of universal outreach, the papacy has a solicitude which extends beyond the confines of the Church's internal life. The pastoral mission of the successor of Peter includes a passionate concern for the world. Since Pius XI, the popes have often explained why they participate in world affairs in a way which differs from that of leaders of the major religions. These explanations highlight the unique nature of the Holy See's position in international law.

In the last century, the bishops of Rome have increasingly expressed their sense of responsibility in this regard. Pope Paul VI referred to this duty of the successors of Peter as one "which flows directly from their mission" and as an "imperative inherent in their office."[14] In his first address to the ambassadors accredited to the Holy See, John Paul II remarked that the Holy See could not "fail to take an interest in the welfare and progress of peoples."[15] Because the primatial office includes love for all dimensions of the person, the pope must be concerned about matters affecting an individual's temporal welfare.[16] Just as no burden of the human family is extraneous to the Church's interest, so is the Apostolic See "in ever closer contact with every expression of human life."[17]

The community of nations accepts the pope as a privileged spiritual spokesman. Most nations approve and, indeed, expect the pope to speak out on international problems. They recognize that in the world there is "hardly any other meaningful source that can claim uncorrupted moral leadership."[18] Even leaders accustomed to the harsh realities of political life acknowledge that the pope's presence among the powerful is on a different plane from their own. Regardless of their personal religious beliefs, world authorities almost invariably confess that meeting with the pope to discuss critical questions of international life comforts them, providing a welcome source of moral and human inspiration.[19]

The juridical status of the Apostolic See furnishes the pope with a platform from which he can intervene persuasively at the international level. Through its various activities, he can foster the Church's mission in its fullness. On the one hand, he provides moral support for the worthy initiatives of government leaders. On the other hand, the Holy See's direct participation in global affairs affords it the opportunity to be an effective spokesman for the Church's positions. The bishop of Rome has a voice with leaders responsible for the political, social, and economic life of peoples. His involvement in the political sphere, however, remains unique. It is always subordinate to the Church's primary and transcendent goal of leading men and women to the kingdom of God.

Instruments of Papal Politics

The pope's influence in the international arena surpasses, of course, what is channeled through the official organs of the Holy See. Entrusted with preaching the gospel, the successor of Peter would continue to teach the Church's social doctrine even if the Holy See were to lose its sovereign status. The religious, moral, and social teachings of the bishop of Rome are, in fact, the primary arm of his diplomatic initiatives.[20] They shape and guide all Vatican socio-political policy.

Diplomatic activity furnishes the pope with the opportunity to have peer relations with world leaders, most of whom are not Catholic. He can address other heads of state face-to-face. If the pope were deprived of the "shield" of the Holy See, it would be difficult for many heads of state, due to pressures in their own countries, to have direct contact with him. On rare occasions, the pope personally writes heads of state on matters of great importance. John Paul II did this in September 1980, before the Madrid Conference, when he addressed the right to religious freedom.[21] He wrote them again in March 1994, communicating his concerns about the International Conference on Population and Development to be held at Cairo.[22] At other times, the pope appeals directly to particular world leaders. On the eve of the Persian Gulf conflict, John Paul II wrote to Presidents Saddam Hussein and George Bush in a last-minute attempt to effect reconciliation.[23] Since he is himself the head of a sovereign entity which they recognize, the pope is at least assured of a courteous hearing.

Among the more routine instruments through which the bishop of Rome now fulfills his responsibilities to the world of diplomacy are his annual messages for the World Day of Peace. As a way of appealing to world leaders on matters pertaining to peace, Pope Paul VI began this practice in 1968. Among the themes treated in recent messages are the need for dialogue (1983), international solidarity (1987), religious freedom (1988), respect for minorities (1989), the environment (1990), the family (1994), and women (1995). The pope also uses his annual New Year address to the diplomatic corps accredited to the Holy See as a forum through which he makes known his views on the

The Shepherd and the Rock

world situation. These discourses survey the bright spots and shadows on the international horizon. Frequently they draw attention to conflicts, abuses of human dignity, and the denial of human rights. In addition, when a new ambassador presents his letters of credence or a head of state visits the Vatican, there are other opportunities for dialogue. On these occasions, the pope expresses his convictions about the particular opportunities and difficulties of a specific country. He also assures its leaders of the Church's willingness to cooperate in all forms of authentic human development. In the presentation of their main arguments, all these speeches and messages draw heavily on the tradition of natural law rather than on the sources of revelation.

Diplomatic Relations

Besides voicing the Church's social doctrine in the international forum, the Apostolic See also establishes diplomatic relations with states. This, too, is a concrete expression of the pope's universal ministry. Official relations enable him to further the welfare of each nation as well as "the common good of humanity."[24] They are a means, wrote Paul VI, "to establish, foster and strengthen relations of reciprocal understanding, mutual coordination" (SOE intro.). Furthermore, diplomatic relations allow the Holy See to help in the promotion of peace among nations and the progress of individual states. When it establishes official relations with a country, the Holy See does so "in the name of the Church,"[25] thereby expressing her universal mission.[26] Diplomatic relations are always with the Holy See, not with Vatican City State. In the past, when some countries, such as the Soviet Union, showed interest in establishing relations with the Vatican as a state, the Holy See staunchly refused such requests. Papal diplomacy, therefore, is independent of the pope's role as the temporal head of Vatican City.[27]

Paul VI believed that diplomatic relations between nations and the Holy See symbolize the Church's awareness of "her spiritual and religious vocation."[28] Their establishment gives the pope an occasion to foster the freedom of religion in the nation concerned and to help assure the legal status of the local churches. In concluding bilateral relations, the Apostolic See also aims to promote the social advancement of the various nations to which the Church is bound.[29] Furthermore, because diplomatic representation is a touchstone of sovereignty, the Holy See continues the practice as a way of reaffirming its autonomy as a subject of international law.

For his part, John Paul II has added a "cultural" reason explaining why the Apostolic See exchanges ambassadors with states. When the Holy See establishes diplomatic relations with a country, this implies that the sovereignty of a people and their culture is more fundamental than that of the state. Essential to that culture is its religious dimension. The Holy See enters into diplomatic relations, said John Paul II, "above all to express its deep esteem for each nation and each people, for its tradition, its culture, its progress in every field." Moreover, it welcomes ambassadors not only as spokesmen for their own governments "but also and above all as representatives of people and nations which, through these political structures, manifest their sovereignty."[30] Official relations of the Holy See, especially with a country where Catholics are the majority, have an "international" and "inter-cultural" character rather than just an "inter-state" one. In addition to the bond of ecclesial communion with the local churches, the pope also establishes an official bond with the whole nation and its culture and not merely with its government.[31] It is appropriate, therefore, that the Catholic Church, through the Holy See, have a relationship with every people and culture.[32]

Commentators are sometimes shocked by the Holy See's willingness to establish official relations with countries whose governments are hostile to religion and to the Catholic Church. Why does the pope do this? Pope John Paul II has proposed an answer. Diplomatic relations between the Holy See and a particular country, he stated, "do not necessarily manifest, on my side, approval of such and such a regime — that is not my business. Obviously, neither do they manifest approval of all its acts in the conduct of public affairs. But they show an appreciation of positive temporal values; a desire for dialogue with those who are legitimately charged with the common good of society."[33] Addressing those who criticize the pope for meeting with certain world leaders, John Paul II has said that "the duty of a Pope is to receive these persons, if this can be of service to a progress in justice and in peace." Moreover, he is "to exhort them, without any compromise whatever, to renounce the means of violence and terrorism."[34]

For their part, countries do not seek diplomatic relations with the Holy See for political or economic support. It can offer neither. More likely, they recognize something specific which only the Apostolic See can provide them. Paul VI articulated some reasons why states seek to exchange envoys. Nations recognize, he believed, the authority which history has accorded the Holy See. They look to it for "an orientation, a moral inspiration, that everyone feels, confusedly sometimes, should animate and guide the life of the Nations and their mutual relationship."[35] The Holy See responds to this need. It both proclaims principles and also takes part in the life of the international community as a member with full rights. However, in keeping with its nature as a spiritual sovereignty, the Holy See never takes the initiative in establishing official relations. It responds to requests from states that come to the Vatican.

With very few exceptions, diplomatic relations are reciprocal. When they are concluded, the Holy See sends a representative to the nation, and the nation, in turn, sends an ambassador to the Holy See. Both parties frequently double up their assignments. Some papal legates, like those to the Caribbean or the Pacific Islands, represent the pope before five nations or more. The same is true for representatives to the Apostolic See. However, in order to emphasize the Holy See's independence from Italy, the one doubling up unacceptable to the Vatican is that with Italy; that is, a nation's ambassador to Italy cannot also be accredited to the Holy See and vice versa.

Since 1950, when only twenty-five countries had missions to the Holy See, the total number of accredited ambassadors has increased sixfold. In 1994, the Holy See had full diplomatic relations with 154 nations, including Angola, Cuba, Egypt, Haiti, India, Israel, Mexico, Nauru, and the United States.[36] From 1848 until 1867, American representatives were accredited to the pope as temporal ruler of the Papal States. Even after the resolution of the Roman Question, however, they were not sent to the Holy See. With the advent of the Second World War in Europe, President Roosevelt appointed Myron Taylor as his personal representative to Pius XII. Finally, in 1984, full diplomatic relations were established between the United States and the Holy See.[37] Besides some Islamic countries, the only major power which does not have any diplomatic relations with the Vatican is China.

This remarkable growth in the number of missions doubtlessly reflects the emergence of many new sovereign countries. It also testifies to the recognized value of the spiritual and moral authority of the Holy See in the international community.[38] The practice of reciprocal diplomatic relations between the Holy See and States is, therefore, an institution which is now more vital than ever.

Concordats

On occasion, the Apostolic See signs a specific type of treaty with a nation state called a "concordat." When Emperor Henry V (†1125) and Pope Callistus II (1119-1124) resolved the investiture controversy by signing the Concordat of Worms in 1122, the first of these agreements was concluded. The Holy See enters into concordats in order to secure the effective presence and freedom of the Church in the country concerned. In endorsing these legal agreements, the pope strengthens the faith of a country's local churches (cf. Lk 22:32).

Since the Second Vatican Council, concordats have recognized the principle that "the political community and the Church are autonomous and independent of each other in their own fields" (GS 76). Consequently, when revisions are being drafted or when new concordats are being drawn up, the Holy See no longer asks that Catholicism be acknowledged as the official religion of the state, as was the case with Italy until 1984. Today concordats typically deal with mixed matters, that is, questions in which both Church and State have a shared interest. These include regulations regarding marriage and its effects, the education of youth, the erection and boundaries of dioceses, the appointment of bishops, the establishment of religious orders, and economic and property matters affecting the Church.[39]

The Fathers at Vatican II affirmed the Church's right to complete control over episcopal appointments. The bishops expressed their hope "that for the future no right or privileges be conceded to the civil authorities in regard to the election, nomination, or presentation to bishoprics" (CD 20). The Code of Canon Law subsequently incorporated their request into its legislation (cf. CIC 377.5). As mandated by the council, the Apostolic See has been able to negotiate successfully for the removal of restrictions on the pope's freedom to name bishops. About a dozen countries, however, still enjoy the right to consultation (*droit de regard*) and can advise Rome about their objections to a candidate. They cannot, however, veto an appointment. At no other time in the Church's history has the bishop of Rome been so free in choosing the members of the episcopal college.[40]

According to the provisions and practices of international law, concordats are negotiated with any well-disposed state. When the Holy See concludes such an agreement, it does so with the sovereignty belonging to it as the representative of the whole

Origins, Development, and Mission of the Papacy

Church. In this case it does not represent the local churches of a nation. This raises the theological question as to whether an ecumenical council headed by the pope, as the holder of supreme authority, might also conclude such an agreement.[41]

Some concordats, such as those signed with Mussolini in 1929, with Hitler in 1933, and with Franco in 1953, have been used to win credibility for unpopular regimes. The Holy See is aware of this. Reflecting on the concordat with Germany in 1933, Pius XII summed up, when the Second World War was over, what he regarded as its benefits. "Although the Church had few illusions about National Socialism," he said, "it must be recognized that the Concordat in the years that followed [1933] brought some advantages, or at least prevented worse evils. In fact, in spite of all the violations to which it was subjected, it gave German Catholics a juridical basis for their defence, a stronghold behind which to shield themselves in their opposition to the ever-growing campaign of religious persecution."[42] With the exception of Ireland, the traditionally Catholic nations in Europe and Latin America regulate many Church affairs by means of concordats with the Holy See. The United States and Canada, however, have no such arrangement.

International Organizations

Especially since the end of World War II, the Holy See has frequently declared its esteem for international organizations which work toward greater solidarity, justice, and peace among peoples and nations. Recent popes have recognized in them a kind of secular counterpart to the Church's unity in catholicity. Paul VI expressed this thought to U Thant, Secretary General of the United Nations. "The universality proper to the Catholic Church," he proposed, "seems in a way to be reflected from the spiritual sphere into the temporal sphere of the United Nations."[43] John Paul II made a similar observation. He affirmed that the Holy See's support for the United Nations "emphasizes the convergence of the aims pursued, each in the sphere proper to it, by your organization with its worldwide nature on the one hand, and by the religious community with a worldwide vocation which is the Catholic Church on the other. The latter is well aware of the specific nature of its possible contribution, which is essentially that of appealing to the conscience of humanity."[44]

As a subject of international law, the Holy See participates in more than a dozen international governmental organizations concerned with moral, social, humanitarian, and cultural affairs. These include full membership in the Conference on Security and Cooperation in Europe (CSCE), and permanent observer status at the United Nations, the Organization of American States, the Council of Europe, FAO, UNESCO, and others. The Holy See is also permanently represented at a host of international non-governmental organizations. Representatives to these bodies express the pope's desire to influence the international community and to share responsibility for its welfare.

The presence of the Catholic Church in international organizations also confirms the Holy See's specific sovereignty. Even more significantly, however, its participation manifests what John Paul II refers to as "the organic and constitutive link which exists between religion in general and Christianity in particular, on the one hand, and culture, on the other hand."[45] Since the Church has been, and is, an essential element of culture, she is fittingly represented in organizations such as UNESCO. Through his delegates, the pope takes part in the discussions of these bodies, regarding them as necessary to "the dialogue of the Church with the cultures of our times."[46]

Because its interest and competence is in the ethical and juridical realm, the Holy See holds itself aloof from exclusively political or military issues. It also observes great discretion with regard to technical problems. A typical Vatican intervention was that of its delegation at the United Nations International Population Conference in 1984. The delegation expressed to the assembly that the reason for the Holy See's participation was "to direct attention in a prophetic manner to the ethical or moral dimensions of what is at stake in population questions."[47] The same was true ten years later at the Cairo Conference. In a 1994 message to a United Nations official, John Paul II reiterated this position: "In accordance with its specific competence and mission, the Holy See is concerned that proper attention should be given to the ethical principles determining actions taken in response to the demographic, sociological and public policy analyses of the data on population trends."[48] Promoting a spirit of openness with all those wishing to go beyond the merely pragmatic or superficial, the Holy See fosters mutual dialogue. Whenever relevant ethical issues are ignored in the international forums, its role is to challenge such omissions, insisting on the moral and spiritual dimensions of the matters discussed by international organizations.

Neutrality and Dialogue

A constant concern of the Holy See's diplomatic activity is the scrupulous attention it pays to its neutrality. By article 24 of the Lateran Treaty, it unilaterally imposed this policy upon itself: "The Holy See, in relation to the sovereignty it possesses also in the international sphere, declares that it wishes to remain and will remain extraneous to all temporal disputes between States and to international congresses held for such objects, unless the contending parties make concordant appeal to its mission of peace; at the same time reserving the right to exercise its moral and spiritual power." Even before the Lateran Pacts, the Holy See had affirmed its neutrality. During the First World War, for example, Benedict XV (1914-1922) refused to call the warring nations by name. He spoke only of facts, never of countries or individual leaders.[49]

American statesman Eugene Rostow commented that the force of the Holy See's diplomacy comes "from its attitude of benevolent neutrality which is an important aspect in the Vatican's diplomatic position and effectiveness."[50] When he was Secretary of State, Cardinal Agostino Casaroli described the singular contribution which the Apostolic See makes to international life because of its impartiality. "Not having any political, territorial or military interests of its own to defend," Casaroli said, "it is in a position to see with greater objectivity the reality and implications of the problems that arise on the international scene."[51] In order to do this effectively, the Holy See remains completely independent of political blocs, maintaining a balanced judgment with regard to all parties. At meetings of international organizations, nearly every intervention of the Holy See repeats this principle of autonomy "which must — in every circumstance and in all international bodies — remain absolute in regard to all the world's States and governmental regimes."[52] The reason for this independence is, says John Paul II, "to serve the common good, the cause of the poor and the oppressed." Accordingly, the Apostolic See is "prepared to listen to all human, religious and political expressions, to open its door to all" who have some responsibility for peoples' welfare.[53] In order to pursue his goals, the pope uses a nonpartisan approach which leaves him free to deal with world leaders from all blocs.

On occasion, it can happen that the interests of the pope and those of a particular country or group of countries coincide. Such was the case when both the West and the Holy See worked for the defeat of atheistic communism. Nonetheless, after the Soviet domination of eastern Europe was consolidated, Pius XII was particularly careful to chart his own course. He refrained from identifying the diplomacy of the Holy See with the West's cause which, he believed, failed to embody Christian ideals sufficiently.[54] Throughout the Cold War between the superpowers, the foundation and goal of the Holy See's international activity remained consistent with its own specific vision.

To be sure, no position of papal diplomacy is more frequently misunderstood than that of the Holy See's neutrality in wartime. By equidistancing himself from both parties in conflict, it appears as if the pope is unwilling to take a moral stand. Nevertheless, this stance, though politically impartial, is far from ethically neutral. He consciously embraces it in order not to aggravate hostilities, to leave the bishops of each country free to take their own stand, and to show the Holy See's willingness to play a conciliatory role in resolving the strife. This neutrality was put to the test during the Second World War and, later, during the Cold War.

The perceived failure of Pope Pius XII to speak out more explicitly against Nazism and anti-Semitism during World War II has occasioned impassioned debate. Jesuit historian Robert Graham has summed up the reasons for the Holy See's neutrality. "In both world wars," he wrote, "publicists and even officials in some countries called on the pope to throw the weight of his religious authority behind their cause — for instance, by expressly condemning certain enemy atrocities and even by declaring their war a just one and excommunicating enemy leadership. In the circumstances an express moral judgment would have served only propagandistic political ends and compromised the Holy See's true religious influence for peace."[55] Through his actions and statements, the Pope, unable to prevent war, tried to stop it from spreading. He was scrupulous in avoiding any gesture which might have worsened the situation or compromised the safety of people in the war-ravaged areas.[56] With regard to Poland, for example, Pius XII once confided the reason for his discreet silence to Montini, the future Paul VI. "We ought to speak words of fire against such things," he avowed, "and the only thing that dissuades us from doing so is the knowledge that if we should speak, we would be making the condition of these unfortunate ones more difficult."[57] During the War, Pius XII was thoroughly consistent, never pronouncing a formal condemnation either against Nazism or communism. He adhered rigidly to the principle of neutrality, nourishing the hope, unrealistic as it turned out, that the Holy See could serve as a mediator between the factions.[58]

Today, the Holy See enjoys considerable prestige in the international community.

This standing owes much to Paul VI, who resolutely advocated its independence vis-à-vis the superpowers, emphasizing its role as the servant of all peoples. His policy was particularly effective in gaining the respect of the newly independent nations which emerged with the collapse of colonialism. Under John Paul II, however, a slight shift in emphasis can be discerned. His public statements are more direct and emphatic than those of his predecessors. During the Gulf War, for instance, John Paul II spoke out repeatedly against Operation Desert Storm. His pleas for dialogue instead of the hurried deadlines for war, however, went unheeded. As an almost solitary voice of opposition to the invasion of Kuwait, he lamented that "the beginning of this war marks a grave defeat for international order and the international community."[59] In an interview in 1993, the Pope asserted that the second phase of the war "was not so much one of defence but of a punitive nature." It thereby failed to meet the traditional criteria for a just war.[60] Throughout the hostilities, John Paul regarded his statements neither as partisan nor as ideological but as appropriate for a servant of peace.

The Holy See usually makes its specific contribution to peace by serving as a "bridge for dialogue." Consequently, as Casaroli commented, this "certainly makes it necessary that the methods and the tone used in assuming a position in the disputes should be such as not to make it impossible to attain the essential aim of the Holy See's pacifying action of concord."[61] Dialogue, founded on truth and respect for the other party, is the privileged instrument that the Apostolic See proposes to the international community. It maintains contacts and holds meetings with world leaders in order to foster mutual understanding among peoples. In his *Message for the 1983 World Day of Peace*, Pope John Paul II pointed out that by its diplomatic relationships the Holy See "seeks to cause dialogue to be adopted as the most suitable means of overcoming differences" (*Message*, 11). Due to its impartiality, the papal delegation at international conferences can be "a faithful interpreter of the concerns and aspirations common to all participants."[62] Within the world community, the Holy See is positioned to act as a leaven for dialogue, promoting trust and peaceful, negotiated settlements to disputes.

Objectives of Papal Diplomacy

By engaging in diplomatic activity, the successor of Peter furthers various aspects of the Church's mission in the world. While nowhere is there a concisely formulated master plan, for the past fifty years the Holy See has invariably pursued the following six objectives in its diplomatic initiatives: the protection of the Church's freedom and religious liberty, the fostering of an ethical vision, the defense of human dignity, the pursuit of peace, the promotion of development and humanitarian initiatives, and the mediation of disputes. Each of these expresses a facet of the papal ministry bearing upon the pope's service to the human family, a function transcending the Church's visible frontiers.

Protection of Church Freedom and Religious Liberty

Traditionally, the pope's primary objective in international affairs has been to defend the Church's liberty, enabling her to accomplish her mission in peace. Papal diplomacy stresses the freedom to practice one's faith, the liberty to nominate bishops without interference, the right to Catholic education, and the defense of marriage and the family. The foremost reason why the Apostolic See maintains contacts with world leaders is, therefore, to secure the religious freedom of all believers, including non-Catholics and non-Christians.[63] The purpose of the Holy See's diplomatic initiatives is, above all, peoples' spiritual welfare.

The Apostolic See assists national episcopates in assuring that Catholics and other believers are free to practice their religion and participate fully in all spheres of their country's life. In recent pontificates, no single theme has been so frequently addressed in the Holy See's interventions at international meetings and in the pope's own teaching. "The right to freedom of religion," John Paul II said to the diplomatic corps, "is so closely linked to the other fundamental rights that it can rightly be argued that respect for religious freedom is, as it were, a touchstone for the observance of the other fundamental rights."[64] Again and again, the Pope has repeated that "religious freedom, an essential requirement of the dignity of every human person, is a cornerstone of the structure of human rights, and for this reason an irreplaceable factor in the good of individuals and of the whole of society, as well as of the personal fulfillment of each individual."[65] Consequently, papal diplomacy adamantly promotes religious liberty and draws the world's attention to its violations. In order to defend this primordial right, the Holy See has undertaken many initiatives. Foremost among its recent contributions is that of successfully inserting the principle of religious freedom in the Final Act of the Helsinki Conference (1975): "respect for human rights and basic freedoms, including freedom of thought, conscience, religion or conviction."[66]

Fostering an Ethical Vision

Because the Holy See situates itself above political, economic, or strategic interests, it serves as a point of reference for all countries, assuming the role of "the conscience of the community of nations."[67] While aware of its limitations, the Holy See feels obliged, Casaroli observed, "to represent in some way all the forces that aim at emphasizing moral values in the conduct of international affairs."[68] In a message to a United Nations session on disarmament, John Paul II wrote that he intended his words to be "the echo of the moral conscience of humanity."[69] With no narrowly political interests to defend, the presence of the Holy See can inspire the level of discussion in world forums to go beyond the merely pragmatic. It "stands in the midst of the nations as a clear moral voice," remarked Archbishop John Quinn of San Francisco, "raising in the international dialogue the vital dimensions of conscience so necessary if there is to be genuine human progress."[70]

The Holy See is combatting the contemporary attempts to resolve global questions without recourse to the objective moral law. It repeatedly stresses that the moral imperatives which are universally valid are essential to the establishment of a more just international order. In their interventions in world affairs, the popes constantly draw on the principles of the natural law as the necessary foundation for authentic human progress.

While they usually refrain from mentioning this law explicitly, they leave no room for doubt about its importance as the basis of all social life.[71] The Vatican's diplomatic activity also reminds the world that Catholics everywhere have a rightful place in the public square and encourages the laity to take part in all fields of human promotion.

What does the Church have to offer the world? In the well-known phrase of Paul VI, she is an "expert in humanity."[72] John Paul II asserted in a speech to diplomats that "the Catholic Church, present in every nation of the earth, and the Holy See, a member of the international community, in no way wish to impose judgments or precepts, but merely to give the witness of their concept of man and history, which they know comes from a divine Revelation. Society cannot afford to forego this original contribution without becoming the poorer for it."[73] In virtue of the Petrine ministry, the pope is the chief guardian of values which contribute to the moral elevation of humanity. Papal diplomacy is, therefore, aimed at fostering those principles which further the international common good. To accomplish this goal, the Apostolic See seeks to enlighten consciences with the truth which comes from God through creation and revelation. Because the Holy See occupies a legitimate place in the international community, the successor of Peter can inspire action in the decision-making centers of governments and international organizations. In them, the pope's voice resounds as a moral force with worldwide extension.[74]

Defense of Human Dignity

In recent years, a particular emphasis of papal diplomacy which has come to the fore is its promotion of human dignity. Attention to human rights began more than a century ago, but it received an enormous boost under John XXIII and Paul VI. As the Holy See's prestige and international status have been consolidated, it has increasingly asserted its role as an advocate of the genuine humanitarian interests for all people.[75]

When the Apostolic See dialogues with leaders or occupies itself with world affairs, such activity is motivated by the Church's mission to be "the sign and the safeguard of the transcendental dimension of the human person" (GS 76). John Paul II reaffirmed this position in his encyclical *Centesimus annus* (1991). The Pope wrote that the Church's "contribution to the political order is precisely her vision of the dignity of the person revealed in all its fullness in the mystery of the Incarnate Word" (*Centesimus annus*, 47). Consequently, the Holy See's diplomatic initiatives attribute an essential importance to defending the dignity and inherent rights of every person. On the one hand, the pope's representatives make a "specific contribution in international assemblies which discuss the safeguarding of human rights and peace." On the other hand, there is also "the action, necessarily more discreet but no less solicitous of the Apostolic See and its representatives in contacts with political authorities of the whole world."[76]

In particular, the Holy See articulates for the international community the moral foundation for the edifice of human rights which originates in the order of creation. It always does so with a certain discretion, aware that in this forum the pope exercises his teaching office less directly than when he addresses the universal Church. Regardless of the international organization concerned, the statements of the Holy See's observers or delegates invariably raise questions about the promotion of human dignity. Delegations habitually cite the Universal Declaration of Human Rights, reaffirming the rights of the person enshrined in this and in other international documents. Through these interventions, the Holy See acts as a kind of "memory," reminding the international community of the obligations it has assumed for guaranteeing basic rights and freedoms.

The Apostolic See also points out failures in this regard. Speaking at the United Nations in 1993, Archbishop Jean-Louis Tauran, Secretary for Relations with States, made a typical intervention: "It is nonetheless painful for the Holy See (and I think, for a great many political leaders) to have to observe that in many places today believers are still subject to serious discrimination. For example, in some countries of Islamic tradition, Christians are not allowed to have a place of worship, nor are they permitted to celebrate in their homes. In other cases, the Pope and the Holy See are prevented from maintaining the normal contact with the Bishops and their faithful that are implicit in the Catholic Church's structure, although these are allowed by the relevant international documents."[77] Both directly and through his spokesmen, the pope has taken upon himself the responsibility of confronting the conscience of the international community. He appeals to it to respect all human rights and to reprimand their violation. Has this policy been successful? According to John Paul II, this persistent commitment to human rights made a "decisive contribution" to the collapse of communism in Europe.[78] Most political commentators would agree with him.

Pursuit of Peace

Among the principal international concerns of all popes, especially since Benedict XV, has been the pursuit of peace. Through its diplomatic activity and its participation in world organizations, the Holy See has been a tenacious advocate of the peaceful settlement of disputes. To counter the skepticism of those who seem resigned to the inevitability of war, the popes have loudly proclaimed that peace is possible. More recently, the Holy See has added the questions of nuclear and non-nuclear disarmament to its agenda of concerns, looking toward a general and controlled disarmament as the final goal toward which nations should be working.[79]

By offering herself as a servant of reconciliation to a world in conflict, the Church makes her own contribution to the pursuit of peace. In his apostolic exhortation *Reconciliatio et paenitentia* (1984), John Paul II explained the work carried out by the Holy See to meet its responsibilities: "The Holy See already endeavors to intervene with the leaders of nations and the heads of the various international bodies, or seeks to associate itself with them, conduct a dialogue with them and encourage them to dialogue with one another, for the sake of reconciliation in the midst of so many conflicts. It does this not for ulterior motives or hidden interests — since it has none — but 'out of a humanitarian concern,' placing its institutional structure and moral authority, which are altogether unique, at the service of concord and peace" (*Reconciliatio et paenitentia*, 25).

The popes, however, have not been content merely to endorse and bless others' work for peace. As the Vietnam War was winding down, Paul VI commented that it was his duty to become an active promoter of peace and pacification, especially where the action of others was lacking or insufficient. Indeed, he remarked that no one had "more responsibility for this before God" than the pope.[80] As a result, the Holy See has sometimes undertaken specific initiatives. In 1971, it adhered to the Treaty on Non-Proliferation of Nuclear Arms. The pope took this step to lend his moral and spiritual authority to building peace. He believed that the treaty was a significant "step forward towards the desired creation of a system of general and complete disarmament under effective international control."[81] For this reason, too, at the request of other nations, the Holy See agreed to take part as a full member in the Conference on Security and Cooperation in Europe.[82]

The moral principles articulated in encyclicals, World Day of Peace messages, and other papal interventions furnish the doctrinal basis for the Holy See's approach to peace. Besides this well-defined teaching, modern popes have also thrown the prestige and moral authority of the Petrine office behind the mobilization of public opinion as a way to avert war and contain conflict.[83] During World War I, Benedict XV made frequent, but unsuccessful, appeals to the belligerents. So, too, did Pius XII during World War II. When addressing the diplomatic corps in 1977, Pope Paul VI summed up the Holy See's mission concerning peace: "As an unflagging defender of peace, we knock at all doors and plead for reasonable agreements affording the possibility of fresh progress."[84]

Promotion of Development and Humanitarian Initiatives

The diplomacy and international activity of the Holy See are also characterized by concern for human development and humanitarian efforts. As John Paul II said, the Church is called to be a good Samaritan "to those who are left abandoned along the path of history."[85] Former American ambassador to the Holy See, Thomas Melady, has commented that during his meetings with Vatican officials the underlining question to him was always the same: "What could we do to be helpful to relieve human suffering?"[86] The diplomatic initiatives of the Apostolic See seek "to make a contribution to strengthening and perfecting the unity of the human family."[87] It participates in international diplomacy to support all efforts which advance the cause of international peace, justice, and development.[88]

Modern popes have treated the Church's responsibilities to human promotion frequently and at length. John XXIII's *Mater et magistra* (1961) and Paul VI's *Populorum progressio* (1967) were the first major papal documents on this theme. Along with the teaching of the Second Vatican Council, these papal documents placed questions of development at the forefront of the Holy See's attention. Repeatedly the popes draw attention to the moral dimension of all authentic development.[89] Furthermore, the Holy See participates in many conferences fostering human development. For his part, the pope praises in his discourses to civil authorities and spiritual leaders the contribution of the vast network of social institutions sponsored by the Church. Of particular concern in the past thirty years is the Holy See's emphasis on the widening gap between the world's developed North and developing South.[90] During the height of the Cold War, John Paul

Origins, Development, and Mission of the Papacy

II referred to this "more fundamental tension ... of the growing contrast between the countries that have had an opportunity to accelerate their development and increase their wealth, and the countries locked in a condition of underdevelopment."[91]

It is also true that the Apostolic See quietly contributes to humanitarian relief programs, especially through the Pontifical Council *Cor Unum*, the curial body which coordinates such activity. It also oversees the disbursal of funds such as those of the John Paul II Foundation for the Sahel.[92] Moreover, in many of the younger churches, papal representatives funnel assistance which the pope makes available for programs of human promotion. These endeavors notwithstanding, the Holy See's major contribution to world development remains that of a spiritual power which encourages international cooperation at all levels.

Mediation of Disputes

In the Middle Ages, the pope assumed the right to settle conflicts between nations. The most famous case resulted in the Treaty of Tordesillas (1494) which temporarily resolved the dispute between Spain and Portugal about the boundaries of their territories in the New World. Pope Alexander VI (1492-1503) drew a line of demarcation, allotting to Spain what was on one side and to Portugal what was on the other. With the rise of nation states in the sixteenth century, however, this mediating role declined. Even so, between 1870-1914 the Holy See was involved in thirteen cases of mediation. The most successful was the resolution in 1885 of the controversy between Germany and Spain over the Caroline Islands.

The Holy See has invariably expressed its willingness to mediate disputes, a policy dependent on its neutrality. Paul VI's message to a United Nations special session on disarmament outlined the classic position: "If you ever think that the Holy See can help overcome the obstacles blocking the way to peace, it will not shelter behind the argument of its 'non-temporal' character nor shy away from the responsibilities that could be involved in interventions that have been desired and asked for."[93] Expressing the same view, Casaroli stated that the Apostolic See is always ready "to offer adversaries the possibility of a discreet, reserved and disinterested intermediary for the beginning of a dialogue which would otherwise be extremely difficult, if not impossible."[94] Moreover, the Holy See's distance from power politics, its moral prestige, and its tradition of civility and fair-mindedness position it very favorably to foster dialogue among parties in conflict.

As a neutral entity, the Holy See is willing to mediate disputes. This is what Pius XII attempted to do during World War II, John XXIII during the Cuban Missile Crisis, and Paul VI during the war in Vietnam. Chile and Argentina called upon John Paul II to arbitrate their conflict over the Beagle Channel. Pleased to have the "opportunity to offer its service,"[95] the Holy See accepted the appeal of the two nations, agreeing to mediate by advocating solutions acceptable to both parties. This prepared the way for the signing of the Treaty of Peace and Friendship in 1984. Unfortunately, petitions for papal mediation have declined in recent years.

Evaluation of Papal Diplomacy

Despite admiration for the pope's stands on particular issues, some writers think that engaging in diplomacy is contrary to the Church's nature. Involvement in diplomatic activity, they believe, runs the risk of assimilating the Church to temporal institutions from which she should be independent. Since the Church's mission is essentially religious, diplomatic activity is held to be either unnecessary or, at worst, harmful. In a 1951 talk to aspiring papal diplomats, the future Paul VI summarized this objection fairly. Critics believe, he said, that the Church should not base her welfare "on links attaching her to powers which have become secular, alien and sometimes even hostile to her." They advocate, Montini continued, that "the Church of our day must expect her strength and prosperity to depend, not on the favour of established powers, but on the word and the power which, by divine institution, she bears in her bosom."[96] Today the same objection is still advanced. As a religious leader, the pope, it is proposed, should discontinue all diplomatic initiatives, limiting himself to the exhortatory preaching of moral principles.

In light of the teaching of the Second Vatican Council, and the separation of Church and State characteristic of modern democracies, other critics contend that the Holy See should cease to conclude concordats. In fact, just the opposite has occurred. Between 1960 and 1994, more than fifty concordats were negotiated. Of the 221 concordats ever signed between the Holy See and a State, 95 are still in effect.[97] In the international arena, the Holy See still favors concordats as a way of providing a legally recognized guarantee of freedom for the Church in certain countries. Because concordats are international treaties between sovereign powers, they survive changes of government. Often they facilitate the Church's mission in situations of political unrest or persecution.

Others complain that the exercise of the traditional diplomacy favored by the Vatican dulls the pope's prophetic ministry. By dialoguing with those in power, they argue, the Holy See is sometimes forced to collaborate with oppressive governments. Allying itself with the *status quo*, it thereby compromises the local churches' efforts to provide a voice for freedom. Before the collapse of the Berlin Wall in 1989, some Catholics in eastern Europe and elsewhere bitterly opposed the Holy See's policy toward Marxist governments (*Ostpolitik*). Through patient negotiation, this strategy tried to gain some concessions for the Church from the regimes in power. When dealing with governments, the Holy See attempted to secure the nomination of bishops to vacant sees as a way of returning to normalcy the Church in these countries. Casaroli, the architect of *Ostpolitik* under Paul VI, has referred to it as a policy of "pastoral prudence." From unfriendly states, it sought partial and imperfect concessions. In his view, the Holy See's limited efforts in no way compromised its long-range objective of restoring full freedom to the Church in the countries concerned.[98]

In a rare allusion to the problems posed by his *Ostpolitik*, Paul VI expressed his opinion on the Holy See's particular method of diplomatic activity. To the college of cardinals, he stated: "If, in some cases, the results of the dialogue seem scanty, insufficient or slow in coming, and if others may see in that a sufficient reason for interrupting it, we consider it, on the contrary, our important duty to proceed with enlightened constancy along a way that seems to us, in the first place, exquisitely evangelical: the way of forbearance, understanding, and charity. We proceed, of course, not without hiding the bitterness and concern we feel at the continuation, or aggravation, of many situations contrary to the rights of the Church or of the human person."[99]

From an ecumenical perspective, Reform theologian Lukas Vischer has pointed out that the special status of the Holy See in international law "obviously presents a difficulty for fellowship and cooperation between churches."[100] Not only do non-Catholic churches have nothing similar, their ecclesiology leads them to conclude that the notion of spiritual sovereignty distorts the nature of the Church. Protestant ecclesiology, he says, regards "the fact that the Holy See is a legal personality of international law as welcome proof of the inextricable confusion of the spiritual and the human in the Roman Catholic Church."[101] Even so, Vischer concedes that the Holy See is a valuable pastoral instrument capable of bearing effective witness to the gospel values of justice and peace.

Other criticisms of papal diplomacy are more superficial. Often they point to the weaknesses inherent in any bureaucracy: favoritism, inefficiency, and careerism. To these are sometimes added negative judgments about the overly Italian and clerical composition of the Holy See's diplomatic corps.

In terms of what is demanded by the divine institution of the Petrine ministry, the pope's involvement in world affairs through diplomatic initiatives could be abolished. For the Church, however, real advantages derive from the pope's involvement in world diplomacy. First, in international forums the Holy See frequently takes firm stands on questions of human dignity and human rights. The prophetic edge of Church teaching, especially in her social doctrine, has not been dulled because of papal diplomacy. If anything, it has been given a wider hearing. Second, the backing given by the Holy See to a national episcopacy often strengthens the bishops to stand together in situations of severe trial provoked by an antagonistic government. A nation which has an ambassador to the Holy See must take the universal Church into account before harassing bishops or faithful within its boundaries. This has often helped to preserve the freedom of local churches which would otherwise have been absorbed or ruthlessly persecuted. Third, the Holy See is a force for keeping alive in the international community religious and ethical principles which serve both society and the Church. The pope, then, makes use of diplomacy, not because it is essential to the Petrine ministry, but because experience has taught the Church that "it is a valuable instrument for the promotion of her mission in the world."[102]

✦

Among all the great world religions, only the Catholic Church, through the Holy See, is recognized as a subject in international law. The existence of the Petrine ministry enables the Church to act forcefully in the international arena. Because of the recognized legal status of the Apostolic See, the pope has a means at his disposal by which he can make the Church's voice heard in international life, and an instrument through which he can protect the rights of the faithful.

The Church's interest in social and political matters goes beyond the commitment of her members in different national communities. She is also involved at the global level. The Apostolic See complements the political and social activity of charismatic individuals, associations, and local churches. It maintains diplomatic relations with over 150 countries and sends representatives to many international organizations. The Holy

See's network of nunciatures, delegations, and observers to international organizations furnishes the pope with an apparatus through which he can exert a moral influence on the world community. Leaders recognize the pope as a great moral authority, even in questions of international life. The community of nations knows that it can rely on the Holy See to defend and promote the great causes of humanity.

Through the participation of the Holy See in world affairs, the Church is a "travelling companion of the nations of the world."[103] While the Petrine ministry is most intimately concerned with the internal life of the Church, it also has a mission to the world. Because of the various initiatives of the Apostolic See, the pope can express the Church's concerns for the hopes and problems of humanity, especially in the fields of education and culture, health care and humanitarian assistance, justice and integral development, human rights and peace. Using the means which tradition and history have placed in his hands, the successor of Peter offers humanity valuable assistance in its struggle against the abuses of human dignity, the horrors of war, the misfortunes of poverty, and the scourge of underdevelopment. The solicitude of Peter's ministry extends beyond the visible frontiers of the Church, embracing all that pertains to the welfare of the human family.

Notes for Chapter fifteen

1. See, for example, John Paul II, *Christifideles laici* (1988), #33; and *Redemptoris missio* (1990), #2-3.
2. Hyginus Eugene Cardinale, *The Holy See and the International Order* (Gerrards Cross: Colin Smythe, 1976), 100.
3. Anthony Rhodes, *The Vatican in the Age of the Dictators: 1922-1945* (New York: Holt, Rinehart and Winston, 1973), 45.
4. John Paul II, Address to the Diplomatic Corps, January 14, 1984, *L'Osservatore Romano*, 5 (January 30, 1984), 7.
5. Luigi Barbarito, "Vatican City, State of," *New Catholic Encyclopedia*, vol. 14 (New York: McGraw-Hill Book Company, 1967), 559.
6. Agostino Casaroli, "The Holy See and the International Community," *L'Osservatore Romano*, 7 (February 13, 1975), 6.
7. Pius XI, Discourse to Priests and Lenten Preachers of Rome, February 11, 1929, *Acta Apostolicae Sedis*, 21 (1929), 108; translation in Cardinale, *The Holy See and the International Order*, 106.
8. Casaroli, "The Holy See and the International Community," 6.
9. Pius XII, *Discorsi e Radiomessaggi di Sua Santità Pio XII*, vol. 11 (Vatican City: Polyglot Press, 1953), 347; translation in Cardinale, *The Holy See and the International Order*, 102.
10. Paul VI, Address to the United Nations General Assembly, October 4, 1965, *The Pope Speaks*, 11:1 (1966), 49.
11. John Paul II, Address to the United Nations General Assembly, October 2, 1979, *L'Osservatore Romano*, 42 (October 15, 1979), 1.
12. Francesco Salerno, "Sede Apostolica o Santa Sede e Curia Romana," in *La Curia Romana nella Cost. Ap. "Pastor Bonus"*, ed. Piero Antonio Bonnet and Carlo Gullo (Vatican City: Polyglot Press, 1990), 71.
13. Arnold Toynbee, "The Holy See and the Work of Peace," *L'Osservatore Romano*, 12 (June 20, 1968), 6.

14. Paul VI, Address to the Diplomatic Corps, January 12, 1970, *L'Osservatore Romano*, 4 (January 22, 1970), 2.
15. John Paul II, Address to the Diplomatic Corps, October 20, 1978, *L'Osservatore Romano*, 44 (November 2, 1978), 3.
16. Paul VI, Address to the College of Cardinals and Roman Curia, December 22, 1975, *L'Osservatore Romano*, 2 (January 8, 1976), 3.
17. John Paul II, Address to the College of Cardinals and Roman Curia, December 22, 1981, *L'Osservatore Romano*, 3 (January 18, 1982), 8.
18. William O. Peterfi, "The Meaning of Papal Diplomacy," *L'Osservatore Romano*, 17 (April 27, 1972), 8.
19. Casaroli, "The Holy See and the International Community," 9.
20. Andrea Riccardi, "L'Internazionale vaticana: scopi, strumenti, limiti," *Rivista Italiana di Geopolitica*, 3 (1993), 36.
21. John Paul II, Letter to the Heads of State on Freedom of Conscience and of Religion, *L'Osservatore Romano*, 3 (January 19, 1981), 12-14.
22. John Paul II, Letter to the Heads of State on the International Conference on Population and Development, *L'Osservatore Romano*, 16 (April 20, 1994), 1.
23. John Paul II, Letters to Presidents Saddam Hussein and George Bush, *L'Osservatore Romano*, 3 (January 21, 1991), 1.
24. Paul VI, Address to the Diplomatic Corps, January 11, 1969, *L'Osservatore Romano*, 4 (January 23, 1969), 1.
25. John Paul II, Address to the Diplomatic Corps, January 15, 1983, *L'Osservatore Romano*, 8 (February 21, 1983), 7.
26. John Paul II, Address to the Diplomatic Corps, January 12, 1981, *L'Osservatore Romano*, 4 (January 26, 1981), 3.
27. Pio Laghi, "The True Nature of Papal Diplomacy," *Origins*, 13:47 (May 3, 1984), 771.
28. Paul VI, Address to the College of Cardinals, June 22, 1973, *L'Osservatore Romano*, 27 (July 5, 1973), 8.
29. John Paul II, Address to the College of Cardinals and Roman Curia, December 22, 1981, *L'Osservatore Romano*, 3 (January 18, 1982), 10.
30. John Paul II, Address to the Diplomatic Corps, January 12, 1979, *L'Osservatore Romano*, 4 (January 22, 1979), 6.
31. John Paul II, Address to the Polish Episcopal Conference, Warsaw, June 14, 1987, *L'Osservatore Romano*, 32 (August 10, 1987), 7.
32. John Paul II, Address to UNESCO, Paris, June 2, 1980, *L'Osservatore Romano*, 25 (June 23, 1980), 10-11.
33. John Paul II, Address to the Diplomatic Corps, October 20, 1978, *L'Osservatore Romano*, 44 (November 2, 1978), 3.
34. John Paul II, Address to the Diplomatic Corps, January 15, 1983, *L'Osservatore Romano*, 8 (February 21, 1983), 8.
35. Paul VI, Address to the College of Cardinals, June 22, 1973, *L'Osservatore Romano*, 27 (July 5, 1973), 8.
36. See official *Liste du Corps Diplomatique près le Saint-Siège* (Vatican City: Polyglot Press, 1994).
37. Robert A. Graham, "Relation between United States of America and the Holy See," *L'Osservatore Romano*, 26 (June 25, 1970), 5.

38. John Paul II, Address to the Diplomatic Corps, January 14, 1984, *L'Osservatore Romano*, 5 (January 30, 1984), 6.
39. Patrick Granfield, *The Limits of the Papacy* (New York: Crossroad Publishing Company, 1987), 75.
40. Riccardi, "L'Internazionale vaticana," 41-42.
41. Carlos Corral Salvador, "Concordato," *Nuovo Dizionario di Diritto Canonico*, ed. Carlos Corral Salvador, Velasio De Paolis, and Gianfranco Ghirlanda (Milan: Edizioni San Paolo, 1993), 240.
42. Pius XII, Address to the College of Cardinals, June 2, 1945; translation in Rhodes, *The Vatican in the Age of the Dictators*, 183.
43. Paul VI, Address to U Thant, July 11, 1963, in *Paths to Peace: A Contribution—Documents of the Holy See to the International Community*, ed. Permanent Observer Mission of the Holy See to the United Nations (Brookfield: Liturgical Publications, 1987), #294, p. 58; cf. Paul VI, Address to the United Nations General Assembly, October 4, 1965, *The Pope Speaks*, 11:1 (1966), 51.
44. Message of John Paul II to Jaime de Pinies, October 14, 1985, in *Paths to Peace*, #346, p. 67.
45. John Paul II, Address to UNESCO, Paris, June 2, 1980, *L'Osservatore Romano*, 25 (June 23, 1980), 10.
46. John Paul II, *Ex corde ecclesiae* (1990), #3.
47. Diarmuid Martin, "The Holy See at the International Conference on Population," *L'Osservatore Romano*, 50 (December 10, 1984), 6.
48. John Paul II, Message to Nafis Sadik, Executive Director of the United Nations Population Fund, March 18, 1994, *L'Osservatore Romano*, 12 (March 23, 1994), 1.
49. Rhodes, *The Vatican in the Age of the Dictators*, 236.
50. Eugene V. Rostow, "The Role of the Vatican in the Modern World," *L'Osservatore Romano*, 9 (May 30, 1968), 4.
51. Agostino Casaroli, "The Papacy and the Challenges of the Modern World," *L'Osservatore Romano*, 24 (September 24, 1984), 6.
52. Alain Lebeaupin, Intervention of the Holy See at the Meeting of Experts on the Peaceful Solution of Controversies (CSCE), *L'Osservatore Romano*, 9 (March 4, 1991), 8.
53. John Paul II, Address to the Diplomatic Corps, January 15, 1983, *L'Osservatore Romano*, 8 (February 21, 1983), 8.
54. Andrea Riccardi, *Il potere del papa da Pio XII a Giovanni Paolo II* (Rome: Laterza, 1993), 106.
55. Robert A. Graham, "Diplomacy, Papal," *New Catholic Encyclopedia*, vol. 4 (New York: McGraw-Hill Book Company, 1967), 883.
56. John Paul II, Apostolic Letter, *On the Occasion of the Fiftieth Anniversary of the Outbreak of the Second World War* (1989), #3.
57. *Actes et Documents du Saint-Siège relatifs à la seconde guerre mondiale*, vol. 1 (Vatican City: Polyglot Press, 1970), #313, p. 455.
58. Riccardi, *Il potere del papa*, 14-16.
59. John Paul II, Address to Officials of the Roman Vicariate, January 17, 1991, *L'Osservatore Romano*, 3 (January 21, 1991), 1.
60. John Paul II, Interview with Jas Gawronski, *L'Osservatore Romano*, 46 (November 17, 1993), 6.

Origins, Development, and Mission of the Papacy

61. Casaroli, "The Holy See and the International Community," 9.
62. Rudolf Kirchschläger, "The Presence of the Holy See as a Factor of Peace in the International Community," *L'Osservatore Romano*, 9 (February 28, 1974), 4.
63. Paul VI, Address to the College of Cardinals and Roman Curia, December 22, 1975, *L'Osservatore Romano*, 2 (January 8, 1976), 2.
64. John Paul II, Address to the Diplomatic Corps, January 9, 1989, *L'Osservatore Romano*, 7 (February 13, 1989), 2-3.
65. John Paul II, *Message for the 1988 World Day of Peace*, intro.; cf. *Message for the 1991 World Day of Peace*, #4-5; *Redemptor hominis* (1979), #17; *Christifideles laici* (1988), #39; *Redemptoris missio* (1990), #39; *Centesimus annus* (1991), #29.
66. Memorandum of the Delegation of the Holy See to the Conference on Security and Cooperation in Europe, June 2, 1992, *L'Osservatore Romano*, 31 (August 5, 1992), 3.
67. Kirchschläger, "The Presence of the Holy See as a Factor of Peace in the International Community," 4.
68. Casaroli, "The Holy See and the International Community," 7.
69. John Paul II, Message to the Second Special Session of the United Nations General Assembly on Disarmament, June 11, 1982, in *Paths to Peace*, #1020, p. 164.
70. John Quinn, "Goals of the Holy See's Diplomacy," *Origins*, 13:34 (February 2, 1984), 572.
71. John Paul II, *Veritatis splendor* (1993), #96-101.
72. Paul VI, Address to the United Nations General Assembly, October 4, 1965, *The Pope Speaks*, 11:1 (1966), 49; cf. *Populorum progressio* (1967), #13.
73. John Paul II, Address to the Diplomatic Corps, January 16, 1993, *L'Osservatore Romano*, 3 (January 20, 1993), 2.
74. Agostino Casaroli, "The Vatican's Position on Issues of War and Peace," *Origins*, 13:26 (December 8, 1983), 435.
75. Riccardi, *Il potere del papa*, 281.
76. John Paul II, *Message for the 1988 World Day of Peace*, #2.
77. Jean-Louis Tauran, Address to the Third Committee of the 48th General Assembly of the United Nations, November 17, 1993, *L'Osservatore Romano*, 48 (December 1, 1993), 7.
78. John Paul II, *Centesimus annus* (1991), #22; cf. Interview of John Paul II with Jas Gawronski, *L'Osservatore Romano*, 46 (November 17, 1993), 6.
79. John Paul II, *Message for the 1987 World Day of Peace*, #8; cf. Apostolic Letter, *On the Occasion of the Fiftieth Anniversary of the Outbreak of the Second World War* (1989), #9; Pontifical Council for Justice and Peace, *The International Arms Trade: An Ethical Reflection* (1994).
80. Paul VI, Address to the College of Cardinals, June 22, 1973, *L'Osservatore Romano*, 27 (July 5, 1973), 8.
81. Audrys J. Backis, Intervention of the Holy See at the Geneva Conference regarding the Treaty on the Non-Proliferation of Nuclear Arms, August 13, 1980, *L'Osservatore Romano*, 41 (October 13, 1980), 5.
82. Agostino Casaroli, "The Holy See and the Problems of Contemporary Europe," *L'Osservatore Romano*, 11 (March 16, 1978), 6.
83. Casaroli, "The Papacy and the Challenges of the Modern World," 6.
84. Paul VI, Address to the Diplomatic Corps, January 15, 1977, *L'Osservatore Romano*, 4 (January 27, 1977), 2.

85. John Paul II, Address to the Diplomatic Corps, January 15, 1983, *L'Osservatore Romano*, 8 (February 21, 1983), 7.
86. Thomas Patrick Melady, "Ten Years of U.S.-Holy See Diplomatic Relations, *The Priest*, 50:1 (1994), 45.
87. John Paul II, Address to the Diplomatic Corps, January 13, 1990, *L'Osservatore Romano*, 5 (January 29, 1990), 1.
88. John Paul II, Address to the Diplomatic Corps, Kampala, February 8, 1993, *L'Osservatore Romano*, 7 (February 17, 1993), 6.
89. See John XXIII: *Mater et magistra* (1961), #205-211, *Pacem in terris*, #36-38; Paul VI: *Populorum progressio* (1967), #14-21; John Paul II: *Sollicitudo rei socialis* (1987), #38, *Redemptoris missio* (1990), #59, *Centesimus annus* (1991), #29.
90. John Paul II, *Sollicitudo rei socialis* (1967), #14; cf. *Redemptoris missio* (1990), #59.
91. John Paul II, *Message for the 1984 World Day of Peace*, #1.
92. See the Statutes of the Foundation, *L'Osservatore Romano*, 30 (July 25, 1988), 5.
93. Message of Paul VI to the First Special Session of the United Nations General Assembly on Disarmament, May 24, 1978, in *Paths to Peace*, #1009, p. 163.
94. Casaroli, "The Holy See and the International Community," 8.
95. John Paul II, Address to the Diplomatic Corps, January 12, 1985, *L'Osservatore Romano*, 4 (January 28, 1985), 6.
96. Giovanni Battista Montini, "Papal Diplomacy as a Means of Representing Christ before the World"; translation in Cardinale, *The Holy See and the International Order*, 297.
97. Carlos Corral Salvador, "Concordati vigenti," *Nuovo Dizionario di Diritto Canonico*, ed. Carlos Corral Salvador, Velasio De Paolis, and Gianfranco Ghirlanda (Milan: Edizioni San Paolo, 1993), 226-227.
98. Agostino Casaroli, "The Holy See between Tensions and Détente," *L'Osservatore Romano*, 9 (March 2, 1978), 10.
99. Paul VI, Address to the College of Cardinals, December 22, 1975, *L'Osservatore Romano*, 2 (January 8, 1976), 2.
100. Lukas Vischer, "The Holy See, the Vatican State, and the Churches' Common Witness: A Neglected Ecumenical Problem," *Journal of Ecumenical Studies*, 11:3 (1974), 618.
101. Vischer, "The Holy See," 621.
102. Cardinale, *The Holy See and the International Order*, 46.
103. Casaroli, "The Holy See and the International Community," 8.

Chapter sixteen
FACING THE FUTURE: 21 THESES ON THE PAPAL MINISTRY

By way of conclusion, I would like to present the following twenty-one theses on the Petrine ministry of the pope. These observations are, in part, a summary of Catholic teaching on the papacy. Even more, however, they are comments on the most significant dimensions of the papal ministry discussed in contemporary theology. Some are conclusions which follow from the book as a whole, but only hinted at in the previous chapters. Others contain suggestions for describing the Petrine office in light of the renewal made possible by modern scriptural, historical, and ecumenical studies and by the Second Vatican Council.

Doubtlessly there are limitations to this approach. First, I make no claim that the theses summarize every point of Catholic teaching. That doctrine, I hope, has already been explained in detail. Second, the numbering of the theses follows no particular order; it does not move from the more to the less important. Third, while Vatican II rounded out Vatican I's doctrine on the papacy, it nonetheless failed to integrate the papal office fully with episcopal collegiality and some of its other ecclesiological insights. The theology of the Petrine ministry is still an uncompleted task and a continuing challenge.

• **THESIS 1**   **The papacy is central to the identity and the faith of Catholics.**

In the third millennium, the papacy will remain a crucial institution for Catholic life. The enduring centrality of this ministry is due to its being a powerful sign of Catholic identity and a dogma of faith.

When Catholics are asked to indicate what they regard as the distinguishing mark of their faith, they invariably point, first of all, to the papacy. The pope is the primary symbol of Catholic self-identity. His pivotal role is confirmed by the emotion-laden responses which he elicits. Peter's successor evokes boundless admiration and curiosity in some, and studied indifference and animosity in others. Even the so-called "anti-Roman complex," what Hans Urs von Balthasar referred to as the "deep-seated anti-Roman attitude within the Catholic Church,"[1] testifies to the papacy's profound roots in the Catholic consciousness. For the world at large the distinctiveness of the Catholic Church also focuses on the papacy. Personal feelings aside, nearly every commentator recognizes that the papal ministry is simply too embedded in the history of the Church and of the West for it to lose its institutional prominence.

It used to be taken for granted that no matter how much Catholics wrangled among themselves about the fine points — the fittingness of the monarchical trappings of the papal office, the electoral procedures, the precise limits of the pope's authority, and so on — they were all fundamentally committed to preserving the papal ministry. While this is undoubtedly still the case for the vast majority of the world's Catholics, an outspoken minority now embraces opinions which contradict Church teaching on the papal office. This anti-Roman attitude is "trying to press toward a point where the objective structures of the Church would be finally surpassed."[2] As history has repeatedly and tragically demonstrated, however, unless such opposition is resolved, it reaches a crossroads, where separation from communion with the pope appears to be the inevitable consequence of holding certain theological positions.

The preceding chapters have explained that, from the doctrinal point of view, the papal ministry belongs to the Church's integral confession of faith. Besides its symbolic significance, the papacy is dogmatically constitutive of Catholic Christianity. There can be no Church without the pope.

- **THESIS 2** **In the third millennium, the papacy will play an increasingly significant role in the life of all Christians.**

Beginning with the pontificate of John XXIII, non-Catholic churches and ecclesial communities have frequently expressed the need for a Petrine ministry and, to a lesser extent, for the papal office. Patrick Granfield remarks that in contrast with the bitter polemics of the past, "the papacy is judged much more benignly today, and with greater openness toward its role as an instrument of unity for the entire Christian community."[3] Whereas ecumenical contacts used to be extremely limited, many churches now seek meetings, conversations, and exchanges with the Holy See. "In the ecumenical movement since the mid-1960s," writes Lukas Vischer, "there has even been something like a de facto recognition of the pope."[4] Whatever their objections to its theology or practice, many Christians now realize that they must live with the papal office. As ecumenical exchanges with the Orthodox, Anglicans, and Lutherans are making clear, the restoration of full visible communion among Christians must in some way include the universal ministry of the bishop of Rome.[5]

Since the Second Vatican Council, Catholics and Orthodox have drawn closer together, recognizing each other as "sister" churches. John Paul II frequently speaks about the need "to hasten the day when the Church can begin once more to breathe fully with her 'two lungs,' the East and the West."[6] Although some direct discussion on the papacy has taken place with the Orthodox, most has been indirect. Dialogue has been fostered by both churches' renewed understanding of an ecclesiology of communion, the role of the local church, and episcopal collegiality. When Patriarch Athenagoras welcomed Paul VI to Istanbul in 1967, he addressed him as "holy brother and successor of Peter."[7] In his salutation, the Patriarch followed the mainstream Orthodox tradition that, although all bishops are successors of Peter, the bishop of Rome is so in a privileged way. Later that year, when Athenagoras returned the Pope's visit and went to Rome, he greeted him as "the venerable Bishop of Rome, who bears the apostolic grace, and is the successor of that great constellation of wise and holy men who bestowed luster on this see (the first in honor and rank in the ordered whole of Christian Churches throughout the world) — men whose holiness and wisdom and whose struggles for the common faith in the undivided Church are a permanent possession and a treasure of the whole Christian world."[8]

Differences regarding the theological foundation of the papal ministry and the way the pope exercises it, however, still exist. To its theology of the local church emphasizing the episcopal ministry and the Eucharist, the East opposes the universalist ecclesiology of the West. Orthodox theologians continue to reject Vatican I's juridical formulation of papal primacy, interpreting its dogma of papal jurisdiction as the culmination of Roman universalism. According to the Orthodox, above the bishop, no higher sacramental or jurisdictional authority exists by divine right. They are wary of any hint that the pope enjoys a higher order of ministry, a situation which they think prevails in the West's monarchical Church structure. The canonical theory which proposes that the papal office is purely jurisdictional and not intrinsically dependent upon episcopal ordination suggests to the East an erroneous ecclesiology.

Based on his view that the historical shape which the primacy has taken in the last two centuries "is not the only possible form," Joseph Ratzinger has proposed a way to resolve the East's objections to papal primacy. He suggests that full communion with the Eastern churches could be restored on the basis of the following principles. First, the West would recognize "the Church of the East as orthodox and legitimate in the form she has always had." Furthermore, "Rome must not require more from the East with respect to the doctrine of primacy than had been formulated and was lived in the first millennium." Second, the East would have to cease opposing "as heretical the developments that took place in the West in the second millennium and would accept the Catholic Church as legitimate and orthodox in the form she had acquired in the course of that development."[9] Ratzinger's proposal furnishes a creative framework within which future Orthodox-Catholic dialogue on the papal ministry can fruitfully take place.

In the coming years, the office of the pope will remain on the agenda of those pursuing unity. This is largely due to the increasing number of non-Catholics who recognize that a common center for Christianity is necessary so that "the faith of Christians can acquire a clear voice amidst the confusing din of differing ideologies."[10] As Christianity effectively becomes worldwide, writes Avery Dulles, the churches appreciate that "the centrifugal forces of social and cultural diversity must be counterbalanced by the centripetal attraction of a symbolic focus of unity."[11] Much progress has been made since Paul VI lamented in 1967 that "the papacy is undoubtedly the most serious obstacle on the ecumenical road."[12] Dialogue will continue because the papacy's place in the hierarchy of truths precludes that it can be simply ignored. Visible unity with other Christians, which is expressed by a shared Eucharist, will come about only if all the parties concerned satisfactorily address Catholic doctrine on the papal ministry.

• *THESIS 3*   **The ministerial structure of the Church is episcopal, primatial, and collegial.**

The Second Vatican Council's teaching on collegiality situated the papacy in a more balanced perspective. While Vatican I safeguarded the uniqueness of the ministry, Vatican II guaranteed the episcopacy. "The Second Vatican Council," wrote von Balthasar, "did not annul the first; it confirmed it; but it brought in all the additions and modifications necessary to establish an overall equilibrium."[13] Thanks to the last ecumenical council, the interdependence of the primacy and the episcopacy in the Church's hierarchical structure can be better appreciated. Moreover, as John Paul II has remarked, "because of this new clarification the erroneous interpretations often made of Vatican I's definition are rejected and the full significance of the Petrine ministry is shown in its harmony with the doctrine of episcopal collegiality."[14]

No renewed vision of the papacy in either theology or practice can, therefore, ignore the significance of Vatican II's emphasis on the divine institution of the episcopacy, the bishops' authoritative teaching role, their responsibility for the welfare of the universal Church, and episcopal collegiality. Each teaching draws into sharper focus the notion that the pope exercises his ministry within the college of bishops. In this framework, the pope appears more as the elder brother among the bishops than as an isolated figure above them. While Peter received a unique charge from Jesus, which distinguished him from the other apostles, it was a service within the community of the Twelve. Collegiality integrates the pope's primatial ministry with the episcopal college, which is one and undivided. Even so, the presence of Peter's successor in the episcopal college entails a certain tension. This give-and-take between the pope's special commission and the collegial co-determination of his office cannot be resolved simply by establishing canonical norms.[15] The fruitful tension arising from collegiality belongs to the mystery of the Church. Granfield observes that this tension "must be cherished as a sign of ecclesial health" which shows the mutual respect that exists between the Roman church and the particular churches.[16]

In varying degrees and in different ways, the spirit of collegiality is expressed by the synod of bishops, the college of cardinals, episcopal conferences, the bishops' *ad limina* visits to Rome, and the pope's pastoral visits to particular churches. These partial realizations of full collegiality manifest the bishops' solicitude for the universal Church in union with Peter's successor. The extent to which these instruments of ecclesial communion derive from the pope's primatial authority or that of the episcopal college remains, at least in part, an open theological question. In light of the Church's tradition, the present canonical regulation of these institutions cannot be regarded as definitive. The experience of collegiality will, no doubt, show that collegial interaction makes papal authority more effective. In the future, these collegial structures will continue to develop in order to manifest more clearly the Church's episcopal, primatial, and collegial structure.

• **THESIS 4**   **The Petrine charism is integrated with the Marian dimension of the Church.**

From the New Testament it is evident, wrote von Balthasar, that "the office of Peter is *one* of several indispensable elements in the ecclesiastical structure, thus freeing it from the pyramid-like isolation to which it consented, partly involuntarily, by permitting itself to be modeled on the pattern of imperial Rome and, partly voluntarily, in reaction to the encroachment of medieval emperors."[17] Peter's mission was intrinsically determined by the callings of others: Mary, John the Baptist, the apostles, the women who followed Jesus, and many more. Recalling the significance of the Marian dimension is a corrective

Origins, Development, and Mission of the Papacy

to the sometimes exaggerated place given to the Petrine ministry in ecclesial life and theology.

In God's plan, the Church's Marian identity is anterior to the founding of the community's institutional structures. It has temporal precedence over the Petrine office.[18] Mary proceeds all others in the plan of salvation, including Peter and the other apostles. The Church begins with her *fiat*, not with Peter's confession of faith. Not only were the apostles born under the burden of sin, their ministry is a means to sanctify the Church, a holiness already fulfilled in Mary. For example, "what Peter receives as 'infallibility' for his office of governing, will be a partial share in the total flawlessness of the feminine, marian Church."[19] Peter always gives way to Mary, because the Marian dimension embraces the Petrine without claiming it as its own.

• **THESIS 5**   **The foundation of the papal office is the unique leadership role which Jesus assigned to Peter.**

Catholic teaching regards the papal office as a personal Petrine service, which receives its justification from biblical revelation. This scriptural witness to Peter's primacy among the apostles and to his responsibilities in the early community is the necessary point of departure for evaluating the legitimacy of all subsequent developments in the historical papacy.[20]

In the major strands of its tradition, the New Testament is familiar with a Petrine tradition which recognizes that Jesus assigned a leadership role to Peter, a function confirmed by the apostle's actions after the ascension and by the early community's peaceful reception of his mission. Christ entrusted this ministry to the Church as a permanent charism, which was to unfold from the biblical witness. Because of Christ's decision, Peter received a special service, a specific function, a pastoral ministry. The deliberate nature of this divine choice becomes even more evident in light of Peter's betrayal, a perfidy which failed to change Jesus' plan of choosing him. Instead, Peter's denial provoked his special prayer for the apostle (cf. Lk 22:31-32).

The New Testament does more than recount the story of the "Peter of history," recording the facts of his life and ministry. It goes beyond historical narration to portray the "Peter of faith." According to the Scriptures, Peter appears not only as the outstanding witness to Christ's earthly and risen life, but also as "the prototype of the guarantor and teacher of the authentic Jesus tradition."[21] He is the symbolic figure of community leadership (cf. Mt 16:18-19) and of pastoral office (cf. Jn 21:15-17). A study of Peter's historical career cannot, therefore, settle the question of the need for a Petrine ministry in the later Church. His continuing mission comes to the fore by studying the trajectory of Petrine images. Opening the possibility for later development, each image points to the continuing importance which the apostolic Church attributed to Peter's ministry.[22]

• **THESIS 6**   **Christ willed that the apostles have successors to their ministry, and among them he intended that Peter would have successors to his specific office.**

Scripture itself furnishes no explicit testimony to Petrine succession. Jesus never said, "I give to you *and to your successors* . . ." Only through the witness of the apostolic community can we can discern the mind of Christ regarding succession to Peter's ministry. By keeping his memory alive in different traditions, the New Testament writers clearly imply that Peter's unique role was to outlive his death.

Theological discussion concerning succession to Peter takes place within the broader context of apostolic succession. Through the succession of bishops, the original apostolic ministry is made present in the Church. The apostolic college continues to exist by means of the episcopal college which is its instrument. Thanks to the Church's sacramentality, the apostles' mission remains. The same is true of the specific ministry in the college assigned to Peter.[23] The transmissible elements in the mission of the original members of the apostolic college point to an equally transmissible office of Peter within the college. Anyone who accepts the existence of an original Petrine primacy and the principle of apostolic succession is similarly compelled to acknowledge the principle of Petrine succession.

Peter's successors exercised their ministry before they explained their reasons for doing so. By the third century, the principle of Petrine succession was clearly formulated, becoming explicit in the tradition. The Church Fathers expressed this *petrinitas* of the Roman bishop by calling him the "vicar" of Peter. They regarded the pope as carrying out the same ministry which Peter first received. Typical of this idea is the formulation of St. Peter Chrysologus (†450). He admonished an adversary to "heed obediently what has been written by the most blessed Pope of the city of Rome; for blessed Peter, who lives and presides in his own see, provides the truth of the faith to those who seek it" (PL 54, 743). The primacy of Peter's successors is, therefore, "something positively intended by God and deriving from the will and institution of Jesus Christ."[24]

- **THESIS 7** **The ministry and martyrdom at Rome of Sts. Peter and Paul laid the foundation for the preeminence of the Roman church in the universal communion.**

A twofold inheritance belongs to the Roman church: the succession of Peter which is the ministry of leadership, and the heritage of Paul which is the special charism of proclaiming the gospel.[25] Pope Paul VI frequently associated the Roman see with both of these apostles. He spoke of Peter and Paul's ministry and martyrdom in Rome as "founding" the church there.[26] John Paul II speaks in a similar fashion. St. Paul, he says, "was always united with Peter, and Peter with him, in this: that God was pleased to reveal in him [Paul] his Son."[27] Both served the same divine truth revealed to them. According to the Pope, God linked the destinies of the two apostles to Rome. "Both were led by Christ to the capital of the empire, which would become the centre of the Church. For each of them the day arrived when their blood would be shed in sacrifice. And thus, from that time on, Rome has remained the city of the definitive witness of the Apostles Peter and Paul."[28] In Rome, the "rock" (Mt 16:18) and the "chosen instrument" (Acts 9:15) sealed their apostolic ministry with their blood.

In recent years, theologians have revived the ancient tradition which recognized St. Paul's contribution to the Petrine ministry. The Apostle to the Nations enjoyed the authority of a prophet. In J. M. R. Tillard's words, "he bore witness to the absolute, radical authority of the Word over everything and everyone, even over him to whom the Lord had committed leadership."[29] The bishop of Rome is not, strictly speaking, the successor to Paul. However, according to John Paul II, the pope is "the heir of Paul, the greatest representative of the early Church's missionary efforts and the wealth of her charisms."[30] Paul's heritage remains in Rome to remind Peter's successor of the transcendence of God's grace over every institution, including the papal ministry. It keeps the pope open to the Spirit, lest his leadership lead to a rigid institutionalization, and open to the nations, lest he be tempted to restrict his ministry only to the Church. According to Tillard, Paul transmits to the primatial ministry of Peter "both an intrinsic limitation (its submission to the permanent newness of the Spirit which his reproaches to Peter himself will recall) and a freedom (the refusal of every myopic fundamentalism)."[31] God has willed that Peter's successor also embody in his ministry the particular gifts of the Apostle to the Nations.

• **THESIS 8** **The tradition of the Roman church as a unique see can be joined to that of Petrine succession, thereby providing a solid theological justification for the pope's universal ministry.**

The church at Rome is the primatial see in the *koinonia*. It owes this primacy to two factors: its bishop succeeds to Peter's ministry in the apostolic college, and it is the see of the apostles Peter and Paul who founded "the greatest and most ancient church known to all."[32] Tillard proposes that the papal ministry is best justified on the grounds of the primacy of the Roman *church*. "It is from this primacy, of *his* local Church in the midst of *all* the Churches that the Bishop of Rome has his primacy in the college of bishops."[33] The Roman see itself, the *sedes*, imparted a certain dignity to the *sedens*, the bishop of the church. The pope's singular power is "attached to the seat of the *potentior principalitatis*" of the Roman church.[34] In many ancient sources, Tillard contends, the recognition of primatial authority is phrased in terms of the church of Rome, held to be the head of all the churches. The "presider in love," which Ignatius described in the salutation of his *Letter to the Romans*, is the whole church at Rome, including its presiding bishop. Therefore, according to Tillard, it is "the primacy and authority of this Church [of Rome] and of this seat which explain those of the bishop, not the reverse."[35]

A Catholic theology of the papacy can benefit from this renewed emphasis on the theological significance of the Roman see. We can grant that, very early on, the other churches recognized Roman primacy because of the uniqueness of this see's dual apostolicity. Nevertheless, it soon became clear that it was not the Roman see as such but its *petrinitas* which gave its bishop his leadership role in the universal Church. Taken alone, Tillard's proposal fails to provide the entire reason for the emergence of papal primacy. Jesus' plan was not to establish the Roman *church* as the rock, key-bearer, and pastor of the whole Church, but Peter and his successors. The bishop of Rome's unique authority does not derive from his church. Christ transmitted the Petrine mission to a person, not to a see.

The primacy of the Roman church can be fully explained only by recourse to the principle of Petrine succession. It is true that later theology sometimes obscured the preeminence of the local church at Rome established by the ministry and martyrdom there of Sts. Peter and Paul. When this insight is integrated with the doctrine of *petrinitas*, the two together provide a solid theological foundation for papal primacy.[36]

- **THESIS 9** **While in theory the primatial see could be relocated, the ancient tradition that the successor of Peter is the bishop of Rome should be maintained.**

Theologians have long debated whether Rome is the necessary see of the Petrine ministry. To be sure, Jesus did not specify the role of Rome in Petrine succession. He entrusted that decision "to historical events in which the divine plan for the Church, the determination of the concrete conditions of Peter's succession, would appear."[37] The theological question is whether the apostle's providentially guided move from Jerusalem to Rome is to be understood as an irreversible decision of the Church.

On the one hand, a universalist ecclesiology emphasizes the primatially-structured episcopal college as the body which possesses apostolic authority in the Church. It regards the pope chiefly as the bishop who is the head of the episcopal college. Taking the college of bishops as its point of departure, this ecclesiology attributes little theological importance to the primacy's historical embodiment in the *Roman* bishop. It therefore leaves open the possibility of dissociating the Petrine ministry from the local church at Rome. As long as there is a head for the college, the successor of Peter need not be the bishop of Rome. For sufficient reason, he could be the bishop of another see and exercise his universal ministry as the head of that local church.[38]

On the other hand, an ecclesiology of communion assigns a theological value to the local church at Rome. It links Petrine primacy to the bishop who is head of the *Roman* church, which is itself a theological reality. This ecclesiology judges any proposal that the pope could be a kind of "super-bishop" in the Church as unfaithful to the ancient tradition. Because Peter was providentially guided in going to the capital of the Empire, the primacy is irrevocably connected to the see of Rome.

Vatican I explicitly refused to take a position on the matter. It remains a disputed question, though most contemporary theologians favor the emphasis on the intrinsic nature of the link between succession to Peter's ministry and succession to the Roman episcopate. Magisterial teaching, expressed in *Romano pontifici eligendo* (1975) and the Code of Canon Law (1983), follows suit. While not proposing a dogma of faith, these documents specify that the universal Church guarantees succession to the Petrine ministry by electing the bishop of the local church at Rome.

- **THESIS 10** **From the ministry which Jesus confided to Peter, the papacy unfolded gradually as a historical institution.**

Whereas an earlier generation of apologists for papal primacy often tried to show that the papacy could be recognized as a distinct ecclesial ministry from the end of the first century, Catholic theologians no longer push so hard to prove this point. They are now more at home with the idea that the papacy evolved gradually from its New Testament foundation in Peter's ministry.

Such a development is parallel to the process by which the Church assembled certain writings into the biblical canon, recognizing them as sacred Scripture. The acceptance of this canon was the work of the Spirit who prompted the Church authorities to acknowledge the inspiration of certain writings. This act of recognition did not, however, create that inspiration. Similarly, only slowly did the bishops of Rome become explicitly aware of their special ministry to the universal Church.

As history unfolded, the Church formulated with increasing clarity the ministerial structure which Christ had provided for her. At the outset, it is possible that the Roman bishops had little idea about what was entailed in succeeding to the see where Peter preached and shed his blood. Similarly, other churches only gradually came to recognize the full import of this office. A lack of an explicit Petrine consciousness does not mean, however, that the Church invented the papacy. On the contrary, Christ provided for, or "instituted," the universal primacy of Peter and his successors. Under the providential guidance of the Holy Spirit, the community discerned ever more profoundly the implications of this ministry. They expressed that realization in concrete structures responding to the "signs of the times."

To admit that human factors contributed to the development of papal primacy is in harmony with the incarnational-sacramental nature of the pilgrim Church. The papacy is neither "just divine" nor "just human." On the one hand, it was not expressly claimed and recognized as a primacy of jurisdiction from the first century onward. On the other hand, it cannot be accounted for by purely historical and human factors. The nucleus of the Petrine ministry comes from Christ, but it is variously embodied according to the Church's needs in a particular era.

• **THESIS 11** Whereas the Petrine ministry originating in Christ's will is of *divine institution*, the historical papacy embodying that responsibility is of *divine design*.

The awareness of the distinction between Peter's original ministry and the pope's historical office has brought with it the need for a clarification in terminology which previous generations did not make. Earlier theology focused on whether the papacy was of "divine institution," where this term meant explicit establishment by Jesus Christ. Catholic theologians defended the papacy's divine institution, while non-Catholics denied it. The ecumenical stalemate produced by this way of dealing with the papacy's theological foundation can, however, be superseded. Dulles sums up the current state of the question: "It seems simplistic to speak of the papacy as having been 'divinely instituted' in the sense that the term would have had in the sixteenth century."[39] Because of their greater awareness of historical development, theologians now distinguish between the Petrine ministry, which Christ himself established, and its historical realizations, which developed under the Spirit's guidance. As an institution which emerged in history, the papacy is inextricably dependent on both historical circumstances and the divine will.

In light of the traditional terminology, two ways of dealing with the meaning of "divine institution" are possible. Theologians such as Karl Rahner extend the meaning of this term to include irrevocable decisions taken by the post-apostolic Church.[40] Such decisions were not necessarily rooted in Christ's explicit word or action. Nonetheless, they are held to express the essential nature of the Church guided in her development by the Holy Spirit. Consequently, they are irreversible. Their permanence in the Church is similar to that of the Scriptures. While the New Testament canon as such was unknown during the apostolic age, once it was determined by post-apostolic authority, it became the Church's permanent and inalienable treasure. The designation "divine institution," therefore, does double duty. On the one hand, it can describe something which Jesus himself directly willed, such as the Eucharist. On the other hand, it can indicate something which was divinely guided in its development, such as the monarchical episcopate. While this provides a satisfactory theological explanation for the origins of institutions directly willed by Christ and those which emerged in the post-apostolic Church, it leaves an unnecessary ambiguity in the terminology: both are described as being of "divine institution."

In order to make the distinction sharper between what Christ explicitly instituted and what later emerged as providentially guided, I suggest an alternative. The theological qualification "by divine institution" should be used to qualify the Petrine ministry, while "by divine design" to qualify the historical papacy.

This terminological clarification has at least three advantages. First, it leaves intact the traditional teaching that the Petrine ministry was directly instituted by Christ. Second, it calls attention to the fact that the papacy gradually emerged over time. The qualification "by divine design" leaves open possibilities for different historical embodiments of Peter's ministry. For example, the pope could exercise his primacy in a more monarchical way at one time, and in a more collegial way at another. Third, the new terminology benefits ecumenical discussion on the papal office. Because an increasing number of official ecumenical dialogues and non-Catholic theologians admit that Christ instituted a Petrine ministry, the distinction emphasizes their mutual agreement. Furthermore, some non-Catholics also recognize that the historical papacy is more than merely a human institution. At least in some sense, they maintain, it expresses God's will for the Church. Although Catholic theologians would give the term "divine design" a fuller meaning than their non-Catholic colleagues, the proposed terminology locates more sharply the specific issues which remain to be resolved.

- **THESIS 12**   **As God's gracious gift, the embodiment of the Petrine ministry in the papal office is a constitutive element of the Church.**

Fidelity to the apostolic tradition demands that the Petrine ministry be carried out by the bishop who is the successor of Peter. According to Christ's mandate and the Spirit's guidance, the primatial ministry is a gift inherent in the Church's divine institution. The papal office cannot be abolished, superseded, or transformed in such a way that it would no longer incarnate the Petrine ministry. God did not give this ministry for a particular, but only limited, period in the Church's life. To maintain that the papacy once served the good of the Church, but might not do so in the future, is contrary to Catholic teaching. Even if its concrete forms developed in response to the community's needs and to historical factors, the papal ministry must endure if the Church is to remain obedient to God's will. The Church is permanently bound to her primatial-episcopal structure.[41]

While non-Catholics are increasingly willing to concede that a Petrine ministry could serve the Church, they do not necessarily identify this service with the office of the bishop of Rome. In the American Lutheran-Catholic ecumenical dialogue on the papacy, the Lutheran participants admitted that "it is God's will that the Church have the institutional means needed for the promotion of unity in the gospel."[42] At the level of international dialogue, they have recognized that "a ministry serving the unity of the Church as a whole is, for Lutherans, in accord with the will of the Lord, but without its concrete form having been fixed once and for all."[43] According to Lutherans, other bodies, such as ecumenical councils, local councils, or the Lutheran World Federation, have at times carried out the Petrine ministry. For their part, the Anglican participants in the international Anglican-Roman Catholic dialogue (ARCIC) admitted the need for a "universal primacy" in the *koinonia*, qualifying it as "appropriately" held by the bishop of Rome.[44]

The acceptance of a ministry of unity, modeled on that of Peter described in the Scriptures but possibly carried out by other bodies, falls short of full Catholic teaching. Neither sociological reasons of expediency nor the venerable tradition that the Roman bishop has discharged the ministry of Peter can completely account for Catholic belief in its providential development. The papacy emerged as an institution positively willed by God rather than as the result of a purely permissive providence.[45]

Consequently, the papal office is more than merely an "appropriate" or "desirable" institution — one possible way of exercising the Petrine ministry.[46] To describe the papacy as fitting, even providential, but "necessary" only in a relative sense, is doctrinally inadequate. An irreversible and divinely-willed link between the ministry of Peter and the office of the pope must be affirmed. Whereas a few theologians, such as Karl-Heinz Ohlig and Hans Küng, maintain that papal primacy is a possibly reversible or temporary ministry,[47] most Catholics rightly reject this position. In truth, the papal office is more than a practical necessity. It corresponds to God's *definitive* will for the Church.

• **THESIS 13**   **Because the office of the pope belongs to the divine plan for the Church, any community not in communion with the Roman see lacks ecclesial fullness.**

Since the papacy is a necessary and permanent ministry in the *koinonia*, a church not in communion with the bishop of Rome lacks the fullness which God wills for it. This follows from the meaning Catholics attribute to the "divine design" of the papacy. Insofar as particular churches interiorly embody the full mystery of the universal Church, they are necessarily in communion with the successor of Peter. According to the Congregation for the Doctrine of the Faith, "the ministry of the successor of Peter as something interior to each particular church is a necessary expression of that fundamental interiority between the universal Church and the particular church" (CN 13). To be particular churches in the fullest sense, they must possess as a constitutive element the bond of communion with the entire episcopal college. Since the universal Church herself contributes to the essential nature of a local church, full ecclesial communion requires acceptance of the pope's Petrine ministry.

A Catholic theology of the local church leads to the same conclusion. The Eucharist is offered by the Church as the organically structured priestly body. The priest who presides at the Eucharist must be in communion with the bishop of the particular church. The bishop, in turn, must be in hierarchical communion with his brothers in the episcopate and their head.[48] Recognition of the papal ministry is necessary to a particular church's complete ecclesial identity and, for this reason, the pope is always mentioned in the Eucharistic prayer.

Only a "full" particular church is in perfect communion with the whole body of churches. Von Balthasar writes that "even where the apostolic reality lacks only one dimension — the Petrine — as in Orthodoxy, we can see its unity profoundly impaired."[49] Thus, any church without the link of communion with Peter's successor is, to a greater or lesser extent, "wounded." At the same time, this situation of imperfect communion also limits the Catholic Church in expressing her diversity, since "divisions among Christians prevent the Church from realizing the fullness of catholicity proper to her" (UR 4).

This Catholic teaching does not entail the "de-churching" of communities lacking perfect communion with the Roman see. Nor does it consider them as non-churches or merely as sociological groupings of Christian believers. Acceptance of the papal office is only one factor determining a community's ecclesial nature. The Catholic Church recognizes the ecclesial reality of the Orthodox churches and of some other churches and ecclesial communities. Nonetheless, because the papacy belongs to the divine design of the universal *koinonia*, a church's ecclesial fullness includes acceptance of the pope's Petrine ministry. Full visible communion with the see of Peter integrates a particular church from within; it does not just complement it from without. This visible unity is not extrinsic to particular churches, as if they could be fully churches without communion among themselves and with the Roman see. The ministry of Peter carried out by the pope belongs to the divinely willed constitution of every particular church.[50]

- **THESIS 14**   **In order to fulfill its specific mission, the Petrine ministry has assumed many different forms in the past and will continue to do so in the future.**

Throughout the ages, the papacy has adopted various structural shapes, fulfilling its Petrine responsibilities in many different ways. There is a long road from the first-century Roman intervention in the church at Corinth to the claims of universal sovereignty advanced by Boniface VIII (†1303) in *Unam sanctam*. For ten centuries the pope held the Papal States, then he was dispossessed of them, and today he exercises temporal sovereignty over the State of Vatican City. That such changes have taken place is consonant with the Church as a living and historical organism. Because the people of God are on pilgrimage, the pope must have the freedom to respond to new challenges, thereby revealing new facets of the Petrine ministry. We must be on guard, therefore, lest we too quickly identify contingent historical forms with what is dogmatically essential to the papal office. In this regard, the Congregation for the Doctrine of the Faith has noted that "the Petrine ministry . . . while preserving its substance as a divine institution, can find expression in various ways, according to the different circumstances of time and place, as history has shown" (CN 18).

The historical papacy changes, but not every development is a permanent acquisition. It may also take some steps that are only temporary. Ratzinger admits that "without a doubt there have been misguided developments in both theology and practice where the primacy is concerned."[51] A particular way of exercising the primacy might well have been the pope's duty for the Church's welfare at one time, without its being so in the future. In the words of Hermann Pottmeyer, "the present juridical and organizational form of the office of Peter is neither the best imaginable nor the only possible realization."[52] Catholic teaching, therefore, is far from demanding unreserved acceptance for every papal practice which has grown up over two millennia.

- **THESIS 15**   **While in theory the nucleus of the Petrine ministry can be distinguished from its various historical forms, this distinction is difficult to apply in practice.**

Despite the difficulties entailed, what is permanent and irreversible in the papal ministry can be distinguished from what is temporary and changeable. John Galvin observes that contemporary Catholic theologies of the papacy reveal a "willingness to distinguish between the principle of a Petrine office and concrete forms of its realization; awareness of the variability of the Petrine office over the course of history and attention to possible further flexibility in the future."[53]

At least in theory, there is an important distinction between what necessarily belongs to the Petrine ministry and how the historical papacy has embodied this. Rahner believed that theologians should "consider more precisely what really is part of the inalienable substance of faith in the doctrine and practice of the Roman primacy and what is not. And in regard to what is not essential, although people cling to it in practice, the Catholic theologians and especially the popes ought to make their position much clearer."[54]

In practice, there is no easy way to apply the theoretical distinction between the nucleus of the ministry of Peter and its embodiment in the office of the pope. The scripturally verifiable Petrine function cannot simply be disembodied to reach a pure "essence" abstracted from all historical forms. This was not the case with Peter and cannot be for his successors. As Cuthbert Rand comments, "it is never going to be possible to produce a doctrine of the papacy which perfectly captures the very essence of the role and so defines exactly how the papacy ought to operate in the future."[55] This task is even more difficult because the Scriptures themselves describe the Petrine ministry using images. While they give direction, the metaphors of rock, holder of the keys, and shepherd cannot furnish a detailed blueprint for all that is entailed in the Petrine service.

It is, of course, in facing the future that the most interesting questions arise. When theologians admit the principle that the papal primacy as it is now exercised can be reformed, they measure it against the Petrine commission given by Christ and expressed in official Church teaching. Historical studies have demonstrated that many powers and rights acquired over the centuries do not belong to the nature of Peter's ministry. If the good of the Church required it, they could be pruned. Innovative ways of discharging the Petrine ministry will undoubtedly be developed in the future.

A creative, if ultimately unacceptable, proposal suggests that the holder of the Petrine ministry need not necessarily be an individual bishop, let alone the bishop of Rome. Paul Misner has argued that the ministry of unity could be carried out by the college of bishops without its head.[56] Rahner and Dulles have advanced a less radical position. Regarding it as desirable to relieve the pope of some of the taxing burden of his office, they recommended a kind of "shared papacy." Rahner unquestionably believed that papal authority was constitutive of the Church. Even so, he proposed that the holder of such authority could be a moral person, that is, a group of individuals.[57] Dulles reached the same conclusion. "In theory," he wrote, "the Petrine function could be performed either by a single individual presiding over the whole Church or by some kind of committee, board, synod, or parliament — possibly with a 'division of powers' into judicial, legislative, administrative and the like."[58] Is this theory of a shared papacy compatible with Church teaching?

The proposed "de-personalization" of the Petrine ministry goes contrary to the defined doctrine that Jesus assigned a unique mission to Peter individually and personally (cf. DS 3055) — and that he intended personal successors to the apostle. The Church is a mystical body of persons, not of functions. Charisms, and the papal ministry is such a charism, are given to individuals. The proposal of a shared papacy smacks of ecclesiological abstraction, failing to take sufficiently into account the radically historical nature of foundational revelation. The ministry entrusted to Peter was personal. Christ did not establish his Church upon an abstract function. Moreover, precisely because the primacy is an episcopal office, it must be carried out by a single individual, after the model of the early Church.

• **THESIS 16** **The specific Petrine ministry of the bishop of Rome should be more clearly distinguished from his duties as patriarch of the West.**

One way of renewing the papacy, which has deep roots in the tradition, would be to disentangle the various "primacies" that have coalesced in the ministry of Peter's successor: diocesan (bishop of Rome), regional (primate of Italy), patriarchal (patriarch of the West), and papal (pastor of the universal Church). The historical form of ecclesial unity is always embodied in local churches, whether of the Western rite or the many Eastern rites. Service to the Church's unity of faith and communion throughout the world belongs to the pope in virtue of his universal primacy.[59] In addition, however, he has a similar responsibility to the Latin rite as patriarch of the West. The pope's jurisdictional

Origins, Development, and Mission of the Papacy

primacy over the whole Church should be more clearly differentiated from his patriarchal authority over the Latin church.

Throughout the first millennium, the pope exercised his primatial prerogatives in the Western patriarchate by consecrating metropolitans, granting the pallium to archbishops, and confirming lower episcopal nominations and ordinations. These functions, however, were not confused with the exercise of his universal primacy as the successor of Peter.[60] Later, when the churches of the East separated from the Petrine see, Rome's patriarchal primacy was mingled with that of its apostolic charge to the whole Church. Since Rome was left as the only patriarchal see in the West, the popes no longer discriminated between their rights and duties as patriarch and those as supreme pastor. In doctrine and practice, the two powers were merged. The bishops of Rome routinely invoked their fullness of power (*plenitudo potestatis*) for all interventions in other churches. Because of these historical factors, many of the functions which the pope currently discharges may well belong to his patriarchal primacy, even though they are commonly attributed to his Petrine ministry.

Congar, Ratzinger, and Tillard think that introducing this distinction into theology and practice would clarify the specific Petrine functions belonging to the pope's apostolic ministry. Because patriarchal authority is "by nature administrative and centralized," it would free the Petrine ministry to fulfill more readily the responsibilities proper to it.[61] This sorting out of the different levels of primatial duties has not yet begun. Even the revised Code of Canon Law for the Latin church fails to attribute any of the pope's tasks to his patriarchal responsibilities. Many roles which the pope now carries out, such as the appointment of bishops, could be more clearly identified as patriarchal rather than as papal. Applying this distinction would doubtlessly make a positive contribution to ecumenical dialogue with the Eastern churches separated from the Roman see. It would clear the way for putting into practice the principle that, when full communion is restored, the bishop of Rome would refrain from exercising his patriarchal authority over the East.

• **THESIS 17**   **The office of the pope is a ministry of service endowed with Christ's authority.**

Before the terminology of "ministry" and "service" became commonplace, Charles Journet recognized that papal authority "is given to the Pope for no other end than the service of the Church.... The Papacy is for the Church, not the Church for the Papacy."[62] The papal office is a pastoral service, which originated in the "birth" of Peter when Simon confessed his faith in Christ (cf. Mt 16:16). According to John Paul II, Peter is "born in the Church and for the Church. He is born for a particular service, to which there corresponds a particular charism." In the Church's journey toward the kingdom of God, she can "bind and loose," because she holds the "keys of the kingdom" (cf. Mt 16:19). Pope John Paul then concluded that "Peter is the first depositary of this power, which is a service (of this service which is a power)."[63]

The Second Vatican Council presented papal primacy as a ministry, and Paul VI developed the idea at length. Because this language lacks authoritarian overtones, it now has a secure place in the theology of the papacy. Pope Paul explained the meaning of papal authority as service. In a Lenten discourse to the Roman clergy, he said: "Is authority domination? Oh no, it is certainly not domination I must exercise over you. Is it the power of ruling, that is, an authority that decides without any other logic than that of impulse or subjective psychology? It is not that either. You know that it is a service. Our authority is ordained to service."[64] Whatever authority the pope exercises is ministerial. In the words of John Paul II, papal power serves the pope's "mission of service to the universal Church, which necessarily entails a corresponding authority precisely because of this service."[65]

Describing the papacy as a ministry reminds the Church that the authority of this ministerial office is spiritual. Von Balthasar recalls that, like all Christian authority, the pope's is "only to be exercised as one . . . undergoes humiliation, only to be exercised for the benefit of others who by it may become strong."[66] The successor of Peter exercises his primacy for the benefit of others so that they might be "strengthened" (cf. Lk 22:32). As a sharing in Christ's messianic mission, Peter's ministry entailed his participation in the sacrificial offering of the Good Shepherd who laid down his life for his sheep (cf. Jn 10:11). By consummating his pastoral service to the Church through martyrdom (cf. Jn 21:18-19), Peter confirmed his ministry and foretold the destiny of his successors. The Church's universal pastoral mission involves, and not only by way of supererogation, a profound sharing in the mystery of the cross. According to Ratzinger, "the primacy is to be understood first of all as witness to the confession of Christ on the basis of witness given personal warranty in martyrdom."[67] This is why the legend of Peter's wish to be crucified upside-down is so significant. In the Petrine ministry, the primacy of authority and of service are complementary.

• **THESIS 18**   **The servant of the servants of God enjoys a primacy of pastoral authority in the universal Church.**

Because the pope has a specific mission in the Church, he has the "power" necessary to carry out effectively the office assigned to him by Christ. Jurisdiction is a power ordained to the service of the community. Lukas Vischer rightly recognizes that "if the pope is to carry out his mission effectively, the office he possesses must have been given to him, and to him alone, by Christ. He must be independent of every other authority and be able to act on his own initiative. He must have direct authority over the entire Church."[68] This authority, often called jurisdiction, is intrinsic to the Petrine ministry, not belonging to it for purely human or historical reasons.[69] Because of the complementary nature of service and jurisdiction, the pope does not exercise authority as secular rulers do.

The First Vatican Council defined the primacy first given to Peter and later exercised by his successors as one of "jurisdiction" (cf. DS 3064). The Fathers used the legal language which Pope Leo the Great had introduced in order to establish solid credentials for papal authority. After Leo, the pope's responsibilities were increasingly described in juridical categories, culminating in the First Vatican Council's definition in *Pastor aeternus*.[70] Without maintaining that this language was the only way of describing papal authority, the bishops declared that Jesus gave Peter a "true and proper primacy of jurisdiction" (DS 3055). This language expressed a profoundly spiritual reality using terms taken from civil law. It created the impression that papal primacy was above all concerned with the efficient government of the universal Church.[71] Johann Auer points out that the term "primacy of jurisdiction" could "mislead one into a view of the Petrine and papal office that places the emphasis too much on legislation, jurisdiction, and administration in the various areas of the Church's life."[72] Today many theologians suggest that another vocabulary might be more suitable for describing the unique nature of the pope's primatial authority. If they can propose an alternative which expresses the same doctrinal meaning, the Church's magisterium could accept such a suggestion.

Canonists still consistently use the language of jurisdiction, while recent conciliar, theological, and papal writings prefer less legal-sounding terms. Vatican II refrained from using the term "jurisdiction," but spoke instead of the hierarchy's sacred "power."[73] In light of the council, Paul VI, too, favored less legal categories, referring to the pope's "primacy of service and of love,"[74] his "pastoral power,"[75] and his "ministry of love and of service on behalf of faith and discipline."[76] John Paul II speaks in the same way. He also systematically avoids the term "jurisdiction," substituting "power" in its place. The Pope has referred to the supreme "pastoral" authority proper to his mission "as a participation in the authority of the one Shepherd and Teacher, Christ."[77] It is evident, says John Paul II, that Jesus entrusted Peter with the keys of the kingdom so that "he might be the minister of his saving power in the Church."[78]

Another response to the theological problems raised by the pope's primacy of jurisdiction has been to shift the discussion away from the nature of papal authority to its purpose. The authority belonging to the papal office is given only to build up the Church (cf. 2 Cor 10:8). Papal jurisdiction is nothing more than the effective power (*potestas*) which God grants to the pope so that he can carry out his responsibilities. Rooted in the sacramentality of the episcopacy, it is unique: the bishop of Rome's pastoral service extends immediately to the universal Church. When jurisdiction is looked at from this viewpoint, it can alleviate the fears of those who oppose what they regard as the pope's supposedly untrammeled authority. Due to the input of ecumenical theology, the ecclesiology of communion, and the doctrine of episcopal collegiality, increasing attention is now being paid to the limits of papal jurisdiction. Even if not formulated canonically, there are real restrictions to the pope's authority: "the natural, divine, and ecclesiastical law; revelation, defined doctrine; and practical circumstances."[79] These limits derive from the nature of the Church and the purpose of the primacy: to strengthen the people of God in faith and communion.

• **THESIS 19**   **As the principal guardian of the Church's faith, the pope teaches authoritatively through his ordinary magisterium and infallibly through his extraordinary magisterium.**

Integral to the pope's ministry as pastor of the universal Church is the doctrinal mission he discharges. As head of the college of bishops, the successor of Peter, says John

Paul II, is "to establish and authoritatively confirm what the Church has received and believed from the beginning, what the apostles taught, what Sacred Scripture and Christian Tradition have determined as the object of faith and the Christian norm of life."[80] Following Peter, who was enlightened by divine revelation to confess Jesus' divine sonship (cf. Mt 16:16-17) and was introduced into the mystery of knowing the Son (cf. Mt 11:27), the bishop of Rome fulfills the Petrine ministry by preaching the gospel with the authority of Christ and under the guidance of the Spirit. This day-to-day teaching ministry depends for its exercise on a divinely given charism.

In certain situations, usually but not exclusively in times of crisis, the Church can make a decisive judgment about her faith and moral teaching. In order to preserve the truth of the gospel, she can define a doctrine to be believed as revealed or to be held definitively. When the Church teaches with this help of the Spirit, she shares in the divine attribute of infallibility or freedom from error. At the heart of Christianity is God's gift of himself to human persons. This communication of divine holiness and truth was given in its fullness to Christ's sacred humanity. Jesus, in turn, communicated this holiness and truth to his Church. Included among the gifts made to the apostles, and to Peter personally among them, was that of teaching without error the truth which God graciously shares with his people.[81] In today's Church, the two subjects which are entrusted with this gift of teaching infallibly are the bishops at an ecumenical council and the pope in making an *ex cathedra* pronouncement.

As the successor of Peter, the pope enjoys a personal charism of teaching infallibly. He can define the Church's belief in order to preserve the people of God from error in matters of faith and morals. When the bishop of Rome exercises his office of "strengthening the brethren" (cf. Lk 22:32) by teaching *ex cathedra*, the faithful are given the certitude that the truth of the gospel is proclaimed in his testimony.[82] Some theologians have suggested that, in the interest of Christian unity, the pope should voluntarily refrain from teaching infallibly in the future.[83] While this charism has been used only once since its definition by Vatican I, when Pius XII defined Mary's Assumption in 1950, the gift of infallibility is inherent in the papal office. Although a pope can choose not to use this charism, every pope must remain free to make an *ex cathedra* statement.

- **THESIS 20**   **The bishop of Rome is the visible center of the communion of churches and the steward of their unity.**

More than unity in the Spirit, ecclesial unity is visibly manifested in the communion of churches. The description of the Church as a communion of particular churches, each headed by a bishop, must also include the pope as the focal point of the universal *koinonia*. Before the Assembly of the World Council of Churches, John Paul II explained that "to be in communion with the bishop of Rome is to give visible evidence that one is in communion with all who confess that same faith."[84] The Second Vatican Council described the pope as "the perpetual and visible source and foundation of the unity both of the bishops and of the whole company of the faithful" (LG 23). As the visible principle and steward of unity, the bishop of Rome works to overcome any separatist and sectarian tendencies in the particular churches. He also promotes the inculturation of the gospel, encouraging the Church to expand the frontiers of her catholicity.[85]

Tillard explains the import of communion with the Roman see: "This Church and its *cathedra* have in the divine *oikonomia* the function of guaranteeing that the communion of all the other Churches and the other *cathedrae* are founded in apostolic unity: a unity of faith, of mission, of sending, of responsibility, of *exousia*, of honour."[86] Within the circle of communion, the bishop of Rome carries out these tasks, neither absorbing nor displacing an individual bishop's pastoral solicitude for his own church. The successor of Peter is the link which unites the bishops with one another, supporting them in their obligation to foster communion with every other church. As the visible center of unity and communion, the pope encourages communication and relations among the churches and their bishops.

The bishop of Rome is the Church's "personified center"[87] who guarantees the stability and cohesion of the *koinonia*. He is the fixed and stable point around which the communion of churches is built up in love. "The Pope must be the Church's heart," said Paul VI, "to make charity circulate, which comes from the heart and goes to the heart. He must be a cross-road for charity, receiving all and loving all."[88] This complex role entails both preserving the Church's unity and stimulating her catholicity so that she will become a more credible sign for the world.

The concept of a "corporate personality" is taken from the social sciences and has long been used in biblical studies. A corporate personality is a particular individual who embodies a group's self-understanding and can represent the whole. In turn, the group recognizes itself in the individual. This idea can be fruitfully applied to the relations between the pope and the other bishops.[89] The successor of Peter "represents" the bishops, and the bishops recognize the confirmation of their episcopal authority in the pope. He speaks and acts for the whole Church as well as for his brother bishops and their churches. Tillard calls the bishop of Rome "the carrier of the conscience of the College of Bishops."[90] As an image of the historical Peter who feeds Christ's sheep, the pope is a symbol of the ideal bishop. What bishops and their flocks believe and live is "summed up" in the bishop of Rome, and his belief and life strengthens them. As head of the episcopal college, the successor of Peter is the cohesive force uniting his brother bishops. Though the pope is always free to exercise his own primatial ministry, his office is nonetheless intrinsically related to the body of bishops with whom he is in communion. Similarly, the bishops cannot operate as a college without the successor of Peter.

The Petrine ministry ensures that the one faith of the Church will be confessed everywhere, and that the liturgy, ecclesiastical discipline, and the apostolate will be lived in full communion with the pope. Not the source of ecclesial unity, the successor of Peter is its guardian, defender, and promoter in the communion of churches. Only the Holy Spirit creates unity, but he uses the pope as a visible instrument, who watches over the Church's unity of faith and communion.

The pope's stature as a commanding religious authority extends beyond the frontiers of Christianity. Because of the Petrine ministry, he is impelled to take an active role in the affairs of the world. John Paul II has said that the pope is to be "not only the centre of the unity of the Church, but also the reference point for the universal desire for brotherhood and international cooperation among peoples, and to give constant proof of a firm will to meet the world. . . . The Holy See tries to go towards the world to meet it and collaborate with it."[91] In international life, the pope's ministry makes it possible for the Church to be an effective sign of hope and salvation, promoting the truths which undergird all social life.

- **THESIS 21**   Because the papal ministry is rooted in the mystery of the Incarnation, the pope is a symbol of Christ to the Church and to the world.

The pope has a particular office within the institutional structure of the Church which is "constituted and organized as society in the present world" (LG 8). Although a given pope might have special charismatic gifts, his authority is not of the prophetic kind belonging to the saints. Nor does he possess the authority of the professional theologian. Installed in his primatial office by rigorous electoral procedures, the pope exercises authority because he is invested with it by God. The papal office belongs to the Church's visible hierarchical structure.

Besides being a society, the Church is also, even primarily, a sacred reality. Therefore her leader, too, must in some way be a sacred figure. As the "prime celebrant of Christianity,"[92] the pope symbolizes both Christ and the Church. In his person, the bishop of Rome makes this twofold authority present and effective.

Consequently, even the contemporary papacy is surrounded by a certain aura of the sacred. In recent years, the popes have simplified the royal-like trappings which came to be attached to their office. Waving ostrich plumes at public ceremonies, kissing the pope's foot, and the papal nobility now belong to the past. Some of these practices and institutions were exaggerated and more appropriate to the court of a temporal sovereign. Even so, due to the uniqueness of his position, a certain awe and reverence still surround the pope. This is conveyed by distinctive dress, forms of address, and other gestures of respect. Precisely as a sacred symbol, the pope touches not just the rational but also the affective side of an individual's experience of the faith. No doubt this sense of the sacred accounts for the pope's religious appeal to the masses even in non-Catholic countries. It also explains the singular teaching value of his gestures. When Paul VI embraced Patriarch Athenagoras on the Mount of Olives, he told believers more about ecumenism than did the statements of the Second Vatican Council. Similarly, John Paul II's visit to the prison cell of his would-be assassin revealed more about forgiveness than his apostolic exhortation on reconciliation. Such symbolic gestures, too, belong to the pope's ministry of confirming the faithful (cf. Lk 22:32). Indirectly, they also manifest the fittingness of referring to him as the vicar of Christ.

The pope, of course, is not a replacement for an otherwise absent Christ. Like all the baptized, he represents Christ to the world. He does so according to the particular mission he has received as chief shepherd of the universal Church. Far from being a title of pretension, the designation "vicar of Christ" makes great demands on the pope to bring Christ's presence to others. In speaking to a group of Colombian peasants, Paul VI linked his own mission as Christ's vicar to Jesus' presence in those whom he was addressing: "And we who have the awesome destiny of being the vicar of Christ in his office of teaching the truth revealed by him, and in his pastoral ministry in the entire Catholic Church — we bow before you, and we wish to recognize Christ in you as if he were once more alive and suffering."[93]

Far from being a mystification of the papal office, the emphasis on its sacramentality saves it from being regarded as merely an administrative or secular function. More than an institution with an unbroken continuity of almost two millennia, the papacy makes Christ present today in the person of his vicar. Christ is the eternal Shepherd who never leaves his flock untended, and through the successor of Peter he continues to watch over and protect his Church. While all ecclesial ministers act in the person of Christ as head of the Church (cf. CCC 875), in virtue of Jesus' command that Peter was to feed his sheep (cf. Jn 21:15-17), the pope does this as the shepherd charged with pastoring the entire Christian community.

Though the bishops at the Second Vatican Council never referred to the pope as a "sacrament," Paul VI developed this theme in his own teaching. Such a sacramental vision suited his twofold intention: to retrieve Leo the Great's understanding of the papal office, and to transcend a juridical presentation of the Petrine ministry. According to Paul VI, the pope is a sacrament of encounter with Christ. He is, first of all, a sign of Christ, his representative. Because the pope is the vicar of Christ, he speaks and acts for him. In the words of Paul VI, "the very voice of Christ himself," reaches listeners "through the lips and ministry of his representative on earth; indeed, Jesus himself speaks with the accent of his vicar."[94] The pope, however, is never to draw attention to himself, since Christ, not his vicar, is the true head of the Church.

In a homily, Pope Paul once rhetorically asked the congregation: "And who am I?" He then answered: "I come to you therefore in the name of the Lord, and I would wish that when you look at me, you would have your thoughts not on my humble person but on him, on Jesus, who is present in my ministry."[95] According to Paul VI, the pope points the way to Christ. Because the vicar of Christ is his living icon, the successor of Peter must make Christ's love present. St. Ambrose (†397) called Peter the "vicar of his love" (PL 15, 1942). Applying this title to the pope, Paul VI said that "he is the witness and the herald of the love that Christ has had and has for us," and "the bearer of the light of the Lord, the light of his burning love."[96] In the same vein, John Paul II has expressly referred to the papal office as "a ministry of love, a service of love, as a response to the eternal and merciful love of God."[97]

***

On the ninth anniversary of his election, Paul VI shared with a public audience some personal reflections on the papal ministry. He wanted to remind the faithful that "it is not our weak and inexpert hand that is at the helm of Peter's bark, but that of the Lord Jesus, invisible but strong and loving." The Pope then cited the following from his notes written some years previously: "Perhaps the Lord has called me to this service not because of any aptitude of mine, not to govern and save the Church from her present difficulties, but to suffer something for the Church, and to make it clear that he, and no one else, guides her and saves her."[98] It is not "flesh and blood" which save, nor any office, but God alone.

The Church, which is built upon Peter's confession and that of his successors, is opposed by the "gates of hell" (cf. Mt 16:18-19). Peter's faith, echoed by his successor, "continues to be the rock against ideologies, against the reduction of the Word to what is plausible in a given age; against submission to the powers of this world."[99] In the great paradox, the "earthen vessel" (cf. 2 Cor 4:7) who fulfills the Petrine ministry has been made into bedrock through the power of God. Forces which seek to overcome this Rock shall not prevail.

Notes for Chapter sixteen

1. Hans Urs von Balthasar, *The Office of Peter and the Structure of the Church*, trans. Andrée Emery (San Francisco: Ignatius Press, 1986), 9.
2. Hans Urs von Balthasar, *Test Everything: Hold Fast to What Is Good*, trans. Maria Shrady (San Francisco: Ignatius Press, 1989), 58.
3. Patrick Granfield, *The Papacy in Transition* (Garden City: Doubleday & Company, 1980), 99.
4. Lukas Vischer, "The Reception of the Debate on Collegiality," in *The Reception of Vatican II*, ed. Giuseppe Alberigo, Jean-Pierre Jossua, and Joseph A. Komonchak, trans. Matthew J. O'Connell (Washington, D.C.: Catholic University of America Press, 1987), 240.
5. See the following dialogues: Orthodox-Roman Catholic Consultation in the United States, "Primacy and Conciliarity," *Origins*, 19:29 (December 21, 1989), 469-472; Comité Mixte Catholique-Orthodoxe en France, "Conclusions du Comité Mixte," in *La primauté romaine dans la communion des églises*, ed. Métropolite Jérémie and André Quélen (Paris: Cerf, 1991), 113-125; Anglican-Roman Catholic International Commission, *The Final Report* (London: SPCK, 1982), 47-98; U.S.A. National Committee, Lutheran World Federation and Bishops' Committee for Ecumenical and Interreligious Affairs, "Differing Attitudes Toward Papal Primacy," in *Papal Primacy and the Universal Church*, Lutherans and Catholics in Dialogue V, ed. Paul C. Empie and T. Austin Murphy (Minneapolis: Augsburg Publishing House, 1974), 9-42; U.S.A. National Committee, Lutheran World Federation and Bishops' Committee for Ecumenical and Interreligious Affairs, "Teaching Authority and Infallibility in the Church," in *Teaching Authority and Infallibility in the Church*, Lutherans and Catholics in Dialogue VI, ed. Paul C. Empie, T. Austin Murphy, and Joseph A. Burgess (Minneapolis: Augsburg Publishing House, 1980), 11-68; and Roman Catholic-Lutheran Joint Commission, "The Ministry in the Church," in *Growth in Agreement: Reports and Agreed Statements of Ecumenical Conversations on a World Level*, Ecumenical Documents II, ed. Harding Meyer and Lukas Vischer (New York: Paulist Press, 1984), 269-271.
6. John Paul II, *Redemptoris mater* (1987), #34.
7. Cited in *Towards the Healing of Schism*, Ecumenical Documents III, ed. E. J. Stormon (New York: Paulist Press, 1987), #173, p. 159.
8. Cited in *Towards the Healing of Schism*, #189, p. 172.
9. Joseph Ratzinger, *Principles of Catholic Theology: Building Stones for a Fundamental Theology*, trans. Mary Frances McCarthy (San Francisco: Ignatius Press, 1987), 199.
10. Joseph Ratzinger, "The Primacy of Peter," *L'Osservatore Romano*, 27 (July 8, 1991), 5.

Origins, Development, and Mission of the Papacy

11. Avery Dulles, *The Catholicity of the Church* (Oxford: Clarendon Press, 1985), 142.
12. Paul VI, Address to the Secretariat for Promoting Christian Unity, April 28, 1967, *The Pope Speaks*, 12:2 (1967), 101.
13. Hans Urs von Balthasar, *Elucidations*, trans. John Riches (London: SPCK, 1974), 99.
14. John Paul II, Discourse, February 24, 1993, *L'Osservatore Romano*, 9 (March 3, 1993), 11.
15. Hermann J. Pottmeyer, "Why Does the Church Need a Pope?" *Communio*, 18:3 (1991), 309.
16. Patrick Granfield, *The Limits of the Papacy* (New York: Crossroad Publishing Company, 1987), 133.
17. Von Balthasar, *The Office of Peter*, 21.
18. John Paul II, Address to the College of Cardinals and Roman Curia, December 22, 1987, *L'Osservatore Romano*, 2 (January 11, 1988), 6.
19. Hans Urs von Balthasar, *New Elucidations*, trans. Mary Theresilde Skerry (San Francisco: Ignatius Press, 1986), 193.
20. Heinrich Fries and Karl Rahner, *Unity of the Churches*, trans. Ruth C. L. Gritsch and Eric W. Gritsch (Philadelphia: Fortress Press, 1985), 65.
21. Pottmeyer, "Why Does the Church Need a Pope?" 308.
22. Edward Yarnold, "Theological Trends: The Papacy I," *The Way*, 19:3 (1979), 221-222.
23. José R. Villar, "El primado del Obispo de Roma en el diálogo católico-ortodoxo," *Diálogo Ecuménico*, 26 (1991), 153-156.
24. Congregation for the Doctrine of the Faith and the Pontifical Council for Promoting Christian Unity, "Response to ARCIC I Final Report," *Origins*, 21:28 (December 19, 1991), 445.
25. John Paul II, Homily, June 29, 1991, *L'Osservatore Romano*, 27 (July 8, 1991), 1.
26. Paul VI, *Vicariae potestatis* (1977), intro.
27. John Paul II, Homily, June 29, 1980, *L'Osservatore Romano*, 30 (July 28, 1980), 11.
28. John Paul II, Homily, June 29, 1994, *L'Osservatore Romano*, 27 (July 6, 1994), 3.
29. J. M. R. Tillard, *The Bishop of Rome*, trans. John de Satgé (Wilmington: Michael Glazier, 1983), 117.
30. John Paul II, Discourse, January 27, 1993, *L'Osservatore Romano*, (February 3, 1993), 11.
31. J. M. R. Tillard, *Church of Churches: The Ecclesiology of Communion*, trans. R. C. De Peaux (Collegeville: Liturgical Press, 1992), 306.
32. Irenaeus, *Against Heresies*, 3.3.3.
33. Tillard, *Church of Churches*, 260.
34. Tillard, *Church of Churches*, 264.
35. Tillard, *Church of Churches*, 284.
36. Roch Kereszty, "Peter and Paul and the Founding of the Church of Rome: Forgotten Perspectives," *Communio*, 15 (1988), 219.
37. John Paul II, Discourse, January 27, 1993, *L'Osservatore Romano*, 5 (February 3, 1993), 11.
38. Dulles, *The Catholicity of the Church*, 138; cf. Granfield, *Papacy in Transition*, 146-147.
39. Avery Dulles, *The Resilient Church* (Garden City: Doubleday & Company, 1977), 117-118.
40. See Karl Rahner, "Basic Observations on the Subject of Changeable and Unchangeable Factors in the Church," in *Theological Investigations*, trans. David Bourke, vol. 14 (London: Darton, Longman & Todd, 1976), 3-23; and "Reflection on the Concept of 'Ius Divinum' in Catholic Thought," in *Theological Investigations*, trans. Karl-H. Kruger, vol. 5 (London: Darton, Longman & Todd, 1966), 219-243.
41. Avery Dulles, "*Ius Divinum* as an Ecumenical Problem," *Theological Studies*, 38 (1977), 702.
42. American Lutheran-Catholic Dialogue, *Differing Attitudes Toward Papal Primacy* (1974), #42, p. 31.

43. International Roman Catholic-Lutheran Commission, "Ways to Community" (1980), in *Growth in Agreement: Reports and Agreed Statements of Ecumenical Conversations on a World Level*, Ecumenical Documents II, ed. Harding Meyer and Lukas Vischer (New York: Paulist Press, 1984), 219.
44. ARCIC, *Authority in the Church I* (1976), #23; *Authority in the Church II* (1981), #9.
45. United States Conference of Catholic Bishops, "Evaluation of the Final Report," *Origins*, 14:25 (December 6, 1984), 412; cf. Tillard, *Church of Churches*, 292-293.
46. See ARCIC, *Authority in the Church I* (1976), #12; American Lutheran-Catholic Dialogue, *Differing Attitudes Toward Papal Primacy* (1974), #40-46.
47. Karl-Heinz Ohlig, *Why We Need the Pope* (St. Meinrad: Abbey Press, 1975), 120-123, 137; Hans Küng, *The Church*, trans. Ray and Rosaleen Ockenden (New York: Sheed and Ward, 1967), 409-413, 476; and Hans Küng, *On Being a Christian* (Glasgow: Collins, 1978), 491, 500.
48. [Unnamed authority], "Church Unity Rooted in Eucharist," *L'Osservatore Romano*, 27 (July 7, 1993), 4.
49. Hans Urs von Balthasar, *In the Fullness of Faith*, trans. Graham Harrison (San Francisco: Ignatius Press, 1988), 99.
50. Congregation for the Doctrine of the Faith, "Observations on the ARCIC Final Report," *Origins*, 11:47 (1982), #B.III.2, p. 755.
51. Joseph Ratzinger, *Church, Ecumenism and Politics*, trans. Robert Nowell (New York: Crossroad Publishing Company, 1988), 77-78.
52. Pottmeyer, "Why Does the Church Need a Pope?" 312.
53. John P. Galvin, "Papal Primacy in Contemporary Roman Catholic Theology," *Theological Studies*, 47 (1986), 287.
54. Karl Rahner, "Pseudo-Problems in Ecumenical Discussion," in *Theological Investigations*, trans. Edward Quinn, vol. 18 (New York: Crossroad Publishing Company, 1983), 43.
55. Cuthbert Rand, "The Universal Pastoral Ministry of the Bishop of Rome: A Roman Catholic Approach," *One in Christ*, 22:1 (1986), 5.
56. Paul Misner, "The Papacy: Three Schools of Thought," *The Ecumenist*, 11 (1973), 54.
57. Karl Rahner, *Vorfragen zu einem ökumenishen Amtsverständnis*, Quaestiones Disputatae, 65 (Freiburg: Herder, 1974), 25-32.
58. Avery Dulles, "Papal Authority in Roman Catholicism," in *A Pope for All Christians?* ed. Peter J. McCord (New York: Paulist Press, 1976), 55.
59. Gustave Thils, *Primauté et infaillibilité du pontife romain à Vatican I*, (Louvain: University Press, 1989), 288-289.
60. Vittorio Peri, "Local Churches and Catholicity in the First Millennium of the Roman Tradition," *The Jurist*, 52:1 (1992), 106.
61. Tillard, *Church of Churches*, 270.
62. Charles Journet, *The Church of the Word Incarnate* (New York, 1955), 423-424.
63. John Paul II, Homily, June 29, 1985, *L'Osservatore Romano*, 27 (July 8, 1985), 6.
64. Paul VI, Discourse, February 10, 1975, *L'Osservatore Romano*, 8 (February 20, 1975), 3.
65. John Paul II, Discourse, February 24, 1993, *L'Osservatore Romano*, 9 (March 3, 1993), 11.
66. Von Balthasar, *Elucidations*, 103.
67. Ratzinger, *Church, Ecumenism and Politics*, 38.
68. Vischer, "Reception of the Debate on Collegiality," 239.
69. Congregation for the Doctrine of the Faith, "Observations on the ARCIC Final Report," #B.III.2, p. 755.

370 ✦ FACING THE FUTURE: 21 THESES ON THE PAPAL MINISTRY

70. Rand, "The Universal Pastoral Ministry of the Bishop of Rome," 16.
71. Klaus Schatz, *La primauté du Pape*, trans. Joseph Hoffmann (Paris: Cerf, 1992), 258.
72. Johann Auer, *The Church: The Universal Sacrament of Salvation*, Dogmatic Theology, trans. Michael Waldstein, vol. 8 (Washington, D.C.: Catholic University of America Press, 1993), 288.
73. Severino Dianich, "Papa: aspetto teologico," *Nuovo dizionario di teologia*, ed. Giuseppe Barbaglio and Severino Dianich, 6th ed. (Milan: Edizioni Paoline, 1991), 1095.
74. Paul VI, Discourse, February 24, 1977, *L'Osservatore Romano*, 10 (March 10, 1977), 12.
75. Paul VI, Discourse, June 17, 1970, *L'Osservatore Romano*, 26 (June 25, 1970), 12.
76. Paul VI, Homily, June 29, 1978, *L'Osservatore Romano*, 27 (July 6, 1978), 3.
77. John Paul II, Discourse, July 1, 1992, *L'Osservatore Romano*, 27 (July 8, 1992), 11.
78. John Paul II, Discourse, November 25, 1992, *L'Osservatore Romano*, 48 (December 2, 1992), 19.
79. Granfield, *Limits of the Papacy*, 76.
80. John Paul II, Discourse, March 10, 1993, *L'Osservatore Romano*, 11 (March 17, 1993), 11.
81. Jean Daniélou, "The Infallibility of the Church," *L'Osservatore Romano*, 3 (January 20, 1972), 3.
82. Congregation for the Doctrine of the Faith, "Observations on the ARCIC Final Report," #B.III.3, p. 755.
83. Granfield, *Limits of the Papacy*, 187-188.
84. John Paul II, Address to the World Council of Churches, Geneva, June 12, 1984, *Origins*, 14:7 (June 28, 1984), 99.
85. Hans Urs von Balthasar, *A Short Primer for Unsettled Laymen*, trans. Mary Theresilde Skerry (San Francisco: Ignatius Press, 1985), 102, 104.
86. J. M. R. Tillard, "The Presence of Peter in the Ministry of the Bishop of Rome," *One in Christ*, 27:2 (1991), 114.
87. Paul VI, Discourse, December 10, 1969, *L'Osservatore Romano*, 51 (December 18, 1969), 12.
88. Paul VI, Discourse, October 27, 1969, *L'Osservatore Romano*, 45 (November 6, 1969), 1.
89. Tillard, *Bishop of Rome*, 157-164.
90. J. M. R. Tillard, "Petrine Office," *New Catholic Encyclopedia*, vol. 18 (Washington, D.C.: Catholic University of America Press, 1989), 375.
91. John Paul II, Address to the College of Cardinals and Roman Curia, December 22, 1980, *L'Osservatore Romano*, 2 (January 12, 1981), 5-6.
92. Andrew Greeley, "Advantages and Drawbacks of a Center of Communications in the Church," *Concilium*, 64 (1971), 327.
93. Paul VI, Discourse to "Campesinos," Bogotá, August 23, 1968, *L'Osservatore Romano*, 23 (September 5, 1968), 4.
94. Paul VI, Discourse, March 13, 1966, *Insegnamenti di Paolo VI*, vol. 4 (Vatican City: Polyglot Press, 1967), 1013.
95. Paul VI, Homily, Bogotá, August 24, 1968, *L'Osservatore Romano*, 23 (September 5, 1968), 8.
96. Paul VI, Discourse, June 2, 1967, *Insegnamenti di Paolo VI*, vol. 5 (Vatican City: Polyglot Press, 1968), 791.
97. John Paul II, Address to the College of Cardinals and Roman Curia, June 28, 1984, *L'Osservatore Romano*, 29 (July 16, 1984), 6.
98. Paul VI, Discourse, June 21, 1972, *L'Osservatore Romano*, 26 (June 29, 1972), 1.
99. Ratzinger, "The Primacy of Peter," 8.

Index

Acacian schism (482-519) 126, 197
Act of Supremacy (1534) 108
Active legation, right of 313-314
Ad gentes (1965) 217, 224, 241, 262
Ad limina discourses 175
Ad limina visits
  meeting with pope 250
  origin of 97, 249
  purpose of 249-250
Adam, Karl 15, 32
Administration of the Patrimony of the Apostolic
    See (APSA) 312
Afanassieff, Nicolas 260
Affective collegiality
  among bishops 218-219, 245-246
  between bishops and pope 230, 234-235, 237,
    238, 240-241, 250, 251, 304, 364
Agostino Trionfo 102
Ailly, Pierre d' 104
Alberigo, Giuseppe 316, 317
Alexander I, Pope, Saint 279
Alexander III, Pope 164
Alexander VI, Pope 9, 338
Alexander VIII, Pope 206
Alexandria, see of 83, 96, 115, 119-121
Alfrink, Bernard, Cardinal 302
Allmen, Jean-Jacques von 285
Ambrose, Saint 82, 366
Anacletus, Pope, Saint 60, 65, 278
Anastasius, Emperor 94
Anglican-Roman Catholic International
    Commission (ARCIC) 62, 310, 356
Anglicans and the papacy 108-109, 356
Anselm of Havelberg 131
Anselm of Lucca, Saint 99
Antichrist, pope as 10, 106-108, 111
Anti-Roman complex 346-347
Antioch
  Peter and Paul at 40-43
  see of 83, 96, 115, 119-121, 145
Apostolic Camera 311-312
Apostolic canon 34 120
Apostolic college 38-39, 54-56, 147, 220-222
Apostolic constitution 174
Apostolic delegate *See* Representative, papal
Apostolic exhortation 174, 240
Apostolic nuncio *See* Representative, papal

Apostolic Penitentiary 309
Apostolic See *See* Holy See
Apostolic Signatura 149, 309
Apostolic succession 54-60, 62, 73, 78-79, 223,
    266, 278, 350, 351
Apostolic visitation 249, 267-268
Apostolica sollicitudo (1965) 238, 239
Aquinas *See* Thomas Aquinas, Saint
Arianism 125
Assumption 72, 174, 194, 201, 204, 363
Athanasius, Saint 64
Athenagoras, Patriarch 347, 365
Auer, Johann 14, 18, 221, 262, 362
Augustine, Saint 28, 169, 294
Avignon 104, 313, 322

Babylonian Captivity (1309-1377) 104
Balthasar, Hans Urs von 26, 77, 148, 213, 229,
    266, 293, 294, 346, 348-349, 357, 361
Barbarito, Luigi 324
Basil, Saint 117, 125
Battifol, Pierre 127
Bea, Augustin, Cardinal 173
Beagle Channel dispute 338
Beal, John 267
Bellarmine, Robert, Saint 109-110, 141, 165, 192,
    292
Benedict XIV, Pope 177
Benedict XV, Pope 177, 311, 331, 336, 337
Bernard of Clairvaux, Saint 101
Beyer, Jean 214
Bishop of the Catholic Church (title) 151
Bishop of Rome (title) 217
Bishops (Episcopacy)
  See also Ad limina visits, Collegiality, Episcopal
    college, Episcopal conference,
  and monarchical episcopate 59-60, 355
  nomination of 98, 272-273, 306, 308, 316-317,
    329, 334, 339, 360
  as successors of the apostles 56-59, 157, 215,
    220-220
  teaching authority of 57-58, 122, 164, 165, 179,
    182, 190-191, 222
  at Vatican I 155-158, 194, 212-214
  at Vatican II 215
  as vicars of Christ 147, 224-225, 304
Bismarck, Otto von, Chancellor 157

371

Bonaventure, Saint 102-103
Boniface I, Pope, Saint 78
Boniface II, Pope 279
Boniface VIII, Pope 95, 103-104, 111, 357
Bossuet, Jacques 192-193
Bouyer, Louis 27, 39, 42, 53, 57, 58-59, 152, 156-157, 221, 258, 270, 293-294, 307
Brown, Raymond E. 20, 37, 39, 44, 46, 61, 62, 258
Bull, papal 174
Burns, Patrick 293

Cabasilas, Nicholas, Archbishop 131
Cajetan, Cardinal (Tommaso de Vio) 292, 294-295
Callistus I, Pope, Saint 81, 83
Callistus II, Pope 329
Canonical mission
  of bishops 224
  of theologians 177
Canonization 307, 308
Cardinal Secretary of State 306
Caroline divines, Anglican 108-109
Casaroli, Agostino 324, 331, 333, 334, 338, 339
Catechism of the Catholic Church 19, 20, 32, 54, 171, 174, 180, 188, 199, 217, 220, 223, 224, 225, 245, 248, 258, 261, 270, 299, 301, 302, 315, 318, 329
Cathedra Petri (Chair of Peter) 76, 77, 81-82, 117, 265, 266
Catholic Reform and the papacy 109-110
  See also Trent, Council of
  and *ad limina* visits 249
  and curia, Roman, reform of 300-301
  and infallibility, papal 192-193
Catholicity, pope as advocate of 248, 250, 264-265, 315, 363-364
Causae maiores 77-78, 123, 301
Celestine I, Pope, Saint 84, 122
Celestine V, Pope, Saint 289
Centesimus annus (1991) 179, 335
Chadwick, Henry 108
Chalcedon, Council of (451) 86, 87, 119-120, 122, 125, 135, 207, 236
Charlemagne 95
Chesterton, Gilbert Keith 294
Chirico, Peter 202, 205
Christus Dominus (1965) 171, 216, 217, 222, 223, 238, 245, 261
Clement I, Pope, Saint 51, 57, 61, 62, 65, 73-74, 88, 278
Clement IV, Pope 132

Code of Canon Law (1917) 151, 213, 241, 301, 311, 315
Code of Canon Law (1983), canons on
  ad limina visits 249
  assent to non-definitive teaching 182
  bishops, teaching authority of 171
  Church as communion 216
  college of cardinals 242-244, 283
  concordats 329-330
  consecrated life 308
  curia, Roman 299, 301
  ecumenical councils 235-236
  episcopal conference 245, 247, 248
  Holy See 304, 323
  impeded see 290-291
  jurisdiction, papal 149-150, 152, 154, 157, 213, 286, 353
  legation, right of 313-314
  papal-episcopal relations 220, 223-224, 228, 229
  particular church 258
  recognitio, papal 269
  representative, papal, duties of 315-316
  reservation, papal 268-269
  resignation, papal 289
  supreme authority of episcopal college 225
  synod of bishops 238-240
  titles, papal 217, 360
Code of Canon Law for the Eastern Churches (1990) 149, 174
College of cardinals
  as collegial body 242, 243-244, 300, 301
  divine right of 243
  and election, papal, role in 152, 281-282, 283-289
  functions of 243-244
  internationalization of 283, 286
  membership of 242-243
  origin of 242-243, 300
  and Roman church 219, 281, 283-286, 291, 300
  as senate of pope 241, 243
Collegial spirit *See* Affective collegiality
Collegiality
  See also Bishops, Episcopal college
  and *ad limina* visits 248-250
  in apostolic Church 38-39, 54-56, 312, 349
  as affective 218-219, 230, 234-235, 237, 238, 240-241, 245-246, 250, 251, 304, 364
  and college of cardinals 241-244
  and corporate personality of pope 364
  and curia, Roman 302, 316-317
  and dispersed episcopate 237

divine right of 235
in early Church 218-219
in East 120
and ecumenical councils 235-237
as effective 234-237, 240-241
and election of pope 283-284
and episcopal conference 244-248
in Leo the Great 87-88
in Middle Ages 219
origins of 217-219
and representative, papal 315-316
and synod of bishops 238-241
at Vatican II 212, 215, 217-218, 220-225, 227, 348-349
and visits, papal 250-252
Cologne Declaration (1989) 318
Commission for Religious Relations with Jews 310
Commissum nobis (1904) 282
Communion, ecclesiology of 215-216, 230, 257, 273, 285, 302, 316, 317, 347, 353, 362
Communionis notio (1992) 216, 261, 262, 263, 357, 358
Communism 332, 336
Conciliarism 104-106, 111, 140, 148, 150, 165, 192, 196, 219, 225, 226, 291, 292
Conclave 282-283, 286-287
Concordat of Worms (1122) 329
Concordats 316, 329-330, 339
Conference on Security and Cooperation in Europe 330, 337
Conference of bishops *See* Episcopal conference
Congar, Yves, Cardinal 32, 58, 98, 123, 126, 164, 180, 192, 227, 229, 293, 360
Congregation for Bishops 308
Congregation for Catholic Education 309
Congregation for the Causes of Saints 308
Congregation for the Clergy 308
Congregation for Divine Worship and the Discipline of the Sacraments 308
Congregation for the Doctrine of the Faith 173, 175-176, 182, 183, 307, 308, 310, 358
  See also Communio notio, Donum veritatis, Mysterium ecclesiae
Congregation for the Evangelization of Peoples 308
Congregation for Institutes of Consecrated Life and Societies of Apostolic Life 308-309
Congregation for Oriental Churches 307, 308
Congregations (*plenaria*) 301, 302, 306-307, 317
Congress of Vienna (1815) 313, 314, 323

Consistory 244, 300, 301
Constance, Council of (1414-1418) 105-106
Constantine, Emperor 52, 93, 96, 97, 119
Constantinople I, Council of (381) 64, 82, 119
Constantinople IV, Council of (869-870) 197
Constantinople, see of 83, 96, 118-119, 120-121, 130-132, 300
Convention of Vienna (1961) 313
Coriden, James 139
Cornelius, Pope, Saint 34-36, 53, 76, 279
Corporate personality, pope as 364
Council for European Episcopal Conferences (CCEE) 245
Council of Latin American Episcopal Conferences (CELAM) 245
Council for the Public Affairs of the Church 302, 306
Counter Reformation *See* Catholic Reform and the papacy
Cullmann, Oscar 14, 16, 32-33, 35, 39, 53
Cunningham, Agnes 73
Curia, Roman
  See also Representative, papal
  authority of 149, 175, 304-305
  collegiality of 304, 307
  documents of 173, 175-176, 180, 183, 307
  and Holy See 304, 322
  internationalization of 301-302, 316
  need for 299, 300-301, 303-304
  organizational structure of 305-312
  origin of 299-301
  and Petrine ministry, participation in 303-305
  reform of, proposals for 316-317
  reforms in, post-Vatican II 301-303
Cwiekowski, Frederick J. 104
Cyprian of Carthage, Saint 76, 81-82, 219, 264, 279
Cyril and Methodius, Saints 128, 178

D'Avanzo, Bishop 142
Damasus I, Pope, Saint 77, 82-83, 84, 125
De ecclesia Christi (Vatican I) 140, 142, 146
De Paolis, Velasio 305
Decretal, papal 87, 114
Decretals of Gratian (*Decretum Gratiani*) 99, 192, 292
Dei Filius (1870) 140
Dei verbum (1965) 12, 50, 72, 166, 169, 170, 188, 191, 200
Deposition of pope 105, 291-293

Origins, Development, and Mission of the Papacy

Dictatus papae 98-100
Dionysius, Bishop 51
Dioscorus, antipope 279
Diplomacy, papal
  See also Holy See; World affairs, pope's role in
  and concordats 316, 329-330, 339
  evaluation of 339-340
  and international organizations 330-331
  objectives of 333-338
  and relations with states 327-329
Diplomatic corps of Holy See 306, 312-316, 317-318, 326, 340
Divine design of historical papacy 353-357
Divine right of papacy 106, 107, 127, 157, 221, 260, 272-273, 284, 304
Donation of Constantine 96, 97
Donatism 294
Donum veritatis (1990) 168, 169, 171, 172, 173, 176, 180, 182, 190, 199, 200
Droit de regard 329
Drucker, Peter 305
Dual apostolicity *See* Peter and Paul, Saints
Dulles, Avery 102, 172, 247, 248, 348, 354, 359

Ecclesia romana 243, 291-292
Eck, John 106
Ecumenical councils
  approval of decrees 236
  in canon law 236-237
  in conciliarism 104-106
  convocation of 226, 236
  and East 121-123
  and judgment of heresy 292-293
  legation, right of 236, 312
  in Leo the Great 86, 122
  in papal monarchy theory 226
  at Vatican I 148-149
Ecumenical dialogue on papacy 285, 310, 347-348, 354-355, 356, 359-360
Edict of Milan (313) 82, 93, 295
Election, papal
  See also Conclave
  acceptance by one elected 288
  by acclamation 287
  candidates eligible for 286
  and college of cardinals, role in 281-282, 283-288, 291
  in conclave 286-287
  by delegation 287
  by designation 278-279
  imperial confirmation of 280
  interference in, by temporal powers 280-281, 282-283
  lay participation in 279-280
  and pre-electoral pacts 282
  reform of, proposals for 283-284
  and Roman community, role in 279-280
  by scrutiny 278-279
  taking of new name 288-289
  veto (*exclusiva*), right of 282-283
Encyclicals
  definition and origin of 177-178
  as disciplinary 179
  as doctrinal 178-179
  exaggerated authority of 179-180
  as exhortatory 179
English Litany (1544) 108
Enlightenment 140
Eno, Robert 59, 61, 62, 122, 125
Ephesus, Council of (431) 84, 120-121, 122, 204
Ephraim, Saint 116
Episcopacy *See* Apostolic succession, Bishops, Collegiality, Episcopal college, Episcopal conference
Episcopal college
  See also Apostolic succession, Bishops, Collegiality, Episcopal conference
  co-responsibility for universal Church 222-223, 229, 238, 241, 246, 304
  corporate authority of 222
  and curia, Roman 222-223, 303-304
  dispersed throughout the world 237
  as one body 220
  pope as head of 146, 152, 154, 217, 221, 228-229, 286, 362-363
  as primatially structured 221, 223-225, 227-228, 230
  as stable group 221-222
  as subject of supreme ecclesial authority 220-221, 226-228
Episcopal conference
  and affective collegiality 245-246
  origin of 244-245
  and relations with Holy See 246-248, 269, 303
  teaching authority of 247-248
Episcopal jurisdiction, papal 150-152, 155-158, 262-263
Eusebius of Caesarea 51, 52, 65, 74, 75, 287
Evaristus, Pope, Saint 65, 278
Ex cathedra statements *See* Infallibility, papal

Extraordinary magisterium *See* Infallibility, papal
Fabian, Pope, Saint 287
False Decretals 96
Farmer, William 40, 43
Febronianism 106, 140
Felix IV, Pope, Saint 279
Filioque 126, 129, 134
Firmilian of Caesarea, Saint 82
Florence, Council of (1431-1445) 102, 109, 133-134, 135, 149, 165, 197
Four Articles of the Gallican Clergy (1682) 193, 206
Franz Joseph, Emperor 282
French Revolution 140, 193
Frequens (1417) 105, 140
Full jurisdiction, papal 123-124, 149-150
Fullness of power *See Plenitudo potestatis*

Gaius, Roman priest 52
Galilei, Galileo 168
Gallicanism 106, 140-141, 142, 146, 148, 201, 202, 206, 219, 225
Galvin, John 358
Gasser, Vincenz Ferrer, Bishop 179, 194, 195, 196, 198, 200, 201, 202, 203, 204, 206
Gaudium et spes (1965) 329, 335
Gelasius I, Pope, Saint 94-95, 97, 101, 110, 191
General Affairs (Secretariat of State, First Section) 306
German bishops, declaration (1875) 157-158
German bishops, pastoral letter (1967) 168
Gerson, John 104
Ghirlanda, Gianfranco 226
Gill, Joseph 134
Gnosticism 57, 78
Graham, Robert A. 332
Granfield, Patrick 139, 155, 207, 215-216, 222, 234, 241, 268, 290, 347, 349
Gratian 101, 165, 192, 292
Gregorian Reform 96-100, 101, 110, 131, 164, 219, 242-244, 249, 251, 265, 267, 280-281, 291-292, 295, 300
Gregory the Great, Pope, Saint 87, 129, 147, 157
Gregory VII, Pope, Saint 96-100, 249, 267
Gregory XIII, Pope 313
Gregory XVI, Pope 177
Gregory of Nazianzus, Saint 125
Grisez, Germain 181
Gulf War 326, 333

Hadrian VI, Pope 288
Haec sancta (1415) 105, 140
Hamer, Jerome 190
Head of episcopal college, pope as 146, 152, 154, 217, 221, 228-229, 286, 362-363
Hebblethwaite, Peter 305, 317
Hegesippus 65
Hennesey, James 315
Henry V, Emperor 329
Henry VIII, King 149
Heresy and loss of papacy 104, 291-293
Hermas, Shepherd of 61-62
Hertling, Ludwig 64, 76, 265
Hierarchical communion 222-225, 246, 247, 250, 252, 253, 260, 262-263, 271, 272, 357
Hill, Edmund 52, 206
Holy Father (title) 101
Holy (Apostolic) See
  See also Curia, Roman; Diplomacy, papal; World affairs, pope's role in
  and defense of human dignity 335-336
  definition of 304, 323
  and diplomatic relations with states 327-329
  and ethics in international order 331, 334-335
  and international organizations 306, 310-311, 330-331, 335-336
  as mediator of disputes 338
  as moral person 323
  neutrality of 331-333
  and promotion of development 337-338
  and pursuit of peace 333, 336-337
  and religious liberty 329, 333-334
  sovereignty of 313-314, 323-325, 327, 330, 331
  as subject of international law, 323-324, 327, 330, 340
  and Vatican City State, relation to 322-324
Hormisdas, Pope, Saint 126, 197
Humanae vitae (1968) 172, 173, 176, 178
Humani generis (1950) 178, 180
Humbert of Silva Candida, Cardinal 130
Hunthausen, Raymond, Archbishop 268

Iconoclasts 117, 126
Ignatius of Antioch, Saint 51, 59, 61, 75-76, 80, 88, 352
Immaculate Conception 72, 194, 202, 204
Immediate jurisdiction, papal 102, 152-154, 156-158, 263, 270, 285
Immensae aeterni Dei (1588) 300-301
Immorality of pope 293-295
Impeccability of pope 188

In forma communi 175
In forma specifica 175, 304
In nomine Domini (1059) 280-281, 282
Indefectibility of Church 189-190, 259, 293-294
Infallibilists (Vatican I) 193, 201
Infallibility, conciliar 191, 192, 363
Infallibility, papal
  attributed to ordinary magisterium 179-180
  basis in Scripture 196, 363
  basis in tradition 196-197
  as charism of assistance 176, 195-196, 363
  conditions for exercise of 201-203, 304
  and consent of Church 206-207
  and consultation 203-206
  definition of 193
  and Marian definitions 204
  misunderstandings of 188-189
  origin of 191-193
  as personal 195, 201-202, 304
  primary objects of 198, 200
  purpose of 194
  reception of, by Church 207
  response of faithful to 200-201
  secondary objects of 198-201
  source of 194-195
  and truth 189
  and Vatican I, debate on 193-194
Infallibility of entire Church 190-191
Innocent I, Pope, Saint 77-78
Innocent III, Pope 101, 111, 131, 288, 292
Innocent IV, Pope 174
Innocent X, Pope 66
International Theological Commission 56, 173, 245, 261, 307
Intervention in a particular church, papal 156-58, 266-273
Irenaeus of Lyons, Saint 57-58, 60, 65, 75, 78-80, 163, 278
Isidore of Seville, Saint 96

Jaki, Stanley L. 15, 35
James (Lord's brother) 36, 41, 42, 53-54, 59
Jedin, Herbert 109
Jerome, Saint 77
Jerusalem
  apostolic council at 36, 42, 46, 74, 122
  see of 53-54, 96, 120-121, 145, 259
Jewel, John, Bishop 108
John 21:15-17
  and Jesus' forgiveness, Peter's love 22-23

  and Peter/pope as pastor 23-25, 28, 44-45, 350, 366
John II, Pope 288
John VIII, Emperor 133
John VIII, Pope 127
John X Camateros, Patriarch 131
John XII, Pope 288
John XXII, Pope 100
John XXIII, Pope 177, 178, 179, 236, 242, 251, 310, 335, 337, 338
John the Baptist, Saint 37, 51, 349
John Chrysostom, Saint 66, 117
John Damascene, Saint 126
John of St. Thomas 292
John of Torquemada 292
John Paul I, Pope 289
John Paul II, Pope
  and Church as communion 216, 317
  and college of cardinals 242, 243, 244
  and collegiality 221, 235, 238, 239, 240, 244
  and curia, Roman 299, 302, 303, 305, 308, 318-319
  and diplomatic relations with states 327-328
  and ethics in international life 334-335
  and Galileo controversy 168
  and Holy See 323, 324, 325, 332, 333, 364-365
  and human dignity, defense of 335
  and humanitarian initiatives 337-338
  and infallibility, papal 199, 205
  and international organizations 330-331
  job description of pope 273
  and jurisdiction, papal 147, 150, 153
  letters to heads of state by 326
  magisterial documents of 172, 174-175, 177-179
  and Orthodox churches, relations with 115, 347
  and particular churches 259, 262, 263, 264
  and Petrine ministry 76, 360, 361, 362, 366
  and pope as custodian of faith 170, 362-363
  and pope as heir of Paul 66, 351, 352
  and synod of bishops 238, 239, 240
  and Vatican II, papacy at 229, 349
  and vicar of Christ, title of 217
  and visits, pastoral 251-252
  and women priests 177
Josephinism 106, 140
Journet, Charles, Cardinal 227, 360
Judge, pope as *See* Supreme judge, pope as; Supreme jurisdiction, papal
Julian of Cos, Bishop 312
Julius II, Pope 251, 288

Jurisdiction, papal
  See also Episcopal jurisdiction, papal; Full jurisdiction, papal; Immediate jurisdiction, papal; Ordinary jurisdiction, papal; Supreme jurisdiction, papal; Universal jurisdiction, papal
  beginning of 151-152, 281, 285, 286
  and East 123-124, 348
  purpose of 145-147, 360, 362
  as service 147-148, 360-361
  terminology of 361-362
Justinian, Emperor 121

Karrer, Otto 42, 54
Kasper, Walter, Bishop 206, 262
Kereszty, Roch 65, 79, 80
Kerkhofs, Jan 316-317
Kerr, Fergus 147
Kloppenburg, Bonaventure 246
Krementz, Philip, Cardinal 146
Küng, Hans 284, 290, 356

Laetentur coeli (1439) 133
Laghi, Pio, Cardinal 268
Lateran III, Council of (1179) 281
Lateran IV, Council of (1215) 132
Lateran Pacts (1929) 322, 324, 331
Lateran Treaty (1929) 323, 331
Laud, William, Archbishop 109
Law of Guarantees (1871) 322
Lay investiture 96, 97, 110, 329
Lécuyer, Joseph 316
Legate, papal *See* Representative, papal
Legation, right of 313-314
Legrand, Hervé 262
Leo the Great, Pope, Saint 64, 66, 84-88, 98, 120, 122, 125, 163, 164, 279, 294, 312, 361, 366
Leo III, Pope, Saint 95
Leo IX, Pope, Saint 130, 251
Leo XIII, Pope 177, 179
Libellus Hormisdae (519) 125-126
Liberian Catalog 60-61
Licet de vitanda (1179) 281
Limits to papal authority 154-158, 269-273, 358, 360, 362
Linus, Pope, Saint 60, 65, 278
Local church, ecclesiology of 118, 120, 122, 123, 215-216, 257-263, 271, 285, 317, 347, 348, 357
  See also Particular church
Lombard, Peter 101
Loomis, Louise Ropes 125

Lubac, Henri de, Cardinal 72, 229, 237, 238, 247, 258, 259, 261, 272, 284-285
Lucius III, Pope 164
Luke 22:31-32
  and Jesus' promise of prayer 21, 86, 350
  and Peter's mission despite weakness 26, 350
  as proof text for papal infallibility 195, 196, 363
  and strengthening the brethren 21, 28, 32, 33, 86, 117, 177, 195, 229, 318-319, 329, 361, 363, 365
Lumen gentium (1964) 55, 57, 58, 102, 147, 148, 154, 157, 162, 169, 176, 180, 182, 183, 190, 195, 197, 198, 199, 205, 207, 215, 216, 217, 218, 220, 221, 224-226, 228, 234, 235, 237, 240, 245, 250, 257-258, 261-263, 265, 269, 304, 363, 365
Luther, Martin 106-108
Lutheran World Federation 310, 356
Lutherans and the papacy 106-108, 347, 356
Lyons II, Council of (1274) 132-133, 197, 281-282

Macaulay, Thomas Babington 9
McDonnell, Kilian 97-98, 195
McManus, Frederick 269
Magisterium, ordinary papal
  assent to 180-182
  assessing degrees of authority of 176-177
  in Catholic Reform 165-166
  as divinely guided 166-167
  in early Church 124-125, 162-164
  in Middle Ages 164-165
  purpose of 170-173
  revision of 168-170
  truthfulness of 167
  and ultramontanists 166
Maistre, Joseph de 140
Marcellinus, Pope, Saint 100
Marcellus II, Pope 288
Marsilius of Padua 100, 104
Martin V, Pope 106
Mary and the papacy 349-350
Matthew 16:18-19
  authenticity of text 13-14
  and binding and loosing 19-20, 28, 81, 95, 360
  and confession of faith by Peter 15-17, 36, 45, 117, 363
  and keys of kingdom 18-19, 23, 81, 106-107, 117, 148, 360
  and rock 15-17, 26, 32, 85, 106, 108, 117, 196
  as proof text for papal infallibility 196
Maximus the Confessor, Saint 124, 126
Meier, John P. 14

Melady, Thomas 337
Melanchthon, Philip 107-108
Mental illness of pope 290-291
Meyendorff, John 116, 119, 126, 130, 260
Michael Cerularius, Patriarch 127, 130
Michelangelo 13, 52
Misner, Paul 359
Monarchy, papal
 in Bellarmine, Robert 109-110
 in Leo the Great 87, 88
 in Middle Ages 96-100, 101-104, 164, 219, 243, 280
 rejection of, by East 118, 131-132, 348
 trappings of 97, 365
Monothelites 126
Montini, Giovanni Battista 332, 339
 See also Paul VI, Pope
Moslems 311
Motu proprio 174
Mysterium ecclesiae (1973) 189, 190, 199, 205
Mystici corporis Christi (1943) 169, 173, 178, 213

National Conference of Catholic Bishops, U.S. 245, 247
Nazism 332
Nero, Emperor 51
Nestorius 122
Nicaea I, Council of (325) 75, 118-120, 236, 312
Nicaea II, Council of (787) 122-123
Nicephorus I, Patriarch, Saint 122-123
Nicetas, Archbishop 131
Nicholas I, Pope, Saint 127-128
Nicholas II, Pope 97, 280-281
Nichols, Aidan 123
Ninety-Five Theses (1517) 106
Nota explicativa praevia (1964) 220, 224, 226, 228, 234
Nunciatures 267, 306, 313, 318, 340-341
Nuncio, papal 314, 316

Occam, William of 104
Office for the Liturgical Celebrations of the Supreme Pontiff 312
Ohlig, Karl-Heinz 356
Optatus of Milevis, Saint 82, 219
Ordinary jurisdiction, papal 153-154, 156-158, 263
Ordinatio sacerdotalis (1994) 170, 174, 177
Origen 108, 116-117
Örsy, Ladislas 167, 304
Orthodox and the papacy
 ecumenical dialogue on 347-348, 357, 360
 and election, papal 285
 and local church, theology of 258, 260, 348
 and Petrine primacy 116, 130
 and Petrine succession 116-117, 130-131, 347
Ostpolitik 339-340

Palamas, Gregory, Archbishop 130
Papal States 95, 96, 103, 140, 251, 300, 301, 313, 317, 322, 323, 328, 357
Particular church
 See also Universal and particular (local) church
 pope's relation to 259-263, 356-357
 relation to universal Church 258-259
 terminology of 257-258
Passive legation, right of 313, 323, 327-329
Pastor aeternus (1870) 139-159, 179, 188, 193-198, 200-202, 204, 206, 208, 212-216, 225, 229, 269, 361-362
Pastor bonus (1988) 147, 149, 174, 175, 246, 250, 264, 270, 299, 301, 302-311, 318
Patriarch of the West, pope as 10, 121, 131-132, 154, 201, 359-360
Patriarchates
 See also Pentarchy
 and episcopal conference 245
 origin of 120, 218
 in theology of East 120-121, 127, 131-132
 in theology of West 121, 359-360
Patrimony of Peter 95
Paul, Apostle, Saint
 See also Peter and Paul, Saints
 confrontation with Peter 41-43
 contribution to Petrine ministry 351-352
 pope as successor to 66, 351-352
 visit to Jerusalem, first 40-41
 visit to Jerusalem, second 41
Paul VI, Pope
 and collegiality 215
 and contraception 172, 176, 178
 and curia, Roman 299, 305, 310
 and ecumenism 348, 365
 and election, papal 278, 282, 283-288, 295
 and episcopal conference 245
 and Holy See, diplomacy of 324-328, 330, 333, 335, 338, 339
 and jurisdiction, papal 155, 362
 and Lyons II, Council of 133
 and ministry, papacy as 148, 360-361
 and Peter, change of name 28

and Peter, relics of 53
and Pius XII 332
and pope as heart of Church 364
and pope as sacrament 366
and pope as vicar of Christ 266, 366
and representative, papal 315
resignation of 290
and Rome as unique city/see 144-145
and synod of bishops 239, 302
visits, pastoral 251
Paulinus of Aquileia, Saint 144
Pavia, Synod of (998) 100
Pelikan, Jaroslav 125
Pentarchy 118, 120-121, 131-132, 134
Pepin I, King 95, 110
Perfect society, Church as 97, 109-110, 146, 314, 323
Perpetuitas See Petrine succession
Peter, Apostle, Saint
 See also Peter and Paul, Apostles, Saints
 in Anglicanism 108
 and the apostles 37-39, 285, 349
 authority to judge of 35
 and beloved disciple 39
 biblical images of 43-46, 350, 358-359
 as bishop of Rome 60-62
 community's prayer for 37
 confession of faith of 17, 45, 116, 117, 164, 350
 as decision maker 34-36
 in East, theology of 116, 130-131
 as guardian of the faith 45-46
 in lists of the Twelve 15-20, 33, 39
 in Lutheranism 106-107
 as leader 33-36, 350
 as martyr 45, 51-52, 79-80, 351, 361
 as miracle worker 34, 39
 as missionary 34, 35-36
 and name, change of 15-16, 28, 288
 prayer of Jesus for 21, 350
 as preacher 33-34, 44-45
 as rock 15-17, 32, 63, 85, 106, 108, 117
 as shepherd (pastor) 22-25, 28, 44-45, 350, 361, 366
 as sinner 25-27, 294
 as spokesman for apostles 25, 38-39
 as strengthening the brethren 21, 28, 32-33, 86-87, 177, 229
 tomb of 52-53, 83-84, 145, 164, 249
 in Vatican I 141-142, 195
 as witness to risen Christ 31-33, 37-38, 350

Peter Damian, Saint 243, 281
Peter Lombard 101
Peter Olivi 192
Peter and Paul, Apostles, Saints
 confrontation at Antioch 41-43
 as founders of Roman church 51, 60, 65-66, 76, 78-80, 94, 115-116, 124, 144-145, 164, 351, 352
 invocation in Church documents of 201
 martyrdom in Rome of 51-52, 60, 65-66, 79-80, 144, 164, 285, 351
Petrine function See Petrine ministry
Petrine ministry
 as constitutive of Church 355-357
 and curia, Roman 303-305
 as distinct from historical papacy 272-273, 358-360
 instituted by Christ 354-355
Petrine succession
 in Anglicanism 109
 in apostolic succession 62-63, 350-351
 in early Church 81-84
 and East 116-118, 131, 134, 347
 and first successors to Peter 65
 in Leo the Great 85-86
 in Lutheranism 106-107
 Peter as bishop of Rome 60-62
 pope as bishop of Rome 143-145, 353
 at Vatican I 142-144
 willed by Christ 62-63, 142-143, 350-351
Petrine texts See John 21:15-17, Luke 22:31-32, Matthew 16:18-19
Petrinitas 81-83, 121, 139
 See also Petrine succession
Philip the Fair, King 103
Photius, Patriarch 116, 127, 128
Pie, Louis François Désiré, Cardinal 206
Pius II, Pope 106
Pius IV, Pope 109
Pius VI, Pope 141, 251
Pius VII, Pope 141
Pius IX, Pope 139-141, 157, 166, 177, 193, 204, 322
Pius X, Pope, Saint 66, 177, 282, 301
Pius XI, Pope 177, 178, 179, 271, 324
Pius XII, Pope
 and Assumption, definition of 174, 201, 204, 363
 and concordat with Germany 330
 and consultation before *ex cathedra* definition 204
 and election, papal 282

and jurisdiction, episcopal 169, 213
and ordinary papal magisterium, role of 180
and Peter, tomb of 52-53
and Rome as unique city/see 144
and Second World War 332, 337, 338
and subsidiarity 271
and Vatican City State 324
Plenitudo potestatis (fullness of authority), papal
  in Bonaventure 102
  in Boniface VIII 103-104
  in canonists, medieval 98-100, 219, 272, 292
  and college of cardinals 243, 291
  and curia, Roman 304
  at Florence, Council of 133-134
  in Innocent III 292
  in Leo the Great 86-87, 294
  at Lyons II, Council of 133
  in Marsilius of Padua 100
  and patriarchal primacy 272, 360
  in Thomas Aquinas 102-103
  at Vatican I 146-147, 148-150, 155
Pontian, Pope, Saint 289
Pontifex maximus (title) 217
Pontifical Academy of Life 312
Pontifical Academy of Sciences 312
Pontifical Academy of Social Sciences 312
Pontifical Biblical Commission 168, 307
Pontifical Council *Cor Unum* 310-311, 338
Pontifical Council for Culture 306
Pontifical Council for the Family 310
Pontifical Council for the Interpretation of Legislative Texts 311
Pontifical Council for Interreligious Dialogue 311, 317
Pontifical Council for Justice and Peace 310
Pontifical Council for the Laity 310
Pontifical Council for Pastoral Care of Migrants and Itinerant Peoples 311
Pontifical Council for Promoting Christian Unity 310
Pontifical Council for Social Communications 311
Pontifical Councils 309-311
Pontifical Ecclesiastical Academy 314
Pope (title) 98, 100-101, 102, 217
Pottmeyer, Hermann 37, 215, 273, 358
Poupard, Paul, Cardinal 306
Power of orders and power of jurisdiction
  in Bonaventure 102
  in canonists, medieval 99, 102
  after Vatican I 213

at Vatican I 14, 152, 157
at Vatican II 169, 223
Prefect, of dicastery 301, 307
Prefecture for the Economic Affairs of the Holy See 312
Prefecture of the Papal Household 312
Primacy of honor (*primus inter pares*)
  and Anglicanism 108-109
  and East 116, 135, 150
  at Vatican I 142, 150
Primate of Italy, pope as 10, 359
Prisoner of the Vatican, pope as 322
Pro-nuncio, papal 314
Provost, James 237, 240, 305, 314
Puzyna, Jan Kozielko, Cardinal 282

Quadragesimo anno (1931) 179, 271
Quatrodeciman controversy 74-75
Quinn, John, Archbishop 334
Quinquennial report 249-250
Quo vadis? legend 52

Rahner, Karl 57, 59, 152, 168, 205, 207, 227, 228, 229, 237-238, 244, 246, 272, 283-284, 293, 355, 358, 359
Rampolla del Tindaro, Mariano, Cardinal 282
Rand, Cuthbert 358
Ranke, Leopold von 9
Ratzinger, Joseph, Cardinal 17, 22, 121, 168, 239, 241, 245, 247, 250, 259, 261, 265, 348, 358, 360, 361
Recognitio 248, 268-269, 308
Reconciliatio et paenitentia (1984) 174, 336
Redemptor hominis (1979) 238
Redemptoris missio (1990) 308
Reformation and the papacy 106-109
Regimini ecclesiae universae (1967) 299, 302
Relations with States (Secretariat of State, Second Section) 306, 336
Representative, papal
  and accreditation, multiple 328
  arguments against 317-318
  and collegiality 315
  as dean of diplomatic corps 313, 314
  as delegate, apostolic 314
  at ecumenical councils 236, 312
  and legation, right of 313-314
  as nuncio 314, 316
  origin of 82, 236, 267, 312-313
  as pro-nuncio 314

The Shepherd and the Rock

responsibilities of 315-316, 338
   after Trent, Council of 267-268, 313, 316
Reservation, papal 268-269
Resignation of pope 289-290, 295
Retirement of pope 290
Roman church (local)
   appeals to 76-78, 81-82, 87, 124-126, 191
   as center of ecclesial communion 219, 363-365
   as defender of orthodoxy 163-164, 191
   in *Dictatus papae* 98
   early interventions of 73-75
   founded by Saints Peter and Paul 60, 65-66, 76, 78-80, 94, 144-145, 164, 285, 351, 352
   in Ignatius of Antioch 75-76
   in Irenaeus 78-80
   as mother and teacher of all churches 100, 131-132, 164
   pope as bishop of 151, 283-286
   primacy of see, not bishop 80-81, 352-353
   reasons for primacy, in East 124-125
Roman curia *See* Curia, Roman
Roman Inquisition 165
Roman pontiff (title) 217, 265
Roman Question (1870-1929) 322, 324, 328
Roman Rota 149, 309
Roman synod 249, 300
Roman Synod (382) 82-83
Roman Synod (495) 101
Roman Synod (769) 280
Romanitas 139, 143-144, 353
   See also Petrine succession
Romano pontifici eligendo (1975) 152, 278, 281, 283, 284, 286-288, 290, 295, 325, 353
Romanus pontifex (1585) 249
Rome, city of
   as center of ancient world 63-64
   Peter's sojourn in 50-53, 351
   as see of Peter's successors 143-145
Roosevelt, Franklin Delano 329
Rostow, Eugene 331
Ryan, Seamus 146, 213

Sacrament, pope as 83-84, 85-86, 101, 265-266, 274, 365-366
Saint Peter's Basilica 13, 52, 322
Salas, Bishop 155
Sapienti consilio (1908) 301
Sardica, Synod of (343-344) 77, 124, 128
Satgé, John de 44
Scheffczyk, Leo 264

Schism (1054) 98, 115, 127, 130
Schmaus, Michael 19
Schmemann, Alexander 115, 124, 129-130
Secretariat of State 302, 305-306, 309
Sensus fidelium 190, 205
Servant of the servants of God (title) 10, 87, 147
Shared papacy 359
Shotwell, James T. 125
Silvester I, Pope, Saint 96, 97, 236, 312
Siricius, Pope, Saint 84, 87
Sixtus V, Pope 249, 300, 301, 302
Smalcald Articles (1537) 107
Sollicitudo omnium ecclesiarum (1969) 84, 313-314, 315, 327
Stapleton, Thomas 165
State of Vatican City *See* Vatican City State
Stephen I, Pope, Saint 81-82
Stephen II, Pope 95, 110
Stickler, Alfons M. 306
Studer, Basilio 83
Súarez, Francisco 192, 292-293
Subsidiarity, principle of 270-272, 317
Substitute (Secretariat of State) 306
Succession, Petrine *See* Petrine succession
Successor of Peter (title) 10, 83-84, 217
Sullivan, Francis A. 55, 168, 172, 180, 198, 199, 205, 292
Supreme authority in Church, holder of
   episcopal college 227-239, 235
   pope alone 226
   as a theological question 225
   two inadequately distinct subjects 226-227
Supreme judge, pope as 76-78, 81-82, 99, 124, 149, 173, 191-192, 309
Supreme jurisdiction, papal 123-124, 148-149, 151, 224, 272
Supreme pontiff (title) 217
Supreme Tribunal of the Apostolic Signatura 309
Sweeney, Garrett 153, 154-155
Synod of bishops
   definition and purpose of 228, 238-239, 252, 349
   election, papal, role in 284
   extraordinary sessions of 238
   ordinary sessions of 238
   papal documents following 174
   reform of, proposals for 240-241
   role of pope in 239-240
   special assemblies of 238
Synod of Bishops (1969) 215
Synod of Bishops (1985) 216, 240, 271

Tauran, Jean-Louis, Archbishop 336
Taylor, Myron 329
Teaching authority *See* Infallibility, papal; Magisterium, ordinary papal
Tertullian 51, 81
Thant, U 330
Theodore of Studios, Saint 117, 126
Theodoret of Cyr, Bishop 66, 125
Theodosius I, Emperor 93
Theological Commission (Vatican II) 155, 198
Thirty-Nine Articles (1563) 108
Thomas Aquinas, Saint 102-103, 172, 192, 264
Thurian, Max 26
Tierney, Brian 104, 105
Tillard, J. M. R. 12, 31, 33, 38, 60, 83-84, 103, 124-125, 148, 151, 163, 166, 178, 189, 205, 212, 215, 222, 248, 265, 270, 352, 360, 364
Titles, papal *See* Bishop of Rome, Holy Father, Patriarch of the West, Pope, Roman pontiff, Successor of Peter, Supreme pontiff, Vicar of Christ, Vicar of Peter
Titular churches 242, 243, 286
Tome to Flavian 86, 122, 125, 164
Toynbee, Arnold 9, 325
Treaty of Tordesillas (1494) 338
Trent, Council of (1545-1563)
 and curia, Roman, reform of 300-301
 and papal primacy 109
Tribunals of the Holy See 149, 301, 305, 309
Tromp, Sebastian 173
Tucci, Roberto 285
Two swords theory 94-95, 97, 103, 110, 129

Ubi periculum (1274) 281-282
Ullmann, Walter 85, 99-100
Ultramontanism 140-141, 166, 193, 212
Unam sanctam (1302) 103-104, 357
Unitatis redintegratio (1964) 127, 135, 263, 357
United Nations 251, 317, 324-325, 330-331, 334, 336, 338
Universal Declaration of Human Rights (1948) 336
Universal jurisdiction, papal
 and East 123-124, 126, 129-130, 134-135
 papal claim to 86-87, 99-100, 101-104, 123-124, 127-128, 129, 135
 at Vatican I, definition of 154
Universal and particular (local) Church
 in East 120, 122, 123-124, 131-132, 260-261, 348
 relationship between 215-216, 258-259, 261-263, 303-304

terminology of 257-258
Universalist ecclesiology 215-216, 219, 257, 258-259, 348, 353

Vacancy in Roman see 289-291
Vacantis apostolicae sedis (1945) 282
Vatican City State
 administration of 323
 origin of 322-324
 pope as head of 10, 323, 357
 relation to Holy See 322-325
Vatican I, Council of (1869-1870)
 background to 139-141
 and consent of Church to *ex cathedra* pronouncements 206
 and consultation prior to *ex cathedra* pronouncements 203-204
 and heresy of pope 293
 and incompleteness of teaching on papacy 158-159, 212-214, 252
 and infallibility, papal 179, 193-203
 interpretation of, in light of Vatican II 139, 214-216, 252, 346, 349
 and jurisdiction, papal 145-147, 148-154, 157-158, 361-362
 and limits to papal authority 154-158
 and magisterium, ordinary papal 166, 179
 and Petrine primacy, institution of 141-142
 and Petrine succession 60, 84, 142-143
 reception of its teaching on papacy 212-216
 and successor of Peter as bishop of Rome 143-144, 353
Vatican II, Council of (1962-1965)
 and assent to ordinary papal magisterium 180
 and authority as service 147-148
 and collegiality 217-218, 225-228, 234-235, 237, 302, 315, 348-349
 and consent of Church to *ex cathedra* pronouncements 206-207
 and consultation prior to *ex cathedra* pronouncements 204-205
 and curia, Roman, reform of 301-303, 309, 316-317
 and episcopacy 215-216, 269, 317
 and hierarchical communion 223-225
 and infallibility, papal, charism of 195
 and infallibility, papal, objects of 198-199
 and interpretation of Vatican I 139, 214-216, 252, 346, 348-349
 and jurisdiction, papal 362

and particular church 257-258, 261, 265, 317
and representative, papal 315, 317
and synod of bishops, institution of 238
and titles, papal 102, 151, 216-217, 220-223
Vatican Library 312
Vatican Radio 312
Vatican Secret Archives 312
Vicar of Christ, bishop as 94, 101, 147, 217, 304
Vicar of Christ, emperor as 95
Vicar of Christ, Saint Peter as 24-25, 28, 46, 62-63
Vicar of Christ, pope as
  See also Sacrament, pope as
  in Bellarmine, Robert 110
  in Boniface VIII 103-104
  at Florence, Council of 102, 133, 197
  in Gelasius I 101
  as holder of supreme authority 226
  in Innocent III 101-102, 292
  in John Paul II 217
  in Paul VI 28, 266, 315, 365-366
  at Trent, Council of 109
  at Vatican I 102, 197, 215
  after Vatican I 214
  at Vatican II 102, 216-217
Vicar of Peter, pope as
  in East 117, 125
  in first millennium 83-84, 85-86, 101, 125, 351
Victor I, Pope, Saint 74-75, 83, 88
Vigilius, Pope 126
Vischer, Lukas 340, 347, 361

Visible center and foundation of unity, pope as 76, 86-87, 102-103, 110, 116, 128, 135, 145-146, 218-219, 230, 247, 248, 250, 261-266, 356-357, 363-365
Visits, pastoral, of pope 173, 175, 250-252, 263, 323
Vries, Wilhelm de 122

Ware, Timothy 128, 129
Wernz, Francis Xavier 291
Wesley, John 10
Western Schism (1378-1417) 104-107
Wicks, Jared 192
World affairs, pope's role in
  through concordats 329-330, 339
  through dialogue 331-333, 339-340, 364-365
  through diplomatic relations with states 327-329
  through international organizations 330-331
  as mediator 338
  through messages 326-327
  and Petrine ministry, relation to 325-326, 335, 365-366
World Council of Churches 363
World Day of Peace, messages for 326, 337

Zephyrinus, Pope, Saint 83
Zinelli, Bishop 151, 152-153, 155, 156, 293
Zizola, Giancarlo 279
Zosimus, Pope, Saint 78

Place The Most Vital Information At Your Fingertips

Catholic Dictionary
Edited by Rev. Peter M.J. Stravinskas, Ph.D., S.T.L.
No. 507, hardcover, $29.95, 500 pp.
This reference tool is the most complete, one-volume guide to Catholic terms and definitions on the market. Includes an easy-to-use pronunciation guide.

Catholic Encyclopedia
Edited by Rev. Peter M.J. Stravinskas, Ph.D., S.T.L.
No. 457, hardcover, $34.95
No. 475, kivar, $29.95, 1,008 pp.
Historically accurate, theologically authoritative, scripturally rich, this encyclopedia highlights 3,000 entries of Catholic teaching and history.

Our Sunday Visitor's Catholic Encyclopedia and Catholic Dictionary on CD-ROM
No. 755, CD-ROM, $49.95/No. 770 on 3.5" HD diskettes, $49.95
Our Sunday Visitor has combined and hyper-linked the entire text for its best-selling **Catholic Encyclopedia** and **Catholic Dictionary** on a single CD-ROM disc. Search any word or phrase and find it instantly. After completing all the searches you desire, combine the files and print your findings.

Available at your local religious bookstore or use this page for ordering:
Our Sunday Visitor • 200 Noll Plaza • Huntington, IN 46750
Please send me the above title(s). I am enclosing payment plus $3.95 per order to cover shipping/handling. Or, MasterCard/Visa customers can order by telephone **1-800-348-2440**.

Name_____
Address_____
City/State_____Zip_____
Telephone(   )_____
Prices and availability subject to change without notice.

A53BBHBP